THE FORGOTTEN PEOPLE

THE FORGOTTEN PEOPLE

Cane River's Creoles of Color

GARY B. MILLS

Revised Edition by Elizabeth Shown Mills

Foreword by H. Sophie Burton

LOUISIANA STATE UNIVERSITY PRESS
BATON ROUGE

Published by Louisiana State University Press
Copyright © 1977, 2013 by Louisiana State University Press
All rights reserved
Manufactured in the United States of America
First printing

DESIGNER: Michelle A. Neustrom
TYPEFACES: Ingeborg, text; Filosofia, display
PRINTER AND BINDER: Maple Press

LIBRARY OF CONGRESS CATALOGING-IN-PUBLICATION DATA

Mills, Gary B.
  The forgotten people : Cane River's Creoles of color / Gary B. Mills ; foreword
by H. Sophie Burton. — Revised edition / by Elizabeth Shown Mills.
     pages cm
  Includes bibliographical references and index.
  ISBN 978-0-8071-3713-0 (pbk. : alk. paper) 1. Creoles—Louisiana—Cane
River Region. 2. Cane River Region, La. —History. 3. Natchitoches Parish (La.)
—History. I. Title.
  F377.N4M54 2013
  976.3'65—dc23
                                                                2013014275

To Hazel Cecilia Rachal Mills,
who taught us to appreciate Cane River and its culture

CONTENTS

CHARTS, TABLES, AND MAPS

FOREWORD TO THE
REVISED EDITION

I t was with great pleasure that I accepted the honor of writing a foreword for the revised edition of Gary Mills's *The Forgotten People.* After its publication, Mills's book stood as the only historical scholarship about the town of Natchitoches for decades. When I set out to write my dissertation, which was a socioeconomic study of colonial Natchitoches, Mills's work was the only well-researched secondary work available. It was lagniappe that Mills's book proved to be well written and engrossing.[1]

Drawing on an abundant array of sources, including official correspondence, court records, notarial documents, and sacramental registers, Mills focuses on Cane River, a district in Natchitoches. He shows how the descendants of the Cane River free people of color, or *gens de couleur libres,* began a colony in the eighteenth century in large part because of the efforts of a black woman named Marie Thérèse, also known by her sobriquet of Coincoin. She had fifteen children, ten of whom were born of her union with a white planter named Claude Thomas Pierre Metoyer. She ceased living with Metoyer about 1786, and less than ten years later three of her sons moved downriver to the Isle Brevelle section of Cane River, where they came to constitute the core of the colony of free people of color. Because the Metoyers worked hard and tended to marry other free people of color, these Cane River Creoles became an economically and socially successful group. Mills follows the community's story into the nineteenth century, showing how their intermediate racial status in Louisiana changed during the first half of the nineteenth century.

At the time of its publication in 1977, *The Forgotten People* was unique among the many historical studies of the colonial and antebellum history of the South and free people of color in particular. Although a few previous studies had focused on free blacks in New Orleans, the free people of color of rural Louisiana had received little attention despite the group's significant numbers and economic importance. Moreover, the majority of work on free people of color tended to focus on the antebellum period alone, while Mills chose to begin in the eighteenth century and follow the story through to the Civil War.

The Forgotten People fits into the larger trend in 1970s colonial and regional historiography that strongly emphasized slavery and related subjects such as free people of color. Mills, like other scholars, had to perform a delicate balancing act while recounting the experiences of the Cane River Creoles. On the one hand, he wanted to show that people living under restrictive legal, social, and cultural circumstances were still active members of society, not passive victims. On the other hand, he had to avoid overemphasizing black and multiracial agency in bondage as this could minimize and thus misrepresent the harsh nature of slavery. Moreover, Mills had a more complicated task than most historians of slavery because many Cane River Creoles actively benefited from the plantation system and became local elites. In the end, Mills skillfully demonstrated how his protagonists, albeit caught in an ambiguous situation, negotiated the succession of slave regimes in Natchitoches with a mixture of dignity and pragmatism.

For decades, The Forgotten People remained the only well-researched history on this important town in northwest Louisiana. Mills's study reshaped the ways in which scholars viewed Natchitoches and inspired more research into free people of color and slaves in Louisiana. I was therefore surprised to find that much of the scholarly community overlooked the book at the time of its publication. While the few contemporary reviewers were complimentary, this lack of attention appears egregious in light of the work's subsequent influence. Perhaps this book escaped the attention of the historical profession because of the abundance of studies of antebellum communities and of free blacks in the late 1970s. Perhaps, more ominously, this book was neglected because it dealt with Louisiana and in particular with the state's non–English-speaking colonial history. Like all histories of French and Spanish colonial regions that later fell under United States sovereignty, Louisiana's history challenged the East Coast and Anglo-Saxon bias within the historical profession, which tended to focus solely on the English colonial experience.[2] Whatever the reasons for the oversight, the handful of critics who did review Mills's book rightfully praised its contributions. One reviewer lauded the work for its "exemplary research," while another scholar noted that it offered a "challenge to the 'two-caste' model of American race relations." Another astute historian praised Mills's focus on "a rural enclave rather than an urban" community.[3] Clearly, however, the impact of Mills's book on the historical profession has grown since its publication, and with good reason.

The Forgotten People challenged the predominant notion that the French and later Spanish town was an outpost devoted to the Indian trade, and showed that the district also became a plantation center. In 1977 the only major publication that dealt with colonial Natchitoches was a compilation of sources edited by Herbert Eugene Bolton.[4] Bolton, who had chosen, translated, edited, and printed a number of important letters and reports to and from Athanase de Mézières, an influential commandant of Natchitoches, was interested in the Spanish borderlands. Because Bolton selected primary documents concerned with trade and Indian relations with Texas, the publication unintentionally fostered the impression that the town was uniquely an Indian trade center. As Bolton's book was published in 1914, twentieth-century historians might be forgiven for assuming that the town was a colony populated by métis, or people of mixed indigenous and French ancestry, because of the strong social ties to local Indian groups. Mills's book stepped into this dearth of research and knowledge about Natchitoches and the Louisiana-Texas frontier and brought to light the existence of the vibrant Cane River community of free people of color. The book raised the tantalizing possibility that the region had much in common with the plantations of lower Louisiana as well as the frontier Indian trade of Texas.[5]

Mills's book also formed part of an important shift in historiography that stressed Louisiana as a colony in its own right within the French colonial world and then the Spanish empire. Before the 1970s, scholarship tended to portray the large population of free people of color in Louisiana as merely one more component of the exceptional and exotic nature of Louisiana. Because of the predominance of British colonial research in the field of history at that time and the status of Louisiana as one of fifty states in the United States, work about this colony had tended to draw parallels with British North America. Such comparisons inevitably led to a view that the Gulf Coast was unusual or singular. Most research avoided this conundrum by ignoring the colonial era and focusing on the antebellum period. As a result, many non–English-speaking regions acquired an undeserved reputation of uniqueness. Scholarship in the 1970s, including Mills's book, began to attribute the differences between the Gulf Coast region—including New Orleans and interior Louisiana—and the rest of mainland North America to the French and Spanish cultural legacies of the colonial period and to study this heritage in its own right. In keeping with the work of his contemporaries, Mills explicitly sought to examine Louisiana as a component of the colonial French and Spanish regimes.[6]

Scholars who examined non–English-speaking colonies as an integral part of their proper empire frequently found the colonies under analysis to be consistent and representative regions, and the results were undeniably more informative to the historical profession. For his part, Mills showed that the treatment of free people of color in Natchitoches differed under French, Spanish, and American rule. While French rule brought a plantation slave society to the region, the advent of Spanish control in Natchitoches facilitated the Cane River community. Upon taking Louisiana from France, Spain established colonial laws and customs in accordance with its own empire. For the governing of slaves and free people of color, Spain overrode the French-imposed *Code Noir* in the face of planter resistance and established codes that were more advantageous to slaves and free people of color. The large class of free people of color existing in Louisiana suggested that colony was more in keeping with other Spanish colonies than with most English colonial slave societies in mainland North America. In addition, Mills demonstrated that life became more difficult for free people of color when Louisiana fell under American administration. To be sure, Mills's focus was less comprehensive than more recent scholarship that locates and studies Louisiana and its peoples as part of the Atlantic World, but his study provided an important step in that direction. This approach alerted other colonial U.S. historians to the different legal, social, cultural, and political ways of non–English-speaking regions that now fall under the jurisdiction of the United States. This type of work showed Louisiana to be a colony worthy of its own historiography and led to a more comprehensive view of North American colonial history.[7]

In the decades after its publication, Mills's book directly inspired a number of studies of Louisiana's colonial people of color and slaves. Kimberly S. Hanger saw the change to Spanish sovereignty in the late 1760s as crucial to the birth of a free black community in New Orleans. L. Virginia Gould looked at free people of color along the Gulf Coast. Like Mills, subsequent scholars found that French and Spanish conditions, laws, and cultures facilitated the rise, growth in numbers, and activities of free people of color. More recently, a trend in scholarship dealing with free people of color focuses on the construction of race during Louisiana's colonial period.[8]

In keeping with Mills's concern with the effects of the successive slave regimes under French, Spanish, and American rule on the lives of free people
of color, newer work on slavery and free people of color challenged the myth
of the distinctiveness of Louisiana and made the colony more prominent in
colonial historiography. Examinations of Louisiana slavery disagreed over
the nature and harshness of Louisiana's slave regimes and provoked a de-
bate. Gwendolyn Midlo Hall argued that the French slave regime was brutal
for enslaved and free Africans, while the Spanish system of slavery was less
harsh in part because of the large influx of Africans who revitalized Louisiana's Afro-Creole culture. Gilbert S. Din undertook a detailed examination of
slavery under Iberian rule, showing that Louisiana's slave regime was consistent with that in other Spanish colonies and suggesting that the application of Iberian slave laws in Louisiana curbed the lives of free and enslaved
blacks. Thomas N. Ingersoll, rejecting cultural explanations of Louisiana's
distinctiveness, argued that the shift in regimes from French to Spanish to
American had little appreciable impact on the colony's social order, which
remained consistently one of brutally enforced white planter control over a
black majority. Daniel H. Usner argued that Louisiana slavery was shaped
more by economic activities than by national laws and customs. Slavery
was less harsh as long as Louisiana's colonial economy amounted to small-
scale exchanges, and it was not until the shift to plantation agriculture in
the 1780s, when the colony became part of the Atlantic World, that slavery
became harsh.[9]

Mills's examination of the Cane River community of Afro-Creoles also
served as an inspiration for studies of manumission as well as the culture,
status, and conditions of life for free people of color in antebellum Louisiana. These books reinterpreted the culture of Afro-Creoles, albeit the focus
tended to be on New Orleans. Judith Kelleher Schafer looked at how slaves
and free people of color employed the legal system, while Caryn Cossé Bell
and others showed that the nineteenth-century protest tradition of Afro-
Creoles brought a multiethnic perspective to race relations. Mills's book
proved to be an important source for Loren Schweninger's large-scale study
of prosperous blacks in the United States because the great majority of affluent free people of color lived in Louisiana. Only in Charleston, New Orleans,
and a few rural areas in South Carolina and Louisiana did blacks acquire
more than modest property holdings before 1830. Moreover, free people of
color in the states of the Lower South remained the largest property-owning
group in the prewar generation.[10]

While *The Forgotten People* was valuable to historians, as it contributed greatly to the knowledge of Louisiana's history in the colonial and antebellum periods, it also addressed a larger audience outside of academia—those interested in Louisiana's rich heritage. In general, these readers are regional history buffs curious to learn about the history of their locality or genealogists who want to know more about their family history and cultural heritage. Aware of this important potential element of his readership, Mills made a deliberate effort to sort out fact from fiction and to provide documentation for his findings. He began by extracting a composite legend of the Cane River community from a group of informants before he undertook his research. He then analyzed traditional historical sources as verification. In the end, he found that much of the tradition had factual roots, although it had been substantially altered by fading memories and active imaginations.

Unlike many professional historians, Mills was aware of the importance of genealogy and perceived a natural congruence between the microcosm of personal family histories and the macrocosm of the wider social and cultural trends that constitute history. His professional pursuit of both history and genealogy was shared by his wife Elizabeth Shown Mills, who has contributed immeasurably to the history of Natchitoches and Louisiana with her publications of primary sources such as censuses, military and tax rolls, and church records.[11] Her work is part of a noticeable and commendable trend in Louisiana's colonial historiography in which independent researchers, genealogists, and local historians locate, translate, and publish primary sources.[12] Elizabeth Shown Mills has now expanded *The Forgotten People* to reflect decades of additional study that she and Gary have done, together and independently, on the Cane River region.

H. SOPHIE BURTON

NOTE ON THE
REVISED EDITION

Creole is a culture, not a color. In 1969, I discovered that culture under the wing of Hazel Cecilia Rachal Mills, a Cane River Creole of French, Native American, and British roots. She took me to Cloutierville and introduced me to her people: Rachals, Brossets, Derbannes, LaCours, Brevelles, and more. As a young student of history, I was intrigued by the fact that, up and down the river, the bearers of those names came in all hues. As a product of "Anglo" America, I was struck by the patterns in which parishioners seated themselves in church—not white on one side and black on the other, but in three groups: black, white, and "in-between." In their homes, I listened to their stories of historic strifes and cultural rivalries—not between black and white but between Creole and Anglo. I mused over their mementoes, savored their gumbo and meat pies, and eventually left. That was when I discovered that no one ever, truly, leaves Cane River. Wherever we go, a part of it goes with us. That part would forever pull me back, seeking to better understand this culture that my mother-in-law Hazel and my husband Gary had passed on to our babies.

In early 1972, Arthur Chopin Watson, a Cane River attorney, called with a proposition. A local legend himself, Arthur shared Gary's roots and our love of history. On our trips back to Cane River, during weekends and school breaks at the university where Gary held his first teaching post, Arthur had opened doors for us, helping us access records that were normally closed and people who were hesitant to discuss their world with strangers. Arthur's new proposition intrigued us. The local preservation society had been given a plantation home steeped in lore. An architectural preservationist already had a team at work on site, and an application had been submitted to the National Register. But Arthur was troubled by the reliance on local legends—

much of it he thought fantastical. Documentation was sorely needed. Were we interested? We were.

Little did we know that project would never end. By the expiration of our short contract, Gary had returned to school to complete his doctorate in history, while I had launched a career as a professional researcher, working with attorneys, biographers, and others interested in yesteryear's people. Cane River's "forgotten people" became the subject of Gary's doctoral dissertation. We expanded our research to archives in France, Spain, Cuba, Canada, and Mexico, as well as all the early settlements across the borderlands and the Mississippi Valley—in short, everywhere from which Cane River's settlers came and many places to which they wandered. The project did not end even in 1977, when LSU Press published the book that evolved from Gary's dissertation, even though his academic research then moved into studies of race relations in the Anglo South. Our Cane River project did not end in 1981, when I completed my own thesis on social and family patterns in colonial Natchitoches. Nor did it end in 1990 when I landed a contract with a major commercial publisher for my historical novel *Isle of Canes*—a contract that carried an intractable provision: one significant story line must be eliminated because, editors contended, no readers would believe that Cane River's beloved black matriarch would, herself, become a slaveowner. But, of course, the past cannot be rearranged to suit preconceived notions. *Isle of Canes* would indeed be rewritten, many times as new research revealed new insight, until its eventual publication by a publisher more committed to preserving the realities of the past.

The project did not end with Gary's death in 2002. Other publications have followed in the wake of new discoveries. At his death, Gary also left one goal unfulfilled: the hope that LSU Press would authorize a revised edition of *The Forgotten People,* a more nuanced and more robust story enriched by all we had discovered since his dissertation of 1974. In 2010, director MaryKatherine Callaway and editor Catherine Kadair offered me that opportunity. Their patience as I first worked through other publication commitments has been a godsend. The revision has proved to be a bigger one than any of us anticipated. Decades of additional research—not only ours, but that of many other scholars working on issues of race, gender, and the intersection of archaeology and history—have provided much new fodder for challenging long-standing assumptions about the complexities of life along Cane River.

This expanded study—nearly two-thirds larger than the original—offers a greatly enriched comparison of the community against their counterparts elsewhere in Louisiana and "Anglo" America. It more sharply defines the issues that confined the lives of Creoles of color and explores the agencies they employed to achieve economic parity. It more fully develops the ethnic and social origins of the families that comprised the community, correcting significant misassumptions made by earlier writers about both the families and the historic properties they left behind. It offers new insight into the roles that the Cane River families played as agents, as well as victims, of America's "peculiar institution"—as well as their efforts to preserve the legal rights of Louisiana's "third caste" and defend the freedom of impoverished members of their class. Many new primary source materials from public archives and private hands in the United States, France, and Spain underpin the perspectives offered in this new edition.

The decades that have passed have also increased our debts to others who have made new research possible or shared their family treasures. Two mentors have passed on: Arthur Watson and his kindred spirit (though not a kinswoman), Dr. Ora V. Watson of the Association for the Preservation of Historic Natchitoches. Some new acquaintances discovered *The Forgotten People* or *Isle of Canes,* sought us out, and then became research colleagues and friends—particularly, Dr. Harlan Mark Guidry and Joseph B. Mullon III. A new cadre of professionals at Natchitoches's Northwestern State University has provided records and photographs or challenged us on thorny issues—especially, Mary Lynn Wernet and Sonny Carter of the Cammie Henry Center; Janet Colson and Louise Llorens of the Louisiana Creole Heritage Center; and Alfred Lemmon and John and Priscilla Lawrence of The Historic New Orleans Collection. All have been valued and generous stewards of history.

This new edition of *The Forgotten People* is offered to a new generation of readers as one small window into a world that history has neglected and a culture that is often misunderstood.

ELIZABETH SHOWN MILLS
HENDERSONVILLE, TENNESSEE
JANUARY 2013

PREFACE

ane River's Creoles of color, despite their fabled "uniqueness," were part of a larger social order long considered peculiar to "Latin" Louisiana.[1] Known as *gens de couleur libres,* the men and women of this society were considered neither black nor white. They successfully rejected identification with any established racial order and achieved recognition as a distinct ethnic group. The diverse cultures that spawned them created an ideology conceived of necessity, nurtured by hope, and carefully guarded against changing mores of society. The status they enjoyed, however, was not entirely of their own making. The growth of this distinctive people was fostered by the attitude of a society still not common to North America.

The fact that most free men or women of color bore some degree of white blood was of little consequence in most of the United States. By law and social custom, the black and the part-black, whether slave or free, were usually relegated to the same social status and frequently displayed the same lifestyle and personal philosophy. The primary exception to this general rule was found in Louisiana, although echoes existed throughout the coastal regions of the Gulf South.

The introduction of African slaves into the New World spawned a complex caste system for Creoles of African descent. In the colonies of France, Spain, and Portugal, special terminology attempted to denote the ratio of African blood held by those who appear in the records. In colonial and antebellum Louisiana, where precision gave way to practicality, the classifications most commonly found in the records are these:

Negro . . . . applied usually to one of full black parentage
Griffe . . . . 3/4 Negro–1/4 white *or* Indio-Negro mixture
Mulatto . . . . . . 1/2 Negro–1/2 white

Quadroon . . . . . 1/4 Negro–3/4 white

Octoroon . . . . . . 1/8 Negro–7/8 white

And, generically, in the Spanish period:

Pardo . . . . light-skinned person of color, percentages uncertain to the scribe

Moreno . . . . dark-skinned person of color, percentages uncertain to the scribe

The degree of privilege or degradation that Louisiana accorded people of color, whether slave or free, frequently depended upon each individual's placement upon this caste scale.

The racial philosophy of the white Creoles who dominated Louisiana society also contained a counterpoint to this caste system. Upon obtaining freedom, a multiracial Creole entered into a separate but complementary racial category—an intermediate class called *gens de couleur libres*. As such, they were accorded special privileges, opportunities, and citizenship rarely granted to counterparts in the English colonies and Anglo-American states.

Preservation of this intermediate class in Louisiana society was contingent upon strict adherence to the caste system by its members. Just as whites entertained feelings of superiority to blacks and slaves, so did Louisiana's *gens de couleur libres*. Often possessing more white blood than black, and quite often on good terms with and publicly recognized by white relatives, most members of this caste in Louisiana were reared to believe they were a race apart. Countless testimonials reveal their inherent pride in their Catholic, French, and Spanish heritage and their identification with that culture rather than their African roots.

Into this complex caste system still another factor injected itself: economic status. Louisiana's legal code provided a wider berth of economic opportunities to free people of color than could be found in any of the other states. As is the case with any given society, *gens de couleur libres* displayed varying degrees of initiative, industry, and aptitude. The extent to which individual members of this class developed their opportunities often determined their degree of social acceptability in society as a whole.

In this economic arena, one sees the most significant difference between the status of *gens de couleur libres* and free people of color elsewhere in North America. In the Anglo-American colonies and states, achieving a greater measure of legal rights and opportunities was typically an *individual* process. Most jurisdictions, prior to the Civil War, refused to fractionally define the line between black and white. As South Carolina's Supreme Court Justice William Harper explained in 1835, "The condition of the individual is not to be determined solely by distinct and visible mixture of negro blood, but by reputation, by his reception into society. . . . [I]t may be well and proper, that a man of worth, honesty, industry, and respectability, should have the rank of a white man, while a vagabond of the same degree of blood should be confined to the inferior caste."[2] Under this construct of "race," many Anglo-American descendants of African slaves became productive and even prominent *white* citizens as they migrated away from their native communities.[3]

In contrast, Louisiana's *gens de couleur libres* achieved a greater measure of legal rights and opportunities as a *class*. However, they enjoyed those rights only so long as they lived within the bounds defined for that class. Their Catholicity and that church's sacramental registers, which functioned as population registers prior to civil vital registration, limited their opportunities to live as white even when their appearance bore no trace of an African forebear. Within New Orleans, a greater range of ethnic diversity and a significantly larger population facilitated a few cross-overs in the colonial era. Elsewhere in the colony and state, merging into the more privileged white class, for those whose appearance might allow it, usually meant abandoning their faith, migrating to a place where they were not known, or both. Prior to the twentieth century, that was an unthinkable option for most *gens de couleur libres*.

As multiracials who achieved a distinct identity through cohesion within a self-sufficient, self-protective community, Cane River's Creoles of color were not unique in the American South. Scholars have identified other "triracial isolate" groups from Maryland and New Jersey to Texas—Melungeons of the Upper South, Lumbees of North Carolina, Brass Ankles of South Carolina, and Redbones of Louisiana, among various interconnected groups whose roots wind back to the seventeenth-century shores of Virginia.[4] They, too, battled for rights of citizenship, as groups. However, the social and legal climates of the societies in which they lived created significant constraints not placed upon *gens de couleur libres* before the Americanization of Louisiana. Like Cane River's Creoles of color, Anglo-America's triracial isolates attempted to build self-sufficient communities to fill their economic and social needs. However, because their emergence predated that of Cane River's denizens by nearly a hundred years, their communities suffered another handicap not felt on Cane River until the twentieth century: population growth that their communities could not economically sustain.

A critical difference between Cane River's *gens de couleur libres* and other triracial groups of the American South was geoeconomic. The hills and mountains where the latter sought refuge as well as livelihood were far less fertile than the loamy bottomland that lined Cane River. The small yeoman farms of the Anglo-rooted triracial communities supported few slaves; the plantations of Cane River required many of them. That economic differential was the primary factor that enabled Cane River's *gens de couleur libres* to sustain themselves *politically* in the increasingly restrictive world of the American South.[5]

In consequence of all these factors, Louisiana's multiracials—as a class—advanced socially, economically, and politically to a level unknown among minorities in North American society. Yet few efforts have been made to examine the depth of their success or the scope of the factors that produced it. As early as 1917 Alice Dunbar-Nelson lamented, "There is no state in the Union, hardly any spot of like size on the globe, where the man of color has lived so intensely, made so much progress, been of such historical importance and yet about whom so comparatively little is known."[6]

Nearly a century has elapsed since that observation was made, but the condition that prompted the remark still exists. Rodolphe Lucien Desdunes's *Nos Hommes et Nos Histoire* was a pioneer work; it had, in fact, already appeared in Canada several years before Nelson pointed to the need for more study of the subject. Desdunes's presentation, however, emphasized the *gens de couleur libres* of the New Orleans area and excluded many worthy Creoles of color who resided in the backcountry of the state.[7]

Desdunes's focus upon New Orleanians remains typical of most studies made of his caste in Louisiana. From Charles B. Rousseve's pioneering *Negro in Louisiana: Aspects of His History and His Literature*[8] to Virginia Dominguez's *White by Definition*[9] and Kimberly Hanger's *Bounded Lives, Bounded Places*[10] (not to mention a host of journal articles, doctoral dissertations, and master's theses across those decades), rural Creoles of color have continued to receive little more than passing reference. The significant exception is Brasseaux, Fontenot, and Oubre's slim study, *Creoles of Color in the Bayou Country*.[11] To some extent, the emphasis upon New Orleans's Creole society is justified, considering that metropolis possessed more men and women of this caste than any city in the nation. But such urban-oriented studies reveal little of the lifestyle of the many rural *gens de couleur libres* and the roles they played in the development of Louisiana as a whole.

An early effort to fill this statewide void was H. E. Sterkx's *Free Negro in Ante-Bellum Louisiana*. Sterkx provided some degree of rural coverage as a much-needed counterpoint to the usual emphasis upon New Orleanians. However, his geographic breadth and the need to cover both blacks and free people of color in vastly different Creole and "American" environments means that only superficial treatment could be given to many aspects of his subject. Sterkx's greatest contribution, thus, was his broad and solid base upon which more in-depth analyses of Louisiana's third caste might be built.[12]

The Forgotten People attempts to fill a portion of this void in three substantive areas. First, the caste barriers that stood between the slave, the free black, and the free man of color in Creole society remain underestimated or misunderstood. Seminal studies have, in some regards, perpetuated misconceptions—Ira Berlin's *Slaves without Masters* being an excellent case at point. Berlin filled a significant need in bringing together a series of less-known publications and unpublished doctoral dissertations into one overarching study. However, his examination of "The Free People of Color in Louisiana and the Gulf Ports" completely ignored the chasm that existed between the black and the part-black in Creole society and treated these two diverse cultures as a single entity.[13] For the past half-century, the prevailing emphasis upon "black brotherhood" has led many scholars, and the public as well, to suppose a historical, ideological bond between all minorities. Presumably, the coloration setting them apart from white Americans has always transcended social and economic differences. This assumption is fallacious—an extension of, and reaction to, the equally unrealistic "one drop" rule imposed by white America in the nineteenth century. The fallacy of this assumption is a point made early at Natchitoches, where Commandant Athanase de Mézières observed, in 1770, a growing cultural riff between "Africans" and "Creoles" of African ancestry, and he worried considerably about the directions that social divide would take.[14]

Second, as Carl N. Degler points out in *Neither Black nor White*, studies in U.S. history have traditionally presented the nonwhite "primarily as a problem, not as a contributor to the making of the society."[15] Subsequent works such as Derek Noel Kerr's dissertation on crime in Spanish Louisiana have continued that theme.[16] The modern focus upon the rich history of minorities is reversing traditional views, and several of the studies discussed above have contributed to the reordering of previously accepted ideas. Much more basic research must be done, however, if the role of Creoles in American history is to be realistically reconstructed.

A third consideration argued by *Forgotten People* is the need to recognize that Americans of slave descent *do* have a traceable ancestry. For too long it has been accepted *de rigueur* that sexual incontinency and a lack of family stability (both of which impede genealogical research) have characterized African American society in America. Fogel and Engerman's controversial *Time on the Cross* blasted this stereotype,[17] but their statistical conclusions were challenged immediately. Herbert Gutman subsequently provided significant evidence, both statistical and anecdotal, to argue the stability of relationships within slave families;[18] and Ann Patton Malone has added a counterpart for Louisiana.[19] Considerable reinforcement, however, is needed before their findings succeed in replacing traditional assumptions. The conduct of slave genealogical research also has been handicapped by a general unawareness of the type and volume of records available. Alex Haley, with the publication of his historical novel *Roots,* sparked an interest in African American genealogy, but subsequent reviews of his work also spotlighted the immense challenges involved.[20] More recent historians and genealogical scholars, publishing in peer-reviewed journals such as the *National Genealogical Society Quarterly,* are now demonstrating the potential that exists.[21]

The Forgotten People's attempt to fill some of these voids is purposefully narrow. It is confined to one family group concentrated in an area roughly thirty miles by five miles in the heart of Louisiana. In another sense, however, it is much broader than any previously presented, for it examines critically every aspect of the private and public lives and feelings of the subject community and relates their development to the progress of the community as a whole. It is hoped that such a detailed examination of the evolution of one minority group—its difficulties, its achievements, its heartaches, and its pride—will make manifest the contributions to society made by minorities and some of the forces that have motivated them.

Cane River's Creoles of color were not entirely unknown to Louisiana scholars when the first edition of this monograph appeared. A major sociological study, Sister Frances Jerome Woods's *Marginality and Identity* discussed the mindset of the community in considerable detail. However, the nature and scope of Woods's work focused upon the contemporaries whom she interviewed. Her coverage of the community's very significant historical role was nominal, and that limitation led to historical inaccuracies that marred an otherwise excellent study of the mid-twentieth-century Creole psyche.[22]

In addition to *Marginality and Identity,* several well-known studies of a historical nature have included references to various individuals of the community and their wealth. None of these, however, have come close to showing the extent of the prosperity of the people of Cane River or the role they played in the maturation of central Louisiana society.

In terms of prosperity, these Creoles of Cane River were not unique in American society. Every southern state had a few men (and, occasionally, women) of color with comparable wealth.[23] Missouri and Louisiana boasted a sizable number. No *individuals* in the Cane River community can be touted as the wealthiest of their class in antebellum society. However, no *family* group yet has been found, in Louisiana or in any other of the United States, which boasted as many prosperous men and women or which retained such a degree of affluence and status for so long a period of time.

Despite the migratory patterns of the past two centuries, the core of this community has remained intact on many of the same plantations their ancestors carved from the Louisiana wilderness more than two hundred years ago. Offshoots of branches that sought opportunities elsewhere after World War II are now returning, reclaiming land their forefathers had lost to post–Civil War poverty and Jim Crow. Descendants also have maintained many of the same values that guided their forefathers and preserved customs lost by most white Creole families. They are still recognized in their region as "the third caste" and still pride themselves on this status. The intensity of their commitment to the core values developed along Cane River has been well expressed by one transplant to Los Angeles, Louis Metoyer, editor of the Creole newspaper *Bayou Talk:*

> "We are one ethnic culture with . . . diverse ethnic inheritances that have enriched our culture over ten generations. All Creoles of today are educators of our culture. [O]ur parents and fore-parents [gave] us their knowledge of our heritage and the desire to be Creoles in our everyday lifestyle. With this knowledge we hold in our hearts the ability to live our culture in our daily lives in this modern-day era."[24]

This commitment to Creole culture in an era in which *Cajun* has become the iconic label for all things Louisianan propelled the 1998 creation of the

Louisiana Creole Heritage Center under the auspices of Northwestern State University at Natchitoches.

In yet another way, the people of the Cane River community are historically significant. As a rule, far fewer historical records exist on minority Americans than on the dominant white class, a factor that undeniably limits the depth of research that can be done. This generalization does not hold for Cane River's Creoles of color. Although many documents have been lost in the course of the past two centuries and many more have strayed to far-flung places, rich troves exist to chronicle almost every aspect of the community's past. There are, in fact, more documents dealing with them in public and private collections than can be found on most white families that settled their area—or the American South, for that matter.

The main challenge to a thorough study of this Cane River community was occasioned by the nature of the people themselves. The social uncertainty that members of this third caste felt from its inception, and especially the events and attitudes that have prevailed since the emancipation of all people of color, have produced a closely knit and reserved society. Betrayals by those they considered their friends cast suspicion on the motives of all "outsiders." More than a few members of the community were hesitant, initially, to talk to writers for fear they might be misrepresented or their statements might be presented in such a way as to offend their family and friends. A few were still afraid that whites in their area would take offense at suggestions of close friendship or even a blood kinship between their ancestors. After the initial release of *Forgotten People* and its favorable reception by white Creole families locally, those relationships are now quite openly embraced.

Still others among Cane River's Creoles of color have shunned whites and non-Creoles who come among them for a much more personal reason: they dislike hearing themselves referred to by terms that have been indiscriminately applied to people of African ancestry, specifically *Negro* and *mulatto*. As will be seen, Cane River's Creoles of color have consistently refused to identify themselves as Negro, and the term *mulatto* is particularly detested by many, despite the fact that it has been a universally applied term from the time the first children of mixed ancestry appeared in the colonies. Because the word *mulatto* has the same etymological base as *mule,* its connotation is especially offensive. Therefore, in the presentation of this study, the feelings of the people will be respected to every extent possible. No confidence will be intentionally betrayed. Offensive nomenclature will be avoided, except in the case of direct quotes from published works of others or from historical records. In the latter case, physical descriptions cannot be replaced with currently preferred language without muddying the evidence trail that will be used by future generations who might prefer still other terms.

With regard to terminology, it must be noted that considerable disagreement exists regarding the exact definition of the term *Creole* and the elements of Louisiana society to which this term should be applied. As Thomas Fiehrer has noted: "'Experts' have continuously volunteered definitions of the ambiguous term in a continuous discourse of defensive identity and cultural nostalgia. Typically, the reference comes down to each participant's real and often imagined neighborhood, group history, or community."[25]

This study uses *Creole* in the manner that prevailed in primary sources of the colonial and antebellum eras: to signify any person born in the colony of ancestry from abroad. (The exception here being Acadian exiles—popularly called Cajuns—who settled in south Louisiana and maintained a distinct ethnic identity.) *Creole* will not be limited here to Louisianans of pure-white descent, to the wealthy aristocracy of the state, or to the residents of the New Orleans–Baton Rouge area exclusively—a restriction popularized by white writers in the late nineteenth century. Nor does it carry the currently popular expectation of at least some African ancestry. The transplants from Europe and Africa who settled amid Louisiana's natives were a polyglot lot; not only the French and Spanish but Germans, Swiss, Irish, Canary Islanders, Roma, and others put down their roots along Louisiana's bayous, where they intermarried and intermixed in every conceivable configuration. Thus the concept that guides this study: *Creole is a culture, not a color.*

In a spirit of respect for the people of the Cane River community and for their story, every effort has been made here to present as objective a view as possible of the socioeconomic history of this exceptional group. Many findings uphold their traditions. Others cast those traditions in a different light or, quite conclusively, disprove them—an outcome that occurs in all families when lore is tested against documentary evidence. Should any inadvertent bias appear, it must be in favor of the society that persevered against such great odds.

ACKNOWLEDGMENTS (1977)

Light is the task where many share the toil.
—HOMER

W hile I would never assert that the completion of this study was a light or easy task, I do humbly admit that the work was lightened immeasurably by the generous assistance given by many of my friends and colleagues. My debt to each of these must be acknowledged.

It was Mr. Arthur Chopin Watson of Natchitoches who sparked my interest in the Cane River Creoles of color. A leading force in Louisiana's development for several decades, Mr. Watson has labored tirelessly to promote and perpetuate the rich heritage of the Cane River area. Without his encouragement and support, as well as that of the Association for the Preservation of Historic Natchitoches and its president, Dr. Ora V. Watson, who funded the initial part of this research, this study never would have materialized.

Special thanks are due to several of my colleagues for assistance, professional criticism, and encouragement. The perceptive and analytical suggestions of Dr. Arvarh E. Strickland of the University of Missouri and Dr. John Marszalek of Mississippi State University proved invaluable in shaping the manuscript. Dr. Jan Vansina of the University of Wisconsin provided vital assistance in pinpointing the African origins of the community's matriarch, and Dr. Jack D. L. Holmes of the University of Alabama at Birmingham generously assisted in locating elusive documents. Deep appreciation also is owed to Professors Roy V. Scott, Harold S. Snellgrove, and Glover Moore of Mississippi State University for their technical guidance throughout all the period in which this study evolved.

Equally vital to this project was the interest, assistance, and cooperation of various descendants of the Cane River community. I must express my

sincerest thanks to Mr. and Mrs. Lewis Emory Jones, Mrs. Lee Etta Vaccarini Coutii, Mr. and Mrs. Tillman Chelettre Sr., and Mrs. Noble Morin, all of
Natchez, Louisiana; to Mr. Hugh LaCour, Sr., of Shreveport, Louisiana; and
to those many others who assisted me in understanding their heritage but
wished to remain anonymous.

I am heavily indebted to Mr. Irby Knotts, the clerk of court for Natchi-
toches Parish, and to his very capable deputies, Mrs. Elaine Smith, Mr. Eddie
Gallien, and Mr. Douglas Knotts, as well as to the pastors of several Roman
Catholic churches of the area: Monsignor Henry F. Beckers, the Reverend
John Cunningham, and the Reverend Russell Lemoyne, former pastors of
the Immaculate Conception Church of Natchitoches; Monsignor Milburn
Broussard of the Church of St. John the Baptist, Cloutierville; and the Reverend William J. McElroy, former pastor of the Church of St. Augustine on
Isle Brevelle. For years these individuals not only patiently tolerated my
persistent presence in their archives but attempted, in every possible way,
to facilitate my use of them.

I also deeply appreciate the contributions of those people who, prompted
by friendship and an interest in history, offered whatever they could in the
way of materials, labor, encouragement, and hospitality: Mr. and Mrs. Robert B. DeBlieux, Mr. and Mrs. E. G. Mahan Jr., Mrs. Arthur C. Watson, Mr.
Francois Mignon, and Mrs. Ora G. Williams, all of Natchitoches; Mrs. Mildred McCoy of the Bayou Folk Museum, Cloutierville; Mr. and Mrs. E. A.
Rachal of Baton Rouge; and Mrs. Rowena E. Mulhern of Rayville, Louisiana.

Much assistance was provided by the staff of Mitchell Memorial Library,
Mississippi State University, and especially by Mrs. Martha Irby of that li-
brary's interlibrary loan department. A special debt is also owed to Mr. John
Price of the Eugene P. Watson Memorial Library at Northwestern State University of Louisiana; Mrs. Connie Griffith, formerly of the Howard-Tilton
Memorial Library at Tulane University; Mrs. Alberta Ducoté of the Louisiana
State Archives and Records Service; and Mrs. Helen Olivier, lands administrator of the Louisiana State Land Office. The staffs of the Louisiana State
University Library, the New Orleans Public Library, the Louisiana State Museum Library, the Office of the Keeper of the Notarial Archives, the Office of
the District Court, and the Catholic Life Center of Baton Rouge also deserve
special thanks for their assistance. Equally appreciated is the unlimited cooperation of the National Archives, Washington, D.C.; the Archivo General
de Indias at Seville; the Bibliothèque Nationale, Paris; and the Archives of
the Departments of Charente-Maritime and the Marne, France.

Foremost is the gratitude that I owe to my research assistant, genealogical consultant, typist, and keenest critic, my wife Elizabeth Shown Mills. Fortunate indeed have I been to have an assistant who is not only willing, versatile, and adept, but who is equally familiar with and interested in the history of the Cane River area.

GARY B. MILLS

UNIVERSITY OF ALABAMA, 1977

THE FORGOTTEN PEOPLE

Prologue

Chicago Tribune
August 1, 1943

Will someone please give me information about a little place called Cane River Lake, Louisiana? It's in the open country. The nearest towns are Natchitoches, Louisiana, and Cloutierville, Louisiana. While on maneuvers we had occasion to pass or travel on the bank of this river, or lake as it is called.

The people there were so nice to us. They gave us coffee and hot biscuits, creole gumbo, filet [*sic*], and rice. They were a bit shy and they spoke French and broken English, and one old lady read eighteenth century French for us in her prayer book and gave us her blessing. They call her Aunt Louise—Looy for short to everyone who knows her.

Their names are all old French names such as Du Pre, Chevalier, LeCaure, Mullon, Sarpy, Laubieu, Metoyer, St. Ville, Rachal, Monette, and Balthazar. They live in an old world, off to themselves, and have their own church, school and places of amusement. When asked who they were, one lady answered in French, "We are the forgotten people of America." That's all we could get out of them. I am on furlough in Chicago for ten days visiting my parents. Will some one please give me this information before I leave? I am very anxious to know as I am called Nosey by all my friends.

Pvt. James Holloway

The "forgotten people" who so intrigued Private Holloway were a legendary community of Creoles who have made the Isle Brevelle area of Louisiana's Cane River country their home for almost two centuries. The origins of this sprawling community are reflected not only in the names the people bear

1

but also in the varied hues that often, but not always, tint their skin. Cane River's "forgotten people" claim a variety of racial origins: French, Spanish, German, English, Indian, and African predominate. Their blend of cultures has been so cultivated that they have long been considered a distinct ethnic group in northwest Louisiana. Neither Caucasian nor Negroid, the families that comprise this community of Creoles had long been known among themselves and by outsiders, simply as "the People," "the people of Isle Brevelle" or, more recently, *Cane River Creoles.*

As with many labels that society places upon people, the place names attached to this community are, in one sense, misleading. Both Cane River, whose first non-native settlers were French soldiers and their wives, and Isle Brevelle, which was settled by a half-French, half-Caddo explorer-turned-farmer who wed the daughter of a French officer and planter, always have been and still are home to all three of Louisiana's historic castes. Private Holloway—like most visitors to the region—was struck and fascinated by the *unexpected:* the in-between caste that defied the stereotypes he had absorbed elsewhere in twentieth-century America.

When cotton was king in the South, Cane River's Creoles of color were noble subjects. Their plantations, stretching for thousands of acres along the Cane and graced by large and stately homes, were tilled by men and women held in bondage according to the custom of the times. But their wealth, prestige, and privilege vanished in the smoke of war and the upheaval of Reconstruction. Their unique status disappeared in the flood of freedmen. The memory of their former prominence faded from the minds of the dominant white society. It was then that the *gens de couleur libres* of Cane River and its best-known isle began to consider themselves the "forgotten people."

Within the confines of their own community, the past has never been forgotten. Indeed, the story of the community's origins and the recollections of life as it was once enjoyed have been proudly, almost religiously, immortalized. From *grandpère* to *demi-fille,* from *marraine* to *filleul,* the legend of their past was handed down, by word of mouth alone, through successive generations.

Like most legends, the story of this Cane River community has taken many variant forms. Every teller of tales does so in his own manner, and the natural infirmities of age often result in a blurring of time and events. In every family, ancestral lines and ethnicities become confused, and the origins and exploits of one lineage are attributed to another. Even greater digression occurred when popular writers of the twentieth century became intrigued with the story of the "forgotten people" and repeated it with their own embellishments—some of which, not surprisingly, have taken on an air of authenticity in tourism venues. The core of the legend is an unusually valid one, and when wheat is sorted from chaff, the reality of their lives sheds significant insight into a chapter of American history that truly has been forgotten. *The Forgotten People* explores that *reality,* reconstructing the history of this community from thousands of documents preserved not only in Louisiana but in the archives of numerous other states and countries to which its records have strayed.

But first, the legend deserves to be presented, as context for the history that follows. Attempting to separate the threads of family history, as originally passed down, from the embroidery of the *étrangers* is an impossibility, and the origins of many versions of the legend have already been explored elsewhere.[1] Beyond this, any attempt to extrapolate from the legend the mindset of the family inevitably falls victim to the biases introduced by many outside chroniclers. All handicaps considered, the gist of the composite legend is this:

⟶✦⟵

The Cane River community, we are told, owes its beginnings to a woman variously called Marie, Marie Thereze, or Coincoin. Of either African or Indian origins and the grandchild of a king, she was from her childhood a slave in the household of the commandant of the Natchitoches post, Sieur Louis Juchereau de St. Denis. The legendary Coincoin was outstanding even as a slave; her natural intelligence, her loyalty, and her devotion to duty soon made her a favored servant in the St. Denis household. Ultimately, these qualifications were to earn for her the one thing she most desired: freedom.

By most accounts, the event that gave her the chance to break the bonds of slavery and take the first step toward becoming the founder of this unique society was the illness of her mistress. Mme. de St. Denis was said to be in bad health, and the local physician could find no cure. Others were brought in from New Orleans, Mexico, and even France; their efforts were to no avail. The family was counseled to accept the will of God. But one member of the household, supposedly, refused to despair. Coincoin, who had gained from her African parents a knowledge of herbal medicines, begged for an opportunity to save the dying mistress whom she loved deeply. In desperation the family yielded to her entreaties, and to the bafflement of the educated physicians she accomplished her purpose. In appreciation, the St. Denis family rewarded her with the ultimate gift a slave can receive.

The gratitude of the St. Denis family, according to the legend, did not end with Coincoin's manumission. Through their influence, allegedly, she applied for and received a grant of land that contained some of the most fertile land in the community. With two slaves given to her by the family and many more whom she was to purchase later, this African woman, lore contends, carved from the wilderness a magnificent plantation.

These accomplishments did not come easily. Coincoin had labored hard as a slave and continued to do so as a free woman. Trees were cut and converted into barrel staves for the West Indian sugar trade. As the land was cleared, tobacco and, supposedly, indigo were planted for exportation to Europe. Indeed, according to legend, Coincoin was the first in the area to recognize the suitability of Natchitoches soil for the cultivation of the lucrative indigo plant. Only this dye, it was said, produced the desired depth of blue for the uniforms of European armies. Other products of a nonagricultural nature were also produced by the former slave. She and her slaves, some accounts aver, went into the woods to hunt native bears, not only for their hides but also for their grease, which was in demand in Europe to lubricate the axles of carriages and artillery pieces.

The center of this emerging agricultural empire, allegedly, was "Yucca Plantation," still extant and now a linchpin of the Cane River National Heritage Area. Here, Coincoin is said to have erected her home and auxiliary plantation buildings, and here again she seems to have exhibited her individuality—constructing her buildings, supposedly, in African style, adapted to Louisiana conditions and native materials.

Coincoin was a family woman, whose actions were calculated to benefit the offspring she left behind. At least one of her daughters, so the story goes, was born into slavery; Coincoin purchased that daughter and the daughter's son in order to give them their freedom. Most of her children, however, were of Franco-African descent, resulting from an alliance with a Frenchman at the Natchitoches post. Not just any Frenchman did she choose to share her life, but a man reputed to be the scion of a noble family, "Thomas" Metoyer. As her children entered adolescence and made their first communion according to religious customs of that time, Coincoin carved for each of them a wooden rosary. At least one such rosary was said to be treasured by her descendants until well into the twentieth century.

Before her death, according to local lore, Coincoin divided her extensive holdings among the children she had borne to Metoyer. For almost a half century following her death, the Metoyers of Cane River enjoyed a wealth and prestige few whites of their era could match. Gracious and impressive manor homes were erected on every plantation, furnished not only with the finest pieces that local artisans could make but also with imported European articles of quality and taste. Private tutors provided the children with studies in the classics, philosophy, law, and music. The young men of many families were sent abroad for the "finishing touches" that only a continental university could provide.

In spite of the racial limbo into which their origins placed them, the men of the family were said to be accepted and accorded equality in many ways by Cane River's white planters. It was not uncommon to find prominent white males at dinner in Metoyer homes (but not their females, a painful slight forced upon them by Louisiana's social codes), and the hospitality was returned. White planters brought their families to worship in the church erected by the community, the only one in its area for many decades. In a time and place in which there were no banking institutions, the Metoyers freely lent and borrowed, advised, and stood in solido with their white friends and neighbors. They were known as "French citizens" long after Louisiana was sold to the United States, and they held themselves aloof from the waves of "red-necked Americans" who settled in the poor pine woods that surrounded the rich Cane River plantations.²

The community was founded by Metoyers, but each successive generation saw the introduction of two or three new family names. Gens de couleur libres *from New Orleans, and allegedly Haiti, settled on the Isle; those whose background passed inspection intermarried with the community. Wealthy white planters of the parish arranged marriages for their own children of color with the offspring of their Metoyer friends. This new genetic input, carefully chosen, did much to protect the core family from the hazards of too-frequent intermarriage.*

For more than a half century this self-contained community flourished on Cane River. The people founded not only their own schools and church but also their own businesses and places of entertainment. The family's patriarch, Grandpère Augustin—the eldest Metoyer son of Coincoin—is said to have served for decades as judge and jury; his word was law and went unquestioned. It was his dream to make of the Isle a place for his people, not merely a home but a refuge from the new influx of greedy Americans who were battling white Creoles for control of Louisiana. By the end of the family's era of afflu-

ence, we are told, Cane River's Creoles of color had almost totally achieved the goal laid out for them by their beloved Grandpère.

A nationwide economic depression and increasingly restrictive legislation cracked the community's economic base in the mid-1800s. Several of their plantations were lost, one of the first of which was "Yucca"—the one now known as Melrose. Legend holds, not surprisingly, that a white man caused its downfall. After the death of Coincoin, some storytellers contended, the central portion of her plantation had been inherited by her son Louis, who in turn had bequeathed it to his son "Louis Jr.," who foolishly cosigned a note for a white planter, as he had often done before. This time, some say, the friend failed to meet his very sizable obligation, "Louis Jr." was held liable for the debt, and his plantation was lost at public auction.

Despite some individual bankruptcies, the community at large prospered until the eruption of the Civil War. Cane River's gens de couleur libres, like other southern planters, are said to have supported the doomed cause of the Confederacy; and they, like most planters, suffered the depredations of war and the financial ruin of Reconstruction. Unlike their white neighbors, however, after Reconstruction their ruin was complete; the reactionary political climate of the Redeemer period throttled their economic opportunities. The "liberation of all men" shackled the people of Isle Brevelle with anonymity; the equality proclaimed by the Union lost for them their special prestige. The community turned inward even more, finding now that they must not only protect themselves against status- and race-conscious whites but also against ambitious black freedmen.

⌀

While the reality of their history strays from much of the lore, both agree on one significant point. Throughout the remainder of the nineteenth century and well into the twentieth, the people of Isle Brevelle nurtured a sense that they were "forgotten people." They were forgotten by their former white friends who now saw all men of color as a threat, forgotten by the American government that had promised so much to Americans of African descent but provided so little, forgotten by a society that sacrilegiously abandoned the French heritage of which the people of Isle Brevelle were so proud, in favor of the American way of life that had brought them nothing but despair.

The Second World War, which thrust Private Holloway into the heart of Cane River country, accompanied a new era for the "forgotten people" of Isle

Brevelle. The new and more mobile society of the twentieth century brought more strangers, often cosmopolitan strangers, into their midst, strangers who were also curious about the origins of the people and who succeeded in obtaining from them answers to questions that Private Holloway did not obtain. Themselves storytellers by profession, many of these outsiders listened with delight to the stories that had been preserved and hastened to repeat them in their own venues. No serious attempt was made to document the stories; on the contrary, more interesting threads of fancy often were interwoven with the fabric of the legend.

Although no longer forgotten, the people of Isle Brevelle have faced a new challenge, a threat against the roots they have proudly cherished. The variations on the theme that developed in the twentieth century contained statements of such obvious fancy that a reaction set in and other writers disclaimed the entire legend as fiction. The survival of this legend as valid oral history is dependent upon its ability to withstand documentation. The chapters that follow present the evidence that chronicles the past of the Cane River people. The story that has emerged is, itself, as phenomenal as any claim of the embroidered legend.

ONE

A Fusion of Roots

In 1714 the intrepid French Canadian Louis Juchereau de St. Denis founded the first military post and colonial settlement in the region now known as northwest Louisiana. It was a strategic location he chose. Situated on the Red River[1] at the site of the Natchitoches Indian village, the post of St. Jean Baptiste des Natchitoches coexisted in harmony with the friendly natives. Located just fifteen miles from the presidio of Los Adaës, the easternmost outpost of Spanish Texas, Natchitoches served as a bulwark against Spanish aggression into French Louisiana and as a convenient base for private and surreptitious trade between the two nations.

The inevitable social intercourse between French, Spanish, and Indian neighbors ultimately affected the ethnic composition of the Cane River community, as well as the region as a whole. The colonial ancestors included at least one commandant each of the Natchitoches and Los Adaës posts; a number of French, Spanish, and German *habitans;* and women of the Caddo, Chitimacha, Lipan Apache, and Natchitoches tribes.

The traditions of the people of Isle Brevelle, relative to their ancestry, contain one fundamental paradox. Of their five primary bloodlines—French, African, Indian, Spanish, and German—it is the French heritage in which they have professed the most pride; yet it is an African woman whom they invariably identify as the nucleus around which their society developed. Proud, aristocratic and, above all, free, the clan considered itself a class apart from those who lived in servitude, but they never lost their admiration or respect for the exceptional black woman who generated their Cane River dynasty.

The African heritage of the people may be traced to the year 1735, when the earliest known progenitor was baptized, as an adult, at the Natchitoches post. Because Roman Catholic Louisiana insisted that all slaves be instructed in the Christian catechism and promptly and regularly administered the sacraments,[2] the fact that this slave was an adult not yet baptized indicates that he was a new arrival in the colony.

The presence of such a slave is particularly curious, in that eight years earlier the French colonial government had suspended the African slave trade. Slaves in the service of the crown were growing older and those still of childbearing years could not reproduce sufficient numbers to satisfy the demands of the swelling colonial population.[3]

Commandant St. Denis, however, was an entrepreneur of the first rank. Few men in the colony were as adept at legal commercial activities or the fine art of smuggling. For three dozen years the ingenious St. Denis had been valued by his French superiors and both respected and feared by the Spanish and Indians for his ability to achieve that which seemed impossible and to procure that which appeared unobtainable.[4] In the 1730s, when fresh supplies of African slaves were by law nonexistent, Commandant St. Denis and another prominent Natchitoches trader with Spanish connections succeeded in procuring several adult blacks.[5]

On December 26, 1735, Pierre Vitry, priest of the Company of Jesus newly assigned to the parish of St. François des Natchitoches, baptized one such slave for the commandant and gave to him the Christian name *François* after the man who had agreed to be his godfather, the surgeon François Goudeau.[6] The African's new master—or his Spanish wife—showed more than common concern for the souls they held in bondage. Thus, less than two weeks after François's baptism, he returned to the small, crude mission church at Natchitoches and wed a young black woman of the St. Denis household named Marie Françoise.[7] Whether the union was one of their own choosing or one mandated by their master is open to interpretation.

Louisiana's ecclesiastical and civil documents note tribal origins for some African slaves who received the sacraments or were involved in legal matters. No such information was recorded for François and Marie Françoise. The only clues to their origins are the African names they gave to five of their eleven children.[8] Contemporary documents created by various members of the St. Denis family refer to Marie Gertrude as Dgimby, Dhimby, Jinby, and Chimba.[9] The second-born child, François Jr., was known by a name written variously in these sources as Choera, Kiokera, and Quioquira.[10] His next-born brother, Jean Baptiste, carried the *dit* Chucha (*var.* Chocras).[11] Marie Thérèse, the second-born daughter, was repeatedly identified as Coincoin,

Quoinquin, KuenKuoin, and numerous other variant spellings,[12] while the tenth child and sixth daughter grew to adulthood using the name Yancdose (*var.* Yancdon).[13]

One leading Africanist historian, consulted in 1973, proposed probable origins for one of Coincoin's parents based on the three African names then known: Coincoin, Dgimby, and Choera. The most conclusive match, he believed, was the name Coincoin, whose phonetic equivalent, KoKwẽ, was used for second-born daughters by those who spoke the Glidzi dialect of the Ewe linguistic group in the Gold Coast–Dahomey region, more specifically the coastal communities of modern Togo.[14] When he made this proposal, he had not been told that Coincoin was indeed the second-born daughter in her sibling group.

Subsequent scholarship questions that linguistic or cultural origin. The classic ethnography apparently consulted by this scholar, Diedrich Westermann's *Die Glidyi-Ewe in Togo,* does carry one (but only one) reference to the name Kɔɔenb (pronounced *Kokwa*) as part of a fold-out genealogy that attributes the name to a second-born daughter. However, closer scrutiny of that genealogy indicates that the mother of that child was unknown but said by offspring to be of different blood (*"anderes blut"*). The fact that the mother's ethnicity is indeterminable raises the likelihood that the name's derivation lies elsewhere.[15] The two additional African names discovered since 1978, together with many additional variants for all five names, have laid the groundwork for a forthcoming study by a team of Africanist anthropologists, linguists, and historians.[16]

Regardless of tribal origins, François, Marie Françoise, or both obviously clung to a birth heritage in the midst of an alien environment. The African names they gave at least some of their children became their "call names" in the community, in obvious preference to the Christian names bestowed upon them by their masters. It has not been possible to reconstruct the life of Dgimby as an adult, but numerous later records exist for a son who perpetuated her African name;[17] and the lives of Coincoin, Choera, Chucha, and Yancdose are mapped in many civil and ecclesiastical documents. For the remainder of their lives, they continued to be known by their African names. Moreover, at least two of Coincoin's sons, and then their offspring, perpetuated her name as late as the fourth generation.[18] Tradition among her descendants also insists that, in addition to the official languages of her time, French and Spanish, she was fluent in an African dialect and that she was well trained by her parents in the native use and application of medicinal herbs and roots.[19]

The retention of some degree of African culture by François or Marie Françoise is typical of the reaction of many blacks transported to colonial America. One authority has concluded that first-generation African slaves "consistently refused to abandon their linguistic tie with their homeland."[20] Those determined to survive in the New World found it necessary to acquire some degree of fluency in the master language, if for no other reason than to be able to understand and follow commands. Yet a fair number seem to have acquiesced only grudgingly to their subjection and stubbornly refused to accept a new name. The most extensive study of the African transportees to Louisiana found "an often successful resistance to socialization through rejection of French names."[21]

Civil and ecclesiastical documents from the colonial and territorial periods record the existence of several such slaves on the Natchitoches frontier. François and Marie Françoise, however, provided a curious variation to the general rule. While they gave African names to at least five of their children (and, logically, the rest as well), there is no indication that they continued to use African names of their own. Various rationales might be proposed, but the evidence suggests one possibility. For Marie Françoise, as with François, no record indicates how the St. Denis family acquired her. Unlike François, there is no baptism for her as an adult at the Natchitoches post. If she had been purchased[22] and baptized prior to the permanent arrival of a priest, that baptism may have been performed by a priest from Los Adaës and recorded in the long-missing registers from that post. She could also have been born into the St. Denis household at Natchitoches and baptized by a Los Adaës pastor. In that case, her failure to use an African name, when her own children carried them, would suggest two things relevant to this study. If born into her mistress's birth household in the Spanish borderlands or Mexico, then she would have been Creolized already and may have felt no cultural affinity for Africa at all. Two, the names given to the couple's children would then, more likely, reflect François's African origin, rather than that of Marie Françoise.

Whatever their origin, the couple provided an example of family solidarity that would characterize their descendants for centuries to come. In this respect, at least partial credit must be given to the particular system of slavery under which they served. One of the inhumane aspects of many slave systems has been the lack of opportunity for bonded men and women to establish permanent relationships and solid family ties. In most eras and locales, slaves have been sold at the will of their master; husbands and wives have been separated, children taken from their parents. In French Louisiana, this evil was somewhat curtailed. Article 43 of the *Code Noir* proclaimed by Governor Jean Baptiste Le Moyne, Sieur de Bienville in 1724 specifically stated:

> Husbands and wives shall not be seized and sold separately when belonging to the same master; and their children, when under fourteen years of age, shall not be separated from their parents, and such seizures and sales shall be null and void. The present article shall apply to voluntary sales, and in case such sales should take place in violation of the law, the seller shall be deprived of the slave he has illegally retained, and said slave shall be adjudged to the purchaser without any additional price being required.[23]

In the first decades of colonial Natchitoches this regulation was generally respected. Thus, from the time of their marriage until their concurrent deaths, François and Marie Françoise were never separated by sale from each other or from their children. As their oldest daughter, Dgimby, matured and became a mother herself, she remained in her parents' household, and the older couple was blessed to experience the day-to-day growth of their first grandchild.

Commandant Louis Juchereau de St. Denis died at the Natchitoches post on June 11, 1744, and was buried within the parish church.[24] In the last years of his life St. Denis had suffered serious financial reverses in his effort to keep the frontier post afloat; but none of those he enslaved had been sold to rectify his finances. As a consequence, he left many debts and nearly three dozen Africans, at least one Indian woman of the Natchez tribe, and her children by an African slave. Because most of his children were minors, his estate was not settled until the last of them reached majority. The first partition of those slaves occurred in September 1756, at which time the Widow St. Denis chose the family of François and Marie Françoise as a substantial part of her share.[25]

Less than two years later, an epidemic struck the St. Denis compound. On April 16, 1758, the Widow St. Denis was buried in the post cemetery; the nature of her death precluded any thought of burying her beside her husband in the parish church. Three days later her slaves François and Marie Françoise were also interred.[26] Their youngest infant, born on Marie Françoise's deathbed, would die eight days later.[27]

Within days the slaves of the St. Denis household were partitioned again, this time among the children and grandchildren of the deceased commandant and his wife. No alternative existed now to separating the orphaned children of François and Marie Françoise. By lot, each of the six heirs drew one or two of the slave children.[28] Marie Thérèse Coincoin and her brother Jean Baptiste Chucha were inherited by Louis Antoine Juchereau de St. Denis, the eldest son of the deceased commandant.[29]

Of the eleven children born to François and Marie Françoise, nine were destined to live and die in the state of anonymity from which few slaves ever escaped. The tenth, Marie Louise *dite* Mariotte, eventually bought her own freedom and that of a daughter, with money earned as a *médicine,* but died in poverty.[30] Only Coincoin could be deemed successful. With loyalty, determination, foresight, ingenuity, and a considerable degree of business acumen, she and one lot of her children challenged the stigma of slavery branded upon them by birth. Engineering their own fate, they would become the respected proprietors of an imposing and, ultimately, legendary plantation operation.

That success was not easily or quickly accomplished. Numerous records contradict the legend that she was given her freedom by the Widow St. Denis, along with a vast grant of land from the king himself. Coincoin was still a slave at the widow's death in 1758 and would remain in bondage for twenty years more. Nothing is known of her life during the first ten of those years, except the fact that she presented seven children to the parish priest for baptism and had two of them sold away from her in violation of the *Code Noir.*[31]

The registers of St. François des Natchitoches clearly reflect the state of religion that shaped Coincoin's mindset as she entered adulthood without parents to guide her. The settlers were Roman Catholic by birth, and Catholicism was the state religion. However, the settlement was fifteen years old before the mother church could provide a priest. In the interim, pastors from the nearby Spanish post of Los Adaës occasionally crossed Red River into the French colony to say mass and administer sacraments; but the piety of the Natchitoches flock suffered from the lack of a spiritual shepherd on a daily basis. When Louisiana's vicar-general dispatched a Capuchin to Natchitoches in 1729, that cleric's tenure was short-lived. He quickly locked horns with Commandant St. Denis, who wanted his first-born son baptized by a Spanish friar, and the Capuchin was "encouraged" to leave. Another five years would pass before an acceptable replacement arrived.[32]

Natchitoches should not, however, be considered Louisiana's wayward child. The colony as a whole suffered from inadequate religious and civil leadership—so much so that one chronicler dubbed it *"sans religion, sans justice, sans discipline, sans ordre, et sans police."*[33]Although Louisiana society underwent considerable improvement throughout the colonial period, organized religion still suffered, especially at Natchitoches. Indeed, for over a century after its settlement—under French, Spanish, and American regimes—there were to be many periods when Natchitoches had no clergyman to baptize its infants, marry its youth, bury its dead, hear confession, or offer regular mass.[34]

During their lives, Commandant and Mme. St. Denis were bulwarks of the local religious congregation, such as it was. They insisted upon the practice of Christian principles among their slaves and saw to it that their slaves were regularly administered the sacraments, when priests were available. Thus, François had been provided with a wife shortly after his arrival at the post, or, possibly, he had been purchased as a husband for their slave Marie Françoise. Most area residents followed the St. Denis example, but religious discipline did not long outlive their hegemony. By the 1760s the parish registers reflect a radical plunge in slave marriages and an explosion of "natural births" to black mothers.[35]

Like most female slaves who reached maturity during this period, Coincoin was not provided with (or forced to choose) a husband by her owners. Nor, apparently, was she encouraged to adhere to the Christian marital codes by which white colonists also had difficulty living. Although the elder St. Denis and wife have been lauded for their piety, some of their children fell short of the parents' example, and the moral laxity they displayed had a significant effect upon their slaves. Indeed, the first six slave infants identified in the parish registers as *mulâtres* were all born into the households of the Widow St. Denis, her sons, and sons-in-law.[36] As historian John Blassingame has pointed out, when members of the self-proclaimed superior race violated with impunity their own code of sexual morality, it is not surprising that their slaves did likewise.[37] Upon reaching maturity Coincoin was left to follow her own spiritual compass.

Economic conditions were in part responsible for the relaxation of Christian precepts that occurred in the slave households of the St. Denis youth. The wealth the commandant had once enjoyed had included slaves of all ages, which made pairing easier for those he held in bondage. His reversal of fortunes, the division of his estate among six heirs, and the trade restrictions imposed upon them under the Spanish political regime that soon followed[38] all reduced the slave holdings of most of the heirs. Louis Antoine, specifically, owned no males of appropriate age with whom he could pair young Coincoin—at the time he owned no male other than her brother—and marriage between slaves belonging to different masters was not a common practice at Natchitoches.

Nonetheless, the institution of slavery in North America vested much of a slave woman's value in her fertility. Coincoin well met expectations. In 1759, the year following her acquisition by the older St. Denis son, the seventeen-year-old girl gave birth to her first child. This daughter, Marie Louise, was described by colonial records as black (i.e., *négritte, negra,* and *négresse*—terms consistently used in her place and time for those of full African ancestry). In 1761, while still the property of St. Denis, Coincoin produced her second daughter; this one, also black, received her mother's Christian name, Thérèse.[39]

At some point between 1761 and 1766 Coincoin and her children became the property of her master's youngest sister, Marie des Nieges de St. Denis, wife of Antonio Manuel de Soto Bermúdez.[40] No record of the conveyance survives. During this period a visiting priest, Fr. Ygnacio María Laba, baptized her third child, Françoise, without specifying the infant's racial composition; subsequent documents, however, would also cite her as black.[41] Two black sons would follow in the next three years: Nicolas "Chiquito" (who would later take the *dit* Coincoin) and Jean Joseph in 1766.[42] The baptismal record of this fifth child indicates an improvement in Coincoin's status. This time she was allowed to choose his godparents: her brother Jean Baptiste, still the slave of Louis Antoine de St. Denis, and one Marie Louise, who could have been either her sister or her eldest, same-name daughter.[43]

Legend insists that Coincoin was emancipated as a reward for saving the life of her dying mistress. No records can be found that effectively support or negate this claim. It is known that her last mistress, Marie de St. Denis (as she called herself, in traditional European fashion, throughout her long marriage to de Soto), was bedridden from the age of forty-five.[44] Several relevant documents also suggest that the hard-nosed daughter of the old commandant held a tender spot in her heart for this slave, who was also her goddaughter. For the remainder of her life the lady was to grant Coincoin and her children a number of favors, and at one point she vigorously

COINCOIN'S FIRST FAMILY

Marie Thérèse Coincoin ——┬—— **Unknown**
b. Aug. *c*23, 1742, Natchitoches
d. *c*1816, Cane River

Marie Louise	**Thérèse Don Manuel**	**Marie Françoise**
b. Sept. 7, 1759	b. Sept. 23, 1761	b. Jul. 1763
Freed 1786–95 by Coincoin	d. Feb. 4, 1831, Opelousas	d. aft. May 31, 1827
(?) Placée of Ant. Coindet	Freed 1790–95 by Coincoin	Freed Jul. 23, 1819, by
No known offspring	*Many offspring, surname*	A. Cloutier
	Victorin	

Remy	**Charles Monette**	**Marie Jeanne**	**Henry**	**Hortense**
b. *c*1779	b. *c*1783	b. *c*1785	b. Oct. 1787	b. 1789–93
	d. May 1827, free	d. young		d. aft. 1815
	Child of Ls. Monet			*Left offspring*

Marie Louise Le Comte
b. Nov. 26, 1781
Child of Ambroise Le Comte
Freed 1835 by son Louis

Louis Monette
b. Dec. 25, 1802
Child of Ls. Monet
Freed 1825 by his
father's widow

Nicolas "Chiquito"
b. 1764–65
d. Apr. 11, 1850
Freed 1793–97 by Coincoin
No known offspring

Jean Joseph
b. Feb. 21, 1766
Purchased by Metoyer, 1776
No proved evidence thereafter

Pierre
b. 1789–93

Marie Jeanne
b. 1797
Left offspring

Thérèse
b. Aug. 20, 1799

Rose
b. 1801
Left offspring

François Nicolas Monette
b. *c*Sept. 1795
Child of Ls. Monet
Free by 1835

Marie Zelia Monette
b. 1820
Slave of Gen. F. Gaiennié
Freed 1835 by her father

defended her slave against detractors. Considering these bonds, possibly the mistress did owe a debt of gratitude for service rendered in one way or another.

The actual accomplishment of Coincoin's freedom, however, is more validly accredited to a happenstance that she may (or may not) have personally leveraged. Toward the end of 1766, there appeared at the Natchitoches post a young Frenchman named Claude Thomas Pierre Metoyer.[45] Together with a friend from La Rochelle, Étienne Pavie, Metoyer had recently emigrated to the colony—not as a soldier or colonial administrator, as some have written, but as an entrepreneur. At Natchitoches, Metoyer and Pavie went into partnership as merchants and taverners, joined the local militia (home guard) as the colonial law required of all able-bodied males, and eventually parlayed their profits into prosperous planting operations.[46]

Tradition among Metoyer descendants, both white and part-white, boasts that he came from a "noble" French family. Records from his French homeland place his family in the merchant class, albeit well-to-do bourgeoisie. He had been born on March 12, 1744, at La Rochelle, where his father had migrated from Rheims in the province of Champagne.[47] Attempts to trace the Metoyer family before Rheims have been unsuccessful. The will Metoyer drew at Natchitoches in 1801 speaks of a chateau of eleven rooms, some miles distant from the town of Rheims, that he had inherited from a late uncle, the priest Jorge Metoyer. Père Metoyer, reportedly, had also bequeathed to him a set of silver flatware and dishes engraved with the family name.[48] All this attests that the Metoyers of Rheims were affluent. However, given that the family name and its variant spellings (Metayer, Mettoyer) translate as "yeoman farmer" or "sharecropper," the traditional claims of nobility do not appear likely.

In a small post the size of Natchitoches, the new merchant would have soon met Mme. de Soto's slave. No accounts of Coincoin's personal characteristics have been found, but her appearance was obviously comely and her personality appealing. She was already twenty-five and the mother of five children, in a society in which feminine beauty was short-lived. Few colonial women could afford imported creams, lotions, and soaps; most rubbed themselves with bear or sheep fat to soften the damage from home-brewed soaps made from lye and ashes.[49] Yet, despite her years and the factors that prematurely aged colonial women, Coincoin was to attract a city-bred Frenchman who was, in fact, two years her junior; and she would hold his affection until well into the fifth decade of her life.

Within months of his arrival, Metoyer had persuaded Mme. de Soto to lease to him her black slave. In payment for her services he promised to provide her room and board, and Coincoin moved into the bachelor's home.[50] In 1771 this arrangement was made illegal when the Cabildo at New Orleans ruled that owners of slaves were henceforth prohibited from hiring them out.[51] As with many such regulations, however, enforcement at posts as distant as Natchitoches was extremely lax. In this instance the parties involved had a double advantage, for the newest commandant at the post was again a brother-in-law of Mme. de Soto, Athanase Christophe Fortunat Mauget de Mézières.[52] The de Soto–Metoyer lease agreement continued after the passage of the new law.

The first children of this French-African alliance were born in January 1768, a set of twins, who would be baptized into the Catholic faith the following week. One circumstance of their baptism was as unorthodox as their parentage. The French and Spanish Catholics of Natchitoches primarily followed the continental custom of having their children named by and for their godparents; and that practice extended to their slaves. Coincoin's father, for example, had been given the baptismal name François by and for his godfather, the surgeon François Goudeau. Pierre Metoyer, born in La Rochelle, likewise carried the Christian name of his godfather, Pierre Draperon. However, Metoyer partially broke with convention in naming his own children. To his first-born son, he gave the name of his own father, Nicolas Augustin; his daughter, he named Marie Susanne, the name borne by the stepmother who had raised him, Marie Susanne Vinault. When the children were presented at the baptismal font a week after their birth, he chose the military officer Maraffret Laissard as godfather of both twins. Perhaps prophetically, the godmothers were the teenaged Marie Louise and Marie Françoise Buard, whose sister Pierre would eventually marry after he set aside his black mistress.[53]

Baptismal records for the parish of Natchitoches are nonexistent for Coincoin's next several childbearing years—specifically between the Christmas season of 1769 and the summer of 1775—even though a priest was in residence for most of that time. A tumultuous, fifteen-year struggle between officers of the church and state at Natchitoches resulted in the clerical abandonment of the parish during Holy Week of 1774. Possibly, the departing priest—as another act of defiance against the commandants he had battled, both of them St. Denis sons-in-law—took sacramental folios with him when he left the colony.[54] Amid the resulting lacunae, three more Metoyer children were born and baptized. As best can be determined from later records, their births were normally spaced, with Louis arriving in 1770, Pierre in 1772, and Dominique in 1774. In January 1776, a newly arrived Spanish priest baptized the sixth Metoyer child, Marie Eulalie. With the discretion convention demanded, Padre Luis de Quintanilla entered into his register the customary statement: "father unknown."[55]

Within a year of his arrival, Fr. Quintanilla also left Natchitoches in a pique, if not a rage. Because no priest was available to take his place, Commandant de Mézières petitioned for his return, and Quintanilla was ordered back upriver. The reason for his 1777 departure is not stated in surviving records, but the letter he took with him upon his return, addressed by Governor Bernardo de Gálvez to the commandant, suggests an explanation. After praising the priest as a worthy man, Gálvez closed with strong advice: "I therefore recommend that you treat him well and protect him as far as you can in order that he may remain willingly in that district."[56] Gálvez did not elaborate as to what protection Quintanilla needed, or from whom he needed it. However, the events of the year to come clearly indicate that his major foes were his own zealousness and his own flock.

By early fall Quintanilla was embroiled in controversy, and his would-be protector, de Mézières, was caught in the middle. Upon Quintanilla's return, he had found Coincoin pregnant again, and his conscience could no longer let him ignore the situation at which his parishioners winked. Her relationship with Metoyer, which so upset Quintanilla, was the frontier's most overt symptom of what contemporary clerics considered a plague: a quasi-marriage custom called *plaçage*. One bishop complained that "a good many inhabitants live almost publicly with colored concubines," and did not even "blush" when they carried their illegitimate offspring "to be recorded in the registries as their natural children."[57] A later judicial decision attempted to explain these extralegal unions: "There were at that time but few of the white women in the colony, and hardly any of equal condition with the officers of the government and of the troops stationed here[;] the inevitable consequence was that these gentlemen formed connections with women of color. This custom coming as it did from the ruling class soon spread throughout the colony."[58]

The factors promoting miscegenation in Louisiana were not unique to the French and Spanish; they also prevailed in the earliest days of the Eastern Seaboard colonies. Commenting on the scarcity of white women in the English provinces, one early historian noted that "the intermixture of races had become so extensive by the end of the colonial period that many mulattoes seem to have lost all the distinguishing physical features of the Negro."[59] Despite drastic efforts to control interracial sex among English subjects, intermixing continued. "The process of miscegenation was part of the system of slavery," another classic authority explains; "the dynamics of race contact and sex interest were stronger than prejudice, theory, law or belief. . . . Every traveler in the South before the Civil War commented on the widespread miscegenation."[60]

Natchitoches reflected that norm. A census of the post taken shortly before Metoyer's arrival identifies, for the "white" class, 127 "men bearing arms," but only 75 females past puberty.[61] (That "white" class also included one free half-African male called *mulata,* one free Indian female identified as such, and several men and women of French and Indian parentage who were routinely treated as white at the post.[62]) This gender imbalance is reflected in the premarital and extramarital pregnancy rate of females at Natchitoches. Premarital conceptions among white women were substantially below the rates reported for comparative societies in the English colonies and abroad; but the baptismal registers of the parish are rife with references to slave children whose fathers were white.[63] In these other cases of miscegenation, the men exercised some discretion. However, Metoyer lived in open plaçage with the black slave of his choice. Thus, they became the prime target in the cleric's crusade to reform public morals.[64]

Two months after his return to the post, Quintanilla filed a formal complaint with Commandant de Mézières:

> Fr. Luis de Quintanilla, Capuchin Religious and Parish curate of the abovesaid Post, has the honor of representing to His Majesty that, perceiving himself compelled by virtue of his ministry to eradicate the vices and relate the scandals as these originate, not having been able after much diligence to place a control on the scandalous concubinage of a Negress named Cuencuen, slave of Dn. Manuel de Soto, hired for many years to the named Metoyer in whose house and company the said Negress has produced (not being married) five or six mulattoes and mulattresses, not including in this number the one with whom she is now pregnant; and as this cannot happen in the house of an unmarried man and an unmarried woman without the public thinking and judging there to be illicit intercourse between the two partners in cohabitation, from which ensues a great scandal and damage to the souls; and according to the mandate

sent to the petitioner by his Superior, the Most Illustrious Senor, Bishop of Cuba, that "in case these concubinages do not cease after apostolic counsel the concubines must deliver themselves to the Royal Court of Justice so that they can be coerced and punished . . . these concubines should make use, Your Reverence, of the apostolic means, they should be persuaded to sanctify their bad concubinage by the union of matrimony and, if after all this, they persist, denounce them, Your Reverence, to the Royal Court of Justice so that they can be forced to do so and the scandal can be removed"—

The petitioner, in consideration of this, denounces to Your Majesty the aforesaid Negress Cuencuen as a public concubine in order that Your Majesty deign to castigate her according to the law, prohibiting her under grave punishment ever to go into the house of the mentioned Metoyer in order to avoid public scandal, having commanded her owner to look after that, so that she not bring more upon herself by similar sins, because of other ways of exposing herself to losing her Negress. Justice, which waits for the conscientiousness of Your Majesty, October 23, 1777.

Fr. Luis de Quintanilla, who is supreme[65]

In response to the curate's request, de Mézières issued a ruling that same day ordering Metoyer to abandon the slave woman, to expel her permanently from his home and his service, never to buy her, and to affirm that he had no desire to cause further scandal or disgrace. In drafting this order, however, the commandant made an error that may well have been intentional. Throughout the months this case dragged on, both Fr. Quintanilla and Coincoin's mistress repeatedly identified her slave solely by her African name—obviously, the name by which she was routinely known in that community. In de Mézières's order, however, he ignored the name by which both the complaints and the rejoinders identified the slave woman and substituted what would be the *official* name—the one under which slaves were baptized. In doing so, he misidentified Coincoin as Marie *Gertrude,* the name of her older sister. Intentionally or not, that misidentification provided a loophole by which Metoyer could continue his relationship with her without being in violation of the commandant's order. Upon receipt of the order, Metoyer made a show of complying, then petitioned de Mézières to release him from the contract he had made with Mme. de Soto, under the terms of which he was to furnish Coincoin's board as payment of the rent for her services.[66]

The Spanish priest thought he had succeeded. The slave woman had been ordered from Metoyer's household, their public concubinage was ostensibly prohibited, and the scandal was theoretically eradicated. Quintanilla's satisfaction, however, was short-lived. Early in 1778 the duties of de Mézières's office as commandant and lieutenant governor sent him to Texas. In February 1778, he posted a letter from the presidio of San Antonio de Bexar, and from there he led an expedition to the Indian nations on the upper Trinity, Brazos, and Red rivers. At least three months passed before he returned to Natchitoches. Meanwhile, Coincoin moved back into Metoyer's home.[67]

In June the outraged Quintanilla greeted the newly returned commandant with a second protest. The first had been directed mainly against Metoyer and had brought no permanent results. This time the priest demanded that Coincoin's owner be commanded to "put away" her slave in her house and forbid any further resumption of this unsanctioned alliance with the Frenchman. Moreover, Quintanilla took this opportunity to castigate Metoyer for his failure to perform his obligations as a "true Christian" and a Catholic; in the two years Quintanilla had been at the post, he swore, Metoyer had not complied with the requirement of annual confession and communion. The curate's denouncement ended with a threat to take the matter to higher authorities, the governor or even the viceroy, if de Mézières (because of his relationship to the recalcitrant Mme. de Soto) was not willing or able to see that justice was done. Again the priest authoritatively signed his protest "Fr. Luis de Quintanilla, who is supreme."[68]

By directly involving Marie des Nieges Juchereau de St. Denis de Soto in this issue, Quintanilla made a grave mistake. This youngest daughter of Natchitoches's founder was a woman whose character was as formidable as her name. The notarial records of the Natchitoches post where she was born, the Opelousas post where she died, and the correspondence files of the contemporary governors all attest her forcefulness and determination. Like her father, Mme. de Soto usually accomplished that which she set out to do.

The basic issue raised by Quintanilla, the "scandalous conduct" of her African slave and this French gentleman, was a trifle in the eyes of Mme. de Soto. Prejudice against the African races did not reach any degree of intensity in French society until the late eighteenth century, and even then, it was short-lived. Until France's 1778 prohibition of marriage between the races, African members of French society were considered more or less "exotic," and even the illustrious Louis XIV reportedly had a Negro mistress.[69]

In true French tradition, Mme. de Soto considered *l'amour* to be a private affair, beyond the understanding of holy priests whose hearts were armored by their vows of celibacy and lives of constant prayer. Scandal, moreover, was not a new experience to the lady; she had weathered her own gales of gossip when she bore a child out of wedlock in 1750.[70] As with other nonconforming girls at the Natchitoches post, the incident had not prevented her from making an acceptable marriage, and she had long since assumed her expected role as a leader of Natchitoches society.

Moreover, Coincoin's mistress was in 1778 a very lonely woman whose life and marriage had been upended by Spanish authority. Her husband, prior to his settlement at the French post, had been secretary to the governor of Texas. Amid accusations of subversive activities, he had deserted to French Louisiana. Because he also had recently married the daughter of the late St. Denis, by which he became the brother-in-law of St. Denis's successor in the commandant's post César de Blanc, de Soto's position in the French colony was secure.[71] The French, after so many years of Franco-Spanish rivalry in the colonies, were not inclined to fault a gentleman for an offense against the Spanish government.

In 1762 Don Manuel's position changed drastically. When Louis XV of France ceded the Louisiana colony to his cousin Charles III of Spain, the country in which de Soto had sought refuge against Spanish justice suddenly came under Spanish control. For seven years, his fate remained in limbo; his 1763 request for a pardon served only as a stopgap measure.[72] In 1769, Spain's military genius, Alexandro O'Reilly, established the first authoritative Spanish regime in Louisiana, and de Soto's political game was lost. Late that year, General O'Reilly reported: "The Viceroy of New Spain has sent me a legal order requesting the arrest of Don Manuel Bermudez de Soto, secretary of the former Governor of the Province of Texas. This man . . . knew the province well and had many friends there, none of whom, however, was of any help to him. Due to my orders he was arrested and delivered to the Commander of the Presidio of Adaes."[73] From Los Adaës, de Soto was transferred to Mexico, where he was to spend nearly a decade in political confinement. In the meantime, his wife was left a *sole feme,* struggling to support her family with only the aid of her flock of children and female slaves.[74]

The affair of the de Soto slave and Pierre Metoyer offered an opportunity for Mme. de Soto to vent her anger against Spanish authorities, and she well exploited it. In a lengthy and scorching redress, directed to de Mézières, she launched a defense of her slave and the man with whom Coincoin had— willingly or not—cast her lot.

Quintanilla's latest charges, according to Mme. de Soto, were "willful" and "inflammatory," designed to "attack her honor and trouble the tranquility of the Post." It should have been obvious to him, in view of the commandant's order of last October barring the slave from Metoyer's home, that Coincoin would not have resumed living with the gentleman even during the commandant's absence. But if Quintanilla chose to believe local wagging tongues rather than her own testimony, then he must consider well the degree of support that she, Mme. de Soto, was providing to Quintanilla's church, as well as the furnace and mill she had donated.[75] Moreover, she was providing a residence for the religious brothers of St. Antoine and had every legal right to require them to work for her in payment for their upkeep.[76]

The fact that Coincoin had produced seven children of mixed blood while living in Metoyer's home and the fact that Metoyer had already purchased four of these children from Mme. de Soto were both irrelevant, the lady argued. Was the Reverend Father ready to accuse all masters whose slaves had produced such children? Moreover, "public belief" in the existence of a plaçage between this couple did not constitute certain knowledge and certainly not legal proof; without proof, Quintanilla had no case. The curate's charge that Metoyer lacked religious devotion was likewise of little import. If Metoyer failed to approach the confessional, he was merely following the example of almost all the post. She, herself, made a practice of leaving mass before the commencement of Quintanilla's tedious and disagreeable sermons, delivered for two to three hours in atrociously mispronounced French idioms and violent, scandalous language.[77]

The Reverend Father also had two faces, the lady challenged. While he preached against avarice, he indulged in it. No longer did he affix to the door of the church, as had been customary, the tax on burials, thereby concealing the fact that he charged more than his predecessors. Indeed, in her view, he followed unfair practices of taxation by which poor people were disproportionately charged, and their taxes were distributed among more fortunate inhabitants whose labors did provide sufficient means upon which to live.[78]

The temerity of the Spanish priest, Mme. de Soto charged, even extended to the encroachment upon civil powers, exercising "with despotism a right that does not belong to him." In support of this charge, she cited a litany of instances in which Quintanilla had, at least in her estimation, meddled in affairs that should not have concerned him[79]—at least some of which were situations in which he had stepped on the lady's toes, rather than overstepped the bounds of his office.[80] In summary, Mme. de Soto requested that de Mézières refer both Quintanilla's charges and her own to his religious superior, the vicar general of the colony.[81]

The only other existing document filed in this case is the curate's reply to the lady's attack. Quintanilla acknowledged receipt of de Mézières's letter informing him of Mme. de Soto's remarks. He was not worried and had no objection to a review of the facts by the vicar general. He did, however, want to know what the commandant intended to do about his sister-in-law, her slave, and the Sieur Metoyer. This time, for the first time, Quintanilla signed his petition in a drastically less confident (or, perhaps, sarcastic) manner: "Your Majesty's attentive servant and chaplain, Fr. Luis de Quintanilla, *humble* Capuchin."[82]

The legal disposition of this case, if it ever occurred, is no longer a matter of record. The events that followed attest Quintanilla's failure to end the Metoyer-Coincoin affair. His mission, in fact, had been doomed from the outset. The commandant to whom he had complained had no inclination to interfere in the private lives of his subjects and well understood the human weaknesses that led to transgressions against the Christian commandments. De Mézières himself fathered and quietly manumitted at least one illegitimate child of color and would eventually succumb to what his contemporaries delicately termed "the pox."[83]

Even so, Quintanilla may be credited with achieving a significant good for Coincoin, albeit not that which he had intended. He envisioned for her the most important goal in any Christian life: salvation of the soul. Tradition among her descendants holds that this was not a consideration she took lightly; her descendants strongly assert that she remained as faithful to Metoyer as any Christian wife was expected to be and that she died a devout Catholic. While assertions of descendants typically reflect their own values more than those of forebears they never knew, their suppositions and values are well grounded in this instance. Coincoin was not Metoyer's wife and, in defiance of Christian precepts, she stayed with him until he left her for another; no evidence suggests she ever strayed from that course.

Although Quintanilla counseled Coincoin and Metoyer to marry, his advice was impractical. Metoyer was French; Coincoin was an African Creole. Had they lived in France and had she not been enslaved, there would have been no legal impediment to the marriage before 1778. However, the *Code Noir* of colonial Louisiana had adopted a more stringent policy, as a means of maintaining the critical caste barrier and power structure between free men and slaves. Any marriage between a white and a black slave would have resulted in the couple's expulsion from the colony.[84] Perhaps Quintanilla was ignorant of the law, or else he placed God's law above Caesar's. In any case, the priest's advice was ignored.

The expulsion of Coincoin from Metoyer's household presented additional problems for Metoyer. The children born to them were legally the property of the mother's owner, the de Sotos. As noted in Quintanilla's first complaint, Metoyer had already purchased four of these children in order to prevent their sale in the event something should happen to their mistress.[85] The children were now legally a part of Metoyer's household, but their mother was not. Reestablishment of a normal family relationship could never be effected as long as Coincoin remained the property of Mme. de Soto and Quintanilla continued his opposition.

Therefore, in July 1778, Metoyer reached an agreement with Mme. de Soto for the purchase of Coincoin and the son who had been born to her since her expulsion, Antoine Joseph. Lacking funds to pay the full price, 1,500 livres, he paid half and assumed responsibility for a financial obligation of Mme. de Soto that equaled the remainder he owed her.[86] Although de Mézières had ordered Metoyer not to purchase the slave woman he had expelled from Metoyer's household, the commandant's order was ignored. He, in turn, reciprocated by ignoring Metoyer's defiance.

The transfer of Coincoin's title enabled the couple to resume their cohabitation; but it presented its own complications. The *Code Noir* further decreed that any master who fathered children by his own slave should suffer the loss of mother and child; both would be sold for the benefit of the hospital and forever denied freedom.[87] Metoyer's alliance with Coincoin had already produced seven children; undoubtedly more would result, and it was obviously not his desire to forfeit Coincoin and the next child born to them. Thus, shortly after the execution of the 1778 purchase, Metoyer called in two friends and neighbors. Taking advantage of the liberal manumission policy of the Spanish government, he declared, in a private document drawn before his friends, that Coincoin and "her" infant son Joseph were henceforth free.[88]

Within a year, the commandant who had shielded Metoyer and Coincoin from the brunt of Quintanilla's wrath was transferred to San Antonio de Bexar to assume the governorship of Texas. There he died, within weeks of his arrival.[89] For the first time in the sixty-five-year history of the Natchitoches post, no member of the St. Denis family controlled frontier affairs. Dubious of prospects under a newly appointed commandant from elsewhere,

Metoyer and the de Sotos arranged to move their households downriver to the post of Opelousas, at the forefront of an exodus by those who sought to escape Quintanilla's overweening ministrations.[90]

Coincoin was now thirty-eight and the mother of twelve children, with three more to come. She was free, but had no money or property of her own. In contrast to many of her counterparts in the city, whose white benefactors gave them homes or other property, Coincoin received nothing at this time except her freedom. She was no longer young, and her legendary success was still many years away. Before its attainment, the freed woman still had a hard row to hoe.

TWO

A Matriarchal Legacy

I n 1778 free nonwhites were relatively rare at the Natchitoches post. The census of 1776, the last one taken before Coincoin's manumission, tallied a total population of 1,021 residents; 430 were nonwhites; but only 8 of these were free. Three of those free people of color died or moved away shortly afterward; by 1785 the post still claimed only eight free nonwhites.[1] Coincoin, Antoine Joseph, and the two additional sons born to her after her manumission constituted half of this free nonwhite population in 1785.[2]

Freedom, initially, had little effect on Coincoin's lifestyle. For at least seven more years she remained with Metoyer under roughly the same status as before Quintanilla's interference. In the meantime, Metoyer did not bother to make public the fact that the woman in his household was no longer his slave and that she remained there by mutual agreement. When their eighth child, Marie Françoise Rosalie, was born in 1780 and when her brother Pierre was born two years later, Quintanilla tersely recorded the baptisms of both, each time identifying their mother as "the slave of Metoyer."[3]

During this period Metoyer executed a series of maneuvers by which he might legally reunite his family and forestall further clerical persecution. In the wake of Manuel de Soto's release from prison in 1779, the two households acquired properties in the more tolerant lower post of Opelousas and prepared to move there. However, citizen removals between settlements in the colony required administrative permission; and those were rarely granted at Natchitoches. A sufficient force of able-bodied men was critical for borderland defense. *Habitans* who abandoned Natchitoches were usually ordered to return by the governor, under threat of arrest and imprisonment.[4] The well-placed de Sotos managed to skirt the prohibition. Metoyer, by necessity or by choice, affected a compromise that allowed him, Coincoin, and their children to remain at Natchitoches without further prosecution.

In April 1780, before the de Sotos' departure, Metoyer purchased his two remaining children whom the lady still owned: Dominique, aged six, and Eulalie, aged four.[5] In September 1780 he sold the *vacherie* (cattle ranch) he had purchased at Opelousas, together with its house (thirty-six feet long), a small cabin for slaves, a stove, a corral, a fenced garden, twenty-one head of cattle with their calves, four bulls, four oxen, one plough, one cart, and fifteen horses.[6] He then petitioned the Natchitoches commandant to grant him land suitable for a plantation, about eight miles below the Natchitoches post on the stretch of Red River then called la Grand Côte (and later, Côte Joyeuse). That petition was successful.[7]

The two children bought in 1780, as with their siblings Metoyer had purchased in 1776, were not freed; however, he soon indicated his intent to do so. He had, by this point, become a man of some means and regularly conducted business in the provincial capital. On one such trip to *la ville,* Metoyer visited a notary to draft a document he apparently did not want to file in the small and gossiping post where he made his home. In February 1783, before the royal notary Leonardo Mazange, Metoyer executed his earliest-known will. A later, public, and less incriminating testament would go into great detail about his family background and his relatives, both living and dead.[8] In this 1783 document, quietly filed in a distant city, Metoyer identified no kin and, contrary to custom, omitted even his place of origin. The document began with the conventional acknowledgment of his faith and his unworthiness, the commendation of his soul to God, and the specifications of desired funeral arrangements. Then, the usually verbose Metoyer wrote one paragraph of uncharacteristic terseness. In its entirety, it stated: "I declare to be a bachelor and not to have any children."[9]

Across the years, writers have extrapolated various motivations from this passage, proposing sentiments from shame to callousness; most have missed the legality that mandated Metoyer's declaration. Under the inheritance laws that prevailed in the colony, and in France where he held other property, had he acknowledged paternity of illegitimate children, Metoyer would have been legally barred from leaving them any of the property for which he and their mother had labored. Denying illegitimate children an inheritance was, indeed, a time-honored means of encouraging "regularity" in marriage and the transmission of family fortunes in most Western nations of that era.[10] With legalities covered, Metoyer proceeded to devote the remainder, and major part, of his testament to arrangements providing for the future needs of the black woman with whom he lived and the multiracial children she had borne during the years they had shared.

First, Metoyer acknowledged the still-private paper by which he had freed Coincoin in 1778. He expressed his wish that the document be as completely binding as it would have been if executed before proper authorities, and he requested that his executors not put any obstacle in the way of her enjoyment of complete liberty. Second, to the six *"mulâtres"* born to Coincoin prior to her purchase and subsequent manumission, he promised freedom upon his death.[11] He also took steps to provide these children with a measure of security. To them and their free-born brothers, he bequeathed a tract of land of five arpents"[12] frontage on both sides of Red River (later Cane River) bordering his own tract that the Spanish crown had granted him—a tract on which he had begun development although no patent had been secured.[13] Finally, Metoyer proclaimed that after his death, should the value of his estate in the colonies exceed the debts he owed, two-thirds of the remainder would go to his kinsmen in France as the law required, and the remaining third should be divided among the multiracial children of Coincoin. As long as she lived, however, Coincoin was to have the use and enjoyment of whatever estate her children inherited from him.[14]

On September 26 of the following year, 1784, Coincoin gave birth to her last child, François. By this time her manumission had become public knowledge.[15] Within three years, she would have her emotional independence as well. Pierre and Coincoin were now in their forties. For Metoyer, age had brought new cares and new wisdom. Enslaved by Catholic morals that apparently weighed more heavily upon his mind and by the deeply ingrained consciousness of his family's social position, he could not free himself to recognize the children he clearly wanted to acknowledge. Now entering the last third of his life, he had no sons to whom he could legally bequeath the fortune he was accumulating. Moreover, the captivating woman whose charms had lifted her from the hopeless station of her birth was now a middle-aged matron, her physical health and sensuality undoubtedly diminished by the fifteen children she had borne.

In July 1785, the couple acquired a new neighbor on the Grand Côte. Jean Délouche, recently arrived from France, petitioned the commandant for a concession of six linear arpents on either side of the river, to a depth of forty, if the twists and turns of the river allowed that much without encroaching upon the claims of a neighbor. The concession was immediately approved,

FAMILY OF COINCOIN AND PIERRE METOYER

Marie Thérèse Coincoin —┬— **Claude Thomas Pierre Metoyer**
b. Aug. *c*23, 1742, Natchitoches | b. Mar. 12, 1744, France
d. *c*1816, Cane River | d. Sept. 30, 1815, Cane River
 | m. Oct. 13, 1788, Marie Thérèse Buard

Nicolas Augustin
b. Jan. 22, 1768
d. Dec. 19, 1856
m. Aug. 22, 1792
Marie Agnes Poissot

- **Marie Modeste**
  1792–d. young

- **J. B. Augustin**
  1795–1855
  m. M. Sus. Anty

- **Marie Louise**
  1797–1847
  m. Flor. Conant

- **J. B. Maxille**
  1798–1830
  m. M. Asp. Anty

- **Auguste Augustin**
  1800–1856
  m. Melite Anty

- **Marie Pompose**
  1802–1856
  m. C. N. Roques

- **Joseph Augustin**
  1804–1851
  m. Ant. Coindet

- **Marie Susette**
  1806–1864
  m. E. Roques, Ls. A.Morin

- **François Gassion**
  1809–1865
  m. Flavie Mézière
  Rosine Carles
  Perine Metoyer

Marie Susanne
b. Jan. 22, 1768
d. Jan. 28, 1838
Plaçages: **Dr. Joseph Conant,
Jean Baptiste Anty**

Plaçage
Dr. Joseph Conant

- **Florentin Conant**
  1794–aft. 1860
  m. M. Lse. Metoyer

Plaçage
Jean Baptise Anty

- **Marie Susette**
  1797–aft. 1860
  m. J. B. A. Metoyer

- **Marie Aspasie**
  1800–aft. 1850
  m. Maxile Metoyer,
  Octave Deronce

- **Marie Arséne**
  1803–1836
  m. Manuel Llorens

- **Unnamed son**
  b. and d. 1805

- **Valsain**
  1806–1814

- **Marie Thérèse Carmelite
  "Melite"**
  1807–aft. 1862
  m. Auguste Metoyer

Louis
b. *c*1770
d. Mar. 11, 1832
m. Feb. 9, 1801
Marie Thérèse Le Comte

- **Jean Baptiste Louis**
  1800–1838
  m. M. Sus. Metoyer
  (dtr. of Pierre II)
  • Théophile Louis

Liaison
Françoise Le Comte
(later placée of J. B. Rachal)

- **M. Louise "Catiche"**
  1790–aft. 1870
  m. F. M. Mulon

- **Marie Rose**
  1793–aft. 1860
  m. J. B. Baltasar
  plaçage: J. A. Coindet
  plaçage: Dr. A. Z. Carles
  liaison: Jas. Hurst, Esq.

Liaison
Madeleine Grappe

- **Thérèse**
  b. 1797
  m. Augustin Cloutier

Liaison
Marie Rosalie
(slave, freed 1831)

- **Joseph St. Cyr**
  b. May 26, 1813
  freed 1831

- **Antoine**
  b. Dec. 6, 1814
  freed 1831

Continued on next page

Pierre II
b. *c*1772
d. June 25, 1833
m. 1802, 1818
Perine Le Comte, Henriette Cloutier

Dominique
b. *c*1774
d. Apr. 30, 1839
m. Jan. 19, 1795
Marguerite Le Comte

Marriage to Perine

— **Marie Susanne**
1804–aft. 1870
m. J. B. Ls. Metoyer

— **Pierre III**
1806–*c*1860–70
m. DesNieges Metoyer
• Perine
m. F. Gass. Metoyer
Joseph E. Dupré

— **Athanase Vienne**
1813–aft. 1860
m. M. Emilie Metoyer

Marriage to Henriette

— **Marie Osite**
1800–aft. 1870
m. J. B. N. Le Court

— **Neres Pierre**
1817–aft. 1901
m. M. Elise Roques

— **Marie Elisa**
1819–aft. 1866
m. Belisaire Llorens

— **J. B. Delores**
1821–d. young

— **Auguste Dorestan**
1823–aft. 1848

— **Dominique**
b. and d. 1796

— **J. B. Dominique**
1797–1850
m. Adelaïde Rachal

— **Joseph Dominique**
1798–1816

— **Marie Susanne**
1801–aft. 1870
m. J. B. Esp. Rachal

— **Marie Perine**
1803–aft. 1830
m. Pre. Miss. Rachal

— **Narcisse Dominique**
1805–aft. 1836
m. M. Ceph. David

— **J. B. Dominique II**
1808–aft. 1860
m. Doralise Dupré

— **Marie Silvie**
1809–aft. 1860
m. J. B. V. Le Court

— **Louis Florentin**
1811–aft. 1870
m. Théotise Chagneau

— **Marie Celine**
1813–*c*1842
m. J. Eloy Le Court

— **Joseph Ozéme**
1815–aft. 1870
m. Catherine David

— **M. Marguerite**
1817–1899
m. Jos. Emanuel Dupré

— **Ambroise Chastain Dominique**
1819–aft. 1870
m. Osine Labaume

— **Marie Cephalide**
1821–*c*1842
m. J. B. Mariotte *dit* St. Ville

— **Marie Louise Théotise**
1824/25–aft. 1851
m. Marin Rachal

— **Marguerite "Zelmie" Artemise**
1826–*c*1850–60
m. F. Vilcour Metoyer

— **Marie Lise**
1828–aft. 1870
m. L. T. B. Le Court

FAMILY OF COINCOIN AND PIERRE METOYER

Marie Thérèse Coincoin ——┬—— Claude Thomas Pierre Metoyer
b. Aug. *c*23, 1742, Natchitoches · b. Mar. 12, 1744, France
d. *c*1816, Cane River · d. Sept. 30, 1815, Cane River
· m. Oct. 13, 1788, Marie Thérèse Buard

Continued

Marie Eulalie
b. Jan. 14, 1776
d. 1788–1801

Antoine Joseph
b. Jan. 26, 1778
d. Oct. 9, 1838
m. Jun. 1, 1801
Pelagie Le Court

M. Françoise Rosalie
b. Dec. 9, 1780
d. bef. 1783

— **Marie Susannne**
1802–1803

— **Marie Aspasie**
1840–*c*1850–60
m. Séraphin Llorens

— **Marie DesNeiges**
1806–aft. 1870
m. Pierre Metoyer III

— **Joseph Jr.**
1807–bef. 1860
m. Doralise Coindet,
Lodoiska Llorens

Separated c1808–17

— **Joseph Zenon**
1818–bef. 1838

— **Marie Elina**
1821–aft. 1867
m. Théophile Louis Metoyer

— **Marie Célina**
*c*1823–1852/53
m. Augustin Maximin
Metoyer

— **St. Sibor Hypolite**
1827–aft. 1861
m. Julie Chevalier

```
┌─────────────────────────┬──────────────────────────────────────────┐
```

Pierre Toussaint
b. Oct. 10, 1782
d. Feb. 17, 1763
Never married

François
b. Sept. 26, 1784
d. Dec. 28, 1862
m. 1804, 1815
Marg. LaFantasy, Arthemise Dupart

```
            ┌──────────────┴──────────────┐
```

By Marg. LaFantasy

  ├— **Marie Adelaïde**
      *c*1805–aft. 1860
      m. Jérôme Sarpy Sr.

  ├— **Joseph François I**
      1807–aft. 1870
      m. Desirée Coton-Maïs

By Artemise Dupart

  ├— **Marie Susette**
      1816–aft. 1850

  └— **Joseph François II**
      aka **Joseph Clervil**
      1819–aft. 1870
      m. M. Cécile Chevalier,
      M. Louise Vienne

and an order of survey was issued eventually by Governor Esteban Miró in March 1787. In the interim, according to the commandant's subsequent certification on the twenty-eighth of that month, part of the land had been sold; the new owner was "Marie Thérèse, free *négresse*."[16] Coincoin had, in fact, already petitioned the Spanish government for title, and on January 18, 1787, the rights to that part of the concession had been changed to her name.[17] No patent was actually issued at that time. A final title required a new survey of her portion, and no surveyor was available on that frontier.

Metoyer apparently supplied the funds for that land, in payment for the years of service Coincoin had now given him as a free woman. In October 1788, he and Coincoin went before the commandant to execute what amounted to a separation agreement. Their older children were to remain his property until he saw fit to manumit them. Coincoin was to receive a stipend of 120 piasters a year to help her support their freeborn children. In a later document, in which she abrogated that agreement in exchange for his manumission of three children who had remained enslaved, Coincoin would specifically say that the annulment applied to her annuity but *not* to her land.[18] Whatever the specifics of their separation agreement, which is no longer on record, Metoyer obviously felt that the land and annuity would suffice for her basic needs and those of their children. It was not an overly generous sum; in Spanish Louisiana the unpretentious rank of military drummer brought an income of 200 piasters annually.[19] Moreover, Metoyer stipulated (and reiterated in later documents) that upon Coincoin's death the property and cash he had donated to her must be divided among the six multiracial children named in the contract. The black offspring whom she had borne before their alliance should not inherit the products of Metoyer's labor.

Having provided somewhat for Coincoin and their children, Metoyer chose a legal wife of his own status, the widow of his old friend from La Rochelle, Étienne Pavie. Ironically, the woman he chose—one whose sisters had, in fact, stood as godmothers to his and Coincoin's first-born twins— bore the same name as his mistress.[20] In October 1788, after legally filing the separation agreement he had executed with Coincoin, Metoyer drew up his contract of marriage with Marie Thérèse Eugénie Buard and exercised extreme caution to protect the rights of Coincoin's children whom he still held in slavery. He clearly specified that those six slaves would not become part of the community property shared with his new wife, and he reserved for himself the right to free them at his discretion.[21]

After his socially approved marriage, Metoyer assumed a place of leadership in the economic, civic, and even ecclesiastic affairs of the community.

As syndic,[22] he took the church census in 1790 and handled the church's preemption claim with the United States Land Office in the early 1800s.[23] His plantations flourished; he enlarged his original grant with the acquisition of a number of tracts; and the census of 1810 declared him to be, by far, the largest slaveholder in the parish, owning 103 men, women, and children.[24] But the greatest blessing that came to him in those years was one he could never have enjoyed with Coincoin. The new Marie Thérèse, considerably younger than her predecessor, gave Metoyer two sons and a daughter he could acknowledge.[25]

In 1788 Coincoin was forty-six years of age. Her life, apparently, had been spent as a house servant. Two decades had been dedicated to serving the Frenchman who desired her and provided her basic temporal needs in return for her service and devotion. Now in the fifth decade of her life, she was a free woman, legally and emotionally, dependent for the most part upon her own abilities and resources for the present and future welfare of her offspring. Despite her age, her apparent inexperience, and a body physically broken by so many childbearings and birthings, Coincoin took to the fields. For the newly freed black woman and her free-born children, those years were lean ones. The mental and financial chasms separating the dependencies of a slave from the responsibilities of a free citizen were not to be bridged in a day or even a year. The acquisition of land thrust upon her the sole responsibility for its success or failure. Other slaves in that era were freed and given land upon which they lived and died in drudging poverty.[26] Coincoin would succeed where the others failed.

Settling into a small cabin on the sixty-eight acres apparently financed by Metoyer, Coincoin began the cultivation of tobacco, an important industry in this Spanish colony. When properly grown and cured, Louisiana tobacco was of such excellent quality that it was used for the famed Havana cigars. The Natchitoches crop, although it represented only a fraction of the total produced in the colony, was noted especially for its superior quality.[27] The dark, aromatic leaves from Natchitoches were the ones Longfellow mentally savored when he penned his *Evangeline:*

> Then from his station aloft, at the head of the table, the herdsman
> Poured forth his heart and his wine together in endless profusion
> Lighting his pipe, that was filled with sweet Natchitoches tobacco . . .

The tobacco industry of Spanish Louisiana was controlled rigorously by specifications designed to maintain that quality. In 1777 Gálvez issued a sev-

enteen-point set of regulations covering every aspect of production, planting, harvesting, shipping, and marketing. Violators faced severe penalties,
whether they acted deliberately or carelessly.[28]

   Meeting these regulations was but a small part of the difficulties faced by
Coincoin in the operation of her farm. Production of the crop was even more
complex than governmental laws. Earlier in the century, Le Page du Pratz
had penned an excellent description of tobacco farming in colonial Louisiana. According to his account, the extremely small seed was first sown very
thinly in a prepared bed of the best soil available, then covered with ashes to
the thickness of a small coin to discourage worms. When each tobacco plant
sprouted four leaves it was transplanted promptly into prepared holes a foot
broad and three feet apart. If the transplanting was not done immediately
after a rain, the seedlings had to be watered.[29]

   Until the young plants fully took root they were lightly covered each day
with leaves plucked the night before, and each plant was examined daily
throughout its growing season to keep it free of caterpillars. Weeding was
a cautious process, with growers taking great care not to touch the hoe to
the plant; at each weeding new earth was pulled to the plant to provide
it with more nourishment. When the plant began to sprout suckers, those
had to be pulled; if permitted to form branches, the leaves would be under-
nourished. Similar care was taken not to let a plant form more than twelve
leaves. At harvest, the leaves were stripped from the stalk, strung, and hung
in the air. When dry they were usually piled in heaps to make them sweat
out still more moisture. At the proper stage of dryness they were rolled into
bundles, wrapped in a cloth, and bound. Twenty-four hours later each cloth
was untied and each bundle rolled still more tightly in order to meet market
regulations.[30]

   Considering the exacting attention each individual plant needed, Coincoin's decision to cultivate tobacco was a surprising choice for a woman
alone, with no slaves and no labor other than that of her small, free-born
children. With experience, her harvest grew until her annual production was
of sufficient size to send her own barge to the New Orleans market. A surviving passport issued to her by Commandant Louis de Blanc in April 1792
granted her barge a pass to New Orleans in company with a bateau belonging to Metoyer. In addition to other commodities, their shipment contained
9,900 *carotes*, or rolls, of tobacco.[31]

   Legend has preserved no details of Coincoin's experiences as a tobacco
planter, but it does report more venturesome endeavors to accumulate capi-

tal. For generations her descendants recounted how their family's matriarch trapped the wild bears in the Natchitoches wilderness and sent bear grease to market in large stone jars supposedly brought from the Mediterranean. Although the exportation of bear grease was a thriving business in early Natchitoches, by the Spanish period it was not widely practiced. According to one authority, the New Orleans market was normally supplied with shipments from the St. Francis river valley.[32] Yet the passport for the 1792 barge sent by Coincoin to New Orleans included shipment of three hundred hides and two barrels of grease. In all probability it was her older sons who did the trapping for Coincoin, for it is definitely known that she did not yet own slaves at this point of her career. Hunting quite possibly was a major source of both food and income for the family. Not only bears but a variety of animals and fowl proliferated in the parish, and Metoyer's 1801 will notes that he was indebted to Coincoin for turkeys she had furnished him.[33]

Local lore of twentieth-century vintage also contends that Coincoin introduced the culture and processing of indigo to the Natchitoches region; and the development of the crop along Red River does indeed date to her era. Edward Nugent and John Kelly, sent out by the new Spanish governor in the winter of 1769–70 to assess borderland conditions, reported that the inhabitants of the post grew only tobacco, corn, and rice, although the soil was "fit for the cultivation of wheat, and barley."[34] By 1775, indigo had been introduced to the region's produce; but Coincoin and Metoyer were then both townspeople, with no agricultural enterprises. Surveys made of their Grand Côte neighborhood in 1794 credit both Metoyer and their neighbor Jean Baptiste Ailhaud de St. Anne with indigo processing sheds; but they show none for Coincoin. At best, she likely grew a small quantity for personal use, as many local planters did.[35]

A highly probable source of income for the freedwoman was the manufacture of medicine. Tradition holds that she was highly skilled in the use and application of medicinal herbs and roots. European-style medicines were perennially short in colonial Louisiana; and much of the colonial production occurred in the northwestern section of the colony, using native plants.[36] Coincoin's younger sister Mariotte is on record as a *médecine,* providing for (at least) slaves and the working class. Coincoin's daughter Thérèse, in the 1790s, was the indispensable nurse of her chronically ill mistress; and Coincoin's daughter Susanne was both a midwife and a nurse.[37] Reason suggests that both Coincoin and her sister learned medicinal skills from their parents, skills that Coincoin then passed to her daughters.

By 1793 Coincoin also had established an efficient planting operation on her farm and moved to extend her holdings. Much unclaimed land still lay within the jurisdiction of the post, and the colonial government encouraged husbandry by freely granting lands of reasonable quantities to deserving heads of household. After putting away her 1793 crop, Coincoin petitioned the commandant for another tract. On May 14, 1794, her petition was answered, with a concession of typical size: twenty arpents' frontage by a depth of forty. The land she chose lay on the west bank of the Old River branch of Red River, about five miles due west of her homestead.[38]

Twentieth-century lore contended that Coincoin was the recipient of a royal grant from "the king himself." Versions of the story variously credit the kings of both France and Spain, place the grant at 1745–50, and suggest that she received it through the influence of her former master. Upon this land, supposedly, she labored alongside her slaves, clearing and developing it, and upon her death that royal grant was divided among her many children. This legend, like most, is rooted in some facts, although the time frame is wildly off and the circumstances were radically misinterpreted.[39]

The statement that Coincoin received a grant "from the King" is one of the most disputed points of her legend. One newspaper feature article, which denied the validity of the legend in general and the existence of any such grant, asserted: "She never received a land grant from the King. . . . I repeat, the King . . . never even knew of the existence of Marie Thereze Coin-coin."[40] The argument is specious. Coincoin received one Spanish patent and one Spanish concession, and all actions of the colonial government were taken in the monarch's name. O'Reilly's land ordinance of 1770, which remained in effect until 1798, specifically stated: "All grants shall be made in the name of the King."[41]

Early versions of the Coincoin legend credited her land grant to the sponsorship of the St. Denis family. However, white patronage was in no way required under Spanish land grant laws; and, by 1793, Coincoin was sufficiently established that she would have needed no intervener. The U.S. Land Office's attachment of the surname Metoyer to her Old River tract has led to speculation that Claude Thomas Pierre Metoyer obtained the patent for her. However, this sole attribution of the Metoyer surname to Coincoin stems from a different cause: a misassumption by a U.S. Land Office clerk with whom she had no contact, as evident from the trail of records relating to this property. The 1794 concession identified the petitioner as "Maria Teresa, *negra libra*," and her 1806 U.S. claim for the tract was filed under that same name. The family friend who filed an affidavit on her behalf with the U.S. Land Office in 1812, Gaspard Bodin, also identified her simply as "Maria Therese"—as did the U.S. deputy surveyor at Natchitoches, Joseph Irwin, in the cover letter by which he submitted Bodin's testimony to the U.S. Land Office register and receiver, Levin Wailes. Again in 1814, when Irwin surveyed the tract, he identified the owner as "Maria Thérèse, a free Négresse." However, most of Coincoin's documents relating to this tract were transmitted with others created by her sons Augustin and Pierre Metoyer. Thus, the U.S. Land Office clerk Lloyd Posey, operating from the Opelousas Land Office, assigned that "family name" to her when he compiled his December 1812 "monthly returns of certificates issued." From that point forward, U.S. land maps and the final patent copied Posey's identification.[42]

Grants made in Spanish Louisiana were basically free, but certain regulations were to be followed by all recipients. A small but immediate cash outlay was required in the form of a surveyor's fee, based upon the actual size of the grant; and no grant was complete until the survey was made. At many posts, the enforcement of this particular requirement was lax and those who lacked the required cash remained in possession of the land without benefit of survey, without a complete title, and without disturbance. Some 75 percent of the grants in the Natchitoches area, by contemporary estimate, remained in this state of legal limbo.[43] Coincoin's concession was one of those.

In other respects, the law was more rigorously enforced. The first matter to be attended was, of necessity, some improvement of the land. Within the first three years of possession, grantees who requested land for farming were to clear the entire front of their tracts to the depth of two arpents and to enclose the front of their land; for the enclosure of the remainder they were to reach an agreement with their neighbors. All grantees were to construct and repair roads, bridges, and embankments where necessary and keep them in good repair—a requirement rigorously enforced, given that it was levied in lieu of taxes. If the lands were used for grazing, all cattle had to be branded. Failure to meet the required conditions would result in the forfeiture of the entire grant.[44]

The land Coincoin chose, however, was not fertile loam for enlarging her planting operation. Rather, it was piney woods for use as a *vacherie,* a grazing range for her cattle. Herding was by then a major industry in central Louisiana, especially in the rolling hills that lay west of Old River. Her choice was a conservative one and an appropriate one for her financial status. Vacheries required no clearage or fencing. Theirs was a society in which crops were fenced, to protect them from animals both domestic and wild, while cattle roamed free; and the mast that carpeted the virgin timberland supplied forage to cattle for most of the year. About 1797, after making the minimal improvements required in the first three years of possession, Coincoin hired a Spaniard named "Jose Maré" (likely José María Torres) to move onto the vacherie for her. For ten years he oversaw her cattle and cultivated a small patch of corn and other crops, to provide for his family needs as well as winter hay for Coincoin's stock. By 1807, however, the Spaniard died or relocated, and no other hirelings were engaged. Coincoin's vacherie was then physically abandoned, although taxes were paid to protect her ownership rights.[45]

In these first years of modest economic growth, Coincoin had one overriding goal: the liberation of her still enslaved children. She had brought fifteen lives into the world. Two of her surviving children, Pierre Toussaint and François, were free from birth. A third free-born, Marie Françoise Rosalie, had not survived infancy; and a fourth, Marie Eulalie, had died in her teens.[46] A fifth, Antoine Joseph, had been bought and freed by his father as a nursing babe, at the same time that Metoyer purchased and privately manumitted Coincoin.[47] Five more children were now the property of their father: Nicolas Augustin, Marie Susanne, Louis, Pierre, and Dominique. For these children, Coincoin had no immediate cause for concern. As long as Metoyer was alive, their enslavement was little more than a legality. Her other children, the black ones, were the ones in need.

Of the five she had borne before Metoyer, one son was also in his possession. On the day in 1776 that Metoyer bought his first four children from Mme. de Soto, he also purchased Jean Joseph, the child Coincoin had been nursing when their relationship began. After that purchase, Jean Joseph dropped from the records of the post. Unless he died as a teen after Coincoin and Metoyer moved beyond convenient access to the parish's burial grounds, history seems to offer only one possibility for his fate. In September 1804, the Marquis de Casa Calvo at New Orleans penned a report to the Spanish Crown in which he wrote of two traders who had left St. Louis for Santa Fe, Jeannot Metoyer and Baptiste LaLande (var. LaBorde).[48] The Spanish agent provided no descriptions for either man, but all these surnames were distinctive to Louisiana's Red River and no other candidate has been found for the Metoyer nicknamed Jeannot other than Coincoin's son Jean.

The other four black children borne by Coincoin presented her with a host of challenges. When Mme. de Soto and her newly returned husband moved their household down Red River to the Opelousas post, they took with them Coincoin's two oldest daughters. The elder, Marie Louise, was subsequently purchased and brought back to the borderlands by Pierre Dolet, a French trader and rancher who had settled at Bayou Pierre, some fifty miles northwest of Natchitoches. In the fall of 1786, Coincoin went to Dolet, proposing the purchase of her daughter. Under the Spanish law of *coartación,* a slave's right to self-purchase, Dolet could not refuse. Because Marie Louise was crippled, the result of a gun accident, her value was set at three hundred piasters, a meager sum for a twenty-seven-year-old female slave. Inasmuch as Coincoin had just begun her planting operation and was of limited means, Dolet also agreed to accept payment in three annual installments. Presumably, the debt was paid on schedule; but nine years would pass before Coincoin could pay a notary to draft formal manumission papers for her firstborn daughter.[49]

As a free woman, Marie Louise apparently remained close to her mother and half-siblings. The extreme commonness of her Christian name and the fact that she shared that name with several members of Coincoin's family make it difficult to track the free Marie Louise with certainty. She was likely the woman of that name who served in 1802 as godmother to an infant of her half-brother Dominique Metoyer, at which time she was described as "a free Negress . . . aunt of the infant."[50] Her age and associations also suggest she was the "Marie Louise Coinde" who served as godmother in 1812 to a child of her niece Marie Rose Metoyer (daughter of Louis) and was buried the next summer (as "Marie Louise Conde, free *moreno*") in the parish cemetery at the stated age of fifty-five—whereupon her French-born, common-law husband entered into a new relationship with Marie Rose.[51]

After completing payment of the debt she had assumed in the purchase of her first daughter, Coincoin planned for the purchase of her second-born. In 1790, young Thérèse was herself almost thirty and the mother of a nine-year-old son. Unlike her own mother, Thérèse had not sought or had not found a man of substance to provide an avenue to freedom. Moreover, her mistress, Mme. de Soto, was now an aging invalid. The future faced by Thérèse was an uncertain one.[52] With proceeds from her 1790 crop, Coincoin set out for Opelousas, a distance of 120 miles by way of prairies and forests—and even further by Red River's twists and bends. With her, she carried just fifty dollars and the infinite hope that spurs mothers to action. Again, she proposed a purchase, with payments to be made on time. Mme. de Soto, the shrewd and hard-biting matron whom few people ever bested, not only accepted the trifling down payment but agreed to a total price for the two slaves that was surprisingly small. The bedridden mistress then personally penned her own deed of sale:

> On this day . . . I, Dona Maria Nieves de St. Denis, legitimate wife of Don Manuel de Soto, in presence of the undersigned witnesses, declare to my Negress named Teresa, for her prompt and faithful service which at all times she has rendered me, and especially rendered me in my infirmities, inasmuch as it is she who has handled everything, I have conceded her the privilege of being sold by me, with her mulatto son Joseph Mauricio of the age of nine years, to her mother Maria Teresa, free Negress, for the sum of seven hundred dollars.[53]

Mme. de Soto did impose one immutable condition, to which Coincoin agreed: Thérèse and her son must continue to serve their mistress until her death. The two would then become Coincoin's property provided they paid the de Soto heirs the remaining debt within a year and a half after Mme. de Soto's demise. In the meantime, to help mother and daughter raise the funds to pay the remaining $650, Mme. de Soto agreed to permit Thérèse to raise cattle in partnership with one Maria del Marger. No explanation was made as to how the young black slave would obtain the necessary stock to enter the cattle business; apparently, the stock or requisite capital was also furnished by Coincoin.[54]

In the years that followed, the physically deteriorating mistress added notations on the document. She mentioned no cash payments; but on two separate occasions she noted a discount to Thérèse and her son, in appreciation for the "continuous and prompt solicitude" they showed in the "protracted infirmities which for almost ten years I have been suffering in this bed without hope of any health."[55] Seven years later, in the summer of 1797, the last rites of the church were finally administered to the dying woman at her home near Opelousas. As promised, the title to Thérèse and José Mauricio went to Coincoin for manumission. A balance of $490 still remained on the debt. The de Soto heirs accepted from Thérèse the payment of six head of cattle, valued at $40, to be applied toward this debt; but no known record reveals how any of them cleared the balance. The following month Thérèse and her son became the property of their mother and grandmother, and by her they were freed.[56]

The circumstances of Thérèse's manumission bear striking resemblance to one facet of the Coincoin legend. In exchange for her solicitous care and nursing abilities, the elder Marie Thérèse—that is, Coincoin—allegedly was "gifted" with her freedom by Mme. de St. Denis. However, the family that preserved this story did not preserve the memory of either a younger Thérèse or a younger Marie de St. Denis, each daughter replicating her mother's name. Over generations, the identities of these same-named women became fused into single personalities, and the story of Thérèse's manumission was inadvertently attributed to her mother.

Ironically, that confusion happened within separate lines of Coincoin's offspring, at both Natchitoches and Opelousas. As a free woman, Thérèse took for a surname the sobriquet favored by her master, Don Manuel. Under that name, Natchitoches documents identify her as one heir of Coincoin's Old River concession that was partitioned after Coincoin's death.[57] Thérèse, however, remained at the Opelousas post, bearing at least two additional children. In 1820 she and her oldest son, Joseph, were both free heads of household in St. Landry Parish. Generations later, Thérèse's great-grandson, Dennis J. Victorian of Lake Charles, would lay claim to the whole of the Old River concession, innocently merging the identity of the two Thérèses. Not so innocently, however, he presented himself as the *sole* heir of "Marie Thérèse" by a fictitious husband "Coin Coin Victorian."[58]

Late in 1794 Coincoin executed another slave purchase and manumission. This fourth beneficiary was also a grandchild, the natural daughter of her still single and still enslaved Metoyer son, Louis. From Widow Jean Baptiste Le Comte, Coincoin purchased for $150 cash a small "mulattress" named "Catiche, or Catherine, age of five years or about." The child's mistress noted that Catiche was already living in Coincoin's home, having been "entrusted to her at the age of two." Three days after the purchase, Coincoin manumitted the child.[59]

Coincoin's varied strategies to free her offspring were sometimes thwarted, and at other times they failed. Two of her children had been taken from her in their childhood: her first-born son Nicolas, called Chiquito, and a daughter who carried down the Christian name of Coincoin's mother, Françoise.[60] In November 1772, while Manuel de Soto was imprisoned in Mexico City, his wife had contemplated a move to the nearby Spanish post of Los Adaës, to live among her mother's people. In preparation, she had bought a tract of farmland there, furnished with a cabin, kitchen, and outbuildings. Lacking cash, she paid for the property with "one small *négrillon*, aged seven."[61] The legalese of that transaction masked multiple problems. First, the *Code Noir* explicitly forbade the sale of prepubescent children away from their mothers—an issue Mme. de Soto likely dismissed under the premise that mother and child would be reunited after her relocation to Los Adaës. Second, the commandant who penned the document, Mme. de Soto's brother-in-law, did not actually name the boy being sold and referenced him generically as "son of the slave Marie Gertrude" (that is, Coincoin's sister). However, it was not the nine-year-old son of Gertrude who was carried off, but Coincoin's Nicolas, age seven as the document stated.[62]

Before Mme. de Soto could move her household, Spanish officials shut down the Los Adaës post and its attached mission. Under the leadership of Nicolas's new master, Antonio Gil y Barbo, the hapless and impoverished Adaësanos embarked on an odyssey through several Texas outposts before they were allowed to settle near the Nacogdoches Indians, with whom the Natchitoches French were in close contact. By 1793, Coincoin or her envoy had visited Nacogdoches and arranged for Nicolas a provisional manumission, likely one similar to those she had negotiated for his older sisters. The Nacogdoches census of that year cites Nicolas as a free *negro,* a native of Natchitoches, aged twenty-five, and unmarried. His quasi-freedom, however, was revoked when Y Barbo fell into political disfavor and was imprisoned. His property was confiscated, and Nicolas was remanded to slavery.[63]

Four harvests would pass before Coincoin had sufficient funds to cover a full payment for Nicolas's freedom. In November 1797, she dispatched her eldest, newly freed, Metoyer son to Nacogdoches to handle the negotiations. Also invoking the right of *coartación,* Augustin arranged for the legal appraisal of his half-brother and proffered, on behalf of their mother, the three hundred pesos that were set as Nicolas's monetary worth. However, Y Barbo's legal representative refused to cooperate, saying he had only the authority to "receive properties that had been seized but not the authority to execute a letter of freedom nor to receive [Nicolas's] value." Nicolas would remain in legal limbo until Y Barbo was released in 1799 under an order of banishment. At that time, the disgraced Spaniard moved his household across the Sabine into what would soon be the Neutral Strip separating American Louisiana from Spanish Texas.[64]

As a free man, Nicolas returned to Natchitoches. Briefly, allegedly, he occupied a piece of backwater timberland, behind the Cane River tracts on which Coincoin's Metoyer sons had begun to settle. But Nicolas was a stranger to his own kin. Coal black to their light brown, and acculturated to Spanish ways rather than the French mores of Cane River, he left the Isle to live among the Hispanic Creoles in the Camptí–Grande Écore community north of Natchitoches. There, Augustin bought for him a tract of land on which Nicolas remained for some two decades, until the land was lost to the counter-claims of white neighbors. In his dotage, Nicolas returned to Cane River, where, in April 1850, Augustin arranged for his burial in the village churchyard at Cloutierville. Of all of Coincoin's children, Nicolas most strongly represented his mother's African heritage. He was the only child to use her African name as a surname past early adulthood; and court testimony describes him as a black man "appearing to be a real African." If he fathered children, their identities remain unknown.[65]

Freedom for Françoise, the second child illegally sold away, would not occur in Coincoin's lifetime. Born in 1763, Françoise had been another casualty of Mme. de Soto's debts and her planned move to Los Adaës. Françoise's purchaser, a French trader named Delissard Jouhannis, resold the girl almost immediately to a neighboring planter named Baptiste Dupré. Her price, 1,200 piasters, was a handsome one for a nine-year-old; and it portended the future young Françoise faced.[66] At sixteen, she became a mother, and ten more birthings would follow across the next two decades. At least several of her children were half-white. At least one of these, daughter Marie Louise born in 1781, was fathered by her mistress's bachelor brother—the soon-to-be wealthy planter Ambroise Le Comte—whose offspring of color by enslaved women both black and red would later intermarry with those of Coincoin.[67] At least two other children of Françoise—Charles, born 1783, and François Nicolas, born 1795—were fathered by Louis Monet, a notoriously harsh and randy master who married Dupré's widow. Those two Monet sons and a grandson whom Louis Monet also fathered by Françoise's Le Comte daughter, would eventually be manumitted through the aid of their mistress Marie Louise (Le Comte) Dupré Monet. The quadroon Louis Monette (as his name was usually rendered) would eventually buy his mother's freedom as well.[68]

Freedom eventually came for Françoise herself, but the means are muddled amid the tangled affairs of the intermarried Duprés, Monets, Le Comtes, and their duplicitous brother-in-law Alexis Cloutier. An 1825 suit against Cloutier by the Dupré heirs charts the Dupré slaves for three to four generations and presents Françoise as the matriarch of twenty-one of them. It makes no reference to her freedom, and the cryptic document by which Cloutier manumitted her on July 23, 1819, merely states that she was "a slave above thirty," without providing any other details. In 1827, as "Marie Françoise, free Negress," she appeared before the Cane River notary Louis Derbanne to report the death of her son Charles Monette. After the inventory valued the young carpenter's property at just $47.25, Derbanne noted that the illiterate "Mademoiselle Marie Françoise" had renounced her son's succession. At the auction held August 21, 1827, none of Coincoin's Metoyer children bid on his chest of carpentry tools, his guns, his old parasol, his seed cotton, or his bed of cypress with a moss mattress. Nor did his mother, who apparently had no funds but would have received the meager proceeds from his sale. Where Françoise made her home thereafter goes unstated in the records. However, the 1830 census household of her half-brother Louis Metoyer and his French-Indian wife Marie Thérèse Le Comte sheltered a number of adult *libres* who were not part of their own nuclear family.[69] Françoise's Monette offspring would become an integral part of the Isle Brevelle clan.

The first six children whom Coincoin bore to Metoyer were technically their father's slaves, but they had long since ceased to be treated as such. As many authorities have demonstrated, slave children of mixed parentage, even when not openly recognized, often received favored treatment and special positions on the plantation.[70] The privileges enjoyed by these Metoyer children were exceptional even to this rule, for they had not only received special treatment from their father but were actually treated as free within the community prior to manumission.

As cases at point, the twins, Nicolas Augustin and Marie Susanne, were only nine years old when they served as godparents at the baptism of their young cousin Nicolas Augustin, the half-French son of Commandant de Mézières's Negro slave, Marie Jeanne. Upon recording their names in the baptismal register, Father Quintanilla identified both young godparents as free.[71] Again in 1795, when Susanne's eldest son, Florentin, was baptized, Quintanilla's successor Juan Delvaux entered into his register that he had baptized a free infant named "Juan Francisco Florentine," son of "Susanne, free mulatress." Godparents were "Louis, free mulatto," and "Coincoin, free Negress."[72]

In 1793 Pierre Joseph Maës, *syndic* of the Grand Côte, compiled a tax list of all free heads of household and free males over the age of fourteen. Coincoin was listed, along with her eldest Metoyer son, who indeed was free by that time. Cited with them was young Pierre Metoyer, now twenty-two but still enslaved. His name was scratched through. Apparently Maës first included him on the list, taking it for granted that he was free, but then was corrected by either Pierre or his mother. This tax list, which purported to include all free male adults or heads of household in the parish, indicated the existence of only one other taxpaying male of color, Coincoin's black neighbor Nicolas *dit* Doclas, who had bought his freedom seven years earlier from Commandant Étienne de Vaugine.[73]

Similarly in 1792, when Coincoin shipped the barge load of tobacco, hides, and bear grease to New Orleans, Commandant Louis de Blanc—a St. Denis grandson who had known Coincoin from his infancy—issued a passport stating that the barge was manned by two free men of color.[74] Inasmuch as Coincoin's sons who actually were free at this time were scarcely old enough to undertake such a voyage, the two boatmen likely were her older sons—technically still the property of their father, whose bateau they also manned on the trip downriver. When Metoyer finally did free his children, he specifically stated that they "were always in a position to gain escape everywhere they found themselves" and had not attempted to do so.[75] Such references attest that the young Metoyers were treated as free at the Natchitoches post long before they legally attained that status.

On August 1, 1792, Metoyer manumitted his eldest son, invoking the privilege he had reserved for himself in his marriage contract with the Widow Pavie. Three weeks later the twenty-four-year-old Augustin wed the free multiracial Marie Agnes Poissot in the parish church.[76] In January 1795, the fourth Metoyer son, Dominique, also decided to marry; and he too was given freedom. Four days later, January 19, Dominique exchanged vows in the chapel of the parish of St. François with another *femme de couleur libre,* the fourteen-year-old French and African Marguerite Le Comte.[77]

In 1801, Metoyer initiated proceedings to free his last three enslaved children, Louis, Pierre, and Marie Susanne. Drafting a new will, radically different from the earlier one of 1782, he reiterated some of the provisions of his marriage contract, noted his right to free his enslaved children at his discretion, and recounted the terms of the annuity agreement that he had made with Coincoin.[78]

It had been his intention, Metoyer stated, that when he deemed it appropriate to free the last of these children, they, their brothers, and their mother should discharge him from the payment of the annual stipend. He was now ready to do so for the three remaining children (who were now past thirty), but their freedom hinged upon one provision. On the day that Coincoin and all of her children annulled the contract, Pierre and Louis would become free and Susanne would receive conditional freedom. In return, if unforeseen events caused the children of his legitimate marriage to become indigent, these children of Coincoin must assist Metoyer's legal family according to their abilities. That latter stipulation, however, was not an expression of Metoyer's personal concern. The prevailing statutes governing manumissions in the late colonial era decreed that all freed slaves must assist their former masters, should the latter become impoverished; failure to do so would entitle the former masters to reclaim ex-slaves as their property.[79]

Metoyer's desire to keep Susanne under his control until his death was indeed a personal issue. Whether he was motivated by a desire to protect her from outside threats or to ensure that she made wise life choices is debatable. He also decreed that after his death Susanne should remain in his household and care for his wife so long as the arrangement was mutually agreeable. Moreover, he specifically charged Susanne with responsibility for the care of his youngest son, François Benjamin, both before and after the death of Mme. Metoyer. In exchange for her continued services, he promised to free both Susanne and the children she had already produced—Florentin, Marie Susanne called Susette, and Marie Aspasie—as well as any other children born to her in the intervening years. Finally, he stipulated that Marie Susanne should receive payment for all midwife duties she performed on his plantation and any other services that justified remuneration.[80]

Metoyer's will of 1801 contains one further clause relative to his still-unacknowledged children by Coincoin. At his death, his young slave Honoré, son of his black slave Salie, should be sold to none other than Dominique, son of Coincoin, at the price set by the estimators of his estate. Metoyer also decreed that Dominique must manumit Honoré prior to his own death. Should Dominique fail to do so, Honoré would revert to Metoyer's estate and would become the inheritance of the legitimate Metoyer heirs. He stated no reason for this special provision, but one is obvious. This child Honoré, whose godmother had been Coincoin, was likely the son of Dominique.[81] No other reason explains the solicitude that the aging Frenchman showed for this child, just one of more than a hundred slaves he then owned.

The conditions set by Metoyer for the manumission of his three children were met in the spring of the year following. In the presence of two witnesses, Coincoin acknowledged that she was now freeing Metoyer of the annuity he had promised her. In final settlement, he would allow her to keep the $1,200 she had already received in annual installments, for her to invest as she deemed advisable. In return, Coincoin released Metoyer from most of the terms of the contract, but she explicitly excluded those that concerned her farm.[82]

Following the execution of this document, Metoyer formally granted freedom to Louis and Pierre. In each document he expressed gratitude for the young man "having always served me faithfully and exactly, always conducting himself to my satisfaction," and stated that he now wished to "recompense him for the good service that he has rendered me, who was in a position to gain escape everywhere that he found himself." In the case of Louis, he further swore that he had already verbally given him liberty on January 1, 1801. Although Metoyer did not state the circumstances that had prompted the verbal promise, they are clear from the pattern he followed in manumitting his other sons. Louis had taken a wife in the parish church, Marie Thérèse Le Comte, the month after his father made him a *statut liber*.[83] In both documents, as with his earlier manumissions of Augustin and Dominique, Metoyer made no acknowledgment of paternity and gave the young men no surname.

The final document executed on this day in May 1802 was the conditional manumission of Marie Susanne. After praising her for always serving him with zeal, fidelity, and exactness, Metoyer raised what had become a recurring theme in documents relating to Coincoin and her offspring: Susanne's medical skills. She had, he swore, saved several lives during various maladies, including those of his wife and all their infants. She had "nourished with her own milk" his youngest son, François Benjamin, and had dry-nursed, reared, and managed his other two children by his legal marriage. Again, he promised that upon his death Susanne and all her children would become free. Because slaves were not legally entitled to any property or money, or even the right to work or sell goods for their own profit without the express permission of their master, Metoyer specifically added that upon his death his heirs and executors would have no claim whatsoever upon any products of Marie Susanne's industry or upon any savings she had managed to accumulate by any talent.[84]

Metoyer's wife died in 1813, thereby freeing Marie Susanne from her father's wish that she serve his spouse after his death. Two years later, Metoyer himself was buried beside his wife in the cemetery of the parish church.[85] Marie Susanne, at the age of forty-seven, finally became a free woman in that fall of 1815.

During the first years of her own freedom, Coincoin had labored with but one goal: to earn the funds necessary to purchase her offspring from the bondage of slavery. Having accomplished that goal, with the exception of her daughter Françoise, the aging black woman did not lessen her toil. Freedom is the most basic requisite of humanity, but a poor freedwoman was still yoked to financial and social servitude. In antebellum plantation society, the passport to real independence was land, slaves, and money. It was these for which Coincoin and her freed children now labored.

No official record reveals exactly when Coincoin first acquired slaves for labor. Her only purchases on record are those executed for the freedom of her children. Apparently, no workers were bought prior to 1790; the church tax list of that year, placing a poll on every free head of household, every free male over fourteen, and every slave, charged her for no slaves. The October 1795 post census of slaveowners attributed five slaves to Coincoin's household, two of whom were likely her still-enslaved, still-single sons Louis and Pierre Metoyer.[86] The others clearly represented Coincoin's entry into the master class, as well as the typical pattern by which colonial settlers built their slave wealth. Her first identifiable acquisition was a Congolese woman named Marguerite, who gave birth in July 1796 to a son Joseph and, the following year, buried a son Jean Baptiste, already three years old. By 1816, Coincoin's holdings had grown to twelve; except for a Congo male named Louis and a Quissay male named Harry, all were offspring of the fertile Marguerite and her oldest daughter. Baptismal records also identify four other children who did not survive until the 1816 accounting.[87] Tradition, as well as several scholarly works, credits Coincoin with many more; but numbers are often exaggerated by the passage of time.[88]

Not surprisingly for a matter so ideologically sensitive, tradition also insists that Coincoin was a genial master. While she purchased other humans and held them in bondage, descendants contend, she never forgot that she herself had once been a slave. Reportedly, she administered no corporal punishment; misbehavior on her plantation was corrected with imprisonment in the "jail" she had erected for that purpose on her property. However, tradition identifies that "jail" as the structure now known as African House, on Melrose Plantation, Isle Brevelle—a property that Coincoin neither owned nor managed.[89] Archaeological excavations on her own Grand Côte lands have revealed no evidence of such a structure.

The only evidence as to how Coincoin treated those she held in bondage are threads drawn from the parish registers. Traditionally, Natchitoches's slavemasters had complied with Catholic doctrine, insofar as it decreed prompt baptisms of all newborn slaves and reasonably prompt catechizing of adult slaves newly imported from Africa or a Western tribe. Most masters had been willing to pay the required fees to bury their dead bondsmen in sacred ground. By the last years of the French regime, however, settlers had virtually abandoned the concept of church-sanctioned slave marriages. By the close of the Spanish regime, most of the post families had moved to outlying plantations beyond reasonable access to the church. In his 1796–1802 annual reports to his bishop, Rev. Pierre Pavie—whose late brother's widow had married Metoyer—repeatedly lamented the impiety of his flock: "Very few of the inhabitants have satisfied their Easter Duty. . . . The great distance of the inhabitants from the church makes it impossible for fathers and mothers to send their infants to instruction classes. . . . I see with sadness that my teachings and my exhortations are for the most part useless with them."[90]

The sacramental registers suggest a compromise of sorts between the pastors of St. François and their scattered flock. Periodically, Pavie and his successors ventured into the outlying settlements, where they baptized backlogs of infants and new imports for almost all the planters. On many of those recorded treks past the Grand Côte, Coincoin dutifully presented Marguerite's latest child for a Christian baptism, or served as godmother for a neighboring child. When Marguerite's son Zenon died in 1797, Coincoin took or sent his body into the parish church for burial in consecrated grounds. She did not, however, urge catechism or conversion upon the three African adults she brought into her household. One of these, the Congolese Louis, sought baptism from a passing priest two years after his arrival, together with Marguerite, who had remained unconverted through at least twelve years under Coincoin's dominion. No evidence exists that the Quissay Harry ever accepted the Catholic faith.[91] While Coincoin obviously held to the Catholic tenet of baptism lest one die outside the grace of God, she clearly respected the rights of her African-born slaves to worship the deity of their choice.

As the Spanish regime gave way to Anglo-American control, Coincoin transitioned into retirement. Her goals had been accomplished, with the exception of freedom for Françoise and that daughter's children. Realistically, that goal held forth little hope under the new regime in which the Spanish concept of *coatarción*, by which she could have forced their emancipation, had been replaced with tighter restrictions upon manumissions. Most of Coincoin's sons, by this point, were established on their own lands; but two remained close at hand: Pierre Jr. and Pierre Toussaint. The former had, before his marriage, obtained a Spanish grant amid his Metoyer brothers, downriver on Isle Brevelle. By December 1806, he had transferred that land to his brother Augustin and returned to the Grand Côte to farm his mother's homestead.[92] When U.S. Land Office officials set up a board at Natchitoches late that month, to accept the "claims" of landholders who now needed an American title, Pierre Jr. made the filings for his mother's property. Documents of 1810 and 1816 continue to place him in charge of both her original farm and her slaves.[93]

Pierre Toussaint was Coincoin's last concern in her old age. This next-to-the-youngest child had not married and had not reached adulthood before the end of the Spanish regime; thus he had not qualified for a Spanish grant. In 1807, after closing down her Old River vacherie, Coincoin made one last purchase—agreeing to pay a neighbor five hundred dollars, before the following March, for a tract of a hundred acres or so adjacent to her farmstead. That tract, already under tillage, became Toussaint's farm; and by 1814 he had accumulated the funds to repay his mother and take title in his own name.[94]

While laboring to build her estate, Coincoin assumed her share of civic responsibility. When in 1790 the church congregation was faced with the necessity of hiring a carpenter to make repairs and enlargements, Pierre Metoyer as syndic took a census of all inhabitants of the region who were served by the church and assessed one *real* for each free head of household, each free male over fourteen, and each slave. Coincoin, at that time, had no free sons old enough to be taxed and owned no slaves. She was assessed one *real,* but she paid two.[95] In 1793 and 1794 still another list was drawn up of all area inhabitants who had made a contribution of labor for the benefit of the parish. Among those who had volunteered to work in the parish cemetery was Coincoin.[96]

Although Coincoin and Metoyer had terminated their affair prior to his marriage in 1788, their separate households remained close. As previously noted, in 1792 they shipped their goods together to the New Orleans market. Further evidence of their continued friendship is provided by the parish records which show Coincoin serving, from time to time, as godmother to Metoyer's slaves. In 1795, for example, the resident priest, Father Delvaux, baptized the infant Juan Bautista Honoré, child of Maria, a slave of Metoyer. Godparents were Coincoin and her Metoyer son Joseph.[97] Some writers have asserted that the children whom Coincoin bore to Metoyer were ashamed of their mother because of her relationship with their father. The records do not support this assertion. Regardless of the circumstances surrounding their births, Coincoin's children clearly maintained their respect for their mother for as long as she lived.

There can hardly be more convincing proof of one individual's regard for another than for that individual to desire the other as a godparent to his own child, as a proxy to guide that child's religious development in the event of parental death. In 1794 the eldest Metoyer son, Augustin, brought his first child to the parish church for baptism; the godmother was Coincoin.[98] From this time until her death more than twenty years later, Coincoin was to serve as godmother to a number of her grandchildren. Among them, several were her namesakes; and her name has been a dominant one in the family through all subsequent generations of her descendants. Tradition also holds that her descendants had masses offered in her memory for more than a half century after her death.[99]

The exact date of Coincoin's death remains unknown. The last records that exist for her are dated in the spring of 1816. On March 9 the old matriarch sold the entirety of her small farmstead to her neighbor, Jean Baptiste Ailhaud de Ste. Anne.[100] On April 20, she presented nine more documents to the parish judge for filing. By the terms of these conveyances, all executed the previous month, Coincoin transferred to her children and grandchildren the twelve slaves she then owned. Each heir who received a slave paid the assessed value, totaling $5,250.[101] At her death, that cash and her Old River grant were amicably divided among her free children, without benefit of probate. Tradition holds that prior to her death Coincoin also divided the land that had been granted to her "by the King" among the children whom she left behind. Later documents relating to this land show that it was divided into ten strips, each with two arpents of frontage on the river by a depth of forty. This tradition is further supported by the 1830 deed of sale from her son Toussaint to his nephew Auguste, in which Toussaint stated that he had acquired the land by "partition made by his mother Marie Thérèse Coincoin between her children."[102]

On December 31, 1817, her son Pierre filed a contract of marriage at Natchitoches with his second wife in which he identified himself as son of the deceased Marie Thérèse *dite* Coincoin.[103] The death of the matriarch, therefore, occurred between April 1816, when she filed her last documents, and December 1817, when Pierre penned his marriage contract.[104] As with Metoyer's legal wife, no record of Coincoin's demise can be found in the fire-damaged fragments that survive for the church burials of that period.

Tradition offers one further detail relevant to Coincoin's death. Near the end of her life, supposedly, she lived alone. Although she was some seventy-four years old, she still insisted upon maintaining her independence, even from her children. Upon learning that his mother was ill, supposedly, Augustin took her to his home to care for her, and it was there she died. When death occurred, descendants say, he took her body the twenty miles or so into Natchitoches for a burial in the cemetery in which her parents, at least two of her children, several of her grandchildren, and Pierre Metoyer were also buried.[105] Tradition also insists that the burial was a fine one, and the wealth her children had attained by this point lends support to the tradition.[106]

Although Coincoin was forced by the laws of society to defy one of the Christian precepts, tradition insists that she was a religious woman. Through the generations her descendants have maintained that their family's matriarch died as a devout Catholic. According to legend she personally taught her children the rosary, and upon the occasion of their first communions she gave to each a chain of wooden rosary beads that she herself had carved.[107] At least one of these was said to be preserved by the family until well into the twentieth century.[108]

Popular versions of the Coincoin legend describe the "fabulous" heritage that she left her children and attempt to explain it in material terms. But it was not a luxurious estate of twelve thousands of acres and one hundred slaves that she bequeathed them, an inheritance whose proceeds would allow them to spend their lives in grand style. A "comfortable" estate, by Cane River standards, would be a more accurate description. It was sizable, before its distribution, consisting of over one thousand arpents of land and, across the years, at least sixteen slaves. If land ownership maps of the period may be used as an acceptable guideline, Coincoin's holdings compared well with those of the white inhabitants of the parish and far exceeded those of the other free people of color. The 1810 census of the parish, the last one taken before her death, shows that only 13 percent of the households had as many or more slaves than Coincoin. Three of these householders who matched or exceeded this number were her children.[109] Even estates of a thousand arpents and sixteen slaves, however, are rendered small when divided among ten heirs.

The Coincoin narrative that took hold along Cane River in the twentieth century portrays a woman significantly different from the one of record. The culture that spawned the narrative was a complex and ideologically tortured world. Cane River remained steeped in memories made painful by a Civil War that had reshaped all lives along its banks. Its families and institutions treasured a trove of historic sites that its disparate populations interpreted in radically different ways. Amid the nation's growing prosperity, the mystic lore of the Old South had spawned a new industry, tourism, in which white-columned manors and moss-draped oaks evoked an idyllic past. But the moral awakening that had begun to prick at white America's conscience, as its citizens of color pressed for civil rights, presented a dichotomy that had to be emotionally bridged for the legacy of the Old South to be preserved.

Coincoin became that bridge. The faded memories cherished by her off-spring provided fodder for writers lured to Cane River by its lore. For some, undoubtedly, the portrayal of a black woman as a plantation mistress eased the moral burden of slavery. For others, recognizing Coincoin as a Cane River founder was a matter of justice, a symbolic acknowledgment of the contributions made by thousands of forgotten blacks whose toil had trans-formed an impoverished, wilderness outpost. For Coincoin's offspring who saw themselves as America's "forgotten people," the presentation of Coincoin as a symbol of success was a just restoration of the respect that Jim Crow America had stripped from them. For a nation of black Americans who had found few role models in their history texts, Coincoin became a historic mother all could embrace. Not surprisingly, the iconic Coincoin became invested with the trappings of success valued by a prosperous, acquisitive twentieth-century America: wealth, grandeur, and power.

Coincoin's legacy was not a vast estate. She created no domain over which her offspring could rule. Archaeologists disagree as whether any building survives as a testament to all that she achieved.[110] But she left an enduring legacy that makes her a powerful icon of the black matriarchal experience upon which much of America is grounded. Industrious and innovative, qui-etly persistent, frugal to a fault, and impelled not by personal ambition but by the needs of her family, Coincoin set an example from which her offspring would draw strength for generations to come. This was the foundation on which her Metoyer sons and daughter would build a unique world along Cane River.

Plate 1. Fort St. Jean Baptiste des Natchitoches, ca. 1742

In 1979, this historic fort was reconstructed in Natchitoches, at its original site, draw-ing upon colonial descriptions and plats. The center building—large by comparison to those around it but cramped by modern standards—was assigned to the commandant as a residence. At the time of Coincoin's birth, the family that occupied the dwelling was headed by Louis Juchereau de St. Denis, the man who held Coincoin's parents in slavery. In the northwest corner stands the church of St. François, where those parents were legally married and Coincoin and her ten siblings were baptized.

Sketch by Auseklis Ozios, image courtesy of Louisiana State Parks

Plate 2. Coincoin's Cabin: An Artistic Rendering

In October 1788, Coincoin was a free woman whose longtime lover and protector had just taken a legal wife. She had borne fifteen children, ten of whom were still minors. Anticipating her separation from Claude Thomas Pierre Metoyer, Coincoin had already petitioned the commandant in November 1786, seeking a concession of land on which she could support her family. Her *requête* was granted. There she would build the cabin that would be her only known home for the rest of her life.

The artist's rendition above—based upon a surveyor's notation and Cane River tradition—depicts the common housing of yeoman families of her place and time, irrespective of their color. The walls would have been bousillage, plastered over upright timbers with crisscrossed bracing. The room with separate entry typically housed a slave, or an enslaved woman and her children, or adult sons. The wide, wrap-around galleries provided an outdoor living space and cooling shade for the interior. Controversy exists as to whether Coincoin's home was the similar structure that still stands and is known today as the Coincoin-Prudhomme House.

Pen sketch by Carrie Starner Mills, owned by the author

Plate 3. Yucca House: Home of Louis Metoyer, ca. 1818–32

In December 1795, Coincoin's still-enslaved son Louis Metoyer filed a *requête* of his own for a tract of downriver land on Isle Brevelle, some ten miles from his mother but adjacent to a concession already made to his older brother Augustin. After the transfer of Louisiana to the United States in 1803, Louis's title was contested by a white planter; in 1818, the Louisiana Supreme Court finally ruled in Louis's favor.

In the wake of that title clearance, apparently, Louis built the home now known as Yucca, as a residence for himself, his wife, their one child, and other dependent kin they took under their wings. In later years, local lore contends, the house was used as a slave hospital, likely by the white family who acquired the property in 1847. Under the twentieth-century ownership of the Henry family, Yucca would be the longtime "writer's residence" of the folklorist Francois Mignon. It still stands today, a prominent feature on the Melrose Plantation grounds.

Pen sketch by Carrie Starner Mills, owned by the author

Plate 4. Melrose

The plantation manor now known as Melrose was begun by Louis Metoyer, a free man of color, shortly before his death in 1832. Its construction was finished by his only legal son, Jean Baptiste Louis Metoyer. Tradition identifies the actual builder as Séraphin Llorens, a free man of color from New Orleans who had settled on the Isle, married Louis Metoyer's niece, and operated there as a carpenter and farmer for over a half century. The original structure consisted of the center section. White owners in the early twentieth century added the two front wings and then brought in, as a rear addition and kitchen, the Marco Givanovich home from lower Rivière aux Cannes.

Melrose is the largest of eight remaining structures on the estate grounds of the similarly named plantation that, since 1974, has been a National Historic Landmark.

Photograph by John C. Guillet, used courtesy of John C. Guillet and Chris Guillet

Plate 5. African House at Melrose Plantation

History remains silent about the origin, purpose, and design of this two-story, mushroom-shaped structure, constructed without the use of a single nail. Neither Louisiana nor other American states offer a specimen of comparable architecture. Some accounts, pointing to the fact that its windows are barred rather than shuttered, describe it as a "jail" for plantation miscreants.

As with other buildings on the grounds that once belonged to Louis Metoyer, this one acquired its name during the twentieth-century Henry regime. The Henry-sponsored folklorist Francois Mignon maintained that the home was built by African slaves imported by Louis Metoyer or (variously) by his mother Coincoin, who drew upon childhood memories of homes in her native Africa. (The latter tale is demonstrably false in every aspect.) The hut's brick walls suggest a possibility that it dates to the time of the bricked "Big House" completed by Jean Baptiste Louis Metoyer in 1833. One architectural study (MacDonald et al., 2006) contends that its construction has no African characteristics and that it more strongly resembles French rural architecture of its era.

Photograph by John C. Guillet, used courtesy of John C. Guillet and Chris Guillet

Plate 6. The Roque House (aka Pacalé's Home)

The hipped roof of the African House—a classic country French feature—is echoed in the Cane River home built about 1803 by an elderly black Creole and associate of Augustin Metoyer. Yves *dit* Pacalé had been baptized at Natchitoches in 1736 as the son of African transplants enslaved by the Derbanne family. After the 1796 death of his half-Indian master, Pierre Derbanne, Pacalé asked for his liberty and the Derbanne heirs complied.

As a freedman, Pacalé first bought his wife, Marie Louise, and then, in 1803, a small tract of land on which he built a home she did not live to enjoy. In 1806 he purchased and manumitted a second wife—Coincoin's apparent sister Gertrude, who would toil within these walls for a dozen years as his wife and then his heir.

Now known as the Roque House, for the last family that inhabited it, the home of Pacalé and Gertrude was moved to the riverfront in Natchitoches in 1967. Extensively restored, it has served as a tourist center and headquarters for the Cane River National Heritage Area Commission.

Photograph by Paul Christiansen, used courtesy of Paul and Kristy Christiansen

Plate 7. The Augustin Metoyer Plantation Home

Anthony Michael Dignowity, a Czech immigrant and doctor who would become the mayor of San Antonio, walked down Isle Brevelle in the mid-1830s. His journal describes his impromptu visit to the "very fine" and "elegant" plantation home of Augustin Metoyer. He was struck by the abundance of silver that furnished a dining table set for sixteen, by the music room from which accomplished and "elegantly dressed" young ladies of color entertained him at mealtime, and by the parlour with its books and periodicals.

The Civil War destroyed the lifestyle that Dignowity described. Reconstruction and Jim Crow destroyed the means to recover. By 1900, the approximate period of the photograph from which this sketch was made, the home of the Isle's beloved Grandpère was in severe decay. It would soon succumb to fire.

Sketch by Deanna Douglas, owned by the author

Plate 8. Front Street, Natchitoches, 1800s

When Dignowity arrived in the "commercial district" of the village of Natchitoches in the mid-1830s, the scene that greeted him was likely this one. The streets were not yet bricked, although some buildings were. When Frederick Law Olmsted arrived in the 1850s and queried local merchants about the "colored planters" of Cane River, these would have been the shops Olmsted visited. In this vignette, the man afoot wears shoes, but Cane River tradition describes another reality of antebellum life where roads were few and unpaved. Those who walked to town were likely to string their "town shoes" around their neck and pause, on the outskirts of the village, to wash their feet in Cane River and don those shoes to make themselves presentable.

The house that Pacalé built stands today on the considerably widened riverbank, roughly in the position of the moss-draped tree.

Pen sketch by Bert Bertrand, based on a theme by Irma Sompayrac Willard,
courtesy of Mr. and Mrs. Bert Bertrand

Plate 9. The Badin-Roque House

This *poteaux-en-terre* home, preserved now by the St. Augustine Historical Society, reflects a style common among yeoman Creole farmers at the turn of the eighteenth to nineteenth centuries. It was likely built by the white Frenchman Gaspard Roubieu, whose heirs sold the property in 1811 to Augustin Metoyer. In the 1856 division of Augustin's succession, it briefly fell to Augustin's eldest son, Jean Baptiste, who, tradition holds, had lived there a while after his 1816 marriage. Shortly after Augustin's death, the Natchitoches bishop acquired the house for reuse as St. Joseph's Convent, a school for young Creole girls of color who could not attend white schools.

Courtesy of the St. Augustine Historical Society

Plate 10. Nicolas Augustin Metoyer and the Church of St. Augustine

Nineteenth-century oil portraits often depict their subjects with a revered item at hand. Here, the patriarch of Isle Brevelle gestures to his most treasured accomplishment: the consecrated Catholic church that he and his brother Louis built adjacent to Augustin's home in 1829. The original chapel no longer remains. A replacement at the original site remains the center of life on Isle Brevelle. Within that newer chapel hangs this portrait of the church's founder.

Portrait by J. Feuille, 1836

Plate 11. Marie Agnes Poissot
(Mme. Augustin Metoyer)
(ca. 1775–1839)

Plate 12. Augustin Paulin Metoyer
(son of Auguste Metoyer
and Melite Anty)
(1829–1836)

As with most wives of her era, Agnes left little to document her life outside the records of her church. Twice in her life, however, she took an uncommon action that left her imprint upon history. In 1784, she sued her mistress (apparently her white father's wife) for mistreatment. About 1836, she also sat for this oil portrait, which, in the twentieth century, would be ineptly restored.

Like the moth atop his hand, Paulin's life was fleeting. His parents had already buried their older child when they commissioned this portrait by Julien Hudson, a New Orleans free man of color, in 1835. Hudson likely added the symbolic moth in the wake of Paulin's death that same year.

Oil by unknown painter, courtesy of Cammie
Henry Research Center, Natchitoches

Creole Boy with a Moth, *by Julien Hudson,*
1835, oil on canvas, courtesy
of a private collection

Plate 13. Auguste Augustin Metoyer
(1800–1855/56)

An Isle Brevelle planter and merchant, Auguste also co-owned a New Orleans mercantile house, Jonau, Metoyer & Co., that served as cotton factor for the Isle.

Oil portrait by J. Feuille, photo courtesy of
Cammie Henry Research Center, Natchitoches

Plate 14. Marie Thérèse
Carmelite "Melite" Anty
(Mme. Auguste A. Metoyer)
(1808–aft. 1860)

Youngest child of the longtime union of Marie Susanne Metoyer and the white Creole planter Jean Baptiste Anty, Melite married her first cousin—the son of her mother's twin.

Oil portrait by J. Feuille, photo courtesy of
Cammie Henry Research Center, Natchitoches

CLOCKWISE:

Plate 15. Thérèsine Carles
(Mme. Florentin Conant Jr.)
(ca. 1825–aft. 1870)

Daughter of Marie Rose Metoyer and the French-born Dr. André Zépherin Carles.

Photo courtesy of Lee Etta V. Coutii

Plate 16. Marie Zéline Le Court
(Mme. Louis Casimere Rachal)
(ca. 1824–aft. 1910)

Born to Coincoin's niece Adelaïde Mariotte and the white Creole Barthélemy Le Court.

Photo courtesy of Joseph B. Mullon III

Plate 17. Joseph Emanuel Dupré
(ca. 1811–bef. 1900)

Son of Adelaïde Mariotte and the white Creole Joseph Dupré III.

Photo courtesy of Lee Etta V. Coutii

Cane River Country

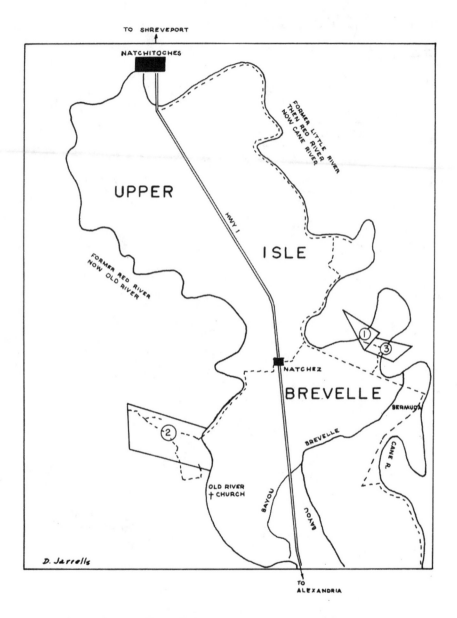

Plantations and Royal Concession of Marie Thérèse Coincoin

1. Donation from Claude Thomas Pierre Metoyer
2. Marie Thérèse's Spanish Land Grant of 1794
3. Marie Thérèse's Purchase of 1807

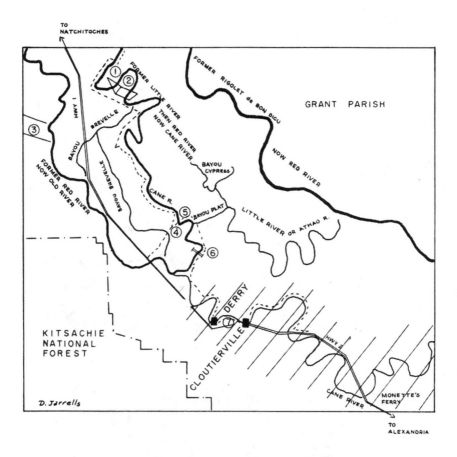

Isle Brevelle—Pinpointing Early Land Grants and Major Points of Interest

1. Homestead given by Pierre Metoyer to Marie Thérèse Coincoin
2. Marie Thérèse Coincoin's purchase of 1807
3. Marie Thérèse Coincoin's Spanish grant of 1794
4. Site of St. Augustine's Church, erected on the 1795 Spanish grant to the Metoyers *de couleur*
5. Melrose Plantation estate grounds, situated on the 1796 Spanish grant to the Metoyers *de couleur*
6. Usual site of 24-Mile Ferry, located on the 1796 Spanish grant to Dominique Metoyer
7. Shallow Lake Cemetery

The slashed area was known in the eighteenth and early nineteenth centuries as Rivière aux Cannes.

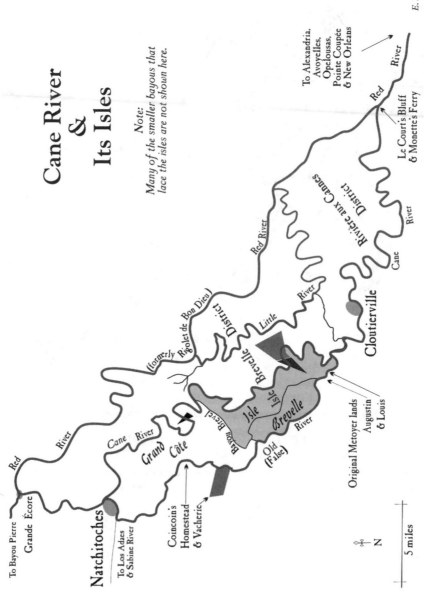

Cane River
&
Its Isles

Note:
Many of the smaller bayous that
lace the isles are not shown here.

E. S. Mills

THREE

Early Development
of the Isle Brevelle Community

I t was the eldest son, Augustin, who led the Metoyers *de couleur* to Isle Brevelle. One by one, his brothers followed and, tract by tract, adjacent lands came under their control by grant, by occupancy, and by purchase. As the years passed, the offspring of Coincoin and Pierre Metoyer were increasingly recognized as a *famille extraordinaire* by denizens of Natchitoches.

The isle to which they are historically attached is not an island, as commonly assumed. Geographically, it is a narrow strip of land, delineated by a waterway that splits, meanders, and joins again. Yet neither the land nor the culture south of Natchitoches can be so tidily defined. The terrain there is a warren of rivers and bayous that created isles within isles. (See map, "Cane River and Its Isles.") Across time, the changing courses of Red River's three channels—and the changing names of not only those channels but also the waterways that snake between them—have confounded many travelers and journalists. The demography has perplexed them even more as settlers of all hues spread their farms and plantations across all three channels of the Red—creating an Isle Brevelle District that encompassed multiple isles.

The earliest survey maps place the isle called Brevelle between the meanders of Old River and Cane River—that is, the two westernmost channels of the Red. Other accounts muddle those bounds. The earliest known description of the isle in American literature was penned by Dr. John Sibley, a New England–born Indian agent whom Thomas Jefferson commissioned to explore the Red River and the Southwest while Lewis and Clark sought a northwest route to the Pacific. Sibley's 1805 report to the president dutifully chronicles his passage from the Red's juncture with the Mississippi up to the town of Natchitoches. But there he planted himself comfortably and fashioned the rest of his report from the secondhand accounts of more adventuresome locals. His description of the terrain below Natchitoches, despite some problems with nomenclature and distances, sketches the geographic and demographic context into which Coincoin's offspring settled:

> After passing the Rapides [modern Alexandria, some sixty river miles below Natchitoches] there are very few settlements to be seen, on the main river, for about 20 miles . . . we arrive then at the Indian villages, on both sides [and then] a large, beautiful plantation of Mr. Gillard . . . on a point of a high pine woods bluff. . . . Six miles above Gillard's . . . [Red] river is divided into two channels, forming an island of about fifty miles in length, and three or four in breadth. The right hand division is called the Rigola [*sic*] de Bondieu [modern Red River], on which are no settlements. . . . The left hand [modern Cane River] is the boat-channel, at present, to Natchitoches. . . . After about 24 miles, we pass a thick settlement and a number of wealthy inhabitants. This is called the River Cane [Rivière aux Cannes] settlement; called so, I believe, from the banks some years ago being a remarkable thick cane-brake.
>
> After passing this settlement of about forty families, the river divides again, forming another island of about thirty miles in length, and from two to four in breadth, called the Isle Brevel, after a reputable old man now living in it, who first settled it. This island is sub-divided by a bayau [*sic*] that communicates from one river to the other, called also Bayau Brevel. The middle division of the river is called Little river [actually, Red River, now Cane River] and is thickly settled, and is the boat-channel: the westward division of the river is called False river [Old River], is navigable, but not settled; the banks are too low; it passes through a lake called Lac Occassa [beyond which, after some miles] you arrive at Natchitoches.[1]

Sibley's narrative disarranges the Isle Brevelle District in two ways that lead researchers astray. First, the watercourse called Little River (var. Rivière Brosset and Attaho) lies to the east of the Cane (the channel Sibley actually traveled). As an offshoot of the Rigolet de Bon Dieu, Little River created two other (unnamed) isles between the Cane and the Rigolet. The district of Isle Brevelle encompassed them all.

Second, Sibley's armchair description of Isle Brevelle more than doubles its length and misses a significant community divide. Bayou Brevelle defines the isle's northern limits. The land above Bayou Brevelle, from the time of its settlement, was known as the Grand Côte, or Côte Joyeuse. It was there that Pierre Metoyer established his plantation and there that he installed Coincoin and their children on the farmstead she developed. Those children, as young adults, pushed south of Bayou Brevelle into the scarcely populated, densely vegetated isle that a few hardy men had but recently tried to tame. Following the custom of the time, by which individual land concessions lay on both sides of a waterway, the lands held by Coincoin's offspring would sprawl across not only Isle Brevelle but the Little River isles as well.

The settler for whom the bayou, the isle, and the district are named was a fitting harbinger of the multiracial community that would grow up around him. Jean Baptiste Brevel Jr. had been born in the far reaches of French Louisiana, the Grand Caddo nation (modern Oklahoma). His mother was a Caddodoque; his Parisian-born father was one of five soldiers stationed at an outpost France maintained within that tribe. After Baptiste's birth, the elder Brevel brought him back to Natchitoches for baptism and, on that same visit to the church, married his son's mother after having her baptized as well. A daughter would be born to them before the death of that native mother who is known only by her baptismal name, Anne. Brevel Sr. would die before either child reached adulthood. Both youth would settle at Natchitoches. There, in 1760, young Baptiste married the daughter of a French officer-turned-planter, Remy Poissot, whose granddaughter of color would marry Augustin Metoyer.[2]

Like the multiracials who came to own most of Isle Brevelle District, Baptiste was a youth torn between two worlds. Partially raised among the Caddo, he would—even after his marriage—travel extensively among South-western tribes, ranging from the Kansas Panis, through Apache and Coman-che lands, to the Pueblo tribes of Santa Fé. As a young man he served in the militia at Natchitoches and spent enough time there to father at least thir-teen children in his first twenty-three years of marriage. Yet he also hunted with the Oklahoma Indians of his birth and served borderland officials as a translator and courier to the Osage of Arkansas. Three years after his mar-riage, he petitioned for and received a concession of land from Daniel Pain, the subdelegate at Natchitoches; his chosen tract was a valuable salt lick near Lake Saline, northwest of the post of Natchitoches.[3] Not until the 1780s did he settle the region that bears his name, choosing a tract that lay on yet another, smaller isle between Bayou Brevelle and Old (False) River.[4]

For eons the lands that formed these isles had been Red River's flood plain. The deposits left behind formed soil of such quality that, after almost

a century of cultivation, the land would still be described as "the most productive cotton growing land in the state" and the "richest cotton growing
portion of the South."[5] But the isles were not easily tamed. Three decades
after Augustin hewed his first tree on the land he had been granted, a visitor
from France described his passage through the Cane River basin this way:

> I had to thread innumerable channels where the tangled roots of lofty
> trees twist themselves into the mud, and a thick underwood renders any
> attempt to penetrate the gloomy recesses of the swamp impossible. [I]
> explored in a boat the labyrinth of bayous. The vegetation is totally dif-
> ferent from what I have experienced; the beautiful live oak trees with
> their quivering leaves and the glassy surface of the water, the waving
> cypress trees, the sweet gum and common oaks, smothered in vines of
> every description. The yellow hickory and clumps of fan-leafed palmetto
> and graceful bamboo can conceal the sturdy trunks of the larger trees,
> which, meeting overhead form an almost impenetrable shade. As we glide
> beneath, bright plumaged birds glance among the branches and vie in
> their plumage with bright colored flowers.[6]

Once cleared of its vines and canopies, the ecosystem of the isles still
inspired rhapsody. Father Yves-Marie LeConniat, a transplanted Frenchman
of the next generation, called the district an "earthly paradise" and described
it to a correspondent as "so rich in lovely vegetation! It overflows with such
a variety of natural beauty, natural produce. We have every species, every
kind of tree, and in the springtime there are flowers in profusion! . . . In the
woods one really breathes pure balmy air. The sight of the multiple variety
of flowers of all different shapes, colors, sizes, is a spectacle to behold! It
inspires a person to get down on his knees in recognition of the Creator of all
its beauty." Father Yves-Marie did acknowledge the ticks or "death-beetles,"
the lizards, the snakes, and the alligators; but in his piety he explained, "The
good God . . . arranged things with balance and equilibrium, the miserable
and disagreeable with the beautiful and the lovely, so that man will not become too attached to any of the things of this world."[7]

Despite the natural advantages the isles offered, the *habitans* of Natchitoches were slow to settle them. Under the French, colonists had clustered
mainly at the village post, where they subordinated agriculture to trade. The
great distance of Natchitoches from central authority and its proximity to
Spanish territory had provided an ideal environment to circumvent restric-

tive trade laws between the two nations, and the commandants of the post not only condoned smuggling but even engaged in the activity themselves.[8]

Realistically, those who chose to settle in the borderlands were not agriculturalists by training or inclination. Most arrived with the military and, as they retired, chose trade. Across the century, within first-generation Euro-Americans, only 23 percent of the men (77 of 324) were farmers or planters. Among their sons, the figure rose to 47 percent. Not until the third generation, and the decade of the 1780s, did farming become the dominant economic activity.[9]

Two factors created the shift in economic interest from which Coincoin's and Metoyer's offspring would profit: one of them onerously governmental and the other intensely personal. First, the administrative change from French to Spanish in the 1760s created new priorities. Trade was stringently curtailed, and a generous land policy was implemented to encourage agriculture.[10] However, governmental regulations had never been taken seriously at Natchitoches. The more influential catalyst for its socioeconomic changes in the late colonial era was a personal reordering of priorities. One reconstitution of its population across five colonial generations concludes: "The desire for family, for legitimate and worthwhile procreation, . . . eventually 'tamed' each woodsman [and] turned individual traders into planters. As their offspring grew to maturity and established their own households, kinship ties were extended. As independent-minded settlers outmigrated to new farms on the fringes of too-civilized areas, their extended families moved with them."[11]

This was the pattern that had driven Metoyer and Coincoin to the Grand Côte and the pattern that drove their sons southward to the isles. Other unconventional families—retired military personnel and traders—had already pushed farther south, bypassing the isles in the 1760s to plant themselves on that stretch of Red River called Rivière aux Cannes, some twenty-four to forty miles from the authority of the post and the watchcare of its pastors. There, these interrelated French—the Le Comtes and Le Courts, the Duprés and Derbannes, and the Cloutier-Monet-Rachal clan—produced their own multiracial branches that would supply spouses for Coincoin's sons and grandchildren.[12]

Of these two offshoot settlements, the isles proved to be the most productive, although few settlers recognized the area's potential at the time. By 1790, the district claimed only twenty-seven free white males over the age of fourteen. The only nonwhites were the forty-nine slaves those households owned.[13] By 1792, Isle Brevelle had attracted its first free nonwhite entrepreneur, Coincoin's sister Mariotte, who farmed her own tobacco field on land provided by her white male companion, Antoine Bergeron.[14] Not until 1795, however, would the name of a landowning person of color appear on the surveys of Isle Brevelle's virgin bottomland.

Nicolas Augustin Metoyer was twenty-seven when the Spanish Crown approved his concession. Three years had passed since his manumission and marriage. He now had a wife and two infants to support. His father, who had provided him with no formal education, did have him trained as a blacksmith; but that was a trade at which, in Augustin's observation at Natchitoches, no man prospered.[15] Economic advancement lay with the land. In the winter of 1794–95, following parental example, Augustin applied for a concession near his aunt Mariotte, toward the bottom of Isle Brevelle; and on May 6, 1795, the colonial government issued him an order of survey and settlement.[16] The 395 acres platted in that survey presented a daunting challenge for a young man with no slaves to help him hack through the vine-covered canopies, uproot the massive live oaks, put the soil under cultivation, and battle the incessant outcroppings of native vegetation that smothered seeds and choked cotton shoots faster than plant hills could be hoed.

Adjacent to Augustin's acquisition lay a large swath of flat caneland much larger than the usual Spanish grant, one that had been conceded in 1789 to an up-and-coming French Creole named Silvestre Bossier. Allegedly, Bossier took three slaves to the tract, opened a road, and cut several acres of cane; but then he abandoned his improvements on the grounds that the land was not worth the cost of building his share of a bridge. He surrendered his order of survey and settlement to the commandant, Louis De Blanc; and, in December 1795, Augustin's younger brother, the still-enslaved Louis Metoyer, petitioned De Blanc for title to the entire tract. Four months later, Governor Estevan Miró issued an order of survey and settlement to Louis for all of the requested land, a tract that eventually would be measured at 912 acres.[17]

It is this land that twentieth-century lore claimed as the core of Coincoin's "empire." Dubbed Melrose by the Irishman who bought Louis's plantation in the 1880s, its surviving structures were declared a National Historic Landmark in 1974—in tribute to Coincoin. They stand today as the heart of the Cane River National Heritage Area, where her legacy is celebrated. However, all contemporary documents that deal with the plantation credit it to Louis, not his mother. In his 1806 memorial to the United States Board of Land Commissioners, Louis stated that he had "presented a petition to Mr. Louis

De Blanc then Commandant of the Post of Natchitoches preparatory to obtaining a 'title in form' . . . that the said commandant certified said land to be
Vacant and on the 18th day of May in the year 1795 the then governor of the
province of Louisiana gave to your Exponant an Order of survey."[18]

Louis's statements were accepted at face value by the land commissioners. However, Article 22 of the *Code Noir* proclaimed that "slaves can have
no right to any kind of property."[19] In May 1796, when Louis supposedly
received this grant, he was still a slave. Not until 1801 did his father verbally manumit him, and not until 1802 did the manumission become legal.[20]
Three possible explanations for this legal contradiction have been proposed
by historical and tourism interests: the land was not actually granted until
after 1802; the land was granted illegally to Louis in 1796; or the land was
actually granted to his free mother, as some versions of her legend contend,
after which she privately transferred the property to her son.

The possibility of backdated paperwork is not implausible on its surface.
As one authority has noted, "When the news of the [Louisiana] Cession was
received [land policy] was thrown to the winds. Spanish administrative officials connived with American speculators in the perpetration of land frauds
by back-dating a large number of blank petitions for grants."[21] In Louis's
case, the fact that no survey was made of the property during the colonial
era might support an argument that his land was a backdated, post-1803
claim. That lack of a survey is a matter he addressed in his affidavit to the
Board of Land Commissioners: the surveyor of his district had become blind
and no replacement had been appointed. Louis also provided the testimony
of a white witness, Antoine Coindet, who swore that Louis held the land by
virtue of a Spanish order of survey and settlement and that he had inhabited and cultivated the land for fifteen consecutive years prior to the date of
Coindet's testimony, November 16, 1811. Coindet, on the other hand, was not
a disinterested party. He was then, apparently, the common-law husband
of Louis's half-sister Marie Louise, and he would soon take one of Louis's
slave-born daughters as his companion. Coindet's relationship to Louis was
not disclosed or even questioned; the United States Land Office accepted his
testimony and ruled that Louis's documentary evidence was valid. Similarly,
the issue of Louis being a slave at the time he supposedly received the grant
was not raised even by Bossier, although he contested Louis's right to its
ownership.[22]

The possibility that Louis was in fact granted the land in 1796 despite his
slave status suggests conspiracy on the part of the commandant. Although

evidence attests that Louis had been treated as free and even identified as such prior to his manumission, it is improbable that the commandant's action was a simple mistake. Free adult Creoles of color were still rare at Natchitoches in 1796; for all of them, manumission papers had been filed with the commandant. Had De Blanc followed protocol in processing Louis's petition for land, he would not have certified the land to be free without determining whether the *homme de couleur* who submitted the petition was a free man. The commandant's motivation for approving an illegal concession to Louis is debatable. Perhaps he did so at the instigation of Louis's influential father. Or he may have done so because, some evidence suggests, Louis Metoyer was Louis De Blanc's godson and namesake.[23]

The third possibility, that the concession was actually made to Coincoin, who then turned it over to her son, seems the only means by which the grant could have been made without subterfuge. At least two arguments have been put forth for this premise. One, Spanish policy did permit multiple concessions, provided that the petitioner possessed at least one hundred head of cattle and two slaves; and several double concessions were granted in the Natchitoches area.[24] Two extant records document other instances in which the aging Coincoin turned over the use of her land to her sons Pierre and Pierre Toussaint, with no rental contract or legal document to ensure herself an income from the property.[25] In such an atmosphere of family cooperation, Coincoin might have sought a grant for her son Louis. This particular proposition has been the most appealing to Coincoin's family, African American historians, and tourism interests alike.

The historical and archaeological record conclusively proves otherwise: the Melrose grant was indeed made to Louis Metoyer, six years before his emancipation. Louis's petition for a concession was one of a pair submitted on the same day and approved simultaneously by De Blanc, authorizing not only Louis but also his brother Dominique to settle land in the Isle District. On May 18, 1796, the governor's office likewise issued two orders of survey and settlement, one to each brother. The already-manumitted Dominique, who was unambiguously eligible for his grant, had no difficulty in finding a surveyor with sufficient eyesight; a survey for his 904 arpents, dated April 15, 1799, was filed with the United States Board of Land Commissioners in support of his title to this land.[26] However, that surveyor, Pierre Joseph Maës, was from the Grand Côte; an adjacent neighbor to both Pierre Metoyer and Coincoin, he was likely well aware of Louis's enslaved status. By not engaging Maës's service, Louis avoided the need to ask the surveyor to certify the illegality De Blanc had arranged. Louis's need to avoid a surveyor also appears to be the reason why the adjacent concession to Augustin also went unsurveyed; surveyors were required to record, on their plats, the legal owners of adjacent land.

Louis's illegal concession was, in fact, not the only one that De Blanc authorized for Coincoin's children. On March 5, 1798, he approved a much smaller concession of 128 acres in the Isle District for Coincoin's fourth Metoyer son, Pierre, according to the claim later filed before the United States Board of Land Commissioners.[27] Young Pierre was then twenty-six, obviously ready to make his own start in life. Like his brother Louis, however, he would not be freed until 1802. Tradition does not argue that his illegal (and unsurveyed) concession, which was located across Bayou Plat from Louis's tract, was actually made to Coincoin.

Legally or otherwise, Coincoin's Metoyer sons received Spanish rights to 2,711 acres of fertile virgin bottomlands along Red River. After the transfer of Louisiana to American authority in 1803, the Board of Land Commissioners accepted claims for the next dozen or so years. During this period, Coincoin's offspring were confirmed in title to a number of additional tracts, all based upon right by occupancy, although the facts of some cases were clearly misrepresented in the interest of the claimant.

Antoine Joseph Metoyer, Coincoin's fifth son, filed a Little River claim for a tract of 640 acres bounding the back side of the Cane River grant given his brother Dominique. According to testimony filed in this claim, Joseph had settled and occupied the land for three consecutive years prior to December 20, 1803, the day the French officials turned Louisiana over to the American government. Joseph's claim was approved and surveyed at 470 acres. But then another was filed by Joseph's wife, Marie Pelagie Le Court, a claim filed under her given name only, with no indication of the family to which she belonged. Her 640-acre claim lay on Old River's Bayou D'Ivrogne (Drunkard's Bayou) in the Kisatchie Forest area south of Natchitoches—some twenty-five miles, by water route, from the tract claimed by her husband. The testimony of the man hired to file affidavits in support of their claims supports the appearance of fraud: Pierre Quierry, a white resident of the parish, testified before the board at Opelousas in the fall of 1813 that both Joseph and Marie Pelagie were heads of households, and made no mention of the relationship between them. However, a reconstruction of the couple's conjugal life explains Marie Pelagie's claim to occupy a separate tract as a head of household. In the first five years after their 1802 marriage, she bore five children, the last of them on November 22, 1807. Between 1818 and 1827, she bore four more. In the eleven years from 1807 to 1818, she bore no children at all. Meanwhile, in 1810, 1813, 1815, and 1817 Joseph fathered children by his slave Marie Rose, before reconciling with his wife. [28]

A similar situation existed with Joseph's brother Pierre. In addition to the claim Pierre filed, his wife Marie Perine Le Comte claimed 640 acres on Old River's Bayou Derbanne, and Quierry testified on her behalf as well. Again, his sworn statement omitted the fact that she was the wife of another claimant and asserted that she, too, was the head of a family. After a considerable dispute over the exact location of her claim and her right to it, Marie Perine's claim was confirmed for 597 acres. As with Joseph and Marie Pelagie, Pierre and Marie Perine appear to have separated early in their marriage, but briefly reconciled before her 1815 death. [29]

Still another claim based upon "occupancy as required by law" was filed by Coincoin's next-to-youngest son, Toussaint. He, too, claimed 640 acres, placing his tract at the juncture of Bayou Blue with "Little River or River Brosset." Supporting his claim was the same family friend, Quierry, who swore that Toussaint, "[who has] inhabited and cultivated the land for fourteen consecutive years preceding said date, is about thirty-four years of age, and the head of a family." [30] Toussaint was actually three years younger, making him seventeen when he set out on his own to "inhabit and cultivate" this land—a plausibility for a rural male in that society. However, neither the church nor civil records of this period show any evidence that Toussaint had a wife or a child. His claim was confirmed, nonetheless, for the amount he had requested.

Adjoining Toussaint's property was an extensive tract of vacant land that was settled by young Jean François Florentin Conant, the eldest son of Toussaint's older sister, Susanne. Upon submitting his claim in 1814, based upon occupancy, Florentin offered the testimony of Michel Papillon, a free multiracial from Opelousas who, like Coincoin, had been a De Soto slave. Papillon swore that Florentin had resided upon and cultivated the land for about ten years. A second witness, Marcellet Martin, offered testimony that Florentin, "[who has] inhabited and cultivated the land for fourteen consecutive years preceding said date, is about thirty-five years of age, and has no family." Martin accurately stated Florentin's marital status but generously overestimated his age. Florentin was born in 1794. If he began to cultivate his land in 1800 as Martin indicated, or even in 1804 as Papillon testified, he was a quite precocious child when he became a planter. His claim was also confirmed for 674 acres.[31]

In addition to these successful claims, two disallowed claims were filed by Coincoin's family with the register and receiver of the land office—one of them clearly valid. Coincoin's sister Mariotte claimed a tract of only two arpents' frontage by a depth of forty on each side of Red (Cane) River, a total of 160 arpents—contending that she had purchased the land from one Antoine Bergeron. The U.S. Land Office rejected her claim, saying she was not able to produce any "document of title, or proof of occupancy."[32] Mariotte's handicap was not a lack of evidence but insufficient skill in navigating legal systems as a freed woman. In 1798, the man with whom she had been coupled for several years did file a deed in her name in the commandant's office, stating that the purchase price would be a year of labor washing his clothes. Indeed, he filed two such documents on her behalf. However, Bergeron died or left Natchitoches soon after; and Mariotte's subsequent attempts to conduct her own business affairs attest to both her excessive trust and her difficulty in communicating with the new English-speaking settlers of the area.[33]

François Metoyer, Coincoin's youngest son, entered a clearly questionable occupancy claim for 640 acres on Bayou Derbanne. He, too, offered Quierry's testimony in support of his claim. According to Quierry, François had used the land as a *vacherie* under the supervision of hirelings for sixteen consecutive years, although he resided on a place he had bought from his brother. Here again, if the claim is to be believed, François went into business for himself at a very tender age. In 1797, the year in which he supposedly began his *vacherie* operation, François was only thirteen. The board forwarded his file to the General Land Office in Washington as a class-nine claim, that is, "land occupied as *vacheries;* and whether with or without evidence of occupancy, ought not, in the opinion of the Register and Receiver, to be confirmed." François's claim was disallowed; and that decision was upheld when he appealed it to the congressional committee that held final authority over land claims generated by the Louisiana Purchase.[34]

Upon the transfer of Louisiana to American authority, Coincoin and her family had presented a total of twenty claims for land. One carried a completed Spanish title—the sixty-eight-acre tract funded by Metoyer—and its validity was not questioned. Eight more sizable claims were based upon land purchases that the Metoyer brothers and their aunt had made along the Cane River channel of Red River. Seven of these were confirmed; the eighth was disallowed. The remaining eleven claims were based upon alleged Spanish titles or upon the right of occupancy. Of the ten that were confirmed, the supporting evidence was valid in only four cases. Coincoin, Augustin, and Dominique received authentic concessions or grants for which they were unquestionably eligible; and there is no evidence of misrepresentation involving Joseph's claim to a tract by right of occupancy. The other six cases, however, reflect the spirit of self-determination that had governed the borderlands since St. Denis's appointment to the commandant's post. The former slaves well followed the examples their masters had set.

In contesting one Metoyer claim, a white neighbor charged: "this . . . is not the first [misrepresentation] of this kind that this family of coloured folks attempt to make."[35] He was correct, but his accusation created a false impression. These questionable claims filed by the Metoyers were by no means the only such claims in the parish or the state. For example, the claim of Brevel's French nephew Jean Baptiste Théodore Grillet for 640 acres, located above Camptí in the northern part of the parish, asserted that Grillet had cultivated the land for fifteen consecutive years, even though he was only twenty-eight at the time of the testimony. The commissioners spotted the discrepancy in the evidence presented to them and disallowed the claim with the observation, "It is very unlikely that the claimant should have established a plantation at thirteen years of age."[36]

Even the complainant who questioned the authenticity of the Marie Perine grant, when it conflicted with his own claim to a portion of the same land, was not without guile. François Roubieu had not only filed his own claims of questionable nature but had assisted his neighbors, including Louis Metoyer, in filing similar claims. Seven years earlier, the U.S. Congressional Committee on Private Land Claims had sent to the House of Representatives a report on a number of petitions submitted by residents of Natchitoches Parish. It was the committee's opinion that "some suspicion [is] thrown over the evidence . . . from the fact that these petitioners seem to have sworn generally for each other. The evidence would seem to convey the idea 'if you will swear for me I will swear for you.'" The committee requested that the Louisiana land office be authorized to collect testimony relative to these doubtful claims for presentation to Congress.[37]

While questionable behavior from a community at large does not exonerate individual responsibility for such actions, it would be disingenuous to censure the ambitious free man or woman of color for employing the same business tactics used by the community's white leaders. This generation of Creoles, white and multiracial, was shaped by an era in which Louisiana had been shuffled like an orphan among three nations. Creoles had learned to resolve their own problems while governments came, went, and struggled for dominance.[38] Across a century, they had been the pawn of distant governments that exploited rather than nurtured its denizens; laws were set by those with little understanding of settlers' lives or needs, especially in backcountry posts such as Natchitoches. There, generations had honed their ability to navigate their own channels through restrictive legislation. Under their latest bureaucratic master, those dynamics had not changed; nor had the self-protective countermeasures devised by the citizenry.

Moreover, this generation of Creoles had grown to maturity in a society in which land was free to any ambitious man who was willing to work it. The restrictive land regulations imposed by the new American government left many young men without a means to make their start in life, including such youths as Jean Baptiste Théodore Grillet and Toussaint and François Metoyer, whose older brothers had received generous concessions from Spain. To the Creoles of Louisiana, the American requirement that citizens must purchase vacant lands from the government undoubtedly seemed more unjust than the expedients they took to accumulate the land they needed to support their families.

An additional irritant to the claimants of land in the new Louisiana territory was the reduction in size of individual holdings that often resulted from the adjustment of claims. As boundary lines were relocated by American surveyors, many landholders found themselves with shrunken bounds. The grant of Augustin Metoyer, for example, had been surveyed by the Spanish at 395 acres; yet the American resurvey allotted him only 157 acres. The 640-acre tract for which Joseph Metoyer filed a claim based on occupancy was surveyed and resurveyed until the boundaries finally decided upon allowed him only 470 acres.[39] To compensate claimants for the shortfall, the U.S. Land Office issued "floats" or "script" for the missing acreage—that is, certificates that could be cashed in for land anywhere in the public domain. By the time the floats were issued, however, most productive land along Cane River had been claimed. Trading the floats for mediocre land at considerable distance from one's farm—land with little resale value and an annual tax liability—was rarely a viable option. A landowner's only recourse, in most cases, was to sell the float to speculators at pennies on the dollar.[40]

Another source of irritation to Natchitoches landholders was the federal requirement that they file their claims with the register and receiver of the federal land office at Opelousas. As late as 1812, the deputy surveyor of the Natchitoches region, Joseph Irwin, wrote to Register Levin Wailes (himself a participant in Georgia's land frauds before his federal appointment to Louisiana)[41] regarding problems faced by Augustin Metoyer and his mother: "The claimants have engaged the bearer to go forward to your Office to prove what he knows respecting the settlements of these two claims. . . . I write this at the request of the claimants who also wish me to state to the Board of Commissioners the Dificulty [sic] they labour under to establish their claims on account of the distance & the Difficulty of finding any person who will leave their habitations to undertake the journey at this season."[42]

The greatest challenge faced by the Metoyers in the establishment of their claims was the one presented to Louis's title by Silvestre Bossier. Although Bossier had been the first concessionaire of the land Louis had been assigned in the Isle Brevelle District, Bossier had forfeited his rights after failing to fulfill requirements exacted of all grantees. In surrendering his order of survey and settlement to the commandant, Bossier had declared that the land was not worth the cost of the half of a bridge that he would have had to build over neighboring Bayou Plat.[43] By 1806 Louis had made substantial improvements upon the tract. Bossier obviously regretted his forfeiture and attempted to regain it. Through unexplained means, he retrieved from the courthouse his surrendered order of survey and settlement and submitted it to the land board as proof of his ownership.

Upon learning of Bossier's actions, Metoyer engaged an attorney, William Murray, to draft for him a memorial setting out the facts regarding Bossier's invalid claim and his own legitimate one. In support of his petition he also secured evidence unusual among the Natchitoches claims: a letter from former commandant De Blanc, who had moved to south Louisiana more than a decade earlier, verifying that Louis was the rightful owner. Despite De Blanc's testimony in which he swore "on my religion, my conscience, and my honor, that this declaration is true, that you may be on your guard against those who now wish to claim those titles . . . having lost all right to them," the Board of Commissioners ruled that Bossier's claim was as valid as Louis's was. The recommendation they forwarded to Washington suggested that Bossier's title be confirmed, on the grounds that no written evidence of abandonment could be provided. It would then remain for the two claimants to settle the issue between themselves or take the matter to court.[44]

In the end, litigation would decide the conflicting claims. Bossier and his heirs filed suit against Louis to have him evicted from the land, and they won in northwest Louisiana's district court. Metoyer appealed to the state supreme court, and in its September 1818 term it overturned the decision of the lower court. Louis Metoyer was adjudged to be the rightful owner, and Bossier was charged with the costs of court.[45]

The adjustment of land claims by the United States government allowed 6,389 acres to Coincoin and her family. Of this, 68 acres—1 percent of the total—had been facilitated by Metoyer when he paid Délouche for his interest in the land so that Coincoin might file for the title. The remaining 6,321 acres, an average of 632 acres per person, had been acquired by Spanish concession or by right of occupancy. This was the foundation on which the family built its future. With industry and frugality, they steadily extended their holdings, purchasing one additional tract after another. At least sixteen such purchases were made prior to Coincoin's death, about 1816, bringing the family's total acreage at that time to 10,846, not counting four tracts of undetermined size.[46]

In 1861 a French-born priest in the parish wrote home to his parents, recounting the wealth of the local planters and the means by which it had been acquired: "With the aid of a negro and a negress, at the most, they started with a little corner in the forest! And now their descendants, despite all their riches are very simple, good affable people."[47] Generally speaking, this rags-to-riches story can be applied to the Metoyers *de couleur*; in one significant respect, however, their situation differed. Coincoin's sons started their labors alone, without either a "negro or a negress," or even children of sufficient age to assist them in clearing their "little corner in the forest."

The first of the brothers to acquire land, Augustin, was also the first to join the slaveholding ranks. Across the years, three distinctly different factors would motivate his slave purchases: a need for labor, the needs of his extended family, and a sense of charity or social justice. His actions of the latter type would expand his influence as a community leader, as well as patriarch of his own kin, and set an example his sons would carry forward throughout the antebellum era.

Living frugally in a small cabin he had erected on his concession, the newly wed Augustin labored for two years to accumulate sufficient capital to purchase his first hand. From a planter of the Rivière aux Cannes settlement, he acquired Antoine, a nineteen-year-old black male, obviously chosen to help clear the live oaks, the locust trees, the gums, and the saw palmettos that blanketed Augustin's concession.[48] From that time forward, the notarial archives of the civil parish chronicle Augustin's advancement into the ranks of Red River's largest slaveowners.

The cash generated by Augustin's and Antoine's toil would not be invested in other laborers for some years to come. In that interim, family needs were Augustin's overriding priority. Both he and his wife Agnes had enslaved siblings. His younger brothers were reaching maturity and needed wives, while the Natchitoches post offered no free women of color for them to court. His still-enslaved brother Louis had already fathered two children, who also needed to be bought from bondage. For the next five years, Augustin focused on these family matters. To the 1798 succession of Widow Pierre Derbanne, he paid 261 piasters for his eight-year-old sister-in-law, the Franco-African Marguerite, whom he immediately freed.[49] In time, she would marry his brother François. By 1800, he had saved another $300 to buy the freedom of Marie Rose, the natural daughter of his brother Louis by the Le Comte slave Françoise.[50] Again the following year, Augustin paid $600 cash for the manumission of the fifteen-year-old Franco-African Marie Perine Le Comte—shortly before her marriage to Augustin's brother Pierre.[51] Similar purchases followed in the years thereafter, with some manumissions executed immediately and others after some passage of time.

Amid the twelve years in which Augustin's slave purchases focused on his family, he made only one non-family acquisition. At the death of his former neighbor, the old parish surveyor Pierre Joseph Maës, the slaves from Maës's plantation went on the auction block. Among them was the apparent slave wife and child of Augustin's Antoine, the eighteen-year-old Jeanne and her two-month-old infant. Augustin arranged to buy the pair. However, slave ownership by people of color was a rarity at Natchitoches in the year 1802, and the civil stature of the young freed Metoyers was still in a state of limbo in which even the use of a surname was a privilege inconsistently granted. Fearing a challenge to his public bidding on slaves from the Maës succession, Augustin arranged for a French Creole friend, Louis Fontenot, to serve as the public front for his purchase. Fontenot successfully bid $851 for Jeanne and her child and then immediately resold the pair to Augustin at the same price. Lacking the cash to pay Fontenot immediately, Augustin gave his note; a second white Creole, Augustin Fredieu, stood *in solido* with Augustin on the $851 debt.[52]

Between 1802 and 1809 Augustin depended upon the natural increase of this couple to enlarge his slave holdings, while he and Antoine likely shared the grueling labor of clearing and tillage with hired hands. His capital, aside from family purchases, was invested exclusively in more land, most of it raw, uncleared, and, thus, cheap. When he returned again to the slave market to expand his labor force, the harvests from his now productive farm had generated a goodly amount of operating cash. He also applied a radically new acquisition policy—one in keeping with the biblical injunction set by Leviticus 25:44: "Slaves male and female, you may indeed possess, provided you buy them from among the neighboring nations." From this point forward, a cultural and ethnic divide would distinguish Augustin's purchases for labor from the more charitable purchases he made as a community agent or benefactor.

By 1809, Anglo-American slave traders were making regular forays up Cane River, offering a variety of bondsmen to willing buyers of any color. Purchases for labor made by Augustin and his siblings were henceforth "English Negroes" or African-born. In June of that year, for example, Augustin purchased from Archibald Phillips of Rapides Parish eight "African Negroes" for $3,500 cash: a male of about twenty, five boys aged about eleven and twelve, and two girls aged eleven to thirteen. Three of the boys were immediately resold to his brother Louis for $1,350.[53] In 1810, he purchased a twenty-year-old male, Harry, from a Virginia trader, followed by a young woman named Charlotte in 1811 from a Tennessee trader. In 1813, he added a family of five: Ned, his wife Ginny, and their children Mima, Jack, and Kitty.[54] Following his mother's example, he would have the children baptized when a priest came to the parish, but he did not compel the adults to adopt his faith.[55]

Most of Augustin's siblings followed his lead, in both their slave purchases and slave baptisms. Two acquisitions made by his sister Susanne attest the ambiguity of the family's status in the new American regime. In 1810 Susanne purchased a young black male for $600 from Thomas Parham, a slave trader of Brunswick County, Virginia. The following year she made a similar purchase from a Tennessee trader named Robert Bell.[56] Undoubtedly, both sellers were unaware that the woman with whom they negotiated was herself still a slave, legally incapable of owning property of any kind. As in the case of her brothers Louis and Pierre, who received Spanish grants while still in bondage, Marie Susanne clearly enjoyed privileges that her community denied to other slaves.

The census of 1810, the first American count taken in Orleans Territory, reflects the economic growth the family had made along Cane River. Augustin Metoyer was listed as the owner of seventeen slaves; Louis had fifteen; the combined household of Pierre Jr. and Coincoin reported twelve; Dominique, eight; François, three; Joseph, two; and Toussaint, one. Together, Coincoin and her children had accumulated fifty-eight slaves in fifteen years. Of the 259 households enumerated on this census, only 166 owned at least one slave. Of the thirteen other free people of color or free blacks who were listed as heads of household, only four owned slaves; they averaged two each—and, notarial records show, those slaves were their own spouse or child. The rise in stature of the Metoyers *de couleur* is even more evident when the *ancien population* of the parish is divided into family groups. Of the 192 surname groups identifiable for the parish, only five owned more slaves than did the Metoyers of color: the Rachals, Lambres, Buards, Prudhommes, and Claude Thomas Pierre Metoyer himself.[57]

The numerous land purchases that Coincoin's offspring made thereafter demanded an increasing number of slaves, and in the subsequent years the Metoyers *de couleur* steadily increased their human capital. Conveyances on record indicate their purchase of at least twenty-two slaves between 1810 and 1817. Natural increase added at least nineteen more during this period.[58] In 1778 Coincoin had been a thirty-six-year-old freed slave with eleven children; she had possessed no home, property, or money. Before her death some thirty-eight years later, she had not only succeeded in obtaining the freedom of almost all those children, but she and they had accumulated an estate of between 11,000 and 12,000 acres of land and at least ninety-nine slaves.

Quantitative counts of slave purchases cannot alone reflect the infinite range of realities those transactions represent. Behind every purchase lies a human story, and each varies in ways that individual documents seldom reveal. One lengthy study of slaveholding by Louisiana's free people of color cites numerous transactions by Augustin Metoyer before concluding, "The Metoyers routinely sold and bought black slaves on a regular basis between relations and acquaintances. In doing so, they showed that they considered black slaves as merely profit making vehicles to realize their wealth."[59] The desire for wealth (or the need for wealth, as subsequent decades made clear) is an undeniable factor. However, a number of the slave transactions of record represent occasions on which Augustin acted as a benefactor, helping other freedmen buy their kin, protecting the economically vulnerable nonwhites along Cane River, or shielding enslaved women from sexual predators.

As a case at point, Augustin executed two separate slave purchases in May and June 1810. In the first transaction, he acquired an eighteen-year-old multiracial Creole girl named Dorothée from Manuel Derbanne, a white Cane River planter. Eleven days later, when a Virginia trader named Thomas Parham passed upriver with a coffle of slaves, Augustin bought a twenty-year-old black male named Harry.[60] On the surface, one might logically assume these two were acquired for their labor. Considering their genders and ages, and the close dates of the two acquisitions, the characterization of Augustin as one who bought slaves as a "profit-making vehicle" might extend to a conclusion that he bought Harry to couple with Dorothée, thereby generating offspring that would enhance his wealth.

The backstory for this pair of purchases suggests a radically different historical perspective. The pivotal character in this episode was Manuel Derbanne, the son of a prominent French and Indian planter on Cane River. Manuel's widowed mother had died in 1798, leaving thirteen slaves; most were black, but two children were said to be "mulatto." Mme. Derbanne's will made two explicit bequests that involved her slaves, but only those two children. The girl Dorothée was to go to her son Joseph. The boy Remy was to go to her son Manuel. The other slaves were left to be disposed of by conventional means: a public auction at which heirs could choose to bid on any item of interest to them.[61] The implication inherent in the widow's bequest follows the pattern of their society: the testator recognized that the slave children were offspring of her sons; thus she bequeathed the children to their fathers, with the expectation that her sons would free their offspring.

Both Joseph and Manuel Derbanne were single males in their twenties when they inherited the children. Both would marry—Joseph in 1802 and Manuel in 1804.[62] Apparently, one of their wives (likely Manuel's, considering the timing) was not happy with the constant presence of her husband's child. To resolve the issue, Joseph and Manuel asked their brother Louis, the Cane River notary, to draft for them a legal exchange: Manuel became the new owner of Dorothée, and Joseph took home Remy.[63]

That exchange did not work well for Joseph and his daughter. In 1809, Manuel became indebted to the Rivière aux Cannes planter Alexis Cloutier. To secure the debt, Manuel was forced to give a mortgage on his slaves— Dorothée included. Joseph retaliated by selling Remy, but did target his buyer carefully. Augustin Metoyer had married Remy's older sister and would, Joseph assumed, manumit Remy when he reached the age prescribed by law. Manuel, meanwhile, failed to raise the funds to repay Cloutier.[64] That failure was seriously exacerbated by the character of the creditor who was about to become Dorothée's new master—a man whose wife charged him with mental and physical abuse, whose relatives sued him for chicanery, and whose slave women had no recourse against his sexual advances.[65]

Shortly before the debt came due, Manuel went to Augustin for help—or Augustin, being apprised of the situation, went to Manuel—and they cobbled together a solution. Manuel had only 60 piasters to put toward the 235-piaster debt. He also owned a note for 101 piasters owed to him by a Cane River neighbor, a note he could assign to Cloutier at a discount. For the balance, Augustin cosigned a new promissory note, agreeing to pay Cloutier that sum, plus interests, if Manuel failed to pay the debt when that new note came due.[66]

The second half of the arrangement was executed the following day. Augustin took title to Dorothée so that her safety would not be compromised again. For her, he not only gave Manuel $200 cash but also promised to deliver, as soon as possible, an even more valuable slave: "a merchantable Negro between fifteen and twenty" years of age. Because Augustin owned no such slave; the men agreed that Dorothée would remain with Manuel until the "merchantable Negro" could be supplied. Eleven days later, the Virginia trader arrived with a coffle of "Anglo" blacks, thereby allowing Augustin to complete his agreement without violating the Leviticus standard he had adopted: slaves purchased for labor could not be one of his own people—that is, Creole and Catholic.[67]

With Dorothée's acquisition, Augustin's family now embraced two enslaved kith and kin who had been purchased for manumission: his wife's brother Remy, newly acquired from Joseph Derbanne, and now Joseph Derbanne's daughter Dorothée. Under the more restrictive regulations of an Americanized Louisiana, however, no slave could be freed before the age of thirty. Proposed manumissions for slaves past that age required masters to file a petition, publish a public notice, and receive judicial approval. When a manumission was authorized, masters had to post a sizable bond, to ensure that the freed man or woman would not become a financial burden upon the public.[68] Both Dorothée and Remy failed the basic test of age.

The legal wait presented Augustin with another moral dilemma. Both additions to his family were past the age at which Creole youth formed marital unions; yet marriage was not a legal option for those who were enslaved. Augustin had been born of a plaçage to parents who could not marry. His wife Agnes had been born of a more casual interracial union. However, from the time his younger brothers settled around him on the isles, Augustin had assumed a patriarchal role grounded in respect for the laws of both church and state. The children Augustin and Agnes had brought into the world had been reared to plan a stable marriage and would fulfill that expectation. The daughters, at least, were expected to be chaste.

By the fall of 1814, Dorothée was twenty-two, in love, and legally incapable of marriage. Weighing her options, as well as his, Augustin chose the venial sin of lying rather than consign her to the mortal sin of violating the Sixth Commandment. He petitioned for her manumission and swore that she was, indeed, past the age of thirty. With perhaps a wink and a nod of his own, the parish judge—whose wife had grown up with Augustin on the Grand Côte—approved the request. Augustin paid the requisite fees, and on November 11, 1814, Dorothée became a free woman. The parental role Augustin had assumed for her did not end with her manumission, however. The man she had chosen, Joseph La Vigne, was also a free multiracial, but a penniless one. When the couple wed three weeks later, Augustin not only served as surety for La Vigne's marriage bond and arranged for a notary to draw up a marriage contract to protect Dorothée's future rights, but also provided 600 piasters for Dorothée to take into the marriage as a financial stake upon which the young couple could build a future.[69]

The patriarchal role Augustin assumed over Cane River in this era generated other slave purchases whose interpretive contexts involve textual layers. In 1813, for example, Augustin acquired a twenty-five-year-old black male named François; the seller was a free black neighbor, Yves *dit* Pacalé, to whom Augustin paid $600. Viewed in isolation, that one document offers no clue to the chain of events that occurred before and after the sale.[70] Pacalé, one of the few Creole black slaves at Natchitoches to use an African name as his *dit* throughout life, had been a slave of the Derbanne family for the first sixty-two years of his life. At the death of Pierre Derbanne's widow in 1798, he asked the heirs to give him his freedom, and they agreed.[71] From a neighbor, he bought a small raw tract of land and built a home. By 1802 he had the funds to buy his wife, Marie Louise; and, under the manumission laws of the colony, he immediately freed her. That wife soon died, and the aging Pacalé saved to buy a new wife, called "Eteroux" in the bill of sale, who was already sixty-five when he purchased and freed her in 1806. With his physical strength waning, he next bought a slave for labor, a young black male named François.[72]

In 1812, the 76-year-old Pacalé approached Augustin Metoyer asking for help. He had a forty-year-old daughter who was still enslaved. Thérèse's owner, the Roubieu brothers, had set a price of $800. Pacalé lacked the money to buy her, but her owners were willing to take a note if someone of substance would guarantee it. Augustin agreed, the purchase was made, and Pacalé advertised his intent to manumit Thérèse. No one in the community objected, and the parish judge approved her manumission. Then the one-year note came due and Pacalé was destitute. He sold his ninety-one acres to a white Creole neighbor, despite the fact that he had already mortgaged the land and his laborer François to Augustin, to cover Augustin's guarantee on the Roubieu debt. Yet the proceeds for the sale of Pacalé's land fell far short of the needed funds. Failure to repay the debt would mean, under manu-mission laws, that his daughter could be seized by the Roubieu brothers and remanded to slavery. Again, Augustin stepped in. He paid the Roubieus for Pacalé's daughter; then, because the young mortgaged male was worth considerably more than the forty-year-old Thérèse, he paid Pacalé an addi-tional $600 to equalize the transaction. Pacalé then made title to Augustin, but Augustin apparently left the man in Pacalé's possession, recognizing that the aged freedman would have no other way of providing a livelihood for himself and the two females he was now supporting. The white Creole purchaser of Pacalé's land also allowed the hapless family to remain in their home and continue tillage of the land. Six years later, Pacalé died, at the age of eighty-two. His land went to the purchaser and his slave moved to Augus-tin's plantation, where he would remain until Augustin's death.[73]

Augustin's role as Cane River's patriarch—not just for his own kin but for less prosperous whites, blacks, and other multiracials—was cemented in that first quarter-century on Isle Brevelle. When the freedwoman Zabelle needed help in purchasing the freedom of her son from the Buard family, she turned to Augustin. When the white Creole planter Jacques La Caze penned a will freeing his two multiracial sons, he named Augustin and Augustin's eldest son as his executors, to ensure that his wishes were followed. When two white males new to the parish accused the aging freedwoman Babet and her daughter Marie Desneiges of physically abusing them, and the women had no witnesses to support their assertion that they had acted only to pro-tect themselves, Augustin and his son successfully mounted the defense that saved the women from the guilty verdict that would have remanded them to slavery and public auction to the highest bidder.[74]

Although the foundations of the Metoyer community in the Isle District were acquired at no monetary cost other than the surveyors' fees, the rapid progress the Metoyers achieved came at the price of thrift and industry, as well as community service. Frequently, the family purchased goods from the probate auctions of deceased neighbors, but luxury items were not among these purchases. Land and slaves were their main capital acquisitions, and profits were reinvested in their planting operations. The only extravagance credited to them during this period was a journey abroad that—tradition claims, but no evidence supports—Augustin supposedly made with his father, touring the cities of France to which he had ancestral ties. This anomaly aside, the Metoyers *de couleur* displayed great frugality during the development of their community, as their mother had done before them. Their way of life was simple at this stage; their homes were modest.

In recalling the first home that Louis Metoyer erected on his grant of land, an elderly descendant of the early twentieth century described it as "an adobe hut, a small house with but one room, built for the most part by his own hands."[75] This home no longer stands; but two other area dwellings of the same type, erected during this period, do survive. Excellent descriptions have been provided by an Isle Brevelle resident of the mid-twentieth century, Father J. J. Callahan:

> The Old Convent [is] said to be the oldest building on the river. The date of its construction is of course unknown, but its appearance does not belie its age. The floor is of hard packed clay, and it has a fire place and chimney of native brick. All the rest is cypress with mud filling. . . . the cypress stanchions remain visible in the adobe screen. In the walls of the Roque house the mud is mixed with deer hair; in the Old Convent with Spanish moss, which is today as strong and durable as when it was inserted. It [the Old Convent, aka Badin-Roque House] is also the most primitive in another sense. It is the only house remaining where there is no attempt at ornamentation. The beams are rough hewn, and the thick boards are just as they were sawed by hand. In later buildings, both boards and beams were hand planed, and every beam that shows in the interior has a bead carved on each side of its face.[76]

Father Callahan's description depicts these earliest homes on the Isle as crude, but the structures were not exceptional. Dr. Sibley's report on the urban dwellings in Natchitoches in 1805 was no more flattering; in his words, the town was "meanly built . . . half a dozen houses excepted."[77]

Typical of a somewhat better class of home in rural colonial Louisiana is a third dwelling that survives on Louis Metoyer's Spanish concession. Dubbed "Yucca House" by twentieth-century occupants, the building employs the same basic construction as was used for the Old Convent and the

Roque House: *poteaux-en-terre.* Logs placed upright in the ground form the framework for the walls. The spaces between the logs are then filled with *bousillage,* a mixture of mud and deer hair or moss. Yet, Yucca House differs in three ways from the more primitive cabins described by Callahan. First, its construction is of a better quality, indicating a greater investment of time and effort. Second, rather than a square one-room cabin, it is an elongated structure of several rooms. Third, its front and back were designed with a spacious veranda extending the full length of the dwelling (although the ends of its back veranda have since been enclosed to form two extra rooms).

The date of the home's construction has been widely debated by archaeological, architectural, historical, and tourism interests. Early-twentieth-century owners, who developed Louis's estate grounds into a retreat for artists and writers, widely touted "Yucca" as Coincoin's plantation and "Yucca House" as the first home built by her as a free woman. The heritage group that later acquired the grounds reverently followed that lead but modified the Coincoin narrative to accommodate historical evidence that the land was a 1796 concession in the name of Coincoin's son. Their stance was also that of the eminent architectural historian they engaged to restore the property and was followed by the Historic American Buildings Survey, which accepted that scholar's judgment. Thus, a new crop of Yucca House literature dated it at 1796–1800.[78] Four subsequent decades of historical research, however, have uncovered no document connecting Coincoin to the property, surveys of the land over the first two decades of Louis's ownership place no structure at that location, and archaeological evidence dates the property to the 1815–20 period.[79]

Dating the construction of Yucca House from its architectural style is problematic because colonial constructions persisted even as new structural forms took hold. Anglo-Americans introduced stacked-log dwellings into Cane River culture in the decade that Coincoin's sons settled their properties. Raised cottages in the West Indian fashion would eventually become Louisiana's symbolic style. However, *poteaux-en-terre* remained the preferred construction along Cane River through several decades of the nineteenth century.[80] One 1812 Anglo-American observer reports that two-story houses were still considered unsafe in Louisiana's "sudden and violent squalls of wind," and that brick was not yet a preferred building material for homes. All houses, this observer added, were partly or entirely "surrounded by arcades or piazzas" for coolness.[81] More to the point—and more controversially—some archaeologists see the one surviving structure on

Coincoin's own farmstead as evidence that *poteau-en-terre* construction persisted at least to the 1830s.[82]

Historical records provide the most definitive evidence. The Louis Metoyer concession on which Yucca stands is divided into two sections— as are the adjacent and nearby properties of Louis's brothers Augustin and Dominique. Louis's land to the west of Cane River, the portion that lies on Isle Brevelle, consisted of a small triangle with only 53 acres. The bulk of his land, 859 acres, lay on the unnamed isle that stretches between the Cane and Little Rivers. Yucca House stands on that more eastern isle. However, the earliest survey of the tract, made in 1814, and two separate surveys of Augustin's neighboring properties made in 1815, all place Louis's home on the small western triangle, just across the property line from Augustin's home. Scarcely a stone's throw separated the two.[83]

The Isle Brevelle (west bank of the Cane) location of Louis's 1814–15 residence is a logical site. In the developmental stage, the neighboring brothers would have shared slaves, tools, and personal assistance. Logic dictates that the first tracts they developed would lie on the same side of the river, eliminating the need to transport slaves, animals, and tools across a surging waterway in order to work each other's lands.

The catalyst for Louis's relocation of his homestead on the unnamed isle to the east of the Cane was likely the 1818 settlement of his legal dispute with Sylvestre Bossier. Twenty-two years had elapsed since Commandant De Blanc had put Louis in possession of the tract. In that interim, Louis and the twenty or so slaves he had accumulated would have thoroughly developed his 53-acre homestead to the west of the river and put much of the east bank's 859 acres under cultivation. Maintaining his base of operations on one bank while most of his daily activities lay on the other would have been highly inefficient. Yet building new slave quarters, barns, and equipment sheds—as well as a new residence—on the east bank would have been an improvident risk until his legal title was secure. Not until the Louisiana Supreme Court vacated Bossier's claim and awarded the property to Louis would it have been feasible for him to reseat himself on the east bank, where Yucca House and other later buildings now stand.[84]

Of those other buildings extant for Louis's plantation, one is unique in Louisiana architecture. That little cabin, two stories high, with only one room on each floor, is dominated by a huge roof that drops low and projects twelve feet on all sides like a giant square toadstool, completely concealing the top story and sheltering the bottom against torrential rains. No columns support the heavy roof. A series of horizontal posts are wedged perpendicularly to the wall and the roof's edge. Without a single nail, these posts have supported the ponderous roof for nearly two centuries. Bars fill the open cavities of its windows, and the absence of a fireplace suggests its use as something other than a residence.[85]

Again, the legend created by the property's early-twentieth-century owners attributes the building to Coincoin. Likening its architectural style to that found in subtropical Africa or the West Indies, they dubbed it the "African House" and spun a story of a Congo-born Coincoin homesick for the land of her birth. In the window bars, they saw evidence that she used the building as a jail.[86] That lore has been disputed by a new generation of architectural historians and archaeologists, who contend that "despite its general aesthetic that invokes for many the 'memory' of a uniquely African form, nothing about this building can be related directly to African tradition. . . . The builders of the African House employed no customary African methods or design principles, but rather those of France." They support their conclusions with comparative illustrations of Gallic farm houses.[87]

Legends aside, one fact is indisputable: by the time the old family matriarch died, a new generation of Metoyers had come to adulthood along Cane River under conditions radically different from those that allowed Coincoin and her children to prosper. Free lands were no longer available. As with the first generation of Euro-settlers on the borderland, individual parents again bore the responsibility of providing children with an economic foothold; but for free people of color in an Americanized Louisiana, those footholds would be far more tenuous. Coincoin had succeeded in providing freedom, not wealth, for most of her children. With no paternal inheritance, her Metoyer offspring had prospered using their own initiative to exploit the small window of opportunity available to them in the late Spanish period. Thus they laid the foundation for the kind of plantation empire that legend has attributed to the family's matriarch.

As new youth began to marry, each was provided with a tract of land, or slaves, or money, or all three, depending upon the assets of the parents and the preferences of the children. One of the first such donations to the new generation was made in 1817 when Augustin's son Maxille married his first cousin, Marie Aspasie Anty, the daughter of Marie Susanne. Augustin gave to the young couple a tract of land with six arpents of frontage "by the depth which it possessed." The tract was located on the lower end of Isle Brevelle between the lands of the white Creole Charles Le Moine and the young couple's uncle, François Metoyer. Augustin also gave the newlyweds $600 in cash, the same sum he had given to Joseph Derbanne's daughter Dorothée at the time of her marriage. On the day of Maxile and Aspasie's marriage contract, the bride's mother made another donation to the couple. Marie Susanne had not long been free, and she had not benefited from free lands during the colonial era. At this early stage of her economic career, her resources were far less ample than those of her twin brother Augustin, but still she made a donation to her daughter and new son-in-law of another $600 in cash.[88]

In subsequent years Augustin, his sister, and their brothers would make many such donations to their numerous progeny. However, even as the family's wealth increased, the generosity of the parents was tempered with moderation. Enough was given to each child to provide a start in life, but no son or daughter was given so great a handout as to weaken their initiative or ambitions. This second generation of Metoyers grew up in households characterized by moderation and industry. Upon reaching maturity each new adult was expected to make his own contribution to the development of their family into a community that could withstand the political and economic changes launched by Louisiana's new regime.

For these new generations, however, wealth would be a necessity, not an indulgence. Their very survival, economic and political, would depend upon the extent to which each new generation sustained the seeds of independence that Coincoin and her children planted on the Grand Côte and the isles below it. Ironically, in the plantation economy of the antebellum South, the independence they would struggle to preserve could be maintained only by depriving others of their freedom. That contradiction would be one the community would struggle with, individually and collectively, until the Civil War and the so-called reconstruction of the South deconstructed the society Coincoin's offspring built along Cane River.

FOUR

Background of the
Major Allied Families

Community expansion was essential for the Metoyers of Isle Brevelle. While Anglo-Protestant America condoned marriages between cousins, the Roman Catholic church proscribed it to the fourth degree. Yet colonial Louisiana provided no means of legal marriage outside the church, and Catholic culture in the new American regime still expected marriage to take place within that church. As a matter of practice, colonial priests seem to have applied marital proscriptions only to their free, white parishioners. Whether this stemmed from disregard or a sense of impracticality is debatable; but the statistics are not. The relatively few couples of color who were legally wed in colonial Natchitoches, free or enslaved, were spiritually united with no apparent effort to discern whether they were biologically related and, if so, how closely.[1]

That laxity continued after the Louisiana Purchase. The diocese of Havana transferred the spiritual welfare of Louisiana to the diocese of Baltimore, which had far too few priests to keep America's western fringe supplied. Meanwhile, Coincoin's youngest children and grandchildren came of age and needed spouses. Cane River's free colored population was expanding; but many were kin, to one degree or another, by blood (consanguinity) or marriage (affinity). Tradition holds that, as the Metoyers entered the social and economic mainstream, a visiting priest warned Augustin of the dangers of intra-family intermarriage and that he, for decades thereafter, brought in new youth from elsewhere. Table 1 provides, in broad brushstrokes, the statistical opportunities they could tap within the parish and the state. However, those statistics do not speak to the difficulty of finding exogamous partners who shared their culture and class and were not legally barred by enslavement or laws against miscegenation.

That dilemma was not unique to Cane River. John Hope Franklin, pointing to marital patterns in North Carolina's Chavis family, quoted a naïve earlier historian who accused that family of inbreeding "to an appalling extent."[2] In context, the situation was neither appalling nor uncommon in any American community where limited population meant a limited choice of mates.[3] Among families such as the Metoyers and the Chavises, however, marital options were further constrained by all those issues other than population density. Despite the long-standing view that early black-activist Bayard Rustin called "the sentimental notion of black solidarity,"[4] strong lines of social demarcation within black and brown America have been the historical norm. Free status, racial composition, religion, economic expectations, political views, and cultural traditions were all important considerations in choosing a mate.

A study of Metoyer marriages of the colonial and antebellum period reveals their challenges, their self-imposed parameters, and their efforts to reconcile one with the other. When Coincoin's children reached maturity, only Augustin found a bride of appropriate age and temperament among the few free people of color available on Cane River. His brothers chose from the larger number of multiracial slave girls, but only after the family accumulated the funds to purchase the freedom of each bride. None of the brothers took for his wife a girl in bondage. Class consciousness was already a part of their psychological makeup.

Table 1. *Population Growth of Louisiana's Free People of Color*

YEAR	METOYER CLAN	PARISH	STATE
1785	8*	8	1,175
1810	52	181	7,585
1820	75	415	10,476
1830	183	532	16,710
1840	—**	657	25,502
1850	362	881	17,462
1860	411	959	18,647

*This figure includes only the members of the nuclear family and their destined spouses who were already free.

**No accurate tabulation can be made of the clan's population for 1840 since one page of the enumeration of Isle Brevelle for that year is missing.

Throughout the decades that followed, the most obvious criterion employed in the selection of spouses—aside from free status—was color. Blacks
were systematically excluded by them in selecting life partners. Again, that
was a characteristic of "aristocratic" families of color. As James Hugo Johnston explained in one of the earliest studies of free nonwhites in the Americas:
"There were agencies that tended to force many of the mulattoes into a caste
apart from the mass of Negro population. When relations of affection existed
between the white father and his mulatto children, such fathers were often
inclined to consider their offspring not as Negroes but as persons of their
blood, and there is evidence that such parents taught their children to consider themselves as better or superior to the members of the servile race."[5]

Religion and culture narrowed even further the choices available to
Coincoin's grandchildren. Discrimination in the larger society advanced
to the point that buying the freedom of a spouse would have endangered
the small social and political toehold the Metoyers had gained. The wave of
opportunity-hungry Americans that flooded into Louisiana after the purchase brought multiracial children they would also free, as well as men of
color born to freedom in the older states. But the religious and cultural divide between them and French-speaking Catholics was one both sides took
seriously.

Economic activity was the sole factor that broadened their opportunities.
Some Creole families of color clustered in other Louisiana settlements—
Rapides, Opelousas, Pointe Coupée, Attakapas, St. Charles, East Baton Rouge,
and Plaquemines—but business and social intercourse appears limited between those areas and Isle Brevelle. New Orleans was the economic center
for all of Louisiana; and, as Metoyer wealth and socioeconomic mobility
increased, it offered the widest choice of peers. Especially after the War of
1812 introduced Cane River's militiamen to more of their counterparts in
the city, a number of New Orleans youths would move upriver and settle on
Isle Brevelle. Even then, they followed the pattern observable in almost all
migratory movements: individuals rarely migrated alone; most moved with
kin. Consequently, the exogamous partners pulled to the Isle from New Orleans were often related before they arrived, thereby limiting marital choices
for the next generation.

Most New Orleanians of color who migrated to the Isle carried old and
proud French names, as well as education. These factors undoubtedly
earned their acceptance into the Metoyer community because, with one sole
exception, none were men of means. Also, with only one known exception,

the New Orleans natives who married on the Isle were male. Part of the reason might be found in a theory advanced by several Louisiana historians: many free women of color in the city, supposedly, disdained alliances with men of their own race as too "limiting." Plaçage with a white man of status offered advantages they could never attain as the wives of free men of color, regardless of how wealthy the nonwhite husbands might be.[6]

Metoyer efforts to achieve marital exogamy also embraced, to a limited extent, male immigrants from France. Being white, none could legally marry women of known African descent, although some such Cane River unions were lifelong commitments. Tradition holds that these quasi-marriages were also discouraged by Augustin Metoyer, as he assumed the mantle of community patriarch. His objection, allegedly, was twofold. First, as a "strict moralist," he strongly discouraged "illicit" unions. Second, he feared that interracial unions would anger the public and endanger the social and political equilibrium that the community strove to maintain amid cycles of limited privileges and outright repression. Late in the nineteenth century, a small few of those unions would be given deathbed blessings by compassionate priests; but if any antebellum cleric defied the law during Louisiana's slave regime, he did not make it a matter of record.[7] Tradition also holds that several of the out-group marriages in the early years on the Isle involved male refugees from Haiti. However, those traditions remain unsupported by evidence; the males identified by those traditions were all, demonstrably, of Louisiana birth.

The most obvious example of Johnston's theory—that a white father's prejudice shaped the social contacts of his children of color—is provided by Susanne, the eldest daughter of Coincoin and Metoyer. Parish records reveal the contemporary presence of no unattached free man of color of appropriate age whom she might have chosen for a spouse. Her father, in whose home she lived and to whom she was inordinately close, clearly discouraged her contacts with male slaves. His efforts to direct the course of her life, however, were not always successful. In the spring of 1793, Susanne was nearly twenty-five and still single. In a society in which 56 percent of all females married in their teens and 80 percent had wed before twenty-five, Susanne's prospects of finding a life partner were rapidly diminishing.[8]

Into that void came a prospect who would have been acceptable to her father: a young doctor named Joseph Conant, from Serrières in the diocese of Lyon. Conant had been lured to New Orleans, apparently, by an uncle of the same name. From there, he journeyed upriver to Natchitoches, where the older Joseph's daughter was married to a wealthy planter and Metoyer neighbor on the Grand Côte.[9] There, the young doctor met Susanne, seduced her, but showed no inclination to accept responsibility for the pregnancy that followed. Susanne's father intervened. In March 1794, two months after the birth of Susanne's son, Metoyer gave Conant, for a token sum, title to a homestead with a *maison de poteaux en terre,* a storehouse, a garden, and auxiliary buildings. Presumably, the intent was for Conant and Susanne to settle into a plaçage. Conant, however, appears to have had little interest in a commitment. That fall, he bought a slave woman to keep his house, an aging black named Victoire for whom he paid 126 piasters—while Susanne apparently stayed on at her father's home, nursing not only her baby but her father's newest infant, Benjamin. The next spring, March 1795, Susanne's infant was finally baptized; but the child was given no surname and his father was recorded as "unknown." Clearly Conant was not willing to publicly acknowledge him. Susanne's brother Louis and her mother Coincoin stood as godparents. If Conant was present at the baptism, he went unmentioned. Seven months later, he sold his land on credit, disposed of the slave woman, and returned to New Orleans.

Conant's departure was a forced one. His sojourn on Cane River had coincided with a regional revolt against Spanish authority. In the course of that unrest—and in the wake of his rejection of Susanne and her son—a pack of prominent insurgents dressed as "ghosts" are said to have "chastised him with a whip." Extant records state no reason for that chastisement. Superficially, the attack by individuals clad in the garb of the political protestors seems to suggest that he opposed their resistance to Spanish authority. Ideologically, that would be a curious stance for a French immigrant living among culturally French insurgents in a small French Creole community. The possibility also exists—given that Conant's attackers were friends and neighbors of Metoyer—that the hooded "ghosts" may have "chastised" Conant for more personal reasons. Conant left the post in the wake of that attack, and subsequently married a French immigrant woman of his own status. Susanne's multiracial son, upon reaching adulthood, would assume Joseph Conant's surname and well-plant it on Cane River.[10]

Within two years, Susanne had made a more compatible match. Jean Baptiste Anty, a shoemaker's son and a planter and ferry owner of moderate means, was twice-widowed but still short of forty. He was also one of those political insurgents, although no known record places him at the "chastisement" of Joseph Conant. His arrangement with Susanne apparently earned the approval of her father, given that she continued to receive special favors from Metoyer while nursing his children and his wife. That plaçage with Anty would be a permanent one. It produced four daughters, all of whom Anty acknowledged to the point of attending their weddings and signing the marriage registers on those occasions.[11]

Susanne's brothers, in all probability, were also guided by their father in their choice of mates. The first three to marry were each manumitted by him just prior to the marriage, a clear indication that the matches enjoyed his approval. All brothers who married would choose free women of color for their wives.

The principal pool of multiracials from which Coincoin's sons chose spouses, as many of their own offspring later did, was a pool that reflected their own origin. It also attested the futility of the efforts made by both the *Code Noir* and Catholic priests to control miscegenation and override caste-based attitudes toward marriage. Particularly in the hinterlands, where vast stretches needed to be settled if Spain was to secure its territory, the economic policies of the state had undermined the church's efforts to keep its flock corralled. The transfer of Louisiana to Spain in the 1760s had forced the retirement of several French officers on the Natchitoches frontier. New restrictions on Indian trade had cut off their profitable lines of commerce within the Texas tribes. The recent resumption of the African slave trade had made agriculture more viable, but productive land in the Natchitoches district was limited. Expansion to the north was impractical, because Red River was jammed for a hundred or more miles by a primordial raft of fallen trees and rotting logs. Expansion to the west held little promise; the Spanish at nearby Los Adaës had long since proved the unproductivity of the piney woods that rose to the west of Red River. Lands east of the Red's three channels were of much the same poor quality. Only the unsettled banks of the Red and the Cane south of Natchitoches offered serious potential for wealth under mid-eighteenth-century agricultural practices.

Those prospects, however, were not the only force that had persuaded a cluster of Natchitoches families to move to the hinterlands. The newly retired Lieutenant Louis Mathias Le Court de Presle, like some other males of the minor *noblesse* who had come to the colony, harbored upper-class French views toward marriage and caste. After twenty years at the post, where women of comparable rank were not available, he was still a bachelor. He had, however, chosen a common alternative: concubinage with a woman the Gallic sense of *class* deemed inappropriate for marriage with men of armorial status. Unlike Pierre Metoyer, Le Court chose a woman who was free and white; Marie Jeanne Le Roy's only shortcoming seems to have been her birth as the daughter of a carpenter by an orphaned teen sent from the Salpetrière.[12] The baptismal acts for Marie Jeanne's first three children, between 1757 and 1763, maintained the fiction that their father was "unknown." Then a spate of moral activism by the parish priest, coinciding with the 1763 discharge of French military personnel in the wake of the colony's transfer to Spain, convinced Le Court to move his family away from the watchcare of the post.[13]

The site Le Court chose was a strategic one. The Red River bluffs, forty miles below Natchitoches, offered not only a vantage point in case of Indian hostility but also fertile land high enough that tobacco crops would be less affected by the river's annual flooding. With him, he took the newly retired corporal Jean Baptiste Le Comte, whose wife, Marguerite Le Roy, was the sister of Le Court's mistress. Soon they would be joined by the sisters' childhood friend, the twice-widowed and thrice-married Marie Louise (Rachal) Cloutier Gallien Charpentier, with young sons by her first two husbands and an orphaned nephew, Louis Monet. Over the next two decades other kith, kin, and displaced Indian traders from the Natchitoches post would join their out-migration: Duprés, Baudoins, Derbannes, and numerous offspring of Marie Rachal's brothers.[14] By the time Coincoin's sons moved down onto Isle Brevelle, those older families and their slaves had already put under cultivation most of the prime land between the bluffs and the Isle—creating the jurisdiction known as Rivière aux Cannes.

There at the bluffs, Le Court subsequently married his mistress, after the volatile priest who had driven them from Natchitoches was, ironically, reassigned to the new military post at the Red River rapids just below Le Court's Bluff. But their community remained outliers in most regards. Their plantations functioned as fiefdoms, operating outside of government control except for, occasionally, matters of inheritance. The church at the rapids soon withered away, and young men who came of age felt little pressure to marry. Concubinage and dalliance with slave women became the norm. Baptisms of children, slave and free, whatever the color, were infrequent. Many of those born in the first two decades cannot be accounted for in any extant records until they emerged as adults at the turn of the century. Manumission of slave children mostly went undocumented, except for two rare wills of the 1780s and 1790s.

Among those slave-born multiracials were the children of Coincoin's daughter Françoise, taken to Rivière aux Cannes as a child by her new master Jean Baptiste Dupré. As she matured, by choice or not, the culture of the district became her own. The children she bore as a Dupré slave would grow up using the names Le Comte and Monette. Three would eventually be freed, intermarry with their Metoyer kin, and become an integral part of their society.[15]

The strength of the bonds for which Isle Brevelle and Cane River became known over the next two centuries was not simply—as often asserted—a manifestation of the "remarkableness" of Coincoin's Metoyer offspring. It was, to a great degree, rooted in the cultural and familial ties knotted by the Le Courts, the Le Comtes, the Rachal clan, and their slaves at Rivière aux Cannes. As Coincoin's sons reached maturity, that district was their frequent haunt. Young Louis Metoyer, years before his manumission, fathered two daughters by one of the Le Comte slaves. Once free, not surprisingly, most of the brothers drew their wives from this pool on lower Cane River.

The first of Coincoin's sons to marry, Susanne's twin Augustin, chose a twenty-two-year-old multiracial named Marie Agnes Poissot. This young freedwoman had been born into the Grand Côte slave household of a half-Chitimacha planter named Pierre Derbanne. Her black mother, Françoise, was the Derbannes' cook. When Agnes was but six years old, a neighboring French-German planter named Athanase Poissot acquired her from Derbanne by offering in exchange a black girl of seven years from the Poissot family holdings. Within two months of this transaction Poissot's aging father, the former lieutenant Remy Poissot, appeared before the commandant and declared Agnes to be free, promising to rear her conscientiously in the love of God and the faith of the Catholic church.[16]

The manumission of Marie Agnes was not accepted well by the Poissot family, particularly not by the wife of young Athanase.[17] Within three years, Poissot the elder had to file a second document in which he repeated his manumission of Agnes and stated at great length that he would go to whatever measures necessary to enforce her freedom over all objections. The manumission was legally recognized, but it appears Mme. Athanase still remained unreconciled to Agnes's freedom and the child's presence in their family. A contemporary index to notarial records of the post indicates that some ten years after this second manumission Agnes filed charges of ill treatment against Mme. Athanase. The actual proceedings of the suit are no longer on file; its particulars and its outcome are left to speculation.[18]

Oral history again proves its weakness in its identification of Augustin's wife. Various writers of the mid-twentieth century, each asserting "tradition," presented Agnes as the daughter of an Indian woman and a French-Canadian "Indian fighter" named Brevelle or Dupré. The basis for the alleged tradition seems to be the genealogical tables compiled in the late nineteenth century by a French priest sent to Isle Brevelle.[19] However, the original records of the various church parishes along the Cane and Red rivers, as well as the civil records of the post, plainly contradict that alleged parentage. Her mother was not Indian and her father was neither Jean Baptiste Brevel (the only man of that name at the post at the time of her birth) nor one of the Dupré brothers. As with many traditions, however, there was a nugget of knowledge tucked inside those layers of confusion. Her mother belonged to a man who was half-Amerindian, Pierre Derbanne; and her father, Athanase Poissot, was both a half-brother of the Duprés and a brother-in-law of Jean Baptiste Brevel.

The identity of Agnes's birth family is doubly important, given that one of her sisters also married a son of Coincoin. The slave girl Marguerite, whom Augustin bought from the Pierre Derbanne estate in 1798 and then freed, was his wife's young sister. Six years later, at the age of fourteen, Marguerite wed Augustin's youngest brother, François. Although records consistently describe Marguerite as "mulatto" while all identify her mother as black, no record hints at the identity of her father. A generation later, her children identified her by the surname La Fantasy, a name found nowhere else in Natchitoches or surrounding parishes. Its literal translation suggests it was chosen to fill a need rather than to denote paternal identity.[20]

The romantic forays that Coincoin's sons made upon Rivière aux Cannes centered upon the Le Comte plantation, which had by that time produced two generations of slave offspring. Corporal Le Comte's marriage had been an unusual one. His teenaged wife, Marguerite Le Roy, bore three children before she turned twenty-one, then bore no others across nearly three decades of marriage. Whether that fact reflected a change in her reproductive health or her conjugal situation is debatable. Her husband, meanwhile, fathered at least two daughters by their slave woman Victoire Marguerite; and their son Ambroise Le Comte would father several more after Corporal Le Comte's death. Widowed in 1782, Marguerite Le Roy never remarried; over the next quarter-century, she would manumit offspring of both her husband and her son, under a variety of circumstances.[21]

In 1795, nineteen-year-old Dominique Metoyer married the fourteen-year-old multiracial Marguerite Le Comte. Whether her father was the aging soldier-turned-planter or his bachelor son goes unstated in the records, but tradition among her offspring holds that Ambroise openly acknowledged her—a probability given that she freely used the Le Comte name throughout both their lives. Marguerite's black mother Marie would remain a Le Comte slave, but the Widow Le Comte freed Marguerite five months before her marriage. Her freedom was, in fact, granted on the same day that Coincoin purchased from the widow the freedom of Catiche, the child whom Louis Metoyer had fathered by Corporal Le Comte's slave daughter, Marie Françoise, called "Fanchon."[22]

Six years later, Augustin reached an agreement with Ambroise Le Comte for the purchase and manumission of another Le Comte slave. The fifteen-year-old Marie Perine was the eldest daughter of the half-French Fanchon. No record identifies her father but he does not appear to have been white, given that all records label Perine a *mulâtresse,* rather than a quadroon. Her widowed mistress had formerly given the girl, twelve years before, to a young grandson, Joseph Dupré. As Dupré's guardian in 1801, Ambroise arranged Perine's transfer to Augustin. Soon after her manumission, Perine wed Augustin's brother Pierre.[23]

The third Metoyer brother to choose a wife from Rivière aux Cannes was Antoine Joseph. His bride, Marie Pelagie Le Court, was the quadroon daughter of Jean Baptiste Le Comte's slave daughter, Marie Madeleine Le Comte. Pelagie was just short of eighteen months when she (but not her mother) was purchased and manumitted by the bachelor Barthélemy Le Court, son of the lieutenant.[24] As the scion of minor nobility, young Barthélemy also chose not to marry. In the years to come, he would produce sizable families by two freedwomen—one of them Caddo and the other French-African. At his demise, he left them his share of his father's estate; but he gave them no education. All would become an integral part of the Metoyer community, but their illiteracy would soon muddle their identity. Civil and church officers who created their records would identify them as La Cours, prompting generations of writers to confuse them with two other area families of that name.[25]

Louis Metoyer, when he eventually married, not only chose a Le Comte offspring but also introduced an Amerindian strain into the family. In colonial and early federal Louisiana, Native Americans occupied an ambivalent social and legal position. According to the decision rendered in the case of *Adéle v. Beauregard,* a free person of color was legally defined as "descended from Indians on both sides, from a white parent, or mulatto parents in possession of their freedom."[26] As free people of color, Native Americans were legally free to marry any other free person of color. If they bore no African blood, the law did not prohibit their marriage to whites. Upon marriage, as a rule, they shared the status of the spouse. On the Louisiana frontier, the free offspring of most Amerindian slaves chose the more privileged path to whiteness. As a consequence, by the end of the colonial era, at least 51 percent of the native-born "white" population of Natchitoches had Native American slave ancestry.[27]

Louis Metoyer's bride was one of those freed slaves, but not one who lived as white. In 1801, when she married Louis, Marie Thérèse was the eighteen-year-old daughter of Ambroise Le Comte by the Le Court slave Thérèse.[28] The mother's tribe, the Canneci—better known as Lipan Apache—roamed the West Texas plains between the Río Grande and the Río Colorado. In describing their nature, Sibley reported: "They are not friendly to the Spanish and generally kill them when they have an opportunity. They are attached to the French; are good hunters [and] very particular in their dress. . . . The women wear a loose robe resembling that of a Franciscan friar; nothing but their heads and feet are to be seen." The Indian agent's 1805 account also noted: "Thirty or forty years ago, the Spaniards used to make slaves of them when they could take them; a considerable number of them were brought to Natchitoches and sold amongst the French inhabitants, at forty or fifty dollars a head, and a number of them are still living here, but are now free. About twenty years ago, an order came from the King of Spain . . . and those that were enslaved [were] emancipated."[29]

Whether Thérèse was brought to Natchitoches on a Spanish leash or whether Le Court de Presle purchased her from the Caddo or another tribe remains debatable. By mid-century the Lipan were in a full-scale war with the Caddo, a nation with whom the lieutenant had both military and trade ties. Whatever chain of misfortunes thrust Thérèse into slavery apparently occurred amid that struggle in the 1760s. At her first appearance on record in 1778, the succession inventory of her mistress, she was described as a thirty-six-year-old *sauvagesse* and the mother of four children aged ten years to two months. The exact birth dates given for each of those children attest their births into the Le Court household and the lieutenant's diligence in recording those births in the absence of a priest. Three more children would follow in the next five years before Thérèse died. When the Spanish eventually outlawed Indian slavery, all her living children would become free; three are traceable as adults.[30]

The marital choices of the children of this Lipan slave epitomized the ambivalence of their racial status. Rosalie, fathered by the Widow Le Comte's son-in-law Louis Monet, married in 1792 a free man of color from Opelousas, Louis Guillory, who is said to be French and Adaës. She settled with him at Le Court's Bluff (by then called Monet's Bluff), where she would spend most of her life in relative poverty.[31] Thérèse Le Comte, the younger daughter who married Louis Metoyer in 1801, would enjoy considerable wealth but limited privilege as a consequence of her marital choice. Their brother Jacques—generally called Jacques Ambroise, without a surname—chose to live as white. His grandfather, shortly before death, had made a donation to the seven-year-old Jacques, consisting of "some mother cows and their young, likewise some mares and their colts." In 1794, Jacques's father Ambroise and his widowed grandmother ratified that donation. Across the next fifteen years, Jacques managed to turn a handsome profit from that small stake or else his father, off the record, provided for him more generously. In 1808, as a man of some means, Jacques eloped to Natchez with the white Creole Marie Silvie Brosset, daughter of the French-born settler Pierre Brosset. Upon their return, they would draft a marriage contract in which Jacques donated $1,000 to his bride; the marriage was then duly blessed by a Catholic priest. Although Jacques had, in 1801, attended the marriage of his sister Thérèse to Louis Metoyer, at which time he identified himself as her brother, he appears not to have associated thereafter with his in-laws of lesser status. His marriage was short lived; both he and Silvie died in 1813, leaving two children who also lived as white. In a twist of historical irony, one of those sons—Louis Metoyer's nephew by marriage—would wed a descendant of Louis's former mistress, Mme. de Soto.[32] In the human color scheme on Cane River, as in most of antebellum America, red plus green (i.e., Native American with money) equaled white. Black plus green did not.

The fifth marriage between a son of Coincoin and a Le Comte slave also illustrated the ambiguity of Amerindian status on Cane River, as well as some of the ways that ambiguity was exploited. In 1817, after the death of his first wife, Perine, Pierre Metoyer Jr. wed Marie Henriette Dorothée Cloutier. Her mother, Dorothée Monet, had been baptized at Rivière aux Cannes by a passing priest in 1778, at which time he identified Dorothée only as the natural daughter of "Margarita," a slave of Jean Baptiste Dupré." The racial composition of neither mother nor child was stated.[33] At Dupré's death in 1781, the inventory of his succession valued the "*Négresse* Margueritte, aged about thirty-five, and her *mulâtresse* daughter, aged about three, named Dorothée," at 1,750 livres. (With regard to Dorothée's ethnicity, it is significant here that Indian slavery had not yet been outlawed in Louisiana and the Duprés had nothing to gain at this point by altering her ethnic identity.) Four years later, his young widow Marguerite Louise Le Comte, whom he had married shortly after she turned twelve, took a new husband: the neighboring planter who had fathered Dorothée, Louis Monet. Their marriage contract, and her subsequent sale to him of her share of Dupré's estate, again itemized "one *Négresse* named Marguerite, a native of Guinea, aged about thirty-five, and her child Dorothée, *mulâtresse*."[34]

After Indian slavery was abolished by the Spanish regime, Dorothée's half-Lipan sister in the Le Court household, Rosalie, became a free woman. As in the case of Jacques and Thérèse Le Comte, no formal manumission was required. Dorothée, as the daughter of a Guinea-born mother, remained in bondage. Her father and master, however, did allow her to use his surname—a highly uncommon practice in their place and time. In 1797, as the "*mulâtresse* slave of Mr. Monet," Dorothée presented two small children to a passing priest for baptism. The younger of those was Marie Henriette, a quadroon daughter Dorothée had borne by her father's cousin, the neighboring planter Alexis Cloutier (himself the brother-in-law of Susanne Metoyer's partner Jean Baptiste Anty). Marie Henriette's baptism, like those of her siblings born during this period, identified their mother Dorothée as a "mulattress."[35]

Within a year, Dorothée's prospects improved immensely and she launched an effort to elevate her status. Her father had already purchased much of Le Court's Bluff from the lieutenant's heirs. Likely encouraged by Louis and Pierre Metoyer's successful petition for their land on Isle Brevelle without having to prove their freedom, Monet petitioned for a concession at the bluffs on behalf of his daughter. By 1798 two nearby tracts had been approved for her. Dorothée immediately converted one of them into operating cash, selling ten arpents' frontage on both sides of the river to Pierre Metoyer's neighbor from the Grand Côte, the surveyor Maës. In that sale, Dorothée not only identified herself as "the natural daughter of Louis Monet," but also asserted that she was a "*métive*."[36]

As a woman of property, Dorothée provided a home for her half-sister and brother-in-law, Rosalie and Louis Guillory. She also entered into a new relationship that was not so much a plaçage as a common-law marriage. In that relationship, she—not he—was the propertied head-of-household. By Étienne Rachal, her father's first cousin, she would bear six children over the next ten years, before Étienne ended the relationship and took a legal wife. At the 1803 baptism of the first of these Rachal children, a set of twins, she again upgraded her status. This time, however, she did not claim to be a *métive;* rather, she borrowed from Rosalie's identity and informed a passing priest that she was "an Indian of the Canneci tribe." Once more, in the baptism of a daughter in 1805, she repeated that claim but never did so thereafter. In the meantime, her father would in 1801–2 tardily rectify his failure to legally manumit her. Following a convention commonly used at the time by white fathers of Natchitoches who feared to risk manumitting their own offspring under Spanish law lest they not be allowed to bequeath property to them, Monet "sold" Dorothée to his friend Manuel Derbanne, and Derbanne then granted her freedom.[37]

The children baptized for Dorothée before her manumission remained in slavery. In 1810 her fifteen-year-old daughter Marie Henriette was purchased from Monet's widow, Marguerite Louise Le Comte, who was by then the wife of the region's new Anglo justice of the peace, James Porter. The purchaser was Coincoin's son Pierre Toussaint Metoyer. The terms were $640 on credit, and Marie Henriette was declared free. Toussaint, apparently, hoped to marry the girl. Henriette, apparently, had other interests. Toussaint soon returned her to her former owner without completing the payment. The following year Henriette's mother, Dorothée, bought her from Mme. Porter for $650 cash and immediately manumitted her.[38]

When Marie Henriette eventually married, the husband she chose was Toussaint's older and newly widowed brother, Pierre. Upon Pierre's death almost two decades later, Marie Henriette remarried. This time, she chose an *homme de couleur libre* who had migrated to the Isle from New Orleans, Émile Dupart. Toussaint remained a bachelor for life. It appears, however, that he held no permanent grudge against Marie Henriette for twice spurning him; there is on record a donation of a slave made to her by Toussaint "in consideration of the love and affection he entertained for Marie Henriette." In all of these records Marie Henriette is described in terms that denote French and African parentage rather than Native American.[39]

Two possible explanations exist for the contradictory racial identifications within the records dealing with Dorothée and Marie Henriette. One theory proposes that Dorothée's mother, Marguerite, was an Indian of the Canneci tribe, sold into slavery at Natchitoches, and that her daughter was subsequently identified as a "*sauvagesse* of the Canneci Nation" by right of bloodline rather than by actual birth within that tribe. After the mother's death, this proposition contends, Monet purchased the child and kept her in subjection, long after the abolishment of Indian slavery, on the pretext that she was of African rather than Indian descent. With no relatives in the area to protect Dorothée's status, some argue, this could easily have been done. When Monet finally manumitted her, proponents argue, her true race was revealed and she was given property by the aging Monet in rectification of the injustice done her.

Evidence does not support this theory. She did indeed have kin who could have reported her plight to authorities if she were being held illegally, including the half-Indian half-sister who had been freed years before her. Moreover, abundant evidence attests that her master was not a man given to regrets on matters of morals or injustices. The weight of the evidence lies with the second explanation. As stated in all records created during the time that Indian slavery was legal, Dorothée's mother Marguerite was a woman from Guinea. Consequently, Dorothée, whom most records identify as a "mulattress," was held in slavery legally. The subsequent effort by her father to upgrade her material status was successful. Her own effort to self-identify as Canneci was not. Meanwhile, to ensure her future rights to the property Monet had assisted her in acquiring, her father arranged to have her manumitted, a legal action he would not have had to take if her mother had been Canneci rather than Guinea. Nor would it have been subsequently necessary to manumit the children Dorothée had borne before her own manumission.

In the case of Dorothée's daughter by Cloutier, exact racial composition was to have little effect upon her status, given that she married two *hommes de couleur libres* and shared the status of her husbands. However, at least one of Dorothée's quadroon sons by Rachal left Natchitoches in the company of a young but poor girl of entirely European parentage and succeeded in establishing, elsewhere, his racial identity as white. His children returned to the parish and assimilated into Anglo and Hispanic families in the pine hills.[40]

In addition to the family of Dorothée, one other branch of the Monet family was unquestionably of African origins. Those individuals were, in fact, directly descended from Coincoin. As noted earlier, Coincoin's black daughter Françoise was sold by Mme. de Soto to a trader. He then resold her at a handsome profit to Jean Baptiste Dupré, the Le Comte son-in-law who was the first master of Dorothée Monet. Françoise would eventually bear children at Rivière aux Cannes. One of those, born in 1782 while Françoise was still the property of Dupré, was a half-French daughter subsequently known as Marie Louise Le Comte.[41]

After Dupré's death and his widow's remarriage to Louis Monet, Monet became the legal owner of that slave child. On Christmas Day, 1802, the twenty-year-old Marie Louise Le Comte gave birth to a quadroon son and named him Louis. Sieur Monet soon died and young Louis, who used the surname of Monette rather than his mother's surname, Le Comte, was inherited by Monet's widow.[42] In December 1824 the still-childless Widow Monet, who was by that time also the Widow Porter, petitioned the Louisiana legislature to permit her to free Louis—her grand-nephew, as well as her husband's son. Although Louis was an adult, he was still short of thirty, the legal age for manumission, Nonetheless, a special bill was introduced in both houses to grant her request and the bill passed. As a free man, Louis did not marry a Metoyer, but he did become their in-law.[43] After the Widow Porter's death, the still-enslaved Marie Louise Le Comte was sold to Pierre Metoyer's grandson-in-law, General François Gaiennié. In April 1834, her son Louis arranged with Gaiennié to buy her freedom for $906.97, payable on time.[44]

One other freed slave of the Le Comte-Dupré-Monet clan, Jean Baptiste Balthasar, personifies several handicaps faced by those who attempt to identify and understand freed slaves: the undependability of "tradition," the ambiguity of Native American status, the fluidity of surnames, and, especially, the hesitancy of many multiracials to assume the family names of their white fathers without explicit consent from those fathers or white kin. About 1807, in the absence of a priest, Balthasar became the common-law husband of Marie Rose Metoyer, the teenaged natural daughter of Louis Metoyer whom Augustin had bought and freed in 1800. The marriage was a brief one. Rose's husband died in 1816, leaving her a widow with two children who thereafter used Balthasar as their surname.

Local lore of the mid-to-late 1900s contended that Balthasar was a native of Haiti, a black who had fought side by side with Toussaint L'Ouverture. Upon his arrival on the Isle, supposedly, he was greeted with suspicion because of the color of his skin; the Cane River community thought it more likely that he was a runaway slave. His story, supposedly, was "checked into" and found to be true. Then, because of the great respect that the Cane River community supposedly had for L'Ouverture—that "great Haitian liberator"—his compatriot Balthasar was accepted into the clan. The source of this tradition, it bears noting, was an informant who struggled deeply to reconcile twentieth-century sensibilities, including respect for black slave ancestry, with the realities faced by her free, multiracial forebears in 1810. More than one of the "traditions" she reported was born of, or shaped by, that personal struggle.[45]

The records created by Jean Baptiste Balthasar and his children contradict the lore. They clearly identify him as a French and Indian child of the

Dupré family, born at Rivière aux Cannes. Jean Baptiste Dupré, just days before his death in 1781, dictated a will in which he provided for his interment, for masses to be said in his memory, for payment of his debts, and for a token twenty-five piasters to be given to the church to pay for those masses. With formalities behind him, his first bequest was liberty to two slave children he described as *griffes*. He described young Balthasar as aged seven and Cécile, nine. He did not name their mother but said she was "a *sauvegesse* of the nation [blank]." None of Dupré's sixteen other slaves of any age, gender, or ethnicity were granted any favor or bequest. In all similar cases documentable for the free multiracials at Natchitoches, and countless cases elsewhere, paternity was the impetus for the manumission. The fact that Dupré labeled them *griffes* (that is, African and Amerindian) rather than *métives* (Amerindian and European) casts a shadow of doubt upon a conclusion that he was their father; but that historical question today should be answerable through Y-line DNA tests.[46]

No Indian female was itemized in the inventory and estimation of Dupré's estate; but other civil and church records briefly tell her story. Catherine, an Indian of unstated and apparently unknown tribe, was baptized in May 1763, at which time she was called an "adult." By the standards of her place and time, one in which girls could marry at age twelve, "adult" simply meant she had reached puberty. When Dupré drafted a marriage contract with Marie Louise Marguerite Le Comte in 1769, he identified Catherine as a childless "young Indian" woman, the only Indian among the eight slaves he owned. In October 1777, an unidentified Indian slave of his household was buried by a passing priest. At that time, Jean Baptiste Balthasar would have been about three years old; his sister Cécile, about five.[47]

As a free adult, Balthasar appears in virtually no records outside those of the church, records that are themselves sporadic. Because of their distance from any house of worship—and the frequent lack of any priest in residence on Red River—one to three years regularly elapsed between clerical visits to Rivière aux Cannes. When sacraments were administered there, Balthasar was invariably present, consistently in company with slaves of the Dupré-Monet household. In 1791, he stood as godfather at the baptism of Florentin, a *"pardo"* child, whom Louis Monet declared free. Monet did not name the child's mother, but the lightness of the child's complexion and the fact that Balthasar shared godparental duties with Susanne Metoyer suggests the mother was likely one of Coincoin's biracial granddaughters whom Monet held in slavery. Again in 1799, when Monet presented for baptism a four-day-old black infant, Balthasar served as godfather. In 1804, he appeared again, this time standing for Rose, a black child of Coincoin's black daughter Françoise. When a priest passed down the river the next year and stopped at the Widow Monet's home, Balthasar stood again for the only slave child offered up that year for baptism. In all such cases, the records describe Balthasar as a man of color, rather than a *nègre*—the term reserved in this place and time for those of dark or black skin, with no known or visible admixture.[48]

Across those two decades, Balthasar fathered three children under circumstances typical for poor men of color along Cane River. His first, born in 1795, was also the first-born child of Monet's daughter Dorothée. The baptismal record of that child, Jean Baptiste Cyriaque, uses the conventional "father unknown." When his mistress later freed Cyriaque at the age of thirty-three, she used no surname for him. But when Cyriaque subsequently married and legitimated the children he had fathered by a freedwoman of the Le Comte family, he informed the priest that his parents were "Baltasar Monet" and "Dorothée Monet."[49] The relationship between Balthasar and Dorothée was a fleeting one, apparently the victim of social mindsets that handicapped free men of color. While both Balthasar and Dorothée were multiracial, Balthasar would superficially seem to hold two advantages over her in their relationship. First, he was free, while Dorothée was not. Second, as a half Indian, he could aspire to acceptance as white if he achieved financial success. As half black, Dorothée could not.[50] Yet she was the one with property and paternal acknowledgment. A permanent relationship with a poor man of color would have resigned her offspring to the "colored" underclass. Consequently, the registration of her first-born, two years after his birth, left his paternity open; and Dorothée moved on to relationships with white males, whereby she and her children could better leverage the advantages her father gave her.

When Balthasar eventually settled into a permanent relationship, he also chose an upwardly mobile path—the best possible option available to him. By 1806, he was clearly entrenched in the family Louis Metoyer had produced at Rivière aux Cannes prior to marriage. In August of that year, Balthasar witnessed the marriage of Marie Louise "Catiche" Metoyer, Louis's teenaged daughter by the still-enslaved Fanchon Le Comte. Soon after, in the absence of a priest, Balthasar set up housekeeping with Catiche's sister, Rose. Their first son, Louis, was born about 1807. A daughter was baptized in 1812 at the age of fifteen months—an occasion on which the passing priest who baptized her there at Monet's Bluff named her father as "Baltasar Monett."[51]

Shortly thereafter, Balthasar died, leaving a deathbed will in which he identified himself only as "Jean Baptiste." He acknowledged "Marie Rose Baptiste" as his wife, named their two children, and left to them each a one-third share of the ten arpents' frontage he owned along the river. When parish officials declared Balthasar's estate "vacant," on the premise that he had died without legal heirs, Louis Metoyer stepped in again to ensure that his daughter and grandchildren did not lose their inheritance. Rose's children by Balthasar never used the Monet surname. After reaching maturity they consistently identified their father as Jean Baptiste Balthasar and themselves as Louis and Rose Balthasar. Their descendants have used Balthasar or Balthazar as a surname through all subsequent generations.[52] Eventually, his young widow formed a new alliance and then another and another, choosing white males of influence in every case—the French immigrants Antoine Coindet and Dr. André Zepherin Carles, then the American attorney-turned-planter James Hurst. The offspring of each union would use that father's surname and would intermarry with their Cane River cousins.[53]

Rose Metoyer's mother, the enslaved "Fanchon" Le Comte, introduced another family line into the Metoyer community. After her youthful romance with Louis Metoyer, Fanchon became the slave placée of a young, white, and single Creole planter with whom she would spend the rest of his known life. Following the pattern of her community, the man of her choice was a Le Comte in-law and a Monet-Cloutier cousin, whose plantation adjoined Ambroise Le Comte's at the point where the Rivière aux Cannes district met the Isle. Jean Baptiste Rachal was the son of Ambroise's aunt Marie Louise Le Roy by her husband Louis Rachal.[54] Their origins was much the same as that of their Le Comte kin. Louis's father, Pierre Rachal, had held the corporal's post before Le Comte. Louis's mother, Marianne Benoist, was a Parisian serving girl temporarily exiled from the household of Louis XV.[55] For a number of years, public records would not acknowledge the plaçage of Jean Baptiste Rachal with Fanchon Le Comte. In the course of time, as Rachal committed himself permanently to his extralegal family, that situation changed. In 1799, he bought his first-born son and freed him, but not the child's mother; apparently the aged Widow Le Comte did not wish to part with Fanchon, her husband's daughter. At the widow's death in 1803, her heirs agreed to sell Fanchon and her latest pair of babies to the children's father; and in 1805, Rachal manumitted them and their infant sister, identifying all the youth as "his own natural children." Four years later, in

November 1809, Rachal freed their mother, stating that "Françoise, mulatto," was aged about thirty-two.[56]

In 1817, the eldest of the quadroon Rachals, Jean Baptiste Espallier, married the proverbial girl next door—Susanne Metoyer, a daughter of Dominique. Young Rachal brought into the marital community 300 piasters, in addition to a tract of five arpents of frontage on both sides of Red River. The land had been acquired two days earlier "from his father," and was valued at another 300 piasters. The bride also received 300 piasters cash from her father, along with land lying between her parental plantation and that of her future spouse. Susanne's tract consisted of only four arpents' frontage on each bank of the river, but was valued at 900 piasters. Apparently, her land was of higher quality or was considerably more improved than that of Rachal. The bride's donation was to be considered an advance on her inheritance. If both tracts of land contained the usual depth of forty arpents on each side of the river, the young couple began their marriage with roughly 600 acres of land and 600 piasters in cash. Upon the death of her father, they would inherit more. Other children of the Rachal plaçage also married members of the Metoyer community. On each occasion Rachal provided them with some degree of financial assistance, although his donations were never as large as those his children's Metoyer spouses received from their parents.[57]

One of the most significant Le Comte lines among Cane River Creoles *de couleur*—the one that actually perpetuated the Dupré name—bound together all the disparate families. They, too, were already Metoyer kinsmen before the first of them took a Metoyer as his wife. They also introduced a third Native American strain, as well as a Spanish one.

Coincoin's younger sister, Marie Louise *dite* Mariotte, had been purchased from the St. Denis family by a neighboring planter, the German-Swiss Gabriel Buard. On the Buard plantation, along the outskirts of the colonial village, she bore several children before she was acquired and manumitted in 1786 by a new arrival at Rivière aux Cannes, a tobacco farmer named Pierre Bouvier.[58] Most of her children would remain in slavery; her efforts to buy their freedom succeeded only once. With proceeds from her work as a *médicine* and her tobacco crops on Bouvier's farm, she approached the Buards on Christmas Eve 1797 to buy the freedom of her youngest daughter. The half-French Marie Adelaïde, whose father goes unstated in the records, had been ten in 1791 when the Widow Buard specifically willed the child to her son Denis. Six years later, Denis (the brother-in-law of Pierre Metoyer) sold Adelaïde to her mother. At that point, Mariotte made a grave mistake. She declared in the purchase document that her daughter would be free at her death—thereby presaging a host of legal problems for her offspring.[59] Those problems would also create a wealth of records by which historians can better understand racial politics in Louisiana.

Between 1798 and 1804, Adelaïde bore three children by unknown white fathers. One eventually married a Metoyer cousin, one married a quadroon son of the freed half-Indian Cécile (Dupré), and one married a free man of color who had migrated upriver from the New Orleans area. After her third child's birth, Adelaïde became the placée of the young Rivière aux Cannes bachelor Joseph Dupré III—a relationship that tightened the tangled familial ties along Cane River. Dupré's mother was a sister of Ambroise Le Comte and, by then, the wife of Alexis Cloutier. She also was the first cousin of Jean Baptiste Rachal. His father's uncle was Jean Baptiste Dupré, who freed and possibly fathered Balthasar and Cécile; his aunt, the wife of Louis Monet. His half-uncle was Athanase Poissot, father of Augustin's wife Agnes. His grandmother, Marie de l'Incarnacion Derbanne, was a quarter-blood Chitimacha whose well-placed grandfathers had been a French administrator and a Spanish lieutenant, respectively. All these kinships would both hurt and help the offspring Adelaïde bore by the young Joseph Dupré, as economic hardships and new racially biased laws unfolded in Louisiana.[60]

As the only surviving child of a well-to-do father, Dupré was a youth of considerable means when he turned twenty-one and set up housekeeping with Adelaïde. Six years into their relationship, he became ill and drafted a deathbed testament, or *donation mortis causa,* to provide for the three children Adelaïde had borne him. That document was carefully crafted, suggesting formal legal counsel. The *Code Civil* that territorial Louisiana had adopted from the colonial regime explicitly stated: "Bastard, adulterous or incestuous children, even duly acknowledged, shall not enjoy the right of inheriting [from] their natural father or mother, . . . the law allowing them nothing more than a mere alimony."[61]

However, the articles of the code that defined these terms left gray areas Dupré attempted to operate within. The code's initial definition of the term *bastard* was explicit on its face: "bastards are such as are born of an illicit union." However, the code also provided for means to elevate their legal status: "Illegitimate children who have been acknowledged by their father are called natural children . . . those whose father is unknown are contradistinguished by the appellation of bastards."[62] Toward this end, Dupré duly acknowledged his children before witnesses. Even so, acknowledgment as a natural child carried its own limits upon heirship:

> Natural children are called to the inheritance of their natural father, who has duly acknowledged them, when he has left no descendants, nor ascendants, nor collateral relations, nor surviving wife. . . . Bastard, adulterous or incestuous children, even duly acknowledged, shall not enjoy the right of inheriting [from] their natural father or mother . . . the law allowing them nothing more than a mere alimony. . . . When the natural father has not left legitimate children or descendants, the natural child or children acknowledged by him, may receive from him by donation . . . *mortis causa*, to the amount of . . . [one] half, if he leaves legitimate brothers and sisters.[63]

Dupré had no wife and no legal children, but he did have one maternal half-brother, born of his mother's remarriage. Threading his way through legal straits, Dupré began his testament by providing the sum of $6,400 to that minor half-brother, Jean Baptiste Sévère Cloutier. Second, he set aside one slave and a small sum of money for Adelaïde, whom he obviously believed to be free. The remainder of his estate, consisting of slaves, land, livestock, and other goods—property calculated to be of roughly equal value as the donation to his brother—was to go to his three children, Philippe Valsain, Marie Doralise, and Joseph Emanuel "Manuel" Dupré. As executor, he appointed his mother's brother, Ambroise Le Comte, rather than his stepfather, Alexis Cloutier—a character judgment that proved prophetic.[64]

Cloutier contested the will. His opposition was clearly financial; disapproval of his stepson's liaison *per se* was not likely, given that Cloutier had already fathered Henriette Cloutier, as well as a son of color (by a different mother) who would marry a daughter of Louis Metoyer. Cloutier, after petitioning the court to appoint him *curator ad litem* of the interests of his minor son, then argued that Dupré's bequest to his family of color was invalid and that young Sévère was the only legal heir. When Sévère died at New Orleans shortly thereafter, Cloutier proceeded to prosecute the case as his minor son's sole heir, asserting that the entire estate of his stepson Joseph Dupré now belonged to him.[65]

Aside from the issue of illegitimacy, the contest centered upon two other grounds: the legality of Dupré's donation to a woman legally defined as his concubine, and the fact that both she and the children were still legally enslaved. With regard to concubines, the code decreed unequivocally that "Those who have lived together in open concubinage, are respectively incapable to make to each other any . . . title, whether *inter vivos* [during their lives] or *mortis causa* [at death]."[66] To rectify this problem, Adelaïde renounced her share in favor of her Dupré children. The second issue was the more fatal one. Cloutier, who was illiterate but legally astute, demanded proof that Mariotte had formally manumitted Adelaïde after purchasing her from Denis Buard. Knowing that she had not done so, Mariotte went before the Rivière aux Cannes notary, her neighbor and Dupré's cousin Louis Derbanne, to make a tardy declaration of freedom for both her daughter and her grandchildren.[67]

Local jurors filtered this stew of laws and transactions through their sense of moral justice and declared the Dupré minors to be the legal heirs. Cloutier appealed that decision to the state supreme court and won a reversal. Thus, in April 1816, Le Comte delivered to Alexis Cloutier $7,000, representing the share of the estate that Dupré had intended to leave his children, plus accrued interest. Adelaïde and her children were left without a home or livelihood. The issue did not end there, however. In 1830, when the youngest Dupré child was just short of the age of majority, a family meeting of his "friends and relatives" deliberated the best course of action that he, as minor legatee of Joseph Dupré, should follow to recover his inheritance. The six "friends and relations" who attended consisted of his older brother and co-heir, Philippe Valsain Dupré, and five of the parish's influential whites: Narcisse Prudhomme (Pierre Metoyer's son-in-law), Narcisse's brother Jean Baptiste Prudhomme (who also fathered children of color), Arnaud Lauvé (a Rachal cousin of Cloutier, as well as a Prudhomme and Buard in-law), Chrisostomé Perot (a cousin of both Joseph Dupré and Augustin Metoyer's wife Agnes), and the parish judge Charles Emmanuel Greneaux.[68]

Acting upon the counsel of these advisors, Dupré's offspring filed suit against Cloutier, requesting that the $7,000 be returned to them. Moreover, they alleged, when their father's plantation of fifteen arpents' frontage on each side of Red (Cane) River had been offered for sale at the customary probate auction, Cloutier had informed the bystanders that he wanted to purchase it for Dupré's children. As a consequence, bystanders had declined to bid against him. Cloutier had entered his bid for $200, was the only bidder, and had then resold the land for $2,000, which he had kept. All matters considered, Dupré's legatees requested a judgment in their favor of those two sums, $7,000 and $2,000, with 5 percent interest from the date of Dupré's death in 1811. Cloutier countered that he had already given to the plaintiffs "several slaves . . . out of respect for the memory of Dupré"[69] and claimed they had already received $5,000 from Dupré's executor. Moreover, Cloutier challenged, they had no right of inheritance at law in the first place. The testator had bequeathed his property to his *children* and since "the Testator was a white man and the Plaintiffs being as they allege themselves persons of colour [they] cannot bring themselves within the term of the will by tracing their paternity."[70]

Cloutier's viewpoint was again rejected by the local jury. The district court's decree of May 1831 ordered Cloutier to pay to Dupré's heirs the sum of $6,687, with 5 percent interest from May 3, 1815, until paid, plus the costs of the suit. That judgment against Cloutier was a tempered one, given that interest then customarily ranged from 8 to 10 percent. This time, Cloutier did not win an appeal. Assuming that he repaid the debt promptly, the sum Dupré's three children were awarded, figured at simple interest, amounted to $14,596. Those youth, however, were not indigent before the receipt of this inheritance. Amid the court proceedings, the youngest son, Manuel, had married Marie Marguerite Metoyer, daughter of Dominique. Mlle. Metoyer entered the marriage with $900 in cash. Dupré listed his assets as $1,300, of which he donated $500 to his future wife.[71] The source of his financial stake goes unstated, but later records attest that he was an enterprising young man.

Amid this legal morass, Adelaïde Mariotte added more knots to Cane River's snarl of kinships. Joseph Dupré's cousin Barthélemy Le Court, after fathering Joseph Metoyer's wife Pelagie in his youth, had remained unmarried. In the interim, he had settled into a plaçage with a *métive* named Ursulle who had been born in the mid-to-late 1770s of unidentified parentage.[72] Barthélemy's father, at that time, owned three female Indians of fertile age: Magdeleine (legal wife of the Indian Capitaine), Thérèse (who was bearing children by Ambroise Le Comte), and Louison (who, in 1778, was said to be aged twenty-four and the mother of two small daughters born in 1772 and 1776). Of the three possibilities, all evidence points to Louison as Ursulle's mother. Magdeleine and Capitaine can be eliminated as parents because of the consistent racial descriptor used for Ursulle: if she had been born to the marriage of two Indians, she would not have been labeled *métive*. The Canneci Thérèse can be discounted because, even though she did bear *métive* children, her children are well identified on the 1778 inventory of Mme. Le Court's succession and baptismal records of the 1770s and 1780s; none were named Ursulle. Similarly, the names Magdeleine and Thérèse were not names that Ursulle passed to her offspring. To the contrary, when Ursulle bore her own first daughter in 1793—with the child's father and his sister Cécile Le Court as godparents—the baby girl was named Marie Louise, the saint's name for which "Louison" was a nickname. More directly, when Ursulle's youngest daughter married sixteen years after Ursulle's death, that girl, who never knew her mother, actually gave her mother's name as "Luison."[73]

Between 1791 and 1811, Ursulle bore ten children to Barthélemy Le Court. As with Thérèse's children by Ambroise Le Comte, Ursulle's Le Court children made widely divergent choices in their spouses. Both Marie Louise and one of her brothers married white Creoles; no record would thereafter apply any hint of color to them. Two other sons of Ursulle married children of Spaniards from Nacogdoches. Three of her sons married Metoyers and Rachals *de couleur.*[74] By 1816, Ursulle had died and Barthélemy had done what males of his society typically did when left with a houseful of young children: he found them a surrogate mother. The woman he chose was Adelaïde, who had remained unattached for several years after Joseph Dupré's death but had recently borne a pair of twins to another white Creole bachelor, Victorin Le Vasseur.[75] By Adelaïde, Le Court would father another three children; they, too, would intermarry with Metoyers and Rachals.[76]

Above the town of Natchitoches sprawled two smaller clusters of freed slaves, only one of whom furnished spouses for the Cane River youth in the antebellum era. Here, quite clearly, caste was a significant factor—not just color and not free-or-slave status, but the kind of social and economic rank that reflected life choices and self-image. The Badins, the oldest enclave, began as *nègres* enslaved by a colonial planter from Thorigne in the diocese of Poitiers. Pierre Badin had arrived at Natchitoches at the end of the French dominion. He purchased, from Le Court de Prelle's mistress, her parental land at the upper end of the Grand Côte, and began planting tobacco with the aid of a slave couple. His legal wife of at least a quarter-century bore him no children. In 1791, three years after her death, he manumitted all twenty slaves in his possession—most of whom were a family unit stemming from that couple of the 1760s. The freedpeople remained with him and took his surname, but their large enclave apparently felt themselves unwelcome amid the Grand Côte plantations based on the institution of slavery. Badin sold his land and relocated in the less populous Camptí community just north of the town of Natchitoches. Shortly before his death as an octogenarian in 1805, Badin drafted a will naming his freed slaves as his legatees.[77]

Across time, the freed Badins had remained black to an unusual extent. Only two *mulâtre* infants had been born among them, and no evidence suggests that they were Badin's children. As free black property owners, the family did not prosper. Badin's bequest, divided among so many heirs, provided little for each to build on. Their offspring across the next half-century would rarely marry, and their illegitimacy rate was inordinately high (the 80–90 percentile).[78] During the upheaval of Reconstruction one descendant, Norbert Badin, would move south to the Isle, where he would eventually buy property and his daughter Zéline, in 1893, would marry a Roques descendant of Coincoin. The one imprint that the Badins left on Cane River was the attachment of their name to the early colonial bousillage home in which the Roques-Badin couple lived a century or so later.[79]

The second north-of-Natchitoches community of freedpeople supplied several spouses for both the Badins and Cane River. Dominated by the biracial Mézières and the triracial Grappes, Trichels, and Davids, their roots mirrored those of the Metoyers, Le Comtes, and Le Courts. The old commandant Athanase de Mézières, whose legal maneuvers had helped Coincoin and Pierre Metoyer circumvent the prosecutorial priest, left offspring from two well-placed marriages. However, his two daughters and the one son who remained at Natchitoches never married. As with Le Court de Presle, they had been reared to reject the idea of wedding beneath their class. All were extremely cognizant of the fact that their aunt was both the wife of the Duke of Orleans and a courtier who escaped imprisonment during the Revolution through the patronage of Napoleon himself. Their mindset toward marriage was frankly explained by one of the commandant's daughters, on her deathbed, to a cleric visiting from New Orleans; and he was sufficiently struck by it to report it to a friend: "Not wanting to make *mésalliances*, they never married."[80]

While the Mézières daughters remained celibate, Athanase Jr. followed the example of his father's friend Le Court: concubinage in lieu of marriage. Like Pierre Metoyer, he chose a black slave as his long-term companion: one Marie Bernarde *dite* Le Noir.[81] He, she, their seven children, and then their grandchildren all lived with his spinster sisters—who not only shared their ownership but also served as godmothers to his offspring. Before Athanase's death, they had freed his children; and his will of 1827 manumitted the four grandchildren remaining in his custody. Having never married, with no living siblings, he bequeathed his estate to his multiracial offspring. Some stayed in the town of Natchitoches; some moved out to family land at

Camptí, near the land to which Pierre Badin had relocated his unorthodox household.[82]

That community—also called Côte Touline—was the same in which Coincoin's eldest son Nicolas Chiquito had settled after his manumission. It was also the locus of a network of triracial families founded by François Grappe *dit* Touline, son of the French soldier and Caddo trader Alexis Grappe by his half-Chitimacha wife Louise Marguerite Guedon.[83] After the death of Alexis, their son François began a plaçage with an enslaved black teenager from the neighboring Trichel plantation. Marie Louise "Rosette," who would be his lifelong companion, had been born at Natchitoches in 1750, as the daughter of an African captive, Romaine Antoine *dit* Souris (slave of the St. Denis son-in-law Jacques de la Chaise), by his young black Creole wife, Catherine—herself the daughter of the African captive Anera and his legal wife Fanchon. At the time Catherine married, she and her parents were enslaved by the German-born trader Henri Trichel and his half-Natchitoches wife, Marie Dumont. Rosette's parents, like Coincoin's parents, benefited for a while from the *Code Noir*'s provision that legally married slaves could not be separated from each other and that mothers could not be separated from their children under the age of fourteen. After a decade of marriage, however, Rosette's father was sent south to the de la Chaise plantation at New Orleans. Rosette was still a toddler. She would barely pass the age of maternal separation before her mother was sold to another New Orleans planter. Shortly before that sale, however, the teenaged Rosette had borne her first child by François Grappe.[84]

By the time Rosalie's master died in 1778, she and François had five children. Three fell by lot to different Trichel heirs. Then, to equalize the inheritance, Rosette and her nursing infant were offered for sale. Young Grappe lacked the 3,000 piasters at which the pair was valued, and mother and child were sold to a neighboring planter for cash that could be distributed among the heirs. Two more children were born to Rosalie before Grappe's *métive* mother provided the funds to reconsolidate his and Rosette's family. At that point, François did what Le Courts had done amid their concubinage of the 1760s and Metoyer had done in the wake of Coincoin's prosecution in 1778–79. He moved his family into the hinterlands beyond the oversight of the Natchitoches priest. That period of residence in extreme northwest Louisiana would also stake his claim to a vast stretch of land after the transfer of Louisiana to the United States.

After the Widow Grappe's death and the arrival at the post of a more lenient pastor, Grappe brought Rosette and their children back to Camptí. There he manumitted them all and executed a donation to them of all his property, inherited and earned. That donation was to take effect at his death. As a quarter-blood Amerindian, legally able to operate as a white or a person of color, he could recognize his half-black children and bequeath his land to them without violating laws against miscegenation. Across the quarter-century thereafter, he also laid a controversial claim to land supposedly given him by the Caddo tribe—some 34,500 acres of land, with a frontage of thirty-six miles along Red River—much of which would fall into the future city of Shreveport. At his death in 1825, the editor of the Natchitoches newspaper eulogized Grappe as "a man of firm spirit [with] a knowledge of many Indian languages [who] possessed more influence upon the numerous tribes . . . West of the Mississippi than any other individual." Describing him as "a man of truth and honor," the editor reported, "He left about eighty children and grandchildren who lived with and about him and no patriarch was ever more respected." The eulogy did not mention the fact that Grappe's offspring were all, under Louisiana law, second-class citizens of color.[85]

Like the Badins, Camptí's multiracial Creoles would not prosper. After Grappe's death, the community lacked cohesion, a sense of unity toward a common goal. As the Americanization of Louisiana increasingly constrained their legal and economic opportunities, each individual family struggled in its own way, with no unifying figure—no Augustin Metoyer—to define strategies, encourage compliance, and publicly battle for their rights. Indeed, none possessed the funds to finance those legal battles. Among their heads of household, women dominated. Like Marie Rose Metoyer and Adelaïde Mariotte, they sought white male protectors to replace their fathers, and despite the respect their family names generated among the Old Guard of Natchitoches, they occupied the fringes of the social fabric of the parish. That respect for the family's origin would resurface temporarily after the war, when political leaders sought a "trustworthy" man of color as a political figurehead and tapped Henri Philippe Mézières—a namesake of his distant kinsman, France's Revolutionary icon Philippe Égalité, Duke of Orleans. But, in northwest Louisiana under the American regime, distant ties to nobility mattered not one whit, certainly not for families of color. By every measure, the community struggled to maintain its economic foothold and its rights.[86]

Commerce, economic or social, was minimal between the Cane River and Camptí societies. Coincoin's roué son Louis Metoyer, while still a slave, had dallied at Camptí at least long enough to father a child by François Grappe's triracial daughter Madeleine. As a young woman, Louis's daughter would leave her mother's family and settle at Rivière aux Cannes as the wife of Alexis Cloutier's biracial son.[87] Sons of Augustin and Dominique would also marry Camptí girls. Extant marriage contracts underscore the disparity in economic status between the two communities. For example, in the wake of the Crash of 1837, Joseph Ozéme Metoyer, son of "Sieur Dominique Metoyer and Dame Marguerite Le Comte," a minor, married Catherine David, the adult daughter of Dame Madeleine Grappe of Camptí. While the groom's property consisted of $300 and a tract of land containing seven arpents' frontage on the river, the bride brought into the community only "a certain number of animals" valued at $100. Joseph Ozéme gave to her a special mortgage on his property to guarantee her dower, according to the custom of that time.[88]

New Orleans offered the third pool of spouses for Coincoin's Cane River offspring. By the end of her life, her children's enterprises had expanded to the point of conducting extensive financial dealings with business houses of *la ville*. Those contacts likely triggered the upriver migration of a dozen or so New Orleanians to Isle Brevelle, where they would contribute significantly to the development of a robust economy as builders, blacksmiths, engineers, hatters, manufacturers, merchants, tailors, and teachers. Most of these transplants were scions of a controversial and highly stereotyped class in the culture of *la ville*.

For two centuries, interracial liaisons have occupied an obligatory, titillating niche in virtually every account of New Orleans. Early writers rhapsodized over café-au-lait quadroons and creamy octoroons, their comely feet and "ankles like angels," portraying them as "some of the most beautiful women that can be seen . . . with lovely countenances, full, dark, liquid eyes, lips of coral and teeth of pearl, long raven locks of soft and glossy hair, sylph-like figures, and such beautifully rounded limbs, and exquisite gait and manner, that they might furnish models for a Venus or a Hebe to the chisel of a sculptor."[89]

Single and ambitious mothers, by these accounts, carefully trained their daughters in the social graces: music, art, literature, dancing, conversation. Many girls were said to be well educated. Above all, supposedly, they were raised in chastity and closely guarded until the day their mother found them a "protector"—a white male who would provide a financial future for them and their offspring. "Quadroon balls," public and semiprivate, were the social grounds on which the girls could be courted, admirers could be assessed by calculating matriarchs, and formal contracts could be arranged. Once a young woman agreed to be "placed," she would be feted by her friends in the manner of a bride. But hers would be a *mariage de la main gauche,* a "left-hand marriage," that typically lasted only so long as she pleased the man who supported her. Her one assurance, if her mother executed a sage contract, was that her offspring would be provided for until they reached maturity and, if they were male, be prepared for a trade. Her greatest hope, according to this narrative, was that her offspring would be light enough to pass as white and escape the subservience of their class.

For two centuries, both moralists and apologists couched the roots of this melodrama in terms of a demographic gender imbalance, rather than European taboos against marriage beneath one's caste. Indeed, the concept of class differences based on something other than color has been antithetical to the American sense of equality—at least among those free and white. Populationwise, there did exist a gender imbalance in most Louisiana settlements during the colonial regime, with white males significantly outnumbering white females. Conversely, among free Creoles of color in the city, females outnumbered males.[90] In the first decade of the 1800s, among the waves of émigrés who arrived at New Orleans from the Caribbean, three of every four were females. Yet the severe shortage of males within *la ville's* colored Creole population did not place a premium on those males. Citing the bittersweet poetry of *Les Cenelles*[91] and other accounts of spurned *hommes de couleur libres,* historians have traditionally held that the city's free women of color rejected marriage to men of color as too limiting. Instead, most supposedly passed through a succession of white lovers before their diminished charms left them with no other choice but a brown or black husband. Meanwhile, their male offspring were, in more privileged cases, sent to France; a few unfortunate ones were said to have ended up in the slave markets. Between those extremes, supposedly, many were placed on plantations in the backcountry of the state, where marriage and the creation of families were possible for men of their class.[92]

Recent scholarship challenges the stereotype as both simplistic and sexist, arguing that the city's free women of color exercised considerable agency over their own bodies and their own fate. Studies have explored the entrepreneurial activities of this class and the extent to which many took the responsibility for their own support. Within that framework, female participation in the sex trade has been presented as a means of self-sufficiency, if not financial advancement.[93]

The effectiveness of this reevaluation remains to be determined. At its core, it basically restates—in a positive light—the premise of earlier historians who presented free women of color as Jezebels lacking control of their libidos and characterized the quadroon balls as "field operations of prostitutes."[94] The reinterpretation, however, projects twentieth-century feminist ideas of sexual liberation upon an eighteenth- to early-twentieth-century Creole culture reared to a different set of moral values. Premarital chastity, parental chaperonage, and connubial exclusivity were—as many contemporaries noted—deeply ingrained into females reared in the Catholic church, at both New Orleans and Isle Brevelle; and transgressors lost respect within both family and society.[95] The tilt of all interpretations seems to pivot on one point: Should plaçage be considered the moral equivalent of marriage in a legal system that arbitrarily forbade marriage between certain classes of people? Most recently, historian Emily Clark argues for a reappraisal more in line with traditional Creole Catholic morés. Quantifying marriage records held by the Archdiocese of New Orleans and the civil parish's notarial archives, she contends that "the city's free women of color got married at the same rate as white women," a finding that includes "young free women of color whose families had been rooted in New Orleans for generations."[96]

The New Orleans youth who migrated to Isle Brevelle represented the institutions of both plaçage and marriage. Contrary to tradition, none have been traced to the Caribbean wave. Most were scions of old-line families within the capital city. Some of their mothers were single at the time of their offspring's removal to Cane River. Some had settled into marriages with *hommes de couleur libres*. Some had formed a lifelong union with one male—white or colored—who had fathered all their children.

The first Cane River transplant from *la ville*, François Maurice Mulon, was a fourth-generation New Orleanian whose French ancestors included the Mississippi River planter Joseph Girardy and the Mobile-based Indian interpreter Louis Forneret. Forneret had taken a legal wife at Mobile in 1764, but she bore him no children in thirty or so years of a tumultuous marriage. Before and during that marriage, he fathered ten acknowledged children by two slave women. About 1785 he relocated in New Orleans with his slave mistress and his multiracial offspring. There, his eldest twin daughters, Felicité Amarante and Catherine Victoire Forneret, became the placées of the French Creole bachelors Maurice and Henry Milon, whose grandparents had come to the colony in the Law regime. At Maurice's death in 1791, his will manumitted the son Felicité had borne him, the young teen François;

Maurice's brother and executor Henri, who lived next door with Felicité's sister Victoire, faithfully executed Maurice's will.[97]

The freed François Mulon surfaced at Natchitoches in August 1806, when he exchanged vows with the sixteen-year-old Catiche Metoyer, Louis's daughter whom Coincoin had bought and freed. Theirs would be a troubled marriage. François and Catiche apparently remained together at least until the next August, at which time they stood together as godparents to a child of Pierre Metoyer and Perine Le Comte. In December 1809, Catiche was not mentioned when Mulon and her sister Rose served as godparents to one of her mother's Rachal children. Over the next five years, Catiche would bear two children, at least one by a French immigrant, Étienne Carle, before reconciling with Mulon and delivering a son who would firmly plant the Mulon name along Cane River.[98]

The multiracial Mulons of New Orleans also contributed two other lines to Cane River, both carrying the surname Dupart. François Mulon's younger sister Victoire Mulon, born about 1780, married a free *mulâtre* named Charles Dupart of New Orleans's prominent Delille Dupart family. By Charles—a slaveowning entrepreneur who variously worked as a hatter, carter, and carpenter—she had six children. In 1815 her eldest, Marie Marguerite Arthemise Dupart, was only fifteen but educated when she arrived on Cane River as a bride-to-be. Her groom, twice her age, was Coincoin's widowed son François, the only Isle Brevelle male to take a city-bred wife. Inasmuch as this marriage took place a few months after the *hommes de couleur libres* of Natchitoches went to New Orleans to assist in the defense of the city against the British, it seems likely that François met Marguerite through François Mulon, in the wake of their participation in that campaign. Marguerite's mother accompanied the girl to Cane River for the wedding. Most of Marguerite's siblings would remain in the city; but her brother Émile Dupart, a blacksmith, joined her on the Isle, where he would marry, successively, Marie Rose Baltasar and Henriette Cloutier.[99]

When Émile arrived on Cane River about 1824, he brought with him a half-brother, Leandre Dupart, the son of Charles by an earlier wife. Leandre's mother, like Émile's mother, defied the historical cliché that free women of color married their male counterparts only when so advanced in years that they could not find white paramours. Charles's first wife, Carlotta "Lolette" Bellair, a multiracial offspring of the well-placed Hubert *dit* Bellair family, was only thirty when she died in 1797, leaving several small children motherless. The middle-aged Charles had then married Victoire

Mulon, scarcely twenty, to help him rear those children. The Cane River wife whom Leandre took in 1825 was an orphan named Marie Jeanne Cécile, a free multiracial and the apparent offspring of Dupré's half-Indian Cécile. As an orphan, Marie Jeanne was the ward of Augustin Metoyer's son Auguste. The marriage contract of Leandre and Marie Jeanne indicates that he expected 500 piasters from the estate of his late mother, who had been a propertied woman of color at New Orleans.[100]

Émile and Arthemise were not the only kin whom Leandre Dupart had when he arrived on the Isle. His maternal cousin Jérôme Sarpy was on Cane River by 1818, the year he married Arthemise Dupart's stepchild, the daughter of François Metoyer. Jérôme's father had been Jean Baptiste de Lille Sarpy, a merchant born at Fumelles, department of Lot-et-Garonne, who had served Natchitoches as a New Orleans-based factor from at least 1789 until his death in 1798. Jérôme apparently arrived on Cane River as an agent of his white half-brother, Jean Baptiste *fils*, who continued the father's business and would actually die at Natchitoches in 1836. Both Jeans found the New Orleans institution of plaçage compatible with their Continental view of concubinage as a sexual outlet until an appropriate marriage was arranged— or as a source of affection when an arranged marriage was not compatible. The elder Sarpy had taken Carlotta Bellair's sister Marthe "Marton" Bellair as his placée before 1785 or so, when their natural son Jérôme was born. His legitimate, same-name son chose the quadroon Marie Josèphe "Pouponne" Diaz, by whom he fathered the revered Henriette DeLille, founder of the New Orleans-based Sisters of the Holy Family.[101]

The pattern set by the Duparts, Mulons, and Sarpys, where kinsmen from New Orleans married kinsmen from Cane River, occurred in two other contemporary cases. In the first, the Llorens brothers Manuel and Séraphin (the latter, a carpenter and engineer) married in 1818 and 1820, respectively, daughters of Susanne Metoyer and her brother Joseph. Their father, a Spanish New Orleanian named Francisco Llorens *dit* Roi, and his French and African placée, Françoise Nivette, had settled at Natchitoches prior to 1808, at which time Francisco witnessed the baptism of an infant born to a young French couple from prominent families. While Llorens's birth family remains to be identified, the status of his earliest contacts at Natchitoches suggests that he was well placed.[102]

The Roques brothers came without their parents but were not without Cane River connections when they arrived. Their uncle Jean Roques, a New Orleans merchant, had married a daughter of Pierre Metoyer's friend and neighbor Manuel Prudhomme. The multiracial Charles Nerestan Roques, who would also open a mercantile store on the Isle, was only twenty when he married Augustin Metoyer's seventeen-year-old daughter Marie Pompose in 1818. His brother Élisée was twenty-three when he married Pompose's fourteen-year-old sister two years later. Their parents—the white Pierre Roques of Montauban in the old French province of Languedoc and Lisette Glapion, free colored—were said in 1818 to be residents of New Orleans. Charles Nerestan specifically named his father in his marriage act; Élisée did not. Whether their father had acknowledged them is an open question. What is evident from the records is that he married in 1795 a woman exceedingly well placed in New Orleans society and apparently fathered two families simultaneously.[103] This circumstance might explain why the Roques brothers had no assets at all when they married on Isle Brevelle. They would, however, well manage the dowries their wives brought into the marriage. In Charles Nerestan's case, his bride's dowry, consisting of an eighteen-year-old "Guineau Negress" valued at 600 piasters and a tract of five arpents' frontage on Isle Brevelle, was valued at 2,100 piasters.[104]

The decade of the 1830s saw a significant reduction in the number of New Orleanians who settled on the Isle. The two who made the most permanent imprint were Firmin Capello Christophe and Louis Morin, both multiracials and both natives of New Orleans. Christophe, a tailor, brought his family to Cane River, including his wife of color Marie Françoise Mayoux. The family was immediately accepted—a not surprising situation, given that their son Charles, born at New Orleans in 1823, had been the godchild and namesake of Charles Nerestan Roques.[105] Morin, who in 1831 wed Augustin Metoyer's daughter Marie Susette, widow of Élisée Roques, was—unlike most of the New Orleans youth who migrated to the Isle to seek their fortunes—a man of property prior to his arrival. His mother, Mme. Sanitte Morin, was also a property owner. According to the marriage contract that Louis Morin filed with Marie Susette on the day of their marriage, Morin owned three tracts of land in *la ville*. Two of these were situated in Faubourg Sainte-Marie above the town and the third in the heart of the city. All were tracts he had personally purchased. He, too, had pre–Cane River ties with other New Orleanians who migrated to the Isle. In 1819, he had served as godfather to a grandchild of Charles Dupart by his first wife, Carlotta Bellair.[106]

Like Christophe, Antoine Coton-Maïs also arrived with a ready-made family, albeit one with a secret that seriously threatened the legal and social status of the Cane River families who accepted him. A native of Illinois, as was his wife Marie Louise de Laure *dite* Bellepeche, Coton-Maïs had first taken his family to New Orleans, at least long enough to baptize one child there. His occupation in that era remains unknown; but, by 1827, he had sufficient funds to establish himself well as a planter at the foot of Isle Brevelle. At his death in the winter of 1839–40, despite the financial depression that gripped the nation, he left an estate valued at $14,150.77, including thirteen slaves. On the surface, his family seemed to be an excellent source of exogamous spouses for Cane River's free multiracials. Between 1827 and 1838, five of his children would marry offspring of the Balthasars, Metoyers, Monets, Mulons, and the Le Comte-Dupré clan.

What the Cane River community tardily discovered—after four of their youth had already taken Coton-Maïs spouses—was that, by law, those new spouses were slaves. In July 1834, their father and legal owner attempted to rectify the problem by filing a manumission paper that granted freedom to his children, though not his wife. Yet, more serious problems remained. The four marriages that had occurred up to that point were themselves illegal; under the laws of Louisiana and other slave states, marriage could not be contracted between a free person and a slave. Moreover, Coton-Maïs's married daughters had already produced ten children who were, by extension, born into slavery and still enslaved. Aside from the stigma, creditors of Coton-Maïs could seize and sell those children.

Facing a considerable amount of community pressure, Coton-Maïs went back to the local notary in December to draft another document. There, he declared that he was freeing ten slave children "for love and affection." He identified them only by first names, generically stated that the group were "children of my daughters." He also left those daughters unidentified, to avoid publicly attaching that stigma of slavery to the free families who had trusted him. Coton-Maïs's solution to the community problem he had created would also have required the complicity of the community notary and justice, who—being made aware that the marriages had been contracted illegally—could have asked for an indictment of each couple. All parties seem to have concluded that good intentions and discretion trumped legalities. All of the marriages had occurred at the altar of a church, all were valid in the eyes of their God, and none would be legally rectified.[107]

One of the last urban youth to settle on the Isle, the schoolmaster-turned-merchant Jean Baptiste Oscar Dubreuil, is one of the few whose origins remain debatable. He also stands apart from all other Creole *de couleur* immigrants to the Isle in one other regard: he is the sole one whom any record labels "black." The census enumerator who applied that label in 1850 did so despite the fact that Dubreuil resided in a home with more than a dozen individuals all of whom the enumerator identified as "mulatto," and the household itself stood in a community in which all other free people of color were also said to be "mulatto."[108] Considering that other documents do use the "mulatto" label for Dubreuil, one might conclude that he was multiracial but noticeably darker than the community into which he married.

Along Cane River, color labels are usually valuable markers for identification, for sorting same-name people, and for determining parentage. At Dubreuil's 1842 marriage to Marie Céline Rachal, daughter of Jean Baptiste Espallier Rachal and Marie Susanne Metoyer, he presented himself as a free man of color and the son of Louis Dubreuil and Julia Talon. That record, unlike its treatment of the bride, does not call him a *legitimate* child. No birthplace is stated for him. Censuses consistently identify him as a native of Louisiana, born about 1817–18. Given the prominence of the name Dubreuil in New Orleans history, descendants have assumed descent from that New Orleans family. Indeed, they have desired one, given that the city's Dubreuils of color produced the revered Henriette DeLille.[109]

However, Louisiana records of the period of Oscar's birth and childhood offer multiple options for him. One man of his father's name lived in the city of Baton Rouge from at least 1812 to 1826. That white male, the merchant Louis St. Croix Chauvet Dubreuil, was of no known connection to the Dubreuils who were in New Orleans by the 1720s; rather, he was an Illinois-born son of a French-born father. At Baton Rouge, he married into the eminent Toutant Beauregard family and fathered several children in the first fifteen years of marriage, before dropping from the Baton Rouge Catholic records in the mid-1820s.[110] The 1830 census seems to offer only one man of similar name, an alleged white, single, and middle-aged Louis Dubreuil who lived alone in New Orleans with one free person of color, a male appropriately aged ten to twenty-four. Meanwhile, however, another Dubreuil family settled in New Orleans from Sainte-Domingue, a family of color headed by one Louis Dubreuil and Marie Jeanne "Sanite" Blanc. Their son Louis Jr. wed there in 1827 and remained for decades; but his bride has in no way been connected to a Julia Talon, and no record of a woman of that name has yet been found in either New Orleans or Baton Rouge.[111]

As the Cane River families expanded, another significant source of exogamous partners was Louisiana's steady supply of émigrés from France. One of the earliest partners, Jacques Antoine Coindet from Île d'Oléron, arrived late in the colonial era. A lifelong bachelor, he progressed through a series of relationships with women of color connected to Coincoin's family. His first son, Jean Noël Coindet, was born in October 1795 to Marie Jeanne, a slave of Pierre Metoyer. His first plaçage appears to have been his union with Marie Louise, a free woman of color (possibly daughter of Coincoin) by whom he had no children. After her death in 1813 and the death of their friend Jean Baptiste Balthasar shortly thereafter, Coindet found solace with Balthasar's young widow, Louis Metoyer's natural daughter Rose. Two daughters would be born to them over the next nine years.[112]

Coindet died leaving no legitimate direct descendants or ascendants, although his siblings left numerous offspring on the Île d'Oléron who were Coindet's forced heirs under Louisiana law. Like Joseph Dupré, Coindet tried to provide for his natural children. First, in 1817, he purchased his then-grown son Noël from Alexis Cloutier, who accommodated him by stipulating in the document that Noël would become free at Coindet's death. Second, in a will made shortly before his death, Coindet bequeathed the remainder of his entire estate to his natural children by Rose. In selecting an executor to see that his wishes were fulfilled, he chose a man he felt would understand his situation: Pierre Metoyer's white son Benjamin. However, neither of Coindet's intentions was carried out as he hoped. Benjamin's co-executor was another French émigré, Jean Jacques Paillette, who, at the time, had gone abroad. Recognizing the legal complexity of the issues involved, young Benjamin chose to delay the executorship until Paillette returned. Coindet's son Noël was not willing to wait; after three months he filed suit—successfully— against Benjamin to gain his freedom immediately. Upon Paillette's return, the executors duly transferred the estate to Coindet's placée (who was Benjamin's own half-niece), putting her in charge of the Coindet plantation and delivering other goods to total $4,878. That settlement was soon contested by Coindet's collateral heirs in France. Their suit was taken to the district court at Natchitoches and was eventually settled in their favor. Rose agreed to repay them the sum she had received from Coindet's estate, plus interest, in three annual installments of $1,650 each.[113]

The Coindet situation was complicated, in the meantime, by the new plaçage Rose had made with another French émigré, Dr. Jean André Zépherin Carles. In 1824 she gave her power of attorney to Carles to assist her in the settlement of Coindet's estate. She also unwisely authorized him to build a home and office on the land her children had inherited from Coindet. When Rose failed to meet one of her annual installments as it fell due, the Coindet heirs seized the land Coindet had left to his children by Rose, along with the house that Carles had built upon the land, and sold both at sheriff's sale.[114] The doctor died in the midst of the litigation, leaving no property. Rose had attained nothing from her alliances with Coindet and Carles, except two children from each plaçage. All were accepted into the Metoyer community. Rose was not left indigent, however. Building upon the estate left her by Balthasar, she had accumulated, by 1830, a total of eleven slaves.[115]

Rose had, by that time, also found a new connubial partner, one who was tallied in her home that year but was not named there. Dr. James Hurst had arrived on Cane River in time to purchase medical equipment and supplies from the December 1827 succession sale of goods left by the recently deceased Carles. He apparently set up practice in Carles's office, on the Coindet property that Rose occupied. His sexual involvement with Rose became a matter of public record in 1835 when the wife he had left behind in North Carolina followed him to Louisiana and discovered him "living in adultery" with Rose. Mrs. Hurst won her suit for divorce, after which he married a French Creole widow. He did not, however, abandon Rose or lose his wandering eye. In 1843 his new wife charged him with impregnating her teenaged daughter and, as evidence of his depravity, invoked his continued relationship with his family of color. His defense on the latter issue was either disingenuous or else he did not take seriously the issue of paternal support: "Certainly I have given occasionally to [Rose Metoyer's] two little daughters, some cloathing of an ordinary quality, little or no provision. I have not given them a fourth part of their support; one family of some of my patrons of my profession has annually paid me more than I have spent for the support of those children."[116]

More typical of the white males involved in Cane River plaçages was Louis Chevalier, a French immigrant from the department of Haute-Loire, who arrived in the United States in 1818. By 1830 he had settled on Isle Brevelle with his common-law wife, a free woman of color named Fanny. Tradition holds that Chevalier came to Cane River as a teacher, possessing a degree from the Sorbonne or an equally prestigious university.[117] The earliest legal record found for him, dated 1832, indicates that he then was a merchant on the Isle and a principal in the firm Chevalier & Oscar; his partner, apparently, was the fellow schoolmaster and merchant Jean Baptiste Oscar Dubreuil, who had not yet begun to use his father's family name.[118] As Chevalier's fortunes increased, he acquired a tract of land across Old River from Isle Brevelle and another on Cane River, where he spent the remainder of his life as a planter.[119] Many documents from the 1830–1850 period indicate a close relationship between Chevalier and the Metoyer community.

Before his death Chevalier drafted a will leaving all of his estate to the seven children he had by his Virginia-born, multiracial placée Fanny. As executors, he named two influential white friends, the brothers-in-law Michael Boyce and Pascalis Roubieu. As with Coindet and Joseph Dupré, Chevalier's will was contested. In Chevalier's case, he actually had a French-born kinsman on the Isle, Dr. Isidore Gimbert, who filed suit on behalf of himself and the collateral heirs in France. Perhaps because of Gimbert's exposure to Cane River's culture, Chevalier's white family was more willing to compromise than Coindet's had been. The Chevalier children received a settlement of $20,000, in addition to the five hundred acres of his Cane River estate that he had purchased in 1851 from the estate of Roubieu's father, François.[120] As a result of this settlement, the Chevalier offspring were among the wealthiest with whom the Metoyers intermarried.

Tradition holds that new bloodlines were introduced into the clan in still one other way. Because of their prosperity, the men of this family formed lasting friendships with many of the leading white planters of the parish, and a small number of these planters were, themselves, the fathers of children of color, in addition to their legal offspring. These solicitous fathers, some of whom acknowledged their children publicly, not only freed the children—according to tradition—but also worried over the possibility of their sons and daughters "going with the blacks." As a solution to this problem, the planters approached their Metoyer friends and arranged marriages between their offspring.

Documentary support of this tradition is not hard to find. For example, in 1841 François Florival Metoyer, son of Jean Baptiste Augustin Metoyer and his wife Marie Susette Anty, wed Marie Thérèse Aspasie Prudhomme. The bride was explicitly identified in the marriage register as the natural daughter of J. B. Prudhomme Jr., a prominent planter on the Côte Joyeuse (the old Grand Côte), by a mother identified only as Marie Pompose. Prudhomme signed the register as a witness to his daughter's marriage, along with the bride's freed brother, Séverin Prudhomme. The bride also signed. That marriage record provides no indication of the mother's status. However, the baptismal record of the three-year-old Marie Thérèse, dated 1826, identifies her as the daughter of Marie Pompose, slave of Prudhomme; and in September 1834, Prudhomme secured the local court's permission to manumit Marie Pompose *dite* Séverine and her three children. A family "Book of Ages" preserved by Aspasie's offspring also uses Sévèrin as Marie Pompose's surname or *dite.* Her racial composition was not specified in any of these records.[121]

By the onset of the Civil War, the community had grown to include families bearing thirty or so different surnames. All of these families possessed multiracial backgrounds similar to that of the Metoyers. No instance has been found on record during this period in which a member of the family group chose a full-black spouse. All spouses came from the general category known as *gens de couleur libres,* men and women with biracial or triracial roots. The full extent of the Amerindian ancestry claimed by those who allied with the Metoyers cannot be determined. The records indicate that five out-group spouses or partners were definitely of Indian lineage and a sixth probably was. Family tradition claims even more. This, in itself, is not unusual. In discussing racial attitudes of nonwhites in American and Brazilian societies, Carl Degler states: "It is not uncommon . . . for a mulatto, though clearly of Negro ancestry, to assert seriously and insistently that all his ancestors were Indians, for Indian blood does not carry the taint that Negro blood does."[122]

To some degree, Degler's generalization holds true in application to Cane River, but exceptions are obvious. Numerous photographs of the early members of the clan depict strong Indian features, even in families whose ancestry cannot be documented to any Indian forebear. One example is provided in the family photograph album of Thérèse (Sarpy) Metoyer, who was born in 1870 to Jérôme Sarpy Jr. and his wife Marie Sylvanie Roques.[123] Early in the album appears the portrait of a well-dressed middle-aged woman with pronounced aboriginal features; this portrait, like the others in the album, carries no identification. Examination of Thérèse's Cane River ancestry, and even that of the wives of her brothers, reveals no known Amerindian. The possibility of Native American ancestry for the Sarpys *de couleur* of New Orleans remains open.

The documentable backgrounds of all the families who allied with the Metoyers, as well as of the Metoyers themselves, also discount another popular generalization: that freed slaves routinely "took" the names of their masters whether or not they bore any relationship to them. One frequently cited authority on Louisiana's *gens de couleur libres* has quoted an earlier writer who broadly asserted: "As a rule free Negro families took the name of their former masters. A large percentage of these in Natchitoches Parish were named Metoyer, one of the old wealthy white Metoyers having freed some of his slaves. The same is true of the Dupré and Rachal families."[124]

On Cane River, most freed multiracials used surnames based on paternity, rather than ownership. In the case of the Duprés, the *gens de couleur libres* who adopted this surname were never the slaves of any master named Dupré. The same holds true in the case of Marie Pelagie Le Court, whose mother was a slave of the Le Comte family; in the case of Marie Thérèse Le Comte, whose mother was a slave of the Le Court family; in the case of Marie Agnes Poissot, whose mother belonged to the Derbannes; and in that of Fanchon Le Comte's children, who used the surnames Metoyer and Rachal although Fanchon was a Le Comte slave. Similar patterns prevailed in the associated community at Camptí, where the enslaved daughter of François Grappe, Madeleine, bore children who used the surnames Metoyer and David; and the freedman Noël used the surname Coindet even though he had been born on a Metoyer plantation and reared by Cloutier, whose sale of him called for his manumission.

A study of all manumitted slaves in this one parish, prior to the Civil War, reveals one sole instance in which freedpeople "took" the name of a white family without a strong indication of a blood tie—that being the Badins, who were manumitted by their widowed, childless master. Freed slaves whose white fathers did not claim them, those whose fathers were black, or those who were not aware of their fathers' identities normally used as a surname the given name of their parent, most commonly their mother. For example, children of the *griffes* Cécile and Balthasar, who were freed by Baptiste Dupré but not acknowledged by him, used Cécile and Balthasar as their surnames. Marie Adélaïde Mariotte, the apparent but unacknowledged daughter of Denis Buard, always identified herself by her mother's *dite*, Mariotte. Coincoin's eldest black son, whose father has never been identified, used her *dite* as his surname.

An analysis of the allied families also reveals that Augustin Metoyer's patriarchal efforts to reduce inbreeding were not successful. A goodly number of other-surnamed families were accepted into the clan; but many of those already bore some relationship to the Metoyers or to each other. Moreover, the numerous progeny that these families produced multiplied faster than the outside society could supply new and "acceptable" matches for. Continued endogamy was inevitable. To a great extent it was desirable, as one twentieth-century informant reported: "Well of course there was lots of marrying back and forth between families! When you check out a family and find they're okay, you stick with them!"[125]

Martin Ottenheimer's sociological study of cousin marriages in the United States contends that the issue was one of little concern in most American states prior to the late nineteenth century and that the intermarriages occurring before then had minimum genetic effect.[126] In Louisiana, enforcement of traditional taboos against intermarriage was left to the church. Along Cane River, clerical inquiries into kinship first appear in 1818, but dispensations from consanguinity in the second and more distant degrees seem to have been routinely granted to whites and multiracials alike from that time forward. In all families, the incorporation of exogamous partners, inside and outside of marriage, had a leveling effect—at least visually. When a newcomer to the region, Dr. J. W. Thomas, enumerated the parish for the census of 1860, he erroneously identified six of Cane River's multiracial households as "white," for a total of thirty-eight individuals. Significantly, Thomas also identified several of the "pure" French households in the area as "mulatto."[127] It is apparent from these mistakes, which were based upon Thomas's personal observation, that a sizable number of Cane River's Creoles of color were actually whiter than an equal number of the documentably white population. The outgroup choices made by the Metoyers and their kin, coupled with their frequent intermarriage, not only preserved but—to a noticeable degree—elevated the original family's level on the Old South's color-based caste scale.

FIVE

In Pursuit of Wealth

The economic activities of Cane River's Creoles spanned a broad spectrum. Farmers, professional men, merchants, tradesmen, and craftsmen, together they formed an almost self-contained society. Plantations that were mainly devoted to the cultivation of cotton also provided foodstuffs for the community. Other supplies were usually purchased from its own merchants. Teachers within the family group instructed each new generation. The people's own craftsmen, both slave and free, supplied the bulk of the skilled labor needed; records of the hiring of outside help are rare.

Coincoin's offspring created a society within a society, and the components of their community differed little from the scheme of the larger economic structure in which they operated. Louisiana's legal codes and moral thought provided considerable flexibility to the various confines legislated for the third caste in pre–Civil rights America. Reviewing the general economic situation of the free man of color in both southern and northern states, one early authority opined:

> The early free negroes are not to be thought of apart from slave negroes. . . . The shifting from one legal category to another left [them] unaltered with respect to fitness for the station they had thereby attained. It did not make them independent of doles from the larders and wardrobes of the whites; it did not essentially change their occupations. . . . Hence in the economic point of view they were not sharply distinguished . . . from those whose status, as the law would have had it, was lower than their own. Their position was anomalous. . . . They themselves were impotent. They went hither and thither as they were impelled.[1]

This negative portrayal has been developed by every subsequent generation of American historians. Louis Gray's depression-era history of southern agriculture concluded:

> Generally speaking, the . . . economic . . . condition of free Negroes was wretched in the extreme. . . . In some respects the position of free Negroes was inferior to that of slaves. The latter enjoyed the advantage of the master's protection; were assured a minimum of subsistence, medical attention, and support in old age; and so long as they were well behaved, were regarded with benevolent toleration.
>
> Free Negroes and poor whites were the outcasts of Southern society, but the former were subject to numerous . . . disabilities not imposed upon the latter. . . . The free Negro was everywhere "regarded with a distrust bordering on apprehension."[2]

A half-century later, another study elaborated: "Because of white prejudice and discrimination, the overwhelming majority of free Negroes were unskilled laborers. Black entrepreneurs found it difficult to obtain capital from white lending institutions. White businessmen were reluctant to employ blacks in skilled or white-collar work, and where they were willing to do so, whites often refused to work with them."[3]

The twentieth century's definitive study of free nonwhites, *Slaves without Masters,* presents an even more dire assessment of the Latin Gulf: "Most French and Spanish settlers remained intensely hostile toward blacks who were free. Like English colonists, they characterized free negroes as indolent, vain, and dangerous. Because they too treasured white dominance, they worried that the presence of so many light-skinned freemen would blur the color line and topple white rule."[4]

Anecdotal evidence to support such generalizations has been easy enough to marshal, especially for Anglo-American states. In 1805 a Maryland law denied free people of color the right to sell corn, wheat, or tobacco without first procuring from a justice of the peace a license certifying that the seller was "an orderly person of good character." Not only did this license have to be renewed annually, but subsequent revisions of the law rendered it applicable to almost all farm products.[5] In Mississippi, after 1831, it was illegal for a free nonwhite to sell goods outside the limits of an incorporated town, whether he acted on his own or as agent for another. In 1856, even within the limits of a town, he was denied the privilege of selling liquor, operating a "grocery" (a grog-shop or drinking house, as opposed to a "green grocery" that sold produce), or keeping a house of entertainment.[6] A North Carolina law of 1861 went so far as to prohibit any free person of color from buying, hiring, or apprenticing slaves or from working in any capacity that would put him in a position of control or management over slaves. Even within the Anglo states, however, there was often a considerable difference between what the law decreed and how it was applied to individuals at the local level.[7]

Inarguably, economic discrimination existed in the Louisiana colony, but on a significantly smaller scale. Incidences or expressions of that asserted "intense hostility" by French and Spanish settlers are not found in the Natchitoches District prior to the arrival of Americans from the Anglo states. Throughout Louisiana, free multiracials and free blacks alike enjoyed a wide latitude of economic liberties. Few limitations had been placed upon their livelihood or their economic competition with whites; and a measure of economic equality persisted throughout the antebellum years. Louisiana's free nonwhites were granted equal protection of property, had the power to make all types of contracts, and could engage in all kinds of business transactions. At least one antebellum entrepreneur of color, a man from Cane River who had ventured elsewhere, firmly declared that he would never live anywhere except in Louisiana. A "colored man," he believed, could make more money in Louisiana than in any of the free states of the North.[8]

Pioneer studies of Louisiana's free nonwhites drew their conclusions from the same template used for the South at large. The distinctions they defined emphasized disparities between urban and rural populations. "Most of the free Negroes in the rural regions," one study opined, "eked out pitiful existences at the sufferance of ever-wary whites," while the *gens de couleur libres* of New Orleans enjoyed "strikingly diverse" economic opportunity.[9] Again, this generalization does not hold true when applied to the rural Creoles of color along Cane River. No local restrictions were placed upon their diversity, and numerous restrictions set by the state legislature were simply not enforced by local authorities. Politically, Natchitoches Parish acquired its share of "ever-wary" whites. Economically, however, Cane River's free multiracial families enjoyed a level of prosperity that belies the general depiction of free rural men who "eked out pitiful existences."

The financial foundation for all families along Cane River was agriculture. In this respect Coincoin's offspring differed little from the rest of the parish or the South as a whole. The staple crop was cotton, the crop favored by the South in general after Eli Whitney's 1793 invention of the cotton gin enabled large-scale processing of the fiber. Much of the labor force, on plantations owned by Coincoin's offspring, was slave labor working under the close supervision of each plantation owner, the common practice of the South's middle-class planters. However, an examination of the family's agricultural activities suggests three distinct factors that accounted in large measure for their success: the quality of the land chosen by the first settlers of the Isle, the efficient use most owners made of it, and their realization that they could never be truly free so long as they were dependent upon the outside world for their livelihood or their survival. Throughout a half-century rocked by economic bubbles, financial panics, depression, inflation, and then war, most of Coincoin's family operated as a self-sufficient community.

The agricultural development of Isle Brevelle paralleled that of Natchitoches Parish in general. The early crops of indigo, tobacco, and sugarcane gave way to cotton. Remnants of these early crops survived, but mainly for home consumption. An indigo sower appears in the 1833 succession inventory of Pierre Metoyer Jr., and a tobacco hook is listed among personal property left by C. N. Roque Jr. in 1854. Many Cane River planters maintained a patch of sugarcane for syrup and as a special treat for the children.[10] Throughout most of their period of affluence, however, the multiracial farmers favored cotton and corn, the first as a cash crop and the second to feed their families, their slaves, and their animals.

A statistical study of farms held by this cohort is hampered by several factors. Censuses of the United States tabulated slaves from 1790. Agricultural data, however, were not gathered by the Bureau of the Census until 1840, and even the figures for that year do not include landholdings. Agricultural schedules of the 1850 and 1860 censuses are much more complete, but other factors, personal and political, had already set Cane River's Creoles *de couleur* on a course of economic decline.

The federal census of 1830, despite its lack of agricultural data, provides a snapshot of slaveholding in the community as compared to the general populace. The 58 slaves Coincoin's offspring had owned in 1810 had increased to 287 by 1830. Of this number, 226 were held by those who bore the surname Metoyer and 61 were owned by those of other surnames. Augustin and his brother Louis led the family that year, with each owning 54 slaves. The 99 people of color who lived in households headed by individuals with the surname Metoyer owned an average of 2.3 slaves for each man, woman, and child. The 3,801 whites in the parish claimed only 3,266 slaves, an average of 0.9 slaves per white. The free families of color who did not descend from Coincoin held an average of 0.2 slaves each.[11]

In other words, the average household in this extended family owned 156 percent more slaves than did the average white of the parish. It held ten and a half times more slaves than the average free person of color who was not part of this family group. Carter Woodson's study of free slaveowners of color throughout the United States in that year reveals that the Metoyers of Cane River owned more slaves than any other free family of color in the nation. While a few colored Americans elsewhere reported more slaves than did any individual Metoyer, no other family group came close to matching the aggregate holdings of those who bore the Metoyer name.[12]

The peak period of Metoyer affluence occurred between 1830 and 1840. Inventories made of several successions (estates) during these years report the size of individual plantations and the extent of their landholdings. Pierre Metoyer Jr., one of the less prosperous of the original brothers, died in 1834 leaving a plantation of approximately 677 acres—after having given land to his seven children at the time of their marriages.[13] The eldest brother, Augustin, who also gave sizable tracts as wedding presents to his many children, divided his remaining holdings between all of them in 1840, after his wife's death. The two plantations he still owned at that time sprawled across 2,134 acres.[14]

Fecundity, far more than racism, posed the critical economic threat to Cane River's multiracial families. As parents divided their holdings between numerous offspring, the inevitable result was a decrease in the size of individual landholdings with each generation. That circumstance is clearly shown by the 1850 agricultural census. Yet the statistics provided there also show that, even in decline, the community held its own in comparison with the population at large. Many family members remained among the largest landholders in the parish. François Gassion Metoyer, son of Augustin, had one thousand acres, all of it "improved"—that is, "cleared and used for grazing, grass, or tillage."[15] Only five other planters in the parish possessed as many improved acres; all were white. No other large-scale planters, white or otherwise, had improved every acre he or she owned. Four other planters of color on the Isle operated enterprises of more than a thousand acres, improved and unimproved combined: François Gassion's older brother Jean Baptiste Augustin, their siblings Joseph Augustin and Susette (Widow Morin), and their brother-in-law Charles N. Roques Sr. Three more kinsmen owned between five hundred and a thousand acres each.[16] The high ratio of improved to nonimproved land also foretold the problems the community faced in subsequent generations. Unimproved land—raw land—represented the opportunity for growth. Cane River families were nearing the practical limits of their ability to expand, physically and economically.

A comparative analysis of their average farm to the parish average, based upon the agricultural statistics of the 1850 census (see Table 2), provides other insight. Larger planters on the Isle stressed the production of their cash crop, cotton, which would bring a flow of money into the Isle, and deemphasized the production of foodstuffs. By purchasing these from their own merchants and truck farmers, they fostered other aspects of their economy. The ratio of slaves to acres of improved land within the extended family also squared with accepted standards. On new ground, the parish average was six acres of cotton and three acres of corn per slave. More acres per slave could be worked if the land had been previously cultivated.[17] The 5,667 acres of improved land owned by Coincoin's offspring in 1850 were tilled by 436 slaves, an average of thirteen improved acres per hand.[18] Of course, not all slaves were field hands, but neither was all improved land planted in these two crops.

A quantitative study of the southern slave-labor force provides a larger econometric framework. Robert Fogel and Stanley Engerman's controversial *Time on the Cross* found that the production of cotton required 34 percent of the labor time of slaves on cotton plantations. The raising of livestock, including the raising of feed, required about 25 percent. Corn for human consumption utilized 6 percent of the time, and the remaining 34 percent, the same amount of time required for cotton production, was devoted to such miscellaneous tasks as the construction of fences and buildings, home manufacturing, domestic work, and the tillage of other crops.[19]

These averages, based on samplings across the South, are at odds with the labor distribution and crop production patterns of cotton plantations on the Isle and some other plantations in central Louisiana. Solomon Northup, a free black from the Atlantic Coast who was enslaved for ten years in nearby Avoyelles Parish, left an account that speaks more clearly to the operation of Red River and Cane River plantations. According to Northup, the agricultural calendar revolved around the two staple crops: "Ploughing, planting, picking cotton, gathering the corn, and pulling and burning stalks, occupies the whole of the four seasons of the year. Drawing and cutting wood, pressing cotton, fattening and killing hogs, are but incidental labors."[20]

Planting season for the cash crop, Northup reports, was March and April. Fields were prepared with ox-drawn plows, turning the soil into rows of six-foot widths. A lighter plow followed, making furrows into which cotton

Table 2. Average Farm within the Community as Compared to Average Farm within Natchitoches Parish, 1850

	AVERAGE FARM IN THE COMMUNITY	AVERAGE FARM IN THE PARISH
Improved acres of land	113.3	84.0
Unimproved acres of land	138.9	172.0
Total acres of land	(252.2)	(256.0)
Value of farm	$1,866	$1,664
Value of implements and machinery	$404	$343
Slaves	9.0	9.0
Horses	3.3	3.4
Mules & asses	2.2	1.2
Oxen	3.4	1.2
Milk cows	4.8	6.0
Beef cattle	4.7	12.0
Swine	6.0	39.0
Sheep	4.2	5.0
Value of animals slaughtered	$30	$61
Ginned cotton (bales)	23.3	18.5
Corn (bushels)	388.9	468.0
Peas & beans (bushels)	1.4	13.7
Irish potatoes (bushels)	.5	4.1
Sweet potatoes (bushels)	22.2	44.3
Butter (pounds)	1.0	35.6
Honey	1.6	9.3
Molasses	*	2.0
Cane sugar (pounds)	*	4.0
Maple sugar (pounds)	*	0.3
Cheese (pounds)	*	0.6
Oats (bushels)	.5	3.8
Rice (pounds)	*	17.1
Garden produce for market (value)	*	$1
Tobacco (pounds)	4.8	5.3
Wool (pounds)	2.0	6.4
Homemade manufactures	$1	$7

*None reported

Based upon manuscript returns of the Seventh Census of the United States, Slave and Agricultural Schedules.

seeds were dropped. Next a harrow was pulled over the rows to cover the seeds. In all, two mules or oxen, three slaves, two plows, and a harrow were used in planting cotton. The cotton sprouted eight to ten days later. Then the first plowing and hoeing began. Not only did grass have to be removed, but the cotton had to be thinned into hills about two and a half feet apart. Two weeks later the seedlings were thinned again, leaving only the strongest and healthiest plant in each hill. Two additional hoeings followed, the last about July 1. Those hoeings were done by slaves paced by a lead worker and driven from behind by a driver or overseer who sported a whip, according to Northup.[21] On Cane River plantations with few or no slaves, that labor was carried out by the farmer (of whatever color), his wife, and their children.

In late August, picking usually began. An average day's work produced 150 to 200 pounds per slave, although a great variation was exhibited by individual pickers. Five hundred pounds per day was not impossible for a slave with exceptionally nimble fingers and a strong back. Four pickings were usually required to clean the stalks, the last coming as late as January. Excessive spring rains that forced replanting could delay the picking season considerably. On the other hand, short crop seasons such as that which occurred in 1841 meant that farmers might finish as much as two months earlier. The cold wave that hit after spring planting in 1841 was, in fact, so severe that it killed much of Cane River's fowl, young cattle, and timber saplings.[22]

Beans, corn, peas, sweet potatoes, and other crops were tended during time not needed for the cotton. The most important of the food crops, corn, was usually planted in February before the onset of the cotton planting season. If February and March were exceptionally cold, the corn did not germinate. Still, most planters gambled and sowed the seed early, lest planting of the cash crop be delayed. In August, after the last cotton hoeing and before picking began, leaves were stripped from cornstalks and laid out to dry for winter use as animal fodder. Ears of corn were turned down on the stalks for protection against rain until the cotton crop was picked. Only after the cotton was gathered was the corn harvested and stored without shucking; those shucks were a natural protection against weevils.

Once the cotton and corn were gathered, preparations began for the next year's production. Stalks were pulled and burned and the fields plowed, turning the debris from one crop into the soil to decompose and enrich the next year's production. Meanwhile, most farm animals were allowed to roam the woods, with minimum care. Milk cows, according to Northup, were worth little since they produced little. Many Louisiana planters, though not those on the Isle, are said to have relied heavily upon the North for cheese and butter.[23]

In most regards, evidence for the Cane River plantations suggests a closer parallel to Northup's account of slave labor usage than to the econometric studies conducted elsewhere. As shown in Table 1, the average farm in the community possessed nine slaves in 1850. If 25 percent of their labor was devoted to the care of the animals and the production of feed for them, as asserted by Fogel and Engerman, then the full-time labor of two slaves and one-fourth of the labor of a third slave would be needed to care for the fifteen livestock the average farm possessed—a stark excess. In 1850, for example, J. B. Augustin Metoyer reported 75 head of cattle as well as 10 work oxen, 30 sheep, and 10 hogs—along with 42 slaves of all ages, who would have been needed to till 500 acres of improved land and clear another 500 acres. In other households, hog raising seems to have been the primary agricultural endeavor. Young Firmin C. Christophe that year reported a stock of 50 hogs, 19 head of cattle, 140 bushels of corn, only 20 acres of improved land, and 340 acres of unimproved land—with only one male slave.[24] Many succession inventories itemized animals "running loose in the woods," as Northup observed, and many cattle and horses were sold at probate auction, sight unseen, for the same reason.

Free-ranging animals were, in fact, the southern norm. As Forrest McDonald and Grady McWhiney have demonstrated, "open range prevailed throughout the South. Animals were simply branded or clipped and turned loose to graze the land—anybody's land, for fencing laws prohibited the enclosure of any space not actually under cultivation and required farmers to fence their crops against the animals of others, rather than the other way around."[25] Indeed, the Census Bureau's 1850 instructions to enumerators called for "no attempt . . . to enumerate or estimate the number of animals on . . . unfenced land."[26]

Crop production for both Cane River and Natchitoches Parish at large also fell short when measured by both of the econometric studies cited above. McDonald and McWhiney, analyzing "representative" samples from the 1850 southern agricultural schedules, calculated 180 pounds of ginned lint as the "average yield per acre." Using their standard base of 400 pounds per bale, the 23.3 bales averaged by multiracial Creole planters on Cane River represent 9,320 pounds on an average farm of 113.3 acres—only 82.5 pounds per acre. The family's production per acre was also slightly lower than the parish averages. The average Natchitoches farmer produced 18.5

bales, or 7,400 pounds, on 84 acres. Yet that parishwide 88.1 pounds per acre in a region populated by wealthy white planters was also significantly lower than McDonald and McWhiney's 1850 figures for the South at large.[27]

Statistics aside, husbandry among Cane River's Creoles of color was not a haphazard enterprise. Nor was it one in which each man learned to farm solely by trial and error or by the guidance of elders. The high value this extended family placed on education was designed not just to enrich itself culturally but to provide its youth with an economic advantage, whatever livelihood they pursued. At least one substantial manual on the latest methods of crop production known in the early nineteenth century has been preserved by descendants, and its pages are well worn.[28]

Although most farming within the community was conducted on an individual basis, partnerships also existed. Auguste Metoyer and his cousin-in-law Jérôme Sarpy, for example, purchased together the plantation of the deceased white neighbor Julien Rachal for $19,300—the land and buildings, with their furnishings (which became Sarpy's residence), but not the slaves.[29] A less amicable partnership was the one formed in 1854 between the New Orleans transplant Hypolite Chevalier and Joseph François Metoyer, son of François, who jointly rented a tract from Louis Monette's widow on lower Cane River. Metoyer supplied the capital and Chevalier supplied the labor; Chevalier was to receive one-third of the crop. The partners ended in court after a dispute concerning the proper division of the cotton and corn they produced.[30] The agreement reached by Athanasite Metoyer (son of Pierre Jr.) and his cousin-in-law Jean Baptiste Cloutier in 1852 reflects a different method of handling the profits. Acting as agent for Vial Girard, a French émigré, *commerçant,* and absentee landowner who resided in Avoyelles Parish, Metoyer agreed to advance merchandise to his less prosperous kinsman. In return, Cloutier promised to produce for Girard that year, on the Frenchman's land, two bales of cotton worth at least $440. Applying here a McDonald-McWhiney statistic, that the average farmhand could produce four and a half bales (1,800 pounds of cleaned lint), then Girard would have exacted 40 percent of Cloutier's cash crop. By 1850, as land became less available for young men coming to adulthood, Cane River's notaries were increasingly called upon to draft land leases for both whites and free people of color, reflecting a variety of sharing schemes.[31]

Leases of whole plantations also took place within the extended family. A typical case was the arrangement between Joseph Augustin Metoyer and his brother François Gassion. The original lease was made in September

1843 and was renewed for three more years in January 1850. The plantation was rented "with all the slaves, horses, mules, cattle, work oxen, and farming utensils thereon, and also all the cattle and horses belonging to the said Joseph and which may be running at large in the woods."[32]

Similar lease agreements were entered into between free people of color and their white neighbors. Contrary to stereotype, the multiracial was often the landlord. The property leased was usually agricultural, but on occasion it included town lots and dwellings. The entrepreneur Auguste Metoyer rented to Louis Gaspard Derbanne, white, a plantation with all fences and buildings for three years beginning January 1, 1835. Derbanne paid three dollars per acre of cultivable land and agreed to return all buildings and fences in good condition at the end of the lease.[33] Another of Auguste's renters, however, did not drive so good a bargain. In March 1839, amid a financial crisis for the country and for Auguste, the Anglo William Townsend agreed to an exorbitant rent of $6.75 per acre, for a term of one year. At the end of the year, Auguste had to take Townsend to court to collect his rent, and the judge considered the price so high that he cut the debt from $338 to $200. Even after the reduction of the rent, Townsend was unable to pay and the sheriff seized and sold a thirteen-year-old slave to satisfy the debt. The implication of the suit was that Auguste considered the white a poor risk and set the rent high to cover that risk and his potential legal bills.[34] A town lease executed in 1844 between one of the several Joseph Metoyers and the French émigré Alexander Pinçon, a notary and justice of the peace, was less problematic. Metoyer rented Pinçon his "lot of ground and buildings" at Cloutierville for one year at the price of fifty dollars. The type of property and its size was not specified.[35]

Basic farm equipment used by Cane River Creoles of all hues tended toward obsolescence. A reluctance to adopt new types of equipment had long been laid on their doorstep. In 1805 a federal agent sent to assess the valleys of the Cane and the Red asserted: "Though Natchitoches has been settled almost one hundred years, it is not more than twelve or fifteen years since they ever had a plow, or a flat to cross the river with, both of which were introduced by an Irish Pennsylvanian, under a similar opposition to the copernican system."[36]

Antebellum inventories of property in the succession records of white and colored planters alike provide an excellent cross section of the types of implements used. Estimators inventoried plows of various types and harrows of wood, some with iron teeth. The assessed values, ranging between fifty cents and a dollar, suggest their rude nature.[37] The assertion that wooden plows were preferred over cast-iron ones throughout Louisiana and the lower Mississippi valley in the 1850s and 1860s appears to hold true for Natchitoches Parish.[38] These implements were pulled by mules, horses, or oxen, depending upon the preference of the individual farmer. Along Cane River, oxen predominated. Other tools inventoried in the various successions included hoes, pickaxes, rakes, scythes, shovels, spades, and saws of various types.

The higher-than-average value of implements and machinery within the community, suggested by the 1850 agricultural census, reflects a high incidence of cotton gins and mills. The base cost of construction for a gin was about $600, the 1836 fee set by Séraphin Llorens to build a gin on the plantation of a white neighbor, F. S. Lattier. In March 1840, the aging Augustin Metoyer owned and operated two such gins, one on the right bank of the river valued at $1,200 and another "with grates" on the left bank worth $2,000. In addition, Augustin's main plantation boasted a "gin for grain" (gristmill) and a "pounding mill." His sister Susanne also erected a gristmill and a cotton gin on the plantation she farmed with her son Florentin Conant. The overall picture provided by the inventories of these two estates is one of unusually progressive operations. By comparison, few planters in the parish at large owned and operated cotton gins, and only three gristmills were tallied in the whole of the parish in 1840.[39]

The operation of a gin was also expensive, even after the initial cost of construction was met. For example, a fire insurance policy taken out by the Jewish planter S. M. Hyams of Natchitoches—a type of record rarely surviving for Cane River, although the policies were common among larger planters— paid $54 for fire insurance on his gin in 1852. Repairs were a continual expense. The 1838 succession of Susanne Metoyer noted a payment of $180 for a repair bill on her gin. When her twin Augustin donated his property to his children in 1840, he specified that the gins were for the use of all of them so long as they contributed their shares to maintenance.[40] Still, the costs of operation and repairs were more than offset by the savings generated. The two gins of Augustin Metoyer and his children would have rendered a saving of $5,764 on the 598 bales of cotton they reported on the 1850 census.[41]

Some planters within this extended family not only used their gins for their own crops but also processed cotton for neighbors, white and multiracial, whose farming operations were not large enough to support a gin. Emanuel Dupré, Valmont Llorens (grandson of Susanne Metoyer), Jean Baptiste Espallier Rachal, and his son Louis Casimere were among those who supplemented their income by ginning and storing cotton for their neighbors.[42]

Most slaves within the community were employed by their owners on their own lands or in their other business enterprises. However, leases of slaves to outside planters as temporary labor did occasionally occur. In 1845, for example, Jacquitte Rachal rented two twenty-eight-year-old slaves, one male and one female, to the wealthy white Charles F. Benoist of the Rachal clan. The price agreed upon was $176 for three years.[43] Other multiracial Creoles rented slaves from white neighbors. In an 1841 agreement between the multiracial Widow Pierre Mission Rachal and the white Widow J. B. Brevelle, Mme. Rachal rented Mme. Brevelle's slave woman for thirty-nine days at a price of fifty cents per day.[44] Slaves were sometimes owned jointly across the color line, as in the case of J. B. Espallier Rachal and his white first cousin, Victor Rachal. For several years, each held a half interest in a slave named Alfred.[45]

In Louisiana, as in most slave societies, the supervision and treatment of slaves were considered the personal prerogatives of each plantation owner, so long as the laws of the state were more or less upheld. Within this framework, slaveholders of color were "damned if they did and damned if they didn't." Those who were kind to their bondsmen risked charges from prejudiced whites such as the one who swore to Olmsted that the Cane River Creoles of color were "a lazy, beastly set—slaves and all on an equality, so-cially—no order or discipline on their plantations, but everything going to ruin."[46] On the other hand, if they treated their slaves with firmness and administered punishment when due, others accused them of being harsh masters "who got out of their slave property all that they could."[47] Neither generalization can be tidily applied to Cane River. As with any other group of slaveowners, Coincoin's offspring who held people in bondage treated them with varying degrees of consideration; and a close examination of their social lives and attitudes clearly belies the statement that slaves were treated as equals.

Family tradition recalled in the 1970s indicted two Cane River ancestors of ill-using their slaves. One, a female, was said to be "mean" to those she held in bondage. In the opinion of the informant, "The good Lord got even with Tante ["Auntie"]; her mansion was burned during the Civil War, her second husband ran through her money, and she was forced to live the rest of her days, bedridden, in one of her slave cabins." Tradition also contends that Coincoin's son François Metoyer was a hard taskmaster, but not neces-

sarily with his own hands. The method he allegedly used to obtain the labor of slaves belonging to others was deceptive. Feigning an interest in the
purchase of certain slaves, supposedly, he would insist upon trying them
before making a final decision. The borrowed slaves would then be put to
work on the worst land he had and at exceptionally exhausting tasks that
he did not want his own slaves to perform. After completing the work he
would return the slaves, claiming they were poor hands not worth purchasing. Allegedly, this ploy was used on his family as well as outsiders. While
his brother Louis was deceived twice, tradition holds, the more perceptive
Augustin saw through his younger brother from the start and refused to let
him have any slaves on trial.[48]

The only evidence for the tradition suggests that François's systemic
problem was a financial one, rather than an abusive or exploitative nature.
In 1834, as the longtime owner of three adult slaves, he acquired two additional ones from his sister Susanne—a thirty-year-old black woman of Anglo
origin and her ten-year-old, locally born, son Victorin—for whom he gave
Susanne a $1,980 mortgage. The mortgage was not paid on time and, in 1837,
the pair reappeared as part of the succession of Susanne's daughter-in-law
Mme. Florentine Conant. At that time, François once again bought Victorin, but not his mother. (In tandem, the details of both purchases suggest
the possibility that Victorin was François's son.) Meanwhile, François also
borrowed $2,466 from Augustin, giving a one-year mortgage on the three
black Creoles he had owned for many years. François paid little on that debt
and—in the wake of the financial crash of 1837—used those same slaves as
collateral for loans from Joseph La Vigne, a free man of color who had married Augustin's ward Dorothée Derbanne.

In 1843, Augustin reached the end of his patience with his younger brother's inability to pay his debts. The matter was not simply one of a character
flaw on François's part or Augustin's more straight-laced view of personal
responsibility. The national economy was still depressed from the Panic of
1837. Suicide was still a significant cause of death throughout America, as
bankruptcies pushed men to the brink of their mental fortitude. On the Isle,
where most men and women borrowed from relatives, one person's failure
to repay hurt his kinsmen and weakened the family as a whole. So it was
that Augustin, the family's patriarch and arbiter, petitioned the court to seize
and sell the mortgaged slaves to pay François's debts. One of those slaves, the
forty-year-old Jacques, was valued then at a mere $10—suggesting hard use
or, at the least, an accident or ailment that had left him with little commer-

cial value. When the court ordered a sheriff's sale of the twice-mortgaged slaves, Augustin took Jacques and his apparent wife, the thirty-three-year-old female Cyde, at the value set by the court's estimators: $10 and $500 respectively. François's grandson Jérôme Sarpy Jr. purchased the third slave, a twenty-five-year-old male priced at $700, and François's debt to Joseph La Vigne was repaid. A similar, concurrent lawsuit by family members who had lent François another $1,700 against a title to young Victorin left the sixty-year-old François with no slave labor to help till his farm. He would eventually repay Augustin for Cyde, but his financial woes would continue and Cyde would, again in 1853, be pledged by François as security for a land lease.[49]

If runaway slaves were indicative of ill treatment, then other family members might stand accused. Louis Metoyer placed an advertisement in the local newspaper in June 1825, offering a reward for "a mulattoe [sic] slave named Charles, aged about 36." The reward offered was one hundred dollars if captured west of the Sabine River and fifty dollars if captured east of the Sabine. When Joseph Augustin Metoyer died in 1851, one of his "Anglo" slaves, a carpenter named Washington, was sold as "having run away once and having bad sight in one eye but otherwise fully guaranteed." The record does not indicate whether he had run away from Joseph or a previous master. By contrast, Joseph also had a twenty-eight-year-old male slave named Bossine who was identified in the succession inventory as a hunter by occupation.[50] If Joseph were so harsh a master that one slave fled his authority, it seems improbable that he would give another slave a gun and send him into the woods.

Numerous legal records supplement the parish's few surviving antebellum newspapers, but no other references to runaways have been found therein.[51] Tradition reports that a few other slaves on the Isle absconded after punishment and joined the triracial "Redbones" who had settled the piney woods west and south of Cane River. Others supposedly abandoned their masters to follow the invading Union army in 1864.[52] One of the latter is documented in the Reconstruction-era files of the Southern Claims Commission, but the man who fled returned five years after the war to settle on the plantation of his former master.[53]

To all appearances, slaves belonging to Cane River's Creoles of color were treated at least as well as those of the region's white planters. Augustin Metoyer and Jérôme Sarpy, tradition avers, had reputations for kindness to those whose lives they controlled in every way. Sarpy, allegedly, insisted that cabins not only be kept clean but be whitewashed twice a year, inside and out, while Augustin is said to have rarely sold a slave.[54]

Here again, documentary evidence adds nuances, both positive and negative, that tradition does not report. Slave sales by Augustin were indeed few. Across six decades, in which he owned a cumulative total of more than a hundred slaves, he executed seven known sales—six of them to family members in situations that could have been designed to unite slave families rather than separate them. His one outside sale occurred in September 1822 when a financial crunch required him to quickly raise a substantial sum. Four adult blacks were sold on a single day for about $2,000, all in cash: three were sold to his brother and brother-in-law; the fourth to a neighboring white Creole widow.[55] Throughout all branches of the family, keeping slaves within the family was the rule rather than the exception—even though, following the law and custom of the time, slaves and other property belonging to a succession would be offered at public auction.

At the sale of belongings left by Pierre Metoyer Jr., for example, only one of his nine slaves went outside the family. That one, a thirty-five-year-old black Catholic woman, was sold to a neighboring Catholic widow. When the succession of Pierre's brother Joseph was auctioned, all of his seventeen slaves were kept in the family. Slave children were clearly parceled with their parents, although Louisiana's law allowed those over ten to be sold separately. Sixteen of Joseph's seventeen slaves went to his multiracial blood relatives and the seventeenth, a twenty-year-old black male, was purchased by a white Creole neighbor whose placée was Joseph's kin. At the death of his sister Susanne, all twenty-one of her slaves were purchased by family members— including a thirty-seven-year-old black male bought by her twenty-one-year-old nephew Gassion, at $1,500, for immediate manumission. When the newlywed Louis Porter died in 1835 leaving a fourteen-year-old widow, one of his three slaves went to her as her share of the estate; the other two were purchased at his succession sale by her uncle and her first cousin. When Espallier Rachal died leaving five slaves, one fell to his white cousin who already held a half-ownership; the other four were purchased by Espallier's multiracial kin. When Charles Nerestan Roque Sr. died in 1859, all of his forty-two slaves were purchased within the family except for one couple, both blacks aged fifty-one, who were purchased by a white neighbor.[56]

Because succession sales were public affairs, routinely attended by males of all ilk who lived within the neighborhood, Cane River's multiracials at times paid a premium for their effort to keep family slaves within the family. Community whites could and did bid up the prices. At the death of Pierre Metoyer Jr., the inventory and estimate of his property valued his nine slaves at $3,250. At the subsequent auction, bidding ran the total up to $5,360.[57] Theoretically, in these cases, heirs benefited from the increased revenue. In reality, because most such slaves were purchased by the heirs, the increased cost of those slaves meant that they had to sell more of the estate's personal goods in order to raise distributable cash to cover the increased value of the slaves. It also meant that kinsmen who purchased the slaves but were not heirs had to have more cash on hand—or assume higher debts—to cover the higher prices.

Slave divisions caused by owner deaths can be interpreted in various ways. When heirs were widely scattered—especially in the older Anglo states where younger generations frequently moved great distances to newly opened lands and slaves were frequently assigned to daughters whose husbands tended to move with the husband's own family—cleavages within slave families were a harsh reality. On Cane River, the problem was ameliorated by two factors. First was the effort to keep husbands and wives together, as well as parents with their prepubescent children. Second, the insularity of the colored Creole families and the extent to which they shared their planting operations also lessened the physical separation that might otherwise result from a sale. Surviving records clearly demonstrate that there were no figurative walls between most of the farms. Not only did their lands adjoin, but census schedules repeatedly show families owning slaves but no slave houses, while their kinsmen next door had slave houses but claimed ownership of no slaves.[58]

These circumstances are easier to visualize against the backdrop of the Creole custom of subdividing family farms among offspring as they matured. The original owner of a plantation built slave cabins in the most efficacious place. When children received a slice of the parental land, together with a slave or so, that slice typically had no slave cabins and the grown child had no immediate need to build any. The family's slaves stayed in place in the already existing "quarters" and continued to work the land they had always worked. On paper, the slaves had new masters. Physically, no change occurred. Not until (or if) the new generation significantly expanded its operation and purchased new slaves from outside the family, or their young slaves matured and created families of their own, would new cabins be constructed for those new slaves on the splinter plantation.

Slave housing on the Isle, generally speaking, exhibited a better standard than either the parish average or the national one. Fogel and Engerman's econometric study of slave life reports that in 1860 the average large plantation enumerated 5.2 slaves per cabin. In Natchitoches Parish that year, the average was four. On plantations belonging to Coincoin's offspring, the average slave dwelling housed only three people.[59] The quarters provided for Cane River slaves were rudimentary, as was most slave housing, and seems to have been typical of that described by Fogel and Engerman for the late antebellum period. Frederick Law Olmsted, the New York travel writer, left descriptions of slave cabins on two large Cane River plantations owned by whites. On the first plantation, cabins were small, one room to a family, built of plank, and chinked with rags and mud. Floors were bare earth, and chimneys were made of sticks and mud. On the second plantation, the slave quarters were larger and each sported a brick chimney and a front gallery. Such accommodations he considered rude but comfortable.[60]

Extant slave cabins on land owned by Coincoin's offspring generally fall into Olmsted's second category. Most measured approximately eighteen by twenty feet and were made of logs chinked with mud. They had plank floors, brick or stone chimneys, and windows. The only dirt-floored cabin recalled by twentieth-century residents of the Isle was built and originally occupied by whites before the Metoyers acquired the land and converted the already hoary dwelling into a Catholic school.[61] No twentieth-century informant, however, reported any recollection of a slave cabin with a chimney of sticks and mud. Fogel and Engerman's assessment—that "such housing is quite mean by modern standards, [but] compared well with the housing of free workers in the antebellum era"[62]—can be validly applied to Natchitoches Parish. In 1860 the farm house of one educated white, a former blacksmith who was that year an overseer owning 640 acres of Red River land himself, was described as "a log house 20 × 18 feet, the [attached] storeroom . . . 12 by 8 feet, 6 feet high." Another room for a hired Negro "was same height, and 10 by 6 feet wide." The master's house and the addition were valued together at $60.[63]

On several Cane River plantations one cabin, larger than the rest, was set aside as a slave hospital. On Louis Metoyer's plantation, after the family built a stately manor house, their original home became the hospital. Another one recalled by older family members in the twentieth century was located just above Emanuel Dupré's 24-Mile Ferry.[64] According to Fogel and Engerman, the hospitalization of slaves served several purposes. The sick were thereby isolated from the well, minimizing contagion. Such special treatment as diets, rest, and medication could be more easily prescribed and administered. Moreover, the immediate confinement and close supervision of those who claimed illness tended to reduce the incidences of feigned ailments.[65]

Parish records do reflect a small number of lame, sickly, and unsound slaves on the plantations of Cane River's multiracial Creoles. The hernias attributed to a few of them attest that heavy manual labor was exacted. However, hernias have always been an occupational hazard among laborers and tradesmen. It was no less so among those employed in gins or on cotton plantations, where slaves loaded produce onto the barges and steamships that stopped at the Isle to pick up goods for the New Orleans market. Along Cane River, physical labor was a risk shared by the masters as well as slaves. Metoyer family tradition pointedly praises François Metoyer for his inordinate strength, specifically his ability to singlehandedly lift bales of cotton, kegs of whiskey, and vats of oil. Allegedly, when the first church was built on the Isle, "he did the raisin' of the church—they needed no jack." Even in the twentieth century, the heavy manual work required of those who continually handled cotton bales routinely resulted in hernias and serious spinal problems.[66]

All retrospective assessments of slavery, whether couched in terms of paternalism, moderation, callousness, or sadism, inevitably incorporate some ideological convictions of the inquirer. The same might be said of historical accounts such as those reported by Olmsted. Even contemporaries who, unlike Olmsted's informant, harbored no racial bias toward people of African descent left stark assessments of the manner in which the institution of slavery created class divides and diminished the humanity of the master class. In the mid-to-late 1830s, a Czech-born engineer named Anthony Michael Dignowity traversed Louisiana repairing cotton gins. He kept a journal of his experiences and impressions, including several pages in which he recorded a visit to Augustin Metoyer's home. At one point, he wrote:

> [I] crossed to what was called the Island. . . . some thirty miles long and from six to eight broad. It was the most fertile land in this part of Louisiana, and was covered with fine plantations, but mostly owned by free negroes and Mulatoes, from French descent. I walked some dozen miles down this Island. The plantation Bells were ringing for Noon, when I arrived to a very fine plantation; all looked elegant, an indication of wealth. I concluded to stop for dinner, and approached a very fine dwell-

ing house. A white headed gentlemanly old Negro man bid me welcome. [After the noon meal] I rested and enjoyed myself this day, in company of the rest of Mr. Matoye['s] family. In the evening I took a stroll about the plantation houses. Adjoining the hospital room, I saw the room containing the stocks and saw two negro slaves confined in them. At a later hour, I could hear the crac[k]s of the overseer's whip. So I saw that the infernal system of bondage was not ameliorated, because the master and the slaves were of the same colour.[67]

Beyond the tangible gauges by which slave treatment is conventionally measured, another suggestion of concern or care that the Metoyers *de couleur* exhibited toward their slaves can be drawn from slave baptismal records. During the 1820s the parish was without a resident pastor for several years. When one priest visited Natchitoches in 1826 he stopped at the larger plantations to baptize whites, free people of color, and slaves who had been born since the last pastoral visit. As the sacraments were administered to the slaves, their names, approximate ages, and sometimes the names of their mothers were written down by him for a later entry into the church registers.

At Metoyer plantations, particularly those of Dominique, Jean Baptiste Augustin, Louis, Susanne, and her son Florentin Conant, priests were given the exact birth dates of each slave child, even though some children were as old as six years. The mother of each child was also identified. By comparison, only three of the white planters of the area gave exact dates for some of their slaves: Dominique Rachal (who provided the information inconsistently), J. B. Lestage, and Sylvestre Rachal. The latter two were both young planters whose holdings were small enough that such information could be maintained with little effort.[68] Either the Metoyers exhibited better than average concern for their slaves as human beings, or they kept a closer inventory of their property.

Cane River slaves held by Creoles of color also received special privileges or bonuses, some of which were not unusual among white planters throughout the South. One of the more common "extras" on southern plantations was a Christmas holiday of varying length, during which some type of festivity was held. According to one authority, the Christmas holidays on cotton plantations usually began on the day before Christmas Eve and ended on New Year's Eve. A dinner and a dance were normally scheduled during this interval, and other activities were sometimes held.[69]

On the plantation of Augustin Metoyer, tradition reports, Christmas celebrations for the slaves centered upon the *papegai*. This ancient French custom, in its continental form, placed parrots or parakeets upon a tall pole as targets for competition among archers. The Cane River French, as with many of their inherited customs, adapted this one to their circumstances and needs. Several days before the festivities began, slaves prepared an effigy of a cow, marked into cuts of meat; that figure was suspended atop a pole. A cow was then butchered. On the night of the celebration, a line was drawn forty yards from the effigy, and the slaves aligned themselves behind it. Taking turns, with the eldest going first, the slaves shot at the effigy, aiming at the choicest sections. Whatever cut of unclaimed meat each slave hit on the effigy was the cut he received from the butchered cow. This beef was a very welcome addition to the pork, cornmeal, potatoes, and vegetables that constituted the usual basis of slave diets in central Louisiana. The customary gift of a bottle of whiskey per slave, along with the usual music and dancing, eased the daily grind of life for those enslaved on Augustin's plantation.[70]

Another common practice the Metoyers followed was the granting of passes for their bondsmen and women to visit other plantations or to go to town. One surviving pass was given by Auguste Metoyer to two of his men, Syphorian and Frank, during the Christmas season of 1850. On the appointed day for their return from George S. Walmsley's house at Cloutierville, the slave Frank had not completed his business. Walmsley wrote a note to Metoyer explaining that Frank "leaves his blanket coat unfinished and has some other little affairs to attend to," that the slave wished to return to Cloutierville on New Year's Day, and that he had no objection to the slave's return if Auguste granted permission.[71]

Cane River's Creoles of color, to a markedly greater extent than their white counterparts, also granted freedom to valued slaves for "good and faithful service" or other cause. In a few cases, kinship or paternity was an obvious motivation. More often, the Metoyers—particularly Augustin and his sons—acted as community benefactors, helping poorer freedmen buy their kin or ambitious slaves buy their freedom. As Louisiana's laws increasingly restricted the emancipation of slaves, the Metoyers devised workarounds, advancing loans and executing paper transactions to hold titles to slaves when colored freedmen of no kinship, as well as white friends, were in danger of losing kinsmen during financial distress. Typically, these were cases in which a mortgaged slave was a child or spouse of an indebted owner, who could not free their loved one under the prevailing law.

Augustin's earliest emancipations were purchases of kinsmen or brides for his brothers, four such purchases between 1795 and 1801.[72] In 1813 he freed his first nonrelative, a sixteen-year-old French and African girl named Dorothée, to whom he had held a title for several years. The following month, "after necessary advertisement for more than forty days, as required by law," with no opposition voiced by others, Augustin granted freedom to another slave of no known kinship. She was said by him to be over thirty years, the minimum age for emancipation. In 1835 he freed a male named Remy, his wife's brother. In the draft of his last will and testament in 1840, he made provisions for the manumission of still another slave, a likely grandchild. Article Seven of that document stated: "I desire and such is my wish that after my death a small mulattress named Lise, belonging to me and now aged about twelve years, will be freed of the bonds of slavery, and as soon as my testamentary executors judge it convenient, provided that the time of her manumission not be allowed to surpass the time when she will have completed her twenty-first year, or as soon after that as it is possible to do it." A decade later, he gave Lise's title to his grandson, François Florival Metoyer, with the understanding that she was to be freed as soon as the law allowed. Other manumissions and purchases for manumission reflect a variety of circumstances.[73]

In many cases, the backstory for each manumission reveals cultural and social nuances that go unstated in any single record. Augustin's emancipation of Dorothée illustrates that point when the documentary trail is fully explored. Dorothée Derbanne was but one year old when her white grandmother died leaving a will in which she bequeathed two slave children specifically to her bachelor sons who had fathered them. Joseph Derbanne was to get Dorothée; his brother Manuel was to get the boy Remy. By 1805, both brothers had married and one of their wives apparently was not happy with daily exposure to her husband's love child. The brothers swapped children; Joseph took Manuel's son Remy, and Manuel took Joseph's daughter Dorothée. By 1810, Manuel fell into debt to Alexis Cloutier—a man so callous that his own aged uncle would soon sue him for misappropriation of resources that were to support the old man in his dotage. Cloutier, in making his loan to Manuel, demanded a mortgage on all the slaves to which Manuel held title. That mortgage included Dorothée, Joseph's daughter, and her personal risk was a significant one. She was now in her mid-teens, and Cloutier was a man who indulged himself freely among the women he held in slavery.[74]

When the debt came due and Derbanne lacked the funds to clear it, Augustin offered to remove Dorothée from harm's way. Because Derbanne could not dispose of a mortgaged slave, Augustin proposed a swap—promising a male slave of higher value, as well as $200 that Derbanne could use toward his debt to Cloutier. Cloutier agreed to the swap and took the cash. Augustin, rather than part with a slave attached to his own household, chose Dorothée's replacement ten days later from a coffle of "Anglo" blacks offered by a Virginia-based slave trader who passed by on the river. The exchange was made and, in June 1810, Augustin took Dorothée home with him. Subsequent evidence suggests that she moved into his home as his ward, not his slave. By 1814, the seventeen-year-old Dorothée was in love with a local freedman named Joseph Tessier *dit* La Vigne. Augustin manumitted her that November, averring inaccurately that she was of legal age to manumit. He also served as La Vigne's surety on the $500 bond the freedman had to post to acquire a marriage license—a bond required in that era of all grooms, not just men of color. Then, he engaged a notary to draft a marriage contract that would protect Dorothée's financial interests at such time as death or incompatibility separated the couple.[75]

A mortgage and sale that Augustin executed with the black freedman Yves *dit* Pacalé carries another nuanced backstory. Pacalé, who was born at Natchitoches six years before Augustin's mother, to African parents of no kin to her, had also been a slave of the Pierre Derbanne family that produced Dorothée. He was past sixty when his master and mistress died. He asked the heirs for his freedom and they gave it to him. For three years, he labored for the funds to buy the freedom of his wife. But then she died, and he saved to buy another: apparently Coincoin's older sister, Gertrude. With his next funds, he bought a young man to help him with physical labor, a French-speaking black like himself. Along the way, he saved enough to buy a neighbor's unimproved land claim, on which he built a house.[76]

Eventually, Pacalé went to Augustin Metoyer and asked to borrow $800, so that he could buy his daughter Thérèse from a white planter. To secure the debt he also offered a mortgage on his land and the one slave he had bought for labor. But then he, like Manuel Derbanne, failed to earn the money to clear the mortgage. Augustin allowed him to sell the encumbered land to a white planter in the neighborhood. However, Pacalé needed a provisional sale, one that would allow him to continue occupancy of the property until death, and that bargain yielded insufficient funds to clear his debt. Augustin deferred the remainder, held the title to Pacalé's slave, but allowed the worker to remain with the old couple who needed his labor. Six years later, Pacalé died at the age of eighty-two. Title to his slave then fell to Augustin, and he remained with the Metoyers until the Civil War.[77]

Pacalé's plight—specifically the image of the aged freedman going hat-in-hand to Augustin's manor house, asking for the loan and then a forbearance—is not without historical irony. Augustin's plantation home would fall to the ravages of time, while the humble cabin Pacalé built on his ninety-one acres would survive. In the twentieth century, it was moved to the riverbank in the town of Natchitoches to serve Cane River as a welcoming center. Similarly, archaeologists question whether fate has preserved any home in which the fabled Coincoin lived, to attest more intimate details of her daily life. But the survival of Pacalé's home offers an opportunity to stand within the walls tended domestically by Coincoin's sister, who lived and died in ignominy.

Evidence attests that Augustin struggled with his own issues of conscience over the moral conflicts his life represented. Most of his manumissions were informal ones made beneath the radar of the law. Reconstructing the evidence also spotlights another ideological nuance that evolved early in the slaveholding experience of Cane River's multiracial Creoles. The purchases that the original brothers and most of their sons made for labor reflected a critical pattern: they were guided not by race, color, or class but by *culture*—i.e., religion, language, and traditions. As a rule, those they bought for labor were imports from Africa or imports from Anglo-Protestant America. Creole purchases rarely occurred, except for a benevolent reason. Here, one sees vestiges of classic "tribal identification." As in continental Africa and among Native Americans, slavery was accepted so long as those slaves came from outside groups, not one's own people.

Eventually, that ideology provided Augustin with means to settle his own conscience. Throughout the first quarter-century of the 1800s, when Natchitoches often lacked a priest in residence, each time a cleric passed along the river Augustin presented for baptism all the infants born into his household since the last pastoral visit. When, in the late 1820s, a priest was again permanently assigned to Natchitoches, Augustin and his brother Louis built a chapel on Augustin's plantation for regular services; but most of the slaves held by their extended family were, by then, of Anglo-Protestant origin. From that point forward, recorded slave baptisms (that is, Catholic baptisms) were few and far between.

The significance was not just a religious one. In 1810 the Louisiana Supreme Court had reached a decision radically different from the policies of other slave states. Ruling in *Adéle v. Beauregard,* the court decreed that a "person of color" was presumed free until and unless evidence was presented otherwise. By comparison, Mississippi's supreme court decreed, "the laws of this state presume a negro *prima facie* to be a slave."[78] For slaves held by Catholic masters everywhere, a major source of evidence was the baptismal registers of their church. Infant baptism, free or slave, represented an official registration of birth. For infants or older slaves baptized into Catholicism, that religious act also created a permanent identification of their civil status.

Evidence suggests that Augustin, as a master, followed the example his mother set. Newly acquired adult slaves, from Africa or the Anglo-American states, were not forced to convert, although some eventually chose to do so. As Protestant slaves came to dominate Augustin's holdings, he extended that policy to their offspring. Because Protestant parents were unlikely to choose a Catholic baptism for their infants, the practical result was that, past the 1820s, slave births were rarely registered for the colored Creole plantations along Cane River. Without a registration, no evidence of their slave status existed, unless and until an inventory was made of the master's property or some circumstance forced their sale.

By 1839 Augustin had clearly begun de facto manumission of undocumented slave children. When his wife's succession was opened that year, the inventory of the estate the two of them held in common included thirty-seven adult slaves. Sixteen of those were women of childbearing age. Yet only four children were inventoried, all infants at the breast—a highly aberrant situation. The 1840 federal census shows that, parishwide, for every slave woman in the census bracket 16–36, there were 1.3 children under the age of ten. With sixteen slave women in that bracket, Augustin's slave holdings should have included some twenty-one children. Yet the inventory he filed with the parish judge claimed only four. The notarial records of the parish offer no deeds, donations, or marriage contracts by which he disposed of those missing children to anyone; and the census households of his offspring do not contain excessive numbers of children to account for the dearth that he reported. Those missing children do not appear in the estate division that he made with his offspring to settle his wife's succession; and no otherwise unidentified slaves of appropriate age are credited to him by the 1850 census or his own succession, when he eventually died in 1856.[79]

De facto manumissions clearly occurred. The only other explanations— that the enslaved females held by Augustin and Agnes had virtually no maternal instinct or sexuality—defy both logic and human nature. Realistically, slave children from the households of any of Cane River's well-known Creoles of color could grow up speaking French fluently, go out into the parish at large using the master's well-known name, and, under *Adéle v. Beauregard,* their freedom was to be assumed.

At least two of Augustin's brothers also granted freedom to slaves on several occasions. Dominique, in 1810, paid $900 for two slaves of no known kinship, Susette, eighteen years of age, and her daughter Marie Madeleine, about one and a half years old—both black, rather than multiracial. The seller, the white Marie Louise (Le Comte) Porter, inserted a stipulation that the child and the mother should be freed after a period of nine years; and that any children born to Susette in that period would be given their freedom at the same time. The circumstances suggest that this conditional sale might have been entered into as a vehicle to circumvent manumission laws—as in the case of Alexis Cloutier's sale of Noël to Antoine Coindet and Louis Monet's sale of Dorothée Monet to Manuel Derbanne, with a required manumission by a certain date. In the case of Susette and Madeleine, their blackness suggests that Mme. Le Comte desired to free them for service or personal goodwill, rather than kinship, and that Dominique agreed to serve as the facilitator through which that freedom could be effected under existing laws.[80]

By 1815, the black Susette had entered into a relationship with a free man of color named Joseph Belanger, by whom she bore a child. At their son's baptism, with Dominique's brother and daughter standing as godparents, the infant was declared free. In 1817, two years ahead of the date required for Susette and Marie Madeleine's manumissions, Dominique petitioned the state to emancipate the pair, received permission, and posted bond guaranteeing that Susette and her children would not become dependent upon the state or the parish for their support. At that point, his bargain with Mme. Le Comte and his recorded associations with the family both seem to have ended. But Metoyer concern for this family of poor ex-freedmen did not end there. In June 1828, Belanger died, without having married Susette. Two months later, Augustin Metoyer's son Auguste petitioned the parish judge for authority to help the woman deal with Belanger's creditors, saying that Belanger had no legal heirs who could take charge and that the property he left had sustained a great deal of damage: a gun, household goods, seven horses, a pair of oxen, and a small tract of land on Isle Brosset worth about $150.[81]

In the meantime, the Metoyer brothers freed other slaves, motivated by a variety of reasons. Dominique granted freedom in 1825 to another woman of no known kinship. This one, Marie Louise, was about thirty-nine years of age; no children were identified for her or included in the manumission. Again, he advertised his intentions to free her in the local newspaper as the law then required, no objection arose from the public, and he posted the required bond. Louis Metoyer, his brother, manumitted at least three slaves in his lifetime. In one case, freedom was granted to the multiracial son of his black slave Maria on the day the child was baptized in 1815. Five years later he emancipated two female slaves together: Baba, about forty-five years old, and Françoise, about fifty-five years of age.[82] A blood relationship between Louis and the manumitted infant might be presumed. In the case of the two older slaves, no relationship can be found, and a romantic interest does not appear likely in view of their ages and the fact that he did not free any of their children.

Past the first generation of multiracial slaveowners, offspring and their spouses continued slave manumissions to the eve of the Civil War. Both benevolence and faithful service appear at play. In 1834, for example, Louis's son Jean Baptiste Louis bought from Francisco Gonzales an eighty-year-old Negro slave named Charles. Gonzales had recently purchased the man from the estate of Louis Barthélemy Rachal, white, and apparently regretted having done so. J. B. Louis reimbursed Gonzales for the twenty dollars the Spaniard had paid down on Charles and agreed to pay Rachal's heirs the remaining ninety dollars. The record attributed no valuable skill to Charles, and his advanced age probably made him a poor investment. No evidence of a relationship has been found between this black man and the Metoyer family. Aside from sympathy as a possible motivator, it is also possible that J. B. Louis already owned a member of Charles's family and had granted his own slave a favor by purchasing the aging relative. In a somewhat different vein, Charles N. Roques Sr., who had married two of J. B. Louis's cousins, remembered two of his slaves in his 1859 last will and testament. A state law passed earlier that year had placed a blanket proscription against all manumissions for any reason. Thus circumvented in his desire to free his slaves Céleste and Reine, Roques specified in his will that these two faithful servants should be emancipated as soon as the law permitted.[83]

None of these incidences individually define the treatment given by the Creoles of color to the slaves who labored for them. Collectively, they do challenge the assertion that slaveowning free people of color were harsher masters than white owners were. Indeed, if any generality can be drawn, it is that the Isle Brevelle families treated their slaves in much the same manner as did whites, possibly no better but certainly no worse. As rising members of the planter class, the Creoles of color worked hard and probably worked their slaves the same; but their business acumen and their periodic acts of charity suggest that they exercised reasonable temperance toward those they held in bondage.

In the earliest days of the family's economic growth, most labor on plantations was performed by the owners and their slaves. As conditions changed and less land became available, especially near the end of the antebellum period, some young men were forced to begin as laborers and overseers. The job of laborer, logically, was the least desired and presented the greatest challenge to advancement. In 1860 the average daily wage for a day laborer in Natchitoches Parish was only $1, with board; a day laborer without board earned $1.25.[84]

Overseers fared somewhat better than laborers. The usual wage for overseers in the Cotton Belt was from four hundred to six hundred dollars per year. Exceptional men could earn as much as two thousand; men of little ability might not gross more than two hundred in cash. In addition, most overseers and their families were provided with food, housing, firewood, and feed for their horses. Occasionally an overseer would be allowed a slave for his own use. Of the seven multiracial overseers employed along Cane River in 1860, two obviously were managers of family operations: George Kirkland for his mother-in-law, Widow Auguste Metoyer; and Théophile Louis Metoyer for his mother, Widow Jean Baptiste Louis. Employers of the other five are uncertain. One who is identified as a planter on the 1860 census later said he was employed during this period as a manager for Auguste Predanes Metoyer (son of Jean Baptiste Augustin), and that after Predanes's death in 1865 he continued in that capacity for the widow. His dual occupation was not uncommon. For example, the white overseer for the nearby Le Comte–Hertzog plantation in 1860, G. E. Spillman, is credited by the census with $7,510 in property; and local records show that he owned 640 acres and one slave.[85]

Records created by and about Cane River's overseers during the late antebellum period reveal one striking variance from the law. As fears of slave revolts rose throughout the South, and agitators argued that people of color would incite revolts, an 1852 Louisiana law called for the presence of at least one white person to every thirty slaves on a plantation.[86] Yet, no known record suggests that Cane River's Creoles of color hired whites as overseers or drivers—or that charges of noncompliance were brought against them.

While agriculture was the foundation of Isle Brevelle's prosperity, economic endeavors were not confined to the soil. In partnership with other free people of color, with whites, or in business alone, they engaged in diverse activities supplemental to the plantation economy. Merchandising, money lending, milling, ginning, blacksmithing, tailoring, and ferrying were common enterprises for the males. Landless females who were self-supporting earned their livelihood almost entirely as dressmakers. Those who owned a small tract of land but lacked sons or slaves to farm it commonly rented out the land and then augmented their income with dressmaking.

Merchants typically operated at the local level, often as a sideline to planting or as a means to acquire capital for a plantation. The earliest known mercantile establishment on the Isle was a partnership formed in the mid-1820s by Auguste Metoyer, his brother-in-law Charles N. Roques, and their cousin-in-law Jérôme Sarpy. Operating as Roques, Sarpy & Company, they carried the conventional dry goods and tobacco, liquor, and foodstuffs until, by mutual consent, the partnership dissolved in September 1827 and held a liquidation sale. Goods were advertised as being "divided into lots to suit planters," and all who were indebted to or had claims against the firm were asked to come forward and settle accounts. The basis for the dissolution appears to be Sarpy's desire to operate his plantation on a full-time basis.[87]

Auguste Metoyer, an especially ambitious entrepreneur, continued in merchandising at multiple levels. Dealing in a variety of goods—from tobacco, whiskey, and wine to food, furniture, and medicines—he served Cane River whites as well as members of his extended family. Most nonperishables offered in his Isle Brevelle store came from New Orleans. A major supplier was the New Orleans firm of Jonau, Metoyer & Company, in which he was a partner. His business associates in the city firm were two whites, Antoine Jonau and Mme. Emilie Jarreau. As cotton brokers, they arranged crop sales, made purchases for their customers, provided credit, and even paid checks written by their clients.[88]

Records of Jonau, Metoyer & Company attest the high quality of the cotton produced by Coincoin's offspring along the Cane. For a sale made in June 1839, the price per pound was 17.5 cents—sharply higher than the average 7.5 cents per pound in June of that year, as reported by one agricultural historian. Another specific comparison is provided by a sale that A. Maurin & Company of New Orleans made for the same planter two months earlier. A shipment of 118 bales went for $7,347, or an average of $62.26 per bale.[89] Although the average per-pound price of this shipment, 14 cents, is significantly lower than the 17.5 cents that Jonau, Metoyer & Company secured, it is still almost twice the southern average for that summer.

The account that Auguste's firm carried for his aunt Susanne Metoyer indicates the broad range of goods it provided, as well as the quality of the goods that Isle Brevelle families could afford. At the time of her death Susanne owed the company for such items as farming supplies, freight for a bicycle ($1.50), "nice dry goods," silk stockings ($1.50 per pair), perfume ($5.75 per bottle), and "workmanship of a gown" ($4.50)—sums that would need to be multiplied by a factor of twenty-five for a modern value. After paying a check for her to C. N. Roques in the amount of $1,430, Jonau, Metoyer & Company recorded a debit for her of $4,470 against credits of $5,442, leaving a balance of $972 to be paid from her estate. Her account with the house of A. Maurin, by way of comparison, shows that she owed $3,755. Other business transactions of Jonau, Metoyer & Company are reflected by the account rendered to the estate of Susanne's daughter-in-law Marie Louise Metoyer, the wife of Florentin Conant, in 1837. Its bill was issued in the amount of $1,728 for the purchase and shipment of furniture—a value of more than $43,000 in modern currency.[90]

After the dissolution of Roques, Sarpy & Company in 1827, Charles Nerestan Roques also continued in business on his own. His son followed him into merchandising, dealing in such items as boots and shoes of Moroccan leather, bags of shot and flintstones, chewing tobacco, cigars and smoking pipes, dishes, lumber and nails, plows, percussion caps, powder, and shotguns. In addition to the usual entries for purchases, the account Roques carried for the white Baptiste Lemoine indicates that the firm had advanced him money to repay loans from other people, including a cotton factor in New Orleans. The presence of eight hundred cigars in the succession inventory of C. N. Roques Jr. has led one study to deduce, incorrectly, that Roques was a cigar maker. Not one of the score of records available locally on Roques contains any reference to his manufacture of this product.[91] Given that cigars and whiskey were two of the best-selling products in most general stores of that era, there seems nothing unusual in the presence of these items on the inventory of goods a merchant left.

Another mercantile house on the Isle began as a partnership between two members of the community and two prominent white planters. The firm apparently opened in 1830 under the name Dupré, Metoyer & Company. Its principals were Emanuel Dupré and his cousin Jean Baptiste Dominique Metoyer, both free men of color; Nicolas Gracia, an immigrant from Dalmatia who operated a Red River ferry in Rapides Parish; and Charles F. Benoist, a white transplant from St. Louis who had married a daughter of the wealthy white planter Julien Rachal. The exact interests of Gracia and Benoist were not specified. Presumably they invested a sum in the business, although it is doubtful that their interest was large. When Dupré married in 1830, his contract of marriage listed his assets at $1,300. The total assets of the firm that same year were tallied at $2,719. The business apparently enjoyed quick success; in 1831 Dupré and Metoyer bought out their white partners and increased their inventory to $3,306.[92]

The activities of all the merchants and entrepreneurs of color on Cane River also attest that the state's increasingly restrictive laws were not locally enforced. An 1856 state law, for example, denied free people of color the right to purchase liquor licenses. Yet the account books of the merchant Oscar Dubreuil reveal that during the last week of 1856 he sold over thirty gallons of whiskey to his credit customers. Here again, one finds no indication that any penalties of the law were exacted against Dubreuil.[93]

Other members of the community who operated as merchants at various times were Auguste Predanes Metoyer, B. Llorens, Charles Dupré, Élisée Roques, Jean Conant, and Vilfried Metoyer.[94] No generalization can be made regarding the efficacy of their enterprises. Some appear to have been quite successful; others, including the risk-loving Auguste Metoyer, eventually lost everything. The credit system on which merchants operated was the usual downfall for those whose businesses failed, as Auguste illustrates. He was a community leader, a benefactor and protector of poor nonwhite neighbors, ambitious, industrious, and seemingly astute. Yet, his business enterprises failed amid the Panic of 1837, generating numerous suits against him in the district court. The Civil War was an equally difficult period for the merchants who operated on the credit system. When Auguste Predanes Metoyer died in 1865, the inventory of his estate included seventeen debts owed to him that were considered worthless. They totaled $1,424. Seven of the debtors were white.[95] By comparison, however, several white merchants of the parish were also forced out of business entirely by the hardships that the war had wrought.[96]

Cane River's Creoles of color not only had extensive interests in mercantile firms, but also operated their own places of entertainment. In 1839, for example, Jean Baptiste Espallier Rachal purchased a billiard hall at Cloutierville from a white cousin, Louis Emanuel Gallien. For $1,100 he acquired a lot with 60 feet of frontage by 120 feet of depth, French measure, with "all the improvements such as the building that is found thereon, constructed as a billiard hall, with all the accessories." Neighbors on all sides were white.[97] In the 1850s and 1860s another multiracial kinsman, Oscar Dubreuil, operated a billiard hall at 24-Mile Ferry, where Emanuel Dupré ran his ferry, a gin, and a mercantile store.[98]

The limited number of craftsmen and mechanics within the clan suggests that most such work was done by slaves. The only known carpenters in the early community were Séraphin Llorens and Philippe Valsain Dupré. The contract work they did for both white and nonwhite planters along the river, especially the work of Llorens, reflected a wide range of skills. Tradition credits Llorens as the architect and builder of most of the Isle's dozen or so "manor houses." Records detail one of the agreements he executed with whites. In 1836, Llorens contracted with F. S. Lattier for the construction of a cotton gin that would both clean and press the cotton into bales. His fee was six hundred dollars, to be paid by a check drawn on a New Orleans bank; the work was to be completed in six weeks.[99]

A building contract held by Llorens and Dupré in 1838 and 1839 involved them in a lawsuit against kinsmen. The two builders and their slaves were felling timber on land they believed to be unclaimed, manufacturing shingles for the construction of a ginhouse, residence, and other plantation buildings. When Auguste Metoyer informed them that they were cutting on land that belonged to him, Llorens and Dupré ignored him. Metoyer filed suit for damages of $500 and posted a bond in that amount. The judge issued a temporary injunction against further cutting until surveyor G. W. Morse could establish the boundary line between Auguste's property and the adjoining unclaimed federal lands. Llorens argued that $500 in damages was unfair, given that he had cut only enough timber to make 35,000 cypress shingles worth $10 per 1,000, for a total of only $350. Still insisting that the land was part of the public domain, Llorens filed a countersuit in the amount of $500. The court eventually ruled in favor of Metoyer.[100]

Among the work credited to Séraphin Llorens is the "big house" on the plantation of Louis Metoyer, the best known of the family's plantation homes that survived into the twentieth century. The much-married Llorens was, by his last wife, father of Hugh Llorens, who assisted in the remodeling of this house for its white owners in the early 1900s. On many occasions, the son Hugh delighted in telling others that he was not the first in his family to work on this house; in fact, his father had been its builder.[101] No building contract has been found for the original construction, but the lack of a written contract was not at all unusual. The proved fact that Llorens did this type of work lends credence to the tradition that he built the house, which came to be called Melrose under white owners of the twentieth century.

By 1860 the number of carpenters in the parish had increased among the white population, but the construction of fine homes had slowed on the Isle. The aging François Forcal was the only remaining builder there among free multiracials. A younger transplant from New Orleans, J. B. Chevalier, still practiced carpentry but had moved to the Camptí area, while Magee Grappe of Camptí, who had newly entered the trade, had sought employment in the town of Natchitoches. All other carpenters in the parish were white. By the outbreak of the Civil War, the building being done on the Isle was mostly handled by slave carpenters. Succession records identify several bondsmen with this skill. For example, the 1837 succession inventory of Marie Louise Metoyer, wife of Florentin Conant, itemizes a slave carpenter, aged thirty-five. The 1851 succession inventory of Joseph Augustin Metoyer noted that the slave named Washington, who had run away once and had poor sight in one eye, was also a skilled carpenter.[102]

Another trade practiced by Cane River's Creoles of color was blacksmithing, the trade in which Augustin had trained as a young man. His brothers may have, as well. The succession inventory of Joseph Metoyer included blacksmithing accouterments sufficient to stock a full shop, including a forge and all its fixtures, a vise, and a turner. His inventory also itemizes a number of small accounts and notes due him by both free people of color and whites. The small accounts suggest some type of business, and no evidence indicates that he was a merchant. His son Joseph Jr. purchased the blacksmithing tools at the succession sale, and the 1860 census would explicitly identify Joseph III as a blacksmith. Apparently the skill was passed from the father through the son to the grandson.[103]

At least two New Orleans transplants pursued the trade in the 1820s and 1830s, Émile Colson and Leandre Dupart. Dupart built and operated a shop on land belonging to François Metoyer at the lower point of the Isle, where he farmed for François while taking smith jobs from the public.[104] The larger Metoyer plantations also operated their own smithies. At the 1827 succession sale of Dr. Jean André Zépherin Carles, Louis Metoyer purchased Carles's forge and blacksmith tools, while Carles's enslaved blacksmith was sold to a white planter. Apparently, Louis had his own skilled smith to operate the equipment he had just purchased. L. S. Prudhomme, a multiracial freedman and in-law from the Côte Joyeuse, was also a blacksmith in 1860. Other Isle planters whose inventories included blacksmithing equipage were Augustin Metoyer, Louis's son Jean Baptiste Louis, and the latter's son, Théophile Louis.[105]

One community trade, tailoring, appears to have been practiced entirely by New Orleanians. At least three such tailors are identifiable between 1830 and 1860, operating concurrently. Firmin C. Christophe Sr., who settled on Cane River during the 1830s, maintained a tailor's shop for three decades. His practice was apparently modest or his business skills limited, given that the 1850 and 1860 censuses place the value of his personal property at only $1,000, the approximate value of his slave.[106] M. B. Llorens, who owned three slaves and was worth $3,000 in 1860, was also a tailor that year. Likely, the slaves owned by these tailors assisted in their craft. Tradition also holds that the versatile Oscar Dubreuil, among his other enterprises, did tailoring for residents of lower Cane River.[107]

Related trades practiced by members of the extended family were those of cobbler, dressmaker, and potter. Louis Villaire Llorens was listed as a shoemaker in 1860. Given that he was only twenty years old and this trade is not previously found on the Isle, it is probable that he was an apprentice of his housemate, Antoine Toures, a shoemaker from France, who shared the home of Louis Villaire's grandmother, Doralise Derbanne (Widow Philippe Valsain Dupré). Five seamstresses were enumerated on the Isle in that same year: Lodoiska Llorens, widow of Joseph Metoyer Jr.; Marguerite Le Comte, widow of Cyriaque Monette; and three of the Monette couple's spinster daughters.[108] Tradition also holds that one member of the community, Adélaïde Mariotte, was skilled in pottery and provided plates, vases, and other crockery for the community. The 1850 and 1860 censuses, the only ones during her life span that asked for occupation, provide none for the aging woman who, it was said, had gone blind.[109]

In a country interlaced with rivers and bayous, ferries were vital to transportation. At least three ferries crossed Cane River on the main road from Alexandria to the town of Natchitoches. As public utilities, each had to be leased annually from the parish at public auction. The highest bidder gave his secured note, due at the end of the year, for the amount of his bid plus the interest. Bidders were required to furnish their own equipage, but the machinery was simple. A hand wrench, attached to a rope or cable that was tied to a sturdy post, sufficed to move flatboats or rafts across the river and back, although considerable animal or human power was also needed to turn the wrench.[110] Passenger rates were set officially and published in the local newspaper. In 1825, fares were set at six and one-fourth cents for one person, twelve and one-half cents for a man and a horse or for a horse and buggy, fifty cents for any four-wheeled vehicle pulled by two horses, and seventy-five cents for a loaded wagon or coach with four horses, including the driver and passengers.[111]

Throughout the 1800s these ferries often were operated by free men of color from Coincoin's family. Monette's Ferry (also called 40-Mile Ferry because it was located that distance from the courthouse in Natchitoches) was operated at times by the family of Louis Monette, Coincoin's great-grandson. The second known ferry on the river was located at the village of Cloutierville, and various members of the family operated it at midcentury. Young Hypolite Metoyer issued an account statement in 1851 to his white neighbor, Charles Molonguet, for twenty-seven crossings by Molonguet, his slave, and Molonguet's apparent employee, Louis Gallien. Crossings made with horse and wagon were billed that year at forty cents each. Crossings made on horseback were then twenty cents, while crossings made on foot were only ten cents.[112]

Several Cane River Creoles of color are known to have operated the 24-Mile Ferry, an important stopover for stagecoaches and a landing for steamboats. Predictably, a thriving community grew up around it. A stage stop, two or three stores, a saloon, and Dubreuil's billiard hall were all established there to meet the needs of the passengers who came through the area. In the 1850s it was operated by Pierre Metoyer III, who owned three pirogues as well as the expected flatboat. His less prosperous multiracial kinsmen provided room and board for stagecoach drivers. Oscar Dubreuil, in addition to being a teacher, merchant, undertaker, tailor, and billiard hall operator, ran the ferry in the 1860s in partnership with Emanuel Dupré. Members of the Dupré family continued to operate the ferry long after the Civil War.[113]

Almost all major occupations found within the parish were also plied on Isle Brevelle. Only in professional fields were multiracials poorly represented —a circumstance to be expected, given legal restrictions on men with African heritage. According to one authority, teaching was the only profession in which a significant number of Louisiana's free people of color were involved,[114] and this generalization held true on the Isle. Also in keeping with the time and place, all known schoolmasters were either males or Catholic nuns.

The area in which Coincoin's family was the least represented, publicly, was the medical profession. Only two physicians of color are known for rural antebellum Louisiana; neither was in Natchitoches Parish.[115] However, the fact that no nonwhite medical practitioner was enumerated on Cane River censuses indicates only that no multiracials held medical degrees. It does not preclude the probability that some of them practiced in the French *médicin* tradition, as Coincoin and Mariotte had done. The procès-verbal of the sale of the estate of Charles N. Roques Jr., in fact, included a set of surgical instruments purchased by Coincoin's grandson Nerestan Pierre Metoyer.[116] As in any rural society, there were also midwives. Claude Thomas Pierre Metoyer's will of 1801 had noted that his daughter, Susanne, was a skilled midwife; and her grandniece, Sidalise (Sarpy) Dupré, is remembered as a *sage-femme* or *accoucheuse*, who delivered many babies on the Isle.[117] Various others in the community were skilled veterinarians.[118]

Almost all activities in which Coincoin's free offspring engaged were economically profitable, but the most significant fortunes were amassed by those who were full-time planters. All those in the first generation gave plantations, slaves, or money to each of their many offspring upon marriage. Even so, they left sizable fortunes. When Pierre Metoyer Jr. died in 1834, his remaining estate was inventoried at $19,969. His sister Susanne was worth $61,600 at her death in 1838, and her nephew Jean Baptiste Louis died the same year leaving an estate valued at $112,761. Dominique, who had supported seventeen children and generously assisted all those who married before his death in 1839, left property inventoried at $42,405. His oldest brother, Augustin, possessed an estate of $140,958 at the time his wife died in 1839, even though a depression was then bankrupting countless Americans. The estates left by these men and women, born in slavery, would carry a current purchasing power of one to three million dollars.[119]

A provocative comparison is provided by the estate of Augustin's white half-brother who died several months prior to the 1839 inventory of Augustin's estate. Their father had been a man of considerable fortune; five years before his death he was the largest slaveholder in the parish, owning 103 bondsmen. At his death, his estate was divided between his three white children: Pierre Victorin, Benjamin, and Elisabeth. His half-white, "natural" offspring received no part of it, in keeping with inheritance laws throughout America prior to the twentieth century. In 1839 Victorin died, leaving an estate whose movables were valued at $3,887 and slaves at $24,801. Meanwhile, Augustin's twin sister Susanne, who began her career as a slave midwife and had wet-nursed their half-brother Benjamin, had died the previous year, leaving movables worth $1,616 and slaves that brought $25,735 at auction. Augustin's estate, inventoried the year following that of his white half-brother, contained movables valued at $8,465.50 and slaves worth $44,560.[120]

The legal fees paid to settle estates of this magnitude were significant. Among the accounts due that were filed in Susanne's succession was a bill from Judge Charles E. Greneaux for $376, representing his share of legal services for filing, recording, and copying succession records. The settlement of the estate of Pierre Jr., the smallest of the successions filed for Coincoin's children, involved stiff legal bills: judge's fees of $293, attorney's fees of $200, and administrator's fees of $499, which together reduced the estate by almost $1,000—or $25,000 in modern purchasing power.[121]

Although the family's prosperity was exceptional among free multiracials of the Old South, it was not unique. Almost every state claimed a few men of color of comparable wealth, while Missouri and Louisiana boasted a number of them. Julius Melbourn of North Carolina, who inherited an estate of $20,000, built it to a peak of $50,000. John Stanley of New Bern, in that same state, began as a barber and amassed a fortune "said at one time" to be worth more than $40,000.[122] An 1858 biographical sketch of Louis Charleville of St. Louis observes: "He was once very wealthy, but his estate has now dwindled down to about $60,000."[123] Antoine Dubuclet of Iberville Parish, Louisiana, was the proprietor of a plantation assessed at $206,400 on the 1860 census, and the total free nonwhite population of New Orleans in 1860 has been valued by various historians as $739,890 to $2,000,000.[124] By comparison, the total assessment of Coincoin's offspring and their spouses in 1860 was $770,545, a figure that supposedly represented 72 percent of the "true" valuation of the property.[125]

Obviously, no Cane River multiracial can be touted as his era's wealthiest free man of color. However, it is rare to find a group, in Louisiana or in any other state, that boasted as many prosperous men and women or retained such a degree of wealth for so long a period of time.

Because of their wealth, the more prosperous planters of the Isle were accepted economically in the highest levels of Natchitoches society. They borrowed and lent cash and stood *in solido* with numerous white counterparts. As early as 1815 Augustin signed as security for a white neighbor, François Lavespère, on a note of $1,085 that Lavespère owed. When Joseph Metoyer died in 1838, the inventory of his estate included a note and account due him by his white half-brother Benjamin.[126]

Similarly, when the estates of the white Mme. Desirée Hertzog and her brother Henry were opened in 1866, they owed $3,000 to the estate of C. N.

Roques Sr. and had owed it for a number of years. A similar debt was owed to the community by their brother Émile. The following year the *Natchitoches Semi-Weekly Times* published a notice of the forthcoming "meeting of the creditors of Émile Hertzog to elect a syndic to represent them in the succession." Jérôme Sarpy Jr. and Nerestan P. Metoyer were elected joint syndics, and two weeks later the parish clerk certified them to act for all claimants against both Émile's succession and that of Mme. Desirée.[127] Given that the creditors of these well-placed white planters included other prominent whites, the election of Sarpy and Metoyer to manage the interests of all attests the respect they enjoyed among the white elite.

The partnership of Sarpy and Metoyer also filed suit that same year against another white, the Isle physician and French émigré Isidore Gimbert. Their legal efforts to recover sums Gimbert owed them were successful. A judgment was declared against the doctor by the court; and the sheriff seized on their behalf and sold at auction three mules, one wagon, and four pairs of wagon harnesses that had belonged to Gimbert.[128]

On the other hand, Cane River's free people of color were frequently advanced sums both small and large by white planters of the area. On occasion the whites took them to court to collect the debts. The inventory of the community that existed between Augustin and Agnes in 1840 indicated that he was indebted to Emanuel Prudhomme, a white planter of the Côte Joyeuse, for $1,500. Despite the depression that then throttled the economy locally and nationally, Augustin paid his note when it fell due. His son, Joseph Augustin, however, signed an 1843 note for $310 in favor of Victor Rachal, a white planter from Cloutierville, and was unable to meet that obligation at its due date ten months later. In 1847, Rachal finally brought suit against Joseph Augustin to collect the sum and won his case in court.[129]

One study of financial interchanges between whites and free people of color has concluded: "Free Negroes frequently engaged in financial and business dealings with White persons. In some instances they borrowed money from White friends and in turn it was not unknown for certain free Negroes to lend money to impecunious White neighbors."[130] The tenor of this observation can be validly applied to Cane River. However, it must not be assumed that the majority of white or multiracial debtors took out loans because they were impoverished. On the contrary, they were often men or women of means, who borrowed for investment purposes when promising opportunities arose and regularly purchased goods on credit as a means of managing cash flow. Most of the debts owed by white friends and neighbors to Cane

River Creoles of color fell into these categories. Rather than rich men helping poor ones, most represented men or women of comparable economic
standing providing mutual assistance.

The aid that Creoles of color provided sometimes caused their downfall.
Not only did they lend to whites and borrow from them but they also acted
in solido for them, signing as security for obligations that whites assumed.
Some would regret their actions. Jean Baptiste Espallier Rachal, for example, agreed in 1835 to act as one of the sureties for a French émigré, Jean
Baptiste Grandchampt, who had married into a tentacle of the sprawling
Brevelle clan. Grandchampt had been named administrator of the solvent
estate of the émigré Pierre Baulos, an in-law of Parish Judge Greneaux.
Grandchampt paid some of the debts of the estate, gave his note for others,
and managed to lose a "large balance" that should have been distributed
among Baulos's debtors and heirs.

When Grandchampt was found to be insolvent, his creditors turned to
his sureties to recover the money owed. Grandchampt's second surety, Espallier's white cousin Sylvestre Rachal, also died amid the legal wrangling.
Sylvestre's widow was forced by one of the creditors to join him in a suit
against Espallier. The local court of probates ruled that the Rachals could
not be held liable for the debt. When the case was appealed by the creditor to the state supreme court, however, that body decreed that Espallier
and Sylvestre's widow must pay the $1,891 due to the Baulos estate and its
creditors.[131]

Incidences such as this cannot be interpreted as evidence that the generosity of the multiracials was systemically exploited by whites whom they
befriended. The opposite situation also occurred, as in the case of Chaler
vs. Birtt and Metoyer. In August 1836, amid a real estate bubble in which
Auguste Metoyer unwisely expanded his enterprises, he borrowed $620
from Jean Baptiste Anty, his aunt Susanne's long-term companion. Auguste
signed two notes at 10 percent interest. Isaac Birtt, a white of the Derbanne
clan who served as bailiff to Cane River's notaries, signed as surety. Then
America's economy collapsed. Auguste could not meet the payment when
it fell due, and Anty died shortly afterward. The administrator of Anty's
estate, another Derbanne offspring named Terence Chaler, filed suit against
both Metoyer and Birtt in 1839. Metoyer did not contest the case; he had no
grounds to do so. Birtt admitted signing *in solido* but insisted that he should
not be held liable and requested a trial by jury. A Connecticut native who had
settled on Cane River on a farm next to Adélaïde Mariotte, Birtt obviously

expected a white jury to rule for him in any suit against people of color. His request was denied, however. The court ordered Chaler to collect from Metoyer the sum due, plus interest and the costs of the suit. Another order was issued simultaneously against Birtt, which was to become effective in the event that Metoyer was not able to pay.[132]

The astuteness that Isle Brevelle's multiracials usually exercised in the conduct of their business was recognized by the larger community in a myriad of other ways. Jacques LaCaze, a white Creole planter on Little River, left a will in which he named Augustin Metoyer and his son Jean Baptiste Augustin as executors, despite the fact that LaCaze left a wife, children, and a number of white relatives who could have handled his affairs. When the white Jesse Smith died about 1841 leaving an estate with no known heirs or administrators but no lack of debtors, the court appointed Auguste Metoyer as its curator. When Jacques Dufrois Derbanne and his wife died in 1849 and 1850, the court appointed two Cane River Creoles of color, Joseph Augustin Metoyer and Emanuel Dupré, to inventory and estimate the Derbanne estate. When estimators were needed for the goods left by the deceased wife of the white Charles Melonguet, the court again appointed Dupré and the white A. G. Rogers; the inventory and estimation was actually drawn up by Dupré. Neither the court order nor the certification of the documents by the white notary made any mention of Dupré's color, although the law specified that nonwhites were to be identified as such in legal records. Even after the Civil War, when Cane River's multiracials had already lost considerable status, Dupré's son Charles was appointed administrator of the estate of a neighboring white planter, Ursin Derbanne. Both of the Derbannes were distant kinsmen of the Duprés; however, the appointments were clearly not made on that basis, considering that both Derbannes had an extremely large network of white kin and in-laws.[133]

The improvement in community status generated by the economic progress of Cane River's Creoles of color is reflected by all the legal documents drafted for them by local notaries. In the family's early years of freedom, when they purchased property or needed other documents executed, they went personally to the office of the notary, or they went to the home of the white citizen with whom they were doing business and the notary joined them there. By the 1820s the situation had reversed. Documents executed on behalf of the Metoyers and their kin, both the rank-and-file and their elite, noted that they were drafted in the homes of the multiracials, to which the notary and other participants went.

In 1823, for example, Louis Metoyer sold to his nephew Jean Baptiste Augustin Metoyer a tract on Red River for $2,200. The notary recorded that the document was "passed at the domicile of Monsieur Louis Metoyer to which I went upon request of the parties."[134] When the transactions involved whites, they also frequently went to the homes of the people of color, as in 1848 when Augustin Metoyer sold to the white Remy McTire of Camptí a tract of land that Augustin owned in the Camptí area. McTire traveled the thirty miles or so downriver to Augustin's home to complete the transaction, and a notary was called to the Isle from Cloutierville to draft the document "dans la domicile d'Augustin Metoyer."[135]

Indisputably, the economic status of Cane River's free multiracials was exceptional in American society as a whole. The conditions of racial tolerance and relative acceptance that persisted in Louisiana certainly influenced their success, but it was by no means the major factor. Toleration never guarantees prosperity, only the right to pursue it. Individuals still bear the responsibility to use their rights to forge their own successes. The people of Isle Brevelle did just that.

The prosperity achieved by the Metoyers and their kin is also explained by several features of their economic profile. The higher percentage of improved land on their plantations clearly demonstrates their determination to maximize opportunities and acquisitions. The broad range of their activities indicates a desire for self-reliance—a recognition of the need to maintain themselves and their standard of living without dependence upon an increasingly restrictive white society. Planter decisions to cultivate the most profitable cash crop, while relying upon their own merchants and truck farmers to supplement food supplies, further reflects their understanding of economic principles and their ability to discern the most profitable course for their community. In general, wise planning, cooperative effort, and unrelenting pursuit of common goals were the main factors that set them apart, economically, from many free people of color in Louisiana.

SIX

The Faith of Their Fathers

Catholicism was—and has remained—the cultural root of the society Coincoin's family created along Cane River. Catholic respect for the sanctity of the family spawned the *Code Noir* provision that allowed Coincoin to grow to maturity in a two-parent household. The concern of a Catholic priest for the souls of the enslaved was the catalyst for Coincoin's manumission. Ultimately her offspring's steady piety and religious leadership would earn for their community much respect that "sheltered it from the ever-increasing restrictions Anglo-Americans introduced into antebellum Louisiana."[1] Theirs was also a devotion purposefully seeded and carefully nurtured by their patriarch, Augustin Metoyer.

The church community the Metoyers created on Isle Brevelle was a rare outcropping in a long season of drought for Catholicism along the Natchitoches frontier. For all the colonial era, the registers of the parish and the civil records of the post reflect incessant tension between clerics, government officials, and the settler class. The last four decades of the century saw most families abandon the post for outlying plantations, seeking not only more economic opportunity but also less control by the parish priest.[2]

As Louisiana's colonial venture limped to a close, the Natchitoches congregation was assigned a new priest, one whose family ties might have led Louisiana's new bishop to hope for reconciliation between the church and its wayward frontier flock. Father Pierre Pavie, born in La Rochelle, was the brother of the late Cane River planter Étienne Pavie.[3] Étienne's widow Marie Thérèse Buard—who would remain Father Pavie's sister-in-law for life by the religious bonds of affinity—had become Pierre Metoyer's wife. Together, the Metoyers, the Buards, and the latter's extended kin were now the hub of Cane River's plantation economy.

Both Father Pavie and his bishop, Luis Peñalver y Cárdenas, were overly optimistic. Pavie's first accounts from the parish, in the wake of Easter 1795, soberly reported the reality he faced: "Very few of the inhabitants have satisfied their Easter Duty. . . . With regard to the catechism that it is necessary to have for children, the major part of the parishioners live a great distance from the post and are not able to come to the instructions that are held for them."[4] Pavie's annual accounts of 1796 and 1797 reflect more dejection than hope; but by 1799 he had a plan. As with his three prior reports, he first noted the failure of the parishioners to satisfy their Easter duties; then he proffered his solution: "I have proposed to the residents of Isle Brevelle to build a small chapel where I can come and say mass several times each year, and where it can be celebrated with more appropriateness than on their plantations, and those settlers from Rivière aux Cannes would be able to come. If this pleases your Reverence, I will make all efforts to succeed in this."[5] Pavie's expectations were reasonable, but he was thwarted by either his parishioners or his bishop. The chapel never materialized. His next annual account, in February 1801, tersely reported: "The residents have not given me the satisfaction I hoped for. . . . I see with sadness that my teachings and my exhortations are for the most part useless with them."[6]

Nearly three decades would pass before Isle Brevelle would have its chapel. When it materialized, it was not the elite white planters along the river who would build that house of worship. It would, instead, be Cane River's Creoles *de couleur,* under the leadership of their patriarch, Augustin Metoyer. The strong presence of religion in Augustin's life can be traced to his childhood. The church register of 1777 shows the nine-year-old Augustin acting as godfather to his cousin and namesake, Nicolas Augustin, a slave of Commandant de Mézières. In 1781 he served as godfather to an Indian slave child of the Sieur Le Court from the lower Rivière aux Cannes. Again in 1783 he sponsored an infant Negro slave of the white widow Mme. Gabriel Buard.[7] By the time Augustin turned twenty-five, he had accumulated a dozen godchildren. From this point on, the registers show him acting regularly in this role. Augustin was, the registers show, godfather to more children than any other contemporary male in the parish.

According to legend, while on Continental travels with his father, Augustin first conceived the idea of a church for his people. According to Rev. J. J. Callahan's history of the parish, "The story goes that Thomas [*sic*] Metoyer had taken his son Augustine [*sic*] to France in 1801 to visit the homeland of his people, which was in the neighborhood of Lyons [*sic*]. It seems the latter was struck by the organization of French villages whose community life centered about the church. It recalled to his mind that there was no church at Isle Brevelle, and so, after his return, he built one in 1803."[8] However, forty years of research have yielded no record of a church or chapel built on the Isle in that year, that decade, or that quarter-century. Indeed, all evidence weighs against it.

The first known chapel on Isle Brevelle was blessed on July 27, 1829, by the curé from Natchitoches, Jean Baptiste Blanc. Upon his return home, Père Blanc penned an official account in his registers:

> The nineteenth day of July of the year 1829. I, the undersigned, pastor of the Church of St. François of Natchitoches, have proceeded to the blessing of a chapel erected on Isle Brevelle on the plantation of Sieur Augustin Metoyer through the care and generosity of the above-named Augustin Metoyer, aided by Louis Metoyer, his brother. The above-named chapel having been constructed to propogate [sic] the principles of our holy religion shall always be considered as a mission of the church of St. François of Natchitoches. The said chapel erected at Isle Brevelle having been dedicated to St. Augustin, shall be considered as under the protection of this great doctor. Done and passed at Natchitoches the twenty-seventh day of July 1829.[9]

Acknowledging the obvious discrepancy between tradition and actual records, Callahan's history rhetorically asks: "If it were built earlier, why had it taken twenty-six years to have it blessed?" Answering his own question, Callahan theorized that the scarcity of priests and the social inferiority of people of color were to blame.[10]

Callahan's account might have differed had he probed his question more deeply. Priests were indeed scarce, but between 1803 and 1829 they made numerous trips to the Isle to perform baptisms and marriages in private homes. Sacramental entries for the fall of 1804 set the pattern for this era. On October 7, Père Pavie baptized six children in the town of Natchitoches, including daughters of both Augustin Metoyer and his brother Joseph. Four weeks later, on November 14–15, "while on a visit to Isle à Brevel, as authorized by Msgr. Leveque," Pavie performed another six baptisms in three different homes—including two children of Augustin's brothers Pierre and Dominique. Both Metoyer children were anointed "at the home of Sieur Pierre Jarri," a white settler of the Isle.[11]

Callahan deemed it natural that priests of the era would go to the home of a white man before they would visit the home of a colored one,[12] and Louisiana's ecclesiastical records do sporadically demonstrate racism or at least pragmatism in matters of race. One of the first acts of Bishop Peñalver y Cárdenas in 1795 was a decree that each parish was to maintain two separate registers for each type of sacrament. One series would be for whites; the other for blacks, Indians, and multiracials, regardless of slave or free status.[13] His dictates were followed at New Orleans, the site of his see, but were less well received in the rural parishes. At Natchitoches, the clergy simply continued their existing habits. A separate baptismal register had been kept for slaves and free people of color since Quintanilla's arrival in the 1770s; but the other registers were racially integrated. In 1802, Father Pavie conceded to a special burial register for slaves but continued to integrate entries for all the free population, regardless of color. The injunction to racially separate marriage registers would be ignored until 1850.

A wave of racism clearly occurred among Catholic townspeople at Natchitoches in the 1840s, apparently as a backlash to initiatives by a new priest. Père H. Figari was appalled to find that seven decades had passed since his predecessors had blessed a slave union and that the registrations of slave baptisms across those decades had routinely dismissed paternity with the formulaic "father unknown." His efforts to reinstate marriage and husbands within the framework of slavery were soon squelched. In 1848, the *marguilliers* (church wardens) of St. François des Natchitoches took matters two steps further with racialized decrees of their own: separate holy-water basins must be used for white and nonwhite parishioners; and all nonwhites were to remain in their seats at the end of Mass until all whites had exited. The protests that ensued soon persuaded the *marguilliers* to rescind the mandate.[14]

Meanwhile, the Natchitoches registers also reveal that priests did go to the Metoyer homes on Isle Brevelle to administer the sacraments, from at least December 1821. On some occasions a Natchitoches-based priest passed by on the river amid an annual or biannual round of outlying communities in the parish. Although the priest often did not state his whereabouts, his movements can be tracked by the identity of the plantation owners whose slaves and children he baptized in clusters. In October 1825 and May 1826, the sacraments were administered on Isle Brevelle by Bishop Louis DuBourg of New Orleans, who stopped there as he traveled upriver to Natchitoches and then again on his return voyage to New Orleans. Both times, he specifically stated that he had performed a cluster of ten baptisms *"in the home* of Augustin Metoyer," with no mention of a chapel.[15]

Evidence suggests that the chapel was likely built in early 1829, in the wintry off-season between crops, when the Metoyer slaves would have been minimally employed. In October 1828, a new priest assigned to Natchitoches blessed the new Church of St. François at Natchitoches; his upriver journey in August had recorded baptisms on Isle Brevelle but no blessing of its chapel. From February 11 through March 19, 1829, Father Blanc conducted his biannual canvass of Cane River plantations, a trek that took him forty miles south to the Rapides Parish line and back upriver, baptizing infants of all colors. Again, he made no mention of a chapel on Isle Brevelle. Four months later, however, he returned to the Isle specifically to bless the Chapel of St. Augustine.[16]

It is also not coincidental that all family marriages prior to the 1829 chapel occurred in the parish church at Natchitoches. Or that four days after the chapel's blessing, the first marriages were blessed therein: a quadruple wedding, representing couples of pure French, Spanish, Indian, and mixed ancestry. Two days after that, a fifth marriage was celebrated in the new chapel,[17] and from that time on the parish registers frequently chronicle sacraments of all types administered in the Chapel of St. Augustine.

Attempting to prove the tradition that the church was built in 1803, Father Callahan offered as evidence a letter belonging to a resident of the Isle. That "memento," which the informant's family was said to have preserved until the mid-twentieth century, has been quoted frequently by subsequent writers. The letter reads:

> Cane River
> State of Louisiana
> Isle Brevelle
> 10 June 1803

Mr. Jerome Sarpy
My dear friend and nephew,

I have just returned from New Orleans, and I suspect that you are anxious to have the news. I'll recount it all. Since you are kept to your bed, and I myself am tired after my trip, I send you my faithful servant John Baptist with this message for you. As you know we lived first under our own French government, then under that of Spain, and now we are under the authority of these new people who speak English and travel in wagons covered in white. As we all know these are unquiet times without repose. We shall all pray to our Creator for his blessings. As you know we have already spoken of building a church, and I am sure that with my brother Louis and his knowledge of building, we shall succeed. I shall give the land to the North of my house for the church and for the cemetery. That is what I have always wished to do since I visited the native land of my father in France; Paris, Marseilles, Lyons, in each one of these cities there are churches in every quarter. In one way or another I am sure that having a house of the good God in our midst, our people will live a better life, will love one another, and will live in harmony. I have heard it said that Father La Salle admired the place that I have chosen for the church. Yes, I have also heard that there have been troubles in Haiti. It seems that up to the present time, Toussaint L'Ouverture is unbeaten. I ask myself for how long. He has come up a long way, from coachman to the position he now holds. He has such love for his people and his land. To lose now would break his heart, both his and that of his beloved country.

I am sure that within a week I shall be able to visit you, when we shall have one of our long discussions. I am certain that the church will be finished by the first of August, and I am very grateful to you personally and to James Dupré for offering the main altar. With the aid of all, I know that we shall succeed. Jerome, I beg you to take good care of yourself, and bridle your impetuous temperament.

May Our Father in Heaven bless you.

I remain

Augustin Metoyer
Yucca Plantation[18]

Father Callahan then asserted: "This letter contains within itself evidence of its own authenticity. It is a personal letter to a friend, whom we know otherwise to . . . have been the husband of a niece of Augustine [*sic*]. Notice also the touch of contemporary history. It was the year in which the United States had taken over the territory of the Louisiana Purchase when the settlers were already beginning to pour through Natchitoches."[19]

As a point of fact, the contents of the letter prove its spuriousness. President Jefferson did not sign the treaty ratifying the purchase until October 21, 1803, and Louisianians were not apprised of the sale until November 30 of that year.[20] After the purchase, Louisiana was known as the Territory of Orleans until statehood was granted in 1812. Augustin Metoyer could not possibly have written a letter from the "State of Louisiana" in June 1803; nor would he have stated in any letter of that date that Louisiana was under American authority.

A second obvious problem in the letter is the reference to the "troubles in Haiti" and the statement that Toussaint L'Ouverture was still unbeaten. The Haitian leader surrendered in Santo Domingo in June 1802. In April 1803, he died in a French prison.[21] News did travel slowly in the early nineteenth century, but it is inconceivable that the latest "news" Augustin supposedly received in New Orleans in June 1803 could have contained the information that Toussaint L'Ouverture was still unbeaten.

Then, too, the date of the letter is seriously contradicted by the personal family information it sets forth. The letter is addressed to "Mr. Jerome Sarpy, my dear friend and nephew." Yet Sarpy did not marry Augustin's niece until 1820, seventeen years after the letter's date.[22] Moreover, the letter sets forth Augustin's hope that having a church in their midst would enable "our people" to love one another and live in harmony. Yet in 1803 the Metoyer settlement consisted only of Augustin and his brothers, all of whom worked together extensively and none of whom had children over the age of ten. The family group was not yet large enough or distinct enough to term it "our people." Nor was the family large enough to need a house of God in its midst to promote harmony between its members.

The letter obviously is contrived. Reasons can only be speculated. The location of the original letter is not known. The Isle resident who provided a copy to Father Callahan states she found the handwritten, English-language copy in an old book given to her many years earlier by her mother.[23] During the period in which the letter first surfaced—the 1930s and 1940s—numerous old books owned by the community were being borrowed and bought by popular writers who visited a nearby plantation. According to one Louisiana historian, at least two of these writers were renowned practical jokers who had once admitted concocting a spurious "historical story" as a joke on an acquaintance. Possibly they invented this letter, after which it was innocently perpetuated by others.[24]

Another series of documents reinforces the conclusion that the Chapel of St. Augustine dates only from 1829. The U.S. land surveys of Isle Brevelle were, for the most part, completed in the 1813–15 period—including those of Augustin Metoyer and his adjacent neighbors, the white Creole François

Lattier and the transplanted Frenchman François Lavespère. Boundaries were firmly established at that time. Significant buildings were noted on each tract's surveys and often cited in the surveys of neighbors as a point of reference for a bead line. None of those surveys mention a chapel.[25] At the time the Chapel of St. Augustine was dedicated, Lavespère's white Creole widow still resided on the tract. Five months later, the widow gave power of attorney to her son-in-law to "act in her stead relative to a certain difference likely to arise between her and Augustin Metoyer, f.m.c., her neighbor, respecting a certain boundary line run between their respective lands."[26] Had the church been built in 1803, with half of it standing on Lavespère's property, neither he nor his wife would have waited twenty-six years to complain about the boundary encroachment. For certain, any such problem would have been discovered and settled when the land surveys were made of these two properties in 1814 and 1815.

That 1829 chapel was both a keystone in Cane River history and a symbol of the faith and culture that guided this society. When the parish church at Natchitoches burned down in 1823, its parishioners went without a house of worship for three years.[27] A special act of the legislature was passed eventually to let the citizens of the parish hold a lottery to raise funds for a new building, not to exceed twenty thousand dollars.[28] While the parishioners did not consider themselves financially able to finance the church, some obviously did not mind risking money in a lottery—nor did their Protestant neighbors. By contrast, Coincoin's offspring took a fertile tract out of production, set it aside for their church and cemetery, and constructed their own house of worship.

One observation by Callahan also remains relevant to the corrected 1829 date. He cites a study of Negro Catholicity and the Jesuit order, asserting that the first church for Catholics of color in the United States was established in 1860 by Bishop Michael O'Connor of Baltimore in a building purchased by the white Catholics of that diocese. Father Callahan disputes this claim: "It is no reflection on the work of Bishop O'Connor [but] the colored Catholics of Isle Brevelle had their own church . . . before that date. . . . And they did not owe their parish to money collected among white Catholics but entirely to themselves."[29]

Undoubtedly, Isle Brevelle's Creoles also prided themselves on the fact that their church was only the third in all of northwest Louisiana.[30] The villagers of Natchitoches had enjoyed a church, intermittently, almost since the founding of the post. The second house of worship in northwest Louisiana cropped up in 1816, when a white resident of Rivière aux Cannes, Alexis Cloutier, built a small chapel on his plantation and donated the grounds to the Roman Catholic "congregation" of his area. His generosity was not without an ulterior motive, however. His chapel was but the first step toward the founding of a town called Cloutierville, which he proposed to be the seat of a new parish he wanted carved from Natchitoches.[31] For four short years, 1825–29, the chapel maintained its own registers; but when Cloutier's ambitions were thwarted the chapel fell into disuse. Not until 1845 did the congregation reorganize as a parish.[32] In that 1829–45 interim, the Isle Brevelle chapel served as the religious center of Cane River.

While Louis Metoyer oversaw the construction on land donated by Augustin, church furnishings were supplied by the community at large. The spurious "1803" letter states that James [Jacques] Dupré donated the altar.[33] Tradition on the Isle more commonly credits the altar to Marie Susette Anty, a daughter of Marie Susanne Metoyer and the wife of Jean Baptiste Augustin Metoyer. Callahan, who apparently considered it politic to embrace all stories told to him by his flock, even when contradictory, asserts this tradition also; he then adds: "They say it cost five hundred dollars, quite a sum for those days, and came from Europe."[34] The altar is said to have been used for over a century, even after the original chapel was twice replaced by newer and larger structures.[35]

Two of the earliest decorations installed in the original chapel were a pair of paintings. The first represented St. Augustine, the patron saint of the man who conceived the church and donated the land for it; the other depicted St. Louis, the patron saint of the chapel's builder. An impressive bell was hung in the belfry above the church's vestibule, one whose resounding tones could be heard the length and breadth of the Isle.[36] The twelve Stations of the Cross bedecked the interior side walls, inspiring the parishioners to contemplate the burdens and sufferings their Lord had endured for them. Each station, it is said, was donated by a different member of the congregation.[37]

In 1836 a New Orleans portrait painter named Feuille captured Augustin in oils as he stood on the columned gallery of his plantation home and gestured to the church of which he was so proud.[38] In this painting we see a traditional white chapel with a single nave covered by a gabled roof on the front of which stood the belfry tower. The roof stretched beyond the walls, creating two broad overhangs that ran the length of both sides. Local lore assigns two purposes to those shelters. Community slaves, who were not allowed to sit inside the small sanctuary with their masters and white parishioners, heard mass through the open windows as they congregated under those side wings. At other times, in the event of rain, the overhangs provided cover for the parishioners' carriages.[39] As the family grew and more interior space was needed for pews, the side wings would be enclosed.[40]

Three years after the painting of his portrait with the chapel, Augustin Metoyer drafted his last will and testament. There, he explained his purpose in organizing this church:

> A portion of land of 3/4 *arpent* of frontage by 1 1/2 *arpent* of depth, situated on the portion of land above given to my children Joseph and Gassion, at its upper part, does not belong to me. The Church of St. Augustin of Natchitoches was built there by me and my family, principally for our usage, except that I desire, and such is my wish that outsiders professing our holy, catholic, apostolic, and Roman religion will have the right to assist at the divine office in the said chapel and shall enjoy, moreover, all the rights and privileges which I and my family are able to have there. After my death I wish that this portion of land continue to be destined for the preservation of the same church and of a cemetery and that it should never be able to be used otherwise, in any manner or under any pretense that may be; with the privilege to my successors of making officers of the said church the Catholic priests who will suit them and not the others.[41]

Augustin's reference to "outsiders" is significant, given that the nonfamily members who attended mass at the chapel were, by and large, white. Integration of Louisiana's churches (particularly the Catholic ones) was the rule rather than the exception in antebellum Louisiana. Normally, however, the whites built the churches and permitted nonwhites to attend. Isle Brevelle reversed that pattern. Creole freedmen created the house of worship, and wealthy white neighbors who had none of their own accepted the Metoyer invitation to commune there.[42]

The presence of these "outsiders" was critical to Augustin, personally and politically. Eight pews in the new chapel, descendants say, were set aside for the exclusive use of his white friends—eight pews directly behind his own, which occupied the place of honor before the statue of the Blessed Virgin.[43] For almost two generations whites regularly used these pews, obviously unperturbed at taking a back seat to a family of color—an unconventional practice even in relatively liberal Creole Louisiana. For Augustin, the establishment of his own church was clearly a mark of prestige, a measure of affluence and position equaled by few of his white contemporaries.

Augustin's seizure of the reigns of religious leadership along Cane River also reflects his perceptive reading of political tea leaves. Those "outsiders" he invited to the Chapel of St. Augustine provided a legal safeguard for his community. As racial tensions mounted in antebellum Louisiana, wary whites looked askance at congregations of free nonwhites for any purpose, religious or otherwise. Such meetings, some argued, provided a convenient cover for plotting slave insurrections—an activity they deemed likely to be instigated by free men of color. By 1850, Louisiana's legislature would bar free nonwhites from incorporating for religious purposes. For the unincorporated throughout the state, including "influential" whites in their religious assemblies thereby became an essential strategy for avoiding suspicion and distrust.[44]

White assumption of control over the affairs at St. Augustine was more than a mere fear or threat. Anglo-Protestant newcomers into northwest Louisiana brought with them intense opposition to both Catholicism and free multiracials.[45] According to Isle tradition, newcomers in the region used various means to "encourage" white Catholics to decamp, thereby leaving the multiracials with no alternative but to close the chapel or accept outside control. On one occasion, family lore contends, a white spy was found in the loft during services. He was removed from the premises by several male members of the congregation and was never seen again. Presumably, that man's disappearance was never linked to the people of St. Augustine's Chapel; local records reflect no charges against them for any such activity.[46]

In retrospect, the failure of the assorted efforts says much about Augustin's standing along Cane River, and it clearly attests the respect that most area whites held for the integrity of his family. Indeed, the spiritual and cultural heritage that the affluent Catholic Creoles *de couleur* shared with white leaders of Louisiana's *ancien régime* created a bond that neither Anglo-Protestant newcomers nor new generations of Americanized Creoles could rend. Along Cane River, as Gary Mills has noted elsewhere, race "would be a far less important factor than faith, heritage, and culture; and that factor was of extreme significance to the welfare of the colony."[47]

Surviving parish registers also reveal that, across the years, priests from as far away as New Orleans and Mexico said mass in the Chapel of St. Augustine. It was Grandpère Augustin, tradition contends, who paid the priests from his own pocket for their trouble and expense. Most of the visiting priests made routine entries in the parish registers, noting the baptisms performed and marriages blessed. A more personal evaluation was left by the Gallic bishop whose evangelization efforts in northwest Louisiana earned him the sobriquet "Louisiana's Joshua in the Land of Promise."[48] During his first pastoral visit to the parish of Natchitoches in 1836, the Most Reverend Antoine Blanc visited the chapel that his younger brother had blessed seven years earlier. Upon his return to Natchitoches he recorded the visit in the parish registers and noted "the condition of decency and cleanliness" he found there.[49]

Bishop Blanc would also shepherd St. Augustine Chapel to the fulfillment of Augustin Metoyer's ultimate goal; and, in the process, he closed out the old patriarch's life. In 1852, at the plea of the Plenary Council of Baltimore, the Holy See created nine new dioceses in the United States, one of which was to serve 22,000 square miles of northwest Louisiana. The see of this new diocese, not surprisingly, was Natchitoches. The new bishop, Auguste Marie Martin, was a protégé of Bishop Blanc and one who shared his mentor's respect for Isle Brevelle's *gens de couleur libres*.[50] In March 1856, Bishop Martin elevated St. Augustine Mission to parish status and assigned his own brother, François Martin, to be its first resident pastor. Together the Martins and Augustin launched plans for a convent under the tutelage of the French Daughters of the Cross.[51] That December, Augustin died peacefully in his sleep, at the age of eighty-eight, having lived to see the fulfillment of what is said to be the greatest wish of his old age: the establishment of a parish and religious school for his people.[52]

Tradition relates one other story relative to Augustin and his church. After its construction or after the establishment of the parish (tradition varies), Augustin supposedly received a special letter of commendation from the pope, which was read to the congregation at high mass. The letter was said to have been preserved by a daughter-in-law, Perine (Metoyer) Metoyer Dupré, until it was destroyed along with many other old and valuable family heirlooms when "Tante" Perine's home burned in the early twentieth century.[53]

The spiritual lives of Augustin's family, indisputably, began and ended in this church. Newborn infants were taken for baptism to St. Augustine's holy font as soon as a priest could be brought to the Isle to administer the sacrament. On rare occasions when death threatened an infant not yet baptized, a family friend or relative would *ondoye* the child, sprinkling it with holy water and blessing it with prayers. Should the sick one survive, a formal baptism still followed in the chapel at the next passing of a priest. At the holy font, each infant was given a saint's name, one carefully chosen to provide the child with a model of Christian behavior that he or she was expected to follow. For most girls, the first name was Marie, in recognition of the most esteemed model of Christian virtue. In keeping with custom, most infants were also named by their godparents—the *parraine* and *marraine* the child would grow to love and respect as dearly as parents. By custom, also, each child's saint's day was celebrated annually, often in lieu of the birthday more commonly celebrated in Protestant society.[54]

Upon reaching puberty, the youth of the Isle received the sacrament of confirmation. From the bishop himself, upon his periodic visits to the parish, the youth received the Holy Spirit. After his visits to the parish in 1836 and 1842, Bishop Blanc noted that he had confirmed a total of fifty-four youth from St. Augustine's Chapel.[55]

Most discussions of the religious views of Louisiana's free people of color contain the usual sensational emphasis upon illicit relations between young women of this class and their white "protectors." The now-classic history of Louisiana's free people of color, for example, discusses this stereotype with a caveat posited as an exception rather than the rule: "Not all free persons of color entered a state of concubinage. Many of them got married and it was *not uncommon* for such persons to have their nuptials performed in the churches of Louisiana."[56] The tenor of this study, like most works on the subject, is that the legitimately married *gens de couleur libres* were an elite minority.

Among Cane River's Creoles of color, traditional Catholic views of morality and sexuality were indeed the rule. Perhaps due to the influence of Grandpère Augustin, who is remembered as a strict moralist, Cane River youths were expected to marry within the church and to pattern their behavior after the strictures of their faith. A sociological study of the Isle Brevelle families reports that 91 percent contracted legal marriages and that most of the remaining 9 percent were youths who died before reaching maturity.[57] A more comprehensive analysis of illegitimacy rates in Natchitoches Parish found a decline within the extended Metoyer clan between 1820 and 1859, from 3 percent to 0 percent, while rates in comparative populations were significantly higher. (White Catholic illegitimacies in that time frame dropped from 14 percent to 4 percent. Within a north Natchitoches community of free multiracials, illegitimacies dropped from 61 percent to 21 percent, while rates among unaffiliated free Negroes and multiracials rose from 85 to 90 percent.)[58]

Only once among the antebellum Metoyers did a parish register cite a newly baptized child as "*père inconnu.*" Even then the child would name her father in later records. By comparison, 48 "father unknown" baptisms were recorded in the north Natchitoches *libre* community, constituting 20 percent of all the illegitimate births there. Among unaffiliated blacks or multiracials, 55 percent of the illegitimate births were deemed "father unknown," and an even larger majority used their mother's surname throughout their lives.[59]

On Isle Brevelle, sexual immorality was constrained by not only church precepts but also community customs. Tradition related by Augustin's daughter-in-law Perine to her husband's niece holds that courting couples were always chaperoned. At dances, girls of good character did not permit boys even to pay for their refreshments. A walk to the edge of the pavilion where lights were low might be countenanced, but no couple dared leave the pavilion unless accompanied by an older woman.[60]

More often than not, marriages were arranged by the parents, who met and decided upon the needs of the couple. In general, the preferences of the young people were considered, but in many cases they were not. An example is said to be Ambroise Sévère Dupré and his wife Sidalise Sarpy. It was Sidalise's sister for whom Sévère really cared, but she was younger than Sidalise. The fathers, Jérôme Sarpy and Emanuel Dupré, conferred and agreed that no younger sister should marry until her older sisters had found husbands. Plans for the wedding were then made, with Sidalise rather than her sister as the bride. The young couple made the best of the situation, reportedly, and remained together for the rest of their lives, even though the marriage was not one of choice on their part.[61]

The marriage of Sévère and Sidalise followed the traditional pattern. The youth of the Isle exchanged matrimonial vows at St. Augustine's altar. After the creation of that mission (and later parish), civil marriages contracted outside the church were uncommonly rare, as were instances of divorce. Some legal separations of bed and board did occur. Those actions did not dissolve the marriages, either legally or civilly, because unions made at the altar of God were expected to last until death. In some cases, the separations protected the dower interests of wives from debts of the husband, particularly in the wake of the Panic of 1837. Otherwise, they allowed incompatible couples to live separate lives in the interest of community harmony.[62]

Church and civil records of the parish reveal that other deviations from the moral code outlined by their religion were the exception rather than the rule. Although each family of color did begin with an illicit liaison between a white male and a woman of color, the families thereafter insisted upon contracting legitimate marriages. For the most part, the community standards were upheld by individual members. Most cases of extramarital or premarital liaisons were relationships between females of the community and white males whom they could not marry; most such liaisons also lasted until death claimed one of the partners.[63]

Historical stereotypes of interracial liaisons as an agency of choice, used by women of color to "lighten" their children, are rarely reflected among Coincoin's offspring. During the antebellum years, when the family enjoyed respect and prestige, the maintenance of their racial composition through selective marriage was sufficient to preserve their distinctiveness, and adherence to Christian precepts was necessary to their own self-respect. Although the situation would change amid the tumult of Reconstruction and Jim Crow, as did all social and economic conditions in Louisiana society, the antebellum generations generally spurned the dishonorable attentions of whites.[64]

Aside from the slave-born Rose Metoyer and Adélaïde Mariotte, Coincoin's granddaughter and niece, records rarely reveal an incidence in which females of the family lived with a succession of white males. Even in such cases, the violation of family standards often had serious impact upon both the consciences and the community standing of the violators. The aging Adélaïde, for example, is said to have been apologetic for her conduct. Apparently fearing that her loved ones would not respect her for the choices she had made, she repeatedly told her children and grandchildren that she "had disgraced herself to uplift her race."[65] Assuming that personal desires might have had a certain amount of influence upon her behavior as well, it is still a measure of the attitude of her peer group that she felt such a compunction to justify her past actions—or that descendants felt the need to apologize for her.

Religious devotion along Cane River was a private as well as a public matter. The rosary was said at home every night before retiring, and the children were always led in their bedtime prayers by an older adult who knelt with them. When the church bell rang the Angelus every morn and eve, men stopped and doffed their hats and women made the sign of the cross.[66] All homes had their little altars, hung prominently on the living room wall. Reflecting the sentiments of the older people recalled from many visits to the Isle, the Louisiana storyteller Harnett Kane wrote: "In each house the altar sparkled beneath the crucifix, and the shrine must be cleaned every day. How would a saint feel if he found dust in which he could write his own name, ahn?"[67]

Although many such altars were purchased later from the family during their periods of need, one little devotional owned by Sidalise (Sarpy) Dupré,

a daughter of Jérôme Sarpy, has been proudly treasured by a granddaughter. Unlike the typical altar found in churches, this home altar resembled
more a wall-hung box, shallow at the top, deep at the bottom. The sparkling
glass front was a door that opened to provide access to the religious articles
stored inside.[68]

All the holy days on the church calendar were faithfully observed, but
the Easter season demanded special devotion. On Holy Thursday and Good
Friday, andirons and pokers were moved from fireplaces on the belief that
iron touching fire on those days would spark evil or disaster. No chickens
or other living things were killed, and meat was not eaten between Good
Friday and Easter Sunday. Nor was any ground plowed; older parishioners
held to the belief that drops of the sacred blood of Jesus would appear in
the freshly turned earth.[69] Good Friday itself was set aside for attending
to religious obligations. The most pressing necessity was the "Easter duty,"
the annual confession and penance expected of every practicing Catholic.
From the confessional, penitents moved to the cemetery behind the church
to clean and decorate the above-ground tombs, as they had done some six
months earlier on All Saints' Day.[70]

Honeysuckle, flowering quince, or other seasonal flowers were placed in
vases on each grave, along with keepsakes of the deceased that the family
had preserved through the years. A lace fan with ivory sticks, a small clock,
a rakish hat, a doll, or a fluttering kite would let departed loved ones know
they had not been forgotten. In the earliest years, lore contends, the graves
were also decorated with bottles, shells, and other miscellanea of interesting shape and color, arranged in decorative patterns or outlining individual
plots—a vestige of African heritage that waned before the twentieth century.[71] Lore does not identify specific families who followed these customs,
but they were likely the ones to whom Callahan referred when he reported
that the ancestors of some families arrived as practitioners or teachers of
voodoo. These newcomers supposedly assumed that their African-based religion would appeal to the Isle Brevelle families, because of their slave origins.
They were mistaken. According to Callahan, their culture made no inroads
in the French Catholic society of Cane River, and the newcomers eventually
converted to the dominant religion.[72]

Easter Sunday was a day of celebration for the entire community. After
mass, coffee was brewed over small fires at the edge of the cemetery, where
the people gathered to socialize and celebrate the end of Lenten fast and
penance. That gaiety would extend through an evening *fais-do-do*. Amid the

chatter in the churchyard, children hid their eggs in the grass around the tombs, while the men gathered with their own gaily decorated eggs, placed their nickel bets, and launched little games of "nip and tuck." Grasping their eggs in the circle formed by the thumb and index finger, each pair of players tapped their eggs together end to end in an effort to crack the opponent's egg while preserving their own intact. By the end of the day, the churchyard would be covered with shells. The parishioners, young and old, would then reconvene in one of their several "mansion houses," decked in their finest, to dance well into the night.[73]

The Easter gathering in the cemetery marked no lack of respect for the dead. To the contrary, it was viewed as a sharing of life once more with loved ones long departed. Louisiana's Creoles, of all hues, have traditionally exhibited a great measure of respect for the deceased. When Mother Hyacinthe LeConniat, Superior of the Daughters of the Cross at Avoyelles, opened a second convent for the girls of Isle Brevelle, she wrote her brother Yves-Marie in France:

> Nothing equals the care rendered to the dead here. . . . The corpse is wrapped well in white silk. The coffin is of perfect workmanship and is painted on the outside. The inside is padded and lined with velvet or satin, with gold tacks keeping the cloth in place. There is another coffin placed in the bottom of the grave; it is not as attractive as the one that holds the corpse. . . . This is naturally correct because it would be senseless to put the fine coffin in the mud. . . . This beautiful coffin which costs the rich 500 or 600 *francs*, is transported in a beautiful carriage or hearse. A man on horseback carries a small cross at the head of the cortege. The family and the friends accompany the body, riding in carriages or on horses. They wear on the arm beautiful bows of black lace which cost $2 or $3 apiece. At the church, which is covered with black, they sing the "Libera Me." No mass. Finally, the burial. All must throw the black crepe into the grave. They erect a fine monument. . . . This sad funeral as I described it to you is first class. If the priest goes to the house to accompany the body to the church, it is $40, and if he does not do this, it is $35. For the second class $25 or $30. For the third class $10 or $15. . . . By means of these stipends the missionary is able to live.[74]

Family funerals were often first-class. The final account rendered by the administrator of the estate of Marie Susanne Metoyer included a payment to the curé of sixty dollars for her burial in 1838.[75] In 1847 the *marguilliers* of the new Church of St. Jean Baptiste at Cloutierville met to establish the tariffs on burials for that parish and set the rates at eighty dollars for a first-class funeral, thirty for a second-class, twenty for a third-class, and ten dollars for a fourth-class.[76] When J. B. Espallier Rachal died not long afterward, his family paid the Reverend G. Guy the full eighty dollars.[77] The hearse to which Mother Hyacinthe referred was furnished to the Isle Brevelle community by the jack-of-all trades Oscar Dubreuil.[78]

Cane River's Creoles of color were buried in four known locations. In the first two decades of the nineteenth century, those who lived near Natchitoches were taken into the town and buried in the cemetery of the parish church there. But their numbers were few. For parishioners who lived more than a few miles from the church, the distance was complicated by a host of other issues. Spring rains brought flooding, heat caused rapid decomposition, and similar factors affected whether it was practical to take a body into the parish cemetery. Family members who lived at the lower end of the Isle found it more convenient to use the consecrated grounds later known as Shallow Lake Cemetery, on the plantation of Ambroise Le Comte. After the dedication of the church and cemetery at nearby Cloutierville, the families at Rivière aux Cannes favored that churchyard.[79]

The 1829 creation of St. Augustine's Chapel changed all these burial patterns. Most family members were thereafter buried behind the chapel, in the heart of their community, even though it was rarely possible to summon a priest before the interment. Augustin, it is said, "officiated" at those private interments. Slaves as a rule were not accorded space in the family's burial ground; their graveyard lay across the road, in the bend of the river, where nothing remains to mark their lives.[80] The motivation for segregating those graves surely included issues of race and status, but faith was a significant factor also. As the Metoyer slaveholdings increased, their slaves were increasingly Protestant; and Protestants of all colors in that time and place preferred their own burial rites and grounds to the "Roman" practices native to Louisiana.

The oldest burials in the cemetery at St. Augustine's Chapel were marked with the iron crosses traditional to French and Spanish Natchitoches. An occasional wooden cross, painted white with black lettering, marked graves of the less affluent. The most striking plots in the cemetery, used even in the twenty-first century, are the above-ground tombs—miniature white houses about five by seven feet, built to shelter the bodies of the most prominent members of the family.[81] In the place of honor nearest the church stands a tomb with a marble door that identifies it as the resting place of Augustin Metoyer and his wife Marie Agnes. After the death of Augustin in 1856 their tomb was twice opened, once in the 1860s for the burial of his favorite son, François Gassion, and then again in the early twentieth century to deposit the last remains of that son's third wife, Perine (Metoyer) Metoyer Dupré.[82]

For more than a century, Catholicity shaped the rhythms of life along the Cane. The Angelus at dawn marked the beginning of each new day; the evening peal of bells from St. Augustine's Chapel brought that day's labor to an end. The calendar of the church determined days of work and days of rest, days of fast and days of feasting. The spiritual ties of godparent to godchild were bonds that held the people together as closely as did ties of blood. The influence their faith held upon these Creoles produced results that earned for Coincoin's family much of the respect that the outside society accorded it.

The religious example instilled by the patriarch Augustin Metoyer would be preserved by the family that continued to revere their Grandpère. At the 1917 dedication of the modern church of St. Augustine, Bishop Cornelius Van de Ven offered accolades to its parishioners:

> I am proud of you, my dear people, and I can without fear of contradiction, give you as a model for my whole Diocese. . . . Your piety, your generosity, have just accomplished an admirable task—admirable not only because of the size and elegance of style of the building, but admirable especially because of the great sacrifices you have imposed on yourselves to realize it. Your predecessors have set a high standard for you which, if you are their true sons and daughters, you are bound to follow. As the language of your ancestors has it, "Noblesse oblige."[83]

The bishop's observation underscores a social and political reality that Augustin clearly foresaw: legal status hinged upon personal behavior as well as race. Five years after his creation of the Chapel of St. Augustine, a South Carolina Supreme Court justice decreed that being Negro or mulatto was not just a matter of being black or brown. Rather, a "man of worth [could] have the rank of a white man, while a vagabond of the same degree of blood should be confined to the inferior caste."[84] Eight decades later, and not long before Bishop Van de Ven's remarks, that mindset still prevailed in many corners of America. A 1906 report to Congress by the director of the U.S. Census Bureau asserted that "race"—as stated by enumerators on the census returns—"reflects local opinion, and that opinion probably is based more upon social position *and manner of life* than upon the relative amounts of blood."[85]

Coincoin's offspring along Cane River never attempted to cross the color line in their home community. Yet, as an Americanized Louisiana increasingly restricted the rights of free multiracials, their *manner of life* would determine the privileges they enjoyed and the prejudice they would suffer. As observed elsewhere, "The astute *homme de couleur libre* who controlled Isle Brevelle was keenly aware that 'his people' must maintain their reputation for piety and devotion to the Catholic faith if they were to survive the new social climate."[86]

SEVEN

Cane River Culture

T he economic and religious underpinnings of the community manifested themselves in many aspects of daily life. Large and stately homes graced the larger plantations. Musical training for the youth nurtured an appreciation of the arts. Education—even university study abroad—equipped each new generation for its role as citizens of distinction. All the graces and amusements enjoyed by affluent white neighbors thrived among Coincoin's offspring, although the social intercourse of the Creoles of color was largely restricted to the confines of their own extended family. The maintenance of law and order was, in their view, their own responsibility. Its enforcement by their leaders kept peace among them and set the standard they observed in society at large.

In appearance, the population was striking. "Latin" might be the most appropriate descriptor. Old and treasured photographs reflect attractive faces of mostly a Gallic model. Although complexions varied, many were fair. Blond and light brown hair was not uncommon; and, in more than one case, eyes were said to have been blue. The perplexity of census takers and their consequent errors are easy to understand. Records created by the Anglo physician engaged by the Census Bureau in 1860 make that point. A newcomer to the parish, John W. Thomas attempted to follow instructions to record race as it *appeared* to him. In doing so, he misidentified at least 4 percent of the population parishwide: at least 76 of its 1,614 families. In twenty-three of those cases, he perceived Cane River's Creoles of color to be "white."[1]

In specific branches of these multiracial families, the various elements of their genetic stock were plainly visible. The portrait of Grandpère Augustin depicts him as pecan colored and solidly built with broad features. His half-brother Nicolas, Coincoin's eldest son, was said in legal testimony to be a black man "appearing to be a real African."[2] Augustin's grandnephew

Barthélemy LeCour, according to a grandson, was "tall, over six feet, with bronze-colored skin, a long nose, and black hair." LeCour, reportedly, never had to shave. When his young grandson questioned why this was so, his Native American heritage was explained to the lad.[3]

In character and personality the people varied just as widely. There was Augustin, long venerated for his wisdom, and his brother François, remembered more than a hundred years after his death as "the strong man." There was Auguste, the risk-taker, who entered every endeavor on a grand scale. There was Rose, the courtesan, who began life as a slave and launched herself with no assets other than her attractiveness, amassed a sizable estate, then ended her life as a servant—a striking contrast to her cousin Perine, a plain and pragmatic woman who, despite her wealth, lived frugally, shared generously, and is well remembered as her family's memory-keeper. There was Oscar, the jack-of-all-trades: merchant, tailor, ferryman, schoolteacher, billiard hall operator, and undertaker. But of them all, the strongest personalities were undoubtedly Augustin and François.

Affectionately called Grandpère by all his extended family, the oldest Metoyer brother was the acknowledged patriarch of the clan. After the death of Metoyer and Coincoin, Augustin became the family head, assuming responsibility for the welfare of all "his people." His word was law, his judgment respected, his person honored. Regardless of how hotly a dispute was waged by individuals within the community, legend holds, when Augustin the arbiter gave his decision, no one dared question it.[4] His reputation for controlling situations and behavior that might reflect negatively upon his community is well supported by existing records. A search of criminal process records for the parish during this period reveals no conviction of a Cane River Creole of color for any infraction of the law.

The reverence accorded Grandpère Augustin extended to the smallest incidents of everyday life. A favorite story on the Isle relates the fondness of the elderly Augustin for sitting on his front gallery, rocking in his favorite chair while he watched passersby on the main road in front of his house. The younger members of the family, with all the haste of youth, tended to gallop down that road; but once in sight of Augustin's house they would rein their horses to a slow trot. Respectfully they approached. Their hats were tipped as they paused to greet him with a *"Bonjour, Grandpère Augustin,"* after which they awaited his customary reply, *"Bonjour, mes enfants."* Once acknowledged, they slowly walked their horses until out of sight, then whipped the animals again into full speed.[5]

While Augustin held the respect of his people, it was his youngest brother who best captured their imagination. Tradition has preserved almost as many anecdotes relating to François as it has of the patriarch himself. Called "Le Point" because his land lay at the point of the lower Isle, François was the free spirit others envied and the model for all youth who wanted to prove their strength and manliness. He was the favorite topic of the old men who sat on the gallery of the community store and swapped stories—and of the young who stopped to listen. One of those youths in his own old age would recall a popular tale of François and a bull, wherein the strongman came upon a raging bull stuck in the mud, physically pulled him out by his horns, and then, when the freed bull snorted at him, shoved him in again with the force of one foot.[6]

François's strength, humor, and quirks were the characteristics most often recalled by twentieth-century admirers. According to legend, he could take two cotton hooks and carry a five-hundred-pound bale as easily as an ordinary man could carry a ten-pound sack of flour. When a foundation block had to be replaced under the Isle Brevelle church, François lifted the structure with seeming ease while a new block was slipped into place; no jack was needed.[7] He was so strong, it is claimed, that he could lift a barrel of whiskey, even though he rarely indulged in stimulants. On one occasion, when he delivered some articles to a Cloutierville resident and was offered a drink, François made an exception to his usual abstinence. A hogshead of whiskey stood nearby, and when the genial host pointed it out, François reached for it. Putting a hand on either side of the staves, just below the top, he "raised the whole hogshead up to the level of his lips, taking one swallow, and then gingerly set it back on the floor without spilling a drop." This youngest son of Coincoin has also been remembered as a plain-living man with no personal pretensions. If he lacked a horse and needed to go to town, he walked—all twenty-four miles from his home to Natchitoches—with his shoes tied around his neck. Upon reaching the bridge at the edge of town, he would wash his feet in Cane River and don his shoes before proceeding up Front Street.[8]

Most members of this community fell between the two extremes marked by Augustin and François. Their health was good, but abstinence from liquor was hardly the reason. Most were conscientious Catholics, but few achieved the same level of personal perfection credited to their patriarch. The formation of their character began in childhood. As children, they were taught to equate age with wisdom. Parents knew what was best for their offspring, their authority should never be questioned, and this respect extended to all legitimate authority. The precept that children should be seen but not heard was strictly followed; when adults visited, the children played outside. All elders were addressed as *Oncle* or *Tante*, whether or not they actually possessed that relationship to the younger person who addressed them. This mark of respect was a lifelong practice, adhered to by adults as well as children.[9]

Self-respect was a core expectation, regardless of economic standing, literacy, or livelihood. Cane River's Creoles of color belied the stereotyped image of nonwhites forced to subsist under white dominance—the shuffling gait, bowed head, subservient demeanor. Most outsiders remarked, sometimes fatuously, upon their "curiously erect" posture, their well-modulated voices, and their personal dignity, even after their wealth and status were lost.[10] François aside, the self-respect instilled from early childhood reflected itself in external trappings: clothes, accessories, horses, and carriages. Family photographs and portraits show stylishly dressed ladies and gentlemen. Succession inventories and merchant account statements attest their taste and their indulgence in the same fine goods enjoyed by wealthy white neighbors. Perfume and silk stockings for the ladies, as well as cologne and beaver hats for the men, were among many luxe items inventoried. Seventy-five-dollar gold watches and hundred-dollar carriages were not just substantial capital purchases but also annually taxable possessions.[11]

Like their white counterparts, the wealthier members of the family indulged their egos in expensively procured oil portraits during the economic boom of the 1830s. Four of those preserved along Cane River have been widely featured in cultural exhibits and historical literature. The 1836 portrait of Augustin, nearly life-sized, and a smaller one of his tignoned wife Marie Agnes have long been identified. Another pair depicts a dapper Creole gentleman and a beautiful young woman, who are believed to be their entrepreneurial son Auguste Augustin and his wife Melite, the daughter of Augustin's twin Susanne.[12] All four paintings were forfeited, amid later destitution, by the descendants who had inherited them. All were acquired by the white chatelaine of Louis Metoyer's historic plantation, who created a Depression-era arts colony on the grounds her family called "Melrose." After viewing the portraits in the mid-twentieth century, a visiting newspaperwoman described them as "the finest collection of paintings of people of color in oil, pastel, and prints, in existence."[13]

The most enigmatic of the Metoyer family paintings is one that surfaced in a Sotheby's catalog in 2001. This exquisite likeness of a young boy in formal attire, one arm folded across his chest, also depicts a multi-hued moth resting lightly on his hand. Thus: the name by which it has come to be known, *Creole Boy with a Moth*. The painting's Cane River roots are well proved. The artist has been identified: a New Orleans–based *homme de couleur libre* named Julien Hudson. The identity of the child and the meaning of the moth have both been matters of speculation. The most recent interpretation of the symbolism, offered by the art historian William Keyse Rudolph, is also useful to the identification of the child: "The use of the moth—like the butterfly, a symbol of the soul—in the little boy's hand offers the tantalizing possibility that this is a memorial portrait."[14]

Two faded photographs of the painting, both taken in the 1930s, appear within scrapbooks created by writers-in-residence at Melrose. The captions for the two are similar; but their small differences are also critical. One page, headed "Mulatto Portraits," presents a photo of the child's painting, pasted alongside that of Marie Agnes; the portraits appear in matching frames. The legend for the child's photo reads "Dominic Metoyer, 1836." The second and rougher photo shares a page with an even more crudely staged photograph of Augustin's portrait. Here, the child's caption, written in a different hand, reads: "Duncan Kirkland's grandfather—Dominique Metoyer."[15]

The date attributed to the child's portrait errs by a year. The painting itself is signed and dated "Julien Hudson, 1835." The time frame, however, is compatible with known evidence for the family, and it, too, points to the identity of the child. The years 1835–36, when all the portraits were painted, marked the apex of the New Orleans career of Auguste Augustin Metoyer. His wealth was soaring in a real estate bubble that would soon burst. In addition to his co-ownership of a New Orleans–based mercantile house and factorship, he was about to expand further with a new plantation and a grand *maison* on the Isle. Commissioning that pair of portraits for himself and his wife Melite—and at least arranging for the portraits of his parents—was an act well in keeping with Auguste's urban lifestyle and upward mobility.

The identity attributed to the child by those captions, created a century after the fact, is demonstrably wrong. Yet the captions are equally valuable for a credible identification. No branch of the Metoyer family had, at that time, a son Dominique of compatible age. A genealogical reconstruction of all the sprawling family left by Coincoin along the river reveals only one prosperous couple with a son of appropriate age who died in the critical time frame: Auguste Augustin and Melite Metoyer. Three children had been born to the couple. A son Nelcourt, born in 1827, had died before 1830. A son

Augustin Paulin, who had been born in June 1829, died in September 1836 at the age of seven—an age and circumstance that parallel the enigmatic 1835 painting. The third child, a daughter Emilie born in 1833, was the only child who would live to adulthood and leave offspring. She was also the only heir to the possessions left by her parents. One of the sons who survived her was John Duncan Kirkland, the individual to whom the older scrapbook entry connects the portrait.[16]

Both errors made by the individuals who created the scrapbook pages— the slight misdating of the painting and the partial misidentification of the child—are common types of errors made by oral history. The uncritical acceptance of the "recollection" that the child was Duncan Kirkland's grandfather, named *Dominique* Metoyer, was also a common practice in past eras. That oral account, when tested against surviving evidence, also yields typical results. Kirkland's maternal grandfather was indeed a Metoyer: not Dominique but Auguste—a grandfather Kirkland never knew, one who died years before his birth. Because Kirkland's mother was effectively an only child, he grew up without the advantage of aunts and uncles and their offspring regaling the youth at family gatherings with memories of that grandfather. On the Isle he certainly had no dearth of cousins to recall family stories of forebears, but those grandfathers of his cousins bore other names—including multiple Dominiques. At the time Kirkland attempted to identify the portrait, he was an elderly man frequently tapped by the denizens of Melrose for both his memories and his mementoes. Whether the inquirer in this case misunderstood him or simply misremembered the details he had related—at whatever later time the scrapbook page was created—the errors were typical. The trail of evidence, on the other hand, is clear. The child in the portrait was Augustin Paulin Metoyer: not Kirkland's mother's *father*, but Kirkland's mother's *brother*.

Both family solidarity and Catholic social values characterized Cane River's Creoles of color across the generations. One traveler of the 1850s inquired about them of the driver of his stagecoach and was sufficiently impressed with the reply that he noted in his journal: "He had often staid [*sic*] over night at their houses, and knew them intimately and he was nowhere else so well treated, and he never saw more gentleman-like people. He appeared to have been especially impressed by the domestic and social happiness he had witnessed in their houses."[17] As in any society or family group, squabbles occasionally occurred, and not all marriages were successful. Yet incidences of mutual assistance are far more prevalent in surviving records—starting with those occasions on which Augustin, his brothers, and his sons purchased freedom for their less fortunate relatives. Among those, the most striking was surely that of Coincoin's son Antoine Joseph Metoyer, who, in 1818, paid six hundred dollars to Ambroise Le Comte for a "mulâtresse named Madeleine, Créole of Natchitoches, aged about fifty, in order to give her liberty." Madeleine was his mother-in-law.[18]

Countless other incidents demonstrate close and protective relationships between members of the community. When Charles N. Rocques Sr. died in 1859, executors of his succession noted that many of the improvements on his plantation were put there by Jérôme Sarpy Jr.[19] When Augustin Cloutier died about 1837 and left his widow, Thérèse Metoyer, and their children without property, the half-Canneci widow of Louis Metoyer gave the Widow Cloutier the use of a house for life. The Widow Metoyer obviously harbored no ill will over the fact that Thérèse was her late husband's illegitimate daughter, and she clearly did not use to her own advantage the legal dictate that illegitimate children were entitled to no share of a father's estate.[20] Valery Barthélemy LeCour, one of the French-Indian youths who married a daughter of Dominique Metoyer, sold his wife's brother the land that his wife had received as a dowry. Looking after this younger sister's interests, J. B. Dominique wrote into the deed of sale the provision that LeCour must immediately invest the money in another tract of land in order to secure her dowry rights and privileges.[21]

Donations occurred frequently. Most children received land or money and sometimes slaves as wedding gifts; but many instances occurred in which the recipients of donations were more distantly related. In 1836, for example, Marie Susette Metoyer, wife of Louis Morin, made a donation to two nieces by marriage. The two daughters whom Marie Susette had borne to her first husband had recently died. From the estate those daughters left, Marie Susette gave $2,443 to Clara Berthe, the daughter of Marie Glapion of New Orleans, and to Marie Elise Rocques, Mme. Morin's godchild, the daughter of Charles Nerestan Rocques.[22]

Family solidarity was also a consequence of the social restrictions the community faced. Because they were not white, they were excluded from most affairs of the white community. Because they were not black, they could not mingle with that class, slave or free, without losing the tenuous legal and social privileges they had managed to achieve. Because they already had accepted into their community, through marriage, the neighboring free people of color who shared their class and caste, they had few options for extending their social intercourse beyond the confines of their extended family. Their menfolk did sometimes mingle socially with white planter neighbors—occasions limited primarily to the hunt, the race, the card game, and the fishing party—but Creole wives and girls did not socialize across the color line. Isolated, they and their homes became insular and, by extension, self-protective.

As with all Creoles, white or colored, dancing was a favorite entertainment, to the consternation of some church officers. The French-born priest who served congregants in the town of Natchitoches as assistant pastor in the 1860s wrote to his parents, expressing his shock at the widespread acceptance of this "evil" that he had found throughout his parish: "The Bishop closes his eyes to any harm done there; that is, whenever the dancing takes place in the family circle, he allows it; he does not censure it. They have succeeded in abolishing the public balls, at least up until now. There are so many reforms to bring about, so many needed."[23] The Catholic-oriented society on Isle Brevelle did restrict its dances to the seasons when the Church permitted festivity. A late-nineteenth-century traveler through the area, after noting that their customs reportedly had not changed in a hundred years, described a traditional affair held on the Isle: "They are fond of dancing, music, and gay dressing. . . . At a dance will be seen a big fire in the yard, and a big pot of gumbo on it, which, with cafe-noir, is served steaming hot to guests at intervals."[24]

A typical dance might be announced to the community by two men in a skiff. While one man rowed up one side of the river and then down the other, his companion would blow a conch shell to draw in those who lived along the banks. As crowds gathered or a head appeared in the back door of a solitary house, the announcer would cup his hands and shout a message such as

> Fais Do-Do!
> Grande danse le soir de Paques à huit heures!
> De la bonne musique, bon temps pour tous!
> Fais Do-Do!
> Au pavilion de Monsieur Monette
> Dimanche à huit heures. Ne manquez pas de venir![25]

The *fais do-do* was the most popular of their dances. Literally, the words mean "go to sleep," but the name was a wry misnomer. To the rhythm of guitars, drums, triangles, and any other instruments available, to the hand-clapping and finger-snapping accompaniment of the spectators, six couples would take the floor for a French version of the American square dance, executing all the graceful moves requested by the man who "called the figures." The quadrille waltz was also popular.[26]

Holidays on Cane River were particularly festive and, here again, family unity set the pattern for celebrations. As children married and were given a tract from a parental plantation, they built small houses near the bigger ones of their parents. A cluster of small homes surrounding the "family mansion" became the pattern. On such holidays as Christmas and Easter, on birthdays, wedding days, and other Church feast days, all children and grandchildren from the smaller homes gathered at the big house for the celebration. A calf or a large "porker" would be barbecued in the yard, then served inside on the vast dining room table with salad, an array of garden vegetables and fruits, coffee, cakes, pralines, and popcorn balls, with wine for the women and whiskey for the men.[27]

Among themselves, Cane River's families were outgoing, sociable, and fun-loving. Sunday was a day for visiting rather than a "day of rest." When their visits took them to see friends at Camptí, Alexandria, or New Orleans, those visits might last for weeks or months. The hospitality of their Camptí relatives was especially memorable; one belle of the antebellum years fondly recalled in her old age a particular Camptí family whom she had frequently visited. When she and the other guests retired for the evening, she related, their clothes were gathered. By the time the guests awoke the next morning, all their garments had been washed, pressed, and hung in their rooms. No matter how many pretty gowns or dresses the girls from Cane River might take with them, they "never needed more than one," because their hosts made certain their clothes were always fresh. The host family, like most of those in the Camptí community, owned no slaves; the overnight toil this hospitality entailed would have been their own.[28]

Within the home, every night was "family night." When the day's work was done, when chickens and children had been fed, families gathered on the veranda—or around the parlor fireplace when the wind blew hard and cold. On those blustery nights the children popped corn over the flickering flames, or the older girls made pralines, and the "old folks" spun their tales of yesteryear, passing on to the young their family's heritage. Once the children were put to bed, the parents might drink together for an hour or so before retiring, the only time when custom permitted the women to indulge in "hard liquor." In some more affluent families, it is said, married couples might also retire to their separate rooms—the master's *chambre* and the mistress's *salle*—a lifestyle luxury that (perhaps due to that cocktail hour) did not noticeably affect the fecundity of the wives.[29]

A variety of other pastimes were popular on the Isle. As elsewhere in the antebellum South, cockfighting and dogfighting were common sports. Both had almost disappeared by the late nineteenth century, but old men were alive then who recalled both fondly. Pepper, they related, would be put under the wings of the chickens to discourage their opponents from pecking them in this vulnerable spot, and soap was rubbed on the birds' necks so that "bill holts" by opposing roosters would be sure to slip.[30] Succession records provide evidence of milder ways in which the people whiled away their leisure hours. In 1854, for example, Nerestan Predanes Metoyer purchased a checker or chess board (a "draft board and men") and a dozen and a half decks of cards from the sale of the estate of Charles Nerestan Rocques Jr., paying $1.50 for the lot.[31]

As implied by Predanes's purchase, card playing was a serious engagement in French Creole culture. The mid-nineteenth-century traveler Frederick Law Olmsted recorded a jaundiced view held by many Anglo-Protestant newcomers to antebellum Louisiana: "The Creoles are inveterate gamblers— rich and poor alike. The majority of wealthy Creoles . . . do nothing to improve their estate; and are very apt to live beyond their income. They borrow and play, and keep borrowing to play as long as they can."[32] Cane River's menfolk were true Creoles who thoroughly enjoyed gambling, but most exercised more prudence than Olmsted's informant allowed them. Succession inventories and agricultural censuses attest that their estates were not neglected, and legal records reveal few within the community who might have gambled beyond their means. One exception is said to have been Emanuel Dupré, who, at one point in his life, was fast working his way through his wife's dowry and inheritance until she resolutely refused to sign over any more property.[33] Reportedly, this was not the end of his gambling, despite his wife's disapproval; but surviving records attest no further breeches of fiscal caution. After the disastrous Civil War, Dupré stood financially at the community's head. While many affluent whites along the river had plunged into poverty and were losing their land for taxes, the 1870 census credits Dupré with real and personal property valued at $16,500.[34]

Two other pastimes popular on the Isle were fishing and horse racing. Some of the fishing parties took place on a grand scale, with seventy to eighty participants, white and colored.[35] Traditionally, the horse races were held at 24-Mile Ferry, where crowds gathered on Sunday afternoons. Refreshment stands offered a wide assortment of foods, such as pies, cakes, anisette, lemonade, and of course coffee. Although the horses usually were not thoroughbreds, many were fast enough to beat the blooded stock of a white neighbor who often raced against them.[36]

Many Cane River women, free and enslaved, were culinary artists. One visiting newspaperman of the nineteenth century swore: "The finest cooks of our State are in Isle Brevelle, and they can beat the San Antonio Mexican making tamales. The Isle Brevelle tamale is made of highly seasoned chopped meats, and meal made from corn treated with lye to remove the husk and pounded in a mortar. Their coffee is unexcelled and if you call at a house, the coffee mill is promptly set agoing, and you are handed a cup of cafe noir, such as you will always remember."[37] This traveler also was impressed with the gumbo, the same "gumbo filet" of which Private Holloway would write many decades later. According to the earlier visitor, "This gumbo is made from boiling fresh meat or game with pulverized leaves and stems of a dwarf sassafras [filé], which grows on the hills, and whither these people go in great numbers at the proper season to gather it."[38]

Food preparation was controlled to a large degree by the seasons. Summer and early fall saw a plentiful supply of fresh garden produce, food that must be preserved to sustain both the free and enslaved families through the long months of winter and spring. One of the most popular methods of food preservation was drying. Beans, peas, and such legumes dried naturally; but pumpkin, okra, peaches, figs, and the other fruits that grew wild along the river were sliced and spread on rooftops to dry. Onions and peppers were hung on strings; root vegetables such as potatoes were often buried.

Winter was the usual season for slaughtering, because cold was needed to protect the meat from spoilage during the processing and aging. Hams and bacon were smoked; other cuts of pork would be cooked and packed in big crocks. So long as lard was poured on top, old-timers reported, the cooked pork never spoiled. Both pork and beef were used to make tasso, a Cane River favorite; cut into cubes, covered with salt and a large quantity of red pepper, the meat was laid out to dry, then packed away in a moisture-proof container.[39]

Health issues were minimal—aside from the region's incessant risks of swamp fevers, the occupational hazards faced by men, and every woman's travails during pregnancy and birthing. When Olmsted appeared in the parish, the first person who mentioned the Creoles of color on Isle Brevelle

swore that "they had sore eyes, and lost their teeth early, and had few children, and showed other scrofulous symptoms, and evidences of weak constitutions." After inquiring extensively and meeting the people themselves,
Olmsted concluded: "This gentleman must have read *De Bow's Review* and
taken these facts for granted, without personal knowledge; for neither my
own observations, nor any information that I could obtain from others at
all confirmed his statement."[40]

Olmsted's informant, however misguided, reflected popular thought.
Even in Jamaica, a prestigious historian in the latter part of the eighteenth
century had recorded as fact his opinion that "some few of them [people
of color] have intermarried with those of their own complexions but such
matches have generally been defective and barren. They seem in this respect
to be actually of the mule-kind, and not so capable of producing from one
another as from commerce with a distinct White or Black."[41] As late as 1927
a Harvard scholar, writing under the headline "New Lights on Evolution,"
repeated the same postulation: "The sterility of hybrids has been long and
even popularly known, as witness the cases of the mule and the mulatto."[42]

Coincoin's offspring, like people of color everywhere, proved the absur-
dity of this generalization. The original six Metoyer brothers all married
multiracial wives and averaged eight children each; one of the brothers,
Dominique, fathered at least seventeen. The census of 1850 reveals that the
average family in the clan had four children living at home; to this number
must be added the children who had died before the census or had already
married. Also, most of the families tabulated were still in their childbearing
years, which meant that their families were not yet complete.[43]

Other chroniclers, somewhat more enlightened, acknowledged that people
of color were just as capable of reproducing their own kind as were members
of any other "race." A West Indian planter of the early nineteenth century
recalled in his journal: "I think it is Long who asserts, that two mulattos
will never have children; but, as far as the most positive assurances can go,
since my arrival in Jamaica, I have reason to believe the contrary, and that
mulattos breed together just as well as blacks and whites." This journalist
diminished his credibility as an astute observer, however, when he added,
"but they are almost universally weak and effeminate persons and thus their
children are very difficult to rear."[44]

Olmsted's first informant in the Cane River area had made essentially the
same argument about the Cane River community. To his credit, the skeptical
journalist inquired further of local residents and came away with an entirely

different view of the physical state of Creoles of color. According to Olmsted, other whites in the parish expressed the opinion that Creoles of color "enjoyed better health than the whites living in their vicinity," and declared that they "could not recollect a single instance of those indications of weak constitution."[45] Contemporary records support the more rational view. The census of 1850, which tabulated incidences of ill health or disability, tallied only twenty such cases for Cane River's multiracial Creoles, approximately 5 percent of their cohort.[46] Most of the extant account statements from doctors of the area were rendered for services to those who were on their deathbeds. Episodic treatments were rare.

Intermarriage between close relatives, especially multigenerational intermarriage, is a practice with some genetic consequences; among those, poor eyesight and mental instability are commonly cited. Yet, for the first seventy years of the community's existence, only one case of insanity and one of blindness are known to have occurred. Neither of the afflicted had incidences of kin-intermarriage within their ancestral lines. In 1842 Philippe Dupré was interdicted by the court as a result of his recent derangement; his brother Emanuel was appointed curator of both Philippe and Philippe's property. As required by law, Emanuel signed a bond guaranteeing honest administration of the estate until his brother regained his mental faculties; a white friend, Dr. Thomas A. Morgan, cosigned as his surety. Whether or not Philippe recovered is unknown; by 1850 he was dead. Neither censuses nor other records mention any case of blindness, but tradition holds that one family member, Philippe's mother, Adelaïde Mariotte, was totally blind in her old age. One case of hermaphroditism is also reported.[47]

Yellow fever and smallpox were constant threats along the river, as throughout the South. The yellow fever epidemic of 1853 wreaked havoc indiscriminately. Among all classes and all colors, many families suffered multiple deaths. Among Creoles of color, the only known victims were Ambroise Azenor Metoyer and his wife, Marie Lilette Sarpy, who died in October that year after the epidemic had begun to wane. A partial list of regional victims was published in a contemporary newspaper, but it included only whites.[48] There were also occasional incidences of smallpox. As was the custom elsewhere by this time, when smallpox ravaged a home, it and all the family's belongings were burned to destroy the causative. Clearly, the population of Natchitoches had learned something about disease management in the decades since the epidemic of 1790, when the Spanish priest de La Vez attended the Natchitoches succession sale of the just-deceased white Creole Marie

Madeleine de La Renaudière and bought her bed—only to be found dead in that bed, and in a state of putrefaction, just eleven days later.[49]

The relatively low incidence of disease is nonetheless surprising when one considers the nature of the country. A northern soldier who spent almost a month in the region during the Civil War wrote in his diary: "Lying in the woods, we begin to be seriously annoyed with the insects and vermin incident to this country. Many of the men are suffering from the effects of the wood-tick, which bore themselves into the flesh, causing inflammation and running sores. Scorpions are not unfrequent [sic] to this region, the sting of which is fatal."[50] Echoing these sentiments, Father Yves-Marie Le Conniat of Natchitoches wrote to his former pastor in France of the "death-beetles," the flies, and the mosquitoes that constantly assailed him. "I really believe," he vowed, "it is in this country that Beezlebub has established his kingdom."[51]

The one feature of Cane River life that most impressed visitors was the quality of the fields and homes. The captain of the steamboat *Dalmau,* which regularly stopped in the area, observed: "The plantations appeared no way different from the generality of those of white Creoles; and on some of them were large, handsome, and comfortable houses."[52] The Czech immigrant Dignowity, whose 1830s-era journal recounts a visit to Isle Brevelle, left the most intimate account of life within the walls of those plantation manors:

> The plantation Bells were ringing for Noon, when I arrived to a very fine plantation; all looked elegant, an indication of wealth. I concluded to stop for dinner, and approached a very fine dwelling house. A white headed gentlemanly old Negro man bid me welcome, and gave me a seat. A little after, a small neatly dressed negro Boy brouth me a porcelain wash beson of cistern water and towels, I made the necessary ablution and presently was invited by the old gentleman to take a glass [of] wine.
>
> Shortly after the bell rang for dinner. I was invited to enter a large and splendidly furnished dinning Room. The old gentleman motioned me to seat, and himself took the head of the table. Several clenly dressed servants wearing white aprons were in attendance, the table glitered with rich and Masive silver plate, and was set for about sixteen persons. I was surprised that no one entered, as I heard music, in adjoining rooms, and singing and talking French, but I was alone at my dinner. The old gentleman was carving, and giving orders to servants. The vians were most excellent and everything to correspond.

I finished my dinner, and was shown to a parlour, and Books and periodicals, and newspapers were laid before me. Then I noticed, that the
rest of the family went to dine. I noticed several elegantly dressed young
ladys, of colour. After dinner was over, I prepared to resume my journey,
when the old gentleman gave me a polite invitation to remain that day
or longer as their guest. I accepted the invitation for that day—but stipulated that I would take my seat at the table with the rest of the family.
This seemed to them a great condescention [act of charitableness], as the
prejudice against colour is in no country so great, as in the U.S. [53]

Of all those "large, handsome, and comfortable houses" built by Coincoin's
offspring, only one survives: the one that Louis Metoyer had begun at the
time of his death in the spring of 1832. Older residents of the late twentieth
century remember six more, all of which were destroyed early in their life-
times: Augustin's manor, leveled by fire about 1900; a similar home belonging to his son Jean Baptiste Augustin; the spacious manor house of Jérôme
Sarpy at the upper end of the Isle (built by the white Julien Rachal Jr. and
replicated in the still-surviving home of Julien's brother-in-law, François
Roubieu); the "eleven-room mansion" of Emanuel Dupré and his wife, Marguerite Metoyer, which stood across from the 24-Mile Ferry; the home of
Oscar Dubreuil at the site of the ferry; and the nearby home of the merchant
Vilfried Metoyer. An eighth large antebellum home, officially described as a
"mansion house," was the residence of Auguste Metoyer and his wife, Melite Anty; this manse was forfeited in a lawsuit before the Civil War. Another large house of the same general style reportedly belonged to Estelle
Morin Metoyer, the granddaughter of Augustin. According to tradition, it
was destroyed during the war, although the postwar damage claims filed by
the Metoyers against the United States do not mention it amid the litany of
losses they reported.[54]

Cane River builders primarily used three construction methods: *bousillage* (an adobe-style mixture of mud and moss or deer hair), *brique-entre-
poteaux* (brick between posts), and round logs chinked with mud. Homes
built during the colonial and territorial periods, described as "cottages" by
the U.S. explorer Thomas Freeman in 1806, were usually of *bousillage*. By
the second decade of the nineteenth century, the two-story manor house of
brique-entre-poteaux had gained in popularity. By the time of the Civil War,
all of the "mansion houses" belonging to the community were constructed in
this fashion. Along Cane River, only the homes of Anglo yeomen and slaves

were built of logs chinked with mud. In later years, most houses and stables were fitted also with equipment to protect them from lightning.[55]

The design of the two-storied manor houses, borrowed from the West Indies, was practical as well as gracious. The bottom floor served as an above-ground basement. Living quarters were installed on the second floor, where the breezes blew cooler and the mosquitoes were less apt to hover. Because houses built along rivers have always faced the threat of floods, the first-floor exterior walls were usually of brick, and brick pillars supported the veranda or *gallerie* that graced the outside of the second floor. A center flight of high, wide steps—as in Augustin's manor and the Rachal house that became home to the Jérôme Sarpy family—typically led to the main living area. Some builders or homeowners preferred smaller staircases at either end of the ground-floor veranda—in the model that has survived on Louis Metoyer's plantation. On many homes the verandas were L-shaped, extending the length of one side as well as the front; in some, those verandas extended down both sides of the home, or even on all four sides as shown in surviving pictures of Jean Baptiste Augustin's "mansion." Bay windows were not uncommon.[56]

Kitchens were detached from the main house, a practice typical across the South. That isolation kept cookfires from heating the living quarters during warm months and prevented kitchen fires from destroying the dwellings. Some estate homes, such as that of Emanuel Dupré, sported a backyard barbecue pit, equipped with a long iron rod on which porkers or calves were speared for cooking. Augustin Metoyer's yard boasted two pigeon houses, appraised at ten times the value of a slave cabin—a feature found on few white plantations of the area.[57]

More affluent homes were graced with a lane of whitewashed oak or cedar trees, a status symbol among planters in both the Latin and Anglo South. Six cedars are said to have lined the entranceway to the Dupré home, and an even larger number led into the estate grounds of the Sarpy plantation. In 1890 the Sarpy manor house—then owned by the entrepreneurial Tennessee-born ex-slave Carroll Jones[58]—was described as "a large and commodious one, being 130 feet long by 80 feet wide. The yard in which it stands contains a fine cedar grove, and overlooking, as it does, the beautiful Cane River it is one of the most beautiful country seats in the parish."[59]

In discussing the homes of this type that he had seen before they were razed in the twentieth century, Callahan wrote: "What called most for ornamentation were the mantels and fireplaces. The wood-work extended from floor to ceiling, and here the craftsman showed his skill. It is all honest wood and honest work. Some of the wood is native, some mahogany. The designs are simple, but elegant. There is no overcharging of ornament, no useless detail. Even now, in some of these old buildings, despite years of neglect, the woodwork of these fireplaces and mantels gives indication of its former beauty."[60] That workmanship is still evident along the river in cottages such as the 1847 home known now as the Lewis Jones House, whose workmanship has been recently described this way:

> This house is finely detailed, with random width beaded boards on the front and side galleries and interior walls, beaded ceiling beams, and several single and double sets of French doors featuring a decorative geometric pattern. French wraparound mantel sets are found in the three front rooms, each with simple pilasters, layered mantel shelf, decorative paneling, cornice, and the lozenge-shaped designs so popular among French Creoles.[61]

Special features in the interior of Cane River homes accommodated them to Louisiana's climate. In many dining rooms, large clover-leaf boards called *punkahs* swung from the ceilings above the long dinner tables. From the punkahs, ropes swagged into easy reach on the perimeter of the rooms. Rhythmic pulls on the ropes—a regular chore for children, free and enslaved— caused the *punkahs* to swing, cooling the diners and fanning the flies from the food.[62]

The interiors of the homes were usually furnished compatibly with their architectural styles. Succession inventories of those who lived in small homes reveal sparse furnishings. Inventories of the larger homes almost all cited articles of quality and taste. The 1837 succession of Mme. Florentin Conant, one of Augustin Metoyer's daughters, reveals that she and her husband had recently purchased new furniture costing $1,728, a serious amount for furnishings in a period when four-poster beds could be purchased for as little as $10. The inventory of her estate also included much other furniture. When J. B. Louis Metoyer died the following year, his furnishings included a mahogany bookcase valued at $60, one of the most expensive bookcases found in any succession inventory, white or nonwhite, in the parish. Most of the furniture in his home was made of mahogany or cherry rather than the more affordable native cypress. When his son Théophile Louis drew up his marriage contract in 1843, the furnishings of his home included a piano.[63]

The probate sale of the succession of C. N. Rocques Sr. in 1859 included a steam bathtub that was purchased by the Widow Jean Baptiste Metoyer for $100 and a stove that was adjudicated to Rocques's widow for $30. A carpet from the Rocques home was bought at the sale by the immigrant French physician Isidore Gimbert; and the inventory of Auguste Predanes Metoyer's home included an iron safe where he kept his valuables. Two clocks, one of them valued at $35, and an organ appear in the estate left by Augustin Metoyer and his wife—likely the organ that provided the music to which Dignowity dined. The succession of C. N. Rocques Jr. inventoried a special set of children's dishes, and numerous successions boasted sterling silver flatwear and serving pieces of the type that impressed Dignowity when set before him by Augustin's servants.[64]

Most of the fine furniture owned by the family passed through successive generations until the reversal of fortunes forced their sale. Pieces that remained in the late twentieth century included a huge oak table with a lazy-susan built into the center, a demitasse set, a marble-top dresser, and a grandfather clock, all of which once belonged to Augustin Metoyer. Another lazy-susan of silverplate is said to have been owned by Jean Baptiste Augustin. An antique pianoforte of rare design that once belonged to the Metoyers was purchased at a 1970 auction for display in the restored manor house of an early family of white planters on the Côte Joyeuse.[65] Recalling the huge old four-poster beds that his family had owned, one twentieth-century descendant offered the following description: "Posts on beds are about eight inches square at the bottom to about 4" × 4" at the top with a canopy (tester) that rests on the four posts. Side rail is about 18 inches wide. There is a large key to lock the side rail to the head and foot boards. The mosquito bar hung from a long rod around the bed inside the tester. The bar rod had rings all along two sides which slipped over the rods so the bar could be pulled back when not in use."[66]

Another descendant recalled that the oldest chairs preserved by her family were straight backed and covered with deer hide; later, cowhide. Her mother had inherited a marble pestle for crushing herbs and spices and an iron clock that "rang so loud you could hear it across the river."[67] An early cypress armoire of the indigenous variety—preserved within the Morin-Roques-Chelettre family—boasted straight, clean lines that complemented its petite size; round wooden pegs held the armoire together without screws or nails; the pegs' perfection marked the work of a proud craftsman.[68]

One of the most treasured items displayed by twentieth-century descendants was a small crystal mug with an ivory bust of Napoleon. Reportedly, there had been eight "brought back from France" by Jérôme Sarpy when "he accompanied Augustin on their last trip abroad." The set was divided when Sarpy died, at which time each of the mugs was said to be inherited by a different child.[69]

Of all the refinements and advantages the people enjoyed, the one they appreciated the most—and the one most critical to the preservation of their freedom and civil rights—was their education. Many of the multiracial Creoles on the Isle possessed a higher level of education than did most whites with whom they did business. Numerous business documents show the signature of a person of color in beautiful, flowing script set beside a white associate's mark of a cross.

Only one of the first-generation Metoyers, Pierre, had been literate. His schooling, likely the tutelage of his father, was the exception to the norm in their era. An 1803 report on affairs in Louisiana complained that there was no college at all in the province, only one public school (at New Orleans), and only a few private schools. "Not more than half of the inhabitants," it was reported, "are supposed to be able to read and write, of whom not more than two hundred perhaps are able to do it well."[70]

Despite the limits of their educational opportunities, the original Metoyer siblings made certain that their children fared better. By whom those early children of the Isle were educated is not known, but Dignowity offers a snippet of insight: "He [M'sieur Metoyer] told me that on account of existing prejudices, him and other planters of negro Blood send their children to be educated in France."[71] Extant evidence partially supports that account. When the second-generation Metoyers came to adulthood, about 1820, all but one of the males were literate. The majority of the females of this second generation, however, could not sign their names; and most other free people of color of Natchitoches Parish with whom they intermarried labored under the same handicap. Of the third generation, all the males and most females were literate. The signature of Widow C. N. Rocques Jr. in 1854 is particularly revealing. Signing a document as guardian of her minor children, she wrote "Marie Anaïs Metoyer, pour moimême et pour enfants mineurs" in script more elegant than that of the notary who drafted the document.[72]

The prejudice of which Augustin spoke was not peculiar to Louisiana. In many antebellum states, teaching a person of color, free or enslaved, to read and write was a crime. In Louisiana such instruction was tacitly tolerated but not publicly encouraged. Public schools came into existence in Louisiana in 1841, but none of them admitted children of color—an ironic restriction considering that Louisiana's first superintendent of education, Alexandre Dimitry, was himself the grandson of a freed slave whose family prominence had allowed him to cross the color line.[73] Those public schools were also slow to take hold in the Louisiana upcountry. The 1850 census of Natchitoches Parish noted the existence of only one public school, with one teacher to whom $320 was paid as an annual salary. The 1860 census enumerated forty public schools, one male (Catholic) college, and one private female academy (also Catholic). None of these schools were located on the Isle, and none accepted students of color.[74] In all cases during this period, the instruction that Cane River's multiracial children received was private.

Tradition holds that one of the earliest teachers on the Isle was the French immigrant Louis Chevalier, who—prior to his arrival on the Isle—had taken a woman of color as his lifelong common-law wife. Chevalier supposedly held a degree from a major European university, perhaps the Sorbonne.[75] No known records prove or disprove this tradition. The earliest identifiable teacher within the community was Nicolas Charles LeRoy, a native of Marseilles, who came to the United States in December 1828 at the age of forty-four, having "crossed the ocean in order to live in a free country and to be more independent."[76]

Arriving in Natchitoches Parish in the early 1830s, LeRoy found employment on Isle Brevelle.[77] By 1841 he had left the community to teach the children of the wealthy white planters on the Côte Joyeuse. LeRoy apparently remained on friendly terms with the multiracial Creoles, even though he had quit their service. A letter he wrote to Auguste Metoyer in 1841 began with "Mon cher Auguste," proceeded to convey his regards for the addressee's wife and daughter, and was signed "votre tout devotée."[78]

The apparent successor to LeRoy was Bernard Dauphin, the first of several free men of color known to have taught on the Isle at various times during the late antebellum years. Dauphin's tenure was not a long one. In 1843, shortly after his marriage to Marie Barbe Mélisine Metoyer, daughter of Jean Baptiste Augustin, he was buried in the Metoyer family cemetery attached to the Chapel of St. Augustine. In his memory, the grieving community carved an epithet on his tomb that reveals not only Dauphin's character, but also something of the values held by the people of the Isle: "Son amour pour la littérature reflechessair les plus rares vertus."[79]

The memorial to Dauphin was appropriate. This gifted young man of letters was one of seventeen Creoles of color whose works appear in the small and rare anthology, *Les Cenelles*. In presenting Dauphin's work, his editor muses: "As to the clarity of thought, as well as the purity of the language, nothing in these selected poems surpasses the excellence of the strophe here produced." That strophe also suggests complications within Dauphin's marriage to his teenaged bride, raising questions for which no known records provide answers:

ADIEUX

Dearest one, why have you
So soon dispelled the transports of my love?
Do you remember the days when you were so enamored
And you promised me a happiness without regret?
Adieu, good-bye, pardon if my faithful heart
Cannot detach itself from you;
I am going to pay today with my life
For the happy day when I received your trust.

> Good-bye, from the celestial vault of heaven
> I will watch over your destiny;
> There will end the unhappiness of life,
> Which already approaches its end;

When tormented by a secret pain,
Your fickle heart will recognize the sorrow
Come, pray to God at my tomb, please
For there you will be reborn to happiness.
And the Eternal One hearing your prayer,
In memory of our past love,
Will place a flower on the marble tomb
Which will cover my dried remains;

> Good-bye from the celestial vault of heaven,
> I will watch over your destiny;
> There will end the unhappiness of life,
> Which already approaches its end.[80]

Other *hommes de couleur libres* followed Bernard Dauphin at the school on Isle Brevelle. Oscar Dubreuil, who taught in the early 1850s, and Firmin C. Christophe Jr., who taught a decade later, were both New Orleanians. Native sons, as well, served as tutors to the youth of the Isle. Émile Chevalier, the oldest son of Louis Chevalier and his placée Fanny, and Oscar Dupré, son of Emanuel Dupré and Marie Marguerite Metoyer, are said to have studied in their childhood under Louis Chevalier and LeRoy. Upon reaching maturity, they became teachers themselves.[81]

In the earliest years, education along Cane River was grounded in the French language and culture. Jean Baptiste Dominique Metoyer and Emanuel Dupré, members of the second generation, were both educated men who penned many surviving documents. Nonetheless, when in 1839 a document was drafted for them in the English language, it was necessary for the notary to attest that he had read the document to them and translated it into French before they signed it. In the next generation, many members of the clan became fluent in both languages. Olmsted's 1853 informant who observed how "well educated" Cane River's Creoles were, also reported that they spoke "French among themselves, but all are able to converse in English also."[82]

In discussing the type of education provided in the Isle Brevelle schools, Callahan described an old, handwritten textbook owned by the late Jean Conant:

The first and larger part . . . is a complete treatise on Bookkeeping, both single and double entry. It explains the theory and gives examples illustrating the whole process. It is the completest treatise in the whole book, evidently important for the education of future planters and merchants. The manuscript is beautifully written; at first sight it looks like a steel engraving. Students got a broad idea of commerce, transactions are noted with Paris, Rouen, Nantes, Metz, Perpignan, as well as with New Orleans and Mexico.

The rest of the manuscript is also important and interesting. The instruction in this part is catechetical. It consists of a series of questions and answers on various subjects. They are so divided as to give a general cultural knowledge. The titles are: The Sphere, Geology, Civics, Astronomy, Geometry, Greek and Roman History. The title, The Sphere, is concerned with the general geography of the globe, the countries of Europe, then particularly France and the United States, as of the time it was written. The list of presidents ends with Jackson. There are only a few torn pages giving examples of arithmetic. The whole course covered what might be called general information from the Great Wall of China to where sugar cane originated and its travels to reach the United States. Many of the questions would stump the college graduate of today. The teacher of those days would make a marvellous quiz-master on television; but I dare say he would not have to give away much money.[83]

Other topically diverse texts used on the Isle included *Civil Code of the State of Louisiana* (1838); Alexandré Dumas, *Mémoires d'un médecin: La Comtesse de Charny* (1856); M. Noel & M. Chapsal, *Leçons d'analyse grammaticale* (1838); A. G. Maillet, *Traité complète des verbes irrégulières, simples et composés de la langue Anglaise* (n.d.); *McGuffey's Third Eclectic Reader* (n.d.); *Le Nouveau Parfait Jardinier; ou, L'Art de cultiver* (1835); *Histoire Romain depuis la fondation de Rome* (1831); *Les Aventures de Télémaque, fils d'Ulysse* (1850); Smith, *English and French Dictionary* (n.d., but published in Paris); and *A Pilgrimage to the Holy Land* (1832).[84]

After the creation of their own schools, the Cane River families continued to send their brightest young men to the North or to France for university study. Among those credited with receiving a year of continental education were Sévère Dupré, Arnould Conant, and Vilfried Metoyer. Young Vilarco Llorens was also sent abroad, it is said, but suffered an acute case of homesickness and returned to Louisiana almost immediately.[85]

Some writers have proposed that whatever organized education existed for Louisiana's free people of color was usually provided by the church.[86] Along Cane River, church schools were a cherished goal but short tenured, once accomplished. In 1856 after Bishop Martin declared the mission of Isle Brevelle to be a parish in its own right, he purchased from a white resident of the Isle a small house and a tract of land on which a school could be established. The Daughters of the Cross, who had established a convent for girls in Avoyelles Parish the year before, were invited to open a branch on the Isle, and the order accepted. Later that year, Mother Superior Hyacinthe LeConniat, of the Avoyelles convent, wrote to her brother in France about the new plans: "Our first mission house will be in Île Brevelle. . . . Father Martin has charge of this mission and the population is all mulatto. These are people of leisure and many of wealth and means. The Bishop bought us a house with sixty acres of land there. It will form a small establishment for three or four Sisters. As soon as the finances of our Bishop permit, he will fix the house, which right now is in mighty poor shape. We will go there when things are repaired."[87]

By January 1858, the school had opened its doors. Mother Hyacinthe again wrote her brother:

> The Île Brevelle house is progressing well. We have already twenty-seven pupils and in the spring we will have forty or fifty more for sure. This is a simple school—a modest school. The students pay $4 a month, that is twenty francs and something. Next year, we will take some boarders. The people of this parish, although they are very rich, are disdained by the white people who do not want the mulattoes in their schools. So, here we will have only mulattoes. These good people gave us $1,100 to $1,200 to build two houses. We have here more land than in Avoyelles. One of the classrooms has been transformed into a chapel. The Blessed Sacrament is reserved there. Father Martin [the bishop's brother, whom he had appointed to St. Augustine Parish] is but one mile from us [and] had the kindness to come three or four times last week to say Mass for us.[88]

The physical work on the school remained unfinished when St. Joseph de l'Île Brevelle opened its doors. The church authorities were still awaiting two thousand pieces of lumber that had been ordered from New Orleans to make not only a floor for the dirt-bottomed structure but also tables for the classrooms, a refectory, some benches, and a partition in the chapel. Two gardens were being laid out as well.[89]

The mission school soon outgrew its accommodations. By 1859 between 120 and 130 girls had enrolled. The nuns had also concluded that the one-mile trek between the convent and the church was much too far a walk to daily mass in the summer heat and winter cold. Again, the islanders raised the funds for a new building, a striking contribution considering the litany of complaints Mother Hyacinthe privately lodged against less generous and more quarrelsome white parents at the Avoyelles school. The new Cane River convent stood next to St. Augustine Church; its enlargement allowed the order to accept as boarders the girls who lived too distant to commute daily. Additional nuns were brought in as enrollment continued to increase.[90]

Through 1862 the school flourished; but war wrought hardships and financial reverses, and the enrollment plummeted at St. Joseph Convent. Federal troops established themselves on Red River and made communication even more difficult between the mother convent at Avoyelles and the mission on Cane River. The mother superior obtained from one general a promise of safe conduct for any provisions she sent to the nuns on the Isle, but the mission convent was doomed. By December 1863, it had closed.[91]

Almost a century later, the resident priest for St. Augustine Parish would observe: "The people of Isle Brevelle have a traditional respect for education."[92] That observation is grounded in a plethora of records. The succession inventories of those who died in the antebellum era itemize many lots of books and other items indicative of their education. The succession of C. N. Rocques Jr. in 1854 included three lots that sold for $3. The number of volumes in each lot was not indicated; but the inventory of property belonging to the schoolmaster LeRoy in that period included six hundred volumes valued at $60, or ten cents per volume. At this rate, Rocques's three lots would have contained some thirty books. Other Rocques tomes included a fifteen-volume set titled *Esprit de Enciclopédie,* which sold for $15 to an inductee into the family, the former Prudhomme slave (and son) Edward Séverin. The inventory and appraisement of the estate of Auguste Predanes Metoyer in 1865 included one lot of books valued at $6, a *Colton's Atlas* at $8, a writing desk, and a secretary.[93]

Although the quantity and value of such private libraries were small by modern standards, they were significant in the mid-nineteenth century. The census of 1870 indicates that in the whole of the parish there were only twenty-three private libraries, including those of lawyers and clergymen, with an average of 107 volumes in each. The five-shelved bookcase that C. N. Rocques Sr. left at his death in 1859, valued at $40.50, would easily have held that number. The $60 bookcase in the 1838 succession of J. B. Louis Metoyer probably held many more.[94] Judging from all the instances in which Metoyer estates included sizable quantities of books, it is quite likely that a large percentage of those private libraries tallied by the 1870 census were located on Isle Brevelle.

Even homes with only a few books were still among the elite minority. According to Olmsted, one fellow traveler in Louisiana informed him that "he might travel several days, and call on a hundred planters, and hardly see in their houses more than a single newspaper apiece, in most cases; perhaps none at all; nor any books except a Bible, and some Government publications, that had been franked to them through the post-office, and perhaps a few religious tracts or school-books."[95]

Placed in a broader context, education was far more than a mere mark of gentility for Cane River's free Creoles of color. It was a critical tool for their survival. Each new generation had to be educated to stay abreast of increasingly restrictive laws imposed after Louisiana's absorption into the United States. The inventories of many successions from the 1820s forward included legal texts. Newspaper subscriptions were not meant to merely grace sitting rooms for guests such as Dignowity; those weekly journals kept Cane River families attuned to public attitudes that threatened their livelihood or their civil rights. Education on a par with that of prominent whites helped them defend their property and the virtue of their females—all issues that form the core of the next chapter.

By and large, Cane River free Creoles of color enjoyed a standard of living comparable to that of well-to-do middle-class white planters of their era. In the view of at least one contemporary observer, the quality of their life actually exceeded that of the very wealthy upper class. Olmsted's traveling companion argued that the middle-class planter worth $40,000 enjoyed a far more gracious life than one worth $300,000—a high mark that Coincoin's offspring never quite achieved. Olmsted, in fact, provides the best and most concise evaluation of the personal lives of Coincoin's offspring that was recorded by any contemporary: "If you have occasion to call at their houses . . . you will be received in a gentlemanly manner, and find they live in the same style with white people of the same wealth."[96]

In 1793, when Augustin Metoyer married and launched his new life on Isle Brevelle, he was a new freedman with a family to support. He had no education, no livelihood other than a laborer's trade that promised no rise beyond the yeoman class, and no property except for the raw land he hoped the Spanish crown would give him in return for his promise to develop it. Within sixty-five years—less than one lifetime—his family vanquished many of the stigmas of slavery, illegitimacy, illiteracy, and poverty.

The various observations that Olmsted recorded, views expressed by all classes from stage driver to merchant to planter to riverboat captain, emphasized the same key considerations: the conduct and lifestyle of the people. Clearly, the basis for their transformation into the ranks of "gentlemen" was their industry, their exemplary behavior, and their prosperity. The fortunes they accumulated, however gained, proved their astute business judgment and won the respect of a society that valued both personal and community betterment. Their wealth enabled them to have their own church, which made influential whites dependent upon their largesse, while impressing the public with their adherence to community standards of morality. Their pursuit of wealth saddled them with serious economic risks, worries, and substantial losses; but their gains bought them more land to support future generations, financed finer homes and accouterments, and earned for them the respect of industrious whites and the envy of less fortunate ones. Most significantly, the wealth of the people brought them education and culture, the two factors that bridged the ethnic chasms between the underclass of Natchitoches Parish and the privileged elite that controlled all matters economic, legal, and social in their society.

EIGHT

Racism and Citizenship

Coincoin's offspring had overcome many handicaps posed by slavery, poverty, illiteracy, and illegitimacy, but they were still *gens de couleur libres*. The most formidable barrier they faced remains to be examined: exercise of the rights of citizenship. What role did they play in a society that measured citizenship by the color of skin? What degree of prejudice did they suffer because of the slave ancestry that their tints and hues attested? What political and social privileges, if any, were allowed them because of their white kinships? Most important, in a society that pitted black against white, where lay the allegiance of these in-between people of Cane River?

In the 1830s, when the community's affluence peaked, a string of court decisions throughout the South underscored the tenuous legal status of those who were free but not white. A Tennessee appellate judge ruling on the conviction of a manumitted slave who had "feloniously and unlawfully" settled in that state, ruled that

> "Free Negroes have always been a degraded race in the United States, having the right . . . of controlling their own actions and enjoying the fruit of their own labor, but deprived of almost every other privilege of the free citizen, and constituting an inferior caste, with whom public opinion has never permitted the white population to associate on terms of equality, and in relation to whom the laws have never allowed the enjoyment of equal rights, or the immunities of the free white citizen."[1]

In the adjacent state of South Carolina, when a free-born man of color was unmercifully beaten and whipped by a white male, an 1832 appeals court judge also hinged his decision on the premise that nonwhites "belong to a degraded caste of society [and] are in no respect on an equality with a white man." Free Negroes, Judge John O'Neill contended, "ought by law to be compelled to demean themselves as inferiors, from whom submission and respect to the whites, in all their intercourse in society ought to be demanded."[2]

O'Neill's prejudice also carried nuances that sketch out the narrow trough within which free nonwhites were expected to channel their lives. Although he opined that "words of impertinence and insolence, addressed by a free negro to a white man, would justify an assault and battery," he also ruled, "No white man [has] the right . . . of correcting at pleasure a free negro. The peace of society is as much broken by an assault upon him as it is upon a white man. Like the latter, he has his passions, and with the means of attack and defense in his possession, if the law refused to protect him, he, too, at last, might be driven to repel force by force."[3]

Such racial discrimination was not confined to the South. Contemporaneously, debates over racial equality in the northern states were spawned by numerous issues, including an ideological battle over universal manhood suffrage. In Pennsylvania, New York, Rhode Island, and elsewhere, legislative opposition raised the specter of Negro and Native American voting. Negroes were denounced as "a peculiar people, incapable . . . of exercising that privilege with any sort of discretion, prudence, or independence." They were deemed a "distinct, inferior caste" that should be given no reason to presume entitlement "to equal rights and equal privileges with the white man, when, by our laws of society, they are not, and cannot be permitted to exercise them." From 1819 forward, virtually every northern state passed laws that denied "Negroes" the right to vote.[4]

"But we are not Negroes!" Cane River's Metoyer clan would have argued. "We are *gens de couleur libres.*" A clear distinction between the two existed among Louisiana's Creoles of color, but this distinction never gained a foothold in North American legal or social thought—except, supposedly, in Louisiana. Decades ago, historian Carl N. Degler reached a conclusion that still expresses conventional thought: "In the United States any person with Negro ancestry has been considered a Negro, even if he appeared to be white. In the days of slavery as later, in the days of legal separation, a Negro was defined in law and in custom as anyone with a certain amount of Negro ancestry— usually one-eighth."[5] Most of Cane River's Creoles of color fell within this legal definition, if only barely.

Occasional jurists, throughout the antebellum South, did argue a legal distinction between "Negro" and "people of color," but they were outliers at the bench and bar. When John Thurmond of Alabama was convicted in 1850 of raping a white woman, he was sentenced under a law that decreed death for any "slave, free negro, or mulatto" deemed guilty of that crime. His conviction was then overturned by the state's supreme court, which surveyed American case law north and south before settling on the most technical definition of *mulatto*: "the offspring of a negress by a white man or of a white woman by a negro." Thurman was, the court pointed out, the son of a white woman by a mulatto and so did not fall within the statutory provision that had been applied to him. The court augmented its ruling with an opinion based not on law but equity: "If the statute against mulattoes is by constriction to include quadroons, then where are we to stop? . . . Are we not bound to pursue the line of descendants, as long as there is a drop of negro blood remaining?"[6]

The irrationality of any degree-of-blood test is argued by historians who have studied racial laws in a global context. Degler, for example, contended that "no other country in the New World, with the exception of Canada, follows the United States in defining a black man as anyone with a measurable amount of Negro ancestry or 'blood.'"[7] That historic difference in racial attitudes between the United States and other contemporary cultures might, in fact, account for occasional inconsistencies found within rulings by southern antebellum courts. Just one year after South Carolina's Justice O'Neill disputed the right of free men of color to show impertinence or insolence toward whites, his colleague on the state's superior bench expressed a radically different view. Ruling in *State v. Cantey,* Justice William Harper decreed that a "vagabond" of color might be "confined to the inferior caste," while a "man of worth" of the "same degree of blood" could "have the rank of a white man."[8] The ideological disparity between those two judicial decisions could pivot on the cultural roots of the two justices: O'Neill was of Irish-American stock, while Harper was a native of the more racially liberal Antigua.[9]

A host of studies since Degler have argued his premise and some have fine-tailored it. Loren Schweninger recites a litany of laws passed across both the Upper and Lower South, laws designed to homogenize everyone with African ancestry. Joel Williamson emphasizes nuances within these laws, asserting: "Far from jumbling all blacks together, lower South Southerners and particularly Deep South Southerners, like their Latin American neighbors, were able to make minute distinctions among mulattoes by degree of mixture."[10]

Ideological discrepancies did exist, not only between regions or states but also within the individual states themselves. In Georgia, the most quixotic and punitive of all states in its treatment of free nonwhites, the 1837 legislature passed a measure designed to protect at least some rights of free persons of color—noting that they were "liable to be taken and held fraudulently and illegally, in a state of slavery, by wicked white men."[11] Just six years later, however, rival ideologues in the legislature pushed for a measure that was not just paternalistic but explicitly degrading. The factions compromised that year with a legislative resolution—not a mandate—declaring that "free negroes are *not citizens* under the Constitution of the United States 'and that Georgia will never recognize such citizenship.'"[12] In the run-up to the Civil War, that stance became statutory law in Georgia, with only two undefined conciliations:

> The free person of color is entitled to no right of citizenship, *except such as are specially given by law.* His status differs from that of the slave in this: No master having dominion over him he is entitled to the free use of his liberty, labor and property. . . . All laws enacted in reference to slaves, and in their nature applicable to free persons of color, shall be construed to include them, *unless specially excepted.*"[13]

Outside the United States, the recognition of a third caste offered a "mulatto escape hatch," as Degler termed it. There, laws created a political and social niche into which people of visible or known color could escape the arbitrary degradation of blackness—a middle ground upon which they could share some of the rights and responsibilities of citizenship.[14] Within continental North America, leanings toward that mindset can be found across the Gulf settlements in the colonial and antebellum years. They would not, however, withstand the acculturation of these regions to Anglo-American ideology as, chunk by chunk, the French and Spanish borderlands were absorbed into the United States.

In custom and law, colonial Louisiana accorded the free man of color most rights of citizenship but drew the line at social equality. This was the society into which Coincoin and her children had been born and the society to which her offspring clung. Long after Louisiana had become a part of the United States, they continued to refer to themselves as "French citizens." Even so, their daily life was delimited by discrimination in matters large and small. At one extreme, for example, interracial marriages had been proscribed from the beginning of the colony, and that ban shaped every contour of the existence Coincoin's offspring lived for generations to come. At the other extreme, petty regulations constantly reminded them that their "citizenship" was second-class. A 1786 ordinance, for example, forbade women of color to show excessive attention to their dress. Feathers, jewelry, caps, and mantillas so popular among stylish Creole ladies were specifically forbidden to women of color, who, the law decreed, must bind their heads at all times in a handkerchief, or *tignon*. While some free multiracials in New Orleans rebelled against such daily injustices, their Natchitoches counterparts chafed in silence.[15]

The Louisiana Purchase of 1803 unleashed a wave of trans-Mississippi migration that would challenge the territory's traditional culture and values. Most newcomers were yeoman farmers from the southern seaboard states, where racial lines had hardened. But the opportunities of the area also enticed hordes of merchants and entrepreneurs out of New York and New England; and a slew of new U.S. forts throughout the territory, including one at Natchitoches, brought military personnel from all parts of the nation. Historian Thomas Fiehrer has well described the reaction of the newcomers at their exposure to the old regime: "The South's creole populations represented an anomaly at best, and a menace at worst. They were attached to a foreign power, an unpopular European Church, a language associated with rationalism, decadence, and revolution, with customs that smacked of scandal, and a cuisine too African to contemplate."[16]

Those who would suffer most from the ensuing clash of ideologies were the members of that intermediary caste. Cane River's Creoles of color and their counterparts across the new Territory of Orleans lost their "escape hatch." From that point forward, retaining their rights to dignity, property, and, ultimately, freedom required legal vigilance. That vigilance required education. That education—as well as the wherewithal to mount legal defenses—required significant discretionary funds and capital reserves. In the agriculturally driven South, that kind of financial leverage came from success in the agri-slave economy. Amid these dynamics, the struggle of the free man of color to survive as free drove a wedge into brown-black relations along Cane River that would persist into the modern era.

Louisiana's *Code Noir* was the target of the first session of the first territorial legislature in 1806. Its replacement limited the privileges of all men of color, slave or free. It tightened immigration laws to prevent an influx of more free people of color from the West Indies. It decreed that those already in Louisiana were to appear before authorities and give proof of their freedom or be classed as runaway slaves. Any free people of color carrying guns were required to carry also their freedom papers.[17]

Many more discriminatory laws would follow. At its second session, the territorial legislature sought to further stanch the increase in Louisiana's free brown population by forbidding manumissions of anyone under the age of thirty. Toward that end, it installed a process designed to impede rather than facilitate freedom—including petitions to the parish judge, a public posting of notification, a thirty-day waiting period, clearance by creditors, and a final hearing.[18] In 1808 the legislature decreed that all public documents referring to free people of color must stigmatize them with the specific words "free man of color," "free woman of color," or the appropriate abbreviation after the surname of the individual.[19] In 1812, when Louisiana was granted statehood, suffrage was limited to whites. During the next half-century, other restrictions would strip the free multiracial of such responsibilities of citizenship as military and jury service and take from him various social and economic privileges.[20]

These measures were not necessarily accepted by the white Creole population. According to one analysis, "When the ancient customs and traditions conflicted with the [new American] code, there were many in Louisiana who sought to evade and nullify the law." Indeed, the conflict between French tradition and American law at one point became so serious that a judge was forced to rule that the "decisions of the courts of France" were no longer legally binding in Louisiana.[21] Obviously, the people of Cane River were not alone when they continued to regard themselves as "French citizens."

The disintegration of legal rights for Louisiana's Creoles of color can be tracked by comparing six benchmarks across the eighteenth and nineteenth centuries: presumption of freedom, the right to bear arms, the right of self-protection, the right to live where one pleased, the right to equal justice before the law, and the question of allegiance to the white-dominated regime.

The right to a presumption of freedom was an issue that the British colonies and their successive states differentially defined for their inhabitants of white, black, or red ancestry. An 1858 summary of prevailing laws, north and south, summarized the distinctions this way:

> The presumption in relation to the Indian is that he is free, and it is incumbent on the party alleging slavery to show his title.
>
> White persons may not be enslaved or held as slaves, except by express statutory enactment. The presumption of freedom arises from the color.
>
> As all the negroes introduced into America were brought as slaves, the black color of the race raises the presumption of slavery, "contrary

to the principles of the common law, which would presume freedom until the contrary is shown." This presumption is extended, in most of the States, to mulattoes or persons of mixed blood, casting upon them the onus of proving a free maternal ancestor. In others, it is confined to the negroes.[22]

With regard to those "mulattoes or persons of mixed blood," the laws of only two Anglo-rooted states distinguished brown from black in the presumption of freedom: "In Virginia and Kentucky," the 1858 legal scholar noted, "one-fourth negro blood presumes slavery, less than that, freedom."[23] The 1715 Maryland law that first linked blackness to the presumption of slavery also set penalties that became the pattern for other colonies and states: nonwhites without free papers on their person were subject to arrest; those who were unable to prove satisfactorily that they were not runaways were returned to their last master or sold into servitude to pay the costs of their detention and trial.[24] The social compact that supported this ideology would not be eradicated by either the Revolution or antislavery legislation. The new state of Connecticut, for example, enacted a constitution that outlawed slavery; yet, for years to come, unprotected children of color would continue to be sold and resold via conveyances that consigned them to servitude "for life."[25]

Officials of the new territory of Orleans sought to bring Louisiana's racial laws into the national fold. For decades thereafter, Louisiana's supreme court had to revisit the demarcation line between slavery and freedom, creating a more nuanced set of bounds for the presumption of freedom in Louisiana. The 1810 decision reached in *Adéle v. Beauregard* was more akin to, but a bit more liberal than, the Virginia-Kentucky doctrine: "Persons of color are presumed free—Negroes otherwise." Indeed, the court ruled, "Considering how much probability there is in favor of the liberty of these [multiracial] persons, they ought not to be deprived of it upon mere presumption."[26] The safeguards of that 1810 ruling, however, would be watered down in 1824 by *English v. Latham,* which decreed that "proof of servile *origin*" trumped that presumption of freedom.[27]

With court protection, Louisiana's free people of color managed to preserve vestiges of their third-caste status, but the challenge continued throughout the antebellum years. In 1845 the court was forced to reaffirm existing case law: "Ever since the case of *Adelle* vs. *Beauregard* it has been the settled doctrine here, that persons of color are presumed to be free. . . . The presumption is in favor of freedom, and the burden of proof is on him who claims the colored person as a slave."[28] Again in 1856, as legal historian Judith Schafer points out, the court's majority reiterated its opinion that "free people of color were totally different from slaves and that the difference was as great as the one between white men and women"—but the decision was not unanimous. The dissent penned by the New Hampshire–born, Amherst-educated Henry M. Spofford argued that "slaves and free persons of color composed 'a single, homogeneous class of beings, distinguished from all others by nature, custom and law. . . . No colored person can be a citizen.'"[29] That yes-you-are but no-you-aren't dichotomy aptly depicts the status of Cane River lives. In the 1984 assessment of Gary B. Mills, Cane River's *gens de couleur libres* held the presumption of freedom, and they were viewed as "worthy and unique *citoyens* of old Louisiana," but they were *citoyens*—not *citizens*. Theirs was an ephemeral world in which they "enjoyed *liberté, fraternité,* and everything else but *égalité*."[30]

The right to bear arms provides another benchmark by which to measure the position of Louisiana slaves and free Creoles of color against the scales of citizenship. In 1757, when Coincoin's black father was arrested amid an investigation of thefts by slaves at the Natchitoches post, his powerful owners defended him as a man they trusted to carry a gun.[31] In that same year, Virginia prohibited free Negroes or part-Negroes from bearing arms, even in the state militia. While they were liable for duty, they must "appear without arms, [to] be employed as drummers, trumpeters, or pioneers, or in such other servile labor as they shall be directed to perform."[32] That policy, adopted by most other Anglo colonies, contrasted starkly with that of Creole Louisiana. When Spain inserted itself into the American Revolution in opposition to England, Louisiana not only outfitted two complete units of free men of color in New Orleans and permitted free nonwhites at the other posts to join local units, but went so far as to arm slaves and give them the opportunity to defend the territory in exchange for their freedom. After the first of their engagements, Governor Bernardo de Gálvez reported to Madrid that these two companies "behaved on all occasions with as much valor and generosity as the white soldiers." At his request, the Crown bestowed medals of honor upon ten of their officers.[33]

Military service, as a privileged obligation of citizenship, was one of the first nonwhite rights targeted after the Louisiana Purchase. Indeed, days before the transfer actually occurred, the Maryland-born general James Wilkinson penned a letter from New Orleans to the secretary of war—one that obviously appraised Louisiana's own ripeness for a Haitian-inspired revolt:

Everything in the city is still tranquil, & I feel no alarm.—but I conjure you sir, as you value the continuation of this tranquility, dispose of a Garrison of 500 Regulars for the place as soon as possible, for indeed I apprehend difficulties from various causes—*The formidable aspect of the armed Blacks & mulattoes, officered & organized, is painful & perplexing*.[34]

Despite at least one recommendation that it was "worth the consideration of the government [that the free brown population] be made good citizens," the new regime proceeded to revise Louisiana's statutes in order to align them more closely with those of the other American states.[35] After first decreeing that "no slave shall, by day or by night, carry any visible or hidden arms, not even with a permission for so doing," the new regime revealed its willingness to take away the rights of free nonwhites as a means of better controlling slaves: "As slaves may declare themselves free, free coloured persons, who carry arms, are expressly directed . . . to carry with them a certificate of a justice of the peace, attesting their freedom, for want of which they shall be subject to the penalty of the nineteenth section of this act"— that is, the seizure and forfeiture of their weapons.[36]

The state of emergency created by British incursions into the Gulf during the War of 1812 temporarily overrode public concerns over armed nonwhites. Louisiana's free men of color were conditionally allowed to form militia units to assist in the defense of the city. When nonwhites in Natchitoches Parish petitioned the governor for a special authorization to form an auxiliary unit of no more than eighty-four men, their request was approved with two caveats. One, they must furnish their own arms and horses. Two, only those who possessed property worth at least one hundred dollars could serve.[37] Given that Coincoin's offspring along Cane River represented 45 percent of the households headed by free people of color in the parish and 73 percent of the property owners who fit that criterion, it is reasonable to assume they also made up most of the patriots who formed this militia unit.[38]

By the 1820s, many southern states were passing even more restrictive gun-control measures aimed at the free nonwhite population. Maryland, in 1824, denied "free Negroes" the privilege of owning firearms. By the outbreak of the Civil War, all southern states had followed suit, Louisiana excepted.[39] The enforcement of Louisiana's less-stringent gun-ownership limitations against nonwhites appears to have been left to the discretion of local officials. Along Cane River, the successions of Creoles of color inventoried guns and ammunition, sometimes in large quantities and often of considerable value. Considering that many of these items were auctioned at succession sales conducted by the parish sheriff and attended by whites, and that many such items were purchased there by other men of color, it is improbable that Natchitoches officials enforced the letter of the law. Too, given the renown of the Metoyers and their kin in the area, it is doubtful that the regulation requiring the possession of freedom papers on one's person while carrying a gun was enforced unless members traveled into other parishes.

Local discretion in the application of laws is also evident from the number of inventories and court papers that reference slaves whose occupation was said to be "hunter." The 1806 Black Code expressly decreed that "inhabitants who keep slaves for the . . . purpose of hunting, shall never deliver to the said slaves any fire arms . . . without a permission by writing, which shall not serve beyond the limits of the plantation of the owners."[40] Even so, Cane River accounts survive of community-wide hunting and fishing parties consisting of white, slave, and free nonwhite planters; and surviving court records for the parish yield no evidence of permissions being sought or granted for the arming of enslaved hunters.

A third benchmark, the right of self-protection, reflects more than any other the struggle of free people of color to maintain some semblance of personal dignity. The South Carolina appeals court ruling that free nonwhites "belong to a degraded caste [and] ought by law to be compelled to demean themselves as inferiors"[41] had its counterpart in contemporary Louisiana law. By the terms of the 1806 legislation, "Free People of Color ought never to insult or strike white people, nor presume to conceive themselves equal to the white, but on the contrary, they ought to yield to them in every occasion, and never speak or answer to them but with respect, under the penalty of imprisonment, according to the nature of the offense."[42]

The black code institutionalized in Louisiana's American regime did not simply pattern itself after that of the older American states. Parts of it were already chiseled in colonial law and culture. One of the earliest Louisiana cases involving a free man of color occurred in 1747, when a free-born "mulatto" named Étienne LaRue, a native of Senegal who had come to the colony as a pilot on the ship *L'Unique,* was gratuitously insulted by three French soldiers on the streets of New Orleans. He responded with a verbal insult of his own, and a brawl ensued in which he attempted to defend himself against a beating by the three soldiers. His self-defense resulted in his arrest by a passing constable. The "well-mauled" man of color would spend eleven days shackled hand and foot in the New Orleans dungeon and pay a fine of

110 livres to the hospital that was said to have attended his attackers.[43] In a twist of historical irony—or, at least, a foreshadowing of ignominies to come—the French soldier who instigated the attack on the man of color, Mathieu Monet, was also the progenitor of many of the Cane River *hommes de couleur libres* who suffered assaults on their own dignity throughout the nineteenth century.[44]

Cane River's Creoles of color were keenly aware of this discriminatory clause in the law. They managed it with the only means available: quiet dignity and strict formality in their dealings with whites. One of the less prosperous members of the community, the "handsome, light coloured young barber" whom Olmsted interviewed on board the steamship *Dalmau,* offered some insight into their personality and attitude: "They rather avoided white people. . . . They were uncertain of their position with them, and were afraid, if they were not reserved, they would be thought to be taking liberties, and would be subject to insults, which they could not very well resent." On the other hand, Olmsted's informant reported, there were some whites whom the people knew quite well and with whom they were very much at ease.[45]

On at least one occasion, a craftsman of the clan was accused of violating this code of interracial behavior. In 1828, Joseph Marie Rabalais, a white resident of Cane River, filed charges of attack and battery against Émile Dupart, a New Orleanian who had married Louis Metoyer's granddaughter. According to Rabalais's accusations, lodged with the Cloutierville justice of the peace Jean Pierre Marie Dubois, he had visited Dupart's blacksmith shop to request five dollars that Dupart owed him. Although his request was polite, Rabalais alleged, Dupart responded with menacing words and actions, advanced toward him, struck him in the face, and knocked his hat to the ground.

Witnesses were present at the alleged affray: Dupart's in-law Jean Baptiste Louis Metoyer and a white neighbor, Lestan Langlois. Both swore under oath that unpleasant words indeed had been exchanged, that Dupart took a step toward Rabalais, and that the latter's hat then fell of its own accord. Neither witness believed that the blacksmith actually struck the white Creole. The extant records in the files of this justice of the peace do not reveal the outcome of the case, but the parish records at Natchitoches indicate no conviction or sentence against Dupart.[46]

Free but poor people of color who were unaffiliated with the Metoyer clan fared less well in their conflicts with whites. Their impotence, when they lacked the wherewithal to defend themselves (as they usually did), was not just a personal problem. It posed a threat to the survival of their class. Any conviction provided both a precedent for limiting the rights of their caste and encouragement to unscrupulous whites who wanted to reduce their numbers through incarceration or reenslavement for alleged offenses. In those cases, leaders of the Cane River community provided both the initiative and the funds to mount the needed defense.

A case at point is that of 1831 when the Anglo newcomer John Penn demanded the arrest of a young woman of the Côte Joyeuse named Marie Desneiges, alleging that she had "abused, assaulted, and beat" him. Marie, at that time, was the legal property of her mother, a free black woman named Babet, who still held her daughter in slavery because Marie had not yet reached the minimum age (thirty years) for legal manumission. Penn, via his attorney Victor Hennessy, pushed this point, insisting that Marie be tried under the penal code that applied to slaves. Because neither Babet nor Marie had the funds to post bail, Marie was incarcerated in the parish jail, awaiting trial. When her plight became news, Jean Baptiste Augustin Metoyer stepped in as agent for the two hapless women. He presented a defense before the parish judge, John C. Carr—an English immigrant who had married into a prominent Creole family of the Côte Joyeuse—and secured a ruling that Marie's arrest was illegal. The case State of Louisiana vs. Marie Desneiges was not prosecuted further. Tradition holds that, in cases such as this, the Metoyer community "settled" with the complainants out of court—using their own financial resources to preserve the freedom of other nonwhites who lived on the margins of economic and political survival.[47]

A fourth benchmark, the right to migrate freely within and across political jurisdictions, was one limited by most American colonies and states. As early as 1717, citizens of New London, Connecticut—a colony that regularly "warned out" white newcomers of limited means lest they become a public charge—petitioned the general assembly to deny free Negroes the right to own property anywhere in the colony.[48] The proposal never became law, but the attempt spoke clearly to the public mindset. By 1793, Virginia had passed legislation that went even further: it entirely barred free people of color from entering its bounds. Most states, north and south, followed suit. Leon Litwack's study of free Negroes north of the Mason-Dixon line concluded that "nearly every northern state considered, and many adopted, measures to prohibit or restrict the further immigration of Negroes."[49]

Colonial Louisiana, like Connecticut and other New England colonies, had its own limits against free movement, albeit for radically different reasons. While New England towns denied "freeman" status to those it feared would become a financial burden, Louisiana's frontier settlements restricted the right to *leave* an outpost where settlers capable of bearing arms were needed.[50] This same need for settlers prompted Spanish Louisiana to welcome all incomers, regardless of color, and to offer generous grants to all free heads of household, whether they were white, black, or multiracial. It was this lenient policy of the colonial Louisiana government that had enabled Coincoin and her children to lay the foundations of the wealth they would enjoy in the Anglo-American regime. As an American territory and state, Louisiana did not adopt legislation that limited ingress or egress to free people of color, although some local efforts were proposed and, in New Orleans, attempted.[51]

Equal justice under the law was never available to free people of color in Louisiana, but it was a benchmark on which they ranked significantly higher than their counterparts elsewhere. Throughout the South and much of the North, free nonwhites were denied the right to testify in court against a white. They were, in fact, prohibited from even instituting a suit against a white in most states before the Civil War.[52] By contrast, Creoles of color were permitted free access to Louisiana's courts of law. Not only were they entitled to defend themselves legally against whites, but they could bring charges against whites as well. Their testimony was accepted in every type of litigation. As late as 1850, the supreme court of Louisiana pointed out that many free people of color were "respectable from [*sic*] their intelligence, industry, and habits of good order. Many . . . are enlightened by education and . . . [are] large property holders." The word of such people, the court decreed, should be accepted without hesitation by any court or jury.[53]

Court records throughout the state attest the persistence with which free people of color defended their rights within this system. Brasseaux and Oubre's study of south Louisiana's bayou country asserts that "prairie Creoles of Color were well aware of their legal rights [and] very aggressive in using the legal system to protect their property and civil rights."[54] Anecdotally, that aggressiveness might also be attributed to Cane River's Creoles of color. However, a statistical analysis of free nonwhite legal actions at Natchitoches in the 1806–45 period for which parish court records survive demonstrates not so much aggression as unwavering resolve. The twenty-seven suits launched by free people of color against whites represented scarcely 2 percent of the court cases filed, while nonwhites ranged from 9 to 14 percent of the free population. The complaints of those free multiracials ranged from debt to false imprisonment, from assault and battery to the destruction of their homes. In slightly over half of the suits, the judgment favored the person of color.[55]

The Natchitoches legal cases also attest class and caste differences in the use of these opportunities. Virtually all the twenty-seven parish court cases in which free people of color were plaintiffs involved the Metoyer clan. Other cases in which the plantiffs were white but the defendants were not typically involved manumitted slaves without supportive family networks. In both the parish and district courts, Coincoin's offspring sued or were sued by whites, gave testimony against whites, swore out complaints against them for unwanted sexual advances, or came to the defense of less fortunate free-colored neighbors. Two extraordinarily expensive litigations occurred across the 1830s and 1840s, both involving Augustin Metoyer and whites who challenged his ownership of property. One or possibly both of them appear to be the basis of the 1853 rumor reported to Olmsted that a Cane River multiracial had expended $40,000 to defend his rights in a case before the local courts.[56]

Metoyer himself launched the first suit in 1832, charging encroachment upon land he had owned for over three decades. He had, records show, bought two adjacent tracts of land soon after his 1797 trip to Nacogdoches to buy the freedom of his half-brother Nicolas. The land was intended, and used, as a place upon which to settle that brother. It lay not on Isle Brevelle, but a few miles north of Natchitoches in the Camptí–Spanish Lake area, where the multiracial DeMézières-Trichel-Grappe community had begun to develop. After the Louisiana Purchase, Metoyer filed the appropriate paperwork with the U.S. Land Office to obtain a U.S. patent, and his title to one of the tracts was confirmed in 1812. The title to the other, like much of the land in that area, remained in limbo until 1829, when the United States finally set the bounds for all tracts in that particular township and range.[57]

Early in 1832, a French immigrant named Alexandre DeBlieux, by then well married and highly placed in the socioeconomic structure of the parish, sent workers upon one of the tracts and refused to withdraw them. Metoyer engaged the legal firm of Boyce & Barry to file suit for $2,000 in damages, plus $500 for the use of the land. Litigation would continue for thirteen years as a morass of claims emerged. DeBlieux presented documents attesting that he had legally leased the land from a New Orleans merchant, Jean Baptiste LePrêtre, who claimed a confirmed title that chained back to the free woman of color Rosette Mézières. Amid their complaints and rejoinders, a third claim to the land was filed by Anglo-French heirs of another early settler of the neighborhood, alleging that the Spanish government had granted the land to their grandfather. Numerous settlers of the region were subpoenaed to attest their knowledge of the tract's occupancy and ownership.[58]

Relatively little of the case file remains. Four surviving documents point to the probable cause of the suit, as well as its outcome. An undated filing by DeBlieux's attorney expressed the opinion that any title Metoyer held to the property would have been "obtained through fraud." However, he quickly added that the fraud was "not on the part of Augustin Metoyer himself but [by] Joseph Irwin, a former Surveyor of the U. States." The second document, a new survey plat created in November 1837, demonstrates a serious error by Irwin, whereupon Irwin's earlier plat of the DeBlieux-Leprêtre-Mézières tract clearly overlay one tract surveyed for Augustin. The third document, dated April 29, 1845, reports the final judgment issued by the court via a warrant notifying Metoyer that "judgment has been rendered against him of nonsuit at his costs." DeBlieux then signed a receipt acknowledging that he was withdrawing from the case file the plat for the tract that was adjudged to be his.[59]

Ironically (or perhaps not), the residence of Coincoin's oldest black son, Nicolas, lay at the heart of the second suit Augustin Metoyer litigated concurrently with his action against DeBlieux. This suit was one Metoyer did not initiate, but it was one he would eventually win. Off and on in his young adulthood, Nicolas had also worked—and occasionally lived on—a tract of cypress land on Little River, at the backside of Augustin's plantation. Nicolas had filed an occupancy claim for the land with the U.S. government; but in 1819, long before the title was confirmed, he sold Augustin his rights to the land and returned to the Spanish Lake community. There, the federal census taker had found him in residence in 1820.[60]

By the twists and turns of the waterways along Isle Brevelle, Nicolas's land also lay at the backside of Little River land confirmed to a white Creole named Auguste Roubieu. Shortly after Augustin launched his suit against DeBlieux, Roubieu died and his brother filed suit against Augustin for encroachment. That suit alleged that a Congressional act of 1832, "commonly called the back concession act," entitled Auguste Roubieu to all unoccupied land at the rear of any riverfront land he legally owned. Indeed, the suit argued that Roubieu had actually "occupied" that back land for ten years. On those grounds, figuratively and literally, his executor and brother François Roubieu had begun construction of a cotton gin. Metoyer countered by engaging a surveyor to run a line between Nicolas's 640-acre tract and the unmeasured land that Roubieu claimed. That survey assigned to Metoyer some 200 acres that Roubieu felt should be his. Roubieu also alleged that Metoyer had removed $5,000 of timber he had no right to take, that the line had been run in such a way as to render worthless the remainder of the Roubieu property, that it had cost Roubieu a sale of yet another tract, and—in his view—justice demanded that Metoyer pay him $10,000 for his "illegal" actions.[61]

Augustin responded with a countersuit, asserting that he had been in quiet and peaceable possession of the land for ten years before François Roubieu took control of Auguste Roubieu's estate and laid claim to the Metoyer land. Moreover, Metoyer charged, Roubieu himself had gone on the land on several occasions and removed great quantities of cypress and other timber for which Metoyer felt he should receive compensation. Metoyer therefore sought an injunction prohibiting Roubieu from committing any further damage. Upon Metoyer's agreement to sign a bond for five thousand dollars, the injunction was issued by the judge.

The cases were consolidated by the district court and remained on the docket for four years. Neighborhood whites and Creoles of color alike were called to testify; several of the whites did so on Metoyer's behalf. Numerous delays were granted to Roubieu, allowing him additional time to settle technicalities that arose in the conduct of his case. In that interim, Roubieu's French Creole attorneys abandoned his cause and took up the prosecution on behalf of of Metoyer. In 1838 an all-white jury that included several of Roubieu's friends and in-laws, including a foreman whose brother was not only Roubieu's overseer but also a witness for Roubieu in the case, ruled in favor of Metoyer. Roubieu filed a motion for a new trial on the technical grounds that the verdict was signed by the foreman after the jury's dismissal, and the motion was granted.

The new trial opened early the following year. After the jury was impaneled, Roubieu noted that a large percentage of the jurors had served during the previous trial and requested their dismissal. His request was granted. Eighteen days into this second trial, the white planter's attorneys apparently convinced him that he had no chance of winning. His counsel moved to have the case dismissed, as in the case of a nonsuit, with their client to pay the costs of trial. That motion was granted as well. Metoyer received no reimbursement for the damages that Roubieu had inflicted upon his property or for the legal expenses he had incurred. On the other hand, he had successfully defended himself against a huge damage suit filed against him by the white neighbor and he had reaffirmed his right to the possession of the property.[62]

In most states, one of the most onerous consequences of denying non-whites the right to testify against whites was the inability to defend the virtue of wives, sisters, or daughters. *Gens de couleur libres* of Louisiana did not suffer this ignominy, and the justice-of-the-peace courts for Cane River clearly show that these Creoles of color did not tolerate disrespect toward their females. On several occasions, they took legal action to protect their young women from the abuse of white neighbors.

In 1829, for example, young Marie Mariotte, who was herself the child of an interracial relationship, filed charges against a white male with whom her mother had once been involved. Specifically, her account alleged that she had been "menaced and threatened by him the day before" while ill in her bed and that he had vowed to "kill three certain persons and to have his satisfaction out of her." The neighborhood justice of the peace ruled that the white male was to post a $100 bond, along with his surety, to guarantee that he would "be quiet and peaceable with every person in the aforesaid State of Louisiana and particularly with Mademoiselle Marie, daughter of Adelaïde Mariotte, f.w.o.c." for a period of six months.[63] Again in 1844 Manuel Llorens filed extensive charges in the same court against another white neighbor who had attempted to force his attentions upon Llorens's young daughter. This time, however, the white was required to post bond in the amount of fifty dollars, and only for a period of three months.[64]

Although Louisiana's free people of color possessed the right to bring suits against whites, to defend themselves against suits by whites, and to bear witness against whites, they were politically impotent in most regards. One authority points out: "Louisiana free Negroes were never allowed direct participation in the affairs of government to the extent enjoyed by white citizens. They were, nevertheless, permitted a kind of left-handed representation through the right of petition."[65] At least once during the antebellum period, the *homme de couleur libre* of Isle Brevelle exercised this right successfully.

In 1817, the white planter Alexis Cloutier, himself the father of several multiracial children who would intermarry with the Metoyers, donated an acre of his Cane River plantation as grounds for a community church. Cloutier's philanthropy, the community discovered, had a financial and political agenda. Cloutier proceeded to divide the surrounding land into lots and put his slaves to labor, laying out several streets in what was to be the new town of Cloutierville.[66] That town, in Cloutier's grand design, would be named the seat of a new parish he hoped to have carved from the extensive boundaries of Natchitoches. Also included in the new parish would be the agriculturally rich Isle Brevelle, which, Cloutier anticipated, would be a critical source of revenue for his new parish. In early 1826 Cloutier's friend, the local senator Placide Bossier, presented to the state legislature several petitions from "his constituents," seeking the division of Natchitoches Parish.[67]

The boundaries of Natchitoches Parish were indeed extensive, covering the whole of northwest Louisiana. Some citizens had to travel more than eighty miles to the parish seat at Natchitoches to conduct official business. Several outlying regions did want to become a separate parish. But the residents of Isle Brevelle, who lived ten to twenty-four miles from the parish seat and had good roads by the standards of their place and time, saw no need to be split off from Natchitoches. More to the point, they already had been taxed for the construction of the parish buildings at Natchitoches and opposed new taxation for the erection of public buildings in a new parish designed only to stroke Cloutier's vanity and fill his coffers.

Within three weeks of Bossier's move, the legislature received a protest petition from the citizens of Isle Brevelle, both white and colored. Bossier, who strongly favored the division, attempted to render the petition impotent by declaring to his colleagues:

> This document, which your committee are at a loss to know by which name to qualify, is signed by twenty-odd persons, the majority of whom . . . [are] free men of colour and other persons having no political rights.
>
> Your committee will forbear making any commentary on the disrespectful terms of this address to the first body politic of this state, nay they will acknowledge that they have given to it all the weight that could have been attached to a petition of our constituents drafted in proper language.[68]

In reporting legislative proceedings, the state's commercial journal repeated Bossier's identification of the signers of the petition as "free men of colour and other persons having no political rights." Moreover, the *Journal* editorialized against the "disrespectful and menacing" action that this class had taken against the legislative body. Its chastisement, which placed a blanket indictment upon the white signers of the petition and unfairly criticized the men of color who did have the legal right of petition, did not go unnoticed along Cane River. A lengthy letter soon appeared in the *Natchitoches Courier* in response to this editorial, signed simply, "An Inhabitant of Isle Brevelle."[69]

The author of this response minced no words. He declared that the signers of the petition from the Isle represented members of both races who possessed "the largest share of taxable property" in the proposed parish. He pointed out that they would carry the burden of the expenses for the institutions of the new parish, just as they had been taxed to pay for the buildings of the existing one. "Such a division," the writer claimed, "would be injurious to their interests, and . . . it was only prayed for by some intriguing persons with the only view of increasing their fortunes."[70]

Those who desired the parish division, the writer asserted, were engaged in racial injustice and chicanery. While they proclaimed that the opinions of free men of color did not matter, they had "employed fraud" to obtain the signatures of those same multiracials on their own petitions for the division. Now that the free people of color had ample opportunity to consider the serious ramifications of the move and had expressed explicit opposition to it, their rights were being challenged by those who previously had courted their support. The *gens de couleur libres* were "to be taxed, and to pay without being consulted or daring to say a word." In closing, the writer of the public protest asserted that the signers of the controversial petition opposing the new parish represented "the *unanimous* wish of the taxable part of its population," both whites and free people of color, and that they had "used the language which free men have the right to use, whenever they think they are about to be wronged by an arbitrary and oppressive measure."[71]

Within a month, the *Courier* published another sharp criticism of Bossier's conduct. This writer, also from Isle Brevelle, accused Bossier of numerous misrepresentations. The senator's statement that the protest petition contained only about twenty-odd signatures, "the majority of which were those of free men of color, enjoying no political rights," was again challenged. There were, this latest writer pointed out, forty signatures in all, and those forty represented all the taxable inhabitants of the Isle, except for three men who were absent at the time. Only fourteen of the forty were actually free men of color, and all fourteen were described as "heads of families . . . respected for their morality, good conduct, and industry, most of them paying very heavy taxes and to whom, although they do not enjoy political rights, we cannot contest that of petitioning." The writer further asserted that the Natchitoches commissioners appointed by the senate the previous year to study the division had not been convened and that one member of the committee, a resident of Rapides Parish, had issued an opinion in their names, a fact that Bossier allegedly attempted to conceal. The senator had, in short, "betrayed the interests of his constituents" on Isle Brevelle.[72]

A weak rebuttal by Bossier sparked another sharp criticism from the author of the first letter to the *Courier*.[73] At the end of May, three months after the submission of the "disrespectful" petition, thirty-nine of its signers submitted to the *Courier* an open letter to Bossier that, beneath a veneer of praise, reeked of sarcasm:

> To what extent, illustrious Senator, are we not indebted to you, for the zeal with which you have defended our rights in a question somewhat delicate, which has lately been agitated in the Senate. . . . What a display of thanks do we not owe you for the friendly advice . . . on the course we ought to pursue, considering our color and our little weight in the political balance. Infatuated as we were . . . we might perhaps have persisted in our folly, with pretensions even to the right of Petition, a right proscribed, and granted even only to characters of influence. . . . We even found ourselves in spite of our prompt repentance, at the threshold of being dragged from our firesides, filed off in detachments, handcuffed . . . and paraded with all the display of criminal misdemeanor. . . . In this critical moment who has saved us? . . . Whose generous voice was heard in our behalf? . . . Come then worthy Representative of a people who are already covered with shame for having had the folly to dare and speak or even think for themselves, on a subject which interested them about which they have no right. . . . Come then and receive the recompense . . . of your fellow citizens of this county on the approaching occasion on which you demand only the right of continuing to extend toward us your fostering care and protection.[74]

The "approaching occasion" to which they referred was the upcoming senatorial election in which Bossier, as the incumbent, enjoyed the endorsement of the state's leading political paper. Despite that journal's claim that Natchitoches could not elect "a more honest senator," the "recompense" Bossier's constituents gave him on election day was a sound defeat. His subsequent contest of the election results was quickly squelched. The parish division proposal had lost its staunchest supporter in the legislature. Moreover, a resident of upper Isle Brevelle won the seat in that election. Not only was he an opponent of the division, but he, Benjamin Metoyer, was the white half-brother of six of those free men of color who had signed the "disrespect-ful" petition.[75]

Upon taking his seat in the house, Metoyer was appointed to a committee to study the proposed division. The majority opinion of this committee ruled against carving up the parish "without some evident necessity, as the expenses of the state are thereby necessarily increased." Because the proposed division also "would be equally injurious to those who petition for, and to those who oppose it," the committee recommended its rejection. Their recommendation was adopted by the house, and the proposal died in the senate as well.[76]

Isle Brevelle's Creoles of color, working hand in glove with their white friends, kin, and neighbors, had won a significant political victory. Realistically, it is doubtful they could have achieved it without the aid of white allies. The two political leaders whose designs they opposed could have easily marginalized them as troublemakers with no political rights, as they had indeed attempted to do. It is also doubtful, on the other hand, that the whites could have succeeded without the free men of color, whose support enabled whites to proclaim their position as the unanimous wish of the taxpaying citizens of the area involved.

The people of Isle Brevelle held the balance of political power in this issue, but the case also illustrates the instability of those "privileges" allowed them as free men of color. Their initial support of the position favored by those in power was not merely accepted but actively sought. When they opposed those in power, the banner of white supremacy was raised against them and allegations of "disrespect" were laid upon them to turn public opinion against their efforts to defend their rights.

A sixth benchmark against which to measure the citizenship accorded to Cane River's Creoles of color is their perceived allegiance to the white-dominated regime. Throughout the antebellum South, this issue—the very crux of antebellum race relations—formed the foundation of most discriminatory laws, as well as the framework for the social opposition to free non-whites as a class. Did their sympathies lie with the whites who "allowed" them freedom or with the enslaved who shared their color? Would they encourage "blood brothers" to revolt and seize freedom, or would they align themselves with white slaveowners to protect the institution of slavery? Southern slaveowners, as a class, held grave doubts about the loyalty of free nonwhites to the prevailing social and economic system; those doubts fueled most of the curtailments of civil rights they imposed upon free nonwhites. Suspicions existed in Louisiana as well. Yet Louisiana also had a deep history in which families of many colors lived cheek and jowl, pursued common lifestyles, held common values, and engaged in mutual assistance. The black code that white Creoles enforced in many parishes still reflected that core trust.

Cane River's Creoles of color typified most in Louisiana in one respect: the significant amount of whiteness they possessed. Of the 17,462 free nonwhites in Louisiana in 1850, only 20 percent were deemed to be of pure African heritage; 80 percent could claim at least some European-American ancestry.[77] The issue of racial affinity undoubtedly caused inner conflict for many of them, as whites expected. "Problems of racial relations are exceedingly complex," one historian observed in the waning days of Jim Crow, "but there can be no more intricate problem than that of the relation of the mulatto to the two races whose blood, in varying proportions, united in his veins."[78]

Along Cane River, as in many areas elsewhere, the conflict was not merely racial; it was also steeped in class. Occupations, incomes, education, and even religion played a role in each person's choice of cultural and political allegiance. Almost inevitably, these factors ruled out any ideological affiliations with blacks or slaves. As James Hugo Johnston concluded from his comparative probe of miscegenation in Virginia: "Some of these people, possessing so much more of white than of Negro blood and with traditions that separated them from the Negro, could not think of themselves as part of the Negro race. With their inheritance and in their peculiar environment, they developed caste attitudes that were very strong and that seem to explain some of the seeming contradictions in Negro life."[79]

In the late colonial era, when the first generation of Metoyer siblings were growing to maturity, much social interaction occurred between them and other people of color—black, part-black, and Native American, free and slave. As the social and economic status of the family progressed, cultural factors cleaved them apart from propertyless or low-income blacks and from slaves of all shades. Ultimately, the last vestiges of Africanness faded from their culture and their lifestyle. The evolution of the community followed closely the pattern theorized by anthropologist Melville J. Herskovitz: "Culture-change differs in degree and intensity with the socio-economic position of the individuals that make up a given Afroamerican society." The various subcultures

Herskovitz examined displayed the same characteristics as those along Cane River: Africanisms disappeared from the social framework of those subcultures as their position advanced in society at large.[80]

The cultural rift between Cane River's third caste and the black slave society they emotionally abandoned was evident in all aspects of their lives. African religious practices were emblems of slavery, not freedom. For three, four, five generations, Coincoin's offspring had bowed their heads and bent their knees before a Roman Catholic altar and baptized their children at the Catholic font. Putting slavery behind them, they had worked beside free whites—yeoman farmers all, helping each other hack a civilization from the deadly canebrakes of Red River's lowlands. Survival in their new world meant alliances with others of free status—men with whom they could partner, men who could lend and borrow on terms of equality to manage cash flow between harvests, men willing to serve as sureties for one another in the daily conduct of business. The quest for survival, progress, and prosperity all aligned Cane River's Creoles of color with free white Creoles, not Africans.

As Anglo-American Protestants settled among them, the cultural rift was then not so much one of color as religion. While most white migrants into the region had little or no personal experience with Roman Catholics, antipapism was deeply ingrained in their social fabric. At one time or another, all thirteen British colonies imposed anti-Catholic legislation; and, in the decades following the admission of Louisiana to the Union, a "Protestant Crusade" of riots, burnings, and violence against Catholic institutions—as well as Catholics personally—raged across most American states. By 1850, over half of Louisiana's population was born outside the state or were the children of Anglo migrants into the state. In the parish of Natchitoches, they settled not so much on Cane River as in the hills surrounding it; but their pervasiveness underscored for *gens de couleur libres* their own dependency upon the goodwill of the white Catholic power structure for survival.[81]

The cultural chasm between Cane River's multiracials and its free blacks or slaves is seen in the social arena. Dancing, for example, was a pastime in which all Creole classes reveled—French, Spanish, German, or African, free or slave. The *style* of dancing was the differentiating factor between the classes. "In Louisiana and the State of Mississippi," one nineteenth-century observer recorded, "the slaves have Sunday for a day of recreation, and upon many plantations they dance for several hours during the afternoon of this day. The general movement is in what they call the Congo dance."[82] The Cane River plantations were no exception, but for the African descendants who lived in the manor houses, the movement was decidedly French; the quadrille waltz and the *fais do-do* replaced the Congo dance.

The unbreachable barrier between the classes of nonwhites on Isle Bre-velle was also evident at the matrimonial altar. In contrast to situations frequently found elsewhere, in no instance did a free Creole of color along Cane River knowingly wed either a black or a slave—the Coton-Maïs epi-sode in which they were caught up unwittingly was the sole exception. Both blacks and slaves represented castes lower on the cultural, social, and eco-nomic scales. Marriage beneath one's caste had been a time-honored taboo in French society, both continental and colonial. It was naturally one the multiracial French of Cane River dared not breach until the Civil War and its aftermath obliterated the last vestiges of the tricaste system that had sup-ported their distinctive identity.[83]

Numerous studies of Louisiana's *gens de couleur libres* have portrayed a social stratification based upon percentages of white "blood." Historian H. E. Sterkx, for example, believed that "the Griffe looked down upon the pure Negro; the Mulatto regarded the Griffe as inferior and in turn was spurned by the Quadroon; while the Octoroon refused any or little social intercourse with those ethnically below himself."[84] More recently, anthropologist Vir-ginia Dominguez, who interviewed elderly Creoles of New Orleans in the late twentieth century, has presented this view as the prevailing mindset both historically and contemporaneously: "Colored Creoles," she argues, "strive for *whitening*. . . . These Creoles impose a value hierarchy on the continuum of physical appearance; the whiter a person is, the better his status, and the blacker he is, the lower his ascribed status. Not uncommon is the case of a child sent to the country to be raised by a grandmother or an aunt away from home, because he is too dark for the family."[85]

While Dominguez presents her work as a study of Creole Louisiana, her reference to "sent to the country" implies the otherwise unacknowledged differences that existed between metropolitan and rural Creoles. Stratifica-tion by skin shade could have been practiced in New Orleans, which boasted thousands of nonwhites. In a country community such as Cane River, such elitism would have been impossible in the antebellum years. The limited size of the population and the interdependence of the multiracials for economic security made stratification by skin color impractical. While "lightness" or "good hair" might have been preferred by some, the fact that all of them bore close and often complicated blood relationships forestalled any such exclusiveness.[86]

The social hierarchy along Cane River, such as it was, was considerably more subtle. Its basis was not so much upon shades of skin as the number of years an individual was removed from slavery—yet another reason why the Coton-Maïs episode threatened the community's status. The attitude was not an uncommon one, as Degler has pointed out: "Just as the white of threatened status may trace his lineage to the Mayflower and seek refuge in the Daughters or Sons of the American Revolution, so the Negro may boast that his family were freed Negroes earlier than others were, or that his parents 'had money.'"[87] This, by and large, was the concept that fueled whatever social discrimination existed among Cane River's multiracial families.[88]

The exclusivity of the community in its intercourse with outgroup non-whites definitely limited its social scope; by law and custom *gens de couleur libres* were prohibited from seeking social equality with whites. In many respects, however, the dictates of both state and society were bent frequently by Creoles, white and colored, who found common bonds in spite of their varying shades of skin.

Degrees of friendship between whites and multiracial Creoles along Cane River can only be measured in relative terms. The most prominent study of Louisiana's Creoles of color concluded that their social status was "just above the slave level." Both legislation and custom in the Creole state, Sterkx argued, "specifically relegated the free Negroes within its borders to an inferior social status and were based primarily upon the idea that such persons were never and could never be equal to White persons just because of their Negro ancestry."[89]

The social intercourse between races along Cane River took place in three areas: gaming, male sports, and concubinages. Mixing in these areas did not equate to social acceptability, however. The subtleties involved in the white code of behavior guarding such interaction were emphasized in 1857 by a New Orleans French Creole who served in the state senate. "If out on a hunt," he swore to his colleagues, "he might set and take refreshments at a free colored man's table, he would never shake hands with one of them because there was social contagion at the touch."[90] Even so, social intercourse between whites and free people of color on Cane River does not appear to have been quite as restrictive or as ambiguous as this observation implies. At all stages of the area's development, records reflect a cordial interchange and mutual acceptance between them and *certain* whites of their area.

The registers of the church provide most surviving evidence of social relations between the clan and its white neighbors. When Dominique and

Marguerite Metoyer took their eldest son into the post for baptism in 1797, the family and friends who accompanied them to act as sponsors for the child were Jean Baptiste Le Comte, Marguerite's twelve-year-old, white, half-brother, and Marie Françoise Himel, a young French and German Creole who had grown up in Coincoin's neighborhood.[91] When Dominique's brother Joseph married Pelagie Le Court in 1801, the friends who stood for him were the white Jérôme Frederic and Antoine Himel.[92] When Louis Metoyer married the half-Indian Thérèse Le Comte that same year, his best man was the white Julien Besson.[93] In 1836 when Eloy Le Court, another youth of French-Indian extraction, married Marie Céline Metoyer, daughter of Dominique, one of the witnesses who signed the church registers was Charles LeRoy, the white immigrant schoolteacher on the Isle.[94] When François Florival Metoyer married Marie Thérèse Aspasie Prudhomme in 1841, the official witnesses at the wedding included one of the most prominent planters of the parish, her father Jean Baptiste Prudhomme Jr.[95] Cane River tradition, in fact, holds that the men of the Prudhomme family were especially close to the Metoyers; church and civil records support that tradition in a variety of ways.

Cross-color friendships are also evident in social compacts created by white Creoles. When Emanuel Brevel and Marie Clarisse Chelettre, white, married in the Chapel of St. Augustine, official witnesses were the groom's father Balthazar and two Creoles *de couleur,* Jérôme Sarpy Jr. and Pierre Metoyer Jr.[96] The marriage of Étienne LaCaze and Caroline LeMoine, white, was also performed in the chapel, at which time the official witnesses were the French and African quadroon Louis Monette and the French and Indian quadroon Cesaire LeCourt.[97] These instances represent only a fraction of such occasions in which the white and nonwhite Creoles of the area stood for each other in the reception of the sacraments.

Legal records of the parish also document interracial fraternization, explicitly or implicitly. Most such records, naturally, pertain to the handful of interracial concubinages that existed, because that form of fraternization was the most likely to create litigation. Yet references to other types of social intercourse, as well as valued family connections, appear in surviving records. In 1838, for example, the seventy-year-old Susanne Metoyer became gravely ill at her home on lower Isle Brevelle and the doctor prescribed leeches. The family member who rode overnight into Natchitoches to purchase them from a local drug firm and paid for them out of his pocket was the fifty-year-old white Narcisse Prudhomme of the Côte Joyeuse, husband of Susanne's white half-sister Elisabeth. Prudhomme would be reimbursed later by the administrator of Susanne's estate, thus creating a record of his participation in the family vigil at Susanne's deathbed.[98]

A more common type of fraternization is the one described by the multiracial Manuel Llorens in 1835. Testifying in a case before the district court, Llorens recalled a fishing party he had attended in 1818 in company with Augustin Metoyer and "seventy or eighty others."[99] Llorens did not mention the race of any of them. However, it is obvious that a goodly number were white, given that the free multiracial adult male population of Isle Brevelle fell considerably short of that number at the time.

Other legal records of the parish reflect situations in which sincere respect obviously existed between members of the two castes, whether or not it included fraternization. For example, in 1840 when Auguste Metoyer was in serious financial difficulty, he received the following from a white planter of the Cloutierville area:

> Rivière aux Cannes
> May 10, 1840

> Mr. Auguste Augustin Metoyer
> I received your letter of yesterday, in which you ask me to join you to go to the Post tomorrow. It is impossible for me to make the trip at this time . . . [to] help in the arrangement of your affair with Baptiste Adlé. I am inclined as much as possible towards your arrangement and because of this I make you the offer of making a $3,000 payment on the property you sold me. For a long time I have been in torment over this affair, it is of importance that we end it.

> Your very devoted
> p^{re} LaCour[100]

Cane River tradition carried down to the twentieth century reported much fraternization between white Creole males—particularly those of the Côte Joyeuse—and multiracial Creole males of comparable economic standing. Dining, card-playing, hunting, fishing, and horseracing are the most commonly mentioned forms of socializing that occurred. One Creole of color, Emanuel Dupré, was later described by his daughter-in-law Sidalise Sarpy as having "nothing but white friends," with the exception of his business partner, Dubreuil. Tradition also holds that the white males not only visited in the homes of their multiracial friends, but that the multiracial males were welcomed in the white homes during the antebellum period. However, that egalitarianism emphatically did not extend to cross-color socialization between their wives and daughters.[101]

The one contemporary travel account that specifically mentions Cane River's Creoles of color cites a variety of white citizens as being on friendly terms with the people and familiar with their hospitality. No informants were identified by name, and the hospitality was spoken of only in generalizations. The informants were also vague about the nature or extent of their social intercourse. They did, however, indicate that the Metoyers generally exercised a considerable degree of prudence and selectivity in fraternizing with whites.[102]

All things considered, the "acceptability," social status, and political trust that Coincoin's offspring enjoyed—or the degree of racism to which they were subjected—depended upon the element of society that judged them. Whites who did not know them well, or those with deeply ingrained notions about the inferiority of "mongrelized races," were prone to indict them. Not uncommon were such broad generalizations as that expressed by James Timothy Flint, the Louisiana-born son of a Massachusetts attorney transplanted upon Red River:

> The mulatto or free born negro as a rule was worthless or in other words he was too lazy to work for himself. The facts are the mixture then as to-day produced a race unfitted or incapacitated to do hard work of any kind. Many of them would marry a slave, and would work with his wife as one, but they were always tractable and peaceably inclined, and yet when freedom came to them all they developed the meanest traits of both races.[103]

Other whites who purported to know Cane River's multiracials, who perhaps envied them their prosperity and were, in turn, disdained by them as "poor white trash," expressed to Olmsted nothing but disrespect for people of color. Similarly, some wealthy whites who were self-made men, *nouveau riche* and unsure of their own social standing, showed considerable ambivalence —offering a semblance of friendship so long as their interests did not conflict. Those whom records and tradition identify as true friends of the Cane River multiracials broadly fall into two categories: the yeoman farmer, content with his lot and basically charitable; and the wealthy planter or merchant, aristocratic although his ancestors might not have been, financially and culturally on a par with the colored Creole elite, and confident of his own social standing. It was the latter class of man who informed Olmsted that the Cane River multiracials were "honest, and industrious, and paid their debts quite as punctually as the white planters and [are] . . . good citizens in all respects."[104]

Treading these straits, few free people of color lived a stable existence in Louisiana or antebellum America. In many states, they were condemned as a class although specific individuals enjoyed community respect. As Gary B. Mills concluded from his study of free people of color in pre–Civil War Alabama: "Wherever whites and free blacks met each other on a one-to-one basis, toleration and often friendship resulted. . . . They did not fear the widow next door . . . or hate the barber with whom they hunted. Instead, it was the vague and theoretical mass of black freedmen that troubled [society]."[105]

Whites who moved to the interior of Louisiana from Alabama and other Anglo-American states exhibited the same reaction to Cane River's Creoles of color. They *tolerated* them as a class. Occasionally friendships developed, and in their public actions they showed signs of respect in everyday ways. Parish officials who created public records routinely called them *M'sieur, Madame,* and *Mademoiselle.* When the white Virginia-born Dr. Thomas A. Morgan and the multiracial Emanuel Dupré were appointed by the parish judge to take the inventory of the estate of the white Mme. Charles Molonguet, for example, Dupré was the party who led the appraisal and penned the documents for the court.[106] When a succession was opened in 1866 to settle the joint affairs of the prominent white widow Fanny (Hertzog) Bossier and her brother Henry Hertzog, the creditors met and elected two planters of color to represent their interests: Jérôme Sarpy Jr. and Nerestan Predanes Metoyer.[107] On the other hand, when the Connecticut-born white Isaac Birt cosigned a note for Auguste Metoyer shortly before the Panic of 1837 and then sought to avoid the debt, he pushed for a jury trial on the premise that a white jury would find in his favor rather than that of the colored man. He was mistaken.[108]

Even under the Americanized black code, Creoles of color, as a class, did enjoy several advantages frequently denied to their counterparts outside Louisiana. One judicial decision explained it this way:

> As far as it concerns everything, except political rights, free people of color appear to possess all other rights of persons, whether absolute or relative. . . . They . . . may take and hold property by purchase, in-

heritance or donation; they may marry, and as a consequence, exercise parental authority over their children; they may be witnesses; they may stand in judgement, and they are responsible under the general designation of "persons" for crimes.[109]

One might also question whether these limited rights would have survived the Anglicization of Louisiana had not so many white Creoles felt a stronger affinity with the Catholic, French-speaking *gens de couleur libres* than with the English-speaking Protestant migrants. That cultural compatibility seems to have significantly delayed the loss of privilege for Cane River's Creoles of color.

Johnston's early study of southern race relations defines the role of America's free nonwhites quite perceptively: "The free mulatto found himself in a peculiar and intricate environment. His happiness and success depended upon his ability to adjust himself to his environment. Had he failed to adjust himself to the intricate social system that surrounded him, he would have been driven from the slave country. The fact that so many of these people prospered in spite of the complications of their lives must be regarded as proof of their individual worth."[110]

Most multiracials along Cane River succeeded in the effort to "adjust to [their] environment." The relative liberalness of colonial Louisiana and the reluctance of white Creoles to change their system provided *gens de couleur libres* with privileges their counterparts in other states did not enjoy. Cane River's families used these privileges, and their quasi-citizenship, to sometimes extralegal advantage. Their business acumen earned them economic equality. Education and cultural accouterments provided a limited degree of male social parity. While the franchise was denied to all men of color in Louisiana, as elsewhere, that legal proscription appears to have been ignored when their support at the ballot box was needed. Sterkx has noted the wink and a nod given by election officials in adjacent Rapides Parish when free men of color from the Ten-Mile Creek appeared at the polls to vote.[111] The same appears to have occurred in Natchitoches as well. In 1913 a prominent, elderly, white attorney from the town of Natchitoches informed readers of the *African Methodist Episcopal Church Review*:

> There was a very large number of these [free people of color] in this Parish, some of the richest people in the Parish. . . . In some instances, there were to be found as many as one hundred and fifty voters in one ward of these free persons of color; their descendants live here yet.[112]

The wealth that reinforced the civil status of the Metoyer clan also divorced them from contemporaries who shared their African heritage but not their freedom. Tenuous bonds of "blood" were irrevocably broken by diverging cultural patterns. Sharp variances in economic progress delineated contrasting courses of behavior. The colored planters of Isle Brevelle certainly did not fit the Sambo image commonly imposed upon the antebellum free man of color. Relatively independent, economically speaking, the Cane River Creole could afford a mien of aloofness and reserve. He had no financial need to efface himself for the sake of harmony with the dominant society on which the poorer man was dependent for a livelihood.

Most significantly, Cane River's *gens de couleur libres* were concerned with their political rights and kept abreast of legislation that affected them.[113] When any white attempted to take advantage of them, they knew their ground and stood it. When the white then took them to court over the issue, they hired counsel and fully defended themselves. When any white infringed upon their rights, they had no qualms about filing suit against that white and trusting the outcome to the judgment of a white jury. When they perceived attempts to exploit them politically, they protested. However limited their citizenship may have been, the Cane River Creoles used it to full advantage. They gave respect to those who earned it and exhibited an expectation that they would, in turn, be respected. By carefully drawing the bounds around their society, they survived and prospered in a system that systematically degraded their class. But that system and those bounds would both be destroyed by a larger sectional conflict over which they had no control.

NINE

Economic and Social Decline

Cane River's Creoles of color prospered steadily until the Panic of 1837, at which point the trend reversed. Their aggregate wealth would continue to increase until the Civil War, reflecting a growing population and economic inflation; but individual holdings in land and slaves, the most significant capital investments they possessed, declined. The extended family numbered 174 members in 1830; by 1860 its population had swelled to 411. In 1830 they owned 276 slaves; by 1850 the number had risen to 436; but in the decade that followed, it declined to 379. While the total population increased 136 percent in the three decades between 1830 and 1860, their slave holdings increased only 37 percent.[1] Landholdings reflected a similar pattern. Federal censuses prior to 1850 did not record the size of farms; but parish-level conveyances and property inventories, together with federal land records, show that in the 1830s their holdings peaked at 18,000 acres. By 1850 this figure had fallen to 12,615, and a decade later a larger population could claim only 7,736 acres.[2]

Despite the decline in individual wealth, relatively few of the core families suffered economic hardship. To the contrary, the average Creole of color on Cane River was still a person of substantial means by any contemporary standard. Viewed against other nonwhites in America, Cane River multiracials appear exceptionally prosperous. John Hope Franklin calculated that the assessed per capita wealth of North Carolina's free nonwhites in 1860 was $34. Among Coincoin's offspring on Cane River, it was $1,875. Out of a total free nonwhite population of 30,463 in 1860 North Carolina, Franklin found only eight who owned any slaves at all and their cumulative holdings amounted to a mere twenty-five slaves. On Cane River, that same year, the census taker credited thirty-one slaves to the household of François Gassion Metoyer alone, while two kinsmen were said to hold more than twenty slaves each.[3]

Population and Slave Holdings of the Community
in Ratio to Parish Totals, 1790–1860

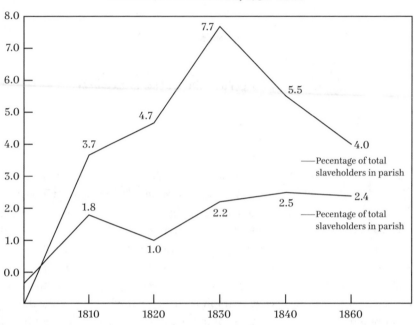

The relatively stable lower line represents the community's total population in relation to the total population of the parish. In 1790, family members constituted less than half of one percent of the area's population. By 1860, the community's population was still only 2.4 percent of the parish total.

Offering sharp contrast, the upper line represents the community's percentage of the total number of slaves owned in the parish. In 1790, the Metoyer clan held no slaves. By 1830 they owned 7.7 percent of the parish's total number of slaves, although they constituted a significantly smaller percentage of the total population. In 1860, despite three decades of declining wealth, the clan still possessed a disproportionately large percentage of the area's slave property.

Studying South Carolina, Larry Koger reported a similar decline in both land ownership and slaveholding among free people of color during the last two decades of the antebellum era. He also found an increase in the extent to which nonwhite testators, discouraged over future prospects for planters of their color, manumitted their bondsmen in their wills instead of bequeathing them to heirs.[4] Loren Schweninger's broader study of black property owners in the South noted a geopolitical pattern: free nonwhites in the border states strengthened their holdings in the late antebellum years, while those in the Lower South struggled to maintain the status they had achieved. In Schweninger's assessment: "In some areas of the Lower South, free persons of color who had previously accumulated more than $2,000 worth of realty either dropped below that level, lost their holdings, or found the political atmosphere so hostile that they decided to leave the United States."[5]

As economic survivors, Cane River's Creoles of color also fared well in comparison to their Louisiana counterparts. Sterkx's statewide study found free nonwhites of Natchitoches to be the wealthiest nonwhites among the rural parishes in 1860, with real and personal holdings totaling "over $750,000" by his calculations. The Metoyer clan possessed most of the wealth in that cohort; their properties, in fact, were assessed at $770,545. By comparison, free nonwhites in St. Landry Parish were said to be worth $640,000; those in Point Coupée claimed only $480,000; and the free men of color in Plaquemines held a combined total of $330,000.[6] No *individual* on Cane River, however, ranked among the state's wealthiest Creoles of color. The two most prosperous multiracials in Natchitoches Parish in 1860—Susanne Metoyer's daughter Susette Anty (Mme. Jean Baptiste Augustin Metoyer) and Susanne's son Florentine Conant—were credited with assessments of $50,000 and $40,000, respectively.[7] By comparison, the Plaquemines Parish widow of Andrew Durnford of Jesuit Bend was credited with real and personal property of $135,000.[8]

Notwithstanding the economic erosion that occurred after 1837, Cane River's multiracial families also compared impressively to Louisiana's white population. The assessed value of the property owned by the eighty-nine core Cane River households in 1860, $770,545, reflected an average estate of $8,658 per family. Parish and state averages were $4,399 and $2,074, respectively. In short, on the eve of the Civil War the average multiracial family in the Metoyer clan was worth twice as much as the average family in the parish and four times as much as the average family in the state. Moreover, the averages provided by the *assessed* valuations given on the 1860 census schedules do not accurately reflect the true worth of any of the individuals. The assessed valuations given that year represented only 72 percent of the "true" valuation of property, placing the actual economic worth of the average Metoyer family at $12,025 and the actual value of the group's real and personal property at $1,070,201—equivalent to roughly thirty million dollars, commodity value, in today's economy.[9]

The decline in opportunities for free multiracial Creoles is more evident from a focus on the have-nots rather than the haves. In 1830, only 18 percent of the households within the extended Metoyer family were landless.

By 1860, 56 percent fell into that category. Theirs was a plight suffered by most free nonwhites in Louisiana, who, according to Sterkx, were forced to earn their livelihood as farm laborers in the fields of others. Roger W. Shugg's classic history of class struggle in Louisiana calculated from the 1860 census that 60 percent of the state's families, of whatever color, were landless. By Shugg's extrapolations, over half the landholdings in Louisiana were farms under fifty acres in size and over half the white inhabitants owned no slaves.[10]

The decline experienced by Cane River's Creoles of color occurred mainly in two time frames: first, the decade following the Crash of 1837; then, the years of Civil War and Reconstruction. Both were eras of widespread destitution in which southerners of all races struggled to survive economically. After both periods, more sagacious whites were able to rebuild. People of color faced significantly different situations.

The depression of the 1830s was not unforeseen by cautious men and women. Toward the end of the economic boom that dominated the 1820s and early 1830s, many predicted a national financial crisis. In January 1837, for example, a north Louisiana physician fretted in his diary: "Property have [sic] taken a very sudden rise here within the last year, caused principally by speculators from Vicksburg coming in to play the same wild game here they did there. Credit is buying everything. How it will end is yet to be determined."[11] In May he answered his own query:

> Every species of property has fallen. The bubble has burst and half the large Merchants in the world have failed and the Banks refused to pay specie. . . . Thousands are thrown out of employment and families want bread, which, with all the necessities of life, has risen to an enormouse price, and no money to buy with, or such as they have is paper depreciated & passing at from 15 to 25 percent discount. . . . even [this] is of no use . . . unless it is the notes of the Pennsylvania U.S. Bank. . . . many farmers owning 100s of 1000s . . . are without the means of buying the necessary food for their slaves and horses.[12]

The financial crisis dragged on for a decade in Louisiana. The spring of 1839 brought a drought; planted seed took months to germinate and then produced poorly. In 1840 land along Cane River was inundated; the wake of the flood brought a drove of caterpillars that ate their way through half the crops. By 1841 cotton fell to less than nine cents a pound. Mercantile houses failed all over the state. By early 1842 most banks were dealing exclusively in specie, depreciating the paper currency issued by states and municipalities. By May of that year, all but four banks in Louisiana had gone broke. Many shared the sentiment of the physician who wailed: "Ruin appears before all who are in debt." True to his fears, hopes of economic recovery in Louisiana were dashed that year when the bud worm destroyed cotton crops south of the Red River. By the summer of 1843, cotton was selling at a new low of four to six cents a pound.[13] Through 1846 the condition of Louisiana's agriculture-based economy remained dire, as the caterpillars, floods, and droughts took their turns wiping out each year's crops.[14]

A few of Cane River's Creoles of color, like many Louisiana planters of the 1830s, had dealt heavily in credit. They were equally unprepared for the decade of disaster that ensued. All experienced economic problems, and some suffered ruin. The records of the district court in this decade chronicle the plight of those who had taken the greatest risks. Litigation rose sharply as planters without funds sued their debtors in hopes of raising money to pay their creditors. The two largest banks in the state, the City Bank of New Orleans and the Union Bank of New Orleans, both of which did extensive business with planters of Natchitoches Parish, filed 275 suits in the district court at Natchitoches during this period. Most defendants were planters of substantial means. Only three of those 275 suits, however, were lodged against members of the Metoyer clan: two against Auguste Augustin Metoyer and one against his brother Joseph Augustin.

Most of that decade's litigation by and against free Creoles of color in the parish involved the more casual, interpersonal lending practices that kept planters afloat. Members of the Metoyer community filed thirteen suits against people who owed them money. They were, in turn, named defendants in thirty-three lawsuits, most for the recovery of debts. Twenty-three of those thirty-three suits were directed against just four members of the clan. Two of these four, Auguste Augustin and Théophile Louis Metoyer, were financially destroyed by the resulting litigation.[15]

The difficulties faced by Auguste heralded the more general decline within the community, in no small part because of the attempts his kinsmen made to keep him afloat. Auguste's financial tentacles spread widely. He was a merchant and factor, the sole owner of one firm located on the Isle and a partner in another firm in New Orleans. He was also an absentee landowner, with some two thousand acres in the area of the Cane and Little rivers. His financial judgment was respected. Various residents of the parish, including

whites, named him as administrator of their estates or gave him their powers of attorney to conduct their business for them. However, he gambled im-
prudently in the inflated real estate market and was seriously overextended
when the financial markets crashed. The credit system under which he and
countless others had operated was the instrument of his defeat.

In January 1837, when prudent men worried over the speculative prices
of real estate, Auguste purchased a Cane River plantation from a white
planter named Baptiste Adlé. For $50,000 he acquired approximately four
hundred acres of land, along with the plantation "mansion house" and its
furnishings, farm buildings, other improvements, and fifteen slaves. Amid
the tightening opportunities for New Orleans's *gens de couleur libres,* perhaps he felt their future would be sounder within the family enclave. Or
perhaps the deaths of two of their three young children had created an emotional void that pulled Auguste and his wife back to the Isle.[16] Whatever
Auguste's reasons, he returned to Cane River and committed himself to a
debt he could not meet. Optimistically, that January 1837, he gave Adlé three
secured notes, each for $16,666.66. The first was due that May; the other two
on March 31 of 1838 and 1839, respectively. Auguste's cousin, Jean Baptiste
Louis Metoyer, cosigned as his surety. Then the nation's financial structure
crashed; Auguste did not meet even the first of his scheduled payments. Adlé
promptly filed suit against both Auguste and his cousin.[17]

In an effort to meet his obligations to Adlé and other creditors while paying his ongoing plantation and business expenses, Auguste sold land that was
not mortgaged—at depression prices. A plantation of 301 acres, for example,
he let go to the white planter Lestan Prudhomme for only $377. His father,
the venerable Augustin, advanced him $23,031; but only $11,700 of that went
to Adlé. A series of writs of seizure were issued against him at Adlé's instigation, but each time Auguste succeeded in obtaining delays. Finally, Adlé
offered to buy back the $50,000 plantation for $18,200, and in May 1843 Auguste accepted the offer. Approximately $20,000 still remained on the debt.[18]

Auguste's personal financial affairs were closely entwined with those of
his wife—the customary circumstance among families of substance. In this
regard, Louisiana's civil law echoed the common law practiced throughout
the rest of America. Wives had no legal identity separate from that of the
husband and were legally barred from managing any property they brought
into the marriage or inherited after the marriage—until and unless they
obtained a judicial separation with the right to manage their own affairs.[19]
Melite sued Auguste for that separation of property, agreeing to forfeit her

right to any inheritance from him should she outlive him. The separation was granted. Then Auguste deeded to her, in December 1843 and February 1844, two parcels equivalent to that which she had inherited.[20] The remainder of his holdings was seized by Adlé. Auguste was left with nothing, but the debt still was not cleared.

The white planter's efforts to recover his losses from others allied with Auguste met with a string of difficulties. Adlé won a local judgment in his favor in the suit he had filed against Auguste's surety, Jean Baptiste Louis Metoyer. However, Jean Baptiste Louis had died during the course of the litigation, and his heirs appealed the judgment to the state's supreme court. The decision of the lower court was reversed, and the heirs were declared not responsible for Auguste's debt. Meanwhile, Adlé had filed suit against Melite and succeeded in obtaining the seizure and sale of the property Auguste had deeded to her; in 1850, however, the supreme court reversed that decision also and ordered the return of her property. Melite then filed her own suit against Adlé for damages amounting to $19,440, representing the rent on slaves and land, the value of a slave lost by death, the loss of crops and building materials, and the "value of a mansion house" removed from the land by Adlé. This suit was also taken to the supreme court, and the final ruling favored the Metoyers.[21]

Auguste, Melite, and their attorneys had skillfully navigated the legal channels open to them. The litigation, however, left the middle-aged Auguste penniless in a society now lacking the opportunities the young Auguste had used to prosper. Melite's dowry and inheritance provided them shelter, a livelihood, and some hope. By the time of Auguste's death in 1859 he had rebuilt his personal estate only to $2,144. That sum, less the expenses of his succession, was assigned to the heirs of Adlé in payment of the balance of the debt. No inheritance was left for his one surviving daughter.[22]

The depression that followed the Crash of 1837 affected most other members of the extended family, if to a lesser degree. Most litigation filed against them represented small sums, such as the suit lodged by the New Orleans brokerage A. Rivarde & Company against Louis Dominique Metoyer in 1842. The brokers had carried forward a balance of $464 on Louis Dominique's account from the previous year and had advanced additional funds to make his crop in 1842. Interest on these sums brought the total due to $1,321. When poor agricultural conditions resulted in a short crop again that year and Louis Dominique sent only fifteen bales of cotton for sale, Rivarde & Company credited his account with the $567 those bales brought in the depressed market and filed suit for the remaining balance. A much smaller suit was instigated against a less well-to-do Metoyer in-law, Charles Coton-Maïs. The court ruled in favor of the creditor and ordered the constable to collect the sum due or seize as much movable property as necessary to pay the $45.96 debt. The constable returned the writ of seizure to the court saying that he had served the notice, the defendant had refused to pay, and he had "not been able to find any movable property to seize."[23]

Similar suits were filed against many citizens of the parish during that decade of want. Some people, both poor and wealthy, planter and trades-man, were financially destroyed; but most managed to survive and began the task of rebuilding their estates. Most of Cane River's Creoles of color also managed to weather the crisis without losing all they owned. None of them, however, escaped without a significant reduction in their estates and a contraction of their lifestyle. Even those who held on to their land and slaves suffered the loss of invested capital, mercantile stock, farm animals, and equipment, as well as creature comforts in their home.

The family's geographic concentration, as well as its fecundity in a pre-contraceptive society, also eroded its financial health. As new generations grew to maturity and the older members of the clan died, original hold-ings were divided and subdivided among their numerous progeny. The de-scription of the small property interest held in 1867 by Auguste and Melite's one surviving child, Emilie (Metoyer) Kirkland, speaks to the plight of the younger generations: "one half of the four-fifth of the piece of a certain tract of land."[24] Opportunities for young adults to purchase additional land had, in fact, reached their limit in the generation of Auguste and Melite, in no small part due to the influx of Americans into Louisiana after the opening of the territory. By the 1830s, almost all land of any value along Cane River and its tributaries was in private hands. The only vacant tracts that remained for sale by the government were in the swamplands and piney-wood hills, acreage that Cane River Creoles of all colors considered worthless.[25] As in-dividuals of the colony fell into debt and their lands were seized, some was purchased at sheriff's sale by family members; but most of the seized farms were taken over by the creditors who held the mortgages.

The geographic confinement of Cane River's multiracials mirrored that of many families in America's older states. As opportunities for expansion became limited, younger generations sought new lands to the west; Loui-siana, itself, was brought into the Union to fill that need. In Natchitoches Parish, many of the younger members of yeoman white families followed that same pattern, pushing into the unsettled areas of northwest Louisiana and crossing the Sabine River to create farms and ranches in eastern Texas.[26] For Creoles of color, this pressure valve for their population explosion was much less practical. Leaving Louisiana for the newly opened lands in Texas would have meant a loss of rights, a loss of status, and an even greater loss of opportunity.

Assessing the economic difficulties faced by Cane River's Creoles of color calls also for comparison to their wealthy white counterparts of the Côte Joyeuse: the close-knit Metoyers, Prudhommes, Buards, and Rouquiers who, up to this point, had displayed strikingly similar patterns of economic development. Those planters suffered the same financial distress during the depression. The growth of their plantations was limited by the same geographic confinement. Their youth also showed little inclination to migrate westward in search of better opportunities. Yet these families sustained the decade's economic assaults far better than the Creoles of color. The political and legal advantages the white families enjoyed are obvious, but two differentials seem primarily responsible for the divergent paths after the 1830s. The white families, by and large, produced fewer offspring, and they enjoyed a larger pool of marital partners from which their children could strengthen their families' fortunes. By comparison, the offspring of the original Metoyer siblings had almost no financial peers with whom to intermarry. The spouses they chose, although they were of similar racial background, were usually of significantly lower economic standing. Each new marriage to an exogamous spouse produced a reduction in per-capita wealth.

The most significant factor that limited the potential of Cane River's multiracials was indisputably the transfer of Louisiana to American authority. Every revision of the *Code Noir,* to align it more closely with American concepts, resulted in less freedom and less opportunity— economically, socially, and politically—for the free person of color. The attitude of the clan toward the new government and the mutual suspicion between them and new Anglo neighbors were also significant factors in the community's decline. For many years following the Louisiana Purchase, as a point of fact, Louisiana's Creole population doubted that the new government would prove to be permanent. Their cultural homeland, France, had given them to Spain, but eventually had taken them back. France had then handed them off to the United States, but many felt—or wanted to believe—that transaction would be rescinded also. The fervor of their hope, continually reinforced by Francophone activities and organizations, left little motivation to adapt to the new culture that subsumed them. By the late antebellum period, the younger members had acknowledged the necessity of learning the English language, but their everyday language and folkways remained French.[27]

Throughout the state, a significant element of distrust developed between the two cultures. Among Coincoin's descendants, tradition contends that they greeted the better class of Americans with the same friendliness they had always shown toward white Creole neighbors and that they were pleased when overtures seemed to be reciprocated. But they learned, too late, that white Creoles and the "new whites" viewed them in vastly different ways. The *Américains,* they concluded, were interested in their friendship only so far as they could profit from it. At a friendly game of cards, according to one family story, the Americans insisted upon high stakes. The Creoles of color, inexperienced with the American game of poker, found they had lost their property rather than the few dollars they had cheerfully lost to white friends and neighbors, in a French game of cards.[28] Accounts of this ilk are invariably difficult to prove or disprove. Legal records rarely indicate the reason a note or mortgage was given. Still, probability suggests that the story has some factual basis.

As the ideological, cultural, and economic conflict between Creoles and Americans increased throughout the state, some of Louisiana's multiracial Creoles sought opportunity in countries where the third caste still held status. In 1844, the *United States Magazine and Democratic Review* lauded the equal rights and status of the free man of color in Latin America and urged Americans of African descent to emigrate:

> In Mexico and in Central America, and in the vast regions still further south, the negro is already a free man—socially as well as politically the equal of the white. Nine tenths of the population there is made up of the colored races; the Generals, the Congressmen, the Presidents are of mixed blood.
>
> Let the emancipated negro find himself on the borders of Mexico and the States beyond, and his fate is no longer doubtful or gloomy. He is near the land of his fellows where equal rights and equal hopes await him and his offspring.[29]

Cane River Creoles showed little enthusiasm for expatriation. Articles of this type were seen for what they typically were: propaganda by whites who sought to rid America of what they considered its "negro problem," by encouraging self-deportation. Unlike the South Louisiana sugar planter Andrew Durnford, members of the Metoyer clan have not been found among supporters of the African colonization movement. Unlike the Donato clan of Opelousas, they have not been found among the multiracial Creoles who created a colony in Vera Cruz.[30] Family tradition alleges that some family members moved to France, as did "one or two to Canada and the island of Martinique." Their names were not recalled. and those self-deportations remain undocumented. One sole account survives inquiry and attests the existence of some political discouragement. "Omar Chevalier and his wife Augusta Dupre" are said to have sought new opportunities in Mexico. There, "Omar" reportedly entered the shipping business, but his career was a short one. Supposedly, he died after the births of two children, and his young wife returned with the children to the Isle.[31] This latter account, as with many family traditions, contains a kernel of truth, albeit wrapped in the usual confusion.

The experience of this one couple speaks to the economic trajectory of the Cane River Creoles in the decades to come. In 1856, Gustave Leon (not Omar) Chevalier married Marie Lida Metoyer (not Augusta Dupré). Their future seemed bright. Gustave's father, the wealthy and aged French-born planter Louis Chevalier, had recently died; he left a significant estate to his children and his placée Fanny. Gustave, at his marriage, was a man of some means. His bride, just sixteen, was the granddaughter of Jean Baptiste Augustin Metoyer; her grandmother, at the next census, would go on record as the wealthiest free woman of color in the parish. Yet Gustave and Lida were discouraged by prospects on the Isle and chose to start their lives elsewhere. A son was born in Tampico in 1860; likely other children were also born and buried there, giving rise to the family story of a tragic death. At the close of the Civil War, they returned to Louisiana—not to the Isle but to New Orleans, where Gustave secured a position as a customs house agent. In 1870, they shared their home with Lida's widowed mother. By 1880, the family had expanded to include a third generation, Lida's octogenarian grandfather Firmin Christophe; but their opportunities and their hopes had died. Gustave, the only employed member of the family, held their household together with whatever he could earn as a peddler.[32]

The Civil War drove Cane River into complete economic, social, and political chaos. It also forced the Creoles of color to reassess their prospects and allegiance. A northern victory promised social and political equality; but the general emancipation of all African Americans, they feared, would eliminate their third-caste status and sow economic upheaval. The public had other fears. For nearly a century, Louisiana's *gens de couleur libres* had been lauded for their patriotism.[33] Now, the unknown that confronted their white neighbors, as hostilities loomed, was the sincerity of that patriotism. Given the tenuous role that free people of color had been allowed in the antebellum regime, did their history of allegiance hinge upon expediency? If so, which side would they now choose?

The sympathies of some Cane River families of color were later questioned, but the community's public face during the conflict favored the Confederacy. If they held opposing views, they discreetly guarded them. They deprived themselves and their children to help maintain Confederate forces. They volunteered their services for whatever uses the Confederacy had for them— so long as it allowed them to maintain their dignity. They ultimately forfeited their slaves and suffered both personal abuse and destruction of their homes, crops, and livestock at the hands of both armies. Their role on the home front differed little from that of white neighbors. Yet the war took a far greater toll on them than it did on any other segment of Natchitoches society.

Cane River's population, white and nonwhite, entered the war in crippling circumstances. After a fairly prosperous decade in the 1850s, the drought of 1860 turned that year's corn crop into "a disastrous failure." One traveler through the parish noted on the eve of the war: "The planter's stock will show their ribs this season, for 'stock never fattens on bought corn,' especially when prices are at the figure that they are and will be hereabout."[34] The outbreak of the conflict totally disrupted the state's economy. Hostilities ended the profitable flow of southern cotton to northern factories. The New Orleans port was blockaded early in the struggle, preventing also the export of Louisiana's principal commodity to foreign markets. Increasing transportation problems created shortages of food and other basic supplies.

Officially, in the wake of the blockade, Louisiana's planters were exhorted to raise provisions rather than cotton. Not only was it critical that each family be self-sufficient, but their food stocks were needed to provision the troops and the indigent families the poorer soldiers had left behind. The sale of surplus food would also generate cash for planters to pay their taxes, and those levies were urgently needed to fund the war. Unofficially, however, opportunists in league with both armies urged planters along the Red and the Cane to keep up the cotton production, to supply a black-market trade in which British and French foreign nationals promised to use their shield of neutrality to ship "white gold" through Mexican ports. Meanwhile, natural disasters continued to plague the parish, and by Christmas 1862 the outlook was grim. "The drought of last summer ruined crops," the local newspaper reported. "Many have no corn to fatten hogs and thus have no meat. No money, but if they did, the price of everything is so high they could buy little."[35]

Despite the shortages, Natchitoches plantations were called upon repeatedly to supply the Confederate troops. Major General Richard Taylor noted in dispatches from the parish that he drew his forage from the families along the Cane River.[36] General Alfred Mouton sent the Confederate officer Felix Pierre Poché into the area to find flour for his troops, an assignment laid upon Poché because of his relations along the river. Theoretically, his ability to tug strings of kinship would encourage personal sacrifice from those families; it also sparked resentment and anger, as goods were taken from those he knew could ill afford to share. In 1864, Confederate General Hamilton P. Bee was also ordered to draw his provision from the plantations along the Cane as long as his cavalry occupied the Red River Valley.[37] That same spring, a Union soldier commented that while the majority of the men in the Cane River area were away fighting the war, the women, children, and slaves were producing foodstuffs on their land to feed "large forces of the enemy."[38]

In addition to supplying forage and foodstuffs, Cane River's Creoles of color were also tapped for state-run labor programs. In October 1862, a gubernatorial directive appeared in the Natchitoches newspaper ordering commitments of labor from all planters. Ostensibly, color, age, or gender did not matter, although the execution of the order would differ according to class and means. First, all were to help harvest the crops of the needy families left behind by volunteers. Beyond that, all men over forty-five years of age and therefore exempted from military duty must donate their labor—and both they and female-headed plantation households had to contribute slaves to build defenses on Louisiana's rivers.[39] November 1862 brought another gubernatorial order, directed specifically to Natchitoches Parish, to furnish 300 male slaves between the ages of eighteen and forty-five for work on the Red River defenses; and the military headquarters of the Western District at Alexandria ordered the Natchitoches police jury to "take immediate steps" to comply. Among the sixteen prominent planters of the parish who sent slaves to labor on the Red River fortifications were four Metoyers of Isle Brevelle.[40] In December, they offered their resources yet again. When a donations drive was held at the Saline Salt Works north of Natchitoches, those who attended agreed to fund a total of 232 bushels. The *Natchitoches Union,* whose foreign-born editor enthusiastically endorsed the "Southern revolution," published a partial list of the donors who contributed thirty-eight of those bushels; at least three of the fifteen names on the list were free people of color.[41]

The one demand that Cane River's *gens de couleur libres* openly resisted was the one that challenged their citizenship. At least five of the Isle's young men of color were forcibly taken to work camps where they were handed a shovel, not a gun, and ordered to labor alongside the drafted slaves. The Morin brothers—Charles Arnould, Charles Bajolia ("Bi-jo") and François ("Pasoose")—were dispatched to Alexandria, while their brother-in-law, Gassion Metoyer Jr., was sent to a labor camp at Shreveport. Charles Arnould labored for a month before his widowed, aging mother paid $500 to A. H. Pierson, a Natchitoches attorney, to obtain an exemption so that he could return home to help operate the family farm. Gassion later attested that he worked at Shreveport for "a month or more" before being excused; how he secured his waiver went unstated. Charles Bajolia and François Morin apparently earned no reprieves. All four men swore later that they contributed their labor under duress.[42] A Dupré cousin was even more candid in a letter he wrote to his wife from the labor camp where he had been assigned. After describing the "squalor" of the camp, he fumed over not only the injustice of his forced labor but also the reversal of caste rolls that were imposed, purposefully and punitively in his view: "We are [now] slaves. . . . The negroes are treated better than we are. We are obliged to do the hardest kind of work and the negro looks on."[43]

Options for personal service to the Confederate cause were limited for Louisiana's *gens de couleur libres*. They were not drafted into the regular army, nor were they allowed to volunteer. Exceptions did occur in western Louisiana, and those exceptions included Cane River's kith and kin at Camptí, but no sons of Cane River itself. The fate of the Camptí volunteers attests the biases that even white Creoles of Natchitoches supported. In late 1864, two years after the first of the Camptí men enlisted, three of them were "discovered" in uniform and in possession of military passes by a Confederate conscription officer. That officer, J. Alphonse Prudhomme, not only knew them but was himself a descendant of the white Pierre Metoyer. Prudhomme confiscated their passes and ordered them to the same labor camp at Alexandria at which Prudhomme's colored cousins, the Morin brothers, were interned. One of the Camptí men, Margil "Magee" Grappe, managed to send word to an influential white friend at Shreveport—ironically an Anglo, albeit one with a French Creole wife. That friend, Peabody Atkinson Morse, convinced Prudhomme's colonel that Grappe, despite having a triracial father, should be considered white because Grappe's mother was a "Mexican white woman." With the colonel's blessing, Grappe was allowed to return to his unit in uniform; but his comrades and cousins of the Perot family, who lacked the white mother, were not accorded the same respect.[44] Most young males of Cane River chose a different course, the only other option offered by the Confederacy. Just one month after Louisiana seceded from the Union, free blacks and tans of New Orleans announced their willingness to "take arms and form themselves into companies for the defence of their homes." They organized within days and were accepted into the Louisiana militia— on the condition that they be officered by whites.[45] At least three of their number would include *hommes de couleur libres* from Cane River: Hypolite Metoyer, Jules Chevalier, and Firmin C. Christophe.[46]

The acceptance of New Orleans's Native Guards into Louisiana's service prompted similar companies to organize in several of the country parishes. By one estimate, some 3,000 Creoles of color had volunteered for home-guard units by early 1862. Two of those country units were formed on Cane River by Coincoin's offspring, soon after the declaration of war.[47] The first, a cavalry squadron called the Augustin Guards, organized under the captaincy of Henry Hertzog, a wealthy white neighbor. The unit soon earned the praise of the white community, not only for its loyalty but also for its ability on the drill field. An observer who attended one drill described the maneuvers:

> The squadron of cavalry, so skillfully trained by Dr. Burdin, was ad-mirable in its uniformity and precision. The firm commands and good cadence of the captain, and the other officers; the intelligent enthusiasm exhibited by all the soldiers; the excellent horsemanship by the squadron; all contributed to amaze the public who had come to attend these maneu-vers. For us who have often attended cavalry drills in Europe, we wonder how, in so little time, these men have been able to attain this degree of perfection.[48]

The Augustin Guards volunteered immediately for field service against the United States. Despite being praised locally as "people who are serving the country loyally and usefully [being] inspired with the same sentiments which aroused their forefathers in 1814 and 1815," their offer of service was refused because of their color.[49]

Cane River's infantry company, the Monette's Guards, was composed of seventy-six men under the direction of Henry Hertzog's brother Hypolite and their in-law Adolphe Prudhomme—the latter, ironically, an uncle of the Confederate conscription officer who was offended at finding the Camptí men of color in a Confederate uniform. The drill performance of the Monette's Guards did not merit quite the same praise the cavalry earned from the *Natchitoches Union:* "The company of infantry, newly formed, has need of practice, but we are convinced that having a little, their drills will be executed with as much precision as in the cavalry." The *Union* editor, despite his tempered enthusiasm, also suggested the two units would make "excellent patrols at the coast and contribute to maintaining the public tranquility." His encouragement was not taken lightly—as a French national in Louisiana, Ernest LeGendre was well known at Natchitoches as a man who had been exiled from his homeland for his own activity in the French Revolution of 1848.[50] Challenged by LeGendre's assessment, the infantrymen did strive to improve. When *Casey's Infantry Tactics for the Instruction, Exercise, and Manoeuvers* appeared on the market the following year, one of them promptly acquired a copy.

Few members of either unit are known by name. Ambroise Sévère Dupré, the owner of *Casey's Infantry Tactics,* served in the Monette's Guards. His father, Emanuel Dupré, was a member of the cavalry squadron. Kinsmen known to have served in one unit or another were three other sons of Emanuel Dupré—Joseph Emanuel, Charles, and Nelson Dominique—along with Augustin Metoyer's grandson Gassion Jr.; and Clémire Metoyer, the great-grandson of François. The youngest member of one or the other Guards is said to have been Clémire's brother Vilfried, who was still short of conscription age when the war ended.[51] Odds are, all able-bodied males of Isle Brevelle and most other *hommes de couleur libres* along the river likely served, given that each unit comprised roughly seventy-five men.

The men in both companies, like all of Louisiana's militiamen of color, were required to furnish their own equipment.[52] Spurred by LeGendre, however, the police jury of Natchitoches appropriated six hundred dollars in March 1862 "to defray the expenses of the volunteers, and their families, composing the company of the free colored persons of this parish, going to New Orleans for the defence of that city." The money was to be given to the captain of the Augustin Guards, Henry Hertzog, for disbursement as needed. In addition to the lump sum appropriated for expenses, each volunteer was to receive a twenty-five dollar bonus—only half the bonus given to white volunteers. Unfortunately, the principal booster of the colored militia, the *Union* editor, died shortly thereafter. On May 1, LeGendre's successor noted that the units still had not departed, although they were scheduled to leave "soon" for New Orleans to join the Native Guards under Colonel Felix Labutut.[53] That assignment never materialized. Two days before that optimistic announcement, New Orleans had surrendered to the Union forces and the city's Native Guards had been disbanded.

The *hommes de couleur libres* would continue to train for another two years, despite rejection by the army that needed them and ridicule from their French-born drillmaster, Dr. Jean Napoleon Burdin. Describing the man's fanaticism, Joseph Dupré later reported, derisively, that Burdin created a "man target" from old clothes stuffed with cotton, perched a hat on the effigy, and scrawled ABE LINCOLN across the "pompous" chest. Week after week, under Burdin's scathing assessment of their skill, they were made to "pass by that thing on horseback and cut at it with our swords."[54] The parish's white home guard, the Chausseurs à Pied, disbanded in 1863; still, the colored militia persisted—even amid the parish's growing reputation as one of Louisiana's "hotbeds of seditious activities." In early 1864, however, their captain died and no qualified white male volunteered to replace him. Dr. Burdin was eager; but the Guards, who had seen numerous displays of irrationality by him, feared to accept him as their officer. Unable to continue without white leadership, they were ordered to disband.[55]

Across the three-and-a-half years of their service, neither the Augustin Guards nor the Monette's Guards saw action against the enemy. Their only known call to service occurred in March 1862, when they were invited to take part in a military funeral held in Cloutierville for one of their white neighbors. Young Felix Chaler had died of typhoid fever at Maysville, Arkansas, in 1861, after distinguished service at the Battle of Oak Hill. Six months later, his body was returned to the Isle. With two white companies of the parish, the two companies of free men of color met and escorted the body to the Church of St. Jean Baptiste for a funeral mass. Captains Pierre Brosset and J. Janin of the white Chausseurs à Pied each fired a farewell shot "into the grave of the hero." The two companies of *gens de couleur libres* then fired their salutes *over* the grave.[56]

Although some members of the Metoyer clan later presented themselves as Union sympathizers, only one is known to have volunteered to fight against the Confederacy. Pierre Felicién Baltasar turned sixteen in February 1861. He was already a year past draft age when the Confederate conscription law was imposed in April 1862; but, of course, he was unwanted. Whether he served in either of the Cane River Guards is unknown.

In June 1863, the state's first Union regiment of Native Guards—reluctantly created ten months earlier by the distrustful commander of occupied New Orleans, General Benjamin "Beast" Butler—launched an aggressive recruitment campaign. Within a week the mails had taken the news upriver. Felicién responded, perhaps enticed by the bounty that was offered: one hundred dollars or 160 acres of land upon enlistment and promised wages of thirteen dollars a month.[57] Whatever his motivation, his action would have been deemed especially traitorous that summer by his neighbors along Cane River. Just weeks before, those black and tan units had reinforced the Union assault upon Fort Hudson, an engagement that claimed the lives of several of Cane River's white sons.

Felicién's experience with the Native Guards, newly renamed the Corps d'Afrique, did not begin well. At the time of his enrollment at Fort Macomb on August 29, 1863, the northern press was lauding the bravery of Louisiana's black volunteers. The corps's own military leaders, however, were unimpressed. The corpsmen were seriously ill equipped in comparison to white troops, and the promised bounty and wages did not materialize. Even worse for morale, Union General Nathaniel Banks, citing "arrogance and self-assertion," was systematically stripping the corps of its nonwhite officers. As he installed whites in their places, many black and tan soldiers deserted, including Felicién. The young man was back within six weeks, however, and his known records report no disciplinary action for the desertion. After several transfers to the 73rd and 91st colored regiments, he would muster out, in November 1865 at New Orleans, as a soldier in Company D, 74th U.S. Colored Infantry.[58]

Postwar, Felicién returned to Cane River, married, and took up farming on a small tract of family land. Amid the community's struggle to rebuild, he appears to have been left unmolested for his Union service. Whether his service was known outside his immediate family remains debatable; no tradition reports it. He clearly did not present himself as a Union veteran in Cane River society, where he, too, battled poverty, the loss of his farm, and an attempt to support his many children as a cobbler. The 1890 census schedule of surviving veterans and their widows does not include him, although he lived at least a decade longer; and his widow, who was also eligible for a Union pension, did not file for one.

Felicién's ability to shield his Union service from public knowledge was aided by the fact that the units in which he served were not part of the Union invasions of Red River. Amid those campaigns of 1863 and 1864, a few free men of color from the parish and a large number of slaves did join the Union ranks, particularly in the spring of 1864. No members of the extended Metoyer family are known to have been among them, although it appears that at least one of their slaves did leave with the troops. The 1890 veterans' census enumerated a man called "Louis Metoyer alias Johnson" who had enlisted in March 1864 and claimed service in the 4th U.S. Cavalry for two and a half years. The free Metoyers, however, included no male of that name, of appropriate age to serve in 1864. Possibly, he was the same former slave recalled as "Henry Johnson Top of the Garden № 9 Come to Town" who, during the early twentieth century, was known along the river as a Union veteran.[59]

The Red River Campaign of March 1864 dealt the death blow to Cane River's economy. The timing could not have been worse, given that the home guard units had just disbanded. A Union force of forty-four thousand, representing all branches of service, amassed at Alexandria. Its publicized mission was to force its way through the north half of the state, seize Shreveport, and open up a transportation route into Texas for Union troops and supplies. In actuality, both its participants and the public viewed it as a "cotton raid for the enrichment of speculators."[60] Its line of march, in March 1864, took 40,000 land troops directly up Cane River Road, from Monette's Ferry, through Cloutierville, through Isle Brevelle, into Natchitoches, and on through Camptí. Along that march, they provisioned themselves off the local farms. As they retreated through the parish a month later, after their defeats at the battles of Mansfield and Pleasant Hill, they swarmed the same route southward—taking their revenge against the people, the homes, the crops, the livestock, and the countryside. The Union campaign failed, but it was the Cane River valley that paid the price, to both armies.

Confederate forces were the first to light the torch along Cane River. Knowing that the Red River Valley harbored the most lucrative cotton stores in Louisiana, Confederate leaders ordered fire brigades up the Red and the Cane, torching many gins and other buildings in which residents and merchants had stored their cotton. Not infrequently, sparks from those burning buildings ignited homes as well. One Confederate soldier who traveled the main road from the lower Isle to Natchitoches recorded in his diary that "the road all the way to Natchitoches . . . was a solid flame. My heart was filled with sadness at the sight of those lovely plantations in flames, and to see the work of honest industry and perseverance of those good old Creole planters destroyed in the twinkling of an eye."[61]

The Union army closely followed the Confederates, and numerous north-
erners would later comment on the state of affairs they found along the
Cane. One soldier observed that the troops "were like the Israelites of old,
accompanied by a cloud (of smoke) by day, and a pillar of fire by night."[62] An
officer later wrote: "No language which I can command can convey to one
not there an idea of the ruin and confusion that we saw. . . . I speak of *ruin*
in connection with the planters' property, and of *confusion* in reference to
the Negroes. The blacks followed us in droves . . . mounted on mules which
they had stolen."[63] The "ruin" on which most of the northern soldiers did not
comment, however, was that which their own forces committed. One of the
few who did make reference to the matter reported that "orders were given
to destroy all property which could not be carried."[64]

The rampage turned even uglier on the Union retreat downriver. War has
always brought plunder and destruction to the invaded, but the vindictiveness vented upon Cane River shocked even the despoilers. Union General
William B. Franklin was "mortified" at the behavior of his fellow soldiers;
later calling their behavior "disgraceful to the army of a civilized nation," he
offered a $500 reward for evidence to convict the guilty parties. One federal
soldier on the march would recall with disgust the incidents that occurred
on their undisciplined retreat and termed it "a lasting disgrace" to the Union
command that committed the atrocities.[65]

Accounts from native southerners were even more graphic. Richard Taylor, a Confederate general who pursued the retreating Federals, later wrote:

> The destruction of this country by the enemy exceeds anything in history.
> For many miles every dwelling-house, every negro cabin, every cotton
> gin, every corn-crib, and even chicken-houses have been burned to the
> ground; every fence torn down and the fields torn up by the hoofs of
> horses and wheels of wagons. . . . In pursuit we passed the smoking ruins
> of homesteads by which stood weeping women and children. Time for the
> removal of the most necessary articles of furniture had been refused.[66]

Henry Watkins Allen, Louisiana's war-time governor, recollected in his
memoirs that "along the river from above Campte to the [foot of Cane River]
. . . the enemy had taken or destroyed nearly every eatable thing, and what
little they left, our own pursuing troops generally appropriated. Thus, those
who had laid up abundant supplies for the season, suddenly found themselves deprived of their last ear of corn and pound of bacon by one army or

the other. Starvation literally stared this part of our population in the face." Reviewing the plight of the *gens de couleur libres,* Allen added: "They have suffered heavily in the war, and, in many instances, have been made the special objects of brutal treatment by the enemy."[67] The governor's assessment was, if anything, understated. Although Cane River's free multiracials were consigned to the race for whose rights the North supposedly fought, they suffered the same devastation wrought upon all white families along the line of march, as well as deliberate excesses at the hands of those who disapproved of the lifestyle maintained by Louisiana's free Creoles of color.

Stories of the vindictiveness of Federal troops toward the families of Isle Brevelle have been rife among their descendants. Tradition speaks of dishes and household utensils purposefully smashed, stolen, or scattered. Food was not only taken but thrown on the ground when not needed by the troops—even the milk for babies. Livestock was slaughtered and left to rot, saddles and harnesses burned. Horses were appropriated, plantation machinery broken, buildings and homes destroyed, and slaves enticed away or driven off when they refused to leave. Family members buried their valuables, just as their white neighbors did. Some items, it is said, were buried in the cemetery and never recovered—including jewelry inherited from Augustin. One resident of Cane River, Barthélemy LeCour, is said to have saved his last barrel of syrup by rolling it three miles to hide it across Little River.

A portion of the Church of St. Augustine was destroyed, reportedly, as well as part of the "eleven room mansion house" of Emanuel and Marguerite Dupré. As proprietors of the Twenty-Four Mile Ferry, the Duprés were particularly vulnerable—their site a magnet for all the retreating forces. Even the portrait of Augustin did not escape the maliciousness of northern troops. One officer, tradition holds, queried the daughter-in-law in whose home the portrait hung: "Was he a slave owner?" When the Creole lady replied, *"Oui, Monsieur,"* the officer drew his sword and slashed it from top to bottom.[68] One Union surgeon gave his own account of the confrontation of cultures in which he expressed his open disdain. Recalling, in his memoirs, the night he spent "upon the fields of a wealthy planter" of color, he remarked: "It was difficult to draw them into conversation, for they were so thoroughly frightened at the advent of the Yankee savages, that they were almost speechless. The boys took great delight in witnessing the panic they had created *among this ignorant people.*"[69] Although this New York–born surgeon noted that most of the wealthy nonwhite planters were "of French extraction," his assessment of the speechlessness of the "ignorant people" made no allowance for the language barrier—or for their justified suspicion that a "wrong" answer would generate more wrath.

The Isle's traditional accounts of wartime experiences are borne out by surviving records. As common with oral history, some accounts have strayed off course, nuances have been lost, and some forgotten details have been replaced with others in ways that do poor justice to the realities these families experienced. One of those traditions, recorded in 1956 by the parish priest, related an incident that typifies the problems with oral accounts. Supposedly, at the time of the war, a white dentist lived upon the Isle—a man patronized by Creoles of all shades. One day he was drilling on an *homme de couleur libre* when, for some inexplicable reason, the man shot him. The dentist died, and the man fled the state—supposedly to Texas—to wait until "things blew over." Eventually he returned and lived out his life on the Isle, without retribution from white neighbors or parish officials.[70] This account, as told, perhaps suggests some degree of community respect for the assailant, but it falls far short of the insight the actual story yields.

The murdered man was Dr. Jean Napoleon Burdin, the French immigrant who trained the Augustin Guards. Burdin was not a dentist but a medical doctor. The "drilling" he did on Cane River residents occurred on the militia field, not in a dental chair. The confrontation itself occurred on the day that the retreating Union forces descended upon the Isle. Hearing news of the approaching swarm, Burdin conceived an ambush, then set out to corral his former militiamen. He caught several of them on their way to and from the funeral of the family's beloved matriarch, Susette Morin. Under the ruse that Jayhawkers were coming, raping and pillaging, he demanded that the men meet him in the churchyard at dusk, with all their kin and their guns. When they pointed out that almost all weapons in the community had been taken by Union forces amid its upriver drive, the frenzied doctor ordered them to arm themselves with axes, hoes, and sticks. Disturbed by his demeanor, they stalled—whereupon Burdin warned that, should any militiaman not show up, he would personally see that the coward's home was burned and his family killed.

The militiamen kept the assignation Burdin ordered, but insisted that the meeting be held in the parish rectory in the presence of the priest. The pastor's intercession failed to calm the doctor. When one former militiaman challenged his orders to attack unarmed, Burdin raged that he would make an example of the man and shot him in the shoulder. At that point, one militiaman whose firearm had survived the Union confiscations returned the fire and felled the doctor before others could be hurt. The rector then offered to take the body home and report the incident to authorities, together with his testimony that the shooting had occurred in self-defense. The day following, Burdin was buried in the parish cemetery and the shooter, upon the advice of the priest, left the parish. When he eventually returned, at war's end, no action was taken against him—not by authorities or by white neighbors.[71]

Years after the close of the war, the U.S. Congress opened three channels through which southern residents who did not support the war might file for reimbursement of approved losses. The French and American Claims Commission was created for French citizens in the United States. such as Burdin. The Mixed Commission of British and American Claims was for British citizens, who to a great extent were merchants engaged in smuggling cotton abroad. The Southern Claims Commission was to serve as a channel through which loyal native-born or naturalized citizens could apply for reimbursement of the contributions they had made to the Union's cause, voluntarily or otherwise. Hundreds of claims were filed in the Red River parishes by French and British nationals, Creoles of all hues, and American-born "Anglos" who swore that they had remained staunch supporters of the Union cause. Some of Cane River's multiracial families were among those who filed for damages; some refused to. Some testified for other claimants, both white and colored. Government investigators interviewed their neighbors of all classes, as well as their former slaves.[72]

The woes laid out in their thousands of documents attest the extent to which Cane River had been ravished. Entering the parish from the south, troops burned a ten-mile swath on the lower Cane before they arrived upon the Isle. Even churches were pillaged by Union forces; aged men—even neutral French nationals—were threatened at gunpoint by soldiers and struck with swords by officers. Between Monette's Ferry and Cloutierville, only two plantations were spared. Testimony in a postwar lawsuit between two white residents of the area reveals that the first plantation burned on the lower Cane was that of Louis Rachal, a free man of color whose cotton gin was the prime target.[73] Rachal did not file a claim, which would have required him to swear his allegiance to the Union cause, although several of his white kin and neighbors of French and Anglo origins did so.

In total, fifty-six claims were filed by Natchitoches Parish residents. In the thirty-six filed with the Southern Claims Commission, all claimants, as required, presented themselves as Union sympathizers. Six of the multiracial applicants who filed with the SCC were core members of Cane River's *gens de couleur* community: Jérôme Sarpy, Emilie Kirkland, the heirs of Susette A. Morin, Gassion Metoyer Jr., and Jean Conant, acting for himself in one case and as guardian of the orphaned children of Auguste Predanes Metoyer in another. From these six families, the U.S. soldiers were said to have taken 40 horses, 16 mules, 141 beef and milk cows, 26 oxen, 16 hogs, 2 sheep, 320 head of fowl, 3,500 bushels of corn, over 400 bottles of wine, and 13,000 pounds of fodder. In addition, soldiers had driven off their wagons and appropriated their harnesses, saddles, chains, flour, sugar, lard, coffee, bacon, pickled beef, and blankets. In making camp, the troops had destroyed the fences that had survived the upriver onslaught and had appropriated, for firewood, over 4,000 cypress fence rails that had been hewn for rebuilding the earlier damages.[74]

Those claimed losses were likely inflated to some extent. Public experience with reimbursement claims against both the government and insurers, even in the nineteenth century, had taught the Cane River residents that any reimbursements they received would be steeply discounted. Expecting a compromise, they probably adjusted their losses upwards. Even so, their claims would not have approached the full extent of their losses. The commissions considered only claims for food and animals that were "officially" appropriated. However, most accounts of the deprivations suffered by Cane River residents, documented and alleged, emphasized that most losses happened amid "useless and wanton destruction of valuable property" by individual soldiers.[75] The six claimants in the Metoyer clan estimated their "officially appropriated" goods at $19,015. A decade and a half after hell descended upon Cane River and blackened its lands, the commission approved 41 percent of the damages sued for and authorized payments totaling $7,716—an average of $1,246 per claimant, with no allowance for accrued interest on the losses.

In describing the carnage and depredations committed around their plantation home, Charles A. and Charles B. Morin informed the commission's investigators that half of their corn was wasted on the ground, trampled by animals, and "scattered through the country." Soldiers slaughtered Jérôme Sarpy's hogs in his yard, carried off the fat ones, and left the leaner ones in the yard to rot. After the troops scattered Gassion Metoyer's animals, he and his stepson Sylvestre Metoyer "went all through the woods . . . and only found one cow."[76]

By happenstance and the quick wit of one man, some Isle Brevelle families fared better than others. The main road from Alexandria to Shreveport followed the course of the Cane through the heart of the clan. The Union forces took this road on their ascent through Natchitoches Parish, and it was on this ascent that most of the depredations on the Isle occurred. On their uncontrolled retreat, Charles B. Morin happened to encounter them just as they approached the Isle—and offered to guide them by way of short-cuts to Cloutierville. His route left the main road and bypassed some of the homes, sparing a few kinsmen the utter destruction that befell others. Not surprisingly, in his later testimony to the Southern Claims Commission, Morin painted his "service" to the Union in a more altruistic light: "In 1864, on the retreat of the army from Mansfield I voluntarily acted as a guide for the Union army, and piloted them by short cuts through the swamps to Cloutierville. The distance around by the main road was 19 miles and the way I took them it was about 9 miles. I was never paid for those services, never asked for any pay, was not compelled to do so, did so voluntarily."[77] In another statement to the commission, Morin couched the incident in a different light that was likely more accurate: "The federal troops took me as a guide on their way down to Alexandria, and turned me loose at Monette's Ferry."[78]

Proof of sympathy for the Union cause was mandatory for all claimants, but the usual "proof"—at Natchitoches and elsewhere across the South—was nothing more than the testimony of other alleged loyalists, the majority of whom also filed claims. Each of the six claimants from the Isle testified for each other, and in one case they bolstered their positions with the testimonies of two white loyalists from Cloutierville. Auguste and Melite Metoyer's daughter, the widowed Emilie Kirkland, brought in the family physician, the Virginia transplant Samuel O. Scruggs, who swore:

> "She was a colored woman, and I took it for granted that her sympathies were with the Union, as were all the free mulatoes [sic] in her neighbor-hood, they could not have been otherwise in as much as they were de-prived of the rights of citizenship, and understood that the successful termination of the war, would guarantee to them both their civil and po-litical rights. . . . All the mulatoes in what is called the Island were looked upon as in sympathy with the Union."[79]

Gervais Fontenot, whose father-in-law Baptiste Adlé had fought a legal battle of many years' duration against Emilie's parents, also testified on her behalf. Fontenot repeated the assertion that she and her deceased husband George Kirkland were loyal supporters of the Union cause, as were "all the colored in that neighborhood."[80] All six claimants, when questioned as to whether they had willingly aided the "enemy," swore they had not. Gassion Metoyer

Jr., for example, complained that the "Rebels" took seven or eight head of horses and mules and about ten head of cattle, in addition to corn and fodder. They had not paid him for the animals, although he was occasionally reimbursed for the feed. In those cases in which the troops did not volunteer payment, he swore, he "dared not ask for payment."[81]

The proclaimed Union sympathies of the community were accepted without reservation by the local resident who had been appointed special commissioner to take testimonies. Louis V. Marye, a French immigrant who had been a grocer in Natchitoches for many years before his retirement, assured the commissioners: "There is very little doubt that all the colored population in the 'Isle Brevelle' settlement were loyal to the Union cause. They were educated and knew that the success of the Union cause would better their social position."[82]

Not without cause, the commissioners in Washington City entertained considerable skepticism. Their experience across the South had demonstrated one consistent sentiment: individuals who had been—in their view—"abused" by the U.S. Army felt entirely justified in making whatever attestations necessary to persuade the U.S. government to pay for all it had stolen or destroyed. Enos Richmond, the special agent sent to Natchitoches by the commission to make an unbiased report, was initially less convinced of the people's loyalty than Marye professed to be. Ultimately, Richmond conceded. While some of the colored claimants "did aid the Confederates by contributions and service," he ruled in the Morin case, they were probably "as loyal as the[y] could be in their situation." His conclusion in the claim of Gassion Metoyer Jr. was much the same: "It is true a few of the free Col'd men in this parish did aid the Confederates by contributions and service. But as for the claimants in this case they did nothing to aid the Confederates further than pay the tax in kind which was required by a Confederate levy."[83]

A review of the testimonies made in these cases supports Richmond's initial doubts. Charles A. Morin, for example, swore to his Union sympathies, but his affidavits also revealed that he had attempted to hide his property from the Union forces. Believing that the Federals were approaching on the east bank of the river, he had hastily driven his herd of cattle to the woods on the west bank. Upon reaching the other side Morin was greeted by another army unit, whereupon he "gladly" gave his cattle to the hungry soldiers.[84] Testifying on behalf of Widow Kirkland, F. Azenor Metoyer attempted to spin his own losses to the advantage of his cousin. He, too, he said, had suffered losses but had not filed a claim for damages because "he did not regret the loss of his slaves and other property . . . [as] he was fully compensated in the benefits he had received in the civil rights obtained and actually declined proving up his claims for these reasons, stating that he . . . willingly gave his property taken from him to the government."[85]

Azenor's testimony does echo the hopes of his family in the wake of the war. His theme is the one that dominated all protestations of loyalty: the expectation that a Union victory would bring improved civil, social, and economic rights. The sincerity of such a hope cannot be doubted. From that standpoint, each individual's loyalty surely was divided in those cataclysmic years. As an educated people who had stayed unusually abreast of legal and economic climates, most of the former *gens de couleur libres* realized that a Union victory would destroy the foundations of their economy, their livelihood, and their special status as a third caste. On the other hand, that status still consigned them to inferiority, whereas the Union seemed to promise equality. In balance, Cane River's multiracials appear to have favored the Confederacy, as tradition holds—after all, it represented their culture and the known conditions through which they had learned to navigate. Yet the crisis that was triggered economically by the South's defeat was clearly tempered, initially, by hope.

The years that lay ahead brought a different reality: economic and social decline, total and irreversible decline for nearly a century. The parish at large was destitute. Flash floods in 1866 submerged the farms and plantations that lined the river; then army worms moved in, destroying the meager crops before they could be harvested.[86] A Freedman's Bureau official reported in January 1868 that the parish treasury was "completely empty; no money paid in for taxes."[87] White planters advertised their fields for rent to anyone who could pay the taxes—no cash rent to be paid; and families of color who had no money to pay for medical care, would be told not to worry—the doctor would be willing to settle for this or that piece of land.[88] By 1870, the value of individual holdings by Cane River's Creoles plummeted from 1860's $8,648 per family to $1,116. In 1860, the average worth per family had been four times the state average, despite the economic bleeding that had already occurred among them. By 1870 the average family worth had fallen to 28 percent below the state average of $1,602. The extent of their losses becomes even more obvious when one considers that the 1870 averages included over 300,000 former slaves who were restarting their lives with little or nothing.[89]

With no capital left to hire free labor and struggling to survive in a destroyed economy, the once-proud *gens de couleur libres* returned to the fields themselves, as their grandfathers and great-grandfathers had done. The

1870 census reveals, among households headed by the Metoyer clan, three times as many farm laborers as there had been just ten years before. Total landholdings had fallen to 5,169 acres, and 67 percent of the households owned no land at all. The total worth of the 121 families in the clan was assessed at $135,098.[90] Augustin Metoyer alone had been worth more than that forty years earlier. Each year that passed eroded more of those holdings, as homes and farms were lost to taxes. The censuses of 1870 and 1880 also attest the toll that the instabilities of war had taken on family structures and traditional values. The number of one-parent households had soared, typically those of young women and small children with no husband-father present. Those conditions, too, set the community's economic course for more downward spirals.

Most crushing of all was the realization that their economic sacrifice had been in vain. The hope of improved status and equal rights that Azenor Metoyer invoked never materialized. For almost a dozen years following the close of the Civil War, "Radical" politicians held control of Louisiana's legislature and chipped away at legal distinctions between white and nonwhite citizens. Nonwhites were enfranchised, miscegenation laws were abolished, public schools were ordered for children of all races, and racial discrimination on public conveyances and in public facilities was outlawed.[91] Application of the letter of the law was not so easily enforced, however. Civil and political privileges in many instances, particularly in Natchitoches Parish, were only token measures.

Coincoin's offspring along Cane River were among the first nonwhites in the parish who registered to vote.[92] Their leaders were active supporters of the National Republican Union Club. The role they were allowed to play in that political organization was also token. One public announcement of a meeting in 1867 reveals the composition of the club. Nine nonwhites attended, including eight from Isle Brevelle: Emanuel Dupré and his son Charles, Jérôme Sarpy Jr., Azenor and F. Metoyer, George Kirkland Jr., and two prewar free men who were not part of the Metoyer clan: François Raphael and Jean Baptiste Vienne (the latter's rejection of his French heritage was evident in the fact that he now styled himself "John B."). Only one nonwhite, the shoemaker Charles LeRoy Jr. from the town of Natchitoches, was identified as a committeeman; all other positions of leadership, the major positions, were held by whites.[93]

Other nonwhites in the parish served in various capacities as minor public servants during the decade of Reconstruction, but their participation by no means represented their numbers. The census of 1870 enumerates 7,312 whites to 10,953 nonwhites in the parish. Yet in the seven years between 1865 and 1871, inclusive, only four of the forty citizens elected to serve terms on the parish police jury were nonwhite. Only one, Théodore Monette, actually came from Cane River's prewar *gens de couleur libres*.[94] Similar tokenism pervaded other local governing agencies. Nerestan Predanes Metoyer, Pierre Jr.'s son, was elected in 1872 to serve as the only nonwhite on the seven-member board of the Immigration Bureau.[95] Five years later an unidentified Metoyer *de couleur* would go on record as a member of the ten-man parish school board.[96]

Even this nominal participation in local government by Cane River's founding Creoles of color was short lived. A predominantly white Democratic legislature took control of the state's government in 1877, and the era of "Redemption" from Reconstruction began. By 1878 white Democrats in Natchitoches Parish were already publicly proclaiming that no one was "worthy to be called white men if they could not do away with fourteen or fifteen radical leaders."[97] From this point forward, no nonwhite in the parish was elected to any public position, and their exercise of civil rights was marked by steady regression. According to the seminal study of reconstructed Louisiana: "Politically, socially, and economically the status of the vast majority of Louisiana [nonwhites] . . . declined for a half-century after 1877. There was to be little or no improvement in their condition for three quarters of a century."[98]

The reversal of political trends after 1877 left most Louisiana freedmen in circumstances at least nominally better than the slavery they had endured before the war. For Cane River's former *gens de couleur libres,* however, the change wrought utter political, financial, and psychological loss. The third caste, for generations to come, existed almost exclusively in its own mind. Instead of elevation to a position of full citizenship and equality, the once influential families of color were now publicly submerged into the new mass of black freedmen—a class and a culture with which they had no identification and one that harbored much resentment toward them. From the Civil War to World War II, the new conflict that brought Union soldiers like James Holloway to their doorsteps, Cane River's Creoles of color were, in their words, America's Forgotten People.

Plate 18. "Daughter of mulatto family returning
home after fishing in the Cane River"

In June 1940, a young photographer with the U.S. Department of Agriculture drove the Red River highway from the plantations of south Louisiana to the fields of Oklahoma. En route, she tarried at Isle Brevelle, capturing relics of a curious world. Rarely did she name her subjects. As her captions on this set of photos show, the labels "mulatto" and "servant" sufficed for her purposes.

That day, Marion Post (later Wolcott) documented the Isle's economic decay. She also captured the spirit of the "forgotten people" Private Holloway would chance upon three years later: impoverished but still proud. The nameless girl-child in this photo had gone fishing to help feed her family, but when she trekked the dirt road that snaked along Cane River, she wore a dress neatly starched and ironed; and both her gaze and her demeanor were unapologetic for being an item of curiosity.

Plate 19. "Son of mulatto servant on John Henry cotton plantation"

The boy-child photographed by Post on that June day of 1940 wears a flared-collared shirt reminiscent of the one sported a century earlier in the elegant oil portrait of his ancestral cousin, *Creole Boy with a Moth*. This shirt is every bit as crisp, but the clipped wings of its collar are a bit more frugal and his sleeves sport no lace cuffs. His hat is tattered; his eyes, wistful. His brow was not yet furrowed, but already it seemed drawn by a too-soon understanding of the world around him.

Plate 20. "Children of mulatto family sitting on steps of very old home built by some prosperous mulattoes, Melrose, Louisiana"

Most grand homes of the Isle were in ruins by 1940. Some that survived were inhabited by offspring of those "prosperous" planters who had built them; but the families were often tenants in their ancestral homes. As day laborers, they lacked the funds for repairs; and the "outsiders" who had bought their lands were merely biding time until the home sites could be leveled and planted.

Post photographed several of these once-gracious showpieces. Their styles differed, but one theme prevailed. All had become obstacles to twentieth-century maximation of farmland. Cotton and corn were planted up to the doorsteps of most, while other front yards had become pastures for cattle, hogs, and sheep.

Plate 21. "One of the mulattoes who works on the John Henry Plantation and is very skilled in woodwork, weaving, and crafts"

Very skilled though he was said to be, this descendant of Cane River's *gens de couleur libres* was reduced to rearing his family in a cabin where the parental bed did daytime duty as front-room seating. "Worker" cabins of this type were typically just fifteen or so feet wide.

From that front porch, this husband and father likely could see the pillared plantation manor he kept repaired for "Miss Cammie" Henry and her son John, in exchange for the servant quarters they supplied. That Henry home, once the seat of Louis Metoyer's plantation, had been occupied by Miss Cammie's family since the 1890s. The Henrys, not the Metoyers, had given the plantation its grand name, Melrose. It was also they, not the Metoyers, whom the Post photos identify as the nexus of Isle Brevelle's economy and social structure.

Plate 22. "Mulatto servant with two of his children in front of home originally built by mulattoes, John Henry cotton plantation"

The "Anglo" American concept of "mulatto" and the one-drop rule that prevailed in 1940 are both starkly evident in this photo. Through the lens of her camera, Post saw a family as white as any of the southerners for whom she felt no racial label was needed. Yet the caption for her photo bore the same pejorative that she applied to this family's kin of darker hue and different phenotypes. The second-class status Post assigned to this trio lay not in the overalls worn by the working-class father, but in someone's readiness to inform a stranger that somewhere in this family's distant past, some forebears had been enslaved.

Plate 23. "Mulatto who is servant and plantation worker on John Henry cotton plantation"

Seventy-five cents a day was the going wage for an adult male farm worker along the Cane when Post encountered this man on whatever daily mission the Henrys had dispatched him. Given his wages, it is likely that the horse he rode was one that belonged to the Henrys—not one that he, himself, could afford. The rope looped over the saddle horn suggests that he tended the plantation's cattle. Like all the Cane River workmen Post asked to pose for her camera, his frame is lean, his bearing is erect, and his eyes are wary.

*Plate 24. "Mulattoes returning from town with
groceries and supplies near Melrose"*

As with the rural poor everywhere in their era, a weekly trip to the plantation store
was an adventure for Cane River families in 1940, one of their few opportunities to
escape the toil of farm work and the heat of kitchens and washpots.

Post, born to far more privileged parentage in New Jersey, was obviously intrigued
by this Sarpy family, whose excursion she would photograph from various angles.
Here, too, she left her subjects nameless, but the barefoot boy would live to describe
that day to an inquisitive reporter (see article, facing page).

"We just worked for food . . ."

"They didn't pay no money. Every week they'd give us a 'white horse' and we'd get on the wagon and go down to the store and buy our groceries for the week."

That was in 1940 in the Cane River area of Natchitoches Parish and the horse John Sarpy referred to isn't the type that is ridden, at least very far. Sarpy was speaking of the small slip of paper his family was paid with instead of hard green cash for five days of working in the fields from sunup to sundown.

The pay for a day's work was 75 cents for men and 50 cents per day for women and children, Sarpy said.

According to Sarpy, who was 13 at the time and sitting at the back of the wagon in the photo . . . the visit to the company store was a weekly event. At the store in nearby Natchez, they could trade the slips of paper for a 25-pound bag of flour . . . and other staples needed to feed the family of 12.

"We stayed on that plantation for two years. The first year, we did day work (as paid laborers) and the second year, we were on shares," he recalled. "We made no money, we just worked for food."

It was in June 1940 that they met Farm Security Administration photographer Marion Post . . . on a return trip from the store . . . to their shack on Cane River.

John Sarpy said the automobile slowed on the narrow, winding road, stopped and then backed up to the wagon. Inside was the photographer and a man. "They stopped, said who they were and explained what they were doing. The lady . . . took four or five pictures. She thanked us, then got back in the car and they left. I've often wondered what became of the pictures," he said in a telephone interview from his Chicago home.

The Sarpy family rode out the lean years of the Great Depression. . . . Sarpy chose to leave the Cane River area. There weren't any jobs. During World War II he moved to Shreveport and worked for the city . . . before he was drafted into the Army. He was wounded during the Korean Conflict. After his discharge from service, Sarpy moved to Chicago where several of his brothers and sisters joined him.

John Sarpy has prospered. Today, he works in a Chicago meat packing plant and owns a three-flat apartment building. Each of his three children has received a good education, and one chose to return to the Natchitoches area. Life has been good for Sarpy in Chicago, but he misses . . . the people of Cane River. "I'm ready to move now. There aren't any better people in the world," he said.

—Keenan Gingles

Plate 25

Epilogue

The twentieth century wrought its own cycles of change along Cane River. As family lands were sliced and slivered among each new generation, few families could subsist on the acreage left to them. Their youth began to disperse, seeking better opportunities in industrial areas. Some settled in North Louisiana's larger towns, Alexandria and Shreveport. Others were drawn to south Texas by the oil booms at Beaumont and Houston. Many sought factory jobs in the North and along the West Coast, particularly in Chicago, Detroit, and Los Angeles. In those distant places, some assimilated into the white population; but most settled in family clusters, creating satellite communities where Creole culture would be preserved. Regardless of where the offshoot families lived or worked, Cane River remained their *home.* Ties to the Isle and its families remained strong, and many of those who died in distant places expressed a last wish to be buried in the cemetery of St. Augustine Parish.

The twentieth century also, eventually, brought progress for those who stayed behind. The first catalyst was a cultural renaissance, of sorts, sparked by a white matriarch of unusual grit. The plantation that had been built by Louis Metoyer—the one his young grandson Théophile Louis had lost for debts in 1847—had passed through a succession of white owners. In 1898, it was inherited by a young planter, John Hampton Henry, who brought his family into the long-neglected manor house. While Henry devoted his time to the redevelopment of the plantation, his wife—the former Carmelite Leudivine Garrett—set out to restore the "estate" to its once stately self. Henry gave the plantation a name, Melrose, in honor of the isle of his immigrant father's birth. But "Miss Cammie," an overseer's daughter from South Louisiana, was drawn to Cane River's French heritage. That was the world she chose to foster, as she developed Melrose into a literary and cultural center.

Fascinated by the families around her, Cammie Henry used their lives as the theme for her endeavors. She also used their needs and talents to create the grand country estate she envisioned. Skilled craftsmen from the Isle restored the buildings for a peasant's pay. They did so, according to their offspring, not for the edification of the landlords but because *Oncle* Louis's home was still, in their hearts, *their* family home. In their times of want, when Miss Cammie showed up with a sack of groceries and offered it for a painting, an armoire, a bookcase, or a four-poster bed, they took consolation in the knowledge that their heirlooms would be preserved in *their* house. At Melrose, with their labor, cabins were restored and turned into writer's cottages and studios, where early Cane River crafts were revived. In the "big house," the library was stocked with works of literature, medicine, and law—family books they had preserved and used to teach their children after schooling became an unaffordable luxury.

With time, Miss Cammie expanded those works into a collection that explored many aspects of Louisiana life and Cane River's past. Records from the parish courthouse found their way to Melrose. The family's oil portraits from the 1830s, including the one of Grandpère Augustin that had been slashed by an enraged Union officer, were "borrowed" for restoration and then hung on the replastered walls of Melrose. Old-timers in the community were regularly visited, not just for their memorabilia but also their memories. Both ended up in a growing collection of scrapbooks that celebrated the river and its people.

Throughout the Great Depression, Melrose was a mecca for writers, painters, and others interested in the arts. Miss Cammie's hospitality was boundless at a time when funding was scarce for those of artistic bent. William Faulkner, Lyle Saxon, Roark Bradford, and other literati of the era visited Melrose, stayed a spell in one or another cottage, and found inspiration in the culture of the Isle. There Saxon penned his *Children of Strangers,* in which he explored his fantasies of a dusky beauty who took lovers from all races. There Harnett Kane was inspired to write his *Plantation Parade,* whose cast of characters included Miss Cammie herself, immortalized as Melrose's "Chatelaine in Shirtwaist."

One of those Cane River visitors, an embodiment of the fictional "man who came to dinner," would spend three decades as Melrose's writer-in-residence —spinning stories as creative as the name he invented for himself: Francois Mignon. Shards of lore, once told to Frank VerNooy Mineah, became full-blown tales, with embellishments spun so well that the informants themselves came to believe the Mignon versions of their past. Amid growing blindness (and a local rumor that he was secretly a son of the Isle, born elsewhere and welcomed home like the prodigal son), Mineah/Mignon entertained Henry friends and newspaper reporters from afar. A favored tale was that of the black lass from the Congo who (in his version) had built "Yucca," the plantation home in which those guests now sipped their coffee. At his prompting, the plantation cook took up a brush and oils left by the New Orleans artist Alberta Kinsey, and—on a roller shade he supplied—she tried her hand at "marking pictures." Thus was born the career of Clementine (Reuben) Hunter, black America's premier primitive painter.

The Henry dominance of Isle Brevelle, like the Metoyer era before it, gave way to time—and a new legend as well. In 1969, at the death of the Henry son who took over the plantation from his widowed mother, Melrose's lands were sold to an agribusiness and the home's artifacts were put at auction. The Metoyer family heirlooms were scattered thereafter among archives, museums, and private owners across the country. One prized item was an exception. When the auctioneer invited bids for Augustin Metoyer's portrait (local lore now holds), the parish priest stepped forward. He told the story of "the people" of his parish and the patriarch who had led them through the turbulence of antebellum Louisiana. He told of the vandalism by Union forces and the damage that one portrait had suffered. He told them about Miss Cammie's offer to restore the painting in return for the privilege of hanging it at Melrose. Then he told all the buyers in their tweeds, and an occasional fur, how his parishioners had labored to raise funds to buy back the painting that, by all rights, belonged to them. He stated the sum they had to offer, and no one bid against him. Father Norbert Rosso then took the painting "home" to St. Augustine Church, where it still hangs above the door, bidding God-speed to all Augustin's offspring as they exit his sanctuary.

Melrose's new owner, Southdown Corporation, donated the estate grounds to the parish's preservation society. The Association of Natchitoches Women for the Preservation of Historic Natchitoches was itself born of Cammie Henry's efforts to preserve the Creole way of life. Under the society's initiative, Melrose's significance to Louisiana's history would be formally recognized. A 1972 application for placement on the National Register of Historic Places would result in Melrose's 1974 designation as a National Historic Landmark. Under the association's development, Melrose's public history would become the story of three invincible women: Coincoin, Cammie, and Clementine. Historians, sociologists, and archaeologists would sift through its records, its legends and, literally, its garbage—probing beneath the layers of twentieth-century fancies in an effort to understand the real lives of Cane River's Creoles of color in a bygone world.

The twentieth century brought not only a renaissance at Melrose but also a rebirth of opportunity for the family that had hacked Melrose from the canebrakes. Coincoin's descendants, today, include physicians, attorneys, college administrators, educators, and professionals of all stripes. Once again, they have provided political leadership to their communities and battled for the civil rights of those with a less advantaged voice. At the local university—a school they were not allowed to attend until the 1970s—they created a Creole Heritage Center to preserve their history and foster public awareness of Creole contributions to America. Some have used their opportunities to reinvest in the lands their forebears lost, returning to family possession most of the 18,000 acres that once comprised the domain of Cane River's Creoles of color.

The Cane River people who took Private Holloway into their homes and touched him with their kindness still exist. The same names still dominate the Isle. The same graciousness is extended to their visitors. Their coffee, tamales, meat pies, and gumbo are even yet the envy of many Creole cooks, and the savory dinners they serve during the area's annual October fair are a lure for connoisseurs who seek to recapture the flavor of the past. The Chapel of St. Augustine has remained the center of community life. The French heritage is still cherished, and the people's pride in the accomplishments of their ancestors still endures. Cane River's Creoles and their countless relatives who have spread from coast to coast are no longer America's "forgotten people."

NOTES

Abbreviations

LLMVC   Louisiana and Lower Mississippi Valley Collection, Special Collections,
            Louisiana State University, Baton Rouge
LSU   Louisiana State University
NCA   Natchitoches Colonial Archives, Natchitoches Parish Courthouse
NCCO   Natchitoches Clerk of Court's Office, Natchitoches Parish Courthouse
NSU   Northwestern State University, Natchitoches
PPC-AGI   Papeles Procedentes de Cuba, Archivo General de Indias, Seville
SCC   Southern Claims Commission

Foreword to the Revised Edition

1. Mills earned his doctoral degree in 1974 at Mississippi State University. *The Forgotten People* was the published version of his dissertation. See *Dissertation Abstracts International* 35 (1975): 5265–66, for Gary B. Mills.

2. The historiographical situation for Louisiana was hardly unique. Many English-speaking scholars of the United States found the regions of the Spanish borderlands—which fell within the modern-day boundaries of the states of California, Arizona, New Mexico, Texas, Mississippi, Alabama, and Florida—daunting.

3. Frederick Stielow, review in *Journal of American History* 65 (Sept. 1978): 453–54; David Steven Cohen, review in *American Historical Review* 83 (Oct. 1978): 1091; Lester C. Lamon, review in *Journal of Southern History* 44 (May 1978): 287–79; Joe Gray Taylor, review in *Alabama Review* 31 (Apr. 1978): 151–53.

4. Herbert Eugene Bolton, ed., *Athanase de Mézières and the Louisiana-Texas Frontier, 1768–1780*, 2 vols. (Cleveland: Arthur Clark Co., 1914). Ross Phares's *Cavalier in the Wilderness: The Story of the Explorer and Trader Louis Juchereau de St. Denis* (Baton Rouge: LSU Press, 1952) was another work furthering the impression that the town was devoted to Indian trade. It focused on Louis Juchereau de St. Denis, the founder and first commandant of Natchitoches.

5. In fact, Natchitoches was a cosmopolitan blend of several frontier social groups and economic activities. While the Indian trade was important, the town became a plantation region by the end of the French era. The truth about interracial alliances between Indians and French

settlers was that only a small group, mostly consisting of the town's elite, formed these ties with Indian tribes and Spanish families during the French era. See H. Sophie Burton and F. Todd Smith, *Colonial Natchitoches: A Creole Community on the Louisiana-Texas Frontier* (College Station: Texas A&M University Press, 2008).

6. Herbert E. Sterkx, *The Free Negro in Ante-Bellum Louisiana* (Rutherford, N.J.: Fairleigh Dickinson University Press, 1972); Donald E. Everett, "Emigrés and Militiamen: Free Persons of Color in New Orleans, 1803–1815," *Journal of Negro History* 38 (Oct. 1953): 377–80; Robert Reinders, "The Decline of the New Orleans Free Negro in the Decade before the Civil War," *Journal of Mississippi History* 24 (Jan. 1962): 88–98; Robert Reinders, "The Free Negro in the New Orleans Economy, 1850–1860," *Louisiana History* 6 (Summer 1965): 273–85; Donald E. Everett, "Free Persons of Color in Colonial Louisiana," *Louisiana History* 7 (Winter 1966): 21–50; Laura Foner, "The Free People of Color in Louisiana and St. Domingue: A Comparative Portrait of Two Three-Caste Slave Societies," *Journal of Social History* 3 (Summer 1970): 406–30; John Blassingame, *Black New Orleans, 1860–1880* (Chicago: University of Chicago Press, 1973).

7. Mills was interested in the ideas put forth by Frank Tannenbaum in *Slave and Citizen: The Negro in the Americas* (New York: A. A. Knopf, 1946). This work posited that free blacks and slaves benefited from the more fluid race relations in French and Spanish colonial Louisiana and suffered under the rigidity of American society. Mills's work bolstered the Tannenbaum thesis as he found that the Cane River Creoles benefited from the Spanish regime and struggled under American rule.

8. Kimberly S. Hanger, *Bounded Lives, Bounded Places: Free Black Society in Colonial New Orleans, 1769–1803* (Durham, N.C.: Duke University Press, 1997); Virginia Meacham Gould, "In Full Enjoyment of Their Liberty: The Free Women of Color of the Gulf Ports of New Orleans, Mobile, and Pensacola, 1769–1860" (Ph.D. dissertation, Emory University, 1991); L. Virginia Gould, "Urban Slavery–Urban Freedom: The Manumission of Jacqueline Lemell," in *More than Chattel: Black Women and Slavery in the Americas,* ed. David Barry Gaspart and Darlene Clark Hine (Bloomington: Indiana University Press, 1996); Carl A. Brasseaux, Keith P. Fontenot, and Claude F. Oubre, *Creoles of Color in the Bayou Country* (Jackson: University Press of Mississippi, 1994); James H. Dormon, ed., *Creoles of Color of the Gulf South* (Knoxville: University of Tennessee Press, 1996); Mary Gehman, *Free People of Color of New Orleans: An Introduction* (New Orleans: Margaret Media, 1994); Guillaume Aubert, "'The Blood of France': Race and Purity of Blood in the French Atlantic World," *William and Mary Quarterly* 61 (July 2004): 439–78; Jennifer M. Spear, "Colonial Intimacies: Legislating Sex in French Louisiana," *William and Mary Quarterly* 60 (Jan. 2003): 75–98.

9. Gwendolyn Midlo Hall, *Africans in Colonial Louisiana: The Development of Afro-Creole Culture in the Eighteenth Century* (Baton Rouge: LSU Press, 1995); Gilbert S. Din, *Spaniards, Planters, and Slaves: The Spanish Regulation of Slavery in Louisiana, 1763–1803* (College Station: Texas A&M University Press, 1999); Thomas N. Ingersoll, *Mammon and Manon in Early New Orleans: The First Slave Society in the Deep South, 1718–1819* (Knoxville: University of Tennessee Press, 1999); Thomas N. Ingersoll, "The Slave Trade and the Ethnic Diversity of Louisiana's Slave Community," *Louisiana History* 37 (Spring 1996): 133–61; Daniel H. Usner Jr., *Indians, Settlers & Slaves in a Frontier Exchange Economy: The Lower Mississippi Valley before 1783* (Chapel Hill: University of North Carolina Press, 1992).

10. Judith Kelleher Schafer, *Becoming Free, Remaining Free: Manumission and Enslavement in New Orleans, 1846–1862* (Baton Rouge: LSU Press, 2003); Caryn Cossé Bell, *Revolution, Romanticism, and the Afro-Creole Protest Tradition in Louisiana, 1718–1868* (Baton Rouge: LSU Press, 1997); Sybil Kein, ed., *Creole: The History and Legacy of Louisiana's Free People of Color*

(Baton Rouge: LSU Press, 2000); Joseph Logsdon and Caryn Cossé Bell, "The Americaniza-tion of Black New Orleans, 1850–1900," in *Creole New Orleans: Race and Americanization*, ed. Arnold R. Hirsch and Joseph Logsdon (Baton Rouge: LSU Press, 1992); Loren Schweninger, "Antebellum Free Persons of Color in Postbellum Louisiana," *Louisiana History* (Fall 1989): 30, 345–64; Loren Schweninger, "Prosperous Blacks in the South, 1790–1880," *American Historical Review* 95 (Feb. 1990): 31–56; Loren Schweninger, *Black Property Owners in the South, 1790–1915* (Urbana: University of Illinois Press, 1990).

11. Among the many works on Natchitoches by or edited by Elizabeth Shown Mills are the following: "Mézières-Trichel-Grappe: A Study of a Tri-Caste Lineage in the Old South," *The Gene-alogist* 6 (Spring 1985): 4–84; *Natchitoches, 1729–1803: Abstracts of the Catholic Church Registers of the French and Spanish Post of St. Jean Baptiste des Natchitoches in Louisiana* (New Orleans, Louisiana: Polyanthos, 1977); *Natchitoches Church Marriages, 1818–1850* (Tuscaloosa: Mills His-torical Press, 1985); *Natchitoches Colonials: Censuses, Military Rolls, and Tax Lists, 1722–1803* (Chicago: Adams Press, 1981); *Natchitoches, 1800–1826: Translated Abstracts of Register Number Five of the Catholic Church Parish of St. François des Natchitoches in Louisiana* (New Orleans: Polyanthos, 1980); "Quintanilla's Crusade, 1775–1783: 'Moral Reform' and Its Consequences on the Natchitoches Frontier," *Louisiana History* 42 (Summer 2001): 277–302; "Religion in Old Natchi-toches, 1714–1864," *Natchitoches Genealogist* (Oct. 1977): 1–7; "Which Marie Louise Is 'Mariotte'?: Sorting Slaves with Common Names," *National Genealogical Society Quarterly* 94 (Sept. 2006): 183–204.

12. Heloise H. Cruzat was an early-twentieth-century researcher who translated and pub-lished documents as well as indexed collections, mostly focusing on French New Orleans. Like-wise, Winston De Ville is a genealogist who has translated and published extensively on many colonial Louisiana posts. Heloise H. Cruzat, trans., "Louisiana in 1724: Banet's Report to the Company of the Indies, Dated Paris, December 20, 1724," *Louisiana Historical Quarterly* 12 (Jan. 1929): 121–33; Winston De Ville, ed., *Marriage Contracts of Natchitoches, 1739–1803* (Nashville?: N.p., 1961); Winston De Ville, comp. and trans., *Natchitoches Documents, 1732–1785: A Calendar of Civil Records from Fort St. Jean Baptiste in the French and Spanish Province of Louisiana* (Ville Platte, La.: Smith Publications, 1994); Katherine Bridges and Winston De Ville, ed. and trans., "Natchitoches and the Trail to the Rio Grande: Two Early Eighteenth-Century Accounts by the Sieur Derbanne," *Louisiana History* 8 (Spring 1967): 239–59.

Preface

1. Since the publication of the first edition of *The Forgotten People* in 1977, scholars have probed other nooks within the American South and identified somewhat comparable groups with similar mindsets. Joel Williamson's *New People: Miscegenation and Mulattoes in the United States* (New York: Free Press, 1980) is a seminal work proposing that the cultural divide was not so much between the Anglo states and Latin Louisiana as between the Upper South and the Lower South. The parallels that Williamson draws between Charleston and Louisiana are strik-ingly similar to those found by the original author of *Forgotten People* in his subsequent, two-decade project reconstituting the lives of free people of color in "Anglo" Alabama vis-à-vis "Creole Mobile." The work of Loren Schweninger, particularly *Black Property Owners in the South,* has also challenged traditional assumptions about the degree of singularity that Louisiana's Creoles of color possessed as a class.

2. *State v. Cantey,* 1835 (2 Hill 614, S.C.).

3. The Fairfaxes and Gibsons of Virginia, as well as the youngest son of Sally Hemings and Thomas Jefferson, Eston Hemings Jefferson, and his offspring are well-known cases at point. For a comprehensive examination of the latter, see Helen F. M. Leary, "Sally Hemings's Children: A Genealogical Analysis of the Evidence," *Jefferson-Hemings: A Special Issue of the National Genealogical Society Quarterly* 89 (Sept. 2001): 165–207.

4. Among triracials of the American South, the Melungeons are by far the best known. Among the academic-press studies, Wayne Winkler's *Walking toward the Sunset: The Melungeons of Appalachia* (Macon, Ga.: Mercer University Press, 2005) offers the most critical examination. The better-known work by N. Brent Kennedy and Robyn Vaughan Kennedy, *The Melungeons: The Resurrection of a Proud People; An Untold Story of Ethnic Cleansing in America,* rev. ed. (Macon: Mercer University Press, 1997), is more grounded in prehistorical speculation than historial evidence. Documentary evidence of the origins of the core families among the Melungeons and other triracial isolates is provided by the historian Virginia Easley Demarce in "'Verry Slitly Mixt': Tri-Racial Isolate Families of the Upper South—A Genealogical Study," *National Genealogical Society Quarterly* 80 (March 1992): 5–35; and DeMarce, "Looking at Legends—Lumbee and Melungeon: Applied Genealogy and the Origins of Tri-racial Isolate Settlements," *National Genealogical Society Quarterly* 81 (March 1993): 24–45.

5. This point is further explored in Elizabeth Shown Mills, "*Isle of Canes* and Issues of Conscience: Master-Slave Sexual Dynamics and Slaveholding by Free People of Color," *Between Two Worlds: Free People of Color in Southern Cultural History,* a special issue of the *Southern Quarterly* 43 (Winter 2006): 158–75, particularly 162–63. In a *Which comes first, the economic chicken or the socio-legal egg?* proposal, Ira Berlin makes a counterpoint in that same set of essays: "The belief that free people of color were more free than colored stood as the basis of the bargain upon which the free people of color's prosperity and sometimes their existence rested." See Berlin, "Southern Free People of Color in the Age of William Johnson," *Between Two Worlds,* 9–17, quote on p. 14.

6. Alice Dunbar-Nelson, "People of Color in Louisiana," *Journal of Negro History* 2 (Jan. 1917): 78.

7. For a translated edition, see Rodolphe Lucien Desdunes, *Our People and Our History,* trans. and ed. Dorothea Olga McCants (Baton Rouge: LSU Press, 1973).

8. Charles B. Rousseve, *The Negro in Louisiana: Aspects of His History and His Literature* (New Orleans: Xavier University Press, 1937).

9. Virginia Dominguez, *White by Definition: Social Classification in Creole Louisiana* (New Brunswick, N.J.: Rutgers University Press, 1993). While Dominguez argues that Creoles no longer exist as a social class, Thomas Fiehrer observes that her findings for "the ancient city" (New Orleans) are "not to be extended willy-nilly to the vast creole region, as Dominguez's title may imply." See Fiehrer, "The Emergence of Pan-Créolité: Louisiana at the Crossroads," *Nanzan Review of American Studies* 17 (1995): 1–28, quote on page 6.

10. Hanger, *Bounded Lives.*

11. Brasseaux, Fontenot, and Oubre, *Creoles of Color in the Bayou Country.*

12. H. E. Sterkx, *The Free Negro in Ante-Bellum Louisiana* (Rutherford, N.J.: Fairleigh Dickinson University Press, 1972).

13. Ira Berlin, *Slaves without Masters: The Free Negro in the Antebellum South* (Oxford: Oxford University Press, 1974).

14. Quoted in Din, *Spaniards, Planters, and Slaves,* 50.

15. Carl N. Degler, *Neither Black nor White: Slavery and Race Relations in Brazil and the United States* (New York: Macmillan, 1971), 7.

16. Derek Noel Kerr, "Petty Felony, Slave Defiance, and Frontier Villainy: Crime and Criminal Justice in Spanish Louisiana, 1770–1803" (Ph.D. diss., Tulane University, 1983).

17. Robert William Fogel and Stanley L. Engerman, *Time on the Cross: The Economics of American Negro Slavery*, 2 vols. (Boston: Little, Brown & Co., 1974).

18. Herbert G. Gutman, *The Black Family in Slavery and Freedom, 1750–1925* (New York: Pantheon Books, 1976).

19. Ann Patton Malone, *Sweet Chariot: Slave Family and Household Structure in Nineteenth-Century Louisiana* (Chapel Hill: University of North Carolina Press, 1992).

20. Alex Haley, *Roots: The Saga of an American Family* (New York: Doubleday, 1976). Haley presented *Roots* as a novelization of his family's history—"faction" supposedly based upon family lore and his genealogical research. Subsequent studies in the fields of journalism, history, and genealogy established that he was not able to retrace his roots prior to the Civil War, either in America or Africa. Nonetheless, *Roots* has encouraged many African Americans to pursue their own ancestral studies, in the course of which they have proved that, at least in America, minority family histories can be reliably reconstructed. Key works that have explored Haley's alleged "documentation" include Mark Ottaway, "Tangled Roots," (London) *Sunday Times*, Apr. 10, 1977 (multiple pages); and Donald R. Wright, "Uprooting Kunta Kinte: On the Perils of Relying on Encyclopedic Informants," *History of Africa* 8 (1981): 205–17. Ottaway, an investigative journalist, focused on Haley's experience in the Gambia and the viability of using griots for family history. Wright, an Africanist historian, deconstructed Haley's supposed African roots. For historical and genealogical analysis of the American portion of *Roots,* see Gary B. Mills and Elizabeth Shown Mills, "*Roots* and the New 'Faction': A Legitimate Tool for Clio?" *Virginia Magazine of History and Biography* 89 (Jan. 1981): 3–26; and Mills and Mills, "The Genealogist's Assessment of Alex Haley's *Roots,*" *National Genealogical Society Quarterly* 72 (Mar. 1984): 35–49. Also insightful for those who seek Cane River roots in Africa is Wright's body of interviews conducted among West African and sub-Saharan griots in the decade prior to *Roots,* and his assessment of their utility, available as *Oral Traditions from the Gambia,* 2 vols. (Athens: Ohio University Center for International Studies, Africa Program, 1979–80).

21. Most of the peer-reviewed African American studies that have appeared in the *National Genealogical Society Quarterly* over the past two decades have been cataloged in the standard "calendars of recent scholarship" published annually by the *Journal of Southern History* and *Journal of American History.* Also exemplary, though not formally peer reviewed, is Paul Heinegg's groundbreaking and encyclopedic *Free African Americans* series (Baltimore: Genealogical Publishing Co., various editions since 1992).

22. Frances Jerome Woods, *Marginality and Identity: A Colored Creole Family through Ten Generations* (Baton Rouge: LSU Press, 1972).

23. Particularly good studies of free colored prosperity and the paths through which this was accomplished exist for South Carolina. Michael P. Johnson and James L. Roark's *No Chariot Let Down: Free People of Color on the Eve of the Civil War* (Chapel Hill: University of North Carolina Press, 2001) chronicles the rise from slavery of the William Ellison family. Larry Koger's *Black Masters: Free Black Slave Masters in South Carolina, 1790–1860* (Columbia: University of South Carolina Press, 1995) broadly studies the experience of this class across the highly diverse regions of the state. Willard B. Gatewood, in *Aristocrats of Color: The Black Elite, 1880–1920* (Bloomington: Indiana University Press, 1990), devotes much of his study to the colonial and antebellum roots of these post–Civil War elite. Adele Logan Alexander, *Ambiguous Lives: Free Women of Color in Rural Georgia, 1789–1879* (Fayetteville: University of Arkansas Press, 1991); Suzanne Lebsock, *The Free Women of Petersburg: Status and Culture in a Southern Town, 1784–*

1860 (New York: W. W. Norton, 1985); and Gould, "In Full Enjoyment of Their Liberty" provide particularly good insight into the lives of females in this class. Henry Wiencek, *The Hairstons: An American Family in Black and White* (New York: St. Martin's, 1999) is notable among a growing number of family-centered histories in which scholars are now probing the complex relationships between the white and multiracial branches of a single family.

24. Louis Metoyer, quoted in Andrew J. Jolivétte, *Louisiana Creoles: Cultural Recovery and Mixed-Race Native American Identity* (Lanham, Md.: Lexington Books, 2007), 41.

25. Fiehrer, "The Emergence of Pan-Créolité," 7.

Prologue

1. For comprehensive analyses of the credibility of legends attributed to the Cane River Creoles, see Elizabeth Shown Mills, "Demythicizing History: Marie Thérèse Coincoin, Tourism, and the National Historical Landmarks Program," *Louisiana History* 53 (Fall 2012): 402–37, which focuses upon the family's historic properties; and E. S. Mills, "Documenting a Slave's Birth, Parentage, and Origins (Marie Thérèse Coincoin, 1742–1816): A Test of Oral History," *National Genealogical Society Quarterly* 96 (Dec. 2008): 245–66, which examines the evidence for Coincoin's identity.

2. For the limits of their roles as citizens, see Gary B. Mills, "*Liberté, Fraternité*, and Everything but *Egalité*: Cane River's *Citoyens de Couleur*," in *North Louisiana*, Vol. 1: *To 1865: Essays on the Region and Its History*, ed. B. F. Gilley (Ruston, La.: McGinty Trust Fund Publications, Louisiana Tech University, 1984), 93–112.

1. A Fusion of Roots

1. The waterways associated with Natchitoches underwent a series of changes during the years covered by this study; those changes affect the interpretation of records and events. French colonial officials built Poste St. Jean Baptiste des Natchitoches adjacent to the Natchitoches tribe, which occupied an "isle" at the upper juncture of two branches of Red River. The western branch was Red River proper; the eastern branch was called Rivière aux Cannes (River at the Canes). In the 1760s, Red River switched to the eastern course and the western course was dubbed Old River, the name it still carries. The "new" Red River was jurisdictionally divided into three settlement districts. The upper ten or so miles, between the post and Bayou Brevelle, became la Grand Côte (later Côte Joyeuse). The next fourteen or so miles, which was surrounded on all sides by waterways—Bayou Brevelle on the upper, Bayou Charette on the lower, and Little River (aka Rivière Brosset) on the east—was dubbed Isle Brevelle. The lower sixteen or so miles, between Isle Brevelle and the point at which Red and Old rivers reunited, became the district of Rivière aux Cannes. In the 1830s, Red River jumped course to the east again, taking over the former Rigolet de Bon Dieu, which it still occupies today. After that last relocation of the Red, the abandoned channel reverted to its original name, rendered in English as Cane River. In the 1930s, it was dammed and renamed Cane River Lake. Throughout this monograph, sites will be identified by the term used in each cited document.

2. B. F. French, ed., *Historical Collections of Louisiana*, 5 vols. (New York: Wiley & Putnam, 1846–53), 3:89. Surviving parish registers for all colonial posts from Mobile to Natchitoches attest that slave baptism was regularly practiced, although slave marriages were viewed more

casually. For colonial and antebellum practices at Natchitoches, see Elizabeth Shown Mills and Gary B. Mills, "Missionaries Compromised: Early Evangelization of Slaves and Free People of Color in North Louisiana," in *Cross, Crozier, and Crucible: A Volume Celebrating the Bicentennial of a Catholic Diocese in Louisiana*, ed. Glenn R. Conrad (New Orleans: Archdiocese of New Orleans, 1992), 30–47.

3. N. M. Miller Surrey, *The Commerce of Louisiana during the French Regime, 1699–1763* (New York: Columbia University Press, 1916), 239–40. Hall, in *Africans in Colonial Louisiana*, chaps. 3 and 5, explores this theme in far more nuanced detail.

4. Burton and Smith, *Colonial Natchitoches*, 15. Considering St. Denis's prominence in the European settlement of Louisiana, he remains remarkably unstudied. His one full-length biography, a romanticized account, is Ross Phares's *Cavalier in the Wilderness*. Also see Ruffin W. Gray, "Louis Juchereau de St-Denis," *Dictionary of Louisiana Biography*, ed. Glenn R. Conrad, 2 vols. (Lafayette: Louisiana Historical Association, 1988), 1:449.

5. Register 1 of St. François Parish (Natchitoches), held today in the successor parish of Immaculate Conception, contains several baptismal entries for adult slaves belonging to the St. Denis family and to Jean Baptiste Derbanne, the half-Chitimacha son of a French explorer and minor official who had participated in St. Denis's travels to Mexico. Like St. Denis, young Derbanne was married to the daughter of a Spanish official, his father-in-law being Lt. José María Gonzales, a sometime commandant of the nearby Spanish post of Los Adaës.

The original registers of this parish are no longer publicly accessible; but translated abstracts for the colonial era are available as E. S. Mills, *Natchitoches, 1729–1803: Abstracts of the Catholic Church Registers of the French and Spanish Post of St. Jean Baptiste des Natchitoches in Louisiana;* E. S. Mills, "Natchitoches Baptisms, 1724–1776: A Supplement," *Natchitoches Genealogist* 7 (April 1983): 6–11; and E. S. Mills, *Natchitoches, 1800–1826.* Other nineteenth-century antebellum sacramental entries from St. François appear in E. S. Mills, *Natchitoches Church Marriages, 1818–1850: Translated Abstracts from the Registers of St. François des Natchitoches, Louisiana.* The subsequent series of nineteenth-century baptismal records by Judy Riffle cover only the "white" registers. Sacramental records from the other church parishes in the civil parish of Natchitoches, used for this Cane River study, are similarly restricted and have not been published. An index to some records of the church established by Coincoin's sons is available as *St. Augustine Catholic Church of Isle Brevelle: Index of Baptismal Records, Book 1, 1852–1889* (Natchitoches, La.: St. Augustine Historical Society, 2000).

6. Mills, *Natchitoches, 1729–1803*, entry 33 (François, bapt. Dec. 26, 1735).

7. Ibid., entry 11 (François and Marie Françoise, Jan. 8, 1736). Note that the sacramental acts are not in numerical sequence. Originally, they were recorded in small folios, by type of sacrament, rather than by date. They were later bound together in a nonchronological order, with dates overlapping across sections and volumes.

8. The children of François and Marie Françoise were as follows: (1) Marie Gertrude *dite* Dgimby, bapt. Nov. 18, 1736; (2) François Jr. *dit* Choera, bapt. Dec. 18, 1738; (3) Jean Baptiste *dit* Chucha, born about 1740; (4) Marie Thérèse *dite* Coincoin, bapt. Aug. 24, 1742; (5) Barnabé, born Sept. 9, 1744, and bur. Sept. 20, 1748; (6) Marie Jeanne *dite* Jeanneton, born about 1746; (7) Marie Louise *dite* Mariotte, born about 1748 or 1749; (8) Bonaventure, bapt. June 18, 1751; (9) Anne Hyacinthe, bapt. Sept. 13, 1753; (10) Louise Marguerite *dite* Yancdose, born 1755 or 1756; and (11) François(e), bapt. Apr. 21, 1758. For these baptisms and burials, see Mills, *Natchitoches, 1729–1803*, entries 48, 111, 225, 269, 279 or 287 (Marie Louise), 305, 392, 523, 565, 677, 824. Also see Succession of St. Denys, docs. 176–78; and Succession of Wife of St. Denys, docs. 203–06, 208, 212. These St. Denis documents were created as part of Natchitoches's colonial notarial records

and, in the twentieth century, bound into volumes that now constitute the Natchitoches Colonial Archives (hereinafter NCA), maintained in the public office of the Clerk of Court, Natchitoches. However, many St. Denis documents were removed from that series prior to binding and, as loose papers, have long been guarded in the private office of the clerk. They and others in that private cache have since been microfilmed as "[Natchitoches] Miscellaneous Archive Records, 1733–1820," microfilm F.T. 565, frames 373–74, Louisiana State Archives, Baton Rouge.

9. Partition of Slaves of St. Denis, Dec. 10, 1756, doc. 176 (3 lists); Aug. 23, 1757, doc. 186 (1 list); ca. 1756–57, doc. 212 (1 list), and ca. 1757–58, doc. 215 (3 lists), NCA.

10. Partition of Slaves of St. Denis, docs. 176, 186, 212, 215, NCA.

11. Partition of Slaves of St. Denis, 1758, unnumbered document, which places "Chucha" (Jean Baptiste) with his sisters "Coincoin" (Marie Thérèse) and Marie Jeanne in Lot 5. A translated typescript of a 1778 document from the estate of Louis Juchereau de St. Denis Jr. renders Chucha's name as "Chocras"; see Laura L. Porteous, trans., "Index to [Abstracts of] the Spanish Judicial Records of Louisiana," *Louisiana Historical Quarterly* 13 (Jan. 1930): 183. While Porteous's work is called an "Index," it offers actual translations and abstracts.

12. St. Denis Successions, docs. 176–78, 203–206, NCA. One recent archaeological study of Cane River questions the identity of François and Marie Françoise as Coincoin's parents, saying "G. B. Mills (1977 [*Forgotten People*]) has argued that she was born in Louisiana of first-generation African parents, rather than being native to Africa, but his claim is based on rather shaky archival evidence." See Kevin C. MacDonald, Aubra L. Lee, and Emma Morley, "The Archaeology of Local Myths and Heritage Tourism: The Case of Cane River's Melrose Plantation," in *A Future for Archaeology: The Past in the Present,* ed. Robert Layton et al. (Walnut Creek, Calif.: Left Coast Press, 2006), 127–42, specifically 128 for quote. However, at that writing, the team of authors had not had access to all the relevant records. The solid trail of evidence for Coincoin's identity was subsequently laid out in Mills, "Documenting a Slave's Birth, Parentage, and Origins (Marie Thérèse Coincoin, 1742–1816)."

13. Marie de St. Denis [Mme. de Soto] to Governor Esteban Miró, Aug. 23, 1780, and May 7, 1782, legajo 195, Papeles Procedentes de Cuba, Archivo General de Indias, Seville (hereinafter cited as PPC-AGI).

14. Dr. Jan Vansina, Department of History, University of Wisconsin, to Gary B. Mills, May 12, 1973.

15. Diedrich Westermann, *Die Glidyi-Ewe in Togo: Züge aus ihrem Gesellschaftsleben* (Berlin: W. de Gruyter, 1935); Dr. Kevin C. MacDonald, Institute of Archaeology, University College London, to Elizabeth Shown Mills, Mar. 7, 2011; also, MacDonald to Mills, email transmitted by Dr. David Morgan, Feb. 9, 2008.

16. The two additional African names and fifteen additional variant spellings from manuscript records, uncovered since 1977 by E. S. Mills, form the basis for a forthcoming study by MacDonald and his colleague Roger Blench of Cambridge, together with Mills and the American archaeologist David Morgan, who has worked extensively on Cane River.

17. Local notarial and court manuscripts created for Dgimby's son François, 1782–1800, spell the name phonetically as Gombeau and Goinbeau. See Joseph Dupré Succession Inventory, Apr. 23, 1782, doc. 2780, NCA; Rex v. François Gombeau, Feb. 25, 1781, doc. 1533, NCA files removed to Melrose Collection (folder 550), Cammie G. Henry Research Center, Northwestern State University, Natchitoches (hereinafter NSU); and Marie Derbanne to son Athanase Dupré, Sale of François *dit* Gombeau, Nov. 8, 1800, doc. 2940, both in "Old Natchitoches Data" (bound typescript, Melrose Collection), 2:72.

18. Mrs. Lee Etta Vaccarini Coutii of Isle Brevelle, the great-great-great-granddaughter of

Marie Thérèse *dite* Coincoin, reported personal recollections of Coinquan Metoyer, son of Neres Pierre, who was given this nickname in memory of his great-grandmother; Mrs. Coutii to author, Mar. 21, 1974. Two of Coincoin's sons also used her African name as a surname in some periods of their lives. Coincoin's one literate son signed his name as Pierre Coinquoin in 1806 records of the U.S. Land Office; see Land Claim of Marie Therese, *négresse libre* (undated but elsewhere set at December 1806), file "OPEL: February 1794," Opelousas Notarial Records Collection, Louisiana State Archives, Baton Rouge. Her black son Nicolas appears under the name Coin Coin in the 1820 U.S. census of Natchitoches Parish, p. 4.

Occasional writers have misidentified this 1820 household as that of Marie Thérèse herself. The previously cited "Archaeology of Local Myths," p. 131, misplaces it at Cedar Bend (on Cane River below Natchitoches), rather than the vicinity of Cedar Bluff, north of Natchitoches. It then offers the census entry as proof that Coincoin was still alive in 1820. To the contrary, when Pierre Metoyer Jr. (aka Coinquoin) drafted a contract of marriage in December 1817 (original document, bound in unpaginated "Marriage & Miscellaneous, Books 2 & 3," Office of the Clerk of Court), he clearly stated that he was the son of *deceased* Marie Thérèse Coincoin. The authors of the archaeological study focused on properties below Natchitoches and were unaware of the existence of Coincoin's black son Nicolas or his settlement above Natchitoches. Nicolas's identity as the "Coin Coin" of the 1820 census is established not just from household data but, more critically, by mapping the landholdings of his census neighbors. That exercise places them adjacent to and surrounding Sections 39 and 75, Township 10N, Range 7W—i.e., Augustin Metoyer's Private Land Claim B1955, which he had exchanged for Nicolas's claim to Sections 68 and 114, T8N R6W, Claim R&R 307. That exchange (documented by affidavits filed in the 1835–40 legal suits of Roubieu v. Metoyer, bundle 59, case 1395, and Metoyer v. Roubieu, bundle 74, case 1473, District Court Files, Clerk of Court's Office, Natchitoches; hereinafter cited as NCCO) enabled Augustin to physically consolidate his property on Isle Brevelle while providing Nicolas with a residence near the community of Spanish settlers from Nacogdoches with whom he had grown to manhood. Some of these points will be developed in later chapters.

19. Interview with Mrs. Coutii, Mar. 24, 1974.

20. John W. Blassingame, *The Slave Community: Plantation Life in the Antebellum South* (New York: Oxford University Press, 1972), 22.

21. Hall, *Africans in Colonial Louisiana,* 166. Also see Gwendolyn Midlo Hall, *Slavery and African Ethnicities in the Americas: Restoring the Links* (Chapel Hill: University of North Carolina Press, 2005).

22. Given that slave importation was banned in 1728 and that Marie Françoise's purchase has not been found in the record of any Louisiana post, if she was purchased after the 1728 cessation then that purchase (as with her husband) likely occurred through trade with the Spanish of Los Adaës. However, her purchase could have occurred at the Natchitoches post before 1732 with no record extant. When Louisiana changed administration in 1732, all records relating to the post were apparently taken back to France. If they survive, they have never been identified.

23. French, ed., *Historical Collections of Louisiana,* 3:94, *Code Noir,* Article 63.

24. Mills, *Natchitoches, 1729–1803,* entry 369 (June 12, 1744).

25. Partition of Slaves of St. Denis, docs. 176 and 186–87, NCA.

26. Mills, *Natchitoches, 1729–1803,* entries 817 (Madame de St. Denis, bur. Apr. 16, 1758 [corrected date]) and 820 (François and Marie Françoise, bur. Apr. 19, 1758).

27. Mills, *Natchitoches, 1729–1803,* entries 677 and 824. These entries muddle the child's identity. The first entry records the baptism of a male child "François," said to be the "son of François and Françoise, slaves of St. Denis." The second act cites the burial "of an infant of Françoise"

but gives no gender. Doc. 208 of Widow St. Denis's succession clarifies the matter; it reports the death of the orphaned *négritte* (i.e., girl child) who had been assigned to the lot just drawn by Marie de St. Denis de Soto, but had died at the age of eight days.

28. In keeping with French succession laws, St. Denis's illegitimate daughter, born of an Indian woman prior to his marriage, was not entitled to a share of the estate. For the evidence that identifies this daughter, see Gary B. Mills and Elizabeth Shown Mills, "Louise Marguerite: St. Denis' Other Daughter," *Southern Studies* 16 (Fall 1977): 321–28. The daughter's surname led Burton and Smith, *Colonial Natchitoches*, 29, to present her as the offspring of St. Denis's legal marriage; however, abundant evidence proves otherwise, and this daughter neither participated in the estate partition nor acquired any of the St. Denis slaves.

29. Succession of Wife of St. Denys, docs. 203–205, 212, 215, NCA.

30. Mills, "Which Marie Louise Is 'Mariotte'?" The original edition of *Forgotten People* mistakenly identified the black Marie Louise *dite* Mariotte as Coincoin's *daughter* Marie Louise, rather than Coincoin's *sister* Marie Louise; and subsequent scholars have followed that lead. The 2006 Mariotte essay separates their identities.

31. These seven births and two sales will be individually discussed later in the narrative.

32. Details of the 1729 dispute between St. Denis and Père Raphaël are found in the affidavit of Barrios y Jáuregui, Nov. 5, 1757, *Bexar Archives Translations,* vol. 32:1–5, Stephen F. Austin State University, Nacogdoches, Texas. Also available as *Bexar Archives Translations,* microfilm edition, 26 reels, Frederick, Md.: University Microfilms [ProQuest], 1989.

33. George Washington Cable, *The Creoles of Louisiana* (New York: Charles Scribner's Sons, 1884), 25.

34. Roger Baudier, *The Catholic Church in Louisiana* (New Orleans: A.W. Hyatt, 1939), 122–29, 147–51, 198–99; also Mills and Mills, "Missionaries Compromised," 30–47.

35. Mills, "Quintanilla's Crusade," surveys the religious roots of the post and analyzes the effectiveness of reforms put into place by the Spanish priest who—as shall be shown in this chapter—stridently targeted Coincoin.

36. Mills, *Natchitoches, 1729–1803*, entries 273 (Pierre Antoine of St. Denis, bapt. Dec. 2, 1746), 283 (Louis of St. Denis, bapt. Sept. 1, 1747), 524 (Antoine of de Mézières, bapt. June 10, 1751), 582 (Géneviève of de Mézières, bapt. Aug. 4, 1754), 595 (Michel of St. Denis, bapt. Mar. 30, 1955), and 646 (Louise Cirena of de Blanc, bapt. Feb. 8, 1757).

37. Blassingame, *The Slave Community,* 82.

38. By the terms of the Treaty of Fontainbleau in 1762, Louis XV of France ceded the Louisiana colony to his cousin, Charles III of Spain.

39. Mills, *Natchitoches, 1729–1803*, entries 713 (Marie Louise, bapt. Sept. 8, 1759) and 462 (Thérèse, bapt. Sept. 24, 1761). For other documents stating a racial category for these daughters, see Marie Thérèse Coincoin to Marie Louise, and Marie St. Denis to Marie Thérèse Coincoin, docs. 2596 and 2804, NCA.

40. Antonio Manuel de Soto Bermúdez's name is rendered many ways by many writers. Some render his name as French, some identify his family name as "Bermudez" and others call it "de Soto." He himself signed his name consistently on multiple documents as Antonio Manuel de Soto Bermúdez—identifying, in Spanish fashion, de Soto as his parental family and Bermúdez as his maternal family. This is the identification used for him herein.

41. Mills, *Natchitoches, 1729–1803*, entry 484 (Françoise, bapt. July 8, 1763). For the first of many records that identify her as black, see Marie Jucheraud de Saint Denys (Mme. de Soto) to Delissard Jouhannis, sale of three slaves, including "Françoise, *négresse* of 7 or 8 years," Dec. 17, 1772, doc. 765, NCA.

42. Mills, *Natchitoches, 1729–1803*, entry 862 (Jean Joseph, bapt. Mar. 29, 1766). Parish registers have a gap during the period of Nicolas's birth. For his identification as a son of Coincoin, see Gil y Barbo to Nicolas Augustin [Metoyer], Sale of slave Nicolas for manumission, in Carmen Leal, *Translations of Statistical and Census Reports of Texas, 1782–1836, and Sources Documenting the Black in Texas, 1603–1803*, 3 rolls (San Antonio: Institute of Texan Culture, 1979), roll 3, frames 826–29. Nicolas's racial composition is consistently described in the Nacogdoches, Texas, censuses of the 1790s as "*negro*, native of Natchitoches" and more explicitly in the 1838 court testimony of a French neighbor at Natchitoches as a "black" man "appearing to be a real African"; see affidavit of Judge C. E. Grenaux in the conjoined cases, Roubieu v. Metoyer and Metoyer v. Roubieu, 1835–40.

43. Mills, *Natchitoches, 1729–1803*, entry 862.

44. In 1779, in the suit Ls. Diard v. Manuel de Soto and wife, Mme. de Soto wrote that she "had been attacked by various maladies for five months, without any improvement in her condition"; see doc. 1434, "[Natchitoches] Miscellaneous Archive Records, 1733–1820," microfilm F.T. 565, frames 373–74. In a 1790 deed, she stated that she had been confined to her bed for ten years or so; Marie St. Denis to Marie Thérèse Coincoin, doc. 2804, NCA.

45. Family tradition among descendants of Coincoin and Metoyer called him "Thomas," rather than "Pierre" as he always identified himself. Their identification of him as "Thomas" was a polite fiction, designed to avoid offending the white offspring of "Pierre." In this same vein, tradition split Claude Thomas Pierre Metoyer into "two brothers," one of whom "married" Coincoin while the other wed a white Creole.

46. Most contemporary merchants at Natchitoches were also taverners. Metoyer's mercantile activities are documented by several notarial acts in NCA: Affidavit of Étienne Pavie, Sept. 14, 1771, doc. 713; Agreement between Merchants, June 13, 1772, doc. 739; Metoyer for de la Chaise v. Bouët Lafitte, Feb. 23, 1776, doc. 1066; Metoyer et al. v. St. Denis, 1774–76, doc. 1219; Metoyer from Joseph Marie Armant, Power of Attorney, May 22, 1778, doc. 1400; Merchant's Bill from Metoyer to Succession of Roche Petit, Nov. 9, 1778, doc. 1430. For his militia (not military) role, see the 1780 and 1782 Spanish militia rosters translated in Mills, *Natchitoches Colonials*, 37–44; in 1780 Metoyer held the noncommissioned post *maréchal de logis* (staff-sergeant). His transition to planter status at Natchitoches is detailed in chapter 2.

47. Metoyer's father, Baptiste Nicolas François Metoyer, was born in the parish of St. Denis de Rheims in 1715, the son of the merchant Jean Metoyer and his wife Françoise Galloteau. At the age of twenty-six, Nicolas François (who, like his son, did not use his first baptismal name) migrated to La Rochelle and established himself in trade there in the parish of Notre-Dame. Two years later he married the twenty-nine-year-old Marie Anne Drapron, a native of Chaignoller, Parish of Dompierre, in the province of Aunis. Mlle. Drapron was also from a merchant family, being the daughter of the deceased merchant François Drapron and his widow, Anne Naudin. At the time of her marriage to Metoyer, Mlle. Drapron was living in the parish of St. Sauveur. Genealogical information on the Metoyer family of France is provided in the baptismal record of Claude Thomas Pierre Metoyer, dated May 14, 1744; in the marriage record of his parents, dated Feb. 20, 1743; and in the burial record of his father, dated May 15, 1766. All are preserved in the *actes civile* of Rheims, Chaignoller, and La Rochelle; photocopies in the possession of the author, provided by the respective departmental archives, do not identify the precise registers from which each photocopy was made.

48. 1801 will of Claude Thomas Pierre Metoyer, folder 728, Melrose Collection.

49. Edwin A. Davis, *Louisiana: A Narrative History* (1961; rpr., Baton Rouge: Claitor's, 1971), 87.

50. Affidavit of Pierre Metoyer to Athanase de Mézières, Rex v. de Soto, doc. 1227, NCA.

51. Works Progress Administration, "Survey of the Federal Archives in Louisiana: Alphabetical and Chronological Digest of the Acts and Deliberations of the Cabildo, 1769–1803," 10 vols. (typescript, New Orleans Public Library, 1934–39), 1:65.

52. Mills, "(de) Mézières-Trichel-Grappe," provides the most complete study of the origin and family connections of Athanase de Mézières and corrects several misassumptions popularized in Louisiana literature.

53. Mills, *Natchitoches, 1729–1803,* entry 921 (Marie Susanne and Nicolas Augustin, bapt. Feb. 1, 1768). For the identity of the godmothers, see ibid., entries 299 and 335.

54. Mills, "Quintanilla's Crusade," 280–81.

55. Mills, *Natchitoches, 1729–1803,* entry 2283 (Marie Eulalie, bapt. Jan. 28, 1776).

56. Quoted in Bolton, ed., *Athanase de Mézières,* 2:134–35; see also Mills, "Quintanilla's Crusade," 282–83.

57. Quoted in Foner, "Free People of Color," 411. *Plaçage* was a system of quasi-marriage common in early Louisiana and the Caribbean, designed to circumvent laws against interracial marriage. Young women of color "placed" themselves (or were placed by parents, guardians, or an occasional owner) in a long-term, monogamous union with a white male who agreed to provide for them and their future children. A few plaçages were formalized with contracts that specified the terms of the relationship and the financial settlement that would govern a breakup, but most plaçages—including all those along Cane River—were informally contracted.

58. *Badillo v. Tio,* 6 King La., 129 (1848).

59. James Hugo Johnston, *Race Relations in Virginia and Miscegenation in the South, 1776–1860* (1937; rpr., Amherst: University of Massachusetts Press, 1970), 190.

60. Tannenbaum, *Slave and Citizen,* 121–23. The varied factors propelling this miscegenation in the Upper and Lower South are well developed by Williamson in his "Genesis" chapter of *New People,* 5–59.

61. Two censuses were actually taken of the Natchitoches post in 1766, one on January 27 and a second on May 6, in preparation for the transfer of Louisiana's administration from France to Spain. The first census showed a 55:54 male-female ratio for adult whites, but was highly flawed. The recount, which includes many provable residents omitted from the first count, shows a 127:75 male-female ratio for "whites." For a published translation of these censuses from the Archivo General de la Nación, Mexico City, and Audencia de Santo Domingo, Archivo General de Indias, Seville, see Mills, *Natchitoches Colonials,* 9–20. For further nuances regarding the male-female sex differential at Natchitoches, see Burton and Smith, *Colonial Natchitoches,* 26–28; and the many statistical quantifications of Antonio Acosta Rodríguez, *La Población de Luisiana Española, 1763–1803* (Madrid: Ministerio de Asuntos Exteriores, 1979). Note, however, that Acosta Rodríguez based his findings for Natchitoches in 1766 on the flawed January return, rather than the May recount.

62. Similar ambiguity existed for *métis* in New Orleans, where "racial identity . . . was very malleable and subjective," according to Hanger, *Bounded Lives,* 15. Hanger's further explication deserves a qualifier: namely, the ambiguity most often happened with individuals whose mothers were Native American, rather than African American. After noting that "a person's racial designation depended on who recorded it, what purpose it served, when it was recorded, and what physical characteristics were considered most relevant," she gives specific examples focused on the malleability of *Indian-ness.*

63. White females of colonial Natchitoches, for example, had an overall illegitimacy rate of only 4 percent, with 11 percent of first-born children arriving less than 8 months after marriage. Comparable figures for "premature" first births in other contemporary societies include

Bristol, R. I. (1740–80), 44–49 percent; Sturbridge, Mass. (1730–99), 25–33 percent; Clayworth, Nottinghamshire, Eng. (1650–1750), 10.2 percent; and Crulai, France (1674–1742), 9.5 percent. See Elizabeth Shown Mills, "Social and Family Patterns on the Colonial Louisiana Frontier," *Sociological Spectrum* 2 (July–Dec. 1982): 233–48, particularly 242–43; and E. S. Mills, "Family and Social Patterns of the Colonial Louisiana Frontier: A Quantitative Analysis, 1714–1803" (New College honors thesis, University of Alabama, 1981), 96–118, which analyzes patterns of morality more finely for the reconstituted colonial population of roughly 2,000 free citizens.

64. Quintanilla also targeted one other female, a free "white" woman of Gypsy origin, whom he accused (with limited success) of prostitution; see Rex v. Babet Varangue et al., 1778, doc. 1308, NCA.

65. Quintanilla to de Mézières, Oct. 23, 1777, Rex v. de Soto, doc. 1227, NCA. Like many of the documents in this collection of notarial records, this numbered "document" is actually a bound file containing numerous individual documents.

66. De Mézières to Metoyer, Oct. 23, 1777, and Metoyer to de Mézières, Oct. 27, 1777, Rex v. de Soto. In identifying Coincoin as Marie Gertrude, de Mézières repeated a mistake he had made once before in a document by which he allowed his sister-in-law to illegally sell Coincoin's first-born son; see Marie St. Denis to Antonio Gil y Barbo, Nov. 17, 1772, doc. 757, NCA.

67. Quintanilla to de Mézières, June 20, 1778, Rex v. de Soto, doc. 1227; Bolton, *Athanase de Mézières*, 2:172, 214–15.

68. Quintanilla to de Mézières, June 20, 1778.

69. Shelby T. McCloy, "Negroes and Mulattoes in Eighteenth-Century France," *Journal of Negro History* 30 (July 1945): 276–92.

70. Mills, *Natchitoches, 1729–1803*, entry 332 (Eleonore de St. Denis, bapt. Nov. 5, 1750).

71. Ibid., entry 711 (de Soto–St. Denis marriage, June 2, 1754); de Soto–St. Denis permission to marry, May 20, 1754, roll 9, frames 497–98, microfilmed Bexar Archives, Barker Texas History Center, University of Texas, Austin. Also Inquiry into the Desertion of "Manuel de Sotto," Jan.–Feb. 1756, roll 9, frames 643–46. For an overview of the de Soto–St. Denis couple who played pivotal roles in Coincoin's life, see Elizabeth Shown Mills, "Marie des Neiges Juchereau de St-Denis," and "Antonio Emanuel de Soto y Bermudes" *Dictionary of Louisiana Biography*, 1:449–50 and 2:755–56. For the commandant who aided in his defection, see Jacqueline O. Vidrine, "César de Blanc," *Dictionary of Louisiana Biography*, 1:223. The sixty-seven-year-old nobleman, after the death of his wife, married Mme. de Soto's teenaged sister, Marie des Douleurs Simone, *dite* "Dolorite"; Mills, *Natchitoches, 1729–1803*, entry 355 (marr., DeBlanc–St. Denis).

72. Manuel Antonio de Soto Bermúdez, Request for Pardon, Los Adaës, E. 3/21/1763–4/8/1763, 010:0160-68, original manuscripts, Bexar Archives, University of Texas Institute of Texan Cultures, San Antonio.

73. David K. Bjork, ed., "Documents Relating to Alexandro O'Reilly and an Expedition Sent Out by Him from New Orleans to Natchitoches, 1769–1770," *Louisiana Historical Quarterly* 7 (Jan. 1924): 23. For the actual Spanish orders upon which de Soto was arrested and transferred to Mexico City, see MX, E. 4/5/1769, 010:0665-66; MX, E. 1/29/1770, 010:0694-98; MX, 7/24/1770, 010:0744; and MX, 8/5/1770, 010:0747-48, Bexar Archives.

74. De Soto's ten-year sojourn in a Mexico City prison ended between July 29, 1778, when his wife executed her last document as a *sole feme* (doc. 1312, NCA), and Apr. 13, 1779, when notice was served "on Mr. Don Manuel in person" at his home, in the case of Louis Diart v. Manuel de Soto & wife, doc. 1434, NCA.

75. This mill that Mme. de Soto furnished the parish was of considerable value, being one of only two or so mills in the entire colony; see Davis, *Louisiana*, 133, citing a 1768 report of

Governor Antonio de Ulla stating the existence of only two mills at that time, one of them at Natchitoches.

76. Marie de St. Denis de Soto to Commandant, June 26, 1778, Rex v. de Soto.

77. Ibid. Mme. de Soto's assessment of Quintanilla's homilies was not unfairly critical. In 1792, after he had been transferred through multiple assignments elsewhere, a colleague called him a prime example of why the Spanish church in Louisiana had poor relations with its French subjects—citing "the ridicule excited in Lent by the sermons of Father Luis de Quintanilla." See Thomas Timothy McAvoy, Lawrence J. Bradley et al., eds., *Records of the Diocese of Louisiana and the Floridas,* 12 microfilm rolls (Notre Dame: University of Notre Dame, 1967), roll 1, for Oct. 20, 1792, Joachim de Portillo to Estevan de Quinoñes.

78. Marie de St. Denis de Soto to Commandant, June 26, 1778, Rex v. de Soto.

79. Ibid.

80. Mme. de Soto and Quintanilla had already locked horns, for example, over the succession of her late brother, Louis Juchereau de St. Denis Jr. Prior to his death, St. Denis had requested the commandant to draft a will for him, leaving his estate to his half-Indian wife, Marie (Derbanne) Barbier, by whom he had no children. De Mézières refused because, under colonial law, St. Denis's siblings or their legitimate offspring (which included de Mézières's daughter by his late wife) would be St. Denis's heirs if he died intestate. After de Mézières's refusal, St. Denis, almost as a dying request, asked the priest to help his wife obtain the inheritance. Quintanilla did just that, thereby earning the enmity of the financially desperate Mme. de Soto, who went to great lengths to have her brother's wish disallowed so that she might inherit a share of the estate. Translated documents relating to this matter are available as Porteous, "Index to [Abstracts of] the Spanish Judicial Records of Louisiana," 177–93. For other conflicts between these antagonists, see Mills, "Quintanilla's Crusade," 283–90.

81. Marie de St. Denis de Soto to Commandant, June 26, 1778, Rex v. de Soto, NCA.

82. Quintanilla to A. de Mézières, June 27, 1778, ibid. Italics added.

83. De Mézières sent his own multiracial son (and probably the child's mother) to New Orleans before the child's baptism; for that son's subsequent marriage as a free man, see Juan Francisco Messiere, Register M3, "Libro Primero de Matrimonios de Negros y Mulatos," p. 10, St. Louis Cathedral, New Orleans. For de Mézières's affliction, see Jack Jackson, *Los Mesteños: Spanish Ranching in Texas, 1721–1821* (College Station: Texas A&M University Press, 1986), 201, n. 42, citing an official discussion of the "diarrhea y Gonorrea" from which de Mézières was then rapidly deteriorating; for that discussion, Jackson cites Domingo Cabello y Robles to Carlos Francisco, Marqués de Croix, Oct. 20, 1779, Bexar Archives. For other perspectives on the political and military affairs that were far more pressing concerns for de Mézières than miscegenation, see Donald E. Chipman and Harriett Denise Joseph, *Notable Men and Women of Spanish Texas* (Austin: University of Texas Press, 1999), 150–77.

84. Article 6 of the *Code Noir* stated: "It must be absolutely prohibited to all white subjects of either sex to contract marriage with any blacks or mulattoes, upon pain of being dishonorably expelled from the Colony." See *Code Noir, ou Loi Municipal Servant de Reglement* (New Orleans: Antoine Boudousquié, 1778), 2.

85. Mme. de Soto to Metoyer, Sale of Slaves, Mar. 31, 1776, doc. 1161, NCA.

86. Marie de St. Denis to Metoyer, Jul. 29, 1778, doc.1312, ibid.; Mills, *Natchitoches, 1729–1803,* entry 2324 (Antoine Joseph, bapt. Feb. 8, 1778).

87. *Code Noir,* Article 10, p. 3.

88. Testament of Claude Thomas Pierre Metoyer, Feb. 26, 1783, Acts of Leonardo Mazange. No. 7 (Jan. 2–Apr. 7, 1783), 188–91, New Orleans Notarial Archives; in this document Metoyer reports the private manumission but does not give an exact date.

89. Bolton, *Athanase de Mézières,* 1:116–22; 2:303–4, 327.

90. For the protracted exodus, see Commandant de Vaugine to Governor, Aug. 9, 1782, identifying removals of the past two years, leg. 195, PPC-AGI. The attempts at relocation were generally not successful.

2. A Matriarchal Legacy

1. De Mézières to Unzaga y Amezaga, Feb. 16, 1776, in Bolton, *Athanase de Mézières,* 2:120–21, reports totals for the census "taken at the beginning of this year." The full enumeration does not appear to exist. For the 1785 statistical totals, see *An Account of Louisiana, Being an Abstract of Documents in the Offices of the Department of State and of the Treasury* (Philadelphia: John Conrad & Co., 1803), 45.

2. H. Sophie Burton, "Free People of Color in Spanish Colonial Natchitoches: Manumission and Dependency on the Louisiana-Texas Frontier," *Louisiana History* 45 (Spring 2004): 173–97, interprets the experiences of most of the free men and women of color at the post. Mills, "Which Marie Louise Is 'Mariotte'?" delves more deeply into the life of the black female who, as an entrepreneur, was second only to her sister Coincoin. For an extended treatment of Jeannot Mulon, the most prominent free male of color in colonial Natchitoches, see Elizabeth Shown Mills, "Jeannot Mulon *dit* La Brun, f.m.c., Colonial Natchitoches, Louisiana," archived at www.bcgcertification.org/skillbuilders/extendedreport.pdf. The life of one other contemporary freedman of historical significance—Yves *dit* Pacalé, whose home was removed to the town of Natchitoches, where it serves as a tourist center—is sketched in Elizabeth Shown Mills and Gary B. Mills, *Tales of Old Natchitoches* (Natchitoches, La.: Association for the Preservation of Historic Natchitoches, 1978), 41–45.

3. Mills, *Natchitoches, 1729–1803,* entries 2383 (Maria Francisca Rosalia, bapt., Dec. 24, 1780) and 2426 (Pedro Todos Santos, bapt., Nov. 10, 1782). The baptismal acts render the names in Spanish, because the priest who recorded them was Iberian and Spanish was then the official language. However, French was the native tongue of both Coincoin and Metoyer; they and their children always rendered their names in French. Hence, their names are rendered in French within this study.

4. See, for example, Commandant de Vaugine to Governor, Aug. 9, 1782, leg. 195, PPC-AGI.

5. Marie de St. Denis to Pierre Metoyer, Apr. 7, 1780, doc. 1473, NCA.

6. Metoyer to François Le Doux, Sept. 19, 1780, doc. 1500, NCA.

7. Metoyer to Commandant, Sept. 1780, doc. 1501, NCA.

8. 1801 Will of Metoyer, folder 728, Melrose Collection.

9. Acts of Leonardo Mazange, Register № 7:188–91, New Orleans Notarial Archives, Although Pierre Metoyer stated in this will that he "had no children," his paternity of Coincoin's children was, and has since been, widely recognized in the area. In 1883, for example, his white granddaughter Mme. Valery Gaiennié made a sworn statement to a family attorney that her grandfather was the father of "a colored son, Augustin Coincoin" and of Augustin's siblings. See "Notes," folder 12, box 2, Safford Collection, Watson Memorial Library, NSU.

10. Mills, *"Isle of Canes* and Issues of Conscience," 167–72, develops this point. Under the prevailing Spanish law, illegitimate children could inherit from their mothers without restriction; but they could inherit from a father, up to one-twelfth of his estate, only if they were born of "a stable concubinage *between persons who could marry each other.*" For an overview of the changing laws toward children of concubinages in Louisiana, which would affect Coincoin's offspring for generations to come, see Robert A. Pascal, "Louisiana Succession and Related Laws and the

Illegitimate: Thoughts Prompted by *Labine* v. *Vincent,*" *Tulane Law Review* 46 (Dec. 1971): 167ff. For the changing laws in France that affected Metoyer's 1783 and 1801 wills, see Matthew Gerber, "The End of Bastardy: Illegitimacy in France from the Reformation through the Revolution" (Ph.D. diss., University of California at Berkeley, 2003).

11. Acts of Leonardo Mazange, Register № 7, 188.

12. An arpent in this place and time was roughly two-thirds of an acre.

13. The complexities of Metoyer's title to this property are developed in Mills, "Demythicizing History."

14. Acts of Leonardo Mazange, Register № 7:189–90. Metoyer's siblings who would have been forced heirs under the laws of France and Louisiana apparently included one brother who also settled in the colony. In his will of 1801 Metoyer referenced a brother at New Orleans to whom he had lent a slave, but did not name him. The 1790 militia roll of the city includes only one Metoyer; and that man's burial record of 1806 confirms that he shared the birth place and year of Pierre Metoyer's only surviving brother. See "Summaria formada sobre un Memorial que intentaban presentar los Milicianos del batallon de la Nueva Orleans . . . 1790," leg. 168e, PPC-AGI; and St. Louis Cathedral Register F6:94 (April 3, 1806, burial of Francisco Metoyer, bachelor, native of La Rochelle), Archdiocesan Archives, New Orleans.

15. Mills, *Natchitoches, 1729–1803,* entry 2489 (François, bapt. Oct. 4, 1784). This entry identifies the mother "Theresa" as a "*free* Negress" and her son as a "free mulato." Again, no father was named.

16. Petition of Jean Délouche, July 6, 1785; certification of Commandant Louis Charles de Blanc, July 12, 1785; order of survey from Estevan Miró, March 28, 1787; and affidavit of De Blanc relative to the sale of the land [n.d.], all in "Louisiana Miscellany Collection, 1724–1837," Manuscripts Division, Library of Congress; available as LC microfilm 17,495 (5 reels), reel 4, frames 1688–89. The actual sale of the land is not on record.

17. Tract Book, T8N R7W, Northwestern District of Louisiana, 17–18, and File A1679, Maria Theresa, Free Negress, in Louisiana State Land Office, Baton Rouge. This land is identified on American survey maps as Sections 18 and 89 of Township 8 North, Range 6 West in the Cedar Bend area of present Cane River on the old Grand Côte.

18. The existence of the separation agreement is noted in the "Index to French Archives," NCA, as Pierre Metoyer to Marie Thérèse Coincoin, Donation, doc. 2119. The actual document is missing. Various terms of the agreement are reiterated in two later documents: Metoyer's 1801 will, Melrose Collection; and Coincoin to Metoyer, Abrogation of Agreement, May 28, 1802, Misc. Book 2:206–7, NCCO.

19. Bolton, *Athanase de Mézières,* 2:122.

20. Mills, *Natchitoches, 1729–1803,* entry 921 (Marie Susanne and Nicolas Augustin, bapt. Feb. 1, 1768; godmothers Marie Louise Buard and Marie Françoise Buard).

21. Metoyer to Marie Thérèse Coincoin, doc. 2119, and Metoyer to Marie Thérèse Buard, doc. 2121, as noted in the colonial "Index to French Archives." Both documents disappeared from the Clerk of Court's Office before the colonial series was bound in the mid-1900s. Metoyer's personal copy of his marriage contract surfaced after the publication of the first edition of *Forgotten People* triggered correspondence from a reader. In the 1950s, one Bob Martin was a teenaged employee of an Alexandria, Louisiana, flower shop whose owner was said to be the remarried widow of Valery Gaiennié Metoyer, a great-great-grandson of Pierre Metoyer and Marie Thérèse Buard. When the owner threw out a box of old French papers, the teenager salvaged them and eventually gave them to his brother, Wayne C. Martin of Houston. Among these papers, Wayne Martin found the personal unrecorded copy of the Metoyer-Buard marriage contract and, in 1991, pro-

vided a photocopy to the Millses. That copy is now archived in the Mills Collection, Cammie G. Henry Research Center.

22. Syndics in Spanish Louisiana were justices of the peace, appointed to office, and were typically established at distances of three leagues apart. At Natchitoches, where settlements were widely scattered, one syndic was assigned to each major outlying settlement. Subordinate to the commandant, they were permitted to hold court and render decisions in small cases and held police authority over roads, taxes, Negroes, and travelers; see *An Account of Louisiana*, 35.

23. "Répartition a L'ocasion de 75 p. que La Comunote de Mes^rs Les habitants son Convenu de Payer a Mr J. B^te Maurin fette le l^r Mars 1790," folder 1, Natchitoches Parish Records, 1734–1916, Department of Archives, Louisiana State University, Baton Rouge. For a more accessible translation, see Mills, *Natchitoches Colonials*, 68–75. For the parish claim handled by Metoyer, see *American State Papers: Documents Legislative and Executive of the Congress of the United States*, 38 vols. (Washington, D.C.: Gales & Seaton, 1832–61), *Public Lands*, 3:195; also Claim 260-873, Congregation of the Roman Catholic Church, for Lot 26, Section 43, Township 9 North, Range 7 West, Louisiana State Land Office.

24. 1810 U.S. Census, Natchitoches Parish, p. 209, line 29. Numerous entries for purchases of land by Metoyer are entered in the "Index to French Archives," NCA; and the "Index to Conveyances, 1800–1880," NCCO.

25. Metoyer's will of 1801 identifies his three legitimate children. For their baptisms, which also identify their parents, see Mills, *Natchitoches, 1729–1803*, entries 1598 and 2005 (dual French and Spanish entries for Pierre Victorin, born Sept. 5, 1789), 2051 (Marie Thérèse Elisabeth, born Nov. 14, 1790), and 2180 (François Benjamin, born July 11, 1794).

26. Burton, "Free People of Color in Spanish Colonial Natchitoches," 173–97.

27. Lewis C. Gray, *History of Agriculture in the Southern United States to 1860*, 2 vols. (1933; rpr., Gloucester, Mass.: Peter Smith, 1958), 1:73.

28. Lawrence Kinnaird, ed., *Spain in the Mississippi Valley, 1765–1794*, Part 1, *The Revolutionary Period, 1765–1781* (Washington, D.C.: U.S. Government Printing Office, 1949), 297–98.

29. Antoine-Simon Le Page du Pratz, *The History of Louisiana* (trans. from the French, London, 1774; rpr., New Orleans: H. S. Harmanson, 1947), 172.

30. Ibid., 172–73.

31. "État de la Cargaison d'un Bateau Apartenant a Pierre Metoyer et d'un Gabarre a Marie Thérèse," Apr. 28, 1792, roll 1, Jack D. L. Holmes Collection (microfilmed documents relating to Natchitoches and adjacent territory from Papeles de Estado and Papeles de Cuba, Archivo General de Indias, Seville), 12 rolls, Northwestern State University Archives.

32. Gray, *Agriculture in the Southern United States*, 1:78; also see Heloise H. Cruzat, trans., "Louisiana in 1724," *Louisiana Historical Quarterly* 12 (Jan. 1929): 122. The most recent studies of the Natchitoches economy note a late-Spanish-era increase in hunting among free Natchitoches males, who hunted buffalo, deer, and bear, and report some slave participation, but do not address the rendition of oil specifically; see Burton and Smith, *Colonial Natchitoches*, 120; and Burton and Smith, "Slavery in the Colonial Louisiana Backcountry: Natchitoches, 1714–1803," *Louisiana History* 52 (Spring 2011): 133–88.

33. Metoyer's will of 1801, Melrose Collection.

34. Report of Eduardo Nugent and Juan Kelly, 1769, in Bjork, "Documents Relating to Alexandro O'Reilly," 34.

35. For indigo production in 1775, see Athanase de Mézières to Unzaga y Amezaga, Feb. 16, 1776, in Bolton, *Athanase de Mézières*, 2:120–21, citing the shipment to market of nine *quintals* (hundred-weights) of indigo and fifteen *fanegas* (about 1,740 pounds) of indigo seed. For the

location of colonial indigo sheds in Coincoin's neighborhood, see surveys by Pierre Joseph Maës for Mr. P^{re} Metoyer, Feb. 9, 1794, File: February 1794; and survey of Maës for Mr Ailhaud Ste Anne, Dec. 10, 1794, File: December 1794; both in Opelousas Notarial Archives Collection, Louisiana State Archives, Baton Rouge. Maës's concurrent survey of Coincoin's homestead, also maintained in the same February 1794 file, places no *indigoterie* on her land.

36. Davis, *Louisiana*, 134. In colonial days, all settlers of the "northwestern section" fell within the Natchitoches jurisdiction—an area roughly 120 miles long by 70 broad that included all or part of the present parishes of Caddo, Claiborne, Webster, Bossier, Lincoln, Sabine, De Soto, Bienville, Winn, Red River, and Grant.

37. Mills, "Which Marie Louise Is 'Mariotte'?" 193; also Rex v. La Costa, doc. 1499 (1785), NCA; and Laura L. Porteous, "Index to [Abstracts of] the Spanish Judicial Records of Louisiana," *Louisiana Historical Quarterly* 26 (Dec. 1943): 897–906. For Thérèse's nursing skills, see Marie St. Denis to Marie Thérèse Coincoin, doc. 2804, NCA. For Susanne, see Metoyer's 1801 will and Metoyer to Marie Susanne, Manumission, Natchitoches Misc. Book 2, 210–11, NCCO.

38. Claim B2146, "Maria Therese, a free Negress," Louisiana State Land Office, Baton Rouge. Also U.S. Serial Patent 437,269, "Marie Therese Metoyer," General Land Office Records, RG 49, National Archives, Washington, D.C. This land is identified on section maps as Section 55 of Township 8 North, Range 7 West, on the west bank of Old River (formerly Red River).

39. For a sampling of the fanciful accounts created by twentieth-century writers, see "Melrose Manor on Cane River Stands as Relic of World's Strangest Empire," *Hammond* (La.) *Progress*, March 25, 1938; D. Garber, "History of Melrose Plantation like Turning Pages of Novel," *Dallas Morning News*, Oct. 21, 1951, p. 8; "Melrose: Home of Famous Louisiana Authors," *Louisiana REA News* (July 1953), 11; Cedric Dover, *American Negro Art* (Greenwich, Conn.: New York Graphic Society, 1960), text at plate 3; Francois Mignon, "Sale of Plantation Biggest in History," *Alexandria Daily Town Talk*, Apr. 21, 1970; Archdiocese of New Orleans, *Clarion Herald*, June 18, 1970, sect. 1, p. 1; Francois Mignon, "Cane River Memo: Melrose Highlights," *Natchitoches Times*, Dec. 19, 1971; Mignon, *Plantation Parade: Plantation Life in Louisiana, 1750–1970, and Other Matter*, ed. Ora G. Williams (Baton Rouge: Claitor's, 1972); "Cluster of Treasures along Cane River: Melrose Makes BIG List," *New Orleans Times-Picayune*, July 2, 1972, p. 19. Some of these claims persist today in "official" literature; see, for example, "African House, Yucca House and Prudhomme-Rouquier House," *National Trust for Historic Preservation* (www.preservationnation.org/travel-and-sites/sites/southern-region/african-house-yucca-house-Prudhomme-Rouquier-House.html), which asserts that the plantation on which these properties stand "was owned by businesswoman Marie Therese Metoyer, a freed slave, who turned the area into a profitable trading post and African community." No known evidence supports the trading post claim.

40. Louis R. Nardini Sr., "Legends about Marie Thereze Disputed by Local Historian and Author," *Natchitoches Times*, Oct. 22, 1972, sect. A, pp. 8–9. A similar article by Nardini, who did not read French or Spanish, considerably misinterprets a number of records relating to other property associated with Coincoin and her children; see "Who Built the Yucca House and Ghana House of Melrose Plantation?" *Natchitoches Times*, July 1, 1973, sect. A, pp. 4–5.

41. "O'Reilly's Ordinance of 1770," *Louisiana Historical Quarterly* 11 (Apr. 1928): 240.

42. For the 1794 concession to "Maria Teresa, *negra libra*" and the 1812 affidavit by Gaspard Baudin, see Claim B2146, File "OPEL: February 1794," Opelousas Notarial Records Collection. For the letter of Joseph Irwin to Levin Wailes, see "Joseph Irwin Correspondence," folder 1806–1849, box 1, Chaplin, Breazeale, and Chaplin Papers, Louisiana State University Special Collections, Baton Rouge. For the December 1812 "monthly return" of Lloyd Posey, Clerk of the Board of Commissioners, see *American State Papers: Public Lands*, 2:866. For the Mar. 29, 1814, survey

by Joseph Irwin, see Claim B2146 (S55 R8N R7W), Louisiana State Land Office. Also see the surveyor general's 1848 consolidated map of all plats in T8N R7W, which renders her name as "Maria Thérèse Metoyer," and Serial Patent file 437,269, dated 1914, issued in the name "Marie Therese Metoyer," both in General Land Office Records, Record Group 49, National Archives.

43. *An Account of Louisiana*, 26–27.

44. "O'Reilly's Ordinance of 1770," 237–40; *An Account of Louisiana*, 38.

45. File B2146, Maria Therese, a free Negress, Louisiana State Land Office. Gray notes that the potential of the cattle industry was recognized and encouraged by officials of Louisiana as early as 1770; see his *Agriculture in the Southern United States*, 1:150. José María Torres is known to have died before 1810, when his daughter filed charges against an Italian immigrant who had settled among them, saying that "with foarce of armes" he and others had "maliciously and willfully batter[ed] and pulled down level with the ground" the house in which she lived with her children and aged mother, leaving all of them homeless. See Marie Gertrude v. Pierre Michel [Zorichi], Parish Court Suits, microfilm roll 7 (1810), NCCO.

46. The 1783 will of Metoyer did not mention Marie Françoise Rosalie, who had been born in 1780; apparently she died within that brief interim. In his will of 1801, Metoyer noted that Marie Eulalie was still alive in 1788 but had since died.

47. Marie de St. Denis to Pierre Metoyer, July 29, 1778, doc. 1312, NCA.

48. Mme. Manuel de Soto to Pierre Metoyer, doc. 1161, NCA. Marquis de Casa-Calvo to His Excellency Don Pedro Ceballos, translated in Louis Houck, *The Spanish Régime in Missouri: A Collection of Documents*, 2 vols. (Chicago: R. R. Donnelly & Sons, 1909), 2:355–58. Houck's editorial notes also speculate that Jeannot Metoyer belonged to the Natchitoches clan.

49. Pierre Dolet to Marie Thérèse, "Old Natchitoches Data," 2:289, Melrose Collection. Hanger, *Bounded Lives*, chap. 1, provides an excellent understanding of *coartación*. See also Marie Thérèse to Marie Louise, doc. 2596, NCA.

50. The first edition of *Forgotten People* erroneously identified Coincoin's daughter Marie Louise as the freed black woman Marie Louise *dite* Mariotte, with whom Coincoin's offspring heavily associated. The identities of these two Marie Louises, one Coincoin's daughter and the other Coincoin's sister, are now separated in Mills, "Which Marie Louise Is 'Mariotte'?" For the 1802 service of Marie Louise as godmother to the daughter of Dominique Metoyer, see Mills, *Natchitoches, 1800–1826*, entry 23. The entry's identification of the godmother as "aunt of the infant" could fit either Coincoin's daughter (a half-aunt) or Coincoin's sister (a great-aunt).

51. Mills, *Natchitoches, 1800–1826*, entry 1734 (bur. of Marie Louise Conde, July 12, 1813); 2099 (bapt. of Marie Rose [Baltasar], 1812, with Marie Louise Coinde as godmother); entry 2406 (bapt. of Marie Antoinette Condé, 1815, daughter of Antoine Condé and Marie Rose Metoyer); and entry 2619 (Marie Doralisse Coindet, bapt. 1818, daughter of Antoine Coindet and Marie Rose Metoyer).

52. Marie St. Denis to Marie Thérèse Coincoin, doc. 2804, NCA.

53. Ibid.

54. Ibid. Maria del Marger, with whom Coincoin arranged a cattle partnership for her daughter Thérèse, has not been identified. One possibility is Coincoin's youngest surviving sister, Marie Marguerite, aka Margarita, whom Mme. de Soto took to Opelousas and gave to her daughter Josepha, wife of Joaquin Ortega. Margarita has been last found on record in the 1784 household of the Ortegas at Pensacola, where Joaquin was artillery commissioner; however, the family had settled in Opelousas by 1790, when Coincoin arranged the partnership. See William S. Coker and G. Douglas Inglis, *The Spanish Censuses of Pensacola, 1784–1820* (Pensacola: Perdido Bay Press, 1980), 43; Recognizance Bond of Joaquin Ortega, Jan. 14, 1782, File OPEL: 1782–75, Opelousas

Notarial Records Collection; and Donald J. Hébert, *Southwest Louisiana Records: Church and Civil Records of Settlers,* vol. 1, *1756–1860,* rev. ed. (Eunice, La.: The compiler, 1976), 438.

55. Marie St. Denis to Marie Thérèse Coincoin, doc. 2804, NCA.

56. Ibid.; St. Landry Catholic Church (Opelousas), Register 1, p. 33 (Aug. 10, 1797).

57. For example, see the deed recorded in Natchitoches Conv. Book 33:133–34, NCCO, whereby an auctioned tract was described as "two arpents front on the right bank of Old River with the depth thereunto belonging, bounded above by lands of Thérèse Don Manuel and below by lands of Joseph Metoyer"; also Théophile L. Metoyer to J. B. Prudhomme, Natchitoches Mortgage Records, 28: 395, NCCO, which used similar verbiage.

58. For Thérèse as an adult at Opelousas, see 1820 U.S. census, St. Landry Parish, stamped p. 426, line 7. For the claim of Thérèse's great-grandson, see affidavit of Dennis J. Victorian, Lake Charles, June 30, 1914, U.S. Serial Patent 437,269, Maria Therese Metoyer, RG 49, National Archives.

59. Marguerite Le Roy, Widow Le Comte, to Marie Thérèse Coincoin; and Marie Thérèse Coincoin to Catiche; docs. 2550 and 2552, NCA. For Catiche's kinship to Coincoin, see Rev. A. Dupré, "Metoyer Family Genealogy," MS, St. Augustine Parish Rectory, Melrose, La. Father Dupré was pastor of St. Augustine Church (the church founded by Coincoin's sons on Isle Brevelle) from 1878 to 1889. His genealogical tables were based upon records in his own parish and registers of St. François (Natchitoches), Nativity Parish (Camptí), and St. Jean Baptiste (Cloutierville), as well as information provided him by the family. Since none of the official registers identify Catiche's parents, it is assumed that Father Dupré's identification of her as Louis's natural daughter was provided by her descendants.

60. Coincoin's daughter Françoise, born 1763, should not be confused with Coincoin's younger daughter Marie Françoise Rosalie, born 1780. Under French Catholic custom of the era, children were named by and for godparents. As a result, living siblings often carried the same names. This practice differed from the more familiar Anglo-American practice of not repeating a child's name unless the older sibling of that name had died. Among Coincoin's fifteen offspring one finds four sets of name duplications: Nicolas and Nicolas Augustin; Françoise and Marie Françoise Rosalie; Jean Joseph and Antoine Joseph; and Pierre and Pierre Toussaint. Similarly, Coincoin's son Dominique had two sons of the exact same name: Jean Baptiste Dominique, *l'aine* (the elder), and Jean Baptiste Dominique, *cadet* (the younger), and another pair named Joseph D. and Joseph O. Augustin Metoyer also gave the name Jean Baptiste to two sons, adding to each a third given name to distinguish between them.

61. Marie St. Denis to Antonio Gil y Barbo, doc. 757, NCA.

62. Ibid. *Code Noir,* article 63. Marie Gertrude's son, François *dit* Dgimby (var. Gimbeau, Gombeau) remained at Natchitoches, where his life is chronicled in various colonial records. For example, see Rex v. François Gombeau, 1781, doc. 550, Melrose Collection; Slave Inventory of Joseph Dupré, 1782, doc. 2780, NCA; and Marie (Derbanne) Varangue [Widow Dupré] to son Athanase Dupré, Sale of François *dit* Gombeau, 1800, doc. 2940, "Old Natchitoches Data," 2:72, Melrose Collection.

63. 1793 Census, Village of Nacogdoches, household 154; in 1792–1809 Censuses of Nacogdoches, Bexar Archives, University of Texas, Austin. Chipman and Joseph, *Notable Men and Women of Spanish Texas,* chap. 9, has a concise summation of the closing of the Los Adaës post and the subsequent life of Gil y Barbo, as it would have affected his slave Nicolas.

64. Leal, *Translations of Statistical and Census Reports of Texas,* roll 3, frames 826–29, Proceedings in effort of "Nicolas Augustin of Natchitoches" to free his "brother" Nicolas Chiquito. The December 1797 census of Nacogdoches enumerates Nicolas as a slave; the next extant census

of that post, taken 1809, does not include him. For the banishment of Y Barbo and his household, see Chipman and Joseph above.

65. Nicolas's first appearance in Natchitoches is that of June 2, 1805, when he served as a godparent in the Grappe-Trichel community at Grande Écore–Camptí; see Mills, *Natchitoches, 1800–1826,* entry 150. For Nicolas's use of his mother's African name as a surname, see 1820 U.S. census, Natchitoches Parish, p. 95, line 65. For the land dealings in which Nicolas was embroiled, see *American State Papers: Public Lands,* 3:199, 237. Also A. Metoyer v. A. L. DeBlieux, Natchitoches District Court Records, bundle 59, no. 1233 (filed May 22, 1833), which involved the Camptí land; and the consolidated suits Roubieu v. Metoyer (May 1835), bundle 59, no. 1395, and Metoyer v. Roubieu (Oct. 1836), bundle 74, no. 1473, which involved Nicolas's original tract in the Isle Brevelle community; all in NCCO.

For Nicolas's burial, see St. John the Baptist Catholic Church (Cloutierville), "Ecclesiastical Burials, A.D. 1847 to A.D. 1906," unnumbered p. 17 (d. April 11, 1850); in this entry, the priest did not identify Nicolas by name; he only stated that he had interred "the body of [blank], brother of Augustin Metoyer, age 85." No surviving cross marks the grave in the parish cemetery. The first edition of *Forgotten People,* published before Nicolas's existence had been discovered, speculated that this unidentified "brother of Augustin" might be the otherwise "lost" brother Jean Joseph, who, in that year 1850, would have been eighty-four.

66. Marie St. Denis to Sr. Delissard Jouhannis, doc. 756, and Sr. de Lisard Jouannis to Jn. Bte. Dupré, doc. 771, NCA. Dupré's wife was a daughter of the previously mentioned Widow Le Comte. Through many generations, the descendants of Coincoin were extraordinarily close to the slaves or freed slaves of the Le Comte family. For detailed charts of the multiracial offspring of the Widow Le Comte's husband and son, and their relationships with Coincoin's offspring, see Elizabeth Shown Mills, *Isle of Canes* (Provo, Utah: Ancestry.com, 2004), xxiii–xxiv.

67. Françoise's offspring are identified in Heirs of Dupré v. Cloutier (1825), Parish Court Suits, microfilm PC.21, NCCO; this file includes several documents that identify Françoise's family at various points in time. For the baptisms of her children, see Mills, *Natchitoches, 1729–1803,* entries 2362 (Remy, 1779), 2404 (Marie Louise, 1781), 2454 (Charles/Carlos, 1784), 2553 (Henri/Henrique, 1787), 3220 (Marie Jeanne, born 1797, bapt. 1799), 3222 (Marie Thérèse, born and bapt. 1799); and Mills, *Natchitoches, 1800–1826,* entry 1929 (Pierre, ca. 1792, bapt. 1804). Baptismal records have not been found for three of Françoise's children named in the court case: Marie Jeanne (born ca. 1785; d. before 1797), Hortense (born ca. 1789–93), and Rose (born ca. 1801). The lack of baptismal records for these three is not remarkable within the interrelated Dupré, Cloutier, Monet, Le Court, and Le Comte families that had, by this time, established plantations some twenty-five to forty miles from the town and church.

68. For the baptism of Louis Monet, the quadroon grandson of Coincoin's black daughter Françoise, see Mills, *Natchitoches, 1800–1826,* entry 1838 (born 1803). For the efforts of his white father's widow (Marie Louise Le Comte) to manumit him, see *Journal of the Senate of the State of Louisiana,* 1825, pp. 25, 27, 46; and *Journal of the House of the State of Louisiana,* 1825, pp. 39, 71, 75, 83. For the freed Louis's purchase and manumission of his mother, also named Marie Louise Le Comte, see folder 396, MS 182, Cane River Notarial Collection, Historic New Orleans Collection, L. Kemper Williams Research Center, New Orleans. The manumission of François Nicolas Monette has not been found, but he was free by Aug. 10, 1834, when he bought the freedom of his fifteen-year-old daughter Marie Zélia from Gen. François Gaiennié; Natchitoches Misc. Book 18:412.

69. Heirs of Dupré v. Cloutier (1825), Parish Court, NCCO. For Françoise as a free woman, see Cloutier to Marie Françoise, Manumission, Natchitoches Conv. Book 8:104, and Succes-

sion of Charles Monette, Natchitoches Succ. Book 6:118-24, NCCO. For her possible residence after Charles's death, see 1830 U.S. census, Natchitoches Parish, stamped p. 69, line 4, Louis "Meytoier."

70. For example, see Foner, "Free People of Color," 413.

71. Mills, *Natchitoches, 1729–1803*, entry 2304 (Nicolas Augustin, 1777). Upon the partition of slaves of Mme. de St. Denis, de Mézières and his wife had inherited Coincoin's sister, Marie Jeanne; see Succession of Wife of St. Denys, doc. 205, NCA.

72. Mills, *Natchitoches, 1729–1803*, entry 2764 (Jean Francisco Florentino [Conant], born 1794).

73. 1793 Natchitoches Tax Roll, folder 703, Melrose Collection, published as Mills, *Natchitoches Colonials*, 88–97, particularly 93. Doclas, a former slave of Joseph Dupré, had been purchased by Commandant de Vaugine, from whom Doclas bought himself and his wife Marianne; see Succession of Joseph Dupré, doc. 2780, and De Vaugine to Doclas, docs. 1856 and 2044, NCA.

74. "État de la Cargaison," roll 1, Holmes Collection.

75. For example, see Pierre Metoyer to Louis, Manumission, in Natchitoches Conv. Book 2:207-08, NCCO.

76. Pierre Metoyer to Nicolas Augustin, Manumission, doc. 2409, NCA; Mills, *Natchitoches, 1729–1803*, entry 3389 (Nicolas Augustin–Agnes, 1792).

77. Pierre Metoyer to Dominique, Manumission, doc. 2584, NCA; Mills, *Natchitoches, 1729–1803*, entry 3401 (Domingo–Marguerite, 1795).

78. 1801 Will of Claude Thomas Pierre Metoyer, Melrose Collection.

79. Ibid. Also Louis Moreau Lislet and Henry Carleton (trans.), *The Laws of Las Siete Partidas Which Are Still in Force in the State of Louisiana,* 2 vols. (New Orleans: James M'Karaher, Printer, 1820), 1:591–93.

80. 1801 Will of Claude Thomas Pierre Metoyer, Melrose Collection.

81. Ibid.; Mills, *Natchitoches, 1729–1803*, entry 2791 (Jean Baptiste Honore, bapt. 1795).

82. Pierre Metoyer to Marie Thérèse Coincoin, "Donation," in Natchitoches Misc. Book 2: 206-7, NCCO. This document is mislabeled. It should read: Marie Thérèse Coincoin to Pierre Metoyer, "Annulment of Donation."

83. Pierre Metoyer to Louis, Manumission, and Pierre Metoyer to Pierre, Manumission, Natchitoches Misc. Book 2: 207-10, NCCO.

84. Pierre Metoyer to Marie Susanne, Manumission, Natchitoches Misc. Book 2, 210-11, NCCO.

85. Dates of death for Metoyer and wife are extracted from their tomb markers in the American Cemetery (formerly the Catholic Cemetery), Natchitoches. As with Coincoin, no record of Mme. Metoyer's burial is to be found in the fire-damaged remnants of St. François Parish's Register 5 and only a fragment remains for Pierre Metoyer's burial entry.

86. "Répartition a L'ocasion de . . . fette le l^r Mars 1790," Natchitoches Parish Records, 1734–1916, Louisiana and Lower Mississippi Valley Collection (hereinafter LLMVC), Special Collections, Hill Memorial Library, LSU; and 1795 census of slaveowners, leg. 201, PPC-AGI; translations of both are published in Mills, *Natchitoches Colonials*, 68–75 and 111–14.

87. For baptisms and burials of slaves born to Coincoin's Marguerite, see Mills, *Natchitoches, 1729–1803*, entries 3148 (Joseph, born 1796), 3252 (Marie Françoise, born 1798), 3305 (Zenon [?], born 1794, died 1797); and Mills, *Natchitoches, 1800–1826*, entries 1847 (Jean Baptiste Hilaire, born 1802), 1888 (Marie Louise, born July 1804), 2001 (Pierre Noel, born December 1805), 2053 (Froisine, born 1807), and 2196 (Marie, daughter of Françoise, born 1814); also Mills, *Natchitoches, 1800–1826*, entry 2060 (Dec. 1809, joint baptism of adults Louis and Marguerite). For the

1816 disposition of Coincoin's slaves prior to her death, see Marie Thérèse Coincoin to [various heirs], Natchitoches Conv. Book 3:524–38, NCCO.

88. Inflated accounts of Coincoin's slaveownership range from fifty to one hundred. Among the most recent, architectural historian Laura Soullière Gates and historian Betje Black Klier both presented Coincoin as the owner of "12,000 acres and (at least) ninety-nine slaves," a pair of assertions that cannot be reconciled with any records. See Laura Soullière Gates, "Frankly, Scarlett, We Do Give a Damn: The Making of a New National Park," *George Wright Forum* 19 (2002): 35; and Betje Black Klier, *Pavie in the Borderlands: The Journey of Théodore Pavie to Louisiana and Texas, 1829–1830* (Baton Rouge: LSU Press, 2000), 15.

The one published resource that should be most reliable, Gwendolyn Midlo Hall's "Louisiana Slave Records, 1719–1820" database, *Ancestry.com* (www.ancestry.com), attributes fourteen slaves to Coincoin in 1816. However, amid data entry, Hall assigned to Coincoin two slaves that were sold by another party but recorded immediately after Coincoin's cluster of documents.

89. Interview with Mrs. Coutii, March 24, 1974.

90. For the quoted passages, see the notes Rev. P. Pavie added to the 1796, 1798, 1799, and 1802 parish censuses, rolls 8 and 9, in McAvoy et al., *Records of the Diocese of Louisiana and the Floridas;* published translations in Mills, *Natchitoches Colonials,* 115–24. For the state of religion at Natchitoches in the decades preceding Pavie's tenure, see Mills, "Quintanilla's Crusade."

91. Mills, *Natchitoches, 1719–1803,* entry 3305 (burial of Zenon [?]), and *Natchitoches, 1800–1826,* 2060 (joint baptism of Louis and Marguerite). Coincoin's religious treatment of her slaves is further explored in Elizabeth Shown Mills, "Marie Thérèse Coincoin (1742–1816): Cane River Slave, Slave Owner, and Paradox," in *Louisiana Women: Their Lives and Times,* ed. Janet Allured and Judith F. Gentry (Athens: University of Georgia Press, 2009), 10–29.

92. For Pierre's 1798 concession, which he conveyed to Augustin prior to filing an American claim, see documents submitted by Augustin, Dec. 28, 1806, and affidavit of Nicolas Gallien, Nov. 16, 1811, in Augustin Metoyer, Claim B1952 (S18 & 95 T7N R6W), Louisiana State Land Office.

93. Affidavit by "Pierre Coinquoin, *mulâtre libre,*" undated [but datable, via a companion document, at Dec. 26, 1806], Claim of "Marie Theresa, a free Negress," File "OPEL: May 1794," Opelousas Notarial Records Collection. See also (a) Louis Verchere to Dominique Rachal, Feb. 1810, doc. 3768, NCA, in which a sale of property adjacent to Coincoin's homestead identifies her son Pierre Jr. as the proprietor of her land; (b) the Aug. 1810 U.S. census, Natchitoches Parish, p. 214, line 18, whereon Coincoin's slaves are attributed to Pierre Jr.; and (c), the Jan. 1, 1816, survey of Coincoin's land, taken two months before she sold it, in which the surveyor states that the Spanish patent had been issued to "Marie Theresa, free Negress," but that the land was now that of "Pierre Metoyer, a man of Colour." For this last document, see Claim A1679 (S18 & 89, T8N R6W), Louisiana State Land Office.

94. Jean La Lande to Marie Thérèse, Natchitoches "Original Conveyance Acts," Book 42, doc. 501; Marie Thérèse Coincoin to Toussaint Metoyer, Natchitoches Conv. Book 3:308–9; and La Lande to Toussaint Metoyer, Apr. 21, 1821, confirmation of sale to Coincoin, Conv. Book 10:41 (clerical copy) and "Original Conveyance Acts," Book 42, original doc. 502. The acquisition, ownership, and disposition of Coincoin's two contiguous tracts on the Grand Côte have been seriously muddled in recent literature produced by the National Historical Landmarks Program. For example, the Historic American Buildings Survey document "Coincoin-Prudhomme House (Maison de Marie Therese)," HABS No. LA-1295, National Park Service, *Heritage Documentation Program* (www.nps.gov/history/hdp/samples/HABS/coincoin/history.pdf), conflates all three of Coincoin's tracts into one sixty-seven-acre farm and asserts that Coincoin sold half of it to her son Toussaint before selling the other half to a neighbor in 1816. For a correction of

the garbled HABS account, with a minutely detailed history of Coincoin's three separate tracts totaling roughly one thousand acres, see Mills, "Demythicizing History."

95. "Répartition a L'ocasion de . . . fette le l^r Mars 1790," for "Grande Cotte" section, Natchitoches Parish Records, 1734–1916, LLMVC, LSU Special Collections; Mills, *Natchitoches Colonials,* 71.

96. "Role de Corvées et Contributions public," Natchitoches Parish Records, 1734–1916, LLMVC, LSU Special Collections; Mills, *Natchitoches Colonials,* 105.

97. Mills, *Natchitoches, 1729–1803,* entry 2791 (Juan Bautista Honoré, bapt. 1795).

98. Ibid., entry 2130 (Maria Modesta Nicolas Agustin [Metoyer], bapt. 1793).

99. Interview with Mrs. Coutii, Mar. 24, 1974. Mrs. Coutii's grandmother, Sidalise (Sarpy) Dupré, the great-granddaughter of Marie Thérèse, was said to be one of those who regularly requested masses to be said for the repose of the soul of their family's matriarch.

100. Marie Thérèse Coincoin to J^n B^{te} Ailhaud Ste. Anne, in Natchitoches Conv. Book 3:522–23, NCCO. HABS No. LA-1295 erroneously reports that the 1816 sale covered only the half of Coincoin's homestead that lay on the "right descending bank."

101. Marie Thérèse Coincoin to [various heirs], ibid., 524–38. Drawing from Hall's database, "Louisiana Slave Records," some writers have elevated the value of Coincoin's slave property to $10,000. That inflated figure results from (a) Hall's attribution to Coincoin of two slaves actually sold by one James Miller, and from (b) Hall's practice of dividing slaves who had been jointly sold into separate database entries with the joint price redundantly attributed to each of them individually. Coincoin's twelve slaves in 1816 were valued at $5,250.

102. Toussaint Metoyer to Auguste Metoyer, Sale of Lands and Slaves, Natchitoches Misc. Book 20:334–35, NCCO.

103. Pierre Metoyer and Marie Henriette, Marriage Contract, Books 2 and 3, Marr. & Misc. (combined), unpaginated, NCCO.

104. A recent archaeological study proposes that Coincoin died after 1820 and was enumerated on that year's census as "Coincoin" living at Cedar Bend (on the Grand Côte below Natchitoches). To the contrary, the "Coincoin" of that census was a male householder—her eldest black son Nicolas "Chiquito" Coincoin, who was enumerated on his farm at Cedar Bluff, north of Natchitoches. The physical location of the male "Coincoin" of 1820 is determined by reconstructing the landholdings of his census neighbors. For the archaeological study, see MacDonald, Lee, and Morley, "The Archaeology of Local Myths," 133; at the time of their writing, MacDonald et al. were not aware that Coincoin had this black son and had not seen the Pierre Metoyer–Marie Henriette marriage contract of 1817 that identifies Pierre's mother as the deceased Marie Thérèse Coincoin.

105. The iron or wooden crosses that would have marked the graves of Marie Thérèse and her children who preceded her in death are no longer extant. Prior to the twentieth century, local burial grounds were commonly "mowed" by cattle, who regularly pushed over the crosses and trampled them into wet soil. The graves of Pierre Metoyer, his wife, and his two white sons are well marked; but the markers are concrete, a medium not used at the time of their deaths— attesting that those markers were erected at a later date to replace lost crosses. The burial grounds used by Natchitoches Catholics from the colonial period through the early 1800s is known today as the American Cemetery.

106. For this part of the Coincoin tradition, see Confidential Source to Francois Mignon, letter, Sept. 3, 1972, Detroit, Michigan. Copy in possession of author. It is also germane to consider that Coincoin's children, by this time, had begun using the Shallow Lake Cemetery on the Ambroise Le Comte plantation at the foot of the Isle.

107. This traditional reference to woodcarving provides a potential link between Marie Thérèse and her African heritage. According to one authority, inhabitants of the Gold Coast,

Dahomey, and Nigeria regions (all three areas inhabited by people of the Ewe linguistic group to which Vansina attributed Marie Thérèse; see note 14 to chapter 1) are noted even today for their highly developed woodcarving skill. Melville J. Herskovits, *The New World Negro*, ed. Frances S. Herskovits (Bloomington: Indiana University Press, 1966), 118.

108. The rosary that Coincoin supposedly carved for her youngest son, François, is the one that older family members recall. Its last owner was said to be his great-grandson, Herman Gassion Metoyer of New Orleans. After Herman's death in 1967, the Isle Brevelle family lost track of the rosary.

109. 1810 U.S. census, Natchitoches Parish. This census, which identifies only heads of household, takes free people of color out of their neighborhood sequence and clusters them at the end of the report. An analysis of each of the few f.p.c. households conclusively places Coincoin and her twelve slaves in the home of her son Pierre, who operated her farmstead. Coincoin's sister Mariotte, with a household that corresponds to Mariotte's known family, appears as a consecutive listing that some writers have misread as "Marie Tte" and, thus, assumed to be Marie Thérèse.

110. A bousillage structure still standing on Coincoin's farmstead has been a source of several archaeological investigations, with opposing conclusions as to whether it might be Coincoin's home. For the origin of the proposal, see Joseph M. Henry, "Marie Therese Coin Coin and Melrose: Discovery of Bousillage Cabin Substantiates True Story," *Natchitoches Times,* Apr. 16, 1978, sect. A, pp. 8–9. For the first study, see Billy Wayne Shaw, "A Ceramic Chronology for the Whittington House Site: 1780–Present" (M.A. thesis, Northwestern State University, 1983). The last published study, by the MacDonald-Morgan team, disagrees; see, primarily, Morgan et al., "Economics and Authenticity." The concurrent HABS No. LA-1295 report, which was heavily influenced by the MacDonald-Morgan work, asserts that the "Coincoin Prudhomme" house "was either rebuilt upon the foundations (possibly using the walls) of the earlier Marie Therese House, or it was an entirely new building constructed by the Prudhomme's [*sic*] on the footprint of the old house during the middle-antebellum era after they purchased the land from Marie Therese Coincoin." (The report does err, here, in its reference to a Coincoin-Prudhomme sale; Coincoin sold her farmstead to Ailhaud Ste. Anne, rather than the Prudhommes.) On the basis of other evidence not cited in the analyses by MacDonald-Morgan and HABS, a new research initiative has reopened the question as to whether the standing structure is Coincoin's home.

3. Early Development of the Isle Brevelle Community

1. *Message from the President of the United States Communicating Discoveries Made in the Exploring of the Missouri, Red River and Washita, by Captains Lewis and Clark, Doctor Sibley, and Mr. Dunbar* (New York: A & G Way, 1806), 79–81.

2. Mills, *Natchitoches, 1729–1803*, entries 9, 41, 119, 229, and 455; Succession of Jean Baptiste Brevel and Appt. of Gabriel Buard, tutors for minors, docs. 148–49, ca. 1754–55, NCA. See also the Sept. 16, 1805, affidavit of Baptiste's sister "Mary Senes" [Marie Louise] Brevell, given amid congressional hearings on the location of the historic boundary between Louisiana and Texas, *Annals of Congress*, 9th Cong., 1st Sess., 1805–1806 (Washington, D.C.: Gales & Seaton, 1852), 1211.

3. The land concession issued to Brevel was assigned doc. no. 396 according to the "Index to French Archives"; the actual document is missing. For the location of the land, see Ory G. Poret, *Spanish Land-Grants in Louisiana, 1757–1802* (Ville Platte, La.: Provincial Press, 1999), 6. For Brevel's interaction with native tribes and his life as a hunter, see *Message from the President*, 79–81; Bolton, *Athanase de Mézières*, 1:181–82; and A. P. Nasatir, ed., "Government Employees

and Salaries in Spanish Louisiana," *Louisiana Historical Quarterly* 24 (Oct. 1946): 933; also Succession of Monmarquet, "who died while on a hunt with Baptiste Brevel and Jeanneau, f.m.c.," 1764, and hunting engagement between Jean Bte. Brevelle and Louis Fonteneau, 1774, docs. 357 and 980, NCA. For his more conventional life at Natchitoches, see 1772 militia roll, doc. 741, NCA; and 1766 French and Spanish censuses of Natchitoches, 1774 census of slaveowners, 1774 tax list of slaveowners, 1790 and 1793 church tax rolls, 1790 and 1793 delinquent tax rolls, 1794 public works roster, and 1795 census of slaveowners, all in Mills, *Natchitoches Colonials*, 9, 16, 28, 32, 35, 74, 76, 81, 97, 100, 103, 112.

4. In 1778, Brevel was not yet in the Isle District; rather, he made his home on parental land at the post of Natchitoches, across the river from the fort; see Joseph Lattier deed, doc. 1423, NCA. He was missed by the canvasser who took the 1787 census of the Natchitoches jurisdiction, likely because he had already moved to the Bayou Brevelle–False (Old) River area. The first colonial roster that cites Isle Brevelle District and enumerates its settlers, a tax roll of 1790, identifies the most prosperous planter as Brevel's brother-in-law Remy Poissot Jr., while enumerating Baptiste Brevel (with property of equal value, apparently an inheritance from the recently deceased Poissot Sr.) in the barely populated False River District; see Mills, *Natchitoches Colonials*, 70, 74.

5. Orton S. Clark, *The One Hundred and Sixteenth Regiment of New York State Volunteers* (Buffalo, N.Y.: Mathews & Warren, 1868), 150; Harris H. Beecher, *Records of the 114th Regiment, N.Y.S.V.* (Norwich, N.Y.: J. F. Hubbard Jr., 1866), 304.

6. Journal of Théodore Pavie, quoted by Robert DeBlieux in *Natchitoches and Louisiana's Timeless Cane River*, photographs by Philip Gould, text by Richard Seale, Robert DeBlieux, and Harlan Mark Guidry (Baton Rouge: LSU Press, 2002), 50.

7. Dorothea Olga McCants, trans. and ed., *They Came to Louisiana: Letters of a Catholic Mission, 1854–1882* (Baton Rouge: LSU Press, 1970), 122–23.

8. Burton and Smith, *Colonial Natchitoches*, and Usner, *Indians, Settlers & Slaves in a Frontier Exchange Economy*, provide excellent insight into borderland trade activities.

9. Mills, "Family and Social Patterns," 52–53, tables 3 and 4. Statistics and patterns presented in this study were drawn from a reconstitution of the colonial population, its family units, and the individual lives of settlers whose migrations were tracked from Europe through French, Spanish, and Anglo-American settlements from Canada to Mexico.

10. Bjork, "Documents Relating to Alexandro O'Reilly," 22; "O'Reilly's Ordinance of 1770," 237–40; Thomas Fiehrer, "The African Presence in Colonial Louisiana: An Essay on the Continuity of Caribbean Culture," in *Louisiana's Black Heritage*, ed. Robert R. Macdonald, John R. Kemp, and Edward F. Haas (New Orleans: Louisiana State Museum, 1979), 3–31. Fiehrer argues that France's restriction of the flow of slaves into Louisiana limited the growth of a plantation economy and encouraged the emergence of a "society of métis and squawmen, barren of town life and religious restraints" (p. 6). That outcome is seen at Natchitoches; but the resumption of the slave trade in 1758 sparked no exodus from trade to agriculture. The tipping point appears to have been the Spanish colonial imposition of stringent controls on trade; it was then that the nexus of free land and a larger supply of slaves convinced the greater number of Natchitoches males that settled agriculture now offered a viable livelihood.

11. Mills, "Family and Social Patterns," 210.

12. The settlement of these lower Cane River families is dated by the marriage of the retired lieutenant (and minor nobleman) Louis Mathias Le Court de Presle to Marie Jeanne Le Roy in Mar. 1765, in the presence of their brother-in-law Jean Baptiste Le Comte. A passing priest found the unmarried couple in residence at a strategic bluff where the channels of Red River converged. When he arrived at Natchitoches, he noted in the parish registers that he had married the Le Court couple and then baptized and legitimated their children. See Mills, *Natchitoches,*

1729–1803, entry 984; also Heirs of Louis Mathias Le Court de Prelle to Louis Monet, sale of Le Court's Bluff, doc. 1848, NCA. The Widow Monet sold this bluff plantation and its forty-seven slaves in 1822 to Alexis Cloutier; see copy filed in the previously cited 1825 Parish Court suit, Heirs of Dupré vs. Cloutier. A later owner of this bluff tract, Robert McAlpin, is alleged to be the prototype of Harriet Beecher Stowe's villainous slaveowner character, Simon Legree; see D. B. Corley, *A Visit to Uncle Tom's Cabin* (Chicago: Laird & Lee, 1893).

13. Répartition a L'ocasion de . . . fette le l^r Mars 1790," Natchitoches Parish Records, 1734–1916, LLMVC, LSU Special Collections.

14. Mills, "Which Marie Louise Is 'Mariotte'?" 195.

15. Blacksmithing bills, penned by Pierre Metoyer for Augustin, appear in several Natchitoches successions of the late colonial era.

16. File B1960, Augustin Metoyer, State Land Office.

17. Memorial of Louis Metoyer, ca. Dec. 28, 1806, in folder OPEL: May, 1796, Opelousas Notarial Records Collection.

18. File B1953, Louis Metoyer, State Land Office; and *Boissier et al. v. Metayer,* 5 Mart. (O.S.) 678ff. (1818). Louis's 1806 affidavit refers to a letter written on behalf of his claim by Commandant De Blanc, by then a resident of Attakapas; but the letter itself was no longer a part of the file when research was done on the first edition of *Forgotten People.* Since then, it surfaced at an auction house and was purchased by a De Blanc descendant, Joseph Darby of Natchitoches. A photocopy shared by Darby is now in the Mills Collection, NSU.

19. French, ed., *Historical Collections of Louisiana,* 3:91.

20. Natchitoches Conv. Book 2:207–8, NCCO.

21. Gray, *Agriculture in the Southern United States,* 2:865.

22. Memorial of Louis Metoyer, File B1953, Louis Metoyer, State Land Office. For Coindet's quasi-marital relations with Coincoin's offspring, see Mills, *Natchitoches, 1800–1826,* entry 2099 (Marie Rose [Baltasar], bapt. 1812, with Marie Louise Coinde as godmother); entry 1734 (Marie Louise Conde, bur. July 12, 1813); entry 2406 (Marie Antoinette Condé, born. 1815, daughter of Antoine Condé and Marie Rose Metoyer); and entry 2619 (Marie Doralisse Coindet, bapt. 1818, daughter of Antoine Coindet and Marie Rose Metoyer).

23. As pointed out by Sophie Burton, "Within a hierarchical society, fictive or ritual kinship such as godparenthood . . . linked people of lower status to those of higher standing. Most *libre* parents strove to choose godparents of equal or preferably higher status in order to allow their children the possibility of gaining privileges." At Natchitoches, the godparental ties between master and slaves clearly generated privileges, as with those already seen with Coincoin and her godmother, Marie Desneiges Juchereau de St. Denis de Soto. All but the last two of Coincoin and Metoyer's children, born in and out of slavery, had godparents from the St. Denis family or other elites at the post. For the quote, see Burton, "Marie Thérèze *dit* Coincoin: A Free Black Woman on the Louisiana-Texas Frontier," in *Nexus of Empire: Negotiating Loyalty and Identity in the Revolutionary Borderlands, 1760s–1820s,* ed. Gene Allen Smith and Sylvia L. Hilton (Gainesville: University Press of Florida, 2010), 104. Natchitoches's baptismal records for the period of Louis's birth have not survived.

24. "O'Reilly's Ordinance of 1770," 239. As cases at point, Jean Baptiste Prudhomme received two grants containing 350 and 766 acres respectively. Sylvestre Rachal's double concession consisted of tracts measuring 322 and 632 acres. Claim files and section maps in the State Land Office reveal a number of similar cases.

25. As previously noted, when Coincoin purchased the La Lande tract on Red River in 1807, she turned it over to her son Toussaint. When her neighbor sold a tract adjacent to her homestead in February 1810, he identified the proprietor of Coincoin's land as her son Pierre; see

Verchere to Rachal, doc. 3768, NCA. When the U.S. deputy surveyor, Joseph Irwin, surveyed her contiguous homestead tract in 1816, he noted that the land was first claimed by Coincoin but was then being claimed by her son Pierre; File A1679, State Land Office.

26. File B1833, Dominique Metoyer, State Land Office; Survey of Land of Dominique Metoyer, folder OPEL: May 1796, Opelousas Notarial Records Collection.

27. File B1952, Augustin Metoyer, State Land Office. Although the land was originally granted to Pierre, the claim for the land was filed with the U.S. Land Office in the name of his brother Augustin, who said he had acquired the tract from Pierre by an exchange of property.

28. File R&R 306, Joseph Metoyer, and File R&R 308, Marie Pelige, State Land Office; Testimony of Pierre Quierry ("Carey"), *American State Papers: Public Lands,* 3:199. For the identity of Joseph's wife and the children she bore, see Mills, *Natchitoches, 1719–1803,* entries 2482, 2880, 3451; and *Natchitoches, 1800–1825,* entries 29, 104, 816, 1117, 1653, 1847, 1887, 2079, 2317. For the baptisms of Joseph's children by his slave Marie Rose "Rosette," see *Natchitoches, 1800–1825,* entries 2303, 2304, 2598, and 2600. Those children born during Joseph's separation from Pelagie were Marie Doralise (1810), Jean Rafael (1813), and twins St. Ville and Jean Baptiste Marville aka Melville (1817).

29. File R&R 309, Marie Perine, State Land Office. For Marie Perine's childbearing record, see *Natchitoches, 1800–1825,* entries 112, 2029, and 2128; for her burial, see ibid., entry 940.

30. *American State Papers: Public Lands,* 3:199; File R&R 310, Toussaint Metoyer, State Land Office.

31. *American State Papers: Public Lands,* 3:195, 199; Mills, *Natchitoches, 1719–1803,* entry 2764 (Juan Francisco Florentine, bapt. Mar. 1, 1795). Miguel Papillon also offers a clue to the *libre* identity of Coincoin's grandson José Mauricio, son of Thérèse. Four years after Papillon's testimony for Coincoin's sons, one "Joseph Therese, f.m.c." sold a tract of land on Bayou Boeuf, St. Landry Parish, saying that his land was bounded on one side by vacant land and on the other side by Michel Papillon; see Judy Riffel, *Calendar of St. Landry Parish, Louisiana, Civil Records,* vol. 1, *1803–1809* (Baton Rouge: Le Comité des Archives de la Louisiane, 1995), 193.

32. *American State Papers: Public Lands,* 3:78, 84.

33. For scattered documents relating to Mariotte's mid-1790s difficulties with Bertrand Mailloche and the English-born agent Richard Sims, see doc. 2877, NCA; folder 710, Melrose Collection; and "[Natchitoches] Miscellaneous Archive Records, 1733–1820," Louisiana State Archives microfilm F.T. 565, frames 486–87. Mills, "Which Marie Louise Is 'Mariotte'?" develops more of her legal and financial difficulties as a freedwoman.

34. *American State Papers: Public Lands,* 3:172, 237; Petition of François Metoyer, presented by Congressman Henry Bullard, Dec. 12, 1832, *Journal of the House of Representatives of the United States, 1832–1833* (Washington, D.C.: Duff Greene, 1832), 42.

35. Fˢ Roubieu to U.S. Land Office, Nov. 20, 1841, at Natchitoches, in File R&R 309, Marie Perine, State Land Office.

36. *American State Papers: Public Lands,* 3:209.

37. Ibid., 5:648.

38. This particular Creole characteristic caused the American government to view Louisiana as a "problem child" even from the beginning. As noted by Foner, "Free People of Color," 421: "The Americans were generally nervous about taking over a territory whose population had seen frequent changes of government, with loyalties torn between France, Spain, and the United States."

39. File B1960, Augustin Metoyer, and File R&R 306, Antoine Joseph Metoyer, State Land Office.

40. Many Natchitoches settlers who filed claims with the U.S. Land Office during the transition to American control found the floats worthless. Nearly a century later, land speculators in the nation's capital contacted local attorneys asking them to track down heirs of individuals for whom floats were still unused. As a result, in the ca. 1900–1905 period at Natchitoches, numerous successions were reopened for settlers of the Louisiana Purchase era. The land speculators paid the attorneys (and the heirs a trifle) for the outstanding floats and consolidated the acreage with similar acquisitions in other parts of the Louisiana Territory; they then exchanged the whole for millions of acres of open timberland in the public domain.

41. S. G. McLendon, *History of the Public Domain of Georgia* (Atlanta: Foote & Davies, 1924), 103.

42. Dec. 9, 1812, at Natchitoches, Joseph Irwin Correspondence, folder 1806–1849, box 1, Chaplin, Breazeale, and Chaplin Papers, LLMVC, LSU Special Collections.

43. *American State Papers: Public Lands,* 3:80.

44. Ibid.; Memorial of Louis Metoyer, folder OPEL: May 1796, Opelousas Notarial Records Collection.

45. *Boissier et al. v. Metayer.*

46. This figure is compiled from the land purchases recorded in the Natchitoches Colonial Archives (which actually extend to 1819) and additional purchases itemized in the claims they submitted to the Board of Land Commissioners for their purchased lands.

47. McCants, *They Came to Louisiana,* 134.

48. François Davion to "Nicolas Augustin," doc. 2740, Mar. 30, 1797, NCA.

49. Augustin Metoyer of Succession of Marie Le Clerc, Widow Derbanne, Sept. 3, 1798, doc. 2857, NCA.

50. Widow Le Comte to "Nicolas Augustin," Nov. 18, 1800, "Old Natchitoches Data," doc. no. 279, Melrose Collection; also Mills, *Natchitoches, 1729–1803,* entry 2749 (Marie Rose, bapt. 1793). Neither the baptismal entry nor the manumission record names Marie Rose's father; family tradition identifies him as Louis, according to Father A. Dupré's genealogical tables for the Metoyers. That tradition is supported by Louis's ongoing presence in Rose's life, in ways found for none of his brothers.

51. Ambroise Le Comte to "Nicolas Augustin," Sale and manumission of Marie Perine, Aug. 24, 1801; copy filed in Claim File R&R 309, Marie Perine, State Land Office.

52. Judicial Sale of Property of Mr. Maës, "English Translations," vol. 1, no. 2992, Melrose Collection.

53. Phillips to Augustin Metoyer, and Augustin Metoyer to Louis Metoyer, June 2, 1809, Natchitoches Misc. Book 1 (Dec. 1806–May 1811): 98–99, NCCO.

54. Parham to Metoyer, Sale of Harry, June 9, 1810, Natchitoches Misc. Book 1 (Dec. 1806–May 1811): 225; Bell to Metoyer, Sale of Charlotte, Mar. 8, 1811, Natchitoches Misc. Book 2 (June 4, 1806–April 28, 1812): 94; Rogers to Metoyer, Sale of Ned, Ginee, Mima, Jack, and Kitty, Aug. 26, 1813, "Old Natchitoches Data," 2:388, Melrose Collection.

55. Mills, *Natchitoches, 1800–1826,* entries 2305–2308 (Marie Pelagie, Marie Celeste, Rose, and Jacques, children of "Jeny," bapt. June 8, 1815), 2368 (Marie "Nete" [Kitty], age 2, daughter of "Guiny," bapt. July 1, 1815), 2413 (L. Silben [Labon], child of Charlotte, bapt. Feb. 11, 1816), and 2522 (Derselin, son of "Jeny," bapt. Jan. 28, 1817). For two decades after the transfer of Louisiana to the United States, Natchitoches was often without a priest. That civil transfer also triggered an ecclesiastical transfer of Louisiana from the Vicar-General of Cuba to the American Diocese of Baltimore, which had insufficient priests to serve the new and heavily Catholic Louisiana Territory.

56. Parham to Marie Susanne, June 1810, Natchitoches Misc. Book 1 (Dec. 1806–May 1811): 225–26; Bell to Marie Susanne, Mar. 1811, Natchitoches Misc. Book 2 (June 4, 1806–April 28, 1812): 94.

57. 1810 U.S. census, Natchitoches Parish; statistical analysis by the authors.

58. Docs. 3331, 3810, 3813, 3814, 3815, 3925, 4150, 4178, 4581, 4582, 4633, 3010, and 3012, NCA; for the natural increase, see the baptismal records published in Mills, *Natchitoches, 1800–1826*.

59. Ellen Yvonne Simms, "Contributing Factors to the Growth of Colored Slave Owners of Louisiana from the Colonial Period to the Nineteenth Century" (graduate seminar paper, Fall 2000, university unidentified), posted online 2003–2008 at *The BlackList Pub* (http://theblacklistpub.ning.com/) but no longer available there. For her characterization of Cane River's "colored slave owners," Simms extensively used the Cane River Notarial Collection held by the Historic New Orleans Collection. Many of the individuals treated in this study as "colored slave owners" of Cane River were actually white; apparently her study assumed that Cane River was an exclusively *libre* community.

60. Derbanne to Metoyer, Sale of Dorothé, May 18, 1810, Natchitoches Misc. Book 1:186–87; Parham to Metoyer, Sale of Harry, June 9, 1810, Natchitoches Misc. Book 1 (Dec. 1806–May 1811): 225, NCCO.

61. Succession of Marie Louise Le Clerc (Widow Pierre Derbanne), doc. 2857, NCA.

62. Mills, *Natchitoches, 1800–1826*, entries 948 (Joseph Derbanne and Catherine Brosset, marr. Nov. 22, 1802) and 954 (Manuel Derbanne and Marguerite Denis, marr. Feb. 2, 1804).

63. Manuel and Joseph Derbanne, Sale and exchange of slaves, June 12, 1805, doc. 3688, NCA.

64. Joseph Derbanne to Metoyer, Sale of Remy, July 14, 1809, Natchitoches Conv. Book 1:97; William Murray to Manuel Derbanne and Augustin Metoyer, Cancellation of mortgage on Dorothé, May 27, 1810, Natchitoches Conv. Book 1:186; and Manuel Derbanne to Augustin Metoyer, Sale of Dorothé, May 28, 1810, Natchitoches Conv. Book 1:186–87; all NCCO. In this period Augustin also manumitted a Creole slave woman of no known kinship and her two children; see Augustin to Marguerite, Jean Baptiste, and Joseph Marie, Manumission, Nov. 3, 1813, doc. 4230, NCA.

65. The character of Alexis Cloutier may be tracked through dozens of contemporary records extant in the church registers, the office of the parish clerk, and the Cane River Notarial Collection. As a starting point, see Marie Lise (Rachal) Cloutier vs. Alexis Cloutier, Her Husband, Parish Court suits (1811), microfilm roll PC.8, NCCO, wherein Mme. Cloutier charged (among other things) that he degraded her in many ways, called her a whore in front of several persons, and "most cruelly whipped her to such a degree as to endanger her life." She petitioned the court to assign her another place of residence and she was authorized to return to her father's home. In another contemporary case—Marie Jeanne, f.w.c. v. Alexis Cloutier and Mary L. Le Compte Porter, Parish Court suits (1810), microfilm PC.7—the petitioner charged that Cloutier had given her freedom "for important services" but, the next year, after she displeased him, he "got her manumission papers back from the clerk" and sold her as a slave to Mme. Porter. When she filed her complaint, the court required her to post security for court costs, in the event that she lost, and she had no funds to do so; that apparently ended her suit against Cloutier, in his favor.

66. William Murray, attorney for Cloutier, to Derbanne and Metoyer, Cancellation of mortgage on Dorothé, May 27, 1810, Natchitoches Conv. Book 1:186, NCCO.

67. Derbanne to Metoyer, Sale of Dorothé, Natchitoches Misc. Book 1:186–87; Parham to Metoyer, Sale of Harry, ibid., 225, NCCO. Researchers who rely upon Hall's convenient slave-sales databases for Louisiana should be aware of a data-entry error. There the two documents involving Dorothée (entry: "Dorotha") appear as a single sale; Augustin is erroneously identified as the

seller, rather than the purchaser; and Dorothée's price is said to be only $200, rather than $200 plus the delivery of an adult male slave in good health. For many of the slave deeds involving the Metoyers, similar discrepancies exist between the database and the original documents filed in the parish courthouse.

68. Judith Kelleher Schafer, "Roman Roots of the Louisiana Law of Slavery: Emancipation in American Louisiana, 1803–1857," in *An Uncommon Experience: Law and Judicial Institutions in Louisiana, 1803–2003,* ed. Judith Kelleher Schafer and Warren M. Billings (Lafayette: Center for Louisiana Studies, 1997), 360–73, esp. 364–65. Also see Mitch Crusto, "Blackness as Property: Sex, Race, Status, and Wealth," bepress Legal Series, Working Paper no. 307, Berkeley Electronic Press, *bepress Legal Repository* (http://law.bepress.com/expresso/eps/307 : 2004); and Charles Vincent, *The African American Experience in Louisiana: From Africa to the Civil War* (Lafayette: Center for Louisiana Studies, 1999).

69. Metoyer to Dorothé, Manumission, Nov. 22, 1814, doc. 4377; Augustin Metoyer to Joseph La Vigne, Security on bond, Dec. 1814, doc. 4383; La Vigne and Dorothé, Marriage contract, Dec. 1814, doc. 4384, all in NCA. For the clerk's recorded copy of Dorothée's manumission, see Natchitoches Conv. Book 3:348, NCCO.

70. Pacalé to Metoyer, May 27, 1813, Natchitoches Conv. Book 3:16–17, NCCO; also "Early Natchitoches Records," Book 1, n.p., Melrose Collection.

71. Yves *dit* Pacalé was born at Natchitoches and baptized there on Jan. 2, 1736, as the son of Jean Baptiste and Marie, two legally married African slaves belonging to the succession of the late subdélégué François Dion des Pres Derbanne. Pacalé was inherited by Derbanne's half-Indian son Pierre, who subsequently became one of the wealthiest planters on Cane River. For the baptism, see Mills, *Natchitoches, 1729–1803,* entry 35. For Pacalé's 1798 manumission, see Succession of Marie Le Clerc (Widow Derbanne), doc. 2857, NCA. The heirs who agreed to give Pacalé his freedom included the previously discussed Joseph and Manuel Derbanne.

72. Marie Derbanne to Yves Pacalis, Sale of slave; and Yves Pascales to Marie Louise, Manumission, 1802, doc. 2979, NCA. The document itself is no longer on file, but descriptive entries appear in the "Index to French Archives." Jean Baptiste Ailhaud Ste. Anne to Pacalé, Sale and manumission of "Eteroux," Jan. 1, 1806, doc. 3324, NCA. The age of "Eteroux," and the fact that Ste. Anne inherited her from the Buard family who owned Coincoin's sister Mariotte and brother François, suggests that "Eteroux" may have been Coincoin's older sister Gertrude *dite* Dgimby. As pronounced by the colonial French, the initial "G" was silent, the "r" was rolled, and the final "de" was elided (thus: Eteru). The name Gertrude was extremely rare at the Natchitoches post; the only ones found on record were a St. Denis daughter and their family slave, Coincoin's sister, who was more commonly called *Dgimby.* (Hall's database, for which access is spelling sensitive, identifies these individuals as *Oteroux* and *Pacals.*)

73. Pacalé to Metoyer, Mortgage, Mar. 20, 1812, doc. 4058, NCA; Roubieu Brothers to Pascalis, Sale of Thérèse, Mar. 20, 1812, 4059, NCA; also Pacalé, Public notice of intent to free Thérèse, Mar. 21, 1812, and Pacalé to "Thérése, *sa fille*" (i.e., "his daughter"), emancipation, May 29, 1812, docs. 4096 and 4097, NCA. Pacallé to Auguste Langlois, Sale of land, May 27, 1813, doc. 4140, NCA; and Natchitoches Conv. Book 3:316–17. Pacallé to Metoyer, Sale of François, May 27, 1813, doc. 4150, NCA; and Natchitoches Conv. Book 3:18.

74. Buard Succession to Zabelle, Sale of Etienne, 1814, doc. 4403, NCA; Will of Jacques La Caze, Natchitoches Succ. file 139-A; State v. Babet and Marie Desneiges, Parish Court, English Translations, 8:219–25, Melrose Collection.

75. Herman de B. Seebold, *Old Louisiana Plantation Homes and Family Trees,* 2 vols. (New Orleans: Pelican Press, 1941), 1:362.

76. J. J. Callahan et al., *The History of St. Augustine's Parish: Isle Brevelle, Natchez, La., 1803–1953; 1829–1954; 1856–1956* (Natchitoches, La.: The parish, 1956), 20. Neither the Roque house nor the "Old Convent" of which Father Callahan wrote was built by the Metoyers. The "Convent," also known as the Badin-Roque House, was apparently erected by a retired lieutenant of the militia, Gaspard Roubieu, who settled a tract of unclaimed land on the isles and lived there with his wife until his death in 1811. At that time the property was acquired by the Metoyer family. The Roque House was the home Pacalé built on his small farm about 1798–1800. In the 1970s, it was moved to the river bank in downtown Natchitoches, where it has been restored and serves as the town's welcome center; see Mills and Mills, "The House That Pacalé Built," in *Tales of Old Natchitoches,* 41–45.

77. *American State Papers: Indian Affairs,* 1:727.

78. Samuel Wilson Jr., School of Architecture, Tulane University, New Orleans, to Gary B. Mills, July 31, 1973. The Millses, who were simultaneously engaged by the preservation society to document the plantation's history, dated the grant to Louis at 1796; Wilson then placed the house's construction as "late eighteenth century" and, more specifically, 1796–1800. The first edition of *Forgotten People* reported Wilson's dating, but noted the "puzzling" incongruity between that date and the historical evidence from 1814–15 land plats that placed Louis Metoyer's dwelling house on the opposite side of the river.

79. For the archaeological evidence at Louis's plantation, see MacDonald, Lee, and Morley, "The Archaeology of Local Myths," 132–34.

80. Carolyn M. Wells, "Domestic Architecture of Colonial Natchitoches" (M.A. thesis, Northwestern State University of Louisiana, 1973).

81. Major Amos Stoddard, *Sketches, Historical and Descriptive, of Louisiana* (Philadelphia: Mathew Carey, 1812), 328–29.

82. The most recent archaeological study places the construction of the house on Coincoin's homestead at the 1820s–30s; see Kevin C. MacDonald, David W. Morgan, and Fiona J. L. Handley, "The Cane River African Diaspora Archaeological Project: Prospectus and Initial Results," in *African Re-Genesis,* ed. Jay B. Haviser and Kevin C. MacDonald (London: University College London Press, 2006), 133. HABS No. LA-1295, p. 6, poses an 1828–47 time frame on the basis of the nails used in the construction. A current initiative, whose work has yet to be published, is challenging both conclusions on the basis of evidence not previously considered.

83. File B1953, Louis Metoyer; File B1960, Augustin Metoyer; and File B 1956, Augustin Metoyer, Louisiana State Land Office.

84. *Boissier et al. v. Metoyer.*

85. Regarding the usage of this building: In light of the prominence of tobacco farming along Cane River (and Coincoin's heavy production of the staple), it is curious that no writer has noted the extent to which the building's construction fits the multi-story tobacco curing sheds described by Antoine-Simon Le Page du Pratz in his colonial memoir, *The History of Louisiana* (1774; rpr. New Orleans: J. S. Harmanson, 1947), 189, particularly.

86. See, for example, the accounts published by Garber, "History of Melrose Plantation like Turning Pages of Novel"; and *Clarion Herald* (the official newspaper of the Archdiocese of New Orleans), June 18, 1970, sect. 2, p. 1.

87. Jay D. Edwards, "Vernacular Vision: The Gallery and Our Africanized Architectural Landscape," in *Raised to the Trade: Creole Building Arts of New Orleans,* ed. Jonn Ethan Hankins and Steven Maklansky (New Orleans: New Orleans Museum of Art, 2002), 66.

88. Augustin Metoyer to Maxile Metoyer and Susanne Metoyer to Marie Aspasie Metoyer [Anty], Donations, Sept. 26, 1817, Natchitoches Conv. Book 6:252–54.

4. Background of the Major Allied Families

1. A study of family and social patterns in colonial Natchitoches, based on a reconstitution of all its free colonial population, found a negligible incidence of intra-kin marriage. As noted there: "A fair number of such dispensations can be found in the records of most Louisiana posts; among the Acadians, who were almost entirely related to each other before their departure from Acadia and their subsequent migration to Louisiana, a large number of dispensations had to be granted late in the colonial period. By contrast, record of only two dispensations from the impediment of consanguinity can be found in colonial Natchitoches; and these two incidences involved two sisters, two brothers, and two pregnancies, as well the prohibitive relationship of first-cousin-once-removed." See Mills, "Family and Social Patterns," 129-30.

For specifics of all known marital dispensations granted elsewhere in colonial Louisiana, see Shirley Chaisson Bouquard, *Marriage Dispensations in the Diocese of Louisiana and the Floridas, 1786-1803* (New Orleans: Polyanthos, 1980). Only two couples of African American ancestry received dispensations anywhere in the colony. All four parties had in common a slave-born grandmother who had been fathered by a white male of considerable prominence. Upon her manumission, she had been allowed to marry, consecutively, three white males of relatively low social status and her offspring lived as white; see Bouquard, *Marriage Dispensations,* 26, 57, and the first four volumes of *Archdiocese of New Orleans Sacramental Records,* where the kinship of these two couples can be specifically traced.

2. John Hope Franklin, *The Free Negro in North Carolina, 1790-1860* (Chapel Hill: University of North Carolina Press, 1943), 183, quoting from James Blackwell Browning, "Free Negro in Ante-Bellum North Carolina," *North Carolina Historical Review* 15 (Jan. 1938): 33.

3. As a case at point, see John M. Kingsbury, "Interconnecting Bloodlines and Genetic Inbreeding in a Colonial Puritan Community: Eastern Massachusetts, 1630-1885," *National Genealogical Society Quarterly* 84 (June 1996): 85-101. Other scholars report similar findings in early modern Britain and British America, where, among families of wealth, first-cousin marriages were a deliberate strategy for economic and community growth. See, for example, Peter Dobkin Hall, "Marital Selection and Business in Massachusetts Merchant Families, 1700-1900," in *The American Family in Social-Historical Perspective,* ed. Michael Gordon (New York: St. Martin's Press, 1978), 101-14; and Lawrence Stone, "The Rise of the Nuclear Family in Early Modern England: The Patriarchal Stage," in *The Family in History,* ed. Charles E. Rosenberg (Philadelphia: University of Penn. Press, 1975), 13-57.

4. Bayard Rustin, "The Role of the Negro Middle Class," *The Crisis* (June-July 1969): 237. Gatewood, *Aristocrats of Color,* demonstrates this class divide in postbellum America, but few existing studies explore it adequately for the antebellum years.

5. Johnston, *Race Relations in Virginia,* 293.

6. Annie Lee West Stahl, "The Free Negro in Ante-Bellum Louisiana," *Louisiana Historical Quarterly* 25 (Apr. 1942): 308, 310, 375.

7. The known blessings of interracial unions by priests along Cane River are recorded in the registers of St. John the Baptist Catholic Church (Cloutierville).

8. Statistics are from Mills, "Family and Social Patterns," Table 14.

9. The presence of two same-named men at New Orleans, from the same French town, has confused many researchers. For a start on the records that separate the two, see *Archdiocese of New Orleans Sacramental Records,* 4:63, 5:369, 6:62; and Alice Daly Forsyth, ed., *Louisiana Marriages: A Collection of Marriage Records from the St. Louis Cathedral in New Orleans during the Spanish Regime and the Early American Period, 1784-1806* (New Orleans: Polyanthos, 1977), 43.

The younger Joseph was born August 24, 1763, son of the surgeon François Conand (*var.* Conant) and his wife Marie Anne Brillac, making him thirty-one during his brief affair with Susanne; a photocopy of his baptismal entry at Serrières has been provided by the Archives Départementales de Ardèche at La Chaumette, without citation of parish, book, or page.

Conant's origin probably explains another "tradition" writers have reported for Isle Brevelle: an assertion that Pierre Metoyer came from Lyon, France. Descendants of Susanne and Conant likely passed down the knowledge of Lyon as his point of origin, but mistakenly attributed it to Susanne's father rather than her son's father.

10. Metoyer to Conant, Sale of land, Mar. 8, 1794, doc. 2518; La Berry Succession to Conant, Sale of Victoire, Nov. 16, 1794, doc. 2564; Conant to Denis Buard, Sale of land, Oct. 31, 1795, doc. 2638; Conant to Louis Rachal *fils,* Sale of Victoire, Nov. 16, 1795, doc. 2640, all in NCA. For baptism of Susanne's son, see Mills, *Natchitoches, 1729–1803,* entry 2764 (Juan Francisco Florentino, born January 1794, bapt. Mar. 1, 1795). For Conant's punishment at the hands of Cane River insurgents during the so-called Ghosts' Revolt of 1795–96, see McAvoy et al., *Records of the Diocese of Louisiana and the Floridas, 1576–1803,* roll 1, José Vasquez Baamonde to Baron de Carondolet, Oct. 21, 1795.

Like most Cane River multiracials, Florentin Conant did not adopt his father's surname until adulthood. As late as February 1819, already aged twenty-four, he was using his mother's surname rather than his father's. See "Inventory General of the Storehouse at Natchitoches, made 18 February 1819," p. 7, for "Flor^in Metoyer," folder "1819: February 18," Original French Records, Natchitoches Parish Museum. The 1820 census was the first to acknowledge his parental name, calling him "Conan Metoyer"; see Natchitoches Parish return, stamped p. 98, line 65.

11. For an example of Anty's acknowledgment of his offspring, see Mills, *Natchitoches, 1800–1826,* entry 720 (Metoyer–Anty, marr., 1816). For Anty's ownership of a ferry, see Commandant to Jean Bte. Anty, Sale of public ferry, 1796, doc. 2662, NCA. For his involvement in Les Revenants, see McAvoy et al., *Records of the Diocese of Louisiana and the Floridas,* roll 1, Luis Carlos De Blanc, certification relative to Delvaux Case, June 21, 1796. The best study of this Cane River revolt is Gilbert C. Din, "Father Jean Delvaux and the Natchitoches Revolt of 1795," *Louisiana History* 40 (Winter 1999): 5–33. Several other white males treated in the present chapter were also involved: Pierre Badin, Pierre Charpentier, Alexis Cloutier, Athanase de Mézières Jr., Athanase Poissot, the Prudhommes, and Mme. de Soto's son and son-in-law.

12. Some details of Le Court de Presle's career have been published in Bolton, *Athanase de Mézières,* and Bill Barron, *The Vaudreuil Papers: A Calendar and Index of the Personal and Private Records of Pierre de Rigaud de Vaudreuil, Royal Governor of the French Province of Louisiana, 1743–1753* (New Orleans: Polyanthos, 1975), 113, 140–51. As a starting point for the family Le Court created and sacramental records on some of his slaves, see the entries in Mills, *Natchitoches, 1729–1803.* The succession of his wife Jeanne Le Roy, opened in November 1777, provides a rare glimpse into life at Le Court's Bluff; see doc. 1285, NCA.

13. A major study of colonial Natchitoches mistakenly presents Le Court as the father in this period of two children by a Native American slave named Jeanne Lisette, who first emerged at Natchitoches as concubine to the soldier-trader Claude Bertrand *dit* Dauphine. According to the authors: "When Bertrand passed away around 1760, Lisette remained [a] slave [of Bertrand's partner Pierre Hauraud] but she struck up a new relationship with a Breton officer and trader named Jean Louis Matthias Le Court de Presle, with whom she had two more daughters. Upon Hauraud's death in 1764, Lisette and her children received their freedom, and Le Court . . . received and distributed the amount destined for Lisette and Bertrand's four [surviving] children." See Burton and Smith, *Colonial Natchitoches,* 59.

To the contrary, Bertrand manumitted Lisette, along with their *three* children, in 1755 (doc. 478, NCA), and he was buried on October 28, 1756 (Mills, *Natchitoches, 1729–1803,* 797). Lisette remained with Hauraud, bearing three more children before Hauraud died. In January 1762, Hauraud set aside 3,000 livres for Bertrand's children, representing Bertrand's half of the partnership (which Bertrand could not legally leave to illegitimate children under Louisiana law), and Le Court was appointed to hold and manage the funds until they reached adulthood. In 1774, when the youngest of the Bertrand children came of age, Le Court paid out the sum due them, not as Lisette's sexual partner or the children's stepfather but as the legally appointed guardian of the minors' finances (docs. 429, 479–80, 576, 1320, NCA).

Correctly identifying Lisette's children and Le Court's involvement with them is critical, given that the authors go on to say, "her [Lisette's] fourth child, Ursule, became the concubine of LeCourt's French creole son Barthelemy" (p. 59). Considering that Lisette's daughter Ursule was born three years after Bertrand's death, if Lisette's post-Bertrand daughters were fathered by the Lieutenant Le Court, and if Barthélemy's placée was Lisette's daughter, then the twenty-year relationship between Barthélemy and his *métive* placée Ursulle would have been an incestuous sibling relationship. The identity of Barthélemy Le Court's Ursulle is addressed later in this chapter.

14. The first census of Rivière aux Cannes, the previously cited return of August 17, 1787, documents the presence of the Le Courts, Le Comtes, Cloutiers, Galliens, and Marie Rachal with her third husband, Pierre Charpentier. Louis Monet was the son of Marie's sister Elisabeth Rachal. Random notarial acts in NCA place these families at Rivière aux Cannes from the 1760s and document the arrivals of the other families soon after the 1787 census. All these families are extensively, but by no means completely, chronicled in the published church records for the post.

15. A genealogical chart filed in the previously cited 1825 case Dupré v. Cloutier outlines all the slave-born offspring of Coincoin's daughter Françoise. The details of their lives can be filled in, to one degree or another, from the published sacramental records, as well as civil records cited later in this chapter.

16. Mills, *Natchitoches, 1729–1803,* entry 3389 (marr., Nicolas Augustin–Agnes, Aug. 22, 1792). Marie Agnes's age at time of marriage is calculated from age and date of death given on tombstone, cemetery of St. Augustine's Church, Isle Brevelle. Also see Pierre Derbanne to Athanase Poissot, doc. 1052; and Remy Poissot to Agnes, doc. 1093, both in NCA. For the occupation of Agnes's mother on the Derbanne plantation, see Succession of Marie Le Clerc, Widow Derbanne, doc. 2857, NCA.

It should be noted that the early church registers accord no surnames to the wives chosen by the Metoyers. The same is true, in fact, of their husbands; on rare occasions the African name of their mother, Coincoin, was used by the priests as an identifying family name for the brothers. As the years passed and the position of the family improved, the community exhibited a change in attitude. The right to particular family surnames was acknowledged in most of the later civil and ecclesiastical records. Marie Agnes's surname, for example, is provided in such later documents as the marriage of Élisée Roques and Marie Susette Metoyer, June 26, 1820, in Mills, *Natchitoches Church Marriages,* entry 47.

17. The wife of Agnes's father, Athanase Poissot, was the young daughter of Mme. Marie de St. Denis de Soto. The charitableness of the mother toward interracial *mésalliances* does not appear to have been inherited by the daughter.

18. Remy Poissot to Agnes, 1775, doc.1357; and Agnes v. Mrs. Athanase Poissot, 1784, doc. 1700, both in NCA.

19. The Brevelle assertion was made by Francois Mignon; see, for example, "A Visit to Melrose Plantation with Francois Mignon," recorded interview, no. B224, in Howard-Tilton Memorial

Library, Tulane University, New Orleans. Agnes's alleged Dupré paternity was asserted by Callahan et al., *History of St. Augustine's Parish,* 13. Mignon, who was blind, apparently drew from his "recollection" of things he had heard. Callahan apparently drew from A. Dupré, "Metoyer Family Genealogy." Father Dupré was of no relation to his same-named parishioners.

20. Mills, *Natchitoches, 1800–1826,* entry 956 (marr., François–Marguerite, July 23, 1804); Augustin Metoyer of Succession of Marie Le Clerc, doc. 2857, NCA. Marguerite La Fantasy's surname is from the 1820 marriage record of her daughter Marie Adelaÿde Metoyer to Jérôme Sarpy, available as Mills, *Natchitoches Church Marriages,* entry 48.

21. Again, the births of the three Le Comte children and thirty or so of their slaves can be tracked in the published church records; unpublished notarial records provide considerably more details. Genealogical charts, with specifics, are provided in the preface to *Isle of Canes.*

22. Mills, *Natchitoches, 1729–1803,* entry 3401 (Domingo–Marguerite, Jan.19, 1795); Marguerite Le Roy [Widow Le Comte] to Marguerite, doc. 2551, NCA. The younger Marguerite's maiden surname is given in such documents as M. Le Comte, tutrix, et al. v. Marie Susanne Metoyer, Natchitoches Succ. Book 12:176–79, NCCO.

23. Le Comte to Augustin, Aug. 24, 1801, copy of sale filed in File R&R 309, Marie Perine, Louisiana State Land Office; Mills, *Natchitoches, 1800–1826,* entry 946 (marr., Pierre–Perine, 1802). The first edition of *Forgotten People,* as with most other writings on the Metoyer family, refers to Perine as Marie Perine Le Comte, that being the surname of her mother; however, no known document actually assigns a surname to Perine and no known record hints at the identity of her father. All that is known about Perine's origin is that the Widow Le Comte, on November 14, 1789, made *two* slave donations, giving one child each to two young grandsons. Joseph Dupré, aged six, was given the three-year-old Perine. Jean Baptiste Le Comte, aged three, was given another three-year-old "mulattress" named Susanne. See docs. 2193 and 2194, NCA.

24. Mills, *Natchitoches, 1729–1803,* entry 2482 (bapt., Pelagie, July 22, 1784); entry 3451 (marr., Antoine Joseph–Marie Pelagie, June 1, 1801). Also, Barthélemy Le Court to Pelagie, doc. 1850, NCA. Pelagie's surname is given in such documents as the marriage of her daughter Marie Aspasie, in Mills, *Natchitoches Church Marriages,* entry 51 (Llorens–Metoyer, Aug. 3, 1820).

25. On the basis of spelling alone, the Cane River Le Courts are frequently but erroneously tied to two other similarly named, nearby families of no kin to themselves or to each other. One Nicolas La Cour of the bishopric of Coutances arrived in Louisiana in 1720 as a laborer for the St. Catherine concession at Natchez; his subsequent home at Pointe Coupée is a historic landmark. Some of his La Cour offspring lived near Le Court's Bluff on Red River, but the two families had distinctly different origins. Similarly, Pierre La Cour, a soldier from the bishopric of Perigueux, came to Natchitoches at the end of the French regime and settled on Cane River, where his children intermarried with the Brevels and other local families; although they lived among the Creoles *de couleur,* no kinships were created. For Nicolas La Cour, a starting point would be Glenn R. Conrad, *First Families of Louisiana,* 2 vols. (Baton Rouge: Claitor's, 1970), 1:113, for the Aug. 20, 1720, roll of the *Loire* bringing workers for St. Catherine; and HABS No. LA-1293. For Pierre La Cour's origin, see La Cour–Verger marriage contract, 1766, doc. 422, NCA.

26. *Adéle v. Beauregard,* 1 Mart. La., 183 (1810).

27. Mills, "Family and Social Patterns," 39.

28. Mills, *Natchitoches, 1729–1803,* entry 3448 (marr., Louis–Thérèse, Feb. 9, 1801). Thérèse's surname is given in such documents as Widow Louis Metoyer to Théophile Metoyer, Natchitoches Conv. Book 30 (Donations): 52, NCCO.

29. *American State Papers: Indian Affairs,* 1:722–23. Cancey, Canneci, and Kancei were variant spellings of the name given to the Lipan Apache by the Caddo Indians of the Natchitoches

region and were, consequently, the names by which the Lipan were known at Natchitoches. F. Todd Smith, *The Caddo Indians: Tribes at the Convergence of Empires, 1542–1854* (College Station: Texas A&M University Press, 1995), 15, 56, 61.

30. Succession Inventory of Marie Jeanne Le Roy, wife of Le Court, Apr. 20, 1778, doc. 1285, NCA. Mills, *Natchitoches, 1729–1803*, entry 2278 (Dorothea, aged one year, bapt. Dec. 29, 1775); entry 2279 (Maria Susana, aged about four, bapt. Dec. 29, 1775); entry 2343 (Rosalia, aged about two, bapt. Dec. 26, 1778); entry 2392 (Marie Celestine, bapt. Apr. 17, 1781); entry 2447 (Marie Thérèse, bapt. Dec. 26, 1783); and entry 2446 (Jacques, born May 25, 1783 [likely 1784], bapt. with Thérèse).

31. Mills, *Natchitoches, 1729–1803*, entry 3394 (Guillori–Rosalia, marr. Nov. 27, 1792). The identity of Rosalie's father is extrapolated from such documents as the 1820 minutes of a family meeting held for Narcisse Monet, minor son of the freedwoman Dorothée Monet. There, the Rivière aux Cannes justice of the peace James F. Porter, who had married Louis Monet's widow, stated: "There being but one of the relations of the said minor in the immediate neighbourhood, I caused her to be called, to wit: Rosalie Louis Guilorie, a free woman of color." Similarly, in her will dated June 9, 1820, Dorothée left five arpents of her land to her "sister Rosalie, Widow Guillorie"; see Conv. Book 8:276, NCCO. Given that Dorothée and Rosalie were born of different mothers, their kinship had to come through a common father. Louis Monet, who manumitted Dorothée and gifted her with land, had no living male kin of his surname when these two slave girls were born. For the Dorothée Monet succession, see Natchitoches Succ. Book 3:22–27, NCCO.

32. Le Comte to "Jacques, f.m.c.," 1794, doc. 2549, NCA; this document states that Jacques was a "*mestif* beyond and free of all slavery." Also Marriage Contract of Jacques Le Compte and Silvia Brossé, with certification by the justice Jonas Davis of Natchez, who performed the couple's civil marriage, June 25, 1808, folder 804, Melrose Collection. Also Succession of "Jacques Ambroise" and Silvie Brosset, Natchitoches Succ. Book 1:145, NCCO. Jacques's succession was well administered by his white half-brother, Jean Baptiste Le Comte, who became the tutor of Jacques's and Silvie's children. For the marriage contract of the Amerindian freedman's son Jacques Tranquillin Le Comte to Marie Céleste La Fitte, the great-great-granddaughter of Mme. de Soto, see Natchitoches Conv. Book 50:63, NCCO.

33. Mills, *Natchitoches, 1729–1803*, entry 2326 (Dorotea, born Oct. 31, 1777, bapt. Mar. 1, 1788).

34. Inventory and estimation of the goods left by deceased Baptiste Dupré, Sept. 1, 1781, p. 15, doc. 1554, NCA; Widow Baptiste Dupré to Louis Monet, 1785, doc. 1831, and Marriage Contract of Louis Monet and Widow Baptiste Dupré, 1785, doc. 1839, NCA.

35. Mills, *Natchitoches, 1729–1803*, entry 2666 (for Dorotea Monet, as godmother, Feb. 6, 1793), entry 3143 (Jean Baptiste, aged two years, bapt. Feb. 22, 1797), and entry 3144 (Henriette, aged two months, bapt. Feb. 22, 1797).

36. Files A1794 and B1702, Dorothée Monet; and Section Map, Township 6 North, Range 4 West, Sections 43, 44, and 71, Louisiana State Land Office; Dorothée to Maës, April 7, 1798, doc. 2838, NCA.

37. Mills, *Natchitoches, 1800–1826*, entries 69–70 (Marie Louise Adeline and Marie Louise Adelaïde, born Feb. 5, 1801; Louis, born Feb. 15, 1803; all bapt. Dec. 4, 1803), entry 171 (Marie Thérèse Rosalie, born July 6, 1805, bapt. Oct. 17, 1805). Dorothée did not repeat her claim to be Indian at the 1809 baptism of her daughter Marie Zéline Rachal; ibid., entry 311. Also see Louis Monet to Manuel Derbanne, Sale of slave Dorothée, and Derbanne to Dorothée, Manumission, 1802, doc. 2962, NCA; "Old Natchitoches Data," 2:40, Melrose Collection. Also Natchitoches Succ. Book 3:22–27, Dorothée Monet (1820); and Alexis Cloutier to Parish Judge, Curator's Bond for

Minor Children of Dorothée Monet, Deceased, Natchitoches Conv. Book 9:34, NCCO. The Dorothée of this Derbanne document should not be confused with Manuel Derbanne's daughter and slave Dorothée, who was conveyed to Augustin Metoyer in 1810.

38. "Mary Louise Le Compte" (Mme. Porter) to Toussaint Metoyer, Natchitoches Misc. Book 1 (Dec. 1806–May 1811): 226; "Marie Louise Le Comte" (Mme. Porter) to Dorothée, doc. 4019, NCA.

39. Marriage Contract, Pierre Metoyer and Marie Henriette, Dec. 3, 1817, Natchitoches Books 2 & 3, Marr. & Misc. (1816–1819): 122; A. P. Metoyer v. Henriette Dupard, Natchitoches District Court Suit 3916; and Toussaint Metoyer to Marie Henriette, Natchitoches Deed Book 30 (Donations): 10–11. The 1850 U.S. census shows the sixty-five-year-old bachelor Toussaint Metoyer living with a seventy-year-old black woman named "Cilese," but that year's census cites no relationships. No free woman of that name has been identified in the parish. She appears to be the Marie Silesie, born into slavery in 1783 as the granddaughter of Coincoin's sister Mariotte—thus Toussaint's first cousin, once removed. See 1850 U.S. census, Natchitoches Parish, pop. sch., stamped p. 49, dwelling/family 874 ("Toucin" Metoyer household).

40. Dorothée's children by Étienne Rachal represent the only known case at Natchitoches in which individuals of African-slave ancestry successfully crossed the color line. See Gary B. Mills, "Monet–Rachal: Backtracking a Cross-Racial Heritage in the Eighteenth and Nineteenth Centuries," *The American Genealogist* 65 (July 1990): 129–42.

41. De Soto to Jouannis, 1770, doc. 765; Jouannis to Dupré, 1770, doc. 771; and Widow Dupré to Monet, 1785, doc. 1831, all in NCA.

42. Monet–Dupré marriage contract, 1785, doc. 1839, and Louis Monet Succession, 1804, doc. 3202, NCA; Mills, *Natchitoches, 1800–1826,* entry 1838 (Louis, bapt. Apr. 10, 1803).

43. *Journal of the Senate of the State of Louisiana,* 1825, pp. 25, 27, 46; *Journal of the House of the State of Louisiana,* 1825, pp. 39, 71, 75, 83; Mills, *Natchitoches Church Marriages, 1818–50,* entry 152 (Monette–Cotton Maye, July 23, 1829). Sterkx, in *The Free Negro in Ante-Bellum Louisiana,* 119, reports Louis's manumission but errs in stating that he was freed by his mother. Louis's mistress and his enslaved, multiracial mother were both named Marie Louise Le Comte.

44. Gaiennié to "Monette," Apr. 1834, folder 396, MS 182, Cane River Notarial Collection. Marie Louise Le Comte, mother of Louis Monette, f.m.c., also had a brother Nicolas who was free by 1835, by means unknown; he is not known to have become a part of the Metoyer community. The 1825 slave genealogical chart in Dupré v. Cloutier names him as Françoise's child. No record names his father, but he openly used the surname Monette. In 1835, Gaiennié described him as a "free *griffe.*" François's only known attachment was with another Le Comte-Monet-Porter-Gaiennié slave, by whom he had a daughter, Marie Zélia Monette, born about 1820; in 1835, François bought his daughter's freedom; see Gaiennié to Monette, Natchitoches Misc. Book 18:412, NCCO.

45. Interview with Mrs. Coutii, June 23, 1974.

46. Will and succession of Jean Baptiste Dupré, Aug.–Sept. 1781, doc. 1554, NCA. Comparative DNA tests have not been made yet by male Y-line descendants of the white Duprés and multiracial Balthasars, to determine whether Jean Baptiste Balthasar did, indeed, have a Dupré father.

47. Mills, *Natchitoches, 1729–1803,* entry 480 (Catherine, bapt. May 24, 1763) and entry 1152 (unnamed Indian slave of Jean Baptiste Dupré, bur. Oct. 29, 1777); Dupré–Le Comte marriage contract, Sept. 7, 1769, doc. 593, NCA. The Jean Baptiste Dupré household at Rivière aux Cannes was missed on the extremely valuable 1787 census, whereon every free person was supposed to be individually named.

48. Mills, *Natchitoches, 1729–1803,* entry 2650 (bapt., Florentin, Dec. 18, 1791), entry 3219 (Théotise, bapt. Oct. 18, 1799); Mills, *Natchitoches, 1800–1826,* entry 1928 (Rose, bapt. aged 3, Nov. 18, 1804) and entry 1981 (Jean Baptiste, bapt. Oct. 17, 1805).

49. Mills, *Natchitoches, 1729–1803*, entry 3143 (bapt., Jean Baptiste, son of Dorothée, Feb. 22, 1797); Marie Louise Marguerite Le Comte, Widow Monette, to Jean Baptiste Cyriaque, Manumission, Aug. 7, 1829, folder 281, Cane River Notarial Collection. At manumission, Widow Monet said she had purchased Cyriaque several years earlier from Alexis Cloutier. Also Mills, *Natchitoches Church Marriages*, entry 375 (Monet–Lecomte marriage and legitimation of children, Nov. 28, 1837).

50. Instances in which someone who was genetically half-black was identified in any record as "white" are extremely rare in pre–Civil War Creole or Anglo America. In the mid-1700s, the half-black daughter of the prominent Louis Chauvin de Lery of New Orleans, despite being allowed to legally marry three white males, was consistently called a *mulâtresse* in the records. The only instance the present writer has found in four decades of ethnic research is the wealthy Barbara (Galphin) Holmes of Barnwell District, South Carolina, the daughter of the Irish-born Indian trader George Galphin by a full-black slave. The 1800 U.S. census marshal classified her and her children as white, although her identity was well-known in her community; and her offspring who left the region and prominently married elsewhere adopted the fiction that her mother was Amerindian. For Galphin's 1782 will, acknowledging several illegitimate children, together with an identification of their mothers and the race of each, see Abbeville County, S.C., probate box 40, pack 898, Clerk of Court's Office, Abbeville.

51. Mills, *Natchitoches, 1800–1826*, entry 973 (Melon–Marie Louise, marr. Aug. 26, 1806); entry 2099 (Marie Rose [Baltasar], bapt. Dec. 6, 1812); entry 1663 (Maria Luisa Cloutier, bapt. Aug. 8, 1822, godparents: Louis Baltasar and Maria Rosa Baltasar).

52. Natchitoches Vacant Successions, roll VS.1 (1813), Will of "Jean Baptiste, f.m.c.," Natchitoches Parish Clerk of Court's Office. In 1830 Balthasar's heirs sold his land to Robert McAlpin, in whose possession it allegedly became the prototype plantation for Harriet Beecher Stowe's *Uncle Tom's Cabin*. For the sale, see Natchitoches Conv. Book 20:325–26.

53. For legal problems created by Marie Rose's subsequent plaçages, see Guillaume Coindet et al. v. Marie R. Metoyer, Natchitoches Parish Court files, case 942; and Succession of Jean André Zepherin Carles, Natchitoches Succ. file 45-B, NCCO; and James Hurst to [unidentified], letter, Jan. 1843, box 4, folder 2, Natchitoches Parish Records, LLMVC, NSU Special Collections. Marie Rose's children by all three are traceable in the previously cited three volumes of published sacramental records for Natchitoches and in the unpublished St. François Church Register 7.

54. Two men of the name Jean Baptiste Rachal lived along Cane River concurrently. One, Jean Baptiste Barthélemy Rachal, was the son of Barthélemy Sr. It was he and his brother Dominique with whom Augustin Metoyer's future wife, the teenaged Agnes Poissot, lived on the Grand Côte after her suit against Mme. Poissot made it impossible for her to remain in the Poissot home. It was apparently Jean Baptiste Barthélemy who fathered her short-lived first-born son (born Aug. 15, 1786; bur. Jan. 21, 1789; Mills, *Natchitoches, 1729–1803*, entries 1434, 1479). The second Jean Baptiste, who never used a patronymic as a middle name, was the son of Barthélemy Rachal Sr.'s brother Louis and lived at Rivière aux Cannes. The extant church records offer a baptismal act for Jean Baptiste, son of Barthélemy (Mills, *Natchitoches, 1729–1803*, entry 883); but the baptismal act for Jean Baptiste, son of Louis, has not survived. Consequently, many researchers in the past have conflated the two men into one. Censuses, tax rolls, and militia lists that had not been uncovered when the first edition of *Forgotten People* went to press, but have since been published in *Natchitoches Colonials*, differentiate between the two men, as does a careful analysis of all the civil records created by each of them.

55. For Rachal's identity as first cousin of Ambroise Le Comte, see his parental marriage in Mills, *Natchitoches, 1729–1803*, entry 727 (marr., Rachal–Roy, Jul. 23, 1753). For the origin of

the Rachal family, see Elizabeth Shown Mills, "European Origins of the Early French Families of Natchitoches, Louisiana," in *Papers of the Sixth Grand Reunion of the Descendants of the Founders of Natchitoches,* ed. Sharon Sholars Brown (Natchitoches, La.: Founders of Natchitoches, 1986), 27–45. For the records of the unusual five-year exile of Mme. Rachal née Marianne Benoist, see "Personnes renfermées en la maison de force de la Salpétrière, bonnes pour les isles," June 27, 1719, Archives de la Bastille, doc. 12692; and "Extrait des Reg^{res} du greffe de la prevosté de l'hotel du Roy et grande prevosté de France," doc. 10659 (1719), Archives de la Bastille, Bibliothèque de l'Arsénal, Archives Nationales, Paris. (Mme. Barbara Allemand of Paris is thanked for uncovering the second document.)

56. Widow Le Comte to J. B. Rachal, 1799, doc. 2913; Heirs of Widow Le Comte to J. B. Rachal, 1803, doc. 3115; J. B. Rachal to "his own natural children," 1805, doc. 3313, all in NCA. The baptisms of the quadroon children of J. B. Rachal and Fanchon (J. B. Espallier, Adelaïde, Pierre Missioni, Marie Astasie, Marie Sidalise, Marie Louise Clarisse, and Antoine Nerestan) can all be found in the three previously cited volumes of published church records for Natchitoches. Also see Alberta Rousseau Ducote, *Early Baptism Records, St. Paul the Apostle Catholic Church, 1796–1824, Avoyelles Parish* (Mansura: St. Paul's Church, 1980), part 2, p. 89, for the 1812 Rachal baptism. Also see Jn. Bte. Rachal *fils* Louis to Marie Françoise, free mulâtress, Donation of land, Oct. 16, 1820, Conv. Book 8:333, NCCO; and Ambroise Lecompte to "Marie Françoise *dite* Fanchon, free mulatress," Sale of land at Rivière aux Cannes, containing 8 arpents on each bank of Red River, bounded on upper and lower by Jn. Bte. Rachal, f.m.c., Nov. 19, 1827, folder 203, Cane River Notarial Collection.

57. Marriage Contract of Jean Baptiste Espallier Rachal and Susanne Metoyer, Mar. 3, 1817, Natchitoches Books 2 & 3, Marr. & Misc. (1816–1819): 43; Jean Baptiste Rachal to J. B. Carteron [i.e., *cuarteron,* quadroon], ibid., 95, and Conv. Book 6:157–58, all in NCCO; Mills, *Natchitoches Church Marriages,* entry 43 (Rachal–Metoyer, Feb. 8, 1820); Marriage Contract of J. B. D. Metoyer and "Adelaïde Françoise," Jun. 17, 1816, Natchitoches Books 2 & 3, Marr. & Misc. (1816–1819): 23; Natchitoches Succ. file 927, J. B. E. Rachal.

58. "Which Marie Louise Is 'Mariotte'?" does not cover her manumission, because the relevant documents had not been pieced together at that time. Known evidence then showed she was a free *médicine* by 1787 and that she, by 1794, was living with one Antoine Bergeon (*var.,* Bergeron) at Rivière aux Cannes. Subsequent research shows that on December 12, 1786, one Pierre Bouvier entered into a slave exchange with Mariotte's owner, the Widow Gabriel Buard. In return for "Marie Louise, a thirty-five-year-old Créole *négresse,*" Bouvier gave a much more valuable slave: a black seventeen-year-old named Madeleine, together with her infant son. (The original document, no. 1840, is missing from the courthouse; a typescript dating the transaction at Dec. 12, 1786, appears in "Old Natchitoches Data," 2:277.) Mariotte remained with Bouvier until his death. After their first three years, he had sufficient funds to purchase a Rivière aux Cannes concession earlier granted at "Ile Derbanne" to Marie (Rachal) Cloutier Gallien Charpentier: sixteen arpents on one bank and five on the other. In less than two years, Bouvier was dead. The inventory of his property taken on Nov. 16, 1792, reveals that Bouvier planted tobacco in partnership with an "associate" Antoine Bergeon (aka Bergeron) and "the free Négresse, Marie Louise." Part of Bouvier's land was purchased at the succession sale by Remi Lambre; Bergeon bought the rest and eventually gave it to Mariotte in exchange for her "laundering his clothes." For Bouvier's land, see Charpentier to Bouvier, Nov. 24, 1789, doc. 2196, and Succession of Pierre Bouvier, Nov. 16, 1792, NCA. For Mariotte's life with Bergeon, see "Which Marie Louise Is 'Mariotte'?"

59. The document whereby Mariotte freed her daughter Marie Adelaïde is not extant; however, it is referred to in a second document, Mariotte to Marie Adelaïde, Donation, in Natchi-

toches Notarial Book 3:302–4. It would also be later detailed in *Lecomte v. Cloutier,* 3 La. 170–77. A tradition that Adelaïde was "pure Indian" has been disproved. Her mother was born to the legitimate marriage of two African slaves. The consistency with which all records identify her as "mulatto" attests that her father was white. The tenor of the legal records strongly suggests that he was the French and German-Swiss Creole, Denis Buard.

60. For Adelaïde's offspring, see Mills, "Which Marie Louise Is 'Mariotte'?" 201–4. All of Joseph Dupré's familial connections to other Cane River families can be reconstructed from the published church registers.

61. *A Digest of the Civil Laws Now in Force in the Territory of Orleans with Alterations and Amendments Adapted into Its Present System of Government* (New Orleans: Bradford & Anderson, 1803), Book 3, Title 1, Chap. 3, Art. 45. This civil code was ratified by the Louisiana legislature and governor in 1808.

62. Ibid., Book 1, Title 1, Chap. 1, Art. 4.

63. Ibid., Book 1, Title 1, Chap. 3, Arts. 45–46; and Title 2, Chap. 2, Art. 14.

64. Philippe Valsain v. Cloutier, Natchitoches District Court Record Book 3:118–26, NCCO.

65. Alexis Cloutier to Augustin [Cloutier], Manumission, 1815, doc. 4528, NCA; Mills, *Natchitoches Church Marriages,* entry 10 ("Clouttier"-Metoyer, Dec. 12, 1818); also Alexis Cloutier to children of Augustin Cloutier, Donation, May 12, 1837, folder "1834: July 3," Original French Records, Natchitoches Parish Museum, Old Courthouse. For the death and burial of Jean Baptiste Sévère Cloutier, see *Archdiocese of New Orleans Sacramental Records,* 10:94 ("Clouctier").

66. *Digest of the Civil Laws* (1803), Book 2, Chap. 2, Art. 10.

67. Louis Derbanne, the quarter-blood Chitimacha who served Rivière aux Cannes as notary and auctioneer, also fathered a slave child, Marie Doralise Derbanne, whom he freed shortly before her marriage to Adelaïde's son, Philippe Valsin Dupré; see Natchitoches Parish Conv. Book 15:138, doc. 1 (Dupré–Derbanne civil marriage, with legitimation of child), NCCO. Fuller details are in Rachal Mills Lennon and Elizabeth Shown Mills, "Mother, Thy Name Is *Mystery*! Finding the Slave Who Bore Philomene Daurat," *National Genealogical Society Quarterly* 88 (Sept. 2000): 211–17; this essay provides the documentary basis for Lalita Tademy's historical novel and family memoir *Cane River* (New York: Time Warner Books, 2001), which centers upon Louis Derbanne's plantation. The plantation name assigned by Tademy ("Rosedew") is a fiction designed to fill an expectation born of stereotype; Cane River planters of this era did not name their lands.

68. *Lecomte v. Cloutier,* 3 La. 170–77. Also Philippe Valsain v. Cloutier, Natchitoches District Court Record Book 3:118–26; Family Meeting of Friends and Relatives of Noel [Emanuel] Dupré, f.m.c., Natchitoches Conv. Book 20:305–6; both in NCCO. The identities and kinships of all those who assisted the Dupré heirs can be assembled from the published church records.

69. Cloutier's claim to have given "several slaves" to the plaintiffs is only partly supported by the records. Only one such donation has been documented; see Alexis Cloutier to Marie Doralise, f.w.c., doc. 4751, NCA. The Marie Doralise of this donation is Marie Doralise (Dupré) Lassize, one of the three heirs to Joseph Dupré. She should not be confused with her sister-in-law Marie Doralise (Derbanne) Dupré, wife of Philippe Valsain Dupré.

70. Philippe Valsain v. Cloutier, Natchitoches District Court Record Book 3:118–26, NCCO. In the interim between the first and second litigations of this case, Louisiana's law had changed somewhat. For the laws applicable in 1830, see Moreau Lislet and Carleton, *The Laws of Las Siete Partidas;* particularly relevant is 1:552–53, Part 4, Law 7(a), which states:

Another way of legitimating natural children, is where a father declares by a writing executed by his own hand, or which he causes to be executed by a notary public, and attested by three witnesses, that he acknowledge[s] such a one for his son, designating him expressly by name. But in such acknowledgement, the father ought not to say he is his natural son; for if he does, the legitimation will have no effect. . . . They who are therein mentioned as being legitimated, can inherit, both the estates of their fathers, and other relations.

Despite Cloutier's claim that his son was Dupré's rightful heir, being Dupré's sole sibling, the court noted the code's provision that "one brother may disinherit another, without cause; and . . . may leave his estate to whomever he pleases, when he has no children, nor other descendants, in the direct line, nor father or other ascendants, provided he do[es] not institute for heir a person of bad life, or who is infamous."

71. Marriage Contract, Emanuel Dupré to Marie Marguerite Metoyer, Natchitoches Misc. Records, Book A, doc. 457, p. 48. Regarding the settlement of this case, also see Adelaïde Mariotte to [her children], Donation, folder "1832:12 March," Original French Records, Natchitoches Parish Museum. The court record does not explain why backdated interest was to begin on May 3, 1815. That date should be the otherwise unrecorded death date of Marie Louise Mariotte—i.e., the date on which her still-enslaved daughter and grandchildren were legally free.

72. Burton and Smith's *Colonial Natchitoches,* 59, misidentifies Ursulle as the daughter of an Indian woman named Jeanne Lisette, whose children by Claude Bertrand *dit* Dauphine were acknowledged by Bertrand before his death. That source also states that Jeanne Lisette, after Bertrand's death, bore two daughters by Louis Mathias le Court de Presle; and that Lisette's daughter Ursulle was the woman of that name who became the concubine of Le Court's son Barthélemy. That reconstruction is disproved in several ways: (1) As discussed in a previous note (chap. 4, n. 13), the elder Le Court did not take Lisette as his concubine; she remained with Bertrand's partner, who appointed Le Court to be the financial guardian of the Bertrand children's inheritance. Hauraud, as the children's "stepfather" and their father's business partner, was not legally qualified to manage their inheritance; doing so represented a conflict of interest that he had to legally address. (2) If Lisette's daughter Ursulle, who was born in 1758, were Barthélemy's same-name placée, she would have been thirty-three when she bore her first child and fifty-three at the birth of her last one—both highly unlikely ages for first and last births in her society. (3) Lisette's daughter Ursulle migrated to New Orleans, where she married one Josef Modena and remained at least until 1794. The published abstracts of her marriage record identify her as "Ursula Dauphine, native of Natchitoches, daughter of Beltran [*sic*] Dauphine and of Juana Dauphine"; see Forsyth, *Louisiana Marriages,* 19; *Archdiocese of New Orleans Sacramental Records,* 4:212 (Moden, Modena), 5:271 (Modin). Jeanne Lisette's Ursulle, born three years after Bertrand's death, apparently believed that her siblings' father was also her own or else she did not want to acknowledge her illegitimacy when she married at New Orleans. In any case, that marriage to Modena, their residence at New Orleans, and her age all disqualify her as the Ursulle who came of age a decade later at Rivière aux Cannes and bore children by Le Court while Mme. Medina was in New Orleans.

73. Succession of Jeanne Le Roy, Mme. Le Court, doc. 1285, NCA; Mills, *Natchitoches, 1729–1803,* entry 2255 ("Marie Louise, Indian, aged three and a half, daughter of Marie Ursulle, Indian of the Caddo nation," bapt. July 6, 1796). This is the only document that identifies Ursulle as a Caddo; no others name a tribe and most cite her as *métive.* For Ursulle's identification as Luison, see Mills, *Natchitoches Church Marriages,* entry 128 (Bask–Lecourt).

74. Ursulle's children by Barthélemy Le Court are easily reassembled from the three volumes of published sacramental records previously cited. In Succession of Barthélemy Le Court, Natchitoches Succ. file 204, NCCO, they were not named as his legal heirs because he had not married

either of their mothers. Like many such fathers, he provided for them prior to his death. The children were also acknowledged by him in such documents as Barthélemy Le Court to [Pierre] Cesaire Brosset, 1814, doc. 4332, NCA, in which he passed to this son-in-law a piece of land adjacent to "Mr. Louis Cesaire Bmy. Lecour, my natural child." They also are identified as his offspring in other documents such as marriage of Marie Tranquilline LeCourt to Thomas Bask, Nov. 5, 1827; Cezaire Le Cour to Gertrude Maurine, July 23, 1829; and Neuville LeCourt to Marie Ositte Metoyer, Feb. 15, 1830, in Mills, *Natchitoches Church Marriages*, entries 128, 154, and 167. For the ethnic status of Ursulle's children see, for example, the family meeting called in May 1822 for minors of Marie Louise Le Court, wife of Pierre Brosset, Natchitoches Succ. file 15, NCCO. For the Brosset family who provided spouses for the *métives* Jacques Le Comte and Marie Louise Le Court, see Elizabeth Shown Mills, "From Chez Bienvenu to Cane River: Four Generations of the Pierre Brosset Family," *Natchitoches Genealogist*, serialized, vols. 11–14 (1986–89).

75. Mills, *Natchitoches, 1800–1826*, entry 2462 (Marie Felony [Felonise] and Marie Emy, bapt. June 27, 1816).

76. Mills, *Natchitoches Church Marriages*, entry 406 (Lecour–Metoyer, May 17, 1838), and entry 633 (Rachal–Lacour, Oct. 4, 1846).

77. Badin's burial record states his age and origin; see Mills, *Natchitoches, 1800–1826*, entry 846. For land and slaveholdings, see January 1766 and May 1766 censuses, the 1774 tax roll and census of slaveowners, and the August 1787 census of Natchitoches in Mills, *Natchitoches Colonials*, 11, 17, 32, 35, 49, as well as numerous baptismal records in the published church registers. Also (all in NCA): Jeanne Le Roy to Pierre Badin, Sale of land, 1760–61, doc. 315; Badin of Marmillion, purchase of slave, 1775, doc. 1047; Badin of Sanchez, Purchase of slave, 1775, doc. 1080; Badin of Borme, Purchase of plantation, 1787, doc. 2032; Pierre Badin to [20 slaves], Manumission, 1791, docs. 2332, 2335–2344; Badin of Widow Grappe's succession, Purchase of land, 1794, doc. 2501; Badin Succession, 1806, docs. 3336, 3394. Also, Will of Marie Serpault, wife of Pierre Badin, 1788, doc. 516, Melrose Collection; and Will of Pierre Badin, Folder 1791: Nov. 15, Original French Records, Natchitoches Parish Museum. Occasional Badin slave baptisms are recorded also in the records of St. Paul the Apostle Church at Mansura, having been conducted at Natchitoches by the Avoyelles priest.

78. Badin statistics are included in Gary B. Mills's analysis of Metoyer illegitimacies with those of comparative communities in the parish; see "Piety and Prejudice: A Colored Catholic Community in the Antebellum South," in *Catholics in the Old South: Essays on Church and Culture*, ed. Randall M. Miller and Jon L. Wakelyn (Macon, Ga.: Mercer University Press, 1983), 171–94.

79. One popular account of the Badin-Roque House, which was used as a convent on the Isle prior to the Civil War, asserts that it "was built in the late 18th century" and "first used as the residence of Jean Baptiste Metoyer, grandson of Marie Thérèse." That grandson, born to Augustin Metoyer in 1795, could hardly have built the property "in the late 18th century." J. B. A. Metoyer did own the property for a few months in 1856, having obtained it in the division of the estate of his father, who had purchased it in 1811 from heirs of the original owner of the tract and the probable builder, the white Gaspard Roubieu. The J. B. A. Metoyer home, which is no longer extant, was a pillared plantation manor standing on land he had owned from the time of his 1816 marriage. For the passage quoted above, see "Badin-Roque House," *Creole Chronicles* 1 (May 2001; rpr., Oct. 2011): 24–25. For J. B. A. Metoyer's ownership of the property and its chain of title before that, see Keiffy to Martin, Natchitoches Conv. Book 49:504–6; and Roubieu to Metoyer, 1811, doc. 4031, NCA.

80. Msgr. Anduze's report of his visit in the unorthodox Mézières household was first published in *Annales de la Propagation de la Foi* 3 (1828): 501–9. It was translated and published

by the late Rev. Dr. J. Edgar Bruns, historian of the Archdiocese of New Orleans, in "Athanase Christophe Fortunat de Mezieres (1721–1779)," *Louisiana Genealogical Register* 32 (March 1985): 3–8, particularly p. 5. According to Bruns, an earlier translation made by Mary Teresa Austin Carroll, *A Catholic History of Alabama and the Floridas* (New York: P. J. Kenedy & Sons, 1908), 251–52, is not reliable.

81. Nothing is known of Marie Bernarde's origin; the only family known for her is a sister named Jeanette Robert, who died at New Orleans shortly before May 15, 1834; Natchitoches Conv. Book 19:436–38, NCCO. The mother of her owner Athanase de Mézières Jr., Pelagie Fazende, was from New Orleans; possibly he inherited Marie Bernarde through the Fazendes.

82. The Mézières *de couleur* are extensively developed in Mills, "(de) Mézières-Trichel-Grappe," 4–18, 21–25, 34–38, 47–49, 55–60.

83. Burton and Smith, in *Colonial Natchitoches,* 29–30, 39, 55, mistakenly present the Camptí Grappes as cousins of the Cane River Derbannes. They reach that conclusion on the basis that the Chitimacha wife of the French administrator Derbanne was called Jeanne de la Grande Terre, while the Chitimacha mother of Louise Marguerite (Guedon) Grappe was called Marianne Thérèse de la Grande Terre. By extrapolation, the authors assumed that "de la Grande Terre" was a family surname and that the two contemporary females must be sisters. However, "la Grande Terre" was a place name, not a family name; it was used by the early French for the Louisiana delta below New Orleans, inhabited by the Chitimacha tribe. Both Jeanne and Marianne Thérèse were among the numerous captives taken by St. Denis and sold into slavery during the 1705–6 war in which the French almost annihilated the tribe. Derbanne and Guedon were two of the French men who bought female captives, fathered children by them, and subsequently freed and married them. Extensive records on both families appear in the published church registers of colonial Natchitoches. For earlier documents, see Register 1, Our Lady Parish, Mobile; also Elizabeth Shown Mills, "François (Guyon) Dion Despres Derbanne: *Premier Citoyen,* Poste St. Jean Baptiste des Natchitoches," *Natchitoches Genealogist* 6 (October 1981): 1–9. No evidence suggests that the two Chitimacha girls were sisters.

84. Mills, "(de) Mézières-Trichel-Grappe," 28–34, 41–46, 54–55. This study reports the 1741 marriage of Souris and Catherine, the births of two daughters in 1748 and 1750, and the circa 1767 sale of Catherine to the New Orleans planter François Hery *dit* Duplanty. Subsequently the author discovered the apparent reason for the births of no children after 1750. Shortly thereafter, the parents were separated and Souris was transferred to the de la Chaise plantation at New Orleans; see Heloise Crozat, trans. and abstr., "Records of the Superior Council of Louisiana," *Louisiana Historical Quarterly* 22 (January 1939): 230, for the Jan. 1753 summons on Sieur Cheval, overseer for de la Chaise, delivered at his house into the hands of the *nègre* "Soury."

85. *Courier des Natchitoches,* Aug. 2, 1825; Caddo Chiefs to President Andrew Jackson, Jan. 28, 1835, copy in Grappe Collection, Centenary College Archives, Shreveport, La.; François Grappe, affidavit, *Annals of Congress,* 9th Cong., 1st Sess., 1805–1806, 1211–18. Also Mills, "(de) Mézières-Trichel-Grappe," 28–34, 41–46, 54–55; Philip C. Cook, "Alexis Grappe: From French Marine to N. La. Frontiersman," *North Louisiana Historical Association Journal* (*NLHA Journal*) 34 (Winter 2003): 34–44; Dayna B. Lee, "François Grappe and the Caddo Land Cession," *NLHA Journal* 20 (Spring–Summer 1989): 53–69; and Bernie Grappe, "F. Grappe: Unique N. La. Frontiersman," *NLHA Journal* 9 (Spring 1978): 65–70.

86. Mills, "(de) Mézières-Trichel-Grappe," for example, analyzes the 1850 planting operation of the wealthiest f.m.c. at Camptí against the "average" multiracial planter along Cane River and the "average" farmer or planter in the parish. The Camptí planter, Joseph Noël Mézières—father of Henri Philippe, the multiracial who became clerk of court during Reconstruction—fell sub-

stantially behind the parish average and immensely behind the average Cane River multiracial. Mills, "Piety and Prejudice," 170–94, delineates other comparisons between the Cane River and Camptí communities.

87. Mills, *Natchitoches, 1729–1803,* entry 2847 (Marie Thérèse Magdeleine, bapt. Oct. 2, 1797); Mills, *Natchitoches Church Marriages,* entry 10 (Cloutier–Metoyer, Dec. 12, 1818).

88. Marriage Contract of Joseph Ozéme Metoyer and Catherine David, "Old Natchitoches Data," 2:113, Melrose Collection. Succession of Narcisse Dominique Metoyer, in Natchitoches Succ. Book 12:175–79, NCCO, identifies his widow as Marie Cephalide David, although no church or civil marriage record seems to be extant. For other intermarriages between the two communities, see Mills, *Natchitoches Church Marriages.*

89. James Silk Buckingham, *The Slave States of America,* 2 vols. (London: Fisher, Son & Co., 1842), 1:358. For the "ankles like angels" analogy, see Samuel Wilson, ed., *Southern Travels: Journal of John H. B. Latrobe* (New Orleans: Historic New Orleans Collection, 1986), 43. Other sensationalized accounts traditionally relied upon are Alexis de Tocqueville, *Journey to America,* ed. J. P. Mayer and trans. George Lawrence (Garden City, N.Y.: Doubleday, 1971); Bernhard, Duke of Saxe-Weimar-Eisenach, *Travels through North America during the Years 1825 and 1826,* 2 vols. (Philadelphia: Carey, Lea & Carey, 1828), particularly 2:58–70; and Harriet Martineau, *Society in America,* 2 vols. (New York: Saunders and Otley, 1837), particularly 2:114–17.

90. Antonio Acosta Rodríguez, in *La Población de Luisiana Española, 1763–1803* (Madrid: Ministerio de Asuntos Exteriores, 1979), provides the best demographic dissection, although his presentation for Natchitoches in 1766 uses only the highly defective January enumeration rather than the corrective one taken in May.

91. Edward Larocque Tinker, ed., *Les Cenelles: Afro-French Poetry in Louisiana* (New York: Colophon, 1930).

92. Traditional interpretations most commonly cited, and still useful as retrospectives, are found in Stahl, "The Free Negro in Ante-Bellum Louisiana," 305–12; Dunbar-Nelson, "People of Color in Louisiana"; Joseph Tregle, "Early New Orleans Society: A Reappraisal," *Journal of Southern History* 18 (Feb. 1952): 20–36; and Donald E. Everett, "Free Persons of Color in New Orleans, 1803–1865" (Ph.D. diss., LSU, 1952).

93. The varied views toward the role of New Orleans women in the institutions of plaçage and quadroon balls are well represented by Randall R. Couch, "The Public Masked Balls of Antebellum New Orleans: A Custom of Masque outside the Mardi Gras Tradition," *Louisiana History* 35 (Fall 1994): 403–31; Liliane Crété, *Daily Life in Louisiana, 1815–1830,* trans. Patrick Gregory (Baton Rouge: LSU Press, 1981); Lois Virginia Meacham Gould, "A Chaos of Iniquity and Discord: Slave and Free Women of Color in the Spanish Ports of New Orleans, Mobile, and Pensacola," in *The Devil's Lane: Sex and Race in the Early South,* ed. Catherine Clinton and Michelle Gillespie (New York: Oxford University Press, 1997), 232–46; Gould, "In Full Enjoyment of Their Liberty"; Monique Guillory, "Some Enchanted Evening on the Auction Block: The Cultural Legacy of the New Orleans Quadroon Balls" (Ph.D. diss., New York University, 1999); Guillory, "Under One Roof: The Sin and Sanctity of the New Orleans Quadroon Balls," in *Race Consciousness,* ed. Judith J. Fossett and Jeffrey A. Tucker (New York: NYU Press, 1997); Kimberly S. Hanger, "Coping in a Complex World: Free Black Women in Colonial New Orleans," in *The Devil's Lane,* ed. Clinton and Gillespie, 218–31; Hanger, "Landlords, Shopkeepers, Farmers, and Slave-Owners: Free Black Female Property-Holders in Colonial New Orleans," in *Beyond Bondage: Free Women of Color in the Americas,* ed. David Barry Gaspar and Darlene Clark Hine (Urbana: University of Illinois Press, 2004), 219–36; Hanger, "Origins of New Orleans's Free Creoles of Color," in *Creoles of Color of the Gulf South,* ed. Dormon, 1–27; Joan M. Martin, "*Plaçage* and the Louisiana

Gens de Couleur Libres: How Race and Sex Defined the Lifestyles of Free Women of Color," in *Creole,* ed. Kein, 64–70; Natasha L. McPherson, "'There was a Tradition among the Women': New Orleans's Colored Creole Women and the Making of a Community in the Tremé and Seventh Ward, 1791–1930" (Ph.D. diss., Emory University, 2011); and Noël Voltz, "Black Female Agency and Sexual Exploitation: Quadroon Balls and Plaçage Relationships" (senior honors' thesis, Ohio State University, 2008).

94. For the prostitute quote, see Henry A. Kmen, *Music in New Orleans: The Formative Years, 1791–1841* (Baton Rouge: LSU Press, 1966), as quoted in Voltz, "Black Female Agency," 2. Historian Joseph Tregle took this tack also, asserting that "free Negro women" of New Orleans "monopolized the task of accommodating the licentiousness of the male part of New Orleans"; see "Early New Orleans Society: A Reappraisal," 34–35.

95. On Isle Brevelle, chaperones in the home and close monitoring at dances remained the norm until after World War II; see Dana Bowker Lee, "The People of the Island: A Living Culture," *Creole Chronicles* 1 (May 2001): 7. As late as the 1970s, in discussing her great-great-grandmother Adelaïde Mariotte, Lee Etta Coutii described the "shame" Adelaïde caused her family because she bore so many children by "so many men, outside of marriage." According to the tradition she reported, Augustin Metoyer had pleaded with Adelaïde, on behalf of the family, to abandon her "immoral" ways. In response, supposedly, Adelaïde had laughed at him, saying she would have as many children by white men as the Lord would give her—then maybe one of them could pass for white; interview with Mrs. Coutii, Apr. 26, 1974.

96. Clark's findings are currently being prepared for publication; for a brief preview, see Carol J. Schlueter, "Historian Unmasks Quadroon Myth," Tulane University, *New Wave,* Aug. 17, 2011 (http://tulane.edu/news/newwave/081711_quadroon.cfm?RenderForPrint=1).

97. "Libertad de Fran[co] Mauricio, Mulato," Feb. 19, 1791, and "Testam[to] de D[n] Luis Forneret," Apr. 19, 1791, both drawn by Francisco Broutin, Notary, New Orleans Notarial Archives. Considerably more historical detail on the interrelated, multiracial Forneret-Girardy-Milon-Dupart family is available in four research reports prepared by Elizabeth Shown Mills for Joseph B. Mullon III, all in Mills Collection, NSU: "Jeannot Milon *dit* LeBrun," Dec. 8, 2005; "Mulon, Milon, Millon of Mobile," Dec. 28, 2005; "Melon (*var.* Mulon, Milon, Millon, etc.) and Forneret," May 21, 2006; and "Mulons of New Orleans and Cane River (var. Melon, Millon): A Genealogical Summary," June 26, 2006. For a synopsis of the Forneret separation proceedings, see Light Townsend Cummins, "Church Courts, Marriage Breakdown, and Separation in Spanish Louisiana, West Florida, and Texas, 1763–1836," *Journal of Texas Catholic History and Culture* 4 (1993): 110, citing "Isabel Alexandre contra Luis Forneret, May 1973, Actos of Quiñones, Vol. 6, f. 134, Orleans Parish Notary Archives." A frequently assumed descent of Cane River Mulons from the intrepid, multiracial Indian interpreter of colonial Natchitoches, Jeannot Mulon *dit* Le Brun, is inaccurate. Jeannot appears to be a collateral kin—a half-brother of the white Maurice Milon, born of a slave belonging to Maurice's maternal grandfather Joseph Girardy.

98. Mills, *Natchitoches, 1800–1826,* entry 973 (marr., Melon–Marie Louise, Aug. 26, 1806), entry 2029 (bapt., Pierre Metoyer, Aug. 16, 1807), entry 2084 (bapt., Marie Sidalise, Dec. 29, 1809), entry 2011 (bapt., Susette, Dec. 6, 1812), entry 2404 (bapt., Alexy Carle, Oct. 29, 1815), entry 1159 (bapt., Louis Milon, Apr. 1, 1819), and entry 1395 (bapt., Marie Felicité Melon, Mar. 25, 1821); Mills, *Natchitoches Church Marriages,* entry 409 (Mullon–Cottonmaïs, May 20, 1838).

99. Mills, *Natchitoches, 1800–1826,* entry 1054 (marr., Metoyer–Marie Arthemise, June 27, 1815); Mills, *Natchitoches Church Marriages,* entry 156 (Duparte–Baltazar, June 25, 1829) and entry 541 (Dupart–Cloutier, Nov. 14, 1842). Émile's occupation as a blacksmith is provided by documents in Dr. Carle's succession, from which Émile rented the forge (Natchitoches Succ. Book

6:129) and by Jʰ Mⁱᵉ Rablés [Rabalé] v. Emile Colson, f.m.c., blacksmith, Aug. 13, 1828, folder 249, Cane River Notarial Collection. See also *Archdiocese of New Orleans Sacramental Records,* 6:196–97; 8:118; 9:127; 10:160–61, 313, 417; 12:271 for other relevant "Millon"–Dupart records available in print. For Charles Dupart's slave ownership, see Glenn R. Conrad, *St. Charles: Abstracts of the Civil Records of St. Charles Parish, 1700–1803* (Lafayette: University of Southwestern La., 1974), 172.

100. *Archdiocese of New Orleans Sacramental Records,* 6:18 (Carlota "Belere," 30, spouse of "Carlos Dupart," bur. Jan. 20, 1797); Marriage Contract, Leandre Dupart and Marie Jeanne Cécille, Natchitoches Conv. Book 14:249, NCCO. In 1819, Charles Dupart, aged sixty-four, hatter, reported the death of his sister Marie Bodaille, daughter of Jean Bodaille and Marie Claude. A *ca.* 1753 birth is given for him on an undated list of freedmen "below the city," attached to a 1770 document, filed in leg. 188-1-2, PPC-AGI. For the *ca.* 1770 list, see Jacqueline K. Voorhies, trans. and comp., *Some Late Eighteenth-Century Louisianians: Census Records, 1758–1796* (Lafayette: University of Southwestern La., 1973), 260. For the 1819 report of death, see Albert L. Robichaux Jr., *Civil Registration of Orleans Parish Births, Marriages, and Deaths, 1790–1833* (Rayne, La.: Hebert Publications, 2000), 104. Also see Dupart's other appearances on pp. 128, 500.

101. *Archdiocese of New Orleans Sacramental Records,* 5:25, records the births of several children to Marthe "Marton" Bellair, Jérôme Sarpy's mother, with Carlotta Bellair a godmother. The baptisms of two of the infants identify their maternal grandmother as "Francisca Belair." The baptism of Jérôme has not been found in the "selected" records made available by the archdiocese; for his age and marriage, see Mills, *Natchitoches Church Marriages,* entry 48 (Sarpy-Metoyer, June 27, 1820). The activities of the white Sarpy merchants, father and son, on Cane River are chronicled in various notarial records such as doc. 2197 (1789), doc. 2504 (1794), doc. 3179 (1804), and doc. 3238 (1805), NCA. The burial of both the father and son identify them as natives of Fumelles in Lot-et-Garonne; see *Archdiocese of New Orleans Sacramental Records,* 6:247 (J. B. Lille Sarpy, father) and the unpublished burial record of the son, J. B. Lille Sarpy at Natchitoches in St. François Parish, Register 15, entry 1836:46 (Oct. 25, 1836). Forsyth's *Louisiana Marriages,* 37, documents the Sarpy-Cavalier marriage. For Henriette DeLille's family identity, see M. Boniface Adams, "The Gift of Religious Leadership: Henriette DeLille and the Foundation of the Holy Family Sisters," in *Cross, Crozier, and Crucible,* 360–74.

102. Mills, *Natchitoches, 1800–1826,* entry 241 (Marcellin Tauzin, bapt. Sept. 20, 1808) and entry 785 (Llorens–Anty, marr. Jan. 29, 1818); Mills, *Natchitoches Church Marriages,* entry 51 ("Llorans"–Metoyer, Aug. 3, 1820). Also Francisco Llorens, curator's bond for children of Françoise Nivette, deceased, 1816, doc. 4691, NCA.

103. *Archdiocese of New Orleans Sacramental Records,* 5:331 (Roch), 6:241 (Roque), and 7:274 (Roch) provide biographical detail on the father. Ibid., 15:179 (Glapion), places the death of Lizette Glapion at Nov. 19, 1823, and identifies her as a fifty-year-old native of New Orleans. Ibid., 13:376 (Roques), documents the marriage of Pierre Roques's brother to Marie Adeline Prudhomme of Natchitoches. Robichaux, *Civil Registrations,* 716, identifies Jean Roques as a merchant. Doc. 3077 (1803), NCA, contains two slave sales in which Emanuel Prudhomme of Cane River identified Jean Ro(c)ques as the dealer through which he had purchased two "brut nègres," one of them a Bambara. See also Mills, *Natchitoches Church Marriages,* entry 6 (Roques-Metoyer, Nov. 3 1818), and entry 47 (Roques-Metoyer, June 26, 1820).

104. Marriage Contract of Charles Nerestan Rocques and Marie Pompose Metoyer, Natchitoches Misc. Books 2 & 3 (1816–1819), no. 87, NCCO.

105. 1850 U.S. Census, Natchitoches Parish, pop. sch., stamped p. 49 recto, dwelling/family 872 (F. Christophe household); Mills, *Natchitoches Church Marriages,* entry 339 (Metoyer-Cris-

tophe, Nov. 3, 1836), entry 552 (Cristophe–Metoyer, Feb. [16?], 1843), and entry 611 (Christophe–Conand, Nov. 18, 1845); *Archdiocese of New Orleans Sacramental Records*, 12:79 (Christoff), 14:84 (Christophe), and 16:85 (Christophe).

106. Mills, *Natchitoches Church Marriages*, entry 198 (Maurin–Metoyer, Jul. 2, 1831); Marie Susette Metoyer Renunciation, Natchitoches Conv. Book 19:268–6, NCCO; Vve Louis Morin to A. Chateigner, procuration, Dec. 30, 1850, folder 1125, Cane River Notarial Collection; *Archdiocese of New Orleans Sacramental Records*, 13:60 (Bricou), for Louis Morin's service as godfather to a child of Henri Bricou and wife Euphrosine Dupart.

107. *Archdiocese of New Orleans Sacramental Records*, 11:99 (Coton-Maye); Mills, *Natchitoches Church Marriages*, entry 118 (Metoyer–Cotton-Maïs, Apr. 26, 1827), entry 152 (Monet–Cotton-Maïs, Jul. 23, 1829), entry 171 (Balthasard–Cotton-Maïs, May 1, 1830), entry 175 (Porter–Cotton-Maïs, Aug. 24, 1830), and entry 409 (Mullon–Cotonmaïs, May 20, 1838). For the identity of Jacques Porter, who married Coton-Maïs's daughter, see also the marriage of his brother Louis Porter, ibid., entry 242 (Porter–Metoyer, May 14, 1833), and his baptism in Mills, *Natchitoches, 1800–1829*, entry 49 (Jacques [Cécile], bapt. Apr. 10, 1803). The American justice of the peace James Porter, who had married the Widow Monet, manumitted his natural son Jacques Porter in 1809; see doc. 3739, NCA. For the death and estate of Coton-Maïs, see Natchitoches Succ. Book 14:41–43, NCCO. For the two Coton-Maïs manumission efforts, see Conv. Book 21: 37–39, and 104, NCCO.

108. 1850 U.S. Census, Natchitoches Parish, pop. sch., stamped p. 49 verso, dwelling/family 883 (Jos. A. Metoyer household); 1860 U.S. Census, Natchitoches Parish, pop. sch., p. 51/479, dwelling/family 420 (Oscar Dubreuil).

109. Mills, *Natchitoches Church Marriages*, entry 531 (Dubreuil–Rachal, June 27, 1842); Succession of J. B. E. Rachal, Natchitoches Succ. file 927. The Dubreuils of color in New Orleans are partially traceable through *Archdiocese of New Orleans Sacramental Records*.

110. *Diocese of Baton Rouge Catholic Church Records* (Baton Rouge: The Diocese, 1978–ca. 2007), 3:280 (Dubreuil), 4:179; 1820 U.S. Census, East Baton Rouge Parish, stamped p. 67, line 4. For Dubreuil's occupation, see Mrs. H. T. Beauregard, "Journal of Jean Baptiste Trudeau among the Arikara Indians in 1795," *Missouri Historical Society Collections* 4 (1912): 10–11.

111. 1830 U.S. Census, Orleans Parish, p. 130, line 15 (Louis "Dubruel"); *Archdiocese of New Orleans Sacramental Records*, 17:126 (Dubreuille, Duvrevil) and 19:122 (Dubreuil).

112. Mills, *Natchitoches, 1729–1803*, entry 3111 (Jean Noël, bapt. Mar. 26, 1796); Mills, *Natchitoches, 1800–1826*, entry 2406 (Marie Antoinette Condé, born 1815, daughter of Antoine Condé and Marie Rose Metoyer) and entry 2619 (Marie Doralisse Coindet, born 1818, daughter of Antoine Coindet and Marie Rose Metoyer). The possibility that Coindet was in a plaçage with Coincoin's daughter Marie Louise is detailed in chapter 3.

113. Guillaume Coindet et al. v. Marie Rose Metoyer, Natchitoches District Court suit no. 942 (1822); also, Noël, a slave v. Benjamin Metoyer, District Court suit no. 502, bundle 16 (1822), both NCCO. For a published abstract of the latter, see University of North Carolina, *Digital Library on American Slavery* (http://library.uncg.edu/slavery/details.aspx?pid=7164), petition 20882213. As a free man, Noël Coindet moved to the Camptí community and intermarried with the Mézières of color; see Mills, *Natchitoches Church Marriages*, entry 141 (Coindet–Mézières, Dec. 29, 1828).

114. Rose Metoyer to J^n A. Z. Carles, D. M., procuration, July 1823, folder 26, and Rose Metoyer to J^n p^{re} M^{ie} Dubois, procuration, July 18, 1828, folder 29a, in Cane River Notarial Collection; Coindet et al. v. Metoyer, District Court, NCCO.

115. For Rose's daughters by Carles, see baptism of Thérèsine, Dec. 20, 1826, in St. François Parish, Register 7 (unpublished); Marriage of Rosine Carles to François Gassion Metoyer in

Dupré, "Metoyer Family Genealogy"; and the marriage of Thérèsine Carles to Florentin Conant Jr. in Mills, *Natchitoches Church Records,* entry 551. For Rose's economic status, see 1830 U.S. Census, Natchitoches Parish, penned p. 60, line 8 (Mary R. "Metyier").

116. Succession of J. A. Z. Carles, Natchitoches Succ. file 45-B, NCCO; *Adams v. Hurst,* 9 La. 243 (March 1836); Jas. Hurst to "Dear Sir," letter dated "Cloutierville Jany. 1843," Box 4, folder 62, Natchitoches Parish Records, LLMVC, LSU Special Collections.

117. The tradition was reported by Mrs. Coutii, Apr. 26, 1974. For Chevalier's origin and date of arrival, see Elizabeth Shown Mills, "Certificates of Naturalization, Natchitoches Parish, Louisiana, 1820–50," *Louisiana Genealogical Register* 21 (Mar. 1974): 73.

118. Chevalier & Oscar to Celestin Cassa, Statement, in Norbert Badin Papers, LLMVC, LSU Special Collections.

119. Section Map, Township 8 North, Range 7 West, State Land Office; 1850 U.S. Census, Natchitoches Parish, pop. sch., stamped p. 63, dwelling/family 1135/1135 (Louis Chevalier household).

120. Succession of Louis Chevalier, Natchitoches Succ. file 752, NCCO.

121. Mills, *Natchitoches Church Marriages,* entry 486 (Metoyer–Prudhomme, Feb. 3, 1841); St. François Parish, Register 7, unpaginated (Nov. 3, 1826, bapt. Marie Thérèse, slave of Prudhomme). J. B. Prudhomme to Marie Pompose alias Séverin and children, Manumission, Natchitoches Conv. Book 21:50, NCCO. Mrs. Coutii in 1974 owned a small leather-bound notebook inherited by her grandfather Ambroise Sévère Dupré that was labeled "Souvenir des Ages." Its earliest entries document Prudhomme's slave mistress and children: "Née Marie Pompose dite Séverin, en Febrier 1805; . . . Né Jean Pierre Cleville dit [*sic*] ce 31 Janvier 1821; Née Marie Thérèse Aspasie, ce 31 Octobre 1823; Né François Edouard, ce 6 Septembre 1832; Né Sylvestre Séverin, ce 30 Novembre 1835." As freedpeople, some of the children used the name Prudhomme and some used Séverin.

122. Degler, *Neither Black nor White,* 167.

123. The family album of Thérèse Sarpy Metoyer was in 1974 owned by Mrs. Rosa (Metoyer) Bernard.

124. D. C. Scarborough (Attorney), Natchitoches, Louisiana, quoted in Calvin Dill Wilson, "Black Masters: A Side-light on Slavery," *North American Review* 181 (Nov. 1905): 691–92, and in Stahl, "The Free Negro in Ante-Bellum Louisiana," 321.

125. Interview with Lela (Grandchampt) Enright, Port Arthur, Tex., June 25, 1971. Mrs. Enright did not descend from the Metoyers; however, she grew up among them and was reared to the same culture.

126. Martin Ottenheimer, *Forbidden Relatives: The American Myth of Cousin Marriage* (Urbana: University of Illinois Press, 1996).

127. 1860 U.S. Census, Natchitoches Parish, statistics drawn by G. B. and E. S. Mills.

5. In Pursuit of Wealth

1. James M. Wright, *The Free Negro in Maryland, 1634–1860* (New York: Columbia University, 1921), 16–17.

2. Gray, *Agriculture in the Southern United States,* 1:523–24.

3. John H. Bracey Jr., August Meier, and Elliott Rudwick, eds., *Free Blacks in America, 1800–1860* (Belmont, Calif.: Wadsworth Publ. Co., 1971), 2.

4. Berlin, *Slaves without Masters,* 110.

5. Wright, *The Free Negro in Maryland,* 101.

6. Charles S. Sydnor, "The Free Negro in Mississippi before the Civil War," *American Historical Review* 32 (July 1927): 770. According to Sydnor, the 1856 Mississippi law forbade free blacks to "sell . . . *groceries* and spirituous liquors." However, his unexplained reference to "groceries" is misleading. The law dealt with alcohol—not food. The "groceries" that free blacks could not operate, under the terminology of the day, were establishments that sold alcohol as opposed to "green groceries," the stores that sold food and produce. Frederick Law Olmsted's 1856 tale of a grocery store (*Journey in the Seaboard Slave States in the Years 1853–1854* [1856; rpr., New York: Negro University Press, 1968], p. 73), for example, explicitly notes that the word *grocery* "in Virginia, means the same thing as in Ireland—a dram-shop." That usage prevailed in countless local-government records and newspaper ads throughout the United States in the nineteenth century; and *OEDonline* (http://www.oed.com/view/Entry/81683?redirectedFrom=grocery#eid) documents its American usage as late as 1946, citing examples from New York to Mexico.

7. Franklin, *The Free Negro in North Carolina,* 161. For localized relaxation of the laws, see such works as Johnson and Roark, *No Chariot Let Down;* Koger, *Black Masters;* Alexander, *Ambiguous Lives;* Gould, "In Full Enjoyment of Their Liberty"; Gary B. Mills, "Miscegenation and the Free Negro in Antebellum 'Anglo' Alabama: A Reexamination of Southern Race Relations," *Journal of American History* 68 (June 1981): 16–34; and G. B. Mills, "Free African Americans in Pre–Civil War 'Anglo' Alabama: Slave Manumissions Gleaned from County-Court Records," *National Genealogical Society Quarterly* 83 (June 1996): 127–42, and (September 1996): 199–214. Mills's conclusions for Alabama are based on his personal extraction of every antebellum legal record filed by or about free people of color in every Alabama courthouse, as well as numerous state, federal, and private resources.

8. Sterkx, *The Free Negro in Ante-Bellum Louisiana,* 201. Olmsted, *Journey in the Seaboard Slave States,* 635, quotes the Cane River entrepreneur. One possibility for this unnamed individual is Hypolite Chevalier, who was then unmarried and was not enumerated on Cane River or in Natchitoches Parish on the 1850 census.

9. Roger A. Fischer, "Racial Segregation in Ante-Bellum Louisiana," *American Historical Review* 74 (Feb. 1969): 929.

10. Gray, *Agriculture in the Southern United States,* 2:688, 757; 1850 and 1860 U.S. censuses, agri. schs.; Successions of Pierre Metoyer and C. N. Roques *fils,* Natchitoches Succ. files 193 and 897, NCCO; Hugh LaCour, Shreveport, La., to author, Mar. 5, 1974 and Apr. 2, 1974; Robert A. Tyson Diary, LLMVC, LSU Special Collections.

11. 1830 U.S. Census, statistics by the authors.

12. Carter G. Woodson, "Free Negro Owners of Slaves in the United States in 1830," *Journal of Negro History* 9 (Jan. 1924): 41–85. In compiling his tabulations of free nonwhite slaveowners in Natchitoches Parish, Woodson omitted the household headed by Rose Metoyer ("Mary R. Metyier"), which contained eleven slaves, four children of color, and one white male, in addition to Rose. Apparently, Woodson assumed that the slaves were the property of the unnamed white male. As discussed in chapter 4, this man (a North Carolinian named James Hurst) was a landless "boarder" in Rose's home.

13. Succession of Pierre Metoyer, f.m.c., Natchitoches Succ. file 193, NCCO; marriage contract of Athanase Vienne Metoyer and Emelia Metoyer, "Old Natchitoches Data," 2:87, Melrose Collection.

14. Augustin Metoyer to his children, 1840, Natchitoches Conv. Book 30 (Donations): 70–78, NCCO.

15. Quoted from J. B. D. De Bow, *The Seventh Census of the United States: 1850, . . . An Appen-*

dix, Embracing Notes upon the Tables of Each of the States (Washington, D.C.: Robert Armstrong, 1853), xxiii, "Instructions to Marshals and Assistants."

16. 1850 U.S. Census, agri. sch., statistics by the authors.

17. Ibid; also Joe Gray Taylor, *Negro Slavery in Louisiana* (Baton Rouge: LSU Press, 1963), 68.

18. 1850 U.S. Census, agri. sch., statistics by the authors.

19. Fogel and Engerman, *Time on the Cross,* 1:42.

20. Solomon Northup, *Twelve Years a Slave,* ed. Sue Eakin and Joseph Logsdon (Baton Rouge: LSU Press, 1968), 130.

21. Ibid., 123–24.

22. Ibid.; for 1841, see Diary of Dr. McGuire, MS, Melrose Collection; and Milton Dunn, "History of Natchitoches," *Louisiana Historical Quarterly* 3 (Jan. 1920), 51. Dunn erroneously attributes this March 1841 winter blizzard to March 1844 but is correct in his depiction of its severity. Northup's subjective citation of 200 pounds per day as the picking average is contradicted by Taylor's quantitative study, which concludes that 150 pounds per day was a more accurate average for adults; see *Negro Slavery in Louisiana,* 65–66.

23. Northup, *Twelve Years a Slave,* 129–31; McGuire Diary, n.d., 1841.

24. 1850 U.S. Census, Natchitoches Parish, agri. sch., p. 479 ("Firmin Cristofe") and p. 485 (J. B. Metoyer); 1850 U.S. Census, slave sch., pp. 929 (J. B. Metoyer) and 931 (F. C. Christophe); statistics by the authors.

25. Forrest McDonald and Grady McWhiney, "The South from Self-Sufficiency to Peonage: An Interpretation," *American Historical Review* 85 (December 1980): 1105–6.

26. The 1850 instructions are quoted from the introduction to William M. Merriam, *Census Reports:* vol. 5; *Twelfth Census of the United States Taken in the Year 1900; Agriculture,* Part 1, *Farms, Live Stock, and Animal Products* (Washington, D.C.: U.S. Census Office, 1902), xv.

27. McDonald and McWhiney, "The South from Self-Sufficiency to Peonage," 1096–97, calculates the southern averages presented in the text. Parish and Cane River statistics were calculated by the authors.

28. *Le Nouveau Parfait Jardinier; ou, L'Art de cultiver* (Paris: Lebigre, 1835), in possession of Mrs. Coutii in 1974.

29. Succession of Julien Rachal, Natchitoches Succ. file 299 and Succ. Book 10:184–94.

30. Chevalier v. Metoyer, Natchitoches District Court suit 4668 (1854), NCCO.

31. Agreement between Jean Baptiste Cloutier and Vial Girard, May 21, 1852, folder 1228, Cane River Notarial Collection; the legibility of the document is extremely poor. 1850 U.S. Census, Avoyelles Parish, pop. sch., stamped p. 117, dwelling/family 186 (Vial Girard, merchant); McDonald and McWhiney, "The South from Self-Sufficiency to Peonage," 1096–97.

32. Joseph Augustin Metoyer to François G. Metoyer, 1850, Natchitoches Misc. Book FW (also lettered E): 170–71, NCCO.

33. Aug^{te} Metoyer to Louis Gaspard Derbanne, Sept. 20, 1834, folder 1336, Cane River Notarial Collection.

34. Metoyer v. Townsend, Natchitoches District Court suit 2468 (1840), NCCO.

35. Joseph Metoyer to Alexander Pinçon, Jan. 20, 1844, folder 719, Cane River Notarial Collection.

36. *Message from the President,* 70.

37. For example, see the successions of the similarly prosperous planters Pierre Metoyer, f.m.c., Natchitoches Succ. file 193, and Louis Barthélemy Rachal, white, Natchitoches Succ. Book 9:4.

38. Leo Rogin, *The Introduction of Farm Machinery in its Relation to the Productivity of Labor in the Agriculture of the United States during the Nineteenth Century* (Berkeley: University of California Press, 1931), 560.

39. F. S. Lattier to Séraphin Llorens, Nov. 1, 1836, folder 472, Cane River Notarial Collection. Also Augustin Metoyer to his children, Natchitoches Conv. Book 30 (Donations): 70–78; Succession of Susanne Metoyer, Natchitoches Succ. file 355; Susanne Metoyer, her Testament, Natchitoches Succ. Book 25:10–11; all NCCO. 1840 U.S. Census, agri. sch., statistics calculated by the authors.

40. S. M. Hyams to Sun Mutual Insurance Co., MS, Chaplin, Breazeale, and Chaplin Papers, LLMVC, LSU Special Collections. Also Augustin Metoyer to his children, Natchitoches Conv. Book 30 (Donations): 70–78; and Succession of Susanne Metoyer, Natchitoches Succ. file 355, NCCO.

41. For the price of cotton, see James Hurst to [unknown], Jan. 1843, in Natchitoches Parish Records, 1734–1916, LLMVC, LSU Special Collections; 1850 U.S. Census, agri. sch., statistics calculated by the authors.

42. Bills for debts owed by whites to these gin owners appear in Succession of Marie A. St. André (Widow François St. Germaine), Natchitoches Succ. Book 20:7; and Succession of Henriette LaCaze and husband Edmond Duthil, Natchitoches Succ. file 803, both NCCO. See also *Dupleix v. Gallien*, 21 La. Ann. 534 (1869), NCCO.

43. Jacquitte Rachal to Ch^s F. Benoist, May 5, 1845, folder 734, Cane River Notarial Collection.

44. Widow J^n B^{te} Brevelle due from Widow P^{re} Mission Rachal, 1841, Original Doc. № 98; in Robert B. DeBlieux Collection, 1974. This collection subsequently was acquired by the Historic New Orleans Collection, where it was rearranged, filmed, and renamed the Cane River Notarial Collection. The Brevelle-Rachal document appears to be omitted from the film; a 1974 photocopy is in the authors' Cane River research files.

45. Succession of J. B. E. Rachal, Natchitoches Succ. file 927, NCCO.

46. Olmsted, *Journey in the Seaboard Slave States,* 633.

47. Wilson, "Black Masters: A Side-light on Slavery," 689; Stahl, "The Free Negro in Ante-Bellum Louisiana," 347.

48. Interview with Mrs. Coutii, Apr. 26, 1974.

49. For the legal wrangling, see François Metoyer Sr. to Susanne Metoyer, June 5, 1834, "No. 337 p. 433," being pages torn from an unidentified courthouse book, in Melrose Collection. Also Augustin Metoyer v. François Metoyer, Natchitoches Dist. Court suit 2826 (1841–44), bundle 118, combined with Florentin Conant v. François Metoyer (1834); also Auguste Metoyer v. F. Metoyer, Dist. Court suit 3046 (1841–42), bundle 137; and Natchitoches Sheriff's Sales Book 33:53–54; all NCCO. For the land lease, see François Metoyer to Vial Gerard, "Nantissement en firme de bail," Apr. 9, 1853, folder 1288, Cane River Notarial Collection.

50. *Natchitoches Courier,* July 19, 1825, and the following six weeks; Succession of Joseph Augustin Metoyer, box 11, folder 47, Natchitoches Parish Records, 1734–1916, LLMVC, LSU Special Collections.

51. Cane River did have a significant runaway problem in 1804. Slaves on the fairly new farms of Coincoin's offspring did not join the flight; but their associates Ambroise Le Comte, Alexis Cloutier, and Louis Derbanne were all affected. For an overview (and sources), see Mills and Mills, *Tales of Old Natchitoches,* 47–50.

52. Interview with confidential source, Apr. 26, 1974. Cane River traditions among families of all hues have branded the "Redbones" as "marauders" and attributed crimes of all ilk to them—including the disposal of at least one Cane River deputy sheriff in a lye pit, as per interview with Lela (Grandchampt) Enright, Aug. 23, 1971. Evidence of the allegations is hard to find, possibly

because most lived in Rapides Parish, whose legal records were destroyed by the Union army on May 1, 1864. The Redbone community's own accounts portray them as hard-scrabble, hard-living southerners of the type historian Grady McWhiney labeled "crackers." For the Redbone perspective, see Webster Talma Crawford's "Redbones in the Neutral Strip . . . and the Westport Fight between Whites and Redbones for Possession of This Strip on Christmas Eve, 1882," undated MS, Melrose Collection; and Shari Miller and Miriam Rich, Mennonite Central Committee, "A History of the Clifton Community; Submitted to the Clifton Community," typescript, Mora, La., March 1983, copy in Melrose Collection. Sterkx, *The Free Negro in Ante-Bellum Louisiana,* 165–69, discusses that ethnic cluster more impartially under the name "Ten Milers." For the rough-edged lifestyle that some of the families represented in the nineteenth century, see Grady McWhiney, *Cracker Culture: Celtic Ways in the Old South* (University, Ala.: University of Alabama Press, 1988).

53. Emilie Kirkland claim, Commission no. 18521, Report no. 5 (1875), Allowed, Records of the Southern Claims Commission, National Archives, Washington, D.C.; digitized online at Ancestry.com's subsidiary for military-related records, *Fold3* (www.fold3.com).

54. Interview with Mrs. Coutii, Apr. 26, 1974.

55. Metoyer to Metoyer, Metoyer to Lemoine, and Metoyer to Anty, Sept. 9, 1821, folders 15–17, Cane River Notarial Collection.

56. Succession sale, Pierre Metoyer, Jan. 2, 1834, "Old Natchitoches Records," 1:27–28, Melrose Collection. Also Succession sale, Joseph Metoyer, Nov. 3, 1838, Natchitoches Succ. Book 11:375–85; Succession sale, Marie Susanne Metoyer, Feb. 15, 1839, Natchitoches Succ. file 355; Succession sale, Louis Porter, Feb. 26, 1835, Natchitoches Succ. Book 8:228; Succession sale, Espallier Rachal, Jul. 2, 1857, Natchitoches Succ. file 927; Succession sale, Charles N. Roques Sr., July 7, 1859, Natchitoches Succ. Book 30:221–28; all in NCCO. The inventory and sale of Susanne's property estimates Lucas's age as thirty, but he was actually thirty-seven, having been baptized as her slave in 1802 at the age of six months; see Mills, *Natchitoches, 1800–1826,* no. 1816 (Joseph Lucas).

57. Succession sale, Pierre Metoyer, "Old Natchitoches Records," 1:27–28, Melrose Collection.

58. The extent of intrafamily slave sales has been developed for the parish at large by Rachal Mills Lennon, "The Slave Trade in Microcosm: Natchitoches Parish, Louisiana," seminar paper, Ph.D. program, Department of History, University of Alabama, 2000; copy in Mills Collection, NSU.

59. Fogel and Engerman, *Time on the Cross,* 1:115; 1860 U.S. Census, slave sch., calculations by the authors.

60. Fogel and Engerman, *Time on the Cross,* 1:116; Olmsted, *Journey in the Seaboard Slave States,* 629–30.

61. Callahan et al., *History of St. Augustine's Parish,* 20; interview with Mrs. Coutii, Apr. 26, 1974; see also the related discussion of the Badin-Roque House (aka "Old Convent") in chapter 3 of the present work.

62. Fogel and Engerman, *Time on the Cross,* 1:116.

63. Christy v. Spillman, in Natchitoches District Court suit 5401 (1860), NCCO; 1850 U.S. Census, Natchitoches Parish, pop. sch., stamped p. 11 verso, dwelling/family 173 (G. E. Spillman); 1860 U.S. Census, Natchitoches Parish, La., pop. sch., p. 53/481, dwelling/family 438 (G. E. Spillman). Spillman in 1860 was overseer for the Le Comte–Hertzog plantation on Cane River at the foot of the Isle; his own land was a few miles to the east on Red River.

64. Hugh LaCour to the Millses, Apr. 5, 1974; interview with Mrs. Coutii, Apr. 26, 1974. Some accounts of the history of Louis Metoyer's plantation claim that the old house called Yucca was

first used as a slave hospital by the white Hertzog family who later owned the plantation, rather than by the Metoyers; see, for example, "Melrose Manor on Cane River Stands as Relic of World's Strangest Empire." However, Metoyer descendants insist that the use of Yucca as a slave hospital was initiated by the Metoyers. The manor house at Melrose was finished by J. B. Louis after the 1832 death of his father Louis, and the family moved from Yucca to the manor at that time. The use of Yucca as a hospital from the mid-1830s is likely, given the documentation that Augustin Metoyer, on the plantation next door, had a hospital for his slaves in that same time frame. The two plantations were comparable in virtually every respect.

65. Fogel and Engerman, *Time on the Cross,* 1:120.

66. Reminiscences of Duncan Kirkland, Jan. 26, 1922, "Natchitoches," vol. 2, Cammie Henry Scrapbooks, Melrose Collection; interview with Mrs. Coutii, June 23, 1973; Jesse Adams, quoted in James G. Andrews, "Let Your Fingers Do the Ginning," *Mid-South,* Nov. 10, 1974, 4–12.

67. Anthony Michael Dignowity Journal, typescript, pp. 67–68; manuscript and typescript owned by great-granddaughter Nancy Walker of Potomac, Maryland. In July 2004, after reading E. S. Mills's newly published *Isle of Canes,* Mrs. Walker contacted the author to report holding an original manuscript journal that discussed a visit to the Isle, and she kindly shared selected pages. Dignowity (1810–1875), after his Louisiana adventures, went on to become a doctor, a businessman, and mayor of San Antonio; but his abolitionist views made him a pariah in antebellum Texas. For overviews of his life, see Clinton Machann and James W. Mendl, *Krásná Amerika: A Study of the Texas Czechs, 1851–1939* (Austin: Eakin Press, 1983); and Estelle Hudson and Henry R. Maresh, *Czech Pioneers of the Southwest* (Dallas: South-West, 1934).

68. St. François Parish, Register 7, Baptisms of Slaves and F.P.C.

69. Taylor, *Negro Slavery in Louisiana,* 128.

70. Interview with Mrs. Coutii, Apr. 26, 1974; Lyle Saxon, *Children of Strangers* (1937; rpr., New Orleans: Robert L. Crager & Co., 1948), 119–22. Although Saxon's work is presented as a novel, it supposedly is based upon actual events in the lives of Coincoin's descendants and purports to portray their lifestyle. Saxon received most of his information from the late Mrs. Zéline Badin Roque of the Badin-Roque House, according to Coutii, who knew both parties. Mrs. Coutii also assumed that Mrs. Roque grew up on Cane River during Augustin Metoyer's lifetime, but that was not the case. Zéline Badin was not born until 1860, four years after Augustin's death, and her family did not move to the Isle until well after the Civil War; see 1860 U.S. Census, Natchitoches Parish, pop. sch., pp. 8–9/434–35, dwelling/family 68 ("Norma Bardo" household), which places the family in the Grappe community above Natchitoches; and the 1870 U.S. Census, Natchitoches Parish, pop. sch., ward 11, stamped p. 464, dwelling 80, family 83 (Norbert Badin household), which places the family amid residents of the Côte Joyeuse. Also see Northup, *Twelve Years a Slave,* 282, for another discussion of Christmas celebrations of slaves in nearby Avoyelles Parish.

71. George S. Walmsley to Aug[te] Metoyer, in Henry Clement Papers, Melrose Collection; Taylor, *Negro Slavery in Louisiana,* 131.

72. Gil y Barbo to Nicolas Augustin [Metoyer], Sale of slave Nicolas for manumission, *Translations of Statistical and Census Reports of Texas,* roll 3, frames 826–29; Nicolas Augustin of Succession of Marie Le Clerc, 1798, doc. 2857, NCA; Widow Le Comte to Nicolas Augustin, "Old Natchitoches Data," 2:279; Ambroise Le Comte to Augustin, in File R&R 309, Marie Perine, Louisiana State Land Office.

73. Augustin Metoyer to Dorothée, Natchitoches Misc. Book 1 (Dec. 1806–May 1811): 225; Augustin Metoyer to mulattress Marguerite, Natchitoches Conv. Book 2:179; Augustin Metoyer to Remy, Natchitoches Conv. Book 21:109; Last Will and Testament of Augustin Metoyer, in

Natchitoches Notarial Book 25:79; Augustin Metoyer to F. Florival Metoyer, Apr. 18, 1851, folder 1157, Cane River Notarial Collection.

74. Will of Marie Le Clerc, 1798, doc. 2857; Derbanne to Derbanne, exchange of slaves, doc. 3688; and Rachal v. Cloutier, 1815, doc. 4496, NCA.

75. Derbanne to Metoyer, Sale of Dorothée, and Cloutier to Derbanne, receipt, May 28, 1810, Natchitoches Misc. Book 1 (Dec. 1806–May 1811): 186–87; Metoyer to Dorothée, Manumission, Nov. 11, 1814, Natchitoches Misc. Book 3:348 and doc. 4377, NCCO; Metoyer to Joseph La Vigne, Security, Dec. 7, 1814, doc. 4383, NCA.

76. For Pacalé's manumission and his chain of purchases, mortgages, emancipations, and sales, see docs. 1798, 2979, 3047, 3324, 3870, 4026, 4058–59, 4096–97, 4099, 4140, and 4150, NCA; also Marie Derbanne, wife of Varangue, to Yves "Pascat," "Old Natchitoches Data," 2:16, Melrose Collection; and Natchitoches Conv. Book 2:23–25, NCCO. The British-born, English-speaking parish judge who penned Pacalé's purchase of Gertrude (doc. 3324) spelled her name phonetically as "Eteroux," having failed to hear the initial "G" or the closing "d" (both of which would have been silent), while catching the rolling "r" that caused him to create an extra syllable in the name. Gertrude was an extremely rare name among both blacks and whites on Cane River. The only three who have been found in the colonial and early federal periods was a daughter of St. Denis (born in 1736), the St. Denis slave child (born about 1741–42) who was named for the master's daughter, and a slave born in 1838 to the J. B. Derbanne household, with a godmother from Los Adaës. J. B. Derbanne moved his family and his slaves to Los Adaës shortly thereafter and did not return. The birth period of the St. Denis slave, Coincoin's sister, matches the age given for "Eteroux" when Pacalé bought her. For the births and baptisms of the two enslaved Gertrudes, see Mills, *Natchitoches, 1729–1803*, entries 48, 100.

77. In buying Thérèse, Pacalé specifically called her his "daughter." However, by custom of the era, he would also have used that term for his wife's daughter. Evidence has not been found to prove whether Thérèse was a daughter of Pacalé by a slave wife or liaison, a daughter of Gertrude by someone else, or a daughter that Pacalé and Gertrude had together in earlier times.

78. *Adéle v. Beauregard*, 1 Mart. La., 183 (1810); also Sydnor, "Free Negro in Mississippi," citing *Randall v. The State*, 12 Miss. 349.

79. Succession of Marie Agnes Metoyer, Natchitoches Succ. file 395; Augustin Metoyer to his children, Natchitoches Conv. Book 30 (Donations): 70–78; Succession of Augustin Metoyer, Natchitoches Succ. file 1009; all NCCO.

80. Marie Louise Le Comte to Dominique Metoyer, 1810, doc. 3779, NCA. Once free, Susette used the surname Le Comte; see Affidavit of Magdeleine Le Comte, free *négresse*, daughter of Susette Le Comte, free *négresse*, Mar. 31, 1828, folders 222–23, Cane River Notarial Collection.

81. Mills, *Natchitoches, 1800–1826*, entry 2352 (Jean Josef Balange, bapt. Dec. 15, 1815, aged 7 months); Metoyer to Susanne and Madeleine, Manumission, 1817, doc. 4791, NCA; Succession of Joseph Bellanger, Natchitoches Succ. Book 6:256–57, NCCO; *Natchitoches Courier*, May 24, 1825.

82. Mills, *Natchitoches, 1800–26*, entry 2318 (Antonio, bapt. June 18, 1815); Louis Metoyer to Baba and Françoise, Manumission, Natchitoches Conv. Book 8:231, NCCO.

83. Francisco Gonzales to J^n B^{te} Louis Metoyer, Natchitoches Conv. Book 19:328; Last Will and Testament, Succession of Charles N. Rocques Sr., Natchitoches Succ. file 1107; both NCCO. Also Paul A. Kunkel, "Modifications in Louisiana Legal Status under Louisiana Constitutions, 1812–1957," *Journal of Negro History* 44 (Jan. 1959): 7.

84. 1860 U.S. Census, Natchitoches Parish, La., social statistics schedule.

85. Gray, *Agriculture in the Southern United States*, 1:546; Jean Conant claim, no. 20088, Report no. 6 (1876), allowed; Records of the Southern Claims Commission. Also 1860 U.S. Census,

Natchitoches Parish, pop. sch., especially p. 49/477, dwelling/family 393 (George Kirkland) and dwelling/family 401 (T. L. Metoyer); and p. 53/481, dwelling/family 438 (G. E. Spillman); and Christy v. Spillman, Natchitoches District Court suit 5401 (1860), NCCO.

86. Dunbar-Nelson, "People of Color in Louisiana," 64.

87. *Natchitoches Courier,* Aug. 28–Oct. 2, 1827.

88. Aug^te Metoyer to various customers, Account Statements, in Henry Clement Papers, Melrose Collection; *Faures v. Metoyer,* 6 Rob. 75 (1843); dissolution of partnership between Antoine Jonau and Dame Blanchard, original document in possession of Mrs. Noble Morin, Natchez, La., 1973; Gray, *Agriculture in the Southern United States,* 2:1027; Succession of Marie Susanne Metoyer, Natchitoches Succ. file 355, NCCO.

89. Succession of Marie Susanne Metoyer.

90. Ibid.; Lawrence H. Officer and Samuel H. Williamson, "Purchasing Power of Money in the United States from 1774 to Present," *Measuring Worth* (www.measuringworth.com/ppowerus); Succession of Marie Louise Metoyer, Natchitoches Succ. file 323, NCCO.

91. Succession of Baptiste Lemoine and Succession of C. N. Rocques *fils,* Natchitoches Succ. files 437 and 897, NCCO; Sterkx, *The Free Negro in Ante-Bellum Louisiana,* 235.

92. Dupré and Metoyer Account Book, LLMVC, LSU Special Collections. Also see Marriage Contract, Emanuel Dupré and Marie Marguerite Metoyer, Natchitoches Misc. Records, Book A:48; and marriage contract of P. V. Dupré and Marie Doralise Derbanne, Misc. Book 15:138; both in NCCO. For Nicola Grazick, aka Gracia, see Declaration Relative to His Birth, 1841, Conv. Book 31:36–37, NCCO; public announcement of lease of "ferry at Colas Gratia's on Red River above the town of Alexandria," *Red River Republican* (Alexandria), November 15, 1851; and death notice of "Nicola Gracia Vidrikin, over a hundred years old, at his residence in this parish," *Louisiana Democrat* (Alexandria), Feb. 29, 1860.

93. Robert C. Reinders, "The Free Negro in the New Orleans Economy, 1850–1860," *Louisiana History* 6 (Summer 1965): 283; [Oscar Dubreuil] Account Book, 1856–1858, MS, LSU Special Collections.

94. 1850 and 1860 U.S. censuses, Natchitoches Parish, pop. schs.; interview with Mrs. Coutii, Mar. 24, 1974; *Natchitoches Courier,* Mar. 13, 1826.

95. Succession of Predanes Metoyer, Natchitoches Succ. file 1360, NCCO.

96. For example, see "Public Auction of Goods of Antoine Marinovich of Cloutierville," *Natchitoches Union,* May 1, 1862, and "Public Auction of Goods of B. Molina, of Natchitoches," ibid., June 12, 1862.

97. Louis Emanuel Gallien to Jean Baptiste Espallier Rachal, Jan. 28, 1839, folder 540, Cane River Notarial Collection.

98. J. E. Dunn, "Isle Brevelle," *Louisiana Populist* (Natchitoches), Feb. 26, 1897; Mrs. Coutii to author, June 5, 1974.

99. Séraphin Llorens to F. S. Lattier, Nov. 1, 1836, folder 472, Cane River Notarial Collection.

100. Metoyer v. Llorice [*sic*] and Dupré, Natchitoches District Court suit 2044 (1839), NCCO.

101. Hugh LaCour to author, Apr. 5, 1974. Mr. LaCour, who reported this tradition, was a grandnephew and namesake of the late Hugh Llorens; Mrs. Coutii, Apr. 26, 1974, believed Hugh Llorens's father to be the builder of most of the "big houses" on the Isle.

102. 1860 U.S. Census, Natchitoches Parish, pop. sch., p. 49/477, dwelling/family 399 (François Forcal); p. 184/614, dwelling/family 1608 (J. B. "Chavieler"); and p. 144/575, dwelling/family 1228 (Magee "Grapple"); Succession of Marie Louise Metoyer and Succession of Joseph Augustin Metoyer, Natchitoches Succ. files 323 and 692. According to Fogel and Engerman's econometric study of slavery (*Time of the Cross,* 1:39), 11.9 percent of slaves were skilled craftsmen (carpen-

ters, blacksmiths, coopers, etc.). The slave inventories of the Cane River clan do not reveal this high an incidence of skilled slaves, but in the absence of a sufficient number of craftsmen among the free population, it seems likely that they possessed more skilled slaves than those that have been documented.

103. Succession of Joseph Metoyer, Natchitoches Succ. file 359, and Succ. Book 11:375–85, NCCO; 1860 U.S. Census, Natchitoches Parish, pop. sch., p. 49/477, dwelling/family 395 ("Jepha" [Joseph] Metoyer).

104. Derbanne v. Metoyer, Natchitoches District Court suit 1097 (1829), NCCO; J^h M^ie Rablés v. Émile Colson, Aug. 13, 1828, folder 249, Cane River Notarial Collection.

105. Succession of Dr. Jean André Zépherin Carles, Natchitoches Succ. Book 6:129; Augustin Metoyer to his children, Natchitoches Conv. Book 30 (Donations): 70–78; Succession of [J. B.] Louis Metoyer, Natchitoches Succ. file 362; marriage contract of Théophile Louis Metoyer to Marie Elina Metoyer, Natchitoches Mortgage Record Book 28:277; all NCCO. Also 1860 U.S. Census, Natchitoches Parish, pop. sch., p. 144/575, dwelling/family 1228 (L. S. Prudhomme).

106. 1850 U.S. Census, Natchitoches Parish, pop. sch., stamped p. 51, dwelling/family 909 ("Firman" Christophe); 1860 U.S. Census, Natchitoches Parish, pop. sch., p. 48/476, dwelling/family 389 ("Firmon Christopher"). In addition to the slave he claimed on the Natchitoches censuses, Christophe was also a property holder and taxpayer in New Orleans in 1860 and 1861; see David C. Rankin, "The Origins of Black Leadership in New Orleans during Reconstruction," *Journal of Southern History* 40 (Aug. 1974): 437.

107. 1860 U.S. Census, Natchitoches Parish, pop. sch., p. 69/497, dwelling/family 612 (M. B. "Florens"). Information on Dubreuil was provided by his granddaughter, Mrs. Armella Rachal, Natchez, La., quoted in Mrs. Coutii to author, June 5, 1974.

108. 1860 U.S. Census, Natchitoches Parish, pop. sch., ward 10, p. 477A, dwelling 478, family 479 (L. V. "Lorance"); dwelling/family 479 (A. "Tourres"). The census taker enumerates these two men as though they lived in separate dwellings, with a female "P. V. Dupree" living between them. In actuality, they shared a dwelling in the small one-street village of Cloutierville. Also see p. 49/477, dwelling/family 395 (Lodoiska S. Metoyer); p. 43/471, dwelling/family 340–341 (Margarett, Eleonore, Paline, and E. Monette). For the life of Doralise, see Lennon and Mills, "Mother, Thy Name Is *Mystery!*" 212–17.

109. 1850 U.S. Census, Natchitoches Parish, pop. sch., stamped p. 52, dwelling/family 933 ("Adalaide Mariot"); 1860 U.S. Census, Natchitoches Parish, pop. sch., p. 52/480, dwelling/family 434 ("Addlaide Nanite"); Mrs. Coutii to author, Mar. 31, 1974. Mrs. Coutii was the great-great-granddaughter of Adélaïde Mariotte.

110. *Natchitoches Union,* Dec. 25, 1862; Hugh LaCour to author, Apr. 5, 1974.

111. *Natchitoches Courier,* Dec. 26, 1825.

112. M. Dunn, "History of Natchitoches," 41 (for Monette Ferry; Dunn errs in identifying the first Louis "Monette" as a Spaniard). Also Hugh LaCour to author, Mar. 5, 1974; Hypolite Metoyer to C. Molonguet, Account Statement, 1851, folder 1130, Cane River Notarial Collection.

113. M. Dunn, "History of Natchitoches," 42, for the stage road passing through 24-Mile Ferry; Succession of Pierre Metoyer Jr., Natchitoches Succ. file 902, NCCO; Succession of Oscar Dubreuil, Natchitoches Succ. file 1255; J. E. Dunn, "Isle Brevelle"; interview with Lewis Emory Jones, Natchez, La., Mar. 16, 1974; Mrs. Coutii to author, June 5, 1974.

114. Sterkx, *The Free Negro in Ante-Bellum Louisiana,* 232–33.

115. Ibid.

116. Succession of Charles N. Rocques *fils,* Natchitoches Succ. file 897, NCCO.

117. 1801 Will of Claude Thomas Pierre Metoyer, Melrose Collection; interview with Mrs.

Coutii, Mar. 24, 1974, who still owned the voluminous manual on midwifery that her grand-mother, Mme. Dupré, used as a guide to her profession.

118. Interview with Tillman Chelettre Sr., Natchez, La., Oct. 12, 1974.

119. Succession of Pierre Metoyer, Natchitoches Succ. file 193; Succession of Dominique Metoyer, file 375; Succession of [J. B.] Louis Metoyer, file 362; Succession of Marie Susanne Metoyer, file 355; Succession of Agnes Metoyer, file 395; all NCCO. Also Officer and Williamson, "Purchasing Power of Money in the United States."

120. Succession of Pierre Victorin Metoyer, Natchitoches Succ. Book 11:393, NCCO. A comparison of Victorin's complete estate with those of his half-siblings is not possible because most of the documents dealing with his succession are no longer on file; only the auction of his movables and slaves has been found on record.

121. Succession of Marie Susanne Metoyer and Succession of Pierre Metoyer, f.m.c., Natchitoches Succ. files 355 and 193, NCCO; Officer and Williamson, "Purchasing Power of Money in the United States."

122. Franklin, *The Free Negro in North Carolina,* 140, 157.

123. Cyprien Clamorgan, *The Colored Aristocracy of St. Louis* (St. Louis: N.p., 1858), 15.

124. Sterkx, *The Free Negro in Ante-Bellum Louisiana,* 208; Erastus Paul Puckett, "The Free Negro in New Orleans to 1860" (M.A. thesis, Tulane University, 1907), 48–49; Reinders, "The Free Negro," 280.

125. 1860 U.S. Census, pop. and social statistics schs.; calculations by the authors.

126. François Lavespère and Wife to Augustin Metoyer, Natchitoches Conv. Book 37, doc. 4534; Succession of Joseph Metoyer, Natchitoches Succ. file 359; both NCCO. The travelogue of Dignowity, the Czech gin repairman who worked the Isle about the time of Joseph's death and visited in Augustin's home, makes clear the fact that the community acknowledged the relationship between the state legislator Benjamin Metoyer and his multiracial half-siblings. Dignowity (typescript, p. 68) wrote: "The name of this gentleman negro was August[in] Matuye; he had a brother, also a wealthy planter, called Benjamin."

127. Succession of C. N. Rocques Sr., Natchitoches Succ. file 1107; Sarpy v. Hertzog, Natchitoches District Court suit 6489 (1866); both NCCO. *Natchitoches Semi-Weekly Times,* Mar. 2, 1867; certification of Jérôme Sarpy Jr., and Nerestan P. Metoyer by J. W. Hamilton, Clerk, in Box 2, Chaplin, Breazeale, and Chaplin Papers, LLMVC, LSU Special Collections.

128. Sarpy and Metoyer v. Gimbert, Natchitoches District Court suit 6336 (1867), NCCO.

129. Succession of Agnes Metoyer, Natchitoches Succ. file 395; Rachal v. Metoyer, Natchitoches District Court suit 3913 (1847), NCCO.

130. Sterkx, *The Free Negro in Ante-Bellum Louisiana,* 56–57.

131. *Gillet v. Rachal,* 9 Rob. 276 (1844).

132. Chaler v. Birtt and Metoyer, Natchitoches District Court suit 1782 (1838), NCCO. On the 1830 census, Isaac Birtt (Burke) was listed erroneously as a free man of color, and was included in Woodson's study of slaveowners of this class. However, the numerous church and civil records that exist for Birtt consistently identify him as white. At his 1831 marriage, he identified himself as a native of Greenwich, Connecticut; see Mills, *Natchitoches Church Marriages,* entry 200. For the erroneous racial identifications, see 1830 U.S. Census, Natchitoches Parish, p. 61 ("Asaac Birt"), and Woodson's derivative, "Free Negro Owners of Slaves in the United States in 1830," 50.

133. Succession of Jacques LaCaze, Natchitoches Succ. file 139; Friend v. Smith, Natchitoches Succ. Book 12:174; Succession of Jacques Dufrois Derbanne and Wife, Natchitoches Succ. file 669; all in NCCO. Also Succession of Mme. Charles Melonguet, May 1850, folder 1101, Cane River Notarial Collection; *Natchitoches Semi-Weekly Times,* Oct. 31, 1866.

134. Louis Metoyer to Jean Baptiste Augustin Metoyer, 1823, Louis Metoyer Document, LLMVC, LSU Special Collections.

135. Augustin Metoyer to Remy MacTaer, Natchitoches Notarial Record Book 39:521–22, NCCO.

6. The Faith of Their Fathers

1. Mills, "Piety and Prejudice," 173.

2. Mills, "Quintanilla's Crusade," develops this theme. Din, "Father Jean Delvaux and the Natchitoches Revolt of 1795," continues the analysis from a political perspective.

3. Mme. A. Bernard, Archivist, Ville de La Rochelle Bibliothèque, to Gary B. Mills, Jan. 15, 1976, enclosing "Liste des Enfants de Joseph Pavie et de Marie-Jeanne Couasse Baptises à Saint-Barthelemy de la Rochelle." Pierre Pavie, baptized June 15, 1741, was the seventh of eighteen children born to the parental marriage; he was just fourteen months younger than his Cane River brother, Étienne, whose widow married Pierre Metoyer.

4. McAvoy et al., *Records of the Diocese of Louisiana and the Floridas,* roll 5, for 1795 report of P. Pavie.

5. Ibid., 1796 report, roll 5; 1797 report, roll 7; 1799 report, roll 8.

6. Ibid., 1801 report, roll 9.

7. Mills, *Natchitoches, 1729–1803,* entry 2304 (Nicolas Augustin, infant slave of de Mézières, bapt. Feb. 9, 1777). This baptismal act asserts that both of the godparents (Nicolas Augustin and Marie Susanne Metoyer) were free. The assertion errs, but it reveals that the nine-year-old twins enjoyed enough liberty that the new priest, Quintanilla, assumed them to be free. Also see ibid., entry 2392 (Marie Celestine, Indian slave of Le Court, bapt. April 17, 1781) and entry 2434 (Jean Baptiste Augustin, *negrito* slave of Buard, bapt. June 22, 1783).

8. Callahan et al., *History of St. Augustine's Parish,* 35. Until the late twentieth century, Coincoin's offspring consistently referred to Claude Thomas Pierre Metoyer as "Thomas," even though he always identified himself as "Pierre." As frequently seen with multiracial, formerly enslaved families elsewhere, they referred to their white ancestor by one of his lesser known names so as not to offend white cousins. Consequently, one version of the legend insists that two Metoyer brothers settled at Natchitoches, one named Pierre and the other named Thomas. Pierre, supposedly, married a French girl at the post and was the progenitor of the white Metoyers of the Grand Côte, while Thomas "married" Coincoin and produced the Metoyers of Isle Brevelle. The assertion that Thomas was from Lyons is inaccurate. As previously shown, the Metoyer "homeland" was actually La Rochelle and, before that, Rheims.

9. St. François Parish, Register 6, p. 116, July 27, 1829.

10. Callahan et al., *History of St. Augustine's Parish,* 37–38.

11. Mills, *Natchitoches, 1800–1826,* entries 101–13.

12. Callahan et al., *History of St. Augustine's Parish,* 37.

13. McAvoy et al., *Records of the Diocese of Louisiana and the Floridas,* roll 1, Nov. 25, 1795, Decree of Bishop Peñalver y Cárdenas.

14. Unlabeled, unpaginated minute book beginning 1848, St. François Parish.

15. For the quote, which appears in both a baptism and a marriage register, see Mills, *Natchitoches, 1800–1826,* entries 1621–48, dated Oct. 1825 and May 27, 1826; also Mills, *Natchitoches Church Marriages, 1818–50,* entry 118 (François Metoyer Jr. to Marie Coton-Mais, Apr. 26, 1827). For other clusters of Metoyer baptisms on Isle Brevelle, none of which mention a chapel, see

Mills, *Natchitoches, 1800–1826*, entries 1153, 1161–62 (Apr. 19, 1819), 1437–40 (Nov. 30, 1821), 1653–56 (Dec. 1, 1821), and 1450–84 (Dec. 16–18, 1821).

16. To track the activities of the Natchitoches priest in 1828 and 1829, see Judy Riffel, trans., *Natchitoches Baptisms, 1817–1840: Abstracts from Register 6 of St. Francis Catholic Church, Natchitoches, Louisiana* (Baton Rouge: Le Comité des Archives de la Louisiane, 2007), pp. 113–22.

17. Mills, *Natchitoches Church Marriages, 1818–50*, entries 152–56.

18. Callahan et al., *History of St. Augustine's Parish*, 36.

19. Ibid.

20. François, Marquis de Barbe-Marbois, *The History of Louisiana, Particularly of the Cession of That Colony to the United States of America*, trans. from the French (Philadelphia: Carey & Lea, 1830), 324, 327–28.

21. Cyril Lionel Robert James, *The Black Jacobins: Toussaint L'Ouverture and the San Domingo Rebellion*, 2nd ed. (New York: Vintage Books, 1963), 330–65.

22. Mills, *Natchitoches Church Marriages, 1818–50*, entry 48 (Sarpy–Metoyer, June 27, 1820).

23. Mrs. Coutii to confidential source, Sept. 1973, copy in possession of author.

24. Davis, *Louisiana*, 380.

25. Files B1806, François Lavespère, and B1960, Augustin Metoyer, State Land Office.

26. Widow François Lavespère to Julien Rachal, in Natchitoches Notarial Book A:38, NCCO.

27. Msgr. Henry F. Beckers, *A History of Immaculate Conception Catholic Church, Natchitoches, Louisiana, 1717–1973* (Natchitoches: Immaculate Conception, 1973).

28. *Journal of the Senate of the State of Louisiana . . . 1826* (New Orleans: State of Louisiana, 1826), 45.

29. Callahan et al., *History of St. Augustine's Parish*, 40. Historical credit as the first church built by and for free people of color in the United States actually goes to the African Meeting House at 46 Joy Street, Boston. Built in 1806 on Beacon Hill under the direction of the African American Rev. Thomas Paul, the original church still stands today and has been a National Historical Landmark since 1973. See Kathryn Grover and Janine V. da Silva, "Historic Resource Study: Boston African American National Historic Site, 31 December 2002," National Park Service, *Boston African American National Historic Site* (http://www.cr.nps.gov/history/online_books/bost/hrs.pdf); also Carol Ann Poh and Robert C. Post, "National Register of Historic Places Inventory-Nomination Form: African Meeting House [aka] African Meeting House, First African Baptist Church," PDF, National Park Service (http://pdfhost.focus.nps.gov/docs/NHLS/Text/71000087.pdf).

30. In the early nineteenth century, all of northwest Louisiana was incorporated into the limits of the church and civil parishes of Natchitoches.

31. Alexis Cloutié(r) to the Roman Congregation, Donation, in Natchitoches Misc. Book 6, doc.142; *Biographical and Historical Memoirs of Northwest Louisiana* (Nashville: Southern Publishing Co., 1890), 317.

32. St. Jean Baptiste Parish (Cloutierville), Baptismal Book 1 and Marriage Book 1; interview with Msgr. Milburn Broussard, Pastor of Church of St. John the Baptist, Aug. 22, 1970; Msgr. Broussard to Gary B. Mills, Mar. 15, 1974.

33. Church and civil records of this period indicate that there was no one at Natchitoches named James or Jacques Dupré, either in 1803 or in 1829.

34. Callahan et al., *History of St. Augustine's Parish*, 42; interview with Mrs. Coutii, Apr. 26, 1974.

35. Supposedly, the original altar was finally replaced in the mid-twentieth century and the old altar was "given away"; its present whereabouts are not known. Interview with confidential source, Apr. 26, 1974.

36. The painting of St. Augustine and the original bell still hang in the modern church; the old painting of St. Louis has been "lost" through the decades.

37. Nine of the twelve members of the clan who donated the Stations of the Cross are said to be Leopold Balthazar, Paul Balthazar, Vilfried Metoyer, Emanuel Dupré, Nemour Sarpy, Neres Pierre Metoyer, Carles "Caloot" Metoyer, Sévère Dupré, and Oscar Dubreuil. Mrs. Coutii to author, May 13, 1974. Most of the named individuals, however, were not born or were mere children at the 1829 construction. Donations by them would necessarily date to a later era.

38. The painter of Augustin's oil portrait is known to history only as "Feuille"; his portraits and miniatures have been dated to 1834–41. He is believed to be a brother of Jean-François Feuille, a New Orleans engraver and printer of the same era. See John A. Mahé and Rosanne McCaffrey, eds., *Encyclopaedia of New Orleans Artists, 1718–1918* (New Orleans: Historic New Orleans Collection, 1987), 133.

39. Interview with Mrs. Coutii, Apr. 26, 1974; Callahan et al., *History of St. Augustine's Parish*, 42.

40. Rev. J. A. Baumgartner, History of St. Augustine Parish, MS, untitled & undated, 5 pp. supplied in 1972 to authors by Arthur C. Watson, attorney for the Association for the Preservation of Historic Natchitoches; copy in possession of E. S. Mills. Baumgartner's tenure on the Isle was 1914–40. It is likely that he prepared this history as "background" for his 1940 successor.

41. Last Will and Testament of Nicolas Augustin Metoyer, in Natchitoches Notarial Book 25:77–80, NCCO.

42. Baumgartner, History of St. Augustine Parish, MS; interview with Mrs. Coutii, Mar. 24, 1974. During the years that St. Augustine was a mission, rather than a parish, the sacraments administered there were recorded at Natchitoches. St. Augustine's registers begin with its designation as a parish in 1856, after which separate registers were maintained for the white and multiracial parishioners.

43. Interview with Mrs. Coutii, Mar. 24, 1974.

44. Stahl, "The Free Negro in Ante-Bellum Louisiana," 357–58, 376.

45. William A. Poe, "Religion and Education in North Louisiana, 1800–1865," in *North Louisiana,* vol. 1: *To 1865,* 113–30, offers much insight into this cultural clash.

46. Interview with confidential source, Apr. 26, 1974; interview with Mrs. Coutii, Mar. 24, 1974; confidential source to Francois Mignon, Sept. 3, 1972, copy in possession of author.

47. Mills, "Piety and Prejudice," 178–79.

48. J. Edgar Bruns, "Antoine Blanc: Louisiana's Joshua in the Land of Promise He Opened," in *Cross, Crozier, and Crucible,* 120–34.

49. St. François Parish (Natchitoches), Register 12, entry 1836:5, Jan. 22, 1836; Baudier, *The Catholic Church in Louisiana,* 346, notes a similar visit in 1842.

50. Elisabeth Joan Doyle, "Bishop Auguste Marie Martin of Natchitoches and the Civil War," in *Cross, Crozier, and Crucible,* 135–44.

51. McCants, *They Came to Louisiana,* passim.

52. Tomb marker, St. Augustine Cemetery, Isle Brevelle; interview with Mrs. Coutii, Apr. 26, 1974, wherein she described Augustin's death as related to her by his daughter-in-law Perine (Metoyer) Metoyer Dupré.

53. Callahan et al., *History of St. Augustine's Parish,* 43; interview with Mrs. Coutii, Apr. 26, 1974. A search of the papal correspondence in the Vatican Archives failed to uncover a copy of the letter; Papal secretary, Archivo Segreto Vaticano, to Gary B. Mills, Apr. 6, 1974.

54. Mrs. Coutii to author, Oct. 5, 1974. For custom and canon law that governed the naming of Catholic children in this era, see the introduction to Donald Attwater, *Names and Name-Days* (London: Burns Oates & Washbourne, 1939).

55. Baudier, *The Catholic Church in Louisiana,* 346, 360.

56. Sterkx, *The Free Negro in Ante-Bellum Louisiana,* 256. Emphasis added.

57. Woods, *Marginality and Identity,* 78.

58. Mills, "Piety and Prejudice," 193, Table 2, citing a statistical analysis by Elizabeth Shown Mills of the four church parishes within the civil parish of Natchitoches.

59. Ibid., 183.

60. Interview with Mrs. Coutii, Apr. 26, 1974; Mrs. Coutii to author, Apr. 25, 1974, crediting Perine (Metoyer) Metoyer Dupré as her source. These same customs are spotlighted in Saxon, *Children of Strangers,* 44–45.

61. Interview with Mrs. Coutii, Apr. 26, 1974.

62. For the few antebellum separations of bed and board, see the District Court files, NCCO.

63. Mills, "Piety and Prejudice," 171–94, discusses many of the nuances of morality along Cane River.

64. For example, refer to the discussion in chapter 8 relative to the legal suits initiated by family members against whites who attempted to violate their females.

65. Interview with Mrs. Coutii, Apr. 26, 1974.

66. Interview with confidential source, Apr. 26, 1974; Mrs. Coutii to author, Apr. 22, 1974.

67. Harnett T. Kane, *Plantation Parade: The Grand Manner in Louisiana* (New York: William Morrow, 1945), 267.

68. Current whereabouts of the altar of Sidalise (Sarpy) Dupré are unknown. Family heirlooms held by her granddaughter Lee Etta Vaccarini Coutii were sold at auction to antique dealers after Mrs. Coutii's death.

69. Hugh LaCour to author, Apr. 22, 1974; Saxon, *Children of Strangers,* 29–31, depicts the same.

70. Mrs. Coutii to author, Apr. 22, 1974; Saxon, *Children of Strangers,* 30–32; Hugh LaCour to author, Apr. 22, 1974.

71. Saxon, *Children of Strangers,* 30–32; Mrs. Coutii to author, Apr. 22, 1974. The Isle Brevelle community, unlike many African descendants in the southern United States, retained almost no other African customs or traditions. This practice of decorating graves with bottles, shells, and mementoes of the dead was a rare vestige. One observer of nonwhite life and customs in the antebellum South recorded: "Negro graves were always decorated with the last article used by the deceased, and broken pitchers and broken bits of colored glass." See Blassingame, *The Slave Community,* 37, who cites Sara A. Torian, ed., "Ante-Bellum and War Memories of Mrs. Telfair Hodgson," *Georgia Historical Quarterly* 27 (Dec. 1943): 350–56. The oldest descendants of the family in the 1970s had no recollection of the practice, although they did recall the days when keepsakes of the departed ones were placed on the graves during religious seasons.

72. Interview with confidential source, Mar. 24, 1974; Callahan et al., *History of St. Augustine's Parish,* 28.

73. Hugh LaCour to author, Apr. 6, 1974; Saxon, *Children of Strangers,* 42–43.

74. McCants, *They Came to Louisiana,* 60.

75. Succession of Marie Susanne Metoyer, Natchitoches Succ. file 355, NCCO.

76. Memorandum of the Marguilliers, Cloutierville, May 9, 1847, folder 985, Cane River Notarial Collection.

77. Succession of J. B. E. Rachal, Natchitoches Succ. file 927, NCCO. By way of comparison, the son of Jean Baptiste Meuillion, a free man of color of Louisiana who is frequently recognized by modern historians for his wealth, paid only 35 piasters for the requiem mass and interment of his father in 1840, according to Sterkx, *The Free Negro in Ante-Bellum Louisiana,* 204.

78. Succession of Oscar Dubreuil, Natchitoches Succ. file 1255, NCCO.

79. Interview with Mrs. Coutii, Mar. 24, 1974; St. John the Baptist Parish (Cloutierville), Burial Book I.

80. Interview with Mrs. Coutii, Mar. 24, 1974.

81. Such tombs were not entirely unique in the parish of Natchitoches; a handful of affluent whites erected similar monuments. Those others, however, have crumbled into decay.

82. Interview with Mrs. Coutii, Apr. 26, 1974. It was Perine (Metoyer) Metoyer Dupré who was responsible, more than anyone, for preserving the legendary stories that the aging Augustin related to her during the years she and her husband cared for him.

83. Callahan et al., *History of St. Augustine's Parish*, 43.

84. *State v. Cantey*, 1835 (2 Hill 614, S.C.).

85. S. D. North, Director, Bureau of the Census, *Special Reports: Supplementary, Analysis, and Derivative Tables; Twelfth Census of the United States, 1900* (Washington, D.C.: Government Printing Office, 1906), 177.

86. Mills, "Piety and Prejudice," 179.

7. Cane River Culture

1. In addition to the twenty-three Creole of color families whom the 1860 U.S. census taker identified as white, he applied the "mulatto" label to fifty-three white families whose ancestry can be traced back to France, Germany, and Spain with no African admixture. An analysis of this census is reported in Elizabeth Shown Mills, "Ethnicity and the Southern Genealogist: Myths and Misconceptions, Resources and Opportunities," in *Generations and Change: Genealogical Perspectives in Social History*, ed. Robert M. Taylor Jr. and Ralph J. Crandall (Macon, Ga.: Mercer University Press, 1986), 89–108, particularly 96. The instructions given to U.S. census takers on the designation of race and other matters have been transcribed online; for Thomas's instructions, see "1860 Census: Instructions to the Marshals," Minnesota Population Center, University of Minnesota, *IPUMSusa* (usa.ipums.org/usa/voliii/inst1860.shtml).

2. Testimony of Judge C. E. Greneaux, Roubieu v. Metoyer (May 1835), case no. 1395, bundle 59; and Metoyer v. Roubieu (Oct. 1836), case no. 1473, bundle 74; consolidated Dec. 1836, District Court Records; NCCO.

3. Hugh LaCour to author, Mar. 5, 1974. Comparisons of racial composition to physical characteristics provide many genetic contrasts. This third-generation Barthélemy Le Court was 2/16 Caddo, 5/16 African, and 9/16 French; no known photograph exists to support the verbal description in the text. Thérèsine Carles (born 1824 of Rose Metoyer and Dr. André Zephérin Carles) was 3/4 French and 1/4 African; her photo (in first section of photos, this volume) reveals light brown hair, and the family reports that her eyes were blue. Emanuel Dupré (born 1807 of Marie Adelaïde Mariotte and Sieur Joseph Dupré) probably possessed the most complicated ancestry among his contemporaries, being 15/32 French, 8/32 African, 6/32 German, 2/32 Spanish, and 1/32 Native American. His photo (section 1) depicts a man with jet-black hair, swarthy complexion, and burly face; likely he defied any one ethnic label. Marie Zéline Le Court, Emanuel's half-sister and Barthélemy III's half-great-aunt, was 5/8 French, 1/4 African, and 1/8 German; her photo (section 1) depicts a woman of mature years with quite fair skin and barely discernible African features. Sephira Dupré (Emanuel's daughter by his half-French and half-African wife Marie Marguerite Metoyer)—to greatly simplify her genetic composition—was roughly 2/3 European and roughly 1/3 African with a barely traceable Native American influence; her complexion was also said to be fair and her hair a soft blond.

4. J. E. Dunn, "Isle Brevelle"; interview with Mrs. Coutii, Mar. 24, 1974.

5. Interview with Mrs. Coutii, Mar. 24, 1974.

6. Hugh LaCour to author, Apr. 6, 1974.

7. Ibid.; Reminiscences of "Duncan Kirkland," Jan. 26, 1922, Natchitoches Scrapbook № 2, Melrose Collection. John Duncan Kirkland was born June 11, 1864, to the marriage of the "Anglo" multiracial George Kirkland and Emilie Metoyer, daughter of Auguste Augustin Metoyer and his wife Melite Anty. For Duncan's birth and baptismal dates, see *St. Augustine Catholic Church of Isle Brevelle, Index of Baptismal Records,* 16, which identifies him simply as "John"; 1870 U.S. census, Natchitoches Parish, La., pop. sch., Ward 11, p. 16, dwell. 126, fam. 133, which identifies him as "Jean D." Kirkland; and his tombstone at St. Augustine Parish Cemetery, where he is memorialized as "John D." Kirkland.

8. Hugh LaCour to author, Apr. 6, 1974; Francois Mignon to author, Apr. 23, 1974.

9. Interview with Mrs. Coutii, Mar. 24, 1974; Mrs. Coutii to author, Oct. 5, 1974.

10. Mrs. Coutii to author, Oct. 5, 1974; Saxon, *Children of Strangers,* 40; Kane, *Plantation Parade,* 269.

11. Succession of Pierre Metoyer, no. 193; Succession of Susanne Metoyer, no. 355; Succession of [J. B.] Louis Metoyer, no. 362; Succession of Dominique Metoyer, no. 375; Succession of Agnes Metoyer, no. 395; Succession of Florentin Conant, no. 1049, all in Clerk of Court's Office, Natchitoches; Succession of Joseph Augustin Metoyer, folder 47, box 11, Natchitoches Colonial Archives Collection, LSU.

12. The earliest notice given to these portraits in the art world appears to be that of Cedric Dover, *American Negro Art* (Greenwich: New York Graphic Society, 1960), 62–65. The identities of Augustin and his wife, as the older couple, are firmly established. Both tradition and Dover (who likely relied on tradition) report that the two younger subjects were grandchildren of Marie Thérèse. Mills and Mills, in their 1972 commission, studied all family members who composed that generation—their ages and wealth in the relevant time frame, their lifestyles, and their residences—and found no viable candidates other than Susanne Metoyer's daughter Marie Thérèse Carmelite "Melite" Anty and husband, the New Orleans–based merchant and factor, Auguste Augustin Metoyer. In the four decades since this identification was first offered, no evidence has emerged to the contrary. The periodic residence of Melite and August in New Orleans, where Auguste's parents would have visited them, would have facilitated sittings with the New Orleans portraitists Feuille and Julien Hudson.

Feuille, who signed one of the portraits, has been a challenge for biographers. According to John A. Mahé II and Rosanne McCaffrey, editors of the *Encyclopaedia of New Orleans Artists, 1718–1918,* 133, his presence in New Orleans is documented at 1834–41, his first name is unknown, and he has been frequently confused with his brother who was a New Orleans engraver in the years 1835–41. Hudson (p. 193) was active in New Orleans during 1831–40. See also William Keyse Rudolph and Patricia Brady, *In Search of Julien Hudson: Free Artist of Color in Pre–Civil War New Orleans* (New Orleans: The Historic New Orleans Collection, 2011). The severe financial depression that followed the Crash of 1837 likely contributed to the end of the Louisiana careers of all three men of art. That economic instability and the time frame of their paintings also help to date the Cane River portraits and identify their subjects.

13. Interview with Mrs. Coutii, Apr. 26, 1974; Garber, "History of Melrose Plantation like Turning Pages of Novel."

14. Quote by Rudolph, in Rudolph and Brady, *In Search of Julien Hudson,* 87; also supporting details from Rudolph to E. S. Mills, emails, Sept. 11–15, 2009.

15. Scrapbooks of Cammie G. Henry and Lyle Saxon, Melrose Collection.

16. Basic evidence for the three children of Auguste and Melite is as follows: (a) *Nelcourt Metoyer,* born September 10, 1827 (St. François Parish, Reg. 7, entries in chronological order); died before the 1830 census; (b) *Augustin Paulin Metoyer,* born June 29, 1829 (Reg. 7), died September 15, 1836 (Reg. 15, "Paul" Metoyer), buried on the Isle; (c) *Emilie Metoyer,* who appears to have been born in New Orleans, about 1833–34, according to a correlation of later census data. For Emilie's son John Duncan Kirkland, the informant for the scrapbook information, see *St. Augustine Catholic Church of Isle Brevelle, Index of Baptismal Records—Book 1, 1852–1889* (Natchitoches: The Society, 2000), 17, for "John" Kirkland, born June 14, 1864, and baptized Aug. 15, 1864, citing Book 1, p. 116; and Kathleen Balthazar Heitzmann and Joseph Metoyer, *The St. Augustine Catholic Church Cemetery Listings* (Catskill, N.Y.: Cane River Trading Co., 2007), 14, for "Kirkland, John D. (Duncan) (14 June 1864 / 28 Nov 1950)."

Paul's death occurred amid a seasonal epidemic—either malaria or yellow fever—that peaked along Cane River in that month of September. The first of the deaths was a New Orleans visitor to the Isle, an eighteen-year-old *homme de couleur libre.* It is probable that Paul's parents left their New Orleans home for the interior as the fever hit the city, thinking they would be safer on the Isle.

17. Olmsted, *Journey in the Seaboard Slave States,* 634.

18. Ambroise LeComte to Joseph Metoyer, doc. 4867 (1818), NCA.

19. Succession of C. N. Rocques Sr., Succ. Book 30: 219, NCCO.

20. Widow Louis Metoyer to St. Cyr Metoyer, Conv. Book 30 (Donations): 85–86, NCCO. In making this donation to St. Cyr, Widow Louis reserved "the buildings thereon" for the use of the young Widow Cloutier during her natural lifetime. Also relevant is Alexis Cloutier to legitimate heirs of Augustin Cloutier, Conv. Book 30 (Donations): 41–42, NCCO. St. Cyr Metoyer, to whom Widow Louis donated these 5 arpents from Louis's domain, appears to be another "natural" child of Louis; Conv. Book 20:413, NCCO, documents Louis's 1831 manumission of "Rosalie, Negro, about 50," with two "mulatto" boys Saint-Cyr and Antoine, aged about 16; Antoine appears to have died in the 1830s. For Louisiana's contemporary law defining legal heirship and the exclusion of illegitimate children from paternal inheritance, see Thomas Gibbes Morgan, comp. and ed., *Civil Code of the State of Louisiana: With the Statutory Amendments, from 1825 to 1853, Inclusive . . .* (New Orleans: Bloomfield & Steel, 1853), Book III, Chaps. II–III, pp. 126–32.

21. Valery Barthelémy LeCour to Jean Baptiste Dominique Metoyer, Misc. Records, Book A (1827–1837): 57, Natchitoches.

22. Donation of Marie Suzette Metoyer to Clara Berthe [Barthe] and Marie Elise Rocques, folder 449, Cane River Notarial Collection.

23. McCants, *They Came to Louisiana,* 134–35.

24. J. E. Dunn, "Isle Brevelle."

25. Saxon, *Children of Strangers,* 22.

26. Ibid., 43; Mrs. Coutii to author, Apr. 15, 1974; Hugh LaCour to author, Mar. 5, 1974.

27. Mrs. Coutii to author, Oct. 5, 1974.

28. Ibid.; Mrs. Coutii to author, Apr. 15, 1974, wherein she referenced her source as a daughter of François Gassion Metoyer and his wife "Tante Perine." Gassion's kinship ties to Camptí resulted from his first and short-lived marriage to Flavie de Mézières, a great-granddaughter of the old commandant whose multiracial offspring settled farms north of Natchitoches at Grande Écore and Camptí. For the 1832 Metoyer-Mézières marriage, see Mills, *Natchitoches Church Marriages, 1818–1850,* entry 215.

29. Mrs. Coutii to author, Oct. 5, 1974.

30. Hugh LaCour to author, Mar. 5, 1974; J. E. Dunn, "Isle Brevelle."

31. Succession of C. N. Rocques *fils*, no. 897, NCCO.

32. Olmsted, *Journey in the Seaboard Slave States*, 649.

33. Marriage contract of Emanuel Dupré to Marie Marguerite Metoyer, Natchitoches Book A, Misc.: 48; and Philippe Valsain v. Cloutier, District Court Records Book 3: 118–26, both NCCO.

34. Interview with Mrs. Coutii, Mar. 24, 1974; 1870 U.S. census, Natchitoches Parish, La., pop. sch., p. 438 (stamped), Ward 10, p. 3, dwelling/family 21.

35. Testimony of Manuel Llorens, Roubieu v. Metoyer, in Natchitoches District Court suit 1395 (1835), NCCO; Hugh LaCour to author, Mar. 5, 1974.

36. Ibid.; J. E. Dunn, "Isle Brevelle."

37. J. E. Dunn, "Isle Brevelle."

38. Ibid.

39. Interview with Mr. and Mrs. Tillman Chelettre Sr., Natchez, La., Oct. 12, 1974.

40. Olmsted, *Journey in the Seaboard Slave States*, 633.

41. Edward Long, *The History of Jamaica*, 3 vols. (London: T. Lowndes, 1774), 2:355, quoted in Edward Braithwaite, *The Development of Creole Society in Jamaica, 1770–1820* (Oxford: Clarendon Press, 1971), 177.

42. Edward C. Jeffrey, "New Lights on Evolution," *Science*, May 13, 1927, 459.

43. 1850 U.S. Census, Natchitoches Parish, La., pop. sch.; calculations by the authors.

44. M. G. Lewis, *Journal of a West India Proprietor, Kept during a Residence in the Island of Jamaica* (1834; rpr. Boston: Houghton Mifflin, 1929), 94–95.

45. Olmsted, *Journey in the Seaboard Slave States*, 633.

46. 1850 U.S. Census, Natchitoches Parish, La., pop. sch.; calculations by the authors.

47. Succession of Philippe Valsain Dupré, an interdict, succ. no. 630, NCCO; Mrs. Coutii to author, Mar. 31, 1974. The incident of hermaphroditism was reported by a confidential source, Apr. 26, 1974, who stated that the individual's abnormality did not prevent her from marrying and leading an otherwise normal life. The census of 1850, which recorded insanity, revealed no instances in the studied population.

48. Interview with Mrs. Coutii, Apr. 24, 1974; Succession of A. A. Metoyer and Wife, no. 841, NCCO; Blaise C. D'Antoni, "Some 1853 Cloutierville Yellow Fever Deaths," *New Orleans Genesis* 35 (June 1970): 261–62.

49. Succession of Fortin née La Renaudière, doc. 2467, and Succession of Padre de La Vez, doc. 2469, NCA.

50. Elias P. Pellet, *History of the 114th Regiment, New York State Volunteers* (Norwich, N.Y.: Telegraph & Chronicle Press Print, 1866), 224.

51. McCants, *They Came to Louisiana*, 122.

52. Olmsted, *Journey in the Seaboard Slave States*, 633.

53. Dignowity Journal, typescript, 67–68. The spellings of the diarist have been left intact, but some punctuation and capitalization are added here for clarity. Dignowity's command of English was uncommonly good for one not a native speaker, but he clearly made a wrong word choice in this passage: that is, his statement that his treatment of the Metoyers as equals seemed to them a great *condescencion*. His act would have been seen as an *acceptance*, but not an act of "looking down" upon them.

54. Interview with Mrs. Coutii, Mar. 24, 1974; Hugh LaCour to author, Apr. 5, 1974. For the plantation manor Auguste purchased just weeks before the Crash of 1837 and lost to sheriff's sale in 1843, see Baptiste Adlé to Auguste Metoyer, Feb. 12, 1837; Auguste Metoyer to J. B. Adlé, May 4, 1843, Notarial Record Book 34 (July 9, 1842–Aug. 14, 1843): 199, doc. 3487; Sheriff's Sales, Book 4:53–55, 68–71; and Metoyer to Adlé, Conv. Book 35:105–8, all in NCCO. Also *Anty v. Adlé,* 9

La. Ann. 490 (1854); and "Natchitoches, 1920, Scrapbook," Melrose Collection. The one surviving "mansion house" on the Isle, that of Louis Metoyer, is known today as Melrose and in 1974 was declared a National Historic Landmark. Since 1971, it has been owned by the Association for the Preservation of Historic Natchitoches. The post–Civil War damage claims filed by Cane River families with the Southern Claims Commission will be discussed at length in chapter 9.

55. For Freeman, see Dan L. Flores, *Jefferson & Southwestern Exploration: The Freeman & Custis Accounts of the Red River Expedition of 1806* (Norman: University of Oklahoma Press, 1984), 118. Stoddard, *Sketches of Louisiana*, 328–29, and McCants, *They Came to Louisiana*, 120, describe Creole housing across the first six decades of the nineteenth century. Cane River lightning rods were described by Hugh LaCour to author, Apr. 5, 1974. For the advent of log cabins in the Natchitoches jurisdiction, see Carol Wells, "Earliest Log Cabins of Natchitoches Parish," *North Louisiana Historical Association Journal* 6 (Spring 1975): 117–22. For a superb documentary analysis of Natchitoches architecture, see Carolyn M. Wells, "Domestic Architecture of Colonial Natchitoches" (M.A. thesis, Northwestern State University, 1973).

56. Hugh LaCour to author, Apr. 5, 1974.

57. Interview with Mrs. Coutii, Mar. 24, 1974; Mrs. Coutii to author, Oct. 5, 1974; Succession of Agnes Metoyer, no. 395, Natchitoches.

58. The history of the Sarpy-Jones home has been muddled by various research efforts. Mrs. Coutii (raised by her grandmother Sidalise Sarpy Dupré, Jérôme's daughter who grew up in the house) emphatically attested in the 1970s that the family home had burned. Some current writings contrarily assert that it is the still-extant house known variously as the Roubieu House, the Flanner House, the Carroll Jones House, and the Richardson House.

The confusion stems from several historical overlaps that were not adequately sorted out. (1) Two identical houses were built on Spanish-era concessions by the white Creole brothers-in-law Julien Rachal Jr. and François Roubieu. (2) These properties were much later acquired, in two separate purchases made in separate centuries, by a father and son. (3) Researchers have merged the identities of those two men: Carroll Jones Sr. (a Tennessee-born freedman of considerable renown for his Civil War activity) and his son John Carroll Jones, who lived a radically different life. For current publications that mistakenly attribute the surviving home to the slave-born Carroll Sr. (all sources with a common origin), see "Carroll Jones House," Northwestern State University, *Louisiana Regional Folklife Program* (http://winhttp.nsula.edu/regionalfolklife/crcc /CarrollJones.html0); Dana Bowker Lee, "The People of the Island," 36, "Carroll Jones House"; and "John Carroll Jones House," National Park Service, *Cane River National Heritage Area* (www .nps.gov/history/nr/travel/caneriver/car.htm).

The hundred or so documents that present a clear chain of evidence for these two dwellings, and sort the men who should be associated with each, will be detailed in a forthcoming study. Here, a clear distinction between the two can be drawn from easily accessible sources:

RACHAL-SARPY-JONES HOUSE. This no-longer-surviving home was built before 1837 by Julien Rachal Jr. on his Spanish-era concession—legally identified on plat maps as *Section 52, T8N R6W*. It was acquired during Reconstruction by the Tennessee-born ex-slave Carroll Jones. A description of the house appears in the autobiography Jones contributed to the 1890 history of northwest Louisiana: "In 1869 he came to this point and located on his present plantation in Ward 9, *eighteen miles* southeast of the city of Natchitoches, which then contained about 1,200 acres of land, but since that time he has made adjoining purchases until he is now the owner of 1,500 acres. . . . Mr. Jones' residence is a large and commodious one, being 130 feet long by 80 feet wide. The yard in which it stands contains a fine cedar grove." See *Biographical and Historical Memoirs of Northwest Louisiana*, 63.

ROUBIEU-FLANNER-RICHARDSON HOUSE. This still-standing home was built shortly after 1837, on *Section 54*, T8N R6W, by Rachal's brother-in-law, François Roubieu. Roubieu died in 1849 and his home and plantation passed to his widow and his daughter Pauline, who shortly thereafter married Dr. Thomas Jefferson Flanner Sr. In 1877, T. J. Flanner Jr. took over the property. He, too, submitted his autobiography to the same 1890 publication. There, he wrote:

> His mother, whose maiden name was Pauline Roubien [Roubieu], was born . . . upon the same plantation now occupied by the subject of this sketch [together with his widowed mother] . . . In 1877 [after extensive travels and professional sojourns elsewhere] he re-turned to the parish of Natchitoches and took charge of [this] plantation, *sixteen miles* southeast of Natchitoches, which he subsequently purchased and which he occupied and managed ever since. It is situated on both the Breville Bayou . . . and Cane River . . . and its improvements are of the best, being one of the most complete in this respect of any plantation on the river, for over $10,000 worth of improvements have been put upon it in the last four years. (*Biographical and Historical Memoirs of Northwest Louisiana, 343*)

Years after the death of Carroll Jones Sr., John Carroll Jones purchased the Roubieu-Flanner property and operated both it and the parental tract until his death in 1938. The National Register, however, attributes the Roubieu-Flanner House to the ex-slave Carroll Jones of Civil War fame, who had no association with it. A surviving photograph of the Rachal-Sarpy-Jones House shows that the two were virtually identical and built in the style of Augustin Metoyer's home.

59. *Biographical and Historical Memoirs of Northwest Louisiana*, 353, "Carroll Jones."

60. Callahan et al., *History of St. Augustine's Parish*, 23.

61. Lee, "The People of the Island," 1:41.

62. Hugh LaCour to author, Apr. 5, 1974.

63. Succession of Marie Louise Metoyer (Mme. Florentin Conant Sr.), no. 323; Succession of [J. B.] Louis Metoyer, no. 362; Théophile L. Metoyer and Marie Elina Metoyer, Marriage Contract, Mortgage Records, 28:276–79; all in NCCO.

64. Succession of Charles Nerestan Rocques Sr., Succ. Book 30:225; Succession of Agnes Metoyer, no. 395; Sucession of C. N. Rocques *fils*, no. 897; and Succession of Predanes Metoyer, no. 1360; NCCO.

65. Francois Mignon to author, Apr. 8, 1974; *Natchitoches: Oldest Settlement in the Louisiana Purchase, Founded 1714* (Natchitoches, La.: Association of Natchitoches Women for the Preservation of Historic Natchitoches, 1973), 49. This piano was relocated to the living room of the home called Cherokee, one of those open for public display during the area's annual tour of homes.

66. Hugh LaCour to author, Apr. 5, 1974.

67. Interview with Mrs. Coutii, Apr. 26, 1974; Mrs. Coutii to author, Apr. 15, 1974.

68. This cypress armoire was owned in 1974 by Armeline Rocques (Mrs. Tillman) Chelettre.

69. Interview with Mrs. Coutii, Apr. 26, 1974; Mrs. Coutii to author, Apr. 15, 1974. The present whereabouts of only one of these mugs is known; the others were said to have been sold by the people to collectors during their years of need.

70. *An Account of Louisiana*, 33.

71. Dignowity Journal, typescript, 68.

72. Succession of C. N. Rocques *fils*, no. 897, NCCO.

73. Alexandre Dimitry, who had married the daughter of the architect of the Washington Monument, Robert Mills, was born at New Orleans on Feb. 6, 1805, to the marriage of the Greek

André Dimitry (Demetrois) and the octoroon Marianne Céleste Dragon. Alexandre's maternal grandfather, the French officer Michel Dragon, had fathered at least one child by Marie Françoise Chauvin de Beaulieu de Montplaisir, an enslaved offshoot of a French-Canadian family that earned wealth and prominence in early colonial Louisiana. Marie Françoise's 1755 baptismal record identifies her as "mulatresse [should be *quadroon*] daughter, aged about eight months, of Marianne Lalande [mulatresse], slave of Mr. Lalande le Conseiller." Marie Françoise's father, François Chauvin de Beaulieu de Montplaisir, went discreetly unmentioned in her baptismal record. The best treatment of this family is provided by Shirley Elizabeth Thompson, *Exiles at Home: The Struggle to Become American in Creole New Orleans* (Cambridge, Mass.: Harvard University Press, 2009), 38–46. See also Patrick Binet, *Cousins des Amériques: France, Québec, Terre-Neuve . . . Saint-Domingue, Louisiane, Illinois, Cuba, etc.; Ascendance et parentèle de Josefa Evelina Muzard, 1835–1913* (France: Biviers, 1998), 541–42. The latter source should be used with caution; the book is impressive in scope, but large chunks of it are lifted, without attribution, from other published works.

74. Statistics drawn by the author from the 1850 and 1860 U.S. censuses reveal that, in 1850, 15.8 percent of the clan's population had attended school within the year (even though the existence of their school was not recorded). Statewide, only 6.9 percent of the nonwhite population had attended school for any time at all during the previous year. Also see J. B. D. De Bow, comp., *Statistical View of the United States* (Washington, D.C.: Beverly Tucker, 1854), 154; Stahl, "The Free Negro in Ante-Bellum Louisiana," 357–59; Blaise C. D'Antoni, "The Catholic Schools of Natchitoches," undated manuscript, Baudier Papers, Archives of the Archdiocese of New Orleans; and Desdunes, *Our People and Our History*, n. 137.

75. All known records for Chevalier, who actually lived west of the Isle on Bayou Derbanne, identify him as a planter rather than a teacher. For his location, see Widow Neville Gallien to Widow Jerome Thomassy, mortgage of land on Bayou Derbanne, bounded on upper by Louis Chevalier, May 16, 1851, folder 1167, Cane River Notarial Collection.

76. Naturalization application of Nicolas Charles LeRoy, Naturalization Records, folder 23, box 6, Natchitoches Parish Records, 1734–1916, LLMVC, LSU Special Collections; Last Will and Testament, Succession of N. C. LeRoy, no. 922, NCCO. In signing his will, LeRoy uniquely appended to his name the identity of which he was most proud: "*Citoyen Americain.*"

77. Succession of Pierre Metoyer, f.m.c., no. 193 (opened 1833), NCCO. The final account of Pierre's administrator reported the settlement of the deceased's account with LeRoy for his teaching services in the local school.

78. 1850 U.S. census, Natchitoches Parish, La., pop. sch., stamped p. 46 verso, dwell. 831, fam. 831, "Chas. Leroi"; also Charles LeRoy to Auguste Metoyer, Apr. 1, 1841, in Auguste Metoyer Papers, LLMVC, LSU Special Collections.

79. Desdunes, *Our People and Our History*, 51–52; Marriage Contract of Bernard Dauphin and Marie Barbe Melisine Metoyer, Natchitoches Conv. Book 32:22; Callahan et al., *History of St. Augustine's Parish*, 29.

80. *Desdunes, Our People and Our History*, 51.

81. Interview with Mrs. Coutii, Mar. 24, 1974; 1850 U.S. census, Natchitoches Parish, La., pop. sch., stamped p. 49 verso, dwell. 883, fam. 883, for Oscar Dubreuil, schoolmaster; 1860 U.S. census, Natchitoches Parish, pop. sch., p. 46, dwell. 379, fam. 379, for F. C. "Christopher," schoolteacher.

82. J. B. D. Metoyer, cadet, to Em^l Dupré, April 16, 1839, folder 553, Cane River Notarial Collection; Olmsted, *Journey in the Seaboard Slave States*, 634.

83. Callahan et al., *History of St. Augustine's Parish*, 30.

84. All these books, once owned by Ambroise Sévère Dupré and his wife Sidalise Sarpy, belonged to their granddaughter, Mrs. Coutii, in the 1970s.

85. Callahan et al., *History of St. Augustine's Parish*, 29; interview with Mrs. Coutii, Mar. 24, 1974.

86. See, for example, Stahl, "The Free Negro in Ante-Bellum Louisiana," 359.

87. McCants, *They Came to Louisiana*, 41, 43; Callahan et al., *History of St. Augustine's Parish*, 32; Baudier, *The Catholic Church in Louisiana*, 409; Sigmond Kieffy to Auguste Martin, in Natchitoches Conv. Book 49:504, NCCO. The home the bishop purchased for the Daughters of the Cross is the one variously known as the "Old Convent" and Badin-Roque House.

88. McCants, *They Came to Louisiana*, 72–73.

89. Ibid., 71–72.

90. Ibid., 83–84, 143; Callahan et al., *History of St. Augustine's Parish*, 32.

91. Baudier, *The Catholic Church in Louisiana*, 432.

92. Callahan et al., *History of St. Augustine's Parish*, 29.

93. Succession of C. N. Rocques *fils*, no. 897; Succession of Nicholas Charles LeRoy, no. 922; Succession of Predanes Metoyer, no. 1360, NCCO. François Edouard Séverin was born Sept. 6, 1832, to Marie Pompose *dite* Séverin, slave of Jean Baptiste Prudhomme, according to the previously cited "Souvenir des Ages," maintained by Ambroise Sévère Dupré. Edouard's sister who used the Prudhomme surname, Marie Thérèse Aspasie (born Oct. 31, 1823 according to "Souvenir des Ages"), also married into the Metoyer family, at which time Sieur Prudhomme attended the marriage and acknowledged his paternity. See Mills, *Natchitoches Church Marriages, 1818–1850*, entry 486.

94. 1870 U.S. census, Social Statistics sch.; also Succession of C. N. Rocques Sr., Succ. Book 30:225, and Succession of [J. B.] Louis Metoyer, no. 362, NCCO.

95. Olmsted, *Journey in the Seaboard Slave States*, 652.

96. Ibid., 634.

8. Racism and Citizenship

1. Thomas Johnson Michie, ed., *The Encyclopedic Digest of Tennessee Reports . . . up to and Including Vol. 115, Tennessee Reports* (Charlottesville, Va.: Michie Co., 1907), 3:226, for *State v. Claiborne* (1838).

2. Robert H. Speers, *Reports of Cases at Law, Argued and Determined in the Court of Appeals and Court of Errors of South Carolina . . . from November 1842 to [May 1844]* (Columbia: A. S. Johnson, 1844), 152–57, quote from p. 155; hereinafter cited as *State v. Harden*, 29 S.C.L. (2 Speers) 152 (1832). This spring term 1832 case was tardily published as a footnote to the 1843 case *State v. Jesse Hill*. For interpretations other historians have made of the Harden case, see H. M. Henry, "The Police Control of the Slave in South Carolina" (Ph.D. diss., Vanderbilt University, 1914), 181–82; and Theodore Brantner Wilson, *The Black Codes of the South* (University, Ala.: University of Alabama Press, 1965), 27.

3. *State v. Harden*, 29 S.C.L. (2 Speers) 152 (1832).

4. Leon Litwack, *North of Slavery: The Negro in the Free States* (Chicago: University of Chicago Press, 1965), 75–79, quote on 76.

5. Degler, *Neither Black nor White*, 101. The first colony to decree that someone must be less than one-eighth black to be treated as white was Virginia in 1705, and it explicitly did so in response to growing concern over interracial sex. The catalyst was a request by John Bunch III,

a young man whose agnatic great-grandfather had been an African import, to marry a white female in Blisland Parish. Although Bunch's father, grandfather, and great-grandfather had all taken white spouses or mates, the Blisland rector refused permission. Young Bunch, one-eighth black, appealed to Virginia's council in August 1705, challenging the application to him of the colony's 1691 statute that forbade a white person to marry a "mulatto." In September, the colony's attorney general issued an opinion that the denial was too punitive in the case at hand but that the meaning of the term *mulatto* was ambiguous under Virginia statutes and should be more clearly defined. In October, in an act issued to "clear all manner of doubts" as to how *mulatto* should be interpreted, the council decreed that "the child of an Indian and the child, grand child, or great grand child, of a negro shall be deemed, accounted, held and taken to be a mulatto." Thus barred from a legal marriage, the couple (John Bunch III and Sarah Slayden) spent their lives in a common-law union sanctioned by their community; and their offspring have lived as white for three subsequent centuries. Significantly to history, the young octoroon who prompted the Virginia law on which most southern states would pattern their definition of whiteness was the seventh great-grandfather of Stanley Anne Dunham, the white mother of President Barack Obama.

For the legislation, see William Waller Hening, *The Statutes at Large; Being a Collection of All the Laws of Virginia from the First Session of the Legislature in the Year 1619*, vol. 3 (Philadelphia: Thomas DeSilver, 1823), 87 (1691), 250–52 (1705); and Henry Read McIlwaine, *Executive Journals of the Council of Colonial Virginia*, 6 vols. (Richmond: Virginia State Library, 1925–66), 3:16. For the evidence of Bunch's ancestry and of Dunham's descent, see Anastasia Harman, Natalie D. Cottrill, Paul C. Reed, and Joseph Shumway's peer-reviewed study, "Documenting President Barack Obama's Maternal African-American Ancestry: Tracing His Mother's Bunch Ancestry to the First Slave in America," archived, *Ancestry.com* (http://c.mfcreative.com/offer/us/obamabunch/PDF/main_article_final.pdf).

6. N. W. Cocke, *Reports of Cases Argued and Determined in the Supreme Court of Alabama during the June Term 1805, and a Part of January Term 1851* (Montgomery, Ala.: J. H. & T. F. Martin, 1851), 276–80. For the case in context, see Mills, "Miscegenation and the Free Negro in Antebellum 'Anglo' Alabama," 29. According to Frank W. Sweet, *Legal History of the Color Line: The Notion of Invisible Blackness* (Palm Coast, Fla.: Backintyme, 2005), 176, Judge Parson's use of the phrase "a drop of negro blood" marks the first time this notorious concept appears in a U.S. appellate court decision.

7. Degler, *Neither Black nor White*, 102.

8. *State v. Cantey*, 2 Hill 614 (SC 1835).

9. See Lawrence Kestenbaum, *The Political Graveyard* (www.politicalgraveyard.com) for William Harper (1790–1847) of South Carolina.

10. Schweninger, *Black Property Owners in the South*, 64–65; Williamson, *New People*, 24.

11. Thomas R. R. Cobb, *A Digest of the Statute Laws of the State of Georgia in Force prior to the Session of the General Assembly of 1851* (Athens, Ga.: Christy, Kelsea & Burke, 1851), 1011.

12. Ibid., 1021. Emphasis in the original.

13. Richard H. Clark, Thomas Read Rootes Cobb, and David Irwin, *The Code of the State of Georgia* (Atlanta: J. H. Seals, 1861), 321. Emphasis added.

14. Degler, in *Neither Black nor White*, uses the "mulatto escape hatch" theory to frame many of his discussions.

15. Charles Gayarré, *History of Louisiana*, 4 vols. (New Orleans: Armand Hawkins, 1903), 3:179. Hanger, *Bounded Lives*, 136–62, provides insight into the restrictions imposed on non-whites in New Orleans and the ways they protested those injustices.

16. Fiehrer, "The Emergence of Pan-Créolité," 9.

17. *Acts Passed at the First Session of the First Legislature of the Territory of Orleans Begun . . . the 25th Day of January [1806]* (New Orleans: Bradford & Anderson, 1807), 126–30, 150–90. If these registration books for free people of color were ever maintained at Natchitoches, no evidence of their existence survives.

18. *Acts Passed at the Second Session of the First Legislature of the Territory of Orleans Begun . . . 12ᵗʰ Day of January [1807]* (New Orleans: Bradford & Anderson, 1807), 82–89.

19. *Acts Passed at the First Session of the Second Legislature of the Territory of Orleans Begun . . . the Eighteenth of January [1808]* (New Orleans: Bradford & Anderson, 1808), 138.

20. Foner, "Free People of Color," 421.

21. For the quote, see Johnston, *Race Relations in Virginia,* 231.

22. Thomas R. R. Cobb, *An Inquiry into the Law of Negro Slavery in the United States of America* (1858; rpr. New York: Negro Universities Press, 1968), 66–67. Cobb prepared this work in an effort to present a moral defense of slavery. He also erred in his own presumption that *all* Africans arriving in America were enslaved. While the vast majority were, some did arrive of their own accord, as with Étienne LaRue, discussed in this chapter.

23. Ibid., 67.

24. *Archives of Maryland,* vol. 75, Thomas Bacon, *Laws of Maryland at Large* (Annapolis: Jonas Green, 1765), 266, para. 20.

25. See Joseph Carvalho III, *Black Families in Hampton, Massachusetts,* 2nd ed. (Boston: Newbury Street Press, 2011), 9, for specific examples.

26. *Adéle v. Beauregard,* 1 Mart. (O.S.) 183 (La. 1810).

27. *English v. Latham,* 3 Mart. (N.S.) 88 (La. 1824).

28. Helen Tunncliff Catterall, *Judicial Cases Concerning American Slavery and the Negro,* 5 vols. (Washington, D.C.: Carnegie Institute, 1932), 3:571.

29. Judith Kelleher Schafer, *Slavery, the Civil Law, and the Supreme Court of Louisiana* (Baton Rouge: LSU Press, 1997), 21. For Spofford's cultural roots, see "Amherst in the Law," *Amherst Graduates' Quarterly* 10 (November 1920): 238–52, specifically 250.

30. Mills, *"Liberté, Fraternité,* and Everything but *Égalité,"* 94.

31. Rex v. Pierrot et al., NCA doc. 186, various dates 1757; scattered unbound documents filmed as "Miscellaneous Archive Records, 1733–1820," Louisiana State Archives microfilm F.T. 565.

32. Hening, *Statutes at Large . . . of Virginia,* 7:95, "An act for the better regulating and disciplining the Militia," April 1757, sect. 7.

33. Quoted in Alice Dunbar-Nelson, "People of Color in Louisiana," part 2, page 374. Hanger, *Bounded Lives,* 119–20, more fully discusses the role of New Orleans nonwhite militia in the Gálvez Campaigns. The Revolutionary-era military rolls presented by Mills, *Natchitoches Colonials,* 39, 43, document the presence of six "people of color used as couriers" among the 126 frontier militiamen who participated in the 1780 Gálvez Campaign: one black slave (Chiq), one Romani (Jean Varangue), and four multiracials. By 1782, that special category was dropped from the rolls, as were five of those men. The sixth, Zacherie [Raymond], had been incorporated into the regular corps of riflemen. Another seven men on these two rolls were multiracial French-Indians who were socially treated as white.

34. Clarence Edwin Carter, ed., *The Territorial Papers of the United States,* 28 vols. (Washington, D.C.: Government Printing Office, 1934–75), vol. 9, *The Territory of Orleans, 1803–1812* (1940), 139. Italics added.

35. Foner, "Free People of Color," 421.

36. Louis Moreau Lislet, *A General Digest of the Acts of the Legislature of Louisiana Passed from the Year 1804 to 1827, Inclusive; and in Force at This Last Period* (New Orleans: Benjamin Levy, 1928), 103–4, for 1806 Black Code, sections 19 and 21.

37. Sterkx, *The Free Negro in Ante-Bellum Louisiana,* 182–84.

38. 1810 U.S. census, Natchitoches Parish; calculations by the authors.

39. Wright, *The Free Negro in Maryland,* 106–7. Bruce A. Clarke, "Laws Designed to Disarm Slaves, Freedmen, and African-Americans," *Old-Yankee.com* (www.old-yankee.com/rkba/racial_laws.html, updated June 11, 2012), provides a table of gun-control laws for the antebellum southern states and, postbellum, all U.S. states; this table cites relevant legal acts in each instance.

40. Moreau Lislet, *General Digest of the Acts of the Legislature,* 104, Black Code of 1806, sect. 20.

41. *State v. Harden,* 29 S.C.L. (2 Speers) 152 (1832).

42. Moreau Lislet, *General Digest of the Acts of the Legislature,* 112, Black Code of 1806, sect. 40.

43. For a judicial analysis of the Monet-LaRue incident, see Henry P. Dart, "A Criminal Trial before the Superior Council of Louisiana, May, 1747," *Louisiana Historical Quarterly* 13 (July 1930): 367–76. For the underlying records, see Heloise H. Cruzat, "The Documents Covering the Criminal Trial of Etienne La Rue, for Attempt to Murder and Illicit Carrying of Arms," *Louisiana Historical Quarterly* 13 (July 1930): 377–90.

44. The soldier Monet was shortly thereafter dispatched to Natchitoches, where he married Elisabeth Rachal. They were the parents of the planter Louis Monet, who lent his name to Monette's Bluff and left multiracial offspring along lower Cane River. As a starting point for Mathieu Monet's connection to Natchitoches, see Mills, *Natchitoches, 1729–1803,* entries 353 and 1093.

45. Olmsted, *Journey in the Seaboard Slave States,* 636.

46. J^h Me Rablés [Rabalais] *contra* Émile Colson, *h.d.c.l.,* Aug. 13, 1828, folder 249, Cane River Notarial Collection.

47. State v. Marie Desneiges ["Desnuges"], typescript, "Old Natchitoches Data," folios 220–24, Melrose Collection. The complainant in this translated transcript is called "John Baptiste Penne." He was, however, an Anglo named John Penn. Also Coutii interview, July 24, 1974.

48. Guocun Yang, "From Slavery to Emancipation: The African Americans of Connecticut, 1650s–1820s" (Ph.D. diss., University of Connecticut, 1999), 243–44.

49. Franklin, *The Free Negro in North Carolina,* 193; Litwack, *North of Slavery,* 64.

50. See, for example, the report of the Natchitoches commandant Étienne de Vaugine to Governor, August 9, 1782, identifying individuals who had moved illegally from the post and must be returned from their new locales, leg. 195, PPC-AGI, Seville.

51. Schweninger, *Black Property Owners in the South,* 64, recounts a New Orleans effort in 1843 to "arrest free persons of color born outside the state." Like many such efforts, it failed for want of enforcement.

52. Herbert Aptheker, ed., *A Documentary History of the Negro People in the United States* (New York: Citadel Press, 1951), 26; Sydnor, "The Free Negro in Mississippi," 7–8.

53. Catterall, *Judicial Cases,* 3:601.

54. Brasseaux, Fontenot, and Oubre, *Creoles of Color in the Bayou Country,* xiii.

55. Microfilms PC.1–PC.49, Office of the Clerk of Court, Natchitoches. The far more voluminous files of the district court have not been quantitatively analyzed.

56. Olmsted, *Journey in the Seaboard Slave State,* 288.

57. Augustin Metoyer v. A. L. DeBlieux, Natchitoches District Court suit no. 1233, bundle 185, filed 22 May 1833. Augustin's two tracts constituted four irregular sections: 39, 41, 75, and 76 at

the juncture of Red River and Bayou Couchinahan (later KeKouen). See Private Land Claims B1955 and 1865, State Land Office. Survey Plat, Township 10 North, Range 7W, Southwestern District Louisiana, December 2, 1829, U.S. General Land Office, RG 49, National Archives. For the period in which Augustin acquired the land from John Horn, see the deposition of Antoine Coindet, November 16, 1811, Claim B1965, Augustin Metoyer, State Land Office. Also see Survey of Geo. W. Morse, February 13, 1847, sects. 39, 75, in B1965, Augustin Metoyer, State Land Office.

58. Metoyer v. DeBlieux, District Court suit no. 1233.

59. Ibid.

60. Roubieu v. Metoyer, Natchitoches District Court suit no. 1395, bundle 59 (May 1835), and Metoyer v. Roubieu, case no. 1473, bundle 74 (October 1836); consolidated Dec. 1836; also Nicolas to Augustin Metoyer, Sale of land on Rivière Athao, Jan. 18, 1819, Conv. Book 7:83–85; all in NCCO. 1820 U.S. census, Natchitoches Parish, p. 4, for black male head-of-household named "Coincoin."

61. Roubieu v. Metoyer and Metoyer v. Roubieu.

62. Ibid. Roubieu's opposition to Metoyer might be deemed personal or financially motivated, rather than a racially charged act, given that Roubieu appears to have fathered and manumitted two quadroon children of his own; see Conv. Book 21:153, NCCO, for his April 15, 1835, manumission of Mulville, aged 5, and Julie, 3—mother not named.

63. Mme. Marie, f.w.o.c., v. Victorin Levasseur, June 30, 1829, folder 278, Cane River Notarial Collection. Parish church records of 1816 explicitly identify Levasseur as the father of twin girls born the previous month to Marie's mother, Adelaïde Mariotte: Marie Felony [Phelonise] Levasseur and Marie Emy [Emeline] Levasseur; see Mills, *Natchitoches, 1800–1825,* entries 2462–2463. Adelaïde also had an older daughter Marie, who was age thirty-one at the time of the complaint; Mills, "Which Marie Louise Is 'Mariotte'?" 202. The 1829 complaint does not clarify which of the three daughters named Marie was the complainant.

64. Manuel Llorens v. Firmin Lattier, 1844, folder 727, Cane River Notarial Collection.

65. Sterkx, *The Free Negro in Ante-Bellum Louisiana,* 170.

66. Alexis Cloutier to the Roman Congregation, Donation, Natchitoches "Book 6–Misc.," doc. 142, NCCO; Germaine Portré-Bobinski and Clara Mildred Smith, *Natchitoches: The Up-to-Date Oldest Town in Louisiana* (New Orleans: Dameron-Pierson Co., 1936), 206; *Journal of the Senate of the State of Louisiana,* 1825, pp. 55–60. Numerous documents in the Cane River Notarial Collection represent sales of lots in Cloutierville that were made by Cloutier in the 1820s; all refer to the various streets laid out on the plat filed with the parish clerk. The actual plat has not been found.

67. *Journal of the House of the State of Louisiana,* 1826, p. 49; *Natchitoches Courier,* March 13, 1826; *Louisiana State Gazette* (New Orleans), Jan. 28, 1826, p. 2, and February 16, 1826, p. 2.

68. *Journal of the Senate of the State of Louisiana,* 1826, 61–62.

69. *Natchitoches Courier,* March 13, 1826.

70. Ibid.

71. Ibid., italics in original.

72. Ibid., April 17, 1826.

73. Ibid., May 1, 1826, and May 8, 1826.

74. Ibid., May 22, 1826.

75. "Placide Bossier," *Louisiana State Gazette* (New Orleans), Jan. 28, 1826, p. 1; *Journal of the Senate of the State of Louisiana,* 1827, pp. 3–4, 20–21.

76. *Journal of the House of the State of Louisiana,* 1827, p. 49; *Natchitoches Courier,* Feb. 27, 1827.

77. De Bow, *Statistical View of the United States,* 83.

78. Johnston, *Race Relations in Virginia*, 296.

79. Ibid., 298.

80. Herskovits, *The New World Negro*, 77.

81. For antipapism, see Roger Daniels, *Coming to America: A History of Immigration and Ethnicity in American Life* (Princeton, N.J.: HarperCollins, 1990), 109, 266–67; and, more generally, Ray Allen Billington, *The Protestant Crusade, 1800–1860: A Study of the Origins of American Nativism* (1938; rpr. Chicago: Quadrangle Books, 1964). For the population statistics, see De Bow, *Seventh Census of the United States: 1850,* xxxvi. For a fuller development of the symbiotic relationship between white and multiracial Catholics in Louisiana, see Randall M. Miller, "Slaves and Southern Catholicism," in *Masters and Slaves in the House of the Lord: Race and Religion in the American South, 1740–1870,* ed. John B. Boles (Lexington: University Press of Kentucky, 1988), 127–52, esp. 133 and 144. One view Miller expresses on the latter page—that the Metoyers of Isle Brevelle "ruthlessly stamped out Africanisms among the slaves and insisted that all men, slave and free, practice their brand of Catholicism"—is supported (p. 233, n. 39) by citations to several works of Gary B. Mills; however, Miller's interpretation is at odds with the conclusions the Millses have reached from their own studies of surviving evidence in original materials.

82. Isaac Holmes, *An Account of the United States of America* (London: Caxton Press for H. Fisher, 1823), 70.

83. After the Civil War, as area whites instituted a binary system that treated the former free Creoles of color on a par with newly emancipated blacks, this attitude did change. To restore some semblance of past order in their lives, their social choices were increasingly affected by the most visible differences between them: skin color and hair texture. Saxon recounts one revealing Cane River song of the early twentieth century about a father whose daughter had brought "disgrace" upon him; it ended with the refrain: "I wouldn't mind the fellow if his skin was yellow, but Mary's run away with a coon." Saxon, *Children of Strangers,* 47.

84. Sterkx, *The Free Negro in Ante-Bellum Louisiana,* 247.

85. Virginia Dominguez, *White by Definition: Social Classification in Creole Louisiana* (New Brunswick, N.J.: Rutgers University Press, 1997), 162; emphasis in original.

86. Woods, *Marginality and Identity,* 46.

87. Degler, *Neither Black nor White,* 168.

88. In the post–Civil War period, when all men of color were suddenly free and allegedly "equal," this conceptual discrimination became even more pronounced. Deprived of their former wealth and status, the clan prided itself—and justified the continuance of its social superiority— upon this factor alone. Indeed, more than one twentieth-century descendant of the family used this one standard as the discriminating factor between their people and members of the black or Negro race. A black or Negro was considered by them to be one whose ancestors were freed by the Emancipation Proclamation, whereas the "old families" were *gens de couleur libres*—free, wealthy property owners and slave owners in antebellum society. For a detailed examination of this social concept within the community, see Woods, *Marginality and Identity,* esp. 53–54, 61, 198–226.

89. Sterkx, *The Free Negro in Ante-Bellum Louisiana,* 240, 283.

90. Ibid., 246.

91. Mills, *Natchitoches, 1729–1803,* entry 2868.

92. Ibid., 3451.

93. Ibid., 3448. Besson was actually one-quarter Chitimacha; but both he and his half-Chitimacha mother lived as white in Natchitoches society and his family intermarried with whites exclusively.

94. Mills, *Natchitoches Church Marriages, 1818–1850,* entry 316.

95. Ibid., entry 486.

96. Ibid., entry 392. Brevel also had Native American ancestry, being one-eighth Caddo; like Besson, his family was considered white at Natchitoches and intermarried with whites exclusively.

97. Ibid., entry 152.

98. Succession of Susanne Metoyer, Natchitoches Succ. file 355, NCCO.

99. Roubieu v. Metoyer, Natchitoches District Court suit no. 1395, NCCO.

100. Henry Clement Papers, Melrose Collection. Because many of Cane River's Creoles of color descended from a family of white Le Courts/LaCours, who openly acknowledged the relationship, it should be noted that the Pierre LaCour in the quoted record did *not* belong to that family and no blood ties fostered his friendship with Auguste Metoyer. Three distinct families of the surname Le Court/LaCour, from three distant areas of France, were among the settlers of early Natchitoches.

101. Interview with confidential source, April 26, 1974; Mrs. Coutii to author, June 5, 1974.

102. Olmsted, *Journey in the Seaboard Slave States,* 636.

103. James T. Flint, "Reminiscences of the Long Ago," p. 2, MS, Melrose Collection. Flint also categorically stated that there existed but one exception to the observations made above: Carroll Jones of Rapides Parish. Jones, after being devastated by the Civil War, settled on Isle Brevelle, converted to Catholicism, rebuilt his fortunes, and soon became one of the most prominent men in the Cane River community. *Biographical and Historical Memoirs of Northwest Louisiana,* 353; interview with Mrs. Coutii, Mar. 24, 1974; interview with confidential source, Apr. 26, 1974.

104. Olmsted, *Journey in the Seaboard Slave States,* 634.

105. Mills, "Miscegenation and the Free Negro in Antebellum 'Anglo' Alabama," 32.

106. Succession of Mme. Charles Melonguet, May 1850, folder 1101, Cane River Notarial Records.

107. Sarpy v. Hertzog, Natchitoches District Court suit 6489 (1866), NCCO.

108. Chaler v. Birt and Metoyer, Natchitoches District Court suit 1782 (1838), NCCO.

109. Quoted in Kunkel, "Modifications in Louisiana Legal Status," 4.

110. Johnston, *Race Relations in Virginia,* 312.

111. Sterkx, *Free Negro in Ante-bellum Louisiana,* 165.

112. D[aniel] C. Scarborough, quoted in "Colored Slave Owners and Traders in the Old Days," *American Methodist Episcopal Church Review* 29 (January 1913): 300–3, particularly p. 302.

113. For example, one of the inherited books treasured by a descendant of Emanuel Dupré in the 1970s was a well-worn 1832 edition of *The Civil Code of Louisiana.*

9. Economic and Social Decline

1. 1830–60 U.S. censuses, Natchitoches Parish, pop. schs.; 1850–60 U.S. censuses, slave schs.; calculations by the authors.

2. 1850–60 U.S. censuses, Natchitoches Parish, agri. schs.; census and land calculations by the authors.

3. Franklin, *The Free Negro in North Carolina,* 17, 157, 159. 1860 U.S. census, Natchitoches Parish, pop. sch., calculations by the authors. Also, 1860 U.S. census, Natchitoches Parish, slave sch., p. 25 (penned), J. B. C. [A.] Metoyer, 23 slaves; p. 26 (penned), F. F. Metoyer, 23 slaves; pp. 26–27 (penned), F. J. [G.] Metoyer, 31 slaves. Numerous others held 12–20 slaves.

4. Koger, *Black Masters,* 138–39.

5. Schweninger, *Black Property Owners in the South,* 112–14.

6. Sterkx, *The Free Negro in Ante-Bellum Louisiana,* 238, for statewide statistics. Metoyer-kin statistics from the 1860 census are calculated by the authors.

7. 1860 U.S. census, Natchitoches Parish, La., pop. sch., p. 45, dwelling/family 366, "Florin Conor," with $5,000 personalty/slaves and $35,000 real estate; also p. 46, dwelling/family 376, [Mme.] "J. B. A. Metoyer," with personalty of $10,000 and $40,000 real estate. This census also asserts that Fanny Chevalier, the 45-year-old multiracial placée of the deceased French-born Louis Chevalier, held $80,000 in personalty and $5,325 in real estate. If accurate, those figures would make her the wealthiest free person of color in the parish. The realty figure shown for her is in line with parish conveyance records and federal land records for the Chevaliers; however, the much larger personalty figure—which represented slaves, household goods, and farm equipment—errs radically. The corresponding slave schedule for that year reports just six slaves for Mme. Chevalier and seven for her son next door. The value of those slaves, in their economy, would have neared $8,000 rather than $80,000. See pop. sch., p. 69, dwelling/family 609, "F. Chevalier"; and slave sch., p. 35, for E. and F. Chevalier. The Natchitoches census taker of 1860, the twenty-five-year-old Anglo newcomer Dr. John W. Thomas, had immense trouble communicating with the French households that he visited.

8. 1860 U.S. census, Plaquemines Parish, La., pop. sch., p. 32, dwelling 231, family 355, "Annette Durnford."

9. Francis A. Walker, *A Compendium of the Ninth Census, June 1, 1870,* 3 vols. (Washington, D.C.: Government Printing Office, 1872), 3: 3, 10, for the differences between assessed and "true" value in 1850–70. Calculations for Cane River censuses by the authors. Calculations for modern currency equivalent drawn from Officer and Williamson, "Purchasing Power of Money in the United States."

10. Sterkx, *The Free Negro in Ante-Bellum Louisiana,* 217; Roger W. Shugg, *Origins of Class Struggle in Louisiana: A Social History of White Farmers and Laborers during Slavery and After, 1840–1875* (Baton Rouge: LSU Press, 1939), 8, 86.

11. McGuire Diary, 13.

12. Ibid., 13–14.

13. Ibid., 19–27; Letter, James Hurst to [unknown], Jan. 1843, in Natchitoches Parish Records, 1734–1916, LLMVC, LSU Special Collections.

14. James L. Watkins, *King Cotton: A Historical and Statistical Review, 1790 to 1908* (1908; rpr. New York: Negro Universities Press, 1969), 197.

15. Calculated by the authors from Index to the Records of the District Court, NCCO, and from the subsequent review of pertinent files.

16. Records to reconstruct the family of Auguste and Melite are incomplete, due to the unavailability for study of most of New Orleans's sacramental records. What is known for their children is this: (a) Nelcourt Metoyer was born September 10, 1827, and died before the 1830 census; for his baptism, see St. François Parish, Reg. 7, entries in chronological sequence. (b) Augustin Paulin Metoyer, born June 29, 1829 (Reg. 7), died September 15, 1836, and was buried on the Isle; see St. François, Reg. 15. (c) Emilie Metoyer appears to have been born in New Orleans, about 1833–34, according to later census data.

17. Auguste Metoyer of Bapt. Adlé, Natchitoches Conv. Book 24:67; Adlé v. Metoyer, District Court Record Book "Oct. 1830–Apr. 1840": 399; both NCCO. When Auguste's financial difficulties began, his white partner in New Orleans, Antoine Jonau, severed their partnership and formed a new business alliance with a well-to-do white matron of that city. Yet, by 1842, Jonau was

bankrupt also. Dissolution of Partnership of Antoine Jonau and Dame Blanchard, Morin Papers (MS in possession of Mrs. Noble Morin, Natchez, La.); also *Faures v. Metoyer,* 6 Rob. 75 (1843).

18. Auguste Metoyer to Lestan Prudhomme, Notarial Record Book 25:351–52; Augustin Metoyer to Children, Donations Book 30:74; Auguste Metoyer to J. B. Adlé, Notarial Record Book 34:199, all in NCCO. Also, *Adlé v. Metoyer,* 1 La. Ann. 254 (1846); and *Adlé v. Anty,* 5 La. Ann. 631 (1850).

19. For the rights of and restrictions upon property-holding wives in Louisiana vis-à-vis the Anglo-rooted states, see Vaughn Baker, Amos Simpson, and Mathé Allain, "*Le Mari Est Seigneur:* Marital Laws Governing Women in French Louisiana," in *The French Experience in Louisiana,* ed. Glenn R. Conrad (Lafayette: Center for Louisiana Studies, 1995), 470–78; and Marylynn Salmon, *Women and the Law of Property in Early America* (Chapel Hill: University of North Carolina Press, 1986). More specifically for Louisiana's traditional law, see *Las Siete Partidas,* trans. Samuel Parsons Scott, vol. 4 of *Family, Commerce, and the Sea: The Worlds of Women and Merchants* (Philadelphia: University of Penn. Press, 2001), 933–34 and 943–44, for Part. IV, Title XI, Laws VII and XXIX. Also Morgan, *Civil Code of the State of Louisiana,* 312–23, for Book III, Title VI.

20. Auguste Metoyer to Melite Anty, Natchitoches Conv. Books 35:64 and 39:606; also see Conv. Book 46:543; all in NCCO.

21. *Adlé v. Anty,* 5 La. Ann 631 (1850); *Adlé v. Metoyer,* 1 La. Ann. 254 (1846); *Anty v. Adlé,* 9 La. Ann. 490 (1854).

22. Succession of Auguste Metoyer, Natchitoches Succ. file 1015, NCCO.

23. Rivarde & Co. v. Metoyer; Natchitoches District Court suit 3603, NCCO; Writ of seizure to William Cannon, constable, on property of Charles Coton-Maïs, undated (but post-Aug. 29, 1845, the date after which interest accrues), folder 849, Cane River Notarial Records.

24. *Natchitoches Semi-Weekly Times,* Mar. 2, 1867.

25. Olmsted, *Journey in the Seaboard Slave States,* 628. Observations on the availability of land are made by the authors from a study of federal tract books and plat maps for the parish.

26. Observations on family and migration patterns among Cane River whites are drawn by E. S. Mills from personal study over four decades; no published study exists yet for these points.

27. Francophone sentiments and organizational news appeared regularly in the newspapers of Louisiana's old French communities—in both New Orleans and the rural parishes. Along Cane River, it was a consistent theme among Creole elders interviewed in the 1970s. McCants, in the introduction to her translated edition of Rodolphe Lucien Desdunes's *Les Cenelles,* notes the persistence of Francophone sentiments among Creoles of color as late as 1896, when a visitor to Louisiana observed, "In their determination to repel all encroachments of the despised *Améri-cains* they remained more French . . . than the Parisians themselves." McCants in Desdunes, *Our People and Our History,* xxii, citing George W. Cable, *Creoles and Cajuns: Stories of Old Louisiana,* ed. Arlin Turner (Garden City, N.Y.: Doubleday, 1959), 1.

28. Interview with Mrs. Coutii, Mar. 24, 1974.

29. "The Re-Annexation of Texas; in Its Influence on the Duration of Slavery," *United States Magazine and Democratic Review* 15 (July 1844): 14.

30. David O. Whitten, *Andrew Durnford: A Black Sugar Planter in Antebellum Louisiana* (Natchitoches, La.: Northwestern State University Press, 1981), 58, 61–62, 103, 125; Brasseaux, Fontenot, and Oubre, *Creoles of Color in the Bayou Country,* 81–85.

31. Mrs. Coutii to author, Apr. 15, 1974; interview with confidential source, Apr. 26, 1974. The Dupré great-great-aunt Augusta, whom Mrs. Coutii thought to be the wife of "Omar" Chevalier, died young. No "Omar" Chevalier has been found in the family.

32. For Gustave Leon Chevalier and Marie Lida Metoyer, see Natchitoches Conv. Book 50:194, marriage contract, 1856, NCCO. Also, 1870 U.S. census, Orleans Parish, La., pop. sch., New Or-

leans, Seventh Ward, p. 86, dwell. 515, fam. 789, Gustave Chevalier household; 1880 U.S. census, Orleans Parish, pop. sch., City of New Orleans, ED 28, p. 13, dwell. 52, fam. 101, Firmin Christophe. One later census record identifies Gustave's brother Hypolite Chevalier, boarding in a white household in the town of Natchitoches, as "born in Mexico" about 1842. That assertion errs. Possibly it reflected an attempt to identify with the Spanish-Mexican culture that became North Louisiana's new "third caste" in the Jim Crow era. See 1880 U.S. census, Natchitoches Parish, pop. sch., ED 28, p. 33, dwell. 154, fam. 185, "Hyp. Chevallier."

33. James G. Hollandsworth Jr., *The Louisiana Native Guards: The Black Military Experience during the Civil War* (Baton Rouge: LSU Press, 1995), 3.

34. J. W. Dorr, "A Tourist's Description of Louisiana in 1860," *Louisiana Historical Quarterly* 21 (Oct. 1938): 1170.

35. *Natchitoches Union*, Nov. 21, 1861, Apr. 17, 1862, and Dec. 18, 1862 (for quoted passage). For the illicit cotton trade along Red River, see Gary B. Mills, "Alien Neutrality and the Red River Campaign: A Study of Cases Heard before the International Claims Commissions," *Southern Studies* 16 (Summer 1977): 181–200; and Gary B. Mills, "Alexandria, Louisiana: A 'Confederate' City at War with Itself," *Red River Valley Historical Review* 5 (Winter 1980): 23–36. Considerably more details are provided in U.S. District Court, Southern District of Illinois, *The United States v. 650 Bales of Cotton, etc.* . . . (Springfield: Bronson & Nixon, Printers, 1865?), a rare publication for which a copy is filed in James Cumming's claim no. 94, Mixed Commission of British and American Claims; Record Group 76, Records of the Boundary and Claims Commissions and Arbitrations, National Archives.

36. Robert N. Scott et al., eds., *War of the Rebellion: A Compilation of the Official Records of the Union and Confederate Armies* (Washington, D.C.: Government Printing Office, 1880–1901), 34: 505, 561.

37. Edwin C. Bearss, ed., *A Louisiana Confederate: Diary of Felix Pierre Poché* (Natchitoches, La.: Northwestern State University Press, 1972), 101; Richard Taylor, *Destruction and Reconstruction: Personal Experiences of the Late War* (New York: D. Appleton & Co., 1890), 181.

38. John Scott, *Story of the Thirty-Second Iowa Infantry Volunteers* (Nevada, Ia.: J. Scott, 1896), 127–28.

39. *Natchitoches Union*, Oct. 9, 1862.

40. Ibid., Nov. 27 and Dec. 11, 1862.

41. Ibid., Dec. 11, 1862. Only the first initial is given for most of the names on this list, making it impossible to determine whether some of the donors were free people of color or white.

42. Suzette A. Morin (decd.) Claim, Commission no. 13578, and Gassion Metoyer Claim, Comm. no. 43576, Southern Claims Commission [hereinafter SCC], Record Group 56, General Records of the Department of Treasury, National Archives.

43. Quoted by Arthur W. Bergeron Jr., "Free Men of Color in Gray," *Civil War History* 32 (Sept. 1986): 254, citing "Alexander S. Dupre to wife, Sept. 29, Oct. 2, 1864, Melrose Collection." The Dupré family at that time had no male named Alexander. Bergeron appears to have mistaken "Ambroise" for "Alexander"; the writer should be Ambroise Sévère Dupré, son of Emanuel. It was Ambroise's widow who reared this book's informant, Mrs. Coutii, and shaped many of her ideas.

44. Bergeron, "Free Men of Color in Gray," 251–53, recounts the Grappe episode. The white conscription officer's kinship to the Metoyer family can be easily tracked through the previously cited volumes of translated church records published by E. S. Mills and Judy Riffel.

45. Hollandsworth, *The Louisiana Native Guards*, 1–2, quoting *New Orleans Daily Picayune*, Apr. 21, 1861.

46. Andrew B. Booth, comp., *Records of Louisiana Confederate Soldiers and Louisiana Confederate Commands*, 3 vols. (New Orleans: State of Louisiana, 1920), 2:325, 332; 3:956. Booth, 1:113,

identifies a Paul Balthasar who may or may not have been from Cane River. Two Paul Balthasars of appropriate age existed in Louisiana at that time: one on Cane River and one in New Orleans; the New Orleans man is the more logical candidate.

47. Bergeron, "Free Men of Color in Gray," 248; John D. Winters, *The Civil War in Louisiana* (Baton Rouge: LSU Press, 1963), 34. Sterkx, *The Free Negro in Ante-Bellum Louisiana*, 213, mistakenly reports only one such unit for Cane River.

48. *Natchitoches Union*, Dec. 26, 1861.

49. Testimonies of Clémire Metoyer and Joseph E. Dupré, Adelaïde Céleste Le Normand Claim, no. 209; French and American Claims Commission Files, Records of the Boundary and Claims Commissions and Arbitrations. Le Normand was the widow of the murdered Dr. Jean Napoleon Burdin. For the quotation, see *Natchitoches Union*, May 1, 1862.

50. *Natchitoches Union*, Dec. 26, 1861; obituary of Ernest LeGendre, *Natchitoches Union*, Feb. 20, 1862.

51. Mrs. Coutii to author, Apr. 15, 1974; interview with Mrs. Coutii, Apr. 26, 1974. Sévère's copy of Casey's manual and Emanuel's cavalry sword were both owned by Mrs. Coutii in the 1970s.

52. Winters, *Civil War in Louisiana*, 35.

53. *Natchitoches Union*, Mar. 27 and May 1, 1862. One circumstance may or may not have affected the Guards on Cane River. Louisiana's legislature, by statute of Feb. 15, 1862, disbanded all existing militia and then reorganized them; but the new law limited participation to white males. By gubernatorial order of March 24, 1862, Native Guard units were reinstated. The five-week interval allowed more than sufficient time for the Cane River units to be informed of the disbanding, but no record has been found to suggest their reaction. For the statute and governor's order, see Hollandsworth, *The Louisiana Native Guards*, 8.

54. Testimony of Joseph E. Dupré, in Adelaïde Céleste Le Normand, French and American Claim no. 209.

55. Gary B. Mills, "Patriotism Frustrated: The 'Native Guards' of Confederate Natchitoches," *Louisiana History* 18 (Fall 1977): 444. Also Testimony of Philippe Poeté in Philippe Poeté (Adm.), French and American Claim no. 399; and testimony of Clémire Metoyer, in Adelaïde Céleste Le Normand, French and American Claim no. 209.

56. *Natchitoches Union*, Jan. 9 and Mar. 6, 1862.

57. For the bounty, see Mary F. Berry, "Negro Troops in Blue and Gray: The Louisiana Native Guards, 1861–63," *Louisiana History* 8 (Spring 1967): 176.

58. The Port Hudson episode and General Banks's rancor toward the black officers of the Corps d'Afrique are extensively explored in Hollandsworth, *The Louisiana Native Guards*, chaps. 5–7. For Felicién specifically, see Compiled Military Service Record, Felician Balthazar (Pvt., Co. A, 20th U.S. Col. Inf., Corps d'Afrique; Co. G, 91st U.S. Col. Inf.; and Co. D, 74th U.S. Col. Inf., La.); Carded Records, Volunteer Organizations, Civil War; Records of the Adjutant General's Office, 1780s–1917, Record Group 94, National Archives. Also, Natchitoches Marriage Book 3, 1866–1869, pp. 117–18, Pierre Felicien Baltasar and Marie Laura Christophe (1866); 1860 U.S. census, Natchitoches Parish, p. 70, dwell. 613, fam. 613, "F. P. Balthzar"; 1870 U.S. census, Natchitoches Parish, pop. sch., Ward 10, p. 4, dwell. 30, fam. 30, "Felicien Balthazard"; 1880 U.S. census, Natchitoches Parish, pop. sch., Ward 9, ED 29, p. 16 [overwritten with 15], no dwelling/family divisions, "Felicien Balthazar"; 1900 U.S. census, Natchitoches Parish, pop. sch., Ward 1, ED 70, sheet 6-B, dwell. 116, "Peter F. Balthasar" (now a cobbler renting a house in the town of Natchitoches); 1910 U.S. census, Natchitoches Parish, pop. sch., Ward 9, ED 92, sheet 37-B, dwell. 628, fam. 598, "Laura Balthazar, widow."

59. 1890 U.S. census, veterans' schedule, Natchitoches Parish; Hugh LaCour to author, Mar. 5, 1974, for recollection of Henry Johnson. According to LaCour, his maternal grandfather, Joseph

Leonard Prudhomme, also fought on the Union side, but that service has not been documented. One "Victor David" is also reputed to have served, but the Davids belonged to the Camptí community of free people of color and no Victor of appropriate age has been found among them.

60. Cloyd Bryner, *Bugle Echoes: The Story of Illinois 47th* (Springfield, Ill.: Phillips Bros., 1905), 99. For the effect that the Red River Campaign had upon the valleys of the Cane and the Red, see Mills, "Alien Neutrality and the Red River Campaign," 181–200; Mills, "Patriotism Frustrated: The 'Native Guards' of Confederate Natchitoches," 437–51; and Mills, "Alexandria, Louisiana: A 'Confederate' City at War with Itself," 23–36.

61. Testimony of Lt. F. L. Grappe, C.S.A., in Charles C. Bertrand, French and American Claim no. 345; Bearss, *A Louisiana Confederate,* 102.

62. John A. Bering and Thomas Montgomery, *History of the Forty-Eighth Ohio Veterans Volunteer Infantry* (Hillsboro, Ohio: Highland News Office, 1880), 129.

63. John M. Gould, *History of the First- Tenth- Twenty-Ninth Maine Regiment* (Portland: S. Berry, 1871), 434.

64. Edward B. Lufkin, *History of the Thirteenth Maine Regiment* (Bridgton, Me.: H. A. Shorey & Son, 1898), 87.

65. Winters, *Civil War in Louisiana,* 365–66; Pellet, *History of the 114th Regiment, N.Y.S.V.,* 229.

66. Taylor, *Destruction and Reconstruction,* 193.

67. Sarah A. Dorsey, *Recollections of Henry Watkins Allen* (New York: M. Doolady, 1866), 279–80, 382.

68. Callahan et al., *History of St. Augustine's Parish,* 27; interview with confidential source, Apr. 26, 1974; interview with Tillman Chelettre, Sr., Oct. 12, 1974; interview with Mrs. Coutii, Mar. 24, 1974; Mrs. Coutii to author, Apr. 15, 1974; Hugh LaCour to author, Feb. 19, 1974. Several Barthelemy LeCours lived on Cane River at the time, the original man of that name having multiple sons, as well as grandsons, who were his namesakes; which of them was recalled in this account is undetermined. The portrait of Augustin remained damaged for three-quarters of a century until the white owner of the former Louis Metoyer plantation offered to have it repaired at her expense in exchange for the right to hang it in that plantation home.

69. Harris S. Beecher, *Record of the 114th Regiment, N.Y.S.V.* (Norwich, N.Y.: J. F. Hubbard Jr., 1866), 304; emphasis added.

70. Callahan et al., *The History of St. Augustine's Parish,* 20–21.

71. For firsthand accounts of the Burdin affair, see the testimony of Clémire and Gassion Metoyer and Charles and Joseph E. Dupré, in Adelaïde Céleste Le Normand (Mme. Burdin), French and American Claim no. 209.

72. For identities of the 478 British claimants, see Donna Rachal Mills, "Civil War Claims Commissions: The Mixed Commission of British and American Claims," *National Genealogical Society Quarterly* 75 (June 1987): 141–52. For the 22,282 American claimants, see Gary B. Mills, *Southern Loyalists in the Civil War—The Southern Claims Commission: A Composite Directory of Case Files Created by the U.S. Commissioner of Claims, 1871–1880 . . .* (Baltimore: Genealogical Publishing Co., 1994). No comparable guide and index has been published to the French and American claims, but the Red River claimants are extensively discussed in Mills, "Alien Neutrality and the Red River Campaign," and Mills, "Alexandria, Louisiana: A 'Confederate' City at War with Itself."

73. Antoine Tourres, Claim no. 229; Charles Bertrand, Claim no. 345; Rev. Jean Marie Beaulieu, Claim no. 468 (also Jean E. Chauvin, adm., for Rev. Thomas Auguste Rebours of Avoyelles, Claim 238), all in French and American Claims Commission; *Dupleix v. Gallien,* 21 La. Ann. 534 (1869).

74. Jerome Sarpy Claim, SCC Comm. no. 43582; Emilie Kirkland Claim, SCC Comm. no. 41317; Suzette A. Morin (decd.) Claim, SCC Comm. no. 13578; Gassion Metoyer Jr. Claim, SCC Comm.

no. 43576; Jean Conant (Tutor for Annie Metoyer and Others) Claim, SCC Comm. no. 43566; Jean Conant Claim, SCC Comm. no. 43565.

75. Claims cited in note 74 above; Beecher, *Record of the 114th Regiment, N.Y.S.V.*, 328; Pellet, *History of the 114th Regiment*, 225.

76. Suzette A. Morin (decd.) Claim, SCC Comm. no. 13578; Gassion Metoyer Jr. Claim, SCC Comm. no. 43576; Jerome Sarpy Claim, SCC Comm. no. 43582.

77. Suzette A. Morin (decd.) Claim, SCC Comm. no. 13578.

78. Ibid.

79. Emilie Kirkland Claim, SCC Comm. no. 41317.

80. Ibid.

81. Gassion Metoyer Jr. Claim, SCC Comm. no. 43576.

82. Emilie Kirkland Claim, SCC Comm. no. 41317.

83. Suzette A. Morin (decd.) Claim, SCC Comm. no. 13578; Gassion Metoyer Jr. Claim, SCC Comm. no. 43576.

84. Suzette A. Morin (decd.) Claim, SCC Comm. no. 13578.

85. Emilie Kirkland Claim, SCC Comm. no. 41317.

86. *Natchitoches Semi-Weekly Times*, May 26, 1866 ("Ruined"), Sept. 12, 1866 ("What we predicted").

87. Susan E. Dollar, *The Freedmen's Bureau Schools of Natchitoches Parish, Louisiana, 1865–1868* (Natchitoches, La.: Northwestern State University Press, 1998), 59, quoting R. C. Buchanan, Asst. Comm. to E. Whittelsey, January 31, 1868.

88. *Natchitoches Semi-Weekly Times*, Feb. 4, 1866, for advertisement by Mrs. Achille Prud-homme offering her 2,000-acre plantation for three years to anyone who would agree to pay the taxes. Interview with Armelina Morin Chelettre, Oct. 12, 1974.

89. 1860–1870 U.S. censuses, Natchitoches Parish, La., pop. and agri. schs.; calculations by the authors; 1860 slave figures for Louisiana drawn from University of Virginia Libraries, *Historical Census Browser*, database (http://mapserver.lib.virginia.edu/php/state.php).

90. Ibid.

91. Germaine A. Reed, "Race Legislation in Louisiana, 1864–1920," *Louisiana History* 6 (Fall 1965): 379–82.

92. Numerous descendants of the Metoyer family, as late as the 1970s, had preserved the registration certificates of their ancestors who registered in 1866 and 1867.

93. *Natchitoches Semi-Weekly Times*, May 22, 1867.

94. Walker, *Compendium of the Ninth Census*, 25; *Biographical and Historical Memoirs of Northwest Louisiana*, 302. The other nonwhite members of the police jury were Emile Silvie, J. B. Vienne, and Charles LeRoy.

95. *Biographical and Historical Memoirs of Northwest Louisiana*, 302. M. B. Llorens also ran for the police jury, on the Republican Ticket, in 1876 but was not elected; an original copy of that year's ballot was in possession of Mrs. Coutii in 1973.

96. Edward Jewett Brown, "History of Education in Natchitoches Parish" (M.A. thesis, Louisiana State University, 1932), 21.

97. Marguerite T. Leach, "The Aftermath of Reconstruction in Louisiana," *Louisiana Historical Quarterly* 32 (July, 1949): 651.

98. Joe Gray Taylor, *Louisiana Reconstructed, 1863–1877* (Baton Rouge: LSU Press, 1974), 507.

BIBLIOGRAPHY

Unpublished Documents, Interviews, and Letters

MANUSCRIPT COLLECTIONS

Church of the Nativity and Chapel of St. Rose, Camptí
 Parish Registers, 1839–1914

Coutii Papers, 1803–1943. In possession of Mrs. Lee Etta Vaccarini Coutii, Isle Brevelle, 1972

Dignowity, Anthony Michael (1810–1875) Journal, *ca.* 1830s. In possession of Nancy E. (Whittemore) Walker, Potomac, Md., 2004

Immaculate Conception Church, Natchitoches, La.
 Registers, Parish of St. François, 1729–1870
 Minutes of the Fabrique, 1849–

Louisiana State University, Baton Rouge, Louisiana and Lower Mississippi Valley Collection, Special Collections
 Badin, Norbert, Papers, 1829–1937, MSS 825
 Bertrand, Charles Jr., Papers, 1866–1928 [1676–1884], MSS 840, 867, 978
 Breazeale, Nita Sims, Family Papers, 1811–1981, MSS 2442
 Breda, Jean Philippe, Family Papers, 1776–1921, MSS 453, 966, 1021
 Carr, J. C. Letter, 1825, MSS 1464
 Chaplin, Breazeale, and Chaplin Papers, 1806–1904, MSS 952, 967, 1028
 Chelette, Attala and Family, 1819–1919, MSS 979
 [Dubreuil, Oscar] Anonymous Daybooks, 1856–1858, MSS 833
 Dupré, Metoyer & Company, Account Book, 1830–1837, 1873, MSS 834
 Lacour Family Papers, 1828, 1831, MSS 849

Metoyer, Adeleda, Papers, 1845–1897, MSS 836

Metoyer, Auguste, Papers, 1835–1846, MSS 834

Metoyer, Louis, Document, 1823, MSS 849

Metoyer Family Papers, 1900–1944, MSS 837, 846

Pre Aux Cleres Plantation Record Books, 1852, 1854, MSS 684

Prudhomme, P. Lestan, Family Papers, 1836–1868, MSS 625, 665

Roque, Pauline, Letter, 1859, MSS 849

Sarpy, Gerome, Documents, 1852, 1876, MSS 849

Tauzin, Marcelin, Family Papers, 1834–1844, MSS 912

Terrell, Miles, and Family, Papers, 1859–1929, MSS 843

Tyson, Robert A., Diary, 1863–1864, MSS 1143

Morin Family Papers. In possession of Mrs. Noble Morin, Isle Brevelle, 1972

Northwestern State University, Cammie Henry Research Center, Natchitoches

Clement, Henry, Papers

Derbanne Collection

Holmes, Jack D. L., Collection

Melrose Collection

Mignon, Francois, Collection

Safford Collection

St. Denis and Other Collection

St. Augustine Catholic Church, Isle Brevelle

Parish Registers, 1856–1900

St. John the Baptist Church, Cloutierville

Parish Registers, 1825–1920

St. Paul the Apostle Catholic Church, Mansura

Parish Registers, 1796–1840

St. Landry Catholic Church, Opelousas, Louisiana

Parish Registers, 1776–1805

Tulane University, Howard-Tilton Memorial Library, New Orleans

"A Visit to Melrose Plantation with Francois Mignon," recorded interview, Melrose, 1967

University of North Carolina, Chapel Hill

Mignon, Francois, Papers, 1853–1980, 1939–80

OFFICIAL RECORDS—UNPUBLISHED

France

Archives d'Aquitaine, Archives de la Gironde, Bordeaux

    Registres de la cathédrale Saint-André (Hertzog)

Archives Départementales de la Charente-Maritime, La Rochelle

    Registres paroissiaux de Fontcouvert and Taillebourg (Brosset)

    Registres paroissiaux de Saint-Denis d'Oléron (Rachal)

Archives Départementales de la Haute Savoie, Annecy

    Registres paroissiaux de Thonon-les-Bains (Buard)

Archives Départementales de Tarn-et-Garonne, Montauban

    Registres paroissiaux de Castelsagrat (Bossier)

Archives Départementales du Calvados, Caen

    Registres paroissiaux de Fimere (Le Court des Presles)

Archives Départementales du Finistère

    Registres paroissiaux de Camaret (Le Court des Presles)

Archives, Mairie de Reims

    Registres paroissiaux de Saint-Denis (Metoyer)

Archives Municipales, Dijon

    Registres paroissiaux de Notre-Dame et St. Médard (Poissot)

Archives Municipales, Marseille

    Registres paroissiaux de Accoules (Anty)

Archives Nationales, Paris

    Archives Criminelles, Greffe du Prévôté de l'Hotel

Archives d'Outre-Mer, Aix-en-Provence

    Colonies, Series C[13]

    Marines, Series B[1,2]

Bibliothèque de l'Arsénal

    Archives de la Bastille (Benoist)

Bibliothèque Nationale

    Dossiers Bleus, Nouveau d'Hozier, Pièces Originales (Le Court des Presles)

Mexico

Archivo General de la Nación, Mexico City

    Ramo de Provincias

Spain

Archivo General de Indias, Seville

    Audencia de Santo Domingo

    Papeles Procedentes de Cuba

United States

Center for Louisiana Studies, Lafayette

  Archives des Colonies

  Archives de la Marine

Historic New Orleans Collection, New Orleans

  Cane River Notarial Collection

Huntington Library, San Marino, Calif.

  Vaudreuil Papers (Pierre de Rigaud, Marquis de Vaudreuil), 1740–1753

Institute of Texan Cultures, University of Texas, San Antonio

  Bexar Archives

Louisiana State Archives, Baton Rouge

  U.S. Land Office Papers

  Opelousas Notarial Records Collection

Louisiana State Land Office, Baton Rouge

  Miscellaneous Land Documents, 1815–1917

  Register's Receipts, Natchitoches

  Township Plats and Sketches, District North of Red River

Louisiana State Museum—Historical Center, New Orleans

  Black Boxes

  Spanish Judicial Records

  Judicial Records of the French Superior Council

  T. P. Thompson Collection

Louisiana State University, Special Collections, Baton Rouge

  Louisiana and Lower Mississippi Valley Collection

    Natchitoches Estate Papers, 1783–1834, MSS 3476

    Natchitoches Parish Legal Documents, 1784–1849, MSS 3729

    Natchitoches Parish Miscellaneous Documents, 1801–1856, MSS 2914

    Natchitoches Parish Papers, 1732–1920, MSS 2917

    Natchitoches Parish Records, 1734–1916, MSS 480, 876, 929, 940, 961

  Louisiana Surveys Collection, MSS 552, 743, 933, 936, 955, 961, 3301

    Natchitoches Parish Surveys, 1681–1801, 1808–1837

Natchitoches Parish, Office of the Clerk of Court, Natchitoches

  Conveyances, 1800–1920 (including Donations, Mortgages, Marriages, Marriage Contracts), Natchitoches Parish Surveys Collection, 1808–1837

  District Court Files & Minutes, 1813–1884

  Judicial Mortgage Records, 1825–1865

  Marriage Registers, 1855–1939

  Miscellaneous Loose Documents (Special Files; personal office, Clerk of Court), 1733–1819

  Natchitoches Colonial Archives (aka Archive Conveyance Records)

  Notarial Registers (incomplete series), 1816–1852

Parish Court Files & Minutes, 1807–1880

Sheriff Sales, 1815–1881

Succession Registers & Packets, 1813–1900

[U.S.] Land Entry Registers, 1806–

Vacant Successions, 1807–1898

New Orleans

    Mortgage Archives

    Notarial Archives

Northwestern State University, Eugene P. Watson Memorial Library, Natchitoches

    Jack D. L. Holmes Collection, Documents Relating to Natchitoches and Adjacent Territory from Papeles de Estado and Papeles de Cuba, Archivo General de Indias, Seville; microfilm, 12 rolls.

Orleans Parish, New Orleans

    Conveyance and Succession Records

    District Court Records

    Orleans Parish Succession Files, New Orleans Public Library

Stephen F. Austin University, Nacogdoches, Texas

    Nacogdoches Archives

Texas State Archives & Library Commission, Austin

    Nacogdoches Archives

Tulane University, Howard-Tilton Memorial Library, New Orleans

    Enrollment Book, Parish of Natchitoches, 1864–1865 (including slaves and free negroes)

United States, Library of Congress (Manuscripts Division), Washington, D.C.

    Archives of Spanish Government of West Florida, 1782–1816

    East Florida Records, 1737–1858

    Louisiana Miscellany Collection, 1724–1837

    Marion Post Wolcott Photograph Collection, Prints & Photographs Division

United States, National Archives, Fort Worth, Texas

    Record Group 21, Records of U.S. District and other Courts in Louisiana

United States, National Archives, Washington, D.C.

    Record Group 29, Bureau of the Census

        Third through Thirteenth Censuses, State of Louisiana, 1810–1910 (Agricultural, Population and Slave Schedules; Social Statistics)

    Record Group 49, General Land Office

        Land Entry Files (Cash, Credit Prior, and Credit Under)

        Private Land Claim Files

    Record Group 56, Records of the Treasury

        Southern Claims Commission Files

    Record Group 76, Boundary and Claims Commissions

        French and American Claims Commission Records

Mixed Commission of British and American Claims
Record Group 205, Court of Claims Section, Department of Justice
Case Files, 1855–1945; Dockets, 1855–1914

PERSONAL INTERVIEWS

Bernard, Rosa Metoyer, Isle Brevelle
Broussard, Msgr. Milburn, St. John the Baptist Church, Cloutierville
Chelettre, Tillman, Sr., and Armeline (Roque) Chelettre, Isle Brevelle
Coutii, Lee Etta (Vaccarini), Isle Brevelle
DeBlieux, Robert B., Natchitoches
Enright, Lela (Grandchampt), Port Arthur, Tex.
Guidry, Harlan Mark, Galveston, Tex.
Jones, Lewis Emory, and Goria (Sers) Jones, Isle Brevelle
LaCour, Hugh, Shreveport
Mignon, Francois, Natchitoches
Morin, Mr. and Mrs. Noble, Natchez, La.
Rachal, Anthony, Xavier University, New Orleans
Rachal, Armella, Cloutierville
Watson, Arthur Chopin, Natchitoches

PERSONAL LETTERS

Archivo Segreto Vaticano, Secretary of, Vatican City, April 6, 1974
Broussard, Msgr. Milburn, Cloutierville, March 15, 1974
Coutii, Lee Etta Vaccarini, Natchez, 1974–1984
Guidry, Harlan Mark, Galveston, Tex., 1982–2013
LaCour, Hugh, Shreveport, 1974–1976
LaCour, Vanue B., Baton Rouge, 1974–1975
Mignon, Francois, Natchitoches, 1972–1974
Mullon, Joseph B., III, Calumet City, Ill., 2004–2013
Vansina, Jan, Madison, Wisc., May 12, 1973
Watson, Arthur Chopin, Natchitoches, 1972–1984
Wilson, Samuel, Jr., New Orleans, July 31, 1973

Published Materials

NEWSPAPERS

Alexandria Gazette & Planters Intelligencer, 1828–1830

Chicago Tribune, August 1, 1943

El Mexicano (Natchitoches), 1813

Louisiana Democrat (Alexandria), 1845, 1860

Louisiana Herald (Alexandria), 1818–1825

Louisiana Messenger & Alexandria Advertiser, 1827

Louisiana Populist (Natchitoches), 1894–1897

Louisiana State Gazette (New Orleans), 1826

Natchitoches Courier, 1825–1827

Natchitoches Populist, 1898

Natchitoches Semi-Weekly Times, 1866–1867

Natchitoches Times, 1872–1873

Natchitoches Union, 1861–1862

Natchitoches Weekly Populist, February 26, 1897

New Orleans Daily Delta, 1846–1853

New Orleans Daily Picayune, 1838–1876

New-Orleans Daily Telegraph, 1845

New Orleans Times Picayune, 1970–1972

Red River Republican (Alexandria), 1847–1853

Weekly Louisiana Gazette (New Orleans), 1825

OFFICIAL RECORDS—PUBLISHED
(INCLUDING GUIDES AND INDICES)

Acts Passed at the First Session of the First Legislature of the Territory of Orleans, 1806. New Orleans: Bradford & Anderson, 1807.

"The African American Community at Oakland: Community and Family Structure." National Park Service. *Cane River Creole National Historical Park: African American History.* http://www.nps.gov/cari/historyculture/african-american-history .htm.

American State Papers: Documents Legislative and Executive of the Congress of the United States. 38 vols. Washington, D.C.: Gales & Seaton, 1832–61.

Acts Passed at the Second Session of the First Legislature of the Terrritory of Orleans Begun . . . 12th Day of January [1807]. New Orleans: Bradford & Anderson, 1807.

Acts Passed at the First Session of the Second Legislature of the Territory of Orleans Begun . . . the Eighteenth of January 1808. New Orleans: Bradford & Anderson, 1808.

An Account of Louisiana, Being an Abstract of Documents in the Offices of the Department of State and of the Treasury. Philadelphia: William Duane, 1803.

Annals of Congress. 9th Cong., 1st Sess. (1805–1806).

Arthur, Stanley Clisby. *Index to the Archives of Spanish West Florida, 1782–1810.* New Orleans: Polyanthos, 1975.

Barron, Bill. *The Vaudreuil Papers: A Calendar and Index of the Personal and Private Records of Pierre de Rigaud de Vaudreuil, Royal Governor of the French Province of Louisiana, 1743–1753.* New Orleans: Polyanthos, 1975.

Benavides, Adán, Jr. *The Béxar Archives, 1717–1836.* Austin: University of Texas Press, 1989.

Bexar Archives Translations. Microfilm edition. 26 reels. Frederick, Md.: University Microfilms [ProQuest], 1989.

Bjork, David K. "Documents Relating to Alexandro O'Reilly and an Expedition Sent out by Him from New Orleans to Natchitoches, 1769–1770." *Louisiana Historical Quarterly* 7 (January 1924): 20–39.

Bolton, Herbert Eugene. *Athanase De Mézières and the Louisiana-Texas Frontier, 1768–1780.* 2 vols. Cleveland: Arthur H. Clark Co., 1914.

Booth, Andrew B., comp. *Records of Louisiana Confederate Soldiers and Louisiana Confederate Commands.* 3 vols. New Orleans: N.p. 1920.

Bouquard, Shirley Chaisson. *Marriage Dispensations in the Diocese of Louisiana and the Floridas: 1786–1803.* New Orleans: Polyanthos, 1980.

Carter, Clarence E., and John Porter Bloom, eds. *The Territorial Papers of the United States.* 28 vols. Washington, D.C.: Government Printing Office, 1934–1975.

Catterall, Helen Tunncliff, ed. *Judicial Cases Concerning American Slavery and the Negro.* 5 vols. Washington, D.C.: Carnegie Institute, 1932.

Civil Code of the State of Louisiana. New Orleans: J. C. de St. Romes, Printer, 1825.

Clark, Richard H., Thomas Read Rootes Cobb, and David Irwin. *The Code of the State of Georgia.* Atlanta: J. H. Seals, 1861.

Cobb, Thomas R. R. *An Inquiry into the Law of Negro Slavery in the United States of America.* 1858; rpr. New York: Negro Universities Press, 1968.

Cocke, N. W. *Reports of Cases Argued and Determined in the Supreme Court of Alabama during the June Term 1850 and a Part of January Term 1851.* Montgomery: J. H. & T. F. Martin, Printers, 1851.

Code Noir, ou Loi Municipal Servant de Reglement. New Orleans: A. Boudousquie, 1778.

Coker, William S., and G. Douglas Inglis. *The Spanish Censuses of Pensacola, 1784–1820.* Pensacola: Perdido Bay Press, 1980.

Compiled Edition of the Civil Codes of Louisiana. Baton Rouge: State of Louisiana, 1940.

Conrad, Glenn R. *First Families of Louisiana.* 2 vols. Baton Rouge: Claitor's Publishing Division, 1970.

———. *St. Charles: Abstracts of the Civil Records of St. Charles Parish, 1700–1803.* Lafayette: University of Southwestern Louisiana, 1974.

Crespi, Muriel. "A Brief Ethnography of Magnolia Plantation: Planning for Cane River Creole National Historical Park." Studies in Archeology and Ethnography, no. 4. National Park Service. *Archaeology Program.* http://www.nps.gov/archeology/pubs /studies/STUDY04A.htm.

De Bow, J. B. D., comp. *Statistical View of the United States. . . .* Washington, D.C.: Beverly Tucker, 1854.

———. *The Seventh Census of the United States: 1850, . . . An Appendix, Embracing Notes upon the Tables of Each of the States.* Washington, D.C.: Robert Armstrong, Public Printer, 1853.

De Ville, Winston. *Calendar of Louisiana Colonial Documents,* vol. 2, *St. Landry Parish, Part One.* Baton Rouge: Louisiana State Archives and Records Commission, 1964.

———. *Louisiana and Mississippi Lands: A Guide to Spanish Land Grants at the University of Michigan.* Ville Platte, La.: Evangeline Genealogical and Historical Society, 1985.

———. *Louisiana Troops, 1720–1770.* Fort Worth: American Reference Publishers, 1965.

———. *Natchitoches Documents, 1732–1785: A Calendar of Civil Records from Fort St. Jean Baptiste in the French and Spanish Province of Louisiana.* Ville Platte, La.: Smith Publications, 1994.

———. "Natchitoches Tax List for 1793." *Louisiana Genealogical Register* 18 (March 1971): 72–73.

———. *Southwest Louisiana Families in 1785: The Spanish Census of the Posts of Attakapas and Opelousas.* Ville Platte, La.: N.p., 1991.

Diocese of Baton Rouge, Catholic Church Records. 22 vols. Baton Rouge: The Diocese, 1978–ca. 2007.

Diocese of Baton Rouge, Catholic Church Records: Pointe Coupée Records, 1770–1900; Individuals without Surnames. Edited by Emilie G. Leumas and Roland Gravois. Baton Rouge: The Diocese, ca. 2007.

Ditchy, Jay K., trans. "Early Census Tables of Louisiana." *Louisiana Historical Quarterly* 13 (April 1930): 205–29.

Forsyth, Alice Daly Forsyth. *Louisiana Marriages: A Collection of Marriage Records from the St. Louis Cathedral in New Orleans during the Spanish Regime and the Early American Period, 1784–1806.* New Orleans: Polyanthos, 1977.

Greenlee, Marcia M., Afro-American Bicentennial Corporation. "National Register of Historic Places Inventory—Nomination Form: Melrose Plantation—Yucca Plantation." Undated, ca. 1974–76. Archived by National Park Service at http://pdfhost.focus .nps.gov/docs/NHLS/Text/72000556.pdf.

Greiner, Meinrad. *The Louisiana Digest, Embracing the Laws of the Legislature of a General Nature, Enacted from the Year 1804 to 1841, Inclusive, and in Force at This Last Period; Also an Abstract of the Decisions of the Supreme Court of Louisiana on the Statutory Law. . . .* New Orleans: Benjamin Levy, 1841.

Grover, Kathryn, and Janine V. da Silva. "Historic Resource Study: Boston African

American National Historic Site, 31 December 2002." National Park Service, *Boston African American National Historic Site*. http://www.cr.nps.gov/history/online _books/bost/hrs.pdf.

Hall, Gwendolyn Midlo. "Louisiana Freed Slave Records, 1719–1820." Database. *Ancestry .com*. http://search.ancestry.com/search/db.aspx?dbid=7382.

———. "Afro-Louisiana History and Genealogy, 1718–1820." Slave-sale database. *Ibiblio: The Public Library and Digital Archive*. http://www.Ibiblio.org/laslave/.

Heacock, Dee, transcriber. "Ambrose LeComte's Account Ledger, 1852–1856 (Pages 37–51)" and "Analysis of LeCompte's Ledger." National Park Service. *Cane River Creole National Historical Park: African American Slavery Archives*. http://www .nps.gov/cari/historyculture/african-american-slavery-archives.htm.

Hébert, Donald J. *Index of New Orleans Confirmations, 1789–1841*. Baton Rouge: Claitor's Publishing Division, 1984.

———. *Southwest Louisiana Records: Church and Civil Records of Settlers, 1750–1900*. 47 print vols. and CD edition. 1974–ca. 2001.

Hening, William Waller. *The Statutes at Large; Being a Collection of All the Laws of Virginia from the First Session of the Legislature in the Year 1619*, vol. 3. Philadelphia: Thomas DeSilver, 1823.

Hill, Roscoe R. *Descriptive Catalogue of the Documents Relating to the History of the United States in the Papeles Procedentes de Cuba Deposited in the Archivo General de Indias at Seville*. Washington, D.C.: Carnegie Institute, 1916.

Historic American Buildings Survey, 1941. Washington, D.C: National Park Service, 1941.

Holmes, Jack D. L. *Honor and Fidelity: The Louisiana Infantry Regiment and the Louisiana Militia Companies, 1766–1821*. Birmingham: N.p., 1965.

Houck, Louis. *The Spanish Régime in Missouri: A Collection of Documents*. 2 vols. Chicago: R. R. Donnelly & Sons, 1909.

Journals of the House of Representatives of the State of Louisiana, 1825–1827.

Journals of the Senate of the State of Louisiana, 1825–1827.

Kennedy, Joseph C. G. *Population of the United States in 1860*. Washington, D.C.: Government Printing Office, 1864.

Kinnaird, Lawrence, ed. *Spain in the Mississippi Valley, 1765–1794*. 3 vols. Washington, D.C.: Government Printing Office, 1949.

Leal, Carmen. *Translations of Statistical and Census Reports of Texas, 1782–1836, and Sources Documenting the Black in Texas, 1603–1803*. Microfilm edition, 3 rolls. San Antonio: Institute of Texan Culture, 1979.

Libro Primero de Confirmaciones de Esta Parroquia de Sn. Luis de la Nueva Orleans: Contener Folios y de Principio al Folio 1. New Orleans: Genealogical Research Society of New Orleans, 1967.

Maduell, Charles R., Jr. *Marriage Contracts, Wills and Testaments of the Spanish Colonial Period in New Orleans, 1770–1804*. Baton Rouge: Claitor's Publishing Division, 1969.

———. *New Orleans Marriage Contracts, 1804–1820: Abstracted from the Notarial Archives of New Orleans*. New Orleans: Polyanthos, 1977.

Martin, François Xavier. *Term Reports of Cases Argued and Determined in the Superior Court of the Territory of Orleans, 1809–1823*. 12 vols. New Orleans: N.p., 1854.

———. *Louisiana Term Reports, or Cases Argued and Determined in the Supreme Court of That State*. 8 vols. New Orleans: Various publishers, 1823–1830.

McAvoy, Thomas Timothy, Lawrence J. Bradley et al., eds. *Records of the Diocese of Louisiana and the Floridas*. Microfilm edition, 12 rolls. Notre Dame, Ind.: University of Notre Dame, 1967.

McCown, Susan. "Melrose Plantation (Yucca Plantation) . . . Written Historical and Architectural Data." HABS No. LA-2-69, September 18, 1985. Library of Congress. *American Memory*. http://memory.loc.gov.

McIlwaine, Henry Read. *Executive Journals of the Council of Colonial Virginia*. 6 vols. Richmond: Virginia State Library, 1925–66.

Menn, Joseph Karl. *The Large Slaveholders of Louisiana, 1860*. New Orleans: Pelican Publishing Co., 1964.

Merriam, William M. *Census Reports: vol. 5; Twelfth Census of the United States Taken in the Year 1900; Agriculture*, part 1, *Farms, Live Stock, and Animal Products*. Washington, D.C.: United States Census Office, 1902.

Message from the President of the United States Communicating Discoveries Made in Exploring the Missouri, Red River and Washita, by Captains Lewis and Clark, Doctor Sibley, and Mr. Dunbar. New York: A. & G. Way, Printers, 1806.

Michie, Thomas Johnson, ed. *The Encyclopedic Digest of Tennessee Reports . . . up to and Including Vol. 115, Tennessee Reports*. Charlottesville, Va.: Michie Co., 1907.

Mills, Elizabeth Shown. "Certificates of Naturalization, Natchitoches Parish, Louisiana, 1820–1850." *Louisiana Genealogical Register* 21 (March 1974): 85–93.

———. *Natchitoches, 1729–1803; Abstracts of the Catholic Church Registers of the French and Spanish Post of St. Jean Baptiste des Natchitoches in Louisiana*. New Orleans: Polyanthos, 1976.

———. *Natchitoches, 1800–1826: Translated Abstracts of Register Number Five of the Catholic Church Parish of St. François des Natchitoches in Louisiana*. 1980; rpr. Bowie, Md.: Heritage Books, 2004.

———. *Natchitoches Church Marriages, 1818–1850: Translated Abstracts from the Registers of St. François des Natchitoches, Louisiana*. 1985; rpr. Bowie, Md.: Willow Bend Books, 2004.

———. *Natchitoches Colonials: Censuses, Military Rolls, and Tax Lists, 1722–1803*. Chicago: Adams Press, 1981.

———. "Natchitoches Militia of 1782." *Louisiana Genealogical Register* 20 (September 1973): 216–18.

Mills, Gary B. *Southern Loyalists in the Civil War—The Southern Claims Commission: A Composite Directory of Case Files Created by the U.S. Commissioner of Claims, 1871–1880*. . . . Baltimore: Genealogical Publishing Co., 1994.

Moore, Thomas O. *Annual Message of Governor Thomas O. Moore to the Twenty-Eighth General Assembly of the State of Louisiana, January, 1864.* Shreveport: N.p., 1864.

Moreau Lislet, Louis. *A General Digest of the Acts of the Legislature of Louisiana: Passed from the Year 1804 to 1827, Inclusive; and in Force at this Last Period.* 2 vols. New Orleans: B. Levy, 1828.

Moreau Lislet, Louis, and Henry Carleton, trans. *The Laws of Las Siete Partidas Which are Still in Force in the State of Louisiana.* 2 vols. New Orleans: James M'Karaher, Printer, 1820.

Morgan, Thomas Gibbes, comp. and ed. *Civil Code of the State of Louisiana: With the Statutory Amendments, from 1825 to 1853, Inclusive.* . . . New Orleans: Bloomfield & Steel, 1853.

National Park Service. "Maison de Marie Thérèse." *Cane River National Heritage Area.* Undated, *ca.* 2004–5. http:www.nps.gov/history/nr/travel/caneriver/mai.htm.

North, S. D., Director, Bureau of the Census. *Special Reports: Supplementary, Analysis, and Derivative Tables; Twelfth Census of the United States, 1900.* Washington, D.C.: Government Printing Office, 1906.

Poret, Ory G. *Spanish Land-Grants in Louisiana, 1757–1802.* Ville Platte, La.: Provincial Press, 1999.

Poret, Ory G., and John Spencer Howell. *Louisiana Land Titles: An Inventory of Land Office Records at the State Archives.* Ville Platte, La.: Provincial Press, 2003.

Porteous, Laura L., trans. "Index to [Abstracts of] the Spanish Judicial Records of Louisiana." *Louisiana Historical Quarterly,* serialized, vols. 6–31 (1923–1948).

Portré-Bobinski, Germaine. *Natchitoches; Translations of Old French and Spanish Documents.* Natchitoches, La.: N.p., 1928.

Price, John Milton. *The Civil War Tax in Louisiana: 1865, Based on Direct Tax Assessments of Louisianians.* New Orleans: Polyanthos, 1975.

Prud'homme, Lucile Keator, and Fern B. Christensen. *The Natchitoches Cemeteries: Transcriptions of Gravestones from the Eighteenth, Nineteenth, and Twentieth Centuries in Northwest Louisiana.* New Orleans: Polyanthos, 1977.

Reports of Cases Argued and Determined in the Supreme Court of Louisiana. 52 vols. New Orleans: Various publishers, 1846–1900.

Reports of Cases Argued and Determined in the Supreme Court of the State of Louisiana. 19 vols. New Orleans: Various publishers, 1831–1841.

Riffel, Judy. *Calendar of St. Landry Parish, Louisiana, Civil Records,* vol. 1, *1803–1819.* Baton Rouge: Le Comité des Archives de la Louisiane, 1995.

———. *Genealogical Selections from the Acts of the Louisiana Legislature, 1804–1879.* Baton Rouge: Le Comité des Archives de la Louisiane, 2005.

———. *Natchitoches Baptisms, 1817–1840: Abstracts from Register 6 of St. Francis Catholic Church, Natchitoches, Louisiana.* Baton Rouge: Le Comité des Archives de la Louisiane: 2007.

———. *Natchitoches Baptisms, 1841–49: Abstracts from Register 9 of St. Francis Catholic Church, Natchitoches, Louisiana.* Baton Rouge: Le Comité des Archives de la Louisiane: 2010.

Robertson, Meritt M., comp. *Reports of Cases Argued and Determined in the Supreme Court of Louisiana.* 12 vols. New Orleans: Various publishers, 1842–1846.

Robichaux, Albert L., Jr., *Civil Registration of Orleans Parish Births, Marriages, and Deaths, 1790–1833.* Rayne, La.: Hebert Publications, 2000.

Ruff, Verda Jenkins. *The Cabildo Records of New Orleans, 1769–1785: An Index to Abstracts in the Louisiana Historical Quarterly.* Ville Platte, La.: Provincial Press, 1997.

St. Augustine Historical Society. *St. Augustine Catholic Church of Isle Brevelle: Index of Baptismal Records, Book 1, 1852–1889.* Natchitoches, La.: The Society, 2000.

Schneider, Elsa L. *Evidence of the Past: Primary Sources for Louisiana History; 1. Cane River Colony.* New Orleans: Historic New Orleans Collection, 1984.

Schweninger, Loren, ed. *A Guide to the Microfilm Edition of Race, Slavery, and Free Blacks,* series 2, *Petitions to Southern County Courts, 1775–1867,* part F, *Louisiana (1795–1863).* A UPA Collection from LexisNexis. *ProQuest.* http://cisupa.proquest.com/ksc_assets/catalog/1543.pdf

———. *Race, Slavery, and Free Blacks,* Series II, *Petitions to Southern County Courts, 1775–1867,* Part F: *Louisiana (1795–1863);* Series: Black Studies Research Sources, Microfilms from Major Archival and Manuscript Collections. Bethesda, Md.: UPA–LexisNexis, n.d. Online edition, University of North Carolina at Greensboro, *Digital Library on American Slavery.* http://library.uncg.edu/slavery.

Scott, Robert N., et al., eds. *The War of the Rebellion: A Compilation of the Official Records of the Union and Confederate Armies.* 130 vols. Washington, D.C.: Government Printing Office, 1880–1901.

Speers, Robert H. *Reports of Cases at Law, Argued and Determined in the Court of Appeals and Court of Errors of South Carolina . . . from November 1842 to [May 1844].* Columbia, S. C.: A. S. Johnson, Printer, 1844.

U.S. Congress. *Report of the Joint Committee on the Conduct of the War: At the Second Session, Thirty-Eighth Congress.* 3 vols. Washington, D.C.: Government Printing Office, 1865.

U.S. District Court, Southern District of Illinois. *The United States v. 650 Bales of Cotton, etc.; . . . Withenbury & Doyle Claimants of 935 Bales of Cotton; Grieff & Zunts, Claimants of 935 Bales of Cotton; G.A. Lemore & Co., Claimants of 830 Bales of Cotton: In Prize.* Springfield: Bronson & Nixon, Printers, 1865.

Voorhies, Jacqueline K., trans. and comp. *Some Late Eighteenth-Century Louisianians: Census Records. 1758–1796.* Lafayette: University of Southwestern Louisiana, 1973.

Walker, Francis A. *A Compendium of the Ninth Census (June 1, 1870).* Washington, D.C.: Government Printing Office, 1872.

Wells, Carolyn M., comp. *Index and Abstracts of Colonial Documents in the Eugene P. Watson Memorial Library.* Natchitoches, La.: Northwestern State University, 1980.

Woodson, Carter G., comp. and ed. *Free Negro Owners of Slaves in the United States in 1830, Together with Absentee Ownership of Slaves in the United States in 1830.* Washington, D.C.: The Association for the Study of Negro Life and History, 1924.

Works Progress Administration. *Survey of the Federal Archives in Louisiana: County-Parish Boundaries in Louisiana.* N.p.: N.p., 1939.

————. *Survey of the Federal Archives in Louisiana: Alphabetical and Chronological Digest of the Acts and Deliberations of the Cabildo, 1769–1803.* 10 vols. N.p.: N.p., 1939.

MEMOIRS, DIARIES, AND OTHER
CONTEMPORARY ACCOUNTS—PUBLISHED

Bacon, Edward. *Among the Cotton Thieves.* Detroit: Free Press Steam Book and Job Printing House, 1867.

Barbe-Marbois, François, Marquis de. *The History of Louisiana, Particularly of the Cession of That Colony to the United States of America.* Trans. from the French. Philadelphia: Carey & Lea, 1830.

Bartlett, Napier. *Military Record of Louisiana, Including Biographical and Historical Papers Relating to the Military Organizations of the State.* New Orleans: L. Graham & Co., 1875.

Bearss, E. C., ed. *A Louisiana Confederate: Diary of Felix Pierre Poché.* Natchitoches, La.: Northwestern State University, 1972.

Beauregard, H. T., Mrs. "Journal of Jean Baptiste Trudeau among the Arikara Indians in 1795." *Missouri Historical Society Collections* 4 (1912): 9–48.

Beecher, Harris H. *Record of the 114th Regiment, N.Y.S.V.* Norwich, N.Y.: J. F. Hubbard Jr., 1866.

Bering, John A., and Thomas Montgomery. *History of the Forty-Eighth Ohio Veterans Volunteer Infantry.* Hillsboro, Ohio: Highland News Office, 1880.

Biographical and Historical Memoirs of Northwest Louisiana. Nashville: Southern Publishing Co., 1890.

Bryner, Cloyd. *Bugle Echoes: The Story of Illinois 47th.* Springfield: Phillips Bros., 1905.

Buckingham, James Silk. *The Slave States of America.* 2 vols. London: Fisher, Son & Co., 1842.

Cartwright, Samuel A. "Diseases and Peculiarities of the Negro Race." *De Bow's Review* 4 (1851): 64–69.

Clamorgan, Cyprien. *The Colored Aristocracy of St. Louis.* St. Louis: N.p., 1858.

Clark, Orton S. *The One Hundred and Sixteenth Regiment of New York State Volunteers.* Buffalo: Printing House of Matthews and Warren, 1868.

Conrad, Glenn R., ed. *Dictionary of Louisiana Biography,* 2 vols. Lafayette: Louisiana Historical Association, 1988.

D'Antoni, Blaise C. "Some 1853 Cloutierville Yellow Fever Deaths." *New Orleans Genesis* 35 (June 1970): 261–62.

Dorr, J. W. "A Tourist's Description of Louisiana in 1860." *Louisiana Historical Quarterly* 22 (October 1938): 1110–1214.

Dorsey, Sarah A. *Recollections of Henry Watkins Allen.* New York: M. Doolady, 1866.

Ewer, James K. *The Third Massachusetts Cavalry in the War for the Union.* Maplewood, Mass.: Wm. G. J. Perry Press, 1903.

Flinn, Frank M. *Campaigning with Banks in Louisiana.* Lynn, Mass.: Thos. P. Nichols, 1887.

French, B. F., ed. *Historical Collections of Louisiana.* 5 vols. New York: D. Appleton & Company, 1851.

Gould, John M. *History of the First-Tenth-Twenty-Ninth Maine Regiment.* Portland: S. Berry, 1871.

Hanaburgh, D. H. *History of the One Hundred and Twenty-Eighth Regiment, New York Volunteers.* Poughkeepsie: Press of the Enterprise Publishing Co., 1894.

Holmes, Isaac. *An Account of the United States of America.* London: Caxton Press for H. Fisher, 1823.

Kneeland, Samuel, Dr. "The Hybrid Races of Animals and Men." *De Bow's Review* 19 (1855): 535–39.

Le nouveau parfait jardinier; ou, L'art de cultiver. Paris: Lebigre, 1835.

Le Page du Pratz, Antoine-Simon. *The History of Louisiana.* Trans. from the French, 1774; rpr. New Orleans: J. S. Harmanson, 1947.

Lewis, M. G. *Journal of a West India Proprietor, Kept during a Residence in the Island of Jamaica.* 1834; rpr. Boston: Houghton Mifflin, 1929.

Long, Edward. *The History of Jamaica.* 3 vols. London: T. Lowndes, 1774.

Lubbock, Francis R. *Six Decades in Texas.* Austin: Ben C. Jones and Co., 1900.

Lufkin, Edwin B. *History of the Thirteenth Maine Regiment.* Bridgton, Me.: H. A. Shorey & Son, 1898.

Martin, François Xavier. *The History of Louisiana from the Earliest Period.* 2 vols. New Orleans: Lyman and Beardslee, 1827; A. T. Penniman, 1829.

McCants, Dorothea Olga, trans. and ed. *They Came to Louisiana: Letters of a Catholic Mission, 1854–1882.* Baton Rouge: LSU Press, 1970.

Northup, Solomon. *Twelve Years a Slave.* Edited by Sue Eakin and Joseph Logsdon. Baton Rouge: LSU Press, 1968.

Olmsted, Frederick Law. *Journey in the Seaboard Slave States in the Years 1853–1854.* 1856; rpr. New York: Negro Universities Press, 1968.

———. *The Cotton Kingdom: A Traveller's Observations on Cotton and Slavery in the American Slave States.* Edited by Arthur M. Schlesinger. New York: Alfred A. Knopf, 1953.

"O'Reilly's Ordinance of 1770." *Louisiana Historical Quarterly* 11 (April 1928): 237–40.

Paris, Comte de (Louis Philippe Albert d'Orléans). *History of the Civil War in America.* 4 vols. Philadelphia: Porter & Coates, 1875–1888.

Pellet, Elias P. *History of the 114th Regiment, New York State Volunteers.* Norwich, N.Y.: Telegraph & Chronicle Press Print, 1866.

Powers, George W. *The Story of the Thirty-Eighth Regiment of Massachusetts Volunteers.* Cambridge, Mass.: Dakin & Metcalf, 1866.

Scarborough, D[aniel] C. "Colored Slave Owners and Traders in the Old Days." *American Methodist Episcopal South Review* 29 (January 1913): 300–3.

Scott, John. *Story of the Thirty-Second Iowa Infantry Volunteers.* Nevada, Iowa: N.p., 1896.

Shorey, Henry A. *The Story of the Maine Fifteenth*. Bridgton, Me.: Press of the Bridgton News, 1890.

Smith, Walter G. *Life and Letters of Thomas Kilby Smith*. New York: G. P. Putnam's Sons, 1898.

Stoddard, Major Amos. *Sketches, Historical and Descriptive, of Louisiana*. Philadelphia: Mathew Carey, 1812.

Stuart, James. *Three Years in North America*. 2 vols. New York: J. and J. Harper, 1833.

Taylor, Richard. *Destruction and Reconstruction: Personal Experiences of the Late War*. New York: D. Appleton and Company, 1890.

Tinker, Edward Larocque, ed. *Les Cenelles: Afro-French Poetry in Louisiana*. New York: Colophon, 1930.

Tunnard, W. H. *A Southern Record: The History of the Third Regiment, Louisiana Infantry*. 1866; rpr. Dayton, Ohio: Morningside Bookshop, 1970.

Willey, Nathan. "Education of the Colored Population of Louisiana." *Harper's New Monthly Magazine* 33 (1866): 246–50.

MONOGRAPHS, DICTIONARIES, DIRECTORIES & ENCYCLOPEDIAS

Acosta Rodríguez, Antonio. *La Población de Luisiana Española, 1763–1803*. Madrid: Ministerio de Asuntos Exteriores, 1979.

Alexander, Adele Logan. *Ambiguous Lives: Free Women of Color in Rural Georgia, 1789–1879*. Fayetteville: University of Arkansas Press, 1991.

Andreu Ocariz. *Movimientos Rebeldes de los Esclavos Negros durante el Dominio Español en Luisiana*. Zaragoza, Spain: Departamento de Historia Moderna, 1977.

Aptheker, Herbert, ed. *A Documentary History of the Negro People in the United States*. New York: Citadel Press, 1951.

Attwater, Donald. *Names and Name-Days*. London: Burns Oates & Washbourne, 1939.

Barr, Juliana. *Peace Came in the Form of a Woman*. Chapel Hill: University of North Carolina Press, 2007.

Baudier, Roger. *The Catholic Church in Louisiana*. New Orleans: A. W. Hyatt, printers, 1939.

Beckers, Henry F., et al. *A History of Immaculate Conception Catholic Church, Natchitoches, Louisiana, 1717–1973*. Natchitoches, La.: n.p., 1973.

Berlin, Ira. *Slaves without Masters: The Free Negro in the Antebellum South*. Oxford: Oxford University Press, 1974.

Billington, Ray Allen. *The Protestant Crusade, 1800–1860: A Study of the Origins of American Nativism*. 1938; rpr. Chicago: Quadrangle Books, 1964.

Blassingame, John W. *The Slave Community: Plantation Life in the Antebellum South*. New York: Oxford University Press, 1972.

Boles, John B., ed. *Masters & Slaves in the House of the Lord: Race & Religion in the American South, 1740–1870*. Lexington: University of Kentucky Press, 1988.

Bracey, John H., Jr., August Meier, and Elliott Rudwick, eds. *Free Blacks in America, 1800–1860.* Belmont, Calif.: Wadsworth Publishing Co., 1971.

Brasseaux, Carl A., Keith P. Fontenot, and Claude F. Oubre. *Creoles of Color in the Bayou Country.* Jackson: University Press of Mississippi, 1994.

Brathwaite, Edward. *The Development of Creole Society in Jamaica, 1770–1820.* Oxford: Clarendon Press, 1971.

Burton, H. Sophie, and F. Todd Smith. *Colonial Natchitoches: A Creole Community on the Louisiana-Texas Frontier.* College Station: Texas A&M University Press, 2008.

Cable, George W. *The Creoles of Louisiana.* New York: C. Scribner's Sons, 1884.

Callahan, J. J., et al. *The History of St. Augustine's Parish; Isle Brevelle, Natchez, La.; 1803–1953; 1829–1954; 1856–1956.* Natchitoches, La.: n.p., 1956.

Carvalho, Joseph, III. *Black Families in Hampton, Massachusetts.* 2nd ed. Boston: Newbury Street Press, 2011.

Chambers, Henry E. *A History of Louisiana.* 3 vols. New York: American Historical Society, 1925.

Chipman, Donald E., and Harriett Denise Joseph. *Notable Men and Women of Spanish Texas.* Austin: University of Texas Press, 1999.

Corley, D. B. *A Visit to Uncle Tom's Cabin.* Chicago: Laird & Lee, 1893.

Daniels, Roger. *Coming to America: A History of Immigration and Ethnicity in American Life.* Princeton, N.J.: HarperCollins, 1990.

Davis, Edwin Adams. *Louisiana: A Narrative History.* Baton Rouge: Claitor's Book Store, 1961.

Degler, Carl N. *Neither Black nor White: Slavery and Race Relations in Brazil and the United States.* New York: Macmillan, 1971.

Desdunes, Rodolphe Lucien. *Our People and Our History.* Translated by Sister Dorothea Olga McCants. Baton Rouge: LSU Press, 1973.

De Ville, Winston. *Opelousas: The History of a French and Spanish Military Post in America, 1716–1803.* Ville Platte, La.: The author, 1986.

Din, Gilbert C. *Spaniards, Planters, and Slaves: The Spanish Regulation of Slavery in Louisiana, 1763–1803.* College Station: Texas A&M University Press, 1999.

Dollar, Susan E. *The Freedmen's Bureau Schools of Natchitoches Parish, Louisiana, 1865–1868.* Edited by Neill Cameron. Natchitoches, La.: Northwestern State University Press, 1998.

Dominguez, Virginia. *White by Definition: Social Classification in Creole Louisiana.* New Brunswick, N.J.: Rutgers University Press, 1993.

Dormon, James H., ed. *Creoles of Color of the Gulf South.* Knoxville: University of Tennessee Press, 1996.

Dover, Cedric. *American Negro Art.* Greenwich: New York Graphic Society, 1960.

Drigon, Claude. *Nobiliare de Normandy.* 2 vols. in 4. Paris: Aubry, Rouen-Caen, Lebrument et Massif, 1863–64.

Flores, Dan L. *Jefferson & Southwestern Exploration: The Freeman & Custis Accounts of the Red River Expedition of 1806.* Norman: University of Oklahoma Press, 1984.

Fogel, Robert William, and Stanley L. Engerman. *Time on the Cross: The Economics of American Negro Slavery.* 2 vols. Boston: Little, Brown & Co., 1974.

Fortier, Alcée. *A History of Louisiana.* 4 vols. New York: Manzi, Joyant & Co., 1904.

———. *Louisiana: Comprising Sketches of Parishes, Towns, Events, Institutions, and Persons, Arranged in Cyclopedic Form.* Madison, Wis.: Century Historical Association, 1914.

Franklin, John Hope. *The Free Negro in North Carolina, 1790–1860.* Chapel Hill: University of North Carolina Press, 1943.

Frazier, E. Franklin. *The Free Negro Family: A Study of Family Origins before the Civil War.* Nashville: Fisk University Press, 1932.

Gatewood, Willard B. *Aristocrats of Color: The Black Elite, 1880–1920.* Bloomington: Indiana University Press, 1990.

Gayarré, Charles E. *History of Louisiana.* 4 vols. New Orleans: Armand Hawkins, 1903.

Gehman, Mary. *The Free People of Color of New Orleans.* New Orleans: Margaret Media, 1994.

Gould, Philip, photographer. *Natchitoches and Louisiana's Timeless Cane River.* Text by Richard Seale, Robert B. DeBlieux, and Harlan Mark Guidry. Baton Rouge: LSU Press, 2002.

Gray, Lewis Cecil. *History of Agriculture in the Southern United States to 1860.* 2 vols. 1933; rpr. Gloucester, Mass.: Peter Smith, 1958.

Greene, Lorenzo Johnston. *The Negro in Colonial New England, 1620–1776.* New York: Columbia University Press, 1942.

Gregory, Hiram F., et al. *The Archaeology of the Badin-Roque House: A 19th-Century Poteau-en-Terre House.* Natchitoches, La.: Northwestern State University Press, 1982.

Gutman, Herbert. *The Black Family in Slavery and Freedom, 1750–1925.* New York: Pantheon Books, 1976.

Haas, Edward F., ed. *Louisiana's Legal Heritage,* Pensacola, Fla.: Perdido Bay Press for the Louisiana State Museum, 1983.

Hall, Gwendolyn Midlo. *Africans in Colonial Louisiana: The Development of Afro-Creole Culture in the Eighteenth Century.* Baton Rouge: LSU Press, 1992.

———. *Slavery and African Ethnicities in the Americas: Restoring the Links.* Chapel Hill: University of North Carolina Press, 2005.

Hanger, Kimberly. *Bounded Lives, Bounded Places: Free Black Society in Colonial New Orleans, 1769–1803.* Durham, N.C.: Duke University Press, 1997.

Heitzmann, Kathleen Balthazar, and Joseph Metoyer. *The St. Augustine Catholic Church Cemetery Listings.* Catskill, N.Y.: Cane River Trading Co., 2007.

Herskovits, Melville J. *The New World Negro.* Edited by Frances S. Herskovits. Bloomington, Ind.: Indiana University Press, 1966.

Hollandsworth, James G., Jr. *The Louisiana Native Guards: The Black Military Experience during the Civil War.* Baton Rouge: LSU Press, 1995.

Hudson, Estelle, and Henry R. Maresh, *Czech Pioneers of the Southwest*. Dallas: South-West, 1934.

Jackson, Jack. *Los Mesteños: Spanish Ranching in Texas, 1721–1821*. College Station: Texas A&M University Press, 1986.

James, Cyril Lionel Robert. *The Black Jacobins: Toussaint L'Ouverture and the San Domingo Rebellion*. 2nd ed. New York: Vintage Books, 1963.

Johnson, Ludwell H. *Red River Campaign: Politics and Cotton in the Civil War*. Baltimore: Johns Hopkins Press, 1958.

Johnson, Michael P., and James L. Roark. *No Chariot Let Down: Free People of Color on the Eve of the Civil War*. Chapel Hill: University of North Carolina Press, 2001.

Johnson, Robert U., and Clarence C. Buel, eds. *Battles and Leaders of the Civil War*. 4 vols. New York: The Century Co., 1887–1888.

Johnston, James Hugo. *Race Relations in Virginia and Miscegenation in the South, 1776–1860*. 1937; rpr. Amherst: University of Massachusetts Press, 1970.

Jolivétte, Andrew J. *Louisiana Creoles: Cultural Recovery and Mixed-Race Native American Identity*. New York: Lexington Books, 2007.

Jordan, Winthrop D. *White over Black: American Attitudes toward the Negro, 1550–1812*. Chapel Hill: University of North Carolina Press, 1968.

Kane, Harnett T. *Plantation Parade: The Grand Manner in Louisiana*. New York: William Morrow, 1945.

Kein, Sybil, ed. *Creole: The History and Legacy of Louisiana's Free People of Color*. Baton Rouge: LSU Press, 2000.

Kennedy, N. Brent, and Robyn Vaughan Kennedy. *The Melungeons: The Resurrection of a Proud People; An Untold Story of Ethnic Cleansing in America*. Rev. ed. Macon, Ga.: Mercer University Press, 1997.

Kerby, Robert L. *Kirby Smith's Confederacy: The Trans-Mississippi South, 1863–1865*. New York: Columbia University Press, 1972.

Klier, Betje Black. *Pavie in the Borderlands: The Journey of Théodore Pavie to Louisiana and Texas, 1829–1830*. Baton Rouge: LSU Press, 2000.

Koger, Larry. *Black Masters: Free Black Slave Masters in South Carolina, 1790–1860*. Columbia: University of South Carolina Press, 1995.

Lagarde, François. *The French in Texas: History, Migration, Culture*. Austin: University of Texas Press, 2003.

Lebsock, Suzanne. *The Free Women of Petersburg: Status and Culture in a Southern Town, 1784–1860*. New York: W. W. Norton, 1985.

Litwack, Leon F. *North of Slavery: The Negro in the Free States*. Chicago: University of Chicago Press, 1965.

Logsdon, Joseph, and Arnold R. Hirsch, eds. *Creole New Orleans: Race and Americanization*. Baton Rouge: LSU Press, 1992.

Louisiana Regional Folklife Program (Region 2). *The Creole Chronicles*. 6 vols. Natchitoches, La.: Northwestern State University, 2001–2004.

Machann, Clinton, and James W. Mendl. *Krásná Amerika: A Study of the Texas Czechs, 1851–1939.* Austin: Eakin Press, 1983.

Mahé, John A., II, and Rosanne McCaffrey, eds. *Encyclopaedia of New Orleans Artists, 1718–1918.* New Orleans: Historic New Orleans Collection, 1987.

Malone, Ann Patton. *Sweet Chariot: Slave Family & Household Structure in Nineteenth-Century Louisiana.* Chapel Hill: University of North Carolina Press, 1992.

McManus, Edgar J. *Black Bondage in the North.* Syracuse, N.Y.: Syracuse University Press, 1973.

McWhiney, Grady. *Cracker Culture: Celtic Ways in the Old South.* University, Ala.: University of Alabama Press, 1988.

Mignon, Francois. *Plantation Parade: Plantation Life in Louisiana, 1750–1970, and Other Matter.* Edited by Ora G. Williams. Baton Rouge: Claitor's, 1973.

Mills, Elizabeth Shown. *Isle of Canes.* Provo, Utah: Ancestry.com, 2004.

Mills, Gary B., and Elizabeth Shown Mills. *Melrose.* Natchitoches, La.: Association for the Preservation of Historic Natchitoches, 1973.

———. *Tales of Old Natchitoches.* Natchitoches, La.: Association for the Preservation of Historic Natchitoches, 1978.

Morrow, Louis Laraboire. *Our Catholic Faith: A Manual of Religion.* Kenosha, Wis.: My Mission House, 1961.

Natchitoches: Oldest Settlement in the Louisiana Purchase, Founded 1714. Natchitoches, La.: Association of Natchitoches Women for the Preservation of Historic Natchitoches, 1973.

Nolan, Charles, ed. *Religion in Louisiana.* Lafayette: Center for Louisiana Studies, 2004.

Painter, Nell Irvin. *Creating Black Americans: African-American History and Its Meanings, 1619 to the Present.* New York: Oxford University Press, 2006.

———. *The History of White People.* New York: W. W. Norton, 2010.

Phares, Ross. *Cavalier in the Wilderness: The Story of the Explorer and Trader Louis Juchereau de St. Denis.* Baton Rouge: LSU Press, 1952.

Portré-Bobinski, Germaine, and Clara Mildred Smith. *Natchitoches: The Up-to-Date Oldest Town in Louisiana.* New Orleans: Dameron-Pierson Co., 1936.

Quarles, Benjamin. *The Negro in the Civil War.* Boston: Little, Brown, 1953.

Ripley, C. Peter. *Slaves and Freedmen in Civil War Louisiana.* Baton Rouge: LSU Press, 1976.

Rogin, Leo. *The Introduction of Farm Machinery in Its Relation to the Productivity of Labor in the Agriculture of the United States during the Nineteenth Century.* Berkeley: University of California Press, 1931.

Rousseve, Charles B. *The Negro in Louisiana: Aspects of His History and His Literature.* New Orleans: Xavier University Press, 1937.

Rudolph, William Keyse, and Patricia Brady. *In Search of Julien Hudson: Free Artist of Color in Pre–Civil War New Orleans.* New Orleans: Historic New Orleans Collection, 2011.

Russell, John H. *The Free Negro in Virginia, 1619–1685*. Baltimore: Johns Hopkins Press, 1913.

St. Augustine Catholic Church, Isle Brevelle, 1803–2003. Natchitoches, La.: The Parish, 2003.

Sarpy, John O. *A Slave, a Frenchman & the Blood of a Saint*. Shreveport, La.: Sarpy Publishing Co., 2001.

Saxon, Lyle. *Children of Strangers*. 1937; rpr. New Orleans: Robert L. Crager & Co., 1948.

Schafer, Judith Kelleher. *Slavery, the Civil Law, and the Supreme Court of Louisiana*. Baton Rouge: LSU Press, 1997.

Schweninger, Loren. *Black Property Owners in the South, 1790–1915*. Urbana: University of Illinois Press, 1990.

Seebold, Herman de Bachelle. *Old Louisiana Plantation Homes and Family Trees*. 2 vols. New Orleans: N.p., 1941.

Shuffelton, Frank. *A Mixed Race: Ethnicity in Early America*. New York: Oxford University Press, 1993.

Shugg, Roger W. *Origins of Class Struggle in Louisiana: A Social History of White Farmers and Laborers during Slavery and After, 1840–1875*. Baton Rouge: LSU Press, 1939.

Smith, F. Todd. *The Caddo Indians: Tribes at the Convergence of Empires, 1542–1854*. College Station: Texas A&M University, 1995.

Smith, Francis J. *Isle Brevelle: St. Augustine Church*. Natchitoches, La.: St. Augustine Church, 1981.

Smith, Gene Allen, and Sylvia L. Hilton, eds. *Nexus of Empire: Negotiating Loyalty and Identity in the Revolutionary Borderlands, 1760s–1820s*. Gainesville: University Press of Florida, 2010.

Sterkx, H. E. *The Free Negro in Ante-Bellum Louisiana*. Rutherford, N.J.: Fairleigh Dickinson University Press, 1972.

Surrey, N. M. Miller. *The Commerce of Louisiana during the French Regime, 1699–1763*. New York: Columbia University Press, 1916.

Swanton, John R. *The Indian Tribes of North America*. 1952; rpr. Grosse Pointe, Mich.: Scholarly Press, 1968.

Sweet, Frank W. *Legal History of the Color Line: The Notion of Invisible Blackness*. Palm Coast, Fla.: Backintyme, 2005.

Tannenbaum, Frank. *Slave and Citizen*. New York: A. A. Knopf, 1947.

Taylor, Joe Gray. *Louisiana Reconstructed, 1863–1877*. Baton Rouge: LSU Press, 1974.

———. *Negro Slavery in Louisiana*. Baton Rouge: Louisiana Historical Association, 1963.

Thompson, Shirley Elizabeth. *Exiles at Home: The Struggle to Become American in Creole New Orleans*. Cambridge, Mass.: Harvard University Press, 2009.

Usner, Daniel H., Jr. *Indians, Settlers & Slaves in a Frontier Exchange Economy: The Lower Mississippi Valley before 1783*. Chapel Hill: University of North Carolina Press, 1992.

Vincent, Charles. *The African American Experience in Louisiana: From Africa to the Civil War.* Lafayette: Center for Louisiana Studies, 1999.

Watkins, James L. *King Cotton: A Historical and Statistical Review, 1790 to 1908.* 1908; rpr. New York: Negro Universities Press, 1969.

Wesley, Charles Harris, and Patricia W. Romero. *Negro Americans in the Civil War: From Slavery to Citizenship.* 3 vols. New York: Publishers Co., 1967.

Westermann, Diedrich. *Die Glidyi-Ewe in Togo: Züge aus ihrem Gesellschaftsleben.* Berlin: W. de Gruyter, 1935.

Whitten, David O. *Andrew Durnford: A Black Sugar Planter in Antebellum Louisiana.* Natchitoches, La.: Northwestern State University Press, 1981.

Wiencek, Henry. *The Hairstons: An American Family in Black and White.* New York: St. Martin's, 1999.

Williams, William H. *Slavery and Freedom in Delaware, 1639–1865.* Wilmington, Del.: Scholarly Resources, 1996.

Williamson, Joel. *New People: Miscegenation and Mulattoes in the United States.* New York: Free Press, 1980.

Wilson, Joseph T. *The Black Phalanx; A History of the Negro Soldiers of the United States in the Wars of 1775–1812, 1861–1865.* Hartford: American Publishing Co., 1888.

Wilson, Theodore Brantner. *The Black Codes of the South.* University, Ala.: University of Alabama Press, 1965.

Winkler, Wayne. *Walking toward the Sunset: The Melungeons of Appalachia.* Macon, Ga.: Mercer University Press, 2005.

Winters, John D. *The Civil War in Louisiana.* Baton Rouge: LSU Press, 1963.

Woodman, Harold D. *King Cotton and His Retainers; Financing and Marketing the Cotton Crop of the South, 1800–1925.* Lexington: University of Kentucky Press, 1968.

Woods, Frances Jerome. *Marginality and Identity: A Colored Creole Family through Ten Generations.* Baton Rouge: LSU Press, 1972.

Woodson, Carter G. *The Education of the Negro prior to 1861: A History of the Education of the Colored People of the United States from the Beginning of Slavery to the Civil War.* New York: G. P. Putnam's sons, 1915.

———. *The Negro in Our History.* Washington, D.C.: Associated Publishers, 1928.

Wright, Donald R. *Oral Traditions from the Gambia.* 2 vols. Athens, Ohio: Ohio University Center for International Studies, Africa Program, 1979–80.

Wright, James M. *The Free Negro in Maryland, 1634–1860.* New York: Columbia University Press, 1921.

ARTICLES & ESSAYS

Adams, M. Boniface. "The Gift of Religious Leadership: Henriette Delille and the Foundation of the Holy Family Sisters." In *Cross, Crozier, and Crucible: A Volume Cel-*

ebrating the Bicentennial of a Catholic Diocese in Louisiana, edited by Glenn R. Conrad, 360–74. New Orleans: Archdiocese of New Orleans, 1993.

"Amherst in the Law." *Amherst Graduates' Quarterly* 10 (November 1920): 238–52.

Andrews, James G. "Let Your Fingers Do the Ginning." *Mid-South,* November 10, 1974.

Arena, C. Richard. "Landholding and Political Power in Spanish Louisiana." *Louisiana Historical Quarterly* 38 (October 1955): 39–54.

"Auction Slated at Plantation." *New Orleans Times-Picayune,* June 4, 1970.

Baker, Vaughn, Amos Simpson, and Mathé Allain. "*Le Mari Est Seigneur:* Marital Laws Governing Women in French Louisiana." In *The French Experience in Louisiana,* edited by Glenn R. Conrad, 470–78. Lafayette: Center for Louisiana Studies, 1995.

Barr, Juliana. "From Captives to Slaves: Commodifying Indian Women in the Borderlands." *Journal of American History* 92 (June 2005): 19–46.

Bergeron, Arthur W., Jr. "Free Men of Color in Gray." *Civil War History* 32 (September 1986): 247–55.

Berlin, Ira. "Southern Free People of Color in the Age of William Johnson." *Between Two Worlds: Free People of Color in Southern Cultural History;* a special issue of the *Southern Quarterly* 43 (Winter 2006): 9–17.

Berry, Mary F. "Negro Troops in Blue and Gray: The Louisiana Native Guards, 1861–63." *Louisiana History* 8 (Spring 1967): 165–90.

Blanton, Mackie J. V., and Gayle K. Nolan. "Creole Lenten Devotions: Nineteenth Century Practices and Their Implications." In *Cross, Crozier, and Crucible: A Volume Celebrating the Bicentennial of a Catholic Diocese in Louisiana,* edited by Glenn R. Conrad, 30–47. New Orleans: Archdiocese of New Orleans, 1993.

Bridges, Katherine. "Natchitoches in 1726." *Louisiana Genealogical Register* 8 (September 1961): 37–39.

Bridges, Katherine, and Winston De Ville. "Natchitoches in 1766." *Louisiana History* 4 (April, 1963): 145–59.

Browning, James Blackwell. "Free Negro in Ante-Bellum North Carolina." *North Carolina Historical Review* 15 (January 1938): 23–33.

Bruns, J. Edgar. "Antoine Blanc: Louisiana's Joshua in the Land of Promise He Opened." In *Cross, Crozier, and Crucible: A Volume Celebrating the Bicentennial of a Catholic Diocese in Louisiana,* edited by Glenn R. Conrad, 120–34. New Orleans: Archdiocese of New Orleans, 1993.

Burns, Francis P. "The Spanish Land Laws of Louisiana." *Louisiana Historical Quarterly* 11 (October 1928): 557–81.

Burton, H. Sophie. "Free People of Color in Spanish Colonial Natchitoches: Manumission and Dependency on the Louisiana-Texas Frontier." *Louisiana History* 45 (Spring 2004): 173–97.

———. "Marie Thérèze *dit* Coincoin: A Free Black Woman on the Louisiana-Texas Frontier." In *Nexus of Empire: Negotiating Loyalty and Identity in the Revolutionary Borderlands, 1760s–1820s,* edited by Gene Allen Smith and Sylvia L. Hilton, 89–112. Gainesville: University Press of Florida, 2010.

Burton, H. Sophie, and F. Todd Smith. "Slavery in the Colonial Louisiana Backcountry: Natchitoches, 1714–1803." *Louisiana History* 52 (Spring 2011): 133–88.

Cheung, Floyd D. "*Les Cenelles* and Quadroon Balls: 'Hidden Transcripts' of Resistance and Domination in New Orleans, 1803–1845." *Southern Literary Journal* 29 (Spring 1997): 5–16.

Clark, Emily, and Virginia Meacham Gould. "The Feminine Face of Afro-Catholicism in New Orleans, 1727–1852." In *Religion in Louisiana,* edited by Charles E. Nolan, 103–33. Lafayette: Center for Louisiana Studies, 2004.

"Cluster of Treasures along Cane River: Melrose Makes BIG List." *New Orleans Times-Picayune,* July 2, 1972.

"Colored Slave Owners and Traders in the Old Days." *African Methodist Episcopal Church Review* 29 (January 1913): 300–3.

Cook, Philip C. "Alexis Grappe: From French Marine to N. La. Frontiersman." *North Louisiana Historical Association Journal* 34 (Winter 2003): 34–44.

Couch, Randall R. "The Public Masked Balls of Antebellum New Orleans: A Custom of Masque outside the Mardi Gras Tradition." *Louisiana History* 35 (Fall 1994): 403–31.

Crusto, Mitch. "Blackness as Property: Sex, Race, Status, and Wealth." bepress Legal Series, Working Paper no. 307, 2004. Berkeley Electronic Press. *bepress Legal Repository.* http://law.bepress.com/expresso/eps/307.

Cruzat, Heloise H. "The Documents Covering the Criminal Trial of Etienne La Rue, for Attempt to Murder and Illicit Carrying of Arms." *Louisiana Historical Quarterly* 13 (July 1930): 377–90.

———, trans. "Louisiana in 1724: Banet's Report to the Company of the Indies." *Louisiana Historical Quarterly* 12 (January 1929): 121–33.

———, trans. and abstractor. "Records of the Superior Council of Louisiana." *Louisiana Historical Quarterly,* serialized vols. 2–27 (1919–44).

Cummins, Light Townsend. "Church Courts, Marriage Breakdown, and Separation in Spanish Louisiana, West Florida, and Texas, 1763–1836." *Journal of Texas Catholic History and Culture* 4 (1993): 97–114.

Daigle, P. Keith. "All in the Family: Equal Protection and the Illegitimate Child in Louisiana Succession Law." *Louisiana Law Review* 38 (Fall 1997): 189–204.

Dart, Henry P. "A Criminal Trial before the Superior Council of Louisiana, May, 1747." *Louisiana Historical Quarterly* 13 (July 1930): 367–76.

Dauphine, James G. "Catholic Education in North Louisiana: The Pre–World War One Foundations of Catholic Life in a Southern Diocese." In *Cross, Crozier, and Crucible: A Volume Celebrating the Bicentennial of a Catholic Diocese in Louisiana,* edited by Glenn R. Conrad, 289–301. New Orleans: Archdiocese of New Orleans, 1993.

De Gournay, P. F. "The F.M.C.'s of Louisiana." *Lippincott's Monthly Magazine* 53 (April 1894): 511–17.

DeMarce, Virginia Easley. "Looking at Legends—Lumbee and Melungeon: Applied Genealogy and the Origins of Tri-Racial Isolate Settlements." *National Genealogical Society Quarterly* 81 (March 1993): 24–45.

———. "'Verry Slitly Mixt': Tri-Racial Isolate Families of the Upper South—A Genealogical Study." *National Genealogical Society Quarterly* 80 (March 1992): 5–35.

Din, Gilbert C. "Father Jean Delvaux and the Natchitoches Revolt of 1795." *Louisiana History* 40 (Winter 1999): 5–33.

Dorr, J. W. "A Tourist's Description of Louisiana in 1860." *Louisiana Historical Quarterly* 21 (October 1938): 1110–1214.

Doyle, Elisabeth Joan. "Bishop Auguste Marie Martin of Natchitoches and the Civil War." In *Cross, Crozier, and Crucible: A Volume Celebrating the Bicentennial of a Catholic Diocese in Louisiana,* edited by Glenn R. Conrad, 135–44. New Orleans: Archdiocese of New Orleans, 1993.

Dunbar-Nelson, Alice. "People of Color in Louisiana." *Journal of Negro History* 1 (October 1916): 361–76; 2 (January 1917): 51–78.

Dunn, J. E. "Isle Brevelle." *Louisiana Populist* (Natchitoches), February 26, 1897.

Dunn, Milton. "History of Natchitoches." *Louisiana Historical Quarterly* 3 (January 1920): 26–56.

DuVal, Kathleen. "Indian Intermarriage and Métissage in Colonial Louisiana." *William and Mary Quarterly,* 3rd ser., 65 (April 2008): 267–304.

Edwards, Jay D. "Vernacular Vision: The Gallery and Our Africanized Architectural Landscape." In *Raised to the Trade: Creole Building Arts of New Orleans,* edited by Jonn Ethan Hankins and Steven Maklansky, 61–94. New Orleans: New Orleans Museum of Art, 2002.

Everett, Donald E. "Free Persons of Color in Colonial Louisiana." *Louisiana History* 7 (Winter 1966): 21–50.

Fiehrer, Thomas. "The Emergence of Pan-Créolité: Louisiana at the Crossroads." *Nanzan Review of American Studies* 17 (1995): 1–28.

———. "The African Presence in Colonial Louisiana: An Essay on the Continuity of Caribbean Culture." In *Louisiana's Black Heritage,* edited by Robert R. Macdonald, John R. Kemp, and Edward F. Haas, 3–31. New Orleans: Louisiana State Museum, 1979.

Fischer, Roger A. "Racial Segregation in Ante-Bellum Louisiana." *American Historical Review* 74 (February 1969): 926–37.

Foner, Laura. "The Free People of Color in Louisiana and St. Domingue: A Comparative Portrait of Two Three-Caste Societies." *Journal of Social History* 3 (Summer 1970): 406–30.

Garber, D. "History of Melrose Plantation like Turning Pages of Novel." *Dallas Morning News.* October 21, 1951.

Gates, Laura Soullière. "Frankly, Scarlett, We Do Give a Damn: The Making of a New National Park." *George Wright Forum* 19 (2002): 32–43.

Gould, Lois Virginia Meacham. "A Chaos of Iniquity and Discord: Slave and Free Women of Color in the Spanish Ports of New Orleans, Mobile, and Pensacola." In *The Devil's Lane: Sex and Race in the Early South,* edited by Catherine Clinton and Michelle Gillespie, 232–46. New York: Oxford University Press, 1997.

Grappe, Bernie. "F. Grappe: Unique N. La. Frontiersman." *North Louisiana Historical Association Journal* 9 (Spring 1978): 65–70.

Gray, Ruffin. "Louis Juchereau de St-Denis." In *Dictionary of Louisiana Biography,* 2 vols., edited by Glenn R. Conrad, 1:449. Lafayette: Louisiana Historical Association, 1988.

Guillory, Monique. "Under One Roof: The Sin and Sanctity of the New Orleans Quadroon Balls." In *Race Consciousness: African-American Studies for the New Century,* edited by Judith J. Fossett and Jeffrey A. Tucker, 67–92. New York: New York University Press, 1997.

Hanger, Kimberly S. "Coping in a Complex World: Free Black Women in Colonial New Orleans." In *The Devil's Lane: Sex and Race in the Early South,* edited by Catherine Clinton and Michelle Gillespie, 218–31. New York: Oxford University Press, 1997.

———. "Landlords, Shopkeepers, Farmers, and Slave-Owners: Free Black Female Property-Holders in Colonial New Orleans." In *Beyond Bondage: Free Women of Color in the Americas,* edited by David Barry Gaspar and Darlene Clark Hine, 219–36. Urbana: University of Illinois Press, 2004.

———. "Origins of New Orleans's Free Creoles of Color." In *Creoles of Color of the Gulf South,* edited by James H. Dormon, 1–27. Knoxville: University of Tennessee Press, 1996.

Harmon, Anastasia, Natalie D. Cottrill, Paul C. Reed, and Joseph Shumway. "Documenting President Barack Obama's Maternal African-American Ancestry: Tracing His Mother's Bunch Ancestry to the First Slave in America." Archived, *Ancestry* .com. http://c.mfcreative.com/offer/us/obama_bunch/PDF/main_article_final.pdf.

Hayes, Blake, and Katie Boarman. "Meatpies, Magnolias and Murals: A New Interpretation Plan for Melrose Plantation." Association for Living History, Farm and Agricultural Museums. *Proceedings of the 2006 Conference and Annual Meeting,* vol. 29, *Interpreting Multiculturalism in the Modern Museum Setting.* http://www .alhfam.org/pdfs/15-Hayes_Boardman.pdf.

Henry, Joseph H. "Discovery of Bousillage Cabin Substantiates True Story." *Natchitoches Times.* April 16, 1978.

Jeffrey, Edward C. "New Lights on Evolution." *Science,* May 13, 1927, 458–62.

Kestenbaum, Lawrence. *The Political Graveyard.* http://www.politicalgraveyard.com.

Kunkel, Paul A. "Modifications in Louisiana Negro Legal Status under Louisiana Constitutions, 1812–1957." *Journal of Negro History* 44 (January 1959): 1–25.

Leach, Marguerite T. "The Aftermath of Reconstruction in Louisiana." *Louisiana Historical Quarterly* 32 (July 1949): 631–717.

Leary, Helen F. M. "Sally Heming's Children: A Genealogical Analysis of the Evidence." *Jefferson-Hemings: A Special Issue of the National Genealogical Society Quarterly* 89 (September 2001): 165–201.

Lee, Dana Bowker. "François Grappe and the Caddo Land Cession." *North Louisiana Historical Association Journal* 20 (Spring–Summer 1989): 53–69.

——— ."The People of the Island: A Living Culture." *Creole Chronicles* 1 (May 2001): 5–8.

Lemée, Patricia. "Ambivalent Successes and Successful Failures: St. Denis, Aguayo, and Juan Rodríguez." In *The French in Texas: History, Migration, Culture,* edited by François Lagarde, 35–45. Austin: University of Texas Press, 2003.

Lennon, Rachal Mills, and Elizabeth Shown Mills. "Mother, Thy Name Is *Mystery*! Finding the Slave Who Bore Philomene Daurat." *National Genealogical Society Quarterly* 88 (September 2000): 201–28.

MacDonald, Kevin C., Aubra L. Lee, and Emma Morley. "The Archaeology of Local Myths and Heritage Tourism: The Case of Cane River's Melrose Plantation." In *A Future for Archaeology: The Past in the Present,* edited by Robert Layton et al., 127–42. Walnut Creek, Calif.: Left Coast Press, 2006.

MacDonald, Kevin C., David W. Morgan, and Fiona J. L. Handley. "The Cane River African Diaspora Archaeological Project: Prospectus and Initial Results." In *African Re-Genesis: Confronting Social Issues in the Diaspora (One World Archaeology),* edited by Jay B. Haviser and Kevin C. MacDonald, 123–44. London: University College London Press, 2006.

Martin, Joan M. "*Plaçage* and the Louisiana *Gens de Couleur Libres:* How Race and Sex Defined the Lifestyles of Free Women of Color." In *Creole: The History and Legacy of Louisiana's Free People of Color,* edited by Sybil Kein, 64–70. Baton Rouge: LSU Press, 2000.

McCloy, Shelby T. "Negroes and Mulattoes in Eighteenth-Century France." *Journal of Negro History* 30 (July 1945): 276–92.

McDonald, Forrest, and Grady McWhiney. "The South from Self-Sufficiency to Peonage: An Interpretation." *American Historical Review* 85 (December 1980): 1095–1118.

"Melrose: Home of Famous Louisiana Authors." *Louisiana REA News* (July 1953): 11.

"Melrose Manor on Cane River Stands as Relic of World's Strangest Empire." Hammond, La., *Progress,* March 25, 1938.

Mignon, Francois. "Cane River Memo: Melrose Highlights." *Natchitoches Times.* December 19, 1971.

———. "Sale of Plantation Biggest in History." Alexandria, La., *Daily Town Talk,* April 21, 1970.

Miller, Randall M. "Slaves and Southern Catholicism." In *Masters and Slaves in the House of the Lord: Race and Religion in the American South, 1740–1870,* edited by John B. Boles, 127–52. Lexington: University of Kentucky Press, 1988.

Mills, Donna Rachal. "Civil War Claims Commissions: The Mixed Commission of British and American Claims." *National Genealogical Society Quarterly* 75 (June 1987): 141–52.

Mills, Elizabeth Shown. "Breathing Life into Shadowy Women from the Past." *Solander* 9 (2005): 21–24.

———. "Deliberate Fraud and Mangled Evidence: The Search for the Fictional Family of Anne Marie Philippe of Natchitoches, Louisiana." *The American Genealogist* 72 (July–October 1997): 353–68.

———. "(de) Mézières-Trichel-Grappe: A Study of a Tri-Caste Lineage in the Old South." *The Genealogist.* Ser. 1, vol. 6 (Spring 1985): 4–84.

———. "Demythicizing History: Marie Thérèse Coincoin, Tourism, and the National Historical Landmarks Program." *Louisiana History* 53 (Fall 2012): 402–37.

———. "Documenting a Slave's Birth, Parentage, and Origins (Marie Thérèse Coincoin, 1742–1816): A Test of Oral History." *National Genealogical Society Quarterly* 96 (December 2008): 245–66.

———. "Ethnicity and the Southern Genealogist: Myths and Misconceptions, Resources and Opportunities." In *Generations and Change: Genealogical Perspectives in Social History,* edited by Robert M. Taylor Jr. and Ralph J. Crandall, 89–108. Macon, Ga.: Mercer University Press, 1986.

———. "European Origins of the Early French Families of Natchitoches, Louisiana." In *Papers of the Sixth Grand Reunion of the Descendants of the Founders of Natchitoches,* edited by Sharon Sholars Brown, 27–45. Natchitoches, La.: Founders of Natchitoches, 1986.

———. "Forgotten People of America." *Ancestry Magazine* (May–June 2004): 16–22.

———. "François (Guyon) Dion Despres Derbanne: *Premier Citoyen,* Poste St. Jean Baptiste des Natchitoches." *Natchitoches Genealogist* 6 (October 1981): 1–9.

———. "From Chez Bienvenu to Cane River: Four Generations of the Pierre Brosset Family." *Natchitoches Genealogist,* serialized, vols. 11–14 (1986–89).

———. "*Isle of Canes* and Issues of Conscience: Master-Slave Sexual Dynamics and Slaveholding by Free People of Color." *Between Two Worlds: Free People of Color in Southern Cultural History;* a special issue of the *Southern Quarterly* 43 (Winter 2006): 158–75.

———. "Jean Delvaux." In *Dictionary of Louisiana Biography,* 2 vols., edited by Glenn R. Conrad, 1:63–64. Lafayette: Louisiana Historical Association, 1988.

———. "Jeannot Mulon *dit* La Brun, f.m.c., Colonial Natchitoches, Louisiana." *Board for Certification of Genealogists.* http://www.bcgcertification.org/skillbuilders/extended report.pdf.

———. "Louis de Quintanilla." In *Dictionary of Louisiana Biography,* 2 vols., edited by Glenn R. Conrad, 1:187–88. Lafayette: Louisiana Historical Association, 1988.

———. "Marie des Neiges Juchereau de St-Denis," and "Antonio Emanuel de Soto y Bermudes." In Glenn R. Conrad, ed., *Dictionary of Louisiana Biography,* 2 vols., 1:449–50 and 2:755–56. Lafayette: Louisiana Historical Association, 1988.

———. "Marie Thérèse Coincoin (1742–1816): Cane River Slave, Slave Owner, and Paradox." In *Louisiana Women: Their Lives and Times,* edited by Janet Allured and Judith F. Gentry, 10–29. Athens: University of Georgia Press, 2009.

———. "Marie Thereze *dit* Coincoin: A Cultural Transfer Agent." In *Four Women of Cane River: Their Contributions to the Cultural Life of the Area,* 1–18. Natchitoches, La.: Natchitoches Parish Library, ca. 1980.

———. "Marie Therese, the Metoyers, and Melrose." In *Proceedings of the Seventeenth Annual Institute of the Louisiana Genealogical and Historical Society,* 13–25. Baton Rouge: The Society, 1974.

———. "Natchitoches Baptisms, 1724–1776: A Supplement." *Natchitoches Genealogist* 7 (April 1983): 6–11.

———. "Quintanilla's Crusade, 1775–1783: 'Moral Reform' and Its Consequences on the Natchitoches Frontier." *Louisiana History* 42 (Summer 2001): 277–302.

——. "Social and Family Patterns on the Colonial Louisiana Frontier." *Sociological Spectrum* 2 (July–December 1982): 233–48.

——. "Which Marie Louise Is 'Mariotte'? Sorting Slaves with Common Names." *National Genealogical Society Quarterly* 94 (September 2006): 183–204.

Mills, Elizabeth Shown, and Gary B. Mills. "Louise Marguerite: St. Denis' *Other* Daughter." *Southern Studies* 16 (Fall 1977): 321–28.

——. "Missionaries Compromised: Early Evangelization of Slaves and Free People of Color in North Louisiana." In *Cross, Crozier, and Crucible: A Volume Celebrating the Bicentennial of a Catholic Diocese in Louisiana,* edited by Glenn R. Conrad, 30–47. New Orleans: Archdiocese of New Orleans, 1993

——. "Slaves and Masters: The Louisiana Metoyers." *National Genealogical Society Quarterly* 70 (September 1982): 164–89.

Mills, Gary B. "Alien Neutrality and the Red River Campaign: A Study of Cases Heard before the International Claims Commissions." *Southern Studies* 16 (Summer 1977): 181–200.

——. "A Portrait of Achievement: Nicolas Augustin Metoyer, f.m.c." *Red River Valley Historical Review* 2 (Fall 1975): 332–48.

——. "Augustin Metoyer" and "Louis Metoyer." In *Dictionary of Louisiana Biography,* 2 vols., edited by Glenn R. Conrad, 1:565.

——. "Cane River Country, 1860–1866." *Proceedings of the Seventeenth Annual Institute of the Louisiana Genealogical and Historical Society,* 1–12. Baton Rouge: The Society, 1974.

——. "Claude Thomas Pierre Metoyer." In *A Dictionary of Louisiana Biography: Ten-Year Supplement, 1988–1998,* edited by Carl A. Brasseaux and James D. Wilson Jr., 154–56. Lafayette: Louisiana Historical Association, 1999.

——. "Coincoin (1742–1816)." In *Black Women in United States History,* 2 vols., edited by Darlene Clark Hine, 1:258–60. Brooklyn: Carlson Publishing, 1990.

——. "Coincoin: An Eighteenth-Century 'Liberated' Woman." *Journal of Southern History* 42 (May 1976): 203–22.

——. "The Faith of Their Fathers." In *Religion in Louisiana,* edited by Charles E. Nolan, 176–91. Lafayette: Center for Louisiana Studies, 2004.

——. "*Liberté, Fraternité,* and Everything but *Egalité:* Cane River's *Citoyens de Couleur.*" In *North Louisiana:* Vol. 1, *To 1865: Essays on the Region and Its History,* edited by B. H. Gilley, 93–122. Ruston, La.: McGinty Trust Fund Publications, Louisiana Tech University, 1984.

——. "Miscegenation and the Free Negro in Antebellum 'Anglo' Alabama: A Reexamination of Southern Race Relations." *Journal of American History* 68 (June 1981): 16–34.

——. "Monet-Rachal: Backtracking a Cross-Racial Heritage in the Eighteenth and Nineteenth Centuries." *The American Genealogist* 65 (July 1990): 129–42.

——. "Patriotism Frustrated: The 'Native Guards' of Confederate Natchitoches." *Louisiana History* 18 (Fall 1977): 437–41.

——. "Piety and Prejudice: A Colored Catholic Community in the Antebellum South."

In *Catholics in the Old South: Essays on Church and Culture,* edited by Jon L. Wakelyn and Randall M. Miller, 171–94. Macon, Ga.: Mercer University Press, 1983.

———. "Shades of Ambiguity: Comparing Antebellum People of Color in 'Anglo' Alabama
and 'Latin' Louisiana." In *Plain Folk of the South Revisited,* edited by Samuel C.
Hyde Jr., 161–86. Baton Rouge: LSU Press, 1998.

Mills, Gary B., and Elizabeth Shown Mills. "Marie Therese and the Founding of Melrose: A Study of Facts and Fallacies." *Natchitoches Times,* July 29, August 5, 12,
19, 1973.

———. "*Roots* and the New 'Faction': A Legitimate Tool for Clio?" *Virginia Magazine of
History and Biography* 89 (January 1981): 3–26.

———. "The Genealogist's Assessment of Alex Haley's *Roots.*" *National Genealogical
Society Quarterly* 72 (March 1984): 35–49.

Morgan, David W., Kevin C. MacDonald, and Fiona J. L. Handley. "Economics and
Authenticity: A Collision of Interpretations in Cane River National Heritage Area,
Louisiana." *George Wright Forum* 23 (2006): 44–61. Archived online, with appendix,
http://www.georgewright.org/231morgan.pdf.

Nardini, Louis R. "Legends about Marie Therese Disputed by Local Historian and Author." *Natchitoches Times,* October 22, 1972.

Ocariz, Juan José Andreu. "The Natchitoches Revolt," Jack D. L. Holmes, trans. *Louisiana Studies* 3 (Spring 1964): 117–32.

"O'Reilly's Ordinance of 1770." *Louisiana Historical Quarterly* 11 (April 1928): 240.

Ottoway, Mark. "Tangled Roots." (London) *Sunday Times,* April 10, 1977.

Ousler, Loree. "Portrait of Carmelite." *Natchitoches Times,* October 11, 1973.

Pascal, Robert A. "Louisiana Succession and Related Laws and the Illegitimate:
Thoughts Prompted by *Labine* v. *Vincent.*" *Tulane Law Review* 46 (December 1971):
167–83.

Poe, William A. "Religion and Education in North Louisiana, 1800–1865." In *North
Louisiana,* Vol. 1: *To 1865: Essays on the Region and Its History,* edited by B. H.
Gilley, 113–30. Ruston, La.: McGinty Trust Fund Publications, Louisiana Tech Uni-
versity, 1984.

Porter, Betty. "The History of Negro Education in Louisiana." *Louisiana Historical
Quarterly* 25 (July 1942): 728–821.

"Preservation Group Given Deed to Melrose Plantation." *New Orleans Times-Picayune,*
January 23, 1972.

Pressly, Thomas J. "The Known World of Free Black Slaveholders: A Research Note
on the Scholarship of Carter G. Woodson." *Journal of African American History*
91 (Winter 2006): 81–87.

Quigley, Bill, and Maha Zaki. "The Significance of Race: Legislative Racial Discrimination in Louisiana, 1803–1865." *Southern University Law Review* 24 (Spring 1997):
145–205.

Rankin, David C. "The Origins of Black Leadership in New Orleans during Reconstruction." *Journal of Southern History* 40 (August 1974): 416–40.

Reed, Germaine A. "Race Legislation in Louisiana, 1864–1920." *Louisiana History* 6 (Fall 1965): 369–92.

Reinders, Robert C. "The Decline of the New Orleans Free Negro in the Decade before the Civil War." *Journal of Mississippi History* 24 (January 1962): 88–98.

———. "The Free Negro in the New Orleans Economy, 1850–1860." *Louisiana History* 6 (Summer 1965): 273–85.

Russ, William A., Jr. "Disfranchisement in Louisiana (1862–1870)." *Louisiana Historical Quarterly* 17 (July 1935): 555–80.

Rustin, Bayard. "The Role of the Negro Middle Class." *The Crisis* 18 (June–July 1969): 237–42.

"St. John the Baptist Catholic Cemetery, Cloutierville, LA." Transcriptions. *Rootsweb.* http://www.rootsweb.com/~lanatchi/Stjohnc.htm.

Schafer, Judith Kelleher. "'Guaranteed against the Vices and Maladies Prescribed by Law': Consumer Protection, the Law of Slave Sales, and the Supreme Court in Antebellum Louisiana." *American Journal of Legal History* 31 (October 1987): 306–21.

———. "Roman Roots of the Louisiana Law of Slavery: Emancipation in American Louisiana, 1803–1857." In *An Uncommon Experience: Law and Judicial Institutions in Louisiana, 1803–2003,* edited by Judith Kelleher Schafer and Warren M. Billings, 360–73. Lafayette: Center for Louisiana Studies, 1997.

Schwarz, Philip J. "Emancipators, Protectors, and Anomalies: Free Black Slaveowners in Virginia." *Virginia Magazine of History and Biography* 95 (July 1987): 317–38.

Schweninger, Loren. "Antebellum Free Persons of Color in Postbellum Louisiana." *Louisiana History* 30 (Fall 1989): 345–64.

Shoen, Harold. "The Free Negro in the Republic of Texas." *Southwestern Historical Quarterly* 39 (April 1936): 292–309; 40 (October 1936): 85–114; (January 1937): 169–99; (April 1937): 267–89; (July 1937): 83–108.

Shugg, Roger Wallace. "Suffrage and Representation in Ante-Bellum Louisiana." *Louisiana Historical Quarterly* 19 (April 1936): 390–406.

Smith, F. Todd. "Athanase de Mézières and the French in Texas, 1750–1803." In *The French in Texas: History, Migration, Culture,* ed. François Lagarde, 46–59. Austin: University of Texas Press, 2003.

Stahl, Annie Lee West. "The Free Negro in Ante-Bellum Louisiana." *Louisiana Historical Quarterly* 25 (April 1942): 301–96.

Sydnor, Charles S. "The Free Negro in Mississippi before the Civil War." *American Historical Review* 31 (July 1927): 769–88.

Taylor, Ethel. "Discontent in Confederate Louisiana." *Louisiana History* 2 (Fall 1961): 410–28.

Thomas, William J. "Louisiana Creole French, Black or White?" *Wichita State University Bulletin* 49 (February 1973): 15–26.

Tikhomirova, Yuliya, and Lucia Desir. "Unspoken Reality: Black Slaveholders prior to the Civil War." *Undergraduate Research Journal for the Human Sciences* 4 (2005), unpaginated; online journal, http://www.kon.org/urc/v4/tikhomirova.html.

Touchstone, Blake. "Voodoo in New Orleans." *Louisiana History* 13 (Fall 1972): 371–86.

Vidrine, Jacqueline O. "César de Blanc." In *Dictionary of Louisiana Biography*, 2 vols., ed. Glenn R. Conrad, 1:223. Lafayette: Louisiana Historical Association, 1988.

Wells, Carol. "Earliest Log Cabins of Natchitoches Parish." *North Louisiana Historical Association Journal* 6 (Spring 1975): 117–22.

Wesley, Charles Harris. "The Employment of Negroes as Soldiers in the Confederate Army." *Journal of Negro History* 4 (July 1919): 239–53.

Williams, Richard H. "General Banks' Red River Campaign." *Louisiana Historical Quarterly* 32 (January 1949): 103–44.

Wilson, Calvin Dill. "Black Masters: A Side-light on Slavery." *North American Review* 189 (November 1905): 685–98.

Woodson, Carter G., ed. "Beginnings of Miscegenation of Whites and Blacks." *Journal of Negro History* 3 (October 1918): 335–53.

———. "Free Negro Owners of Slaves in the United States in 1830." *Journal of Negro History* 9 (January 1924): 41–85.

Wright, Donald R. "Uprooting Kunta Kinte: On the Perils of Relying on Encyclopedic Informants." *History of Africa* 8 (1981): 205–17.

Wringle, Ken. "Up from Slavery." *Washington Post*. May 12, 2002, F:1–2. Archived online, http://www.washingtonpost.com.

THESES, DISSERTATIONS, AND PAPERS

Brown, Edward Jewett. "History of Education in Natchitoches Parish." M.A. thesis, Louisiana State University, 1932.

Constantin, Roland Paul. "The Louisiana 'Black Code' Legislation of 1865." M.A. thesis, Louisiana State University, 1956.

Cook, Philip C. "François Grappe: Profile of a North Louisiana Creole." Paper, Louisiana Historical Association annual conference. Natchitoches, March 1979.

Crawford, Webster Talma. "Redbones in the Neutral Strip . . . and the Westport Fight between Whites and Redbones for Possession of This Strip on Christmas Eve, 1882." Undated MS. Melrose Collection, Cammie G. Henry Research Center, Northwestern State University, Natchitoches.

D'Antoni, Blaise C. "The Catholic Schools of Natchitoches." Undated. Baudier Papers, Archives of the Archdiocese of New Orleans.

Delphin, Terrel. "The Creole Struggle and Resurrection: Our Story as Told by Creoles." Undated, Creole Heritage Center, Natchitoches.

Dupré, Rev. A. "Metoyer Family Genealogy." Undated, ca. 1880–89. St. Augustine Parish Rectory, Melrose.

Everett, Donald E. "Free Persons of Color in New Orleans, 1803–1865." Ph.D. diss., Tulane University, 1952.

Gallien, Charles Stanley. "Melrose: A Southern Cultural and Literary Center." M.A. thesis, Northwestern State University of Louisiana, 1966.

Gerber, Matthew. "The End of Bastardy: Illegitimacy in France from the Reformation through the Revolution." Ph.D. diss., University of California at Berkeley, 2003.

Gerona, Carla. "'He Did Not Know What Other Things His Wife Did' (or Did He?): Women, Kinship, Laws, and Lawlessness on the East Texas Borderlands." Paper, Georgia Workshop in Early American History and Culture, University of Georgia, January 28, 2008.

Gould, Lois Virginia Meacham. "In Full Enjoyment of Their Liberty: The Free Women of Color in the Gulf Ports of New Orleans, Mobile, and Pensacola, 1769–1860." Ph.D. diss., Emory University, 1991.

Henry, H. M. "The Police Control of the Slave in South Carolina." Ph.D. diss., Vanderbilt University, 1914.

Hobratsch, Ben Melvin. "Creole Angel: The Self-Identity of the Free People of Color of Antebellum New Orleans." M. A. thesis, University of North Texas, 2006. *UNT Digital Library.* http://digital.library.unt.edu/ark:/67531/metadc5369/.

Hymes, Valery. "A History of Navigation of the Red River from 1815 to 1865." M.A. thesis, Louisiana State University, 1939.

Kerr, Derek Noel. "Petty Felony, Slave Defiance, and Frontier Villainy: Crime and Criminal Justice in Spanish Louisiana, 1770–1803." Ph.D. diss., Tulane University, 1983.

Lee, Dayna Bowker. "Indian Slavery in Lower Louisiana during the Colonial Period, 1699–1803." Bound typescript, *ca.* 1989. Watson Memorial Library, Northwestern State University, Natchitoches.

Lennon, Rachal Mills. "The Slave Trade in Microcosm: Natchitoches Parish, Louisiana, 1845–55." Seminar paper, Ph.D. program. Department of History, University of Alabama, 2000. Archived online, http://www.findingsouthernancestors.com/download/slavetrade.pdf.

McPherson, Natasha L. "'There was a Tradition among the Women': New Orleans's Colored Creole Women and the Making of a Community in the Tremé and Seventh Ward, 1791–1930." Ph.D. diss., Emory University, 2011.

Metoyer, Patricia Heisser, and Luke Metoyer Sr. "The Grace of Coincoin: The Role of an African Woman's Spirituality and Its Impact on Creole Culture." Paper, Creole Studies Conference, Oct. 23–25, 2003, New Orleans.

Miller, Shari, and Miriam Rich, Mennonite Central Committee. "A History of the Clifton Community, Submitted to the Clifton Community." Typescript, Mora, La., March 1983. Copy in Melrose Collection, Cammie G. Henry Research Center, Northwestern State University, Natchitoches.

Mills, Elizabeth Shown. "Family and Social Patterns of the Colonial Louisiana Frontier: A Quantitative Analysis, 1714–1803." New College honors' thesis, University of Alabama, 1981.

Morgan, David W., and Kevin C. MacDonald. "Myth, Archaeology, and History: Interpreting the Story of Cane River's Marie Thérèse Coincoin." Paper, Louisiana Historical Association, Monroe, Louisiana, March 20, 2009.

Pastor, Lori Renee. "Black Catholicism: Religion and Slavery in Antebellum Louisiana." M.A. thesis, Tulane University, 2005.

Puckett, Erastus Paul. "The Free Negro in New Orleans to 1860." M.A. thesis, Tulane University, 1907.

Reddick, Lawrence D. "The Negro in the New Orleans Press, 1850–1860: A Study in Attitudes and Propaganda." Ph.D. diss., University of Chicago, 1939.

Shaw, Billy Wayne. "A Ceramic Chronology for the Whittington [Coincoin] House Site: 1780–Present." M.A. thesis, Northwestern State University, 1983.

Vincent, Charles. "Negro Leadership in Louisiana, 1862–1870." M.A. thesis, Louisiana State University, 1966.

Volz, Noël. "Black Female Agency and Sexual Exploitation: Quadroon Balls and Plaçage Relationships." Senior honors' thesis, Ohio State University, 2008.

Wells, Carolyn M. "Domestic Architecture of Colonial Natchitoches." M.A. thesis, Northwestern State University of Louisiana, 1973.

Yang, Guocun. "From Slavery to Emancipation: The African Americans of Connecticut, 1650s–1820s." Ph.D. diss., University of Connecticut, 1999.

INDEX